Frommer's

6th
Edition

Washington & Oregon

by Karl Samson & Jane Aukshunas

D0905882

Macmillan • USA

ABOUT THE AUTHORS

Karl Samson moved to the Northwest from the East Coast in 1990 after writing *Frommer's Seattle & Portland*. Since then he has been busy exploring the region; in fact, he's now hard at play researching *Frommer's Great Outdoors Guide: Northwest*. He is also the author of Frommer guides to such far-flung destinations as Costa Rica, Nepal, Arizona, and Nashville & Memphis.

Karl is assisted by **Jane Aukshunas,** who has also lived in the Northwest for several years now, and who is intrigued by the unique landscapes, contemporary art and design, and cuisine of her new home.

MACMILLAN TRAVEL

A Simon & Schuster Macmillan Company
1633 Broadway
New York, NY 10019

Find us online at **http://www.mcp.com/mgr/travel** or
on America Online at Keyword: **SuperLibrary.**

ISBN 0-02-860705-8
ISSN 1051-6806

Editor: Lisa Renaud
Production Editor: Matt Hannafin
Editorial Assistant: Reid Bramblett
Design by Michele Laseau
Digital Cartography by Ortelius Design and Stephen Martin

SPECIAL SALES

Bulk purchases (10+ copies) of Frommer's travel guides are available to corporations at special discounts. The Special Sales Department can produce custom editions to be used as premiums and/or for sales promotion to suit individual needs. Existing editions can be produced with custom cover imprints such as corporate logos. For more information write to: Special Sales, Simon & Schuster, 1633 Broadway, New York, NY 10019.

Manufactured in the United States of America

Contents

11   The Columbia Gorge & Mount Hood   312

12   The Oregon Coast   333

List of Maps

AN INVITATION TO THE READER

In researching this book, we discovered many wonderful places—hotels, restaurants, shops, and more. We're sure you'll find others. Please tell us about them, so we can share the information with your fellow travelers in upcoming editions. If you were disappointed with a recommendation, we'd love to know that, too. Please write to:

Karl Samson & Jane Aukshunas
Frommer's Washington & Oregon, 6th Edition
Macmillan Travel
1633 Broadway
New York, NY 10019

AN ADDITIONAL NOTE

Please be advised that travel information is subject to change at any time—and this is especially true of prices. We therefore suggest that you write or call ahead for confirmation when making your travel plans. The authors, editors, and publisher cannot be held responsible for the experiences of readers while traveling. Your safety is important to us, however, so we encourage you to stay alert and be aware of your surroundings. Keep a close eye on cameras, purses, and wallets, all favorite targets of thieves and pickpockets.

WHAT THE SYMBOLS MEAN

✪ Frommer's Favorites

Hotels, restaurants, attractions, and entertainment you should not miss.

⑤ Super-Special Values

Hotels and restaurants that offer great value for your money.

The following abbreviations are used for credit cards:

AE	American Express	EU	Eurocard
CB	Carte Blanche	JCB	Japan Credit Bank
DC	Diners Club	MC	MasterCard
DISC	Discover	V	Visa
ER	enRoute		

The Best of Washington & Oregon

Planning a trip to the Northwest involves making lots of decisions, so we've tried to give you some direction. We've traveled both states extensively and have chosen what we feel are the very best that Washington and Oregon have to offer—the places and experiences you won't want to miss. Most are written up in more detail elsewhere in this book; this chapter will give you an overview and get you started.

1 The Best Natural Attractions

- **Mount Rainier National Park** (WA): With its glaciers and easily accessible alpine meadows, Mount Rainier is Washington's favorite mountain. Mountaineers train here for assaults on high peaks all over the world. Sunrise and Paradise are the two best vantage points for viewing the massive bulk of Mount Rainier, and from these locations you'll also find some of the best hiking trails. See Chapter 7.
- **Mount St. Helens National Volcanic Monument** (WA): Mount St. Helens is slowly recovering from the 1980 volcanic blast that turned one of the Cascades' most beautiful peaks into a scarred landscape of fallen trees and fields of ash. Several visitor centers relate the events of the eruption and what has been happening on the mountain since. See Chapter 7.
- **Olympic National Park** (WA): In the park are the only rain forests in the contiguous United States, and they comprise a fascinating ecosystem—a living plant stakes out almost every bit of space, from towering Sitka spruce trees to mosses and lush ferns. And the park also preserves miles of pristine, fog-shrouded beaches and beautiful alpine and subalpine scenery dotted with lush meadows. Shy Roosevelt elk also populate the park. See Chapter 8.
- **Columbia Gorge National Scenic Area** (OR): Carved by ice-age floods that were as much as 1,200 feet deep, the Columbia Gorge is a unique feature of the Northwest landscape. Waterfalls by the dozen cascade from the basalt cliffs of the gorge. Highways on both the Washington and Oregon sides of the Columbia River provide countless memorable views. See Chapter 11.
- **The Oregon Coast:** Rocky headlands, offshore islands and haystack rocks, natural arches, sea caves full of sea lions, giant sand

dunes, and dozens of state parks make this one of the most spectacular coast-lines in the country. See Chapter 12.

- **Crater Lake National Park** (OR): Crater Lake, at 1,932 feet deep, is the deep-est lake in the United States, and its sapphire-blue waters are a bewitchingly beautiful sight when seen from the rim of the volcanic crater that forms the lake. See Chapter 14.

2 The Best Outdoor Activities

- **Sea Kayaking in the San Juan Islands** (WA): Emerald islands, clear water, remote campsites that can only be reached by boat, orca whales, and bald eagles lure sea kayakers to the San Juan Islands. You can paddle the islands on your own or go out with a guide for a few hours or a few days. See Chapter 6.
- **Cross-country Skiing in the Methow Valley** (WA): This valley on the east side of Washington's North Cascades has more than 90 miles (150km) of groomed trails, making it one of the premier cross-country ski destinations in the coun-try. See Chapter 7.
- **Windsurfing at Hood River** (OR): Winds that rage through the Columbia Gorge whip up whitecapped standing waves and have turned this area into the windsurfing capital of the United States, attracting windsurfers from around the world. See Chapter 11.
- **Fishing for Salmon on Oregon's Coastal Rivers:** There is something primor-dial and improbable about pulling a 50-pound salmon from the waters of a river that's only a few yards wide. It is just this thrill that has seduced the anglers of the Northwest. See Chapter 12.
- **Bicycling the Oregon Coast:** With U.S. 101 clinging to the edge of the continent for much of its route through Oregon, this road has become the most popular cycling route in the Northwest. The entire coast can be done in about a week, but there are also plenty of short sections that make good day trips. See Chapter 12.
- **Fly Fishing for Steelhead on the North Umpqua River** (OR): Made famous by Zane Gray, the North Umpqua is the quintessential steelhead river (though it's open to fly fishing only for part of its length). The river and the elusive steel-head offer a legendary fishing experience. See Chapter 14.
- **Mountain Biking in Bend** (OR): Outside the town of Bend, in central Or-egon, dry ponderosa pine forests are laced with trails that are open to mountain bikes. Routes pass by several lakes and along the way there are great views of the Sisters, Broken Top, and Mount Bachelor. See Chapter 15.

3 The Best Beaches

- **Third Beach, Olympic National Park** (WA): It's difficult to pick the best beach in the national park, since they are almost all so ruggedly beautiful, but Third Beach, at the end of a 1¹/₂-mile trail, is one of our personal favorites. Here you can listen to the calls of the eagles and gulls and contemplate the sheer vast-ness of the Pacific. See Chapter 8.
- **Cannon Beach/Ecola State Park** (OR): With the massive monolith of Hay-stack Rock rising up from the low-tide line and the secluded beaches of Ecola State Park just south of town, Cannon Beach offers all the best of the Oregon coast. See Chapter 12.

- **Oswald West State Park** (OR): It's a 15-minute walk down to the beach at this state park south of Cannon Beach, which keeps the sands from ever getting too crowded. The crescent-shaped beach is on a secluded cove backed by dense forest. This also happens to be a favorite surfing spot. See Chapter 12.
- **Bandon** (OR): It's difficult to imagine a more picturesque stretch of coastline than the beach in Bandon. Haystack rocks rise up from sand and sea as if strewn there by some giant hand. Motels and houses front this scenic beach, which ensures its popularity no matter what the weather. See Chapter 12.
- **Sunset Bay State Park** (OR): Almost completely surrounded by sandstone cliffs, this little beach near Coos Bay is on a shallow cove. The clear waters here get a little bit warmer than unprotected waters elsewhere on the coast, so it's sometimes possible to actually go swimming. See Chapter 12.

4 The Best Hikes

- **Trails out of Sunrise:** The Sunrise area, on the northeast flanks of Washington's Mount Rainier, offers fabulous unobstructed views of both the mountain and Emmons Glacier, the largest glacier in the contiguous 48 states. From Sunrise more than a dozen trails of different lengths head off to viewpoints and lakes. Take your pick. See Chapter 7.
- **Cascade Pass Trail:** This is the single most popular and rewarding hike in North Cascades National Park, WA. Before you even start hiking there are stupendous vistas of jagged granite peaks all around, and as you climb up to the pass, the views just get better. The energetic can continue up to the foot of a glacier. See Chapter 7.
- **Trails out of Hurricane Ridge:** Hurricane Ridge is the most easily accessible alpine region of Olympic National Park, WA, and from here and nearby Obstruction Peak there are several possible hikes of varying durations that will give you a glimpse of a superb part of the Olympic wilderness. See Chapter 8.
- **Eagle Creek Trail:** This trail on the Oregon side of the Columbia Gorge follows the tumbling waters of Eagle Creek and passes two spectacular waterfalls in the first 2 miles. Along the way, the trail climbs up the steep gorge walls; in places, it's cut right into the basalt cliffs. See Chapter 11.
- **Timberline Trail:** As the name implies, this trail starts at the timberline, near the famous lodge of the same name. Because this route circles Mount Hood, OR, you can start in either direction and make a day, overnight, or multiday hike of it. Paradise Park, its meadows ablaze with wildflowers in July and August, is a favorite for both day hikes and overnight trips. See Chapter 11.
- **Deschutes River Trail:** The Deschutes River, which flows down from the east side of the Cascades, passes through open ponderosa pine forest to the west of Bend, OR. Paralleling the river, and passing tumultuous waterfalls along the way, is an easy trail that's popular with hikers, mountain bikers, and joggers. See Chapter 15.

5 The Best Scenic Drives

- **Chuckanut Drive:** This road winds south from Bellingham, WA, through the Chuckanut Mountains, which rise straight up from the waters of Samish Bay; across the waters lie the San Juan Islands. The sunsets are spectacular. There are several good seafood restaurants along the way where you can sample fresh oysters, on the half shell or in a creamy oyster stew. See Chapter 6.

- **The North Cascades Highway:** Passing through the most rugged and spectacular mountains in the Northwest, this highway was not opened until 1972 because of the difficulty of building any sort of road through Washington's glacier-carved North Cascades. See Chapter 7.
- **Historic Columbia River Highway:** Opened in 1915 to allow automobiles access to the wonders of the Columbia Gorge, this narrow, winding highway east of Portland, OR, climbs up to the top of the gorge for a scenic vista before diving into the forests, dotted with waterfalls. See Chapter 11.
- **Gold Beach to Brookings:** No other stretch of U.S. 101 along the Oregon coast is more breathtaking than the segment between Gold Beach and Brookings. This remote coastline is dotted with offshore islands, natural rock arches, sea caves, bluffs, and beaches. Take your time, stop at the many pull-offs, and make this a leisurely all-day drive. See Chapter 12.
- **Crater Lake Loop Drive:** Circling the massive caldera that holds Crater Lake is this scenic drive along the rim. Along the way are numerous pull-offs where you can gasp in astonishment at the sapphire-blue waters and the ever-changing scenery. See Chapter 14.

6 The Best Bed-and-Breakfast Inns

- **The Inn at Swifts Bay** (Lopez Island, WA; ☎ 360/468-3636): Though the superb breakfasts here alone would be enough to qualify this place as one of the best B&Bs in the region, the secluded setting on laid-back Lopez Island makes this a superb getaway spot. See Chapter 6.
- **Loganita by the Sea** (Lummi Island, WA; ☎ 360/758-2651): Lummi Island, out of the San Juan Islands mainstream, is a tranquil hideaway, and this century-old island estate captures the feel of a bygone, and more relaxed, era. Spacious lawns surround the inn and the views across the water are as expansive as you'll find anywhere in the Northwest. See Chapter 6.
- **Ann Starrett Mansion** (Port Townsend, WA; ☎ 360/385-3205): This is *the* premier Victorian B&B in the Northwest. The outrageously ornate Queen Anne–style mansion is packed to the rafters with antiques. Staying here will feel a bit like staying in a museum. See Chapter 8.
- **Ziggurat** (Yachats, OR; ☎ 541/547-3925): A boldly styled contemporary pyramid-shaped home built right on the beach, this is the Oregon coast's most visually stunning B&B. Its setting, near one of the breathtaking stretches of coast, makes this place a winner. See Chapter 12.
- **Sylvia Beach Hotel** (Newport, OR; ☎ 541/265-5428): Taking literature as its theme and decorating its rooms to evoke different authors—from Edgar Allan Poe to Dr. Seuss—the Sylvia Beach Hotel is the most original B&B in the Northwest. The fact that it's only a block from the beach is just icing on the cake. See Chapter 12.
- **Old Stage Inn** (Jacksonville, OR; ☎ 541/899-1776 or 800/US-STAGE): Located on the outskirts of Jacksonville, which is a designated National Historic District, this inn offers luxurious accommodations in a restored 1857 Greek revival farmhouse. In the front parlor, a baby grand piano, fireplace, and gaming table hold promises of long relaxing evenings. See Chapter 14.

7   The Best Small Country Inns

- **The Inn at Langley** (Whidbey Island, WA; ☎ 360/221-3033): The setting alone, overlooking the Saratoga Passage, would be enough to rank this place firmly among the best small inns in the region. Japanese-influenced styling, soaking tubs with water views, and fireplaces all add up to a romantic retreat. See Chapter 6.
- **La Conner Channel Lodge** (La Conner, WA; ☎ 360/466-1500): Set on the shore of the Swinomish Channel, this inn is steeped in Northwest styling. River rocks and weathered wood siding lend an air of age to the exterior, which is brightened by lovely perennial gardens. In the guest rooms, balconies, fireplaces, fir accents, and slate floors yield an unexpected sophistication. See Chapter 6.
- **Columbia Gorge Hotel** (Hood River, OR; ☎ 541/386-5566 or 800/ 345-1921): Built in 1915 to handle the first car traffic up the Columbia Gorge, this mission-style hotel commands a stunning view across the gorge and is surrounded by colorful gardens. The breakfasts are legendary. See Chapter 11.
- **Tu Tu Tun Lodge** (Gold Beach, OR; ☎ 541/247-6664): Though some might think of this as a fishing lodge, it's far too luxurious for anglers to keep to themselves. A secluded setting on the lower Rogue River guarantees tranquillity, and choice guest rooms provide the perfect setting for forgetting about your everyday stress. The dining room serves excellent meals. See Chapter 12.
- **Stephanie Inn** (Cannon Beach, OR; ☎ 503/436-2221 or 800/633-3466): Combining the look of a mountain lodge with a beachfront setting in Oregon's most artistic town, the Stephanie Inn is a romantic retreat that surrounds its guests with unpretentious luxury. See Chapter 12.
- **Channel House** (Depoe Bay, OR; ☎ 541/765-2140 or 800/447-2140): Situated on the cliff above the channel into tiny Depoe Bay, this small lodge offers one of the most striking settings on the Oregon coast. The contemporary design includes guest rooms made for romance—a hot tub on the balcony, a fire in the fireplace, and an unsurpassed view out the windows. See Chapter 12.
- **Steamboat Inn** (Steamboat, OR; ☎ 541/498-2411): Oregon's North Umpqua River is legendary for its steelhead fishing and this is where you stay if you want to return to elegance and comfort after a day of fishing. The word is out on this inn, and many guests now show up with no intention of casting a fly into the river's waters. They'd rather just sit back and watch the river flow. See Chapter 14.

8   The Best Historic Hotels & Lodges

- **Captain Whidbey Inn** (Whidbey Island, WA; ☎ 360/678-4097 or 800/ 366-4097): This unusual inn was built in 1907 of local madrona-tree logs, which give it a thoroughly unique appearance. The island's seafaring history is evoked throughout the inn, and the seat in front of the lobby's beach-stone fireplace is a wonderful spot to while away a gray afternoon. See Chapter 6.
- **Roche Harbor Resort** (San Juan Island, WA; ☎ 360/378-2155 or 800/ 451-8910): Established in 1886 as part of a limestone business, this is the oldest hotel in all the San Juan Islands. The shimmering white clapboard buildings, surrounded by colorful manicured gardens, have a timeless appeal, with porches

that wrap around both floors of the hotel and overlook the old-fashioned marina. See Chapter 6.

- **Paradise Inn** (Mt. Rainier National Park, WA; ☎ 360/569-2275): Perched high on the slopes of Washington's Mount Rainier, this classic mountain lodge was built in 1917, and though it's a bit faded from hard use, it's always packed throughout its short May to October season. See Chapter 7.
- **Timberline Lodge** (Mount Hood, OR; ☎ 503/231-7979 or 800/547-1406): Built by the WPA during the Great Depression, this stately mountain lodge is a showcase for the skills of the craftspeople who created it, with a grand stone fireplace, exposed beams, and wide plank floors. The views of Mount Hood's peak, and of the Oregon Cascades to the south, are superb. See Chapter 11.
- **Crater Lake Lodge** (Crater Lake National Park, OR; ☎ 541/594-2511): Though only a small portion of the original structure was salvaged during its reconstruction, it still maintains the feel of a classic mountain lodge, with a stone fireplace and ponderosa pine–bark walls in the Great Hall. The setting, high above jewel-like Crater Lake, is breathtaking. See Chapter 14.

9 The Best Resorts

- **The Inn at Semiahmoo** (Blaine, WA; ☎ 360/371-2000 or 800/822-4200 in the U.S., 800/631-4200 in Canada): Located on a spit of land looking across the water to Canada, this beach resort offers a chance to get away from it all and still get in a few rounds of golf or a few tennis matches. See Chapter 6.
- **Sun Mountain Lodge** (Winthrop, WA; ☎ 509/996-2211 or 800/572-0493): Set on a mountaintop above the Methow Valley in the Washington Cascades, this four-season resort has miles of cross-country ski trails, hiking and mountain-biking trails, a lake with boat rentals, and views that just won't quit. See Chapter 7.
- **Skamania Lodge** (Stevenson, OR; ☎ 509/427-7700 or 800/221-7117): Golf with a very distracting view of the Oregon side of the Columbia Gorge is what makes this modern but rustic retreat east of Portland a popular weekend getaway spot. See Chapter 11.
- **Salishan Lodge** (Gleneden Beach, OR; ☎ 541/764-3600 or 800/452-2300): This place has long been the quintessential Oregon coast resort and offers accom-modations set amid the lush forest and plenty of holes of golf. The only drawback is that the beach is a bit of a hike. See Chapter 12.
- **Black Butte Ranch** (Sisters, OR; ☎ 541/595-6211 or 800/452-7455): This former ranch offers wide-open views and a world unto itself. The Three Sisters peaks are the backdrop for golf, horseback riding, canoeing, tennis, and numerous other activities. See Chapter 15.
- **Sunriver Lodge & Resort** (Bend, OR; ☎ 541/593-1221 or 800/547-3922): Popular in both summer for golfing and family vacations and in winter for skiers spending time on the slopes of Mount Bachelor, this resort offers so much to do that it's really a sort of summer camp for families. Bicycle trails wind for miles through the property. See Chapter 15.

10 The Best Restaurants

- **Dahlia Lounge** (Seattle, WA; ☎ 206/682-4142): Though crab cakes are the all-time favorite dish at this popular restaurant, chef Tom Douglas lets his culinary creativity range the globe, translating what he finds into quintessentially northwestern dishes. See Chapter 5.

- **Fuller's** (Seattle, WA; ☎ 206/447-5544): This elegant and refined restaurant in the Sheraton Seattle Hotel has managed to maintain its enviable reputation for many years now, despite changes in chefs. Dishes are beautifully presented and draw on the bounty of the Northwest for their inspiration. See Chapter 5.

- **Rover's** (Seattle, WA; ☎ 206/325-7442): This little cottage restaurant in an unassuming neighborhood east of downtown Seattle is a stage for the French-Northwest culinary fusions of chef Thierry Rautureau. Every course here surprises with flavors both subtle and bold. See Chapter 5.

- **The Herbfarm** (Fall City, WA; ☎ 206/784-2222): This restaurant, located east of Seattle near Issaquah, in the Cascade foothills, started out as a roadside herb farm but has since grown to become one of the most highly acclaimed restaurants in the Northwest. See Chapter 5.

- **Bay Cafe** (Lopez Island, WA; ☎ 360/468-3700): Small and casual, this cafe on quiet Lopez Island has become a local institution that sums up the Lopez experience. Fresh seafood and local wines combine for memorable meals. See Chapter 6.

- **The Shoalwater Restaurant** (Seaview, WA; ☎ 360/642-4142): Located on the tourist-clogged Long Beach Peninsula, this restaurant succeeds in conjuring up an atmosphere far removed from the reality outside the door. Seek out the dishes made with cranberries, which are grown locally. See Chapter 8.

- **Genoa** (Portland, OR; ☎ 503/238-1464): Genoa serves Italian fare like you've never tasted before. Many a Mediterranean restaurant could take a few lessons here. The seven-course dinners are feasts for the eyes and mouth, and the handful of tables assure very personal service. See Chapter 10.

- **Wildwood** (Portland, OR; ☎ 503/248-WOOD): At the head of a new wave of Portland restaurants that have been garnering the sort of publicity once reserved for Seattle restaurants, Wildwood immerses diners in an ethos of urban chic. The menu draws on all that's current in culinary trends. See Chapter 10.

- **Zefiro Restaurant & Bar** (Portland, OR; ☎ 503/226-3394): For several years now this little restaurant has been the most popular dining spot in Portland—the place to be seen. The menu is primarily Mediterranean in focus and the decor is minimalist. See Chapter 10.

- **Chateaulin** (Ashland, OR; ☎ 541/482-2264): Though the raison d'être of Ashland may be Shakespeare, it is memories of the French cuisine at Chateaulin that many theater-goers recall most fondly after they have left town. The dishes are hearty and the decor is theatrically country French. See Chapter 14.

11 The Best of Northwestern Cuisine

- **Smoked Salmon:** Smoked salmon has been a staple of the Northwest diet for thousands of years, and though salmon runs have been decimated, you can still get smoked salmon (sometimes made from Alaskan or farm-raised fish) all over the region. The very best comes from Karla's Smoke House in Rockaway Beach, OR.

- **Dungeness Crab:** Smaller than an Alaska king crab but larger than a Maryland blue crab, the Dungeness crab is a hefty crustacean with thick legs and plenty of meat. You'll find it prepared any number of ways in the region's restaurants, but you can also buy whole cooked crabs in grocery stores at very reasonable prices. At the Pike Place Market in Seattle, fish markets will pack your crab on ice in a container that you can take on a plane. They'll also ship it almost anywhere in the United States.

- **Pinot Noir:** Oregon's Willamette Valley produces some of the best pinot noir wine in the world. At wineries in the Dundee and Newberg area, you can taste a variety of these oak-aged wines and decide which ones you like. Personally we're not big pinot noir fans, but those produced at Lange Winery in Dundee are superb, though very pricey.

- **Berries:** Wild blackberries are ubiquitous in the Northwest and find their way into scrumptious pies, jams, jellies, and juices. Many superior cultivars have also been developed, and during the summer you can find marionberries, boysenberries, loganberries, ollalieberries, red raspberries, golden raspberries, and others at farmstands, in groceries, and on restaurant menus.

- **Aplets & Cotlets:** These unusual gummy candies are sold in gourmet shops all over the country, and in the town of Cashmere, near Leavenworth, WA, you can tour the kitchens where they're made. If you do make it to Cashmere, don't miss an opportunity to try some of the unusual flavors that are available here at the factory.

- **Hazelnuts:** Oregon is known the world over for producing the best hazelnuts, which are also known as filberts. We like smoked hazelnuts, but roasted and salted ones are good, too. These nuts are at their very best when mixed with chocolate.

- **Wild Mushrooms:** Everyone knows that it rains a lot in the Northwest, but what you might not know is that there's an upside to all that rain—mushrooms. The Northwest has such an abundance of wild mushrooms that the past few years have seen the equivalent of mushroom wars between mushroom hunters. Morels and chanterelles are the most common and show up frequently on restaurant menus.

12   The Best Microbreweries

- **Pacific NW Brewing Company** (Seattle, WA; ☎ 206/621-7021): Located in the heart of the Pioneer Square historic district, this big, busy pub feels as if it has been here since logs skidded down nearby Yesler Way. Its cask-conditioned ales are generally excellent. See Chapter 5.

- **Thomas Kemper Brewery** (Poulsbo, WA; ☎ 360/697-1446): This pub isn't very large and is a bit out of the way, but that hasn't stopped the folks living on the west side of Puget Sound from making it their favorite spot for a pint. Fruit-flavored ales are the summer specialty. See Chapter 5.

- **Grant's Pub** (Yakima, WA; ☎ 509/575-2922): Located in a restored railroad depot in downtown Yakima, which is hops country as well as wine country, this pub specializes in Scottish-style ales. See Chapter 9.

- **Bridgeport Brewery & Brewpub** (Portland, OR; ☎ 503/241-7179): Since it's the oldest brewpub in Portland, you could say this is the place that got the Northwest taps flowing. It's housed in the oldest industrial building in the city, a warehouse with a very medieval look. Don't miss the cask-conditioned ales. See Chapter 10.

- **Edgefield Brewery** (Troutdale, OR; ☎ 503/669-8610): Housed in the former county poor farm, this pub is part of a complex that includes a B&B, a hostel, restaurants, and a movie theater. There's always a wide selection of McMenamin brothers ales on tap. See Chapter 11.

- **Cornelius Pass Roadhouse** (Hillsboro, OR; ☎ 503/640-6174): Located 15 miles west of Portland, this brewpub is owned by the same people who created the Edgefield Brewery and is housed in an old farmhouse. On summer afternoons and evenings, the picnic tables all around the big shady yard are packed with people happily downing pints and noshing on pub grub. See Chapter 10.

13   The Best Museums

- **Seattle Art Museum:** An outstanding collection of Northwest Coast Native American art and artifacts is the highlight of this museum, but the African art exhibit is equally impressive. The 20th-century art collection includes a respectable exhibition of works by regional artists. See Chapter 5.
- **Museum of Flight** (Seattle, WA): As the home of Boeing, Seattle has played a historic role in the history of flight, and this museum reflects this heritage with its diverse collection of planes. The location, adjacent to Boeing Field, allows visitors to watch planes taking off and landing as they study the museum displays.
- **Columbia Gorge Interpretive Center** (Stevenson, OR): With historical photos, quotations from pioneers, and exhibits on various aspects of historic and prehistoric life in the Columbia Gorge, this museum serves as a valuable introduction to one of the Northwest's scenic wonders. See Chapter 11.
- **Oregon Trail Interpretive Center** (north of Baker City, OR): The lives of pioneers, who gave up everything to venture overland to the Pacific Northwest, are documented at this evocative museum. Set atop a hill in sagebrush country, the museum overlooks wagon ruts left by pioneers. See Chapter 15.
- **High Desert Museum** (Bend, OR): With its popular live-animal exhibits, this is more a zoo than a museum, but exhibits also offer glimpses into the history of the vast and little-known desert that stretches from the Cascades eastward to the Rocky Mountains. See Chapter 15.

14   The Best Places to Discover Northwest Native American Culture & History

- **Suquamish Museum** (Poulsbo, WA): This museum, across the Puget Sound from Seattle, features an exhibit that presents local Native American history through the eyes of Chief Sealth, for whom Seattle is named. See Chapter 5.
- **Makah Museum** (Neah Bay, WA): This museum is located on the northwesternmost tip of the Olympic Peninsula and contains artifacts recovered from a nearby archaeological site. In the museum are totem poles, dugout canoes, and even a mock-up of a native longhouse complete with smoked salmon hanging from the rafters. See Chapter 8.
- **Yakama Indian Nation Cultural Center** (Toppenish, WA): The museum at this cultural center provides a glimpse into the history and the culture of the Yakama people who for thousands of years roamed this region, following the natural cycles of the seasons. See Chapter 9.
- **Horsethief Lake State Park** (east of the Dalles on the Washington side of the

Columbia River): This park overlooks the site of the Celilo Falls, which were the most prolific salmon-fishing grounds on the river before they were flooded by the waters behind the Dalles Dam. In the park are Native American petroglyphs that date back hundreds of years. See Chapter 11.

- **The Museum at Warm Springs** (on the Warm Springs Reservation in central OR): This modern museum houses an outstanding collection of artifacts from the area's Native American tribes. See Chapter 15.
- **Favell Museum of Western Art and Indian Artifacts** (Klamath Falls, OR): This museum houses an absolutely amazing assortment of Native American artifacts, including thousands of arrowheads, spear points, and other stone tools. See Chapter 14.

15 The Best Family Attractions

- **Enchanted Village and Wild Waves** (Federal Way, WA): Kids of all ages have a blast at this combination water park and children's amusement park south of Seattle. See Chapter 5.
- **Point Defiance Park** (Tacoma, WA): This gigantic city park at the north end of Tacoma packs in more fun stuff for kids to see and do than a family could ever hope to pack into one day. There's a zoo, a storybook land, a reconstructed historic trading fort, and an old-time logging camp. See Chapter 6.
- **Oregon Coast Aquarium** (Newport, OR): This modern aquarium is the biggest attraction on the coast. Tufted puffins and sea otters steal the show, but tidepools, jellyfish tanks, and a giant octopus all contribute to the appeal of this very realistically designed public aquarium. See Chapter 12.
- **Sea Lion Caves** (on the OR coast north of Florence): This massive cave is home to hundreds of Steller sea lions that lounge on the rocks of this protected cave beneath busy U.S. 101. See Chapter 12.
- **West Coast Game Park Safari** (Bandon, OR): The opportunity to pet wild animal babies, including leopards and bears, doesn't come often, so it's hard to pass up this roadside attraction on the southern Oregon coast. See Chapter 12.
- **Wildlife Safari** (Winston, OR): This drive-through wildlife park south of Roseburg provides a chance to get close to wild animals with no bars. The setting is even reminiscent of the African plains. See Chapter 14.

16 The Best Small Towns

- **La Conner** (WA): Surrounded by tulip fields and filled with art galleries and interesting shops, this former fishing and farming town gets jammed on weekends, but if you stop by on a weekday or in the off-season, you can easily be seduced by the vintage charm. See Chapter 6.
- **Leavenworth** (WA): Done over as a Bavarian village, this town in Washington's Cascades is popular in both winter and summer. You can get all the bratwurst and sauerkraut you could ever want and pick up a cuckoo clock as well. Sure, it's tacky, but at least it's well done. See Chapter 7.
- **Port Townsend** (WA): Late in the 19th century, this town on the Olympic Peninsula was poised to become the region's most important city, but when the

railroad passed it by, it slipped into obscurity. Today Port Townsend is obscure no more. With block after block of Victorian homes and a waterfront setting, it has become a favorite weekend destination for Seattleites. See Chapter 8.

- **Cannon Beach** (OR): This little town on the Oregon coast is well on its way to becoming another Carmel or Mendocino. There's a stunning stretch of beach, the downtown is full of art galleries and crafts shops, the weatherbeaten cottages and modern beach houses are surrounded by colorful flower gardens, and there are good restaurants and hotels. What more could you ask for? See Chapter 12.

- **Ashland** (OR): At six hours from either San Francisco or Portland, Ashland seems an unlikely cultural mecca, but that's exactly what it is. All summer long the town stays packed with theater-goers who come to see Shakespeare performed under the stars at the Oregon Shakespeare Festival. B&Bs and good restaurants fill the town, at the center of which is a beautiful park. See Chapter 14.

- **Jacksonville** (OR): Founded as a gold-mining town in 1851, Jacksonville is one of the best-preserved historic towns in the Northwest. Its stately Victorian homes and old brick commercial buildings have almost all been restored. The annual Britt Festivals each summer stage performances by musicians and dancers of international acclaim. See Chapter 14.

17 The Most Interesting Historical Sites

- **Chief Sealth's Grave** (Suquamish, WA): Chief Sealth, for whom the city of Seattle is named, is buried in a mission cemetery just west of Bainbridge Island. The grave is topped both with a stone and Suquamish wood carvings. With its many offerings left by visitors, the grave has the feel of a shrine. See Chapter 5.

- **San Juan Island National Historic Park:** Dedicated to preserving the history of San Juan Island's forgotten Pig War (that never was), this park affords a look at what life was like for soldiers stationed in this remote location in Washington more than 100 years ago. See Chapter 6.

- **Fort Clatsop National Memorial** (Astoria, OR): This small log fort is a reconstruction of the fort that explorers Lewis and Clark built during the winter of 1805–06. Costumed interpreters bring the history of the fort to life. See Chapter 12.

- **Granite** (near Baker City, OR): This weatherbeaten ghost town in the Blue Mountains is left over from a gold rush that brought miners to this region in the late 1800s. The schoolhouse, general store, and bordello are still standing and are identified with signs. See Chapter 15.

- **Oregon Trail Wagon Ruts** (Baker City, OR): It's hard to believe that something as ephemeral as a wagon rut can last more than 150 years, but the trail left by the thousands of pioneers who followed the Oregon Trail cut deep into the land. Among other places, you can see ruts near the Oregon Trail Interpretive Center. See Chapter 15.

- **Kam Wah Chung Museum** (John Day, OR): This unusual little museum is way off the beaten track, but is well worth a visit if you're anywhere in the vicinity. The museum preserves the home, office, and apothecary of a Chinese doctor who ministered to the local Chinese community in the early part of this century. See Chapter 15.

18   The Best Offbeat Attractions

- **Seattle Underground Tour** (Seattle, WA): The jokes are bad and the history isn't the stuff of your high school textbooks, but this tour beneath the sidewalks of Seattle provides an opportunity to delve into the dark underside of the city. See Chap-ter 5.
- **Ye Olde Curiosity Shop** (Seattle, WA): Curious it is, with two-headed calves, mummies, shrunken heads, and much, much more. This shop is a long-time fixture of the Seattle waterfront and does a brisk business in cheap souvenirs. See Chapter 5.
- **Dick and Jane's Spot** (Ellensburg, WA): Fans of folk art won't want to miss this colorful conglomeration of artworks made from found objects. The art is all on display in Dick and Jane's yard. See Chapter 9.
- **The Oregon Vortex and House of Mystery** (Gold Hill, OR): Bring the kids here before they learn too much science and they'll be convinced that they have visited one of the most mysterious places on earth. See Chapter 14.
- **Where's the Art? The Church of Elvis** (Portland, OR): This odd little place is far more than an altar of Elvis worship; it's a cathedral of kitsch. If your sense of humor is warped, you'll love this place. See Chapter 10.

Getting to Know Washington & Oregon

2

Washington and Oregon, the upper left-hand corner of the nation, are together an amalgam of American life and landscapes; within their boundaries these two states reflect a part of almost every region of the country. Take a bit of New England's rural beauty: covered bridges, steepled churches, and familiar place names such as Portland and Springfield. Temper the climate to that of the upper South to avoid harsh winters. Now bring in some low rolling mountains like the Appalachians; rugged, glaciated mountains like the Rockies; and even volcanoes, as in Hawaii. Add a river as large and as important as the Mississippi, with paddlewheel steamers. Toss in a coastline as rugged as California's and an island-filled inland sea that offers as many sailing opportunities as the coast of Maine. Of course there would have to be sagebrush and cowboys and Indians. Even the deserts of the Southwest and the wheat fields of the Midwest could be added. The wine country of California would be a nice touch, and so would some long sandy beaches. On top of all this there should be a beautiful city, one with hills and a waterfront like those in San Francisco. Mix all of these things together and you have a portrait of the Northwest.

1 The Natural Environment

Together the two states of Washington and Oregon encompass a vast area that contains within its boundaries an amazing diversity of natural environments—not only lush forests, but also deserts, glacier-covered peaks, grasslands, alpine meadows, and sagebrush-covered hills. Together these diverse environments support a surprisingly wide variety of natural life that has evolved to fill the many niches created by Northwest geography.

The Pacific Northwest coastline stretches for 450 miles from northern California to the tip of the Olympic Peninsula, and much of this length is only sparsely populated. Consequently, the shore provides a habitat not only for large populations of seabirds such as cormorants, tufted puffins, and pigeon guillemots, but also several species of marine mammals. The largest and most impressive marine mammals to frequent these shores are the more than 20,000 Pacific gray whales that visit Northwest shores between December and April as they make their annual migration south to their breeding grounds off Baja California. These whales can often be seen from shore at various points along the Washington and Oregon coasts, and numerous whale-watching tours operate along this stretch. More frequently spotted, however, are harbor seals and Steller's and California sea lions, which are frequently seen lounging on rocks. Sea Lion Caves and Cape Arago State Park, both on the Oregon coast, are two of the best places to spot sea lions. Off the remote beaches of the Olympic Peninsula, there's also a small population of sea otters.

Giving the coastline its characteristic rugged look are two mountain ranges—the Coast Range in Oregon and the Olympic Mountains in Washington. However, even more than mountains, rain gives these coastlines their definitive character. As moist winds from the Pacific Ocean rise up and over the coastal mountain ranges, they drop their moisture as rain and snow. In the northwest corner of Washington state, on the western slopes of the Olympic Mountains, rain falls not by the inch but by the foot. Rainfall here can exceed 12 feet! This tremendous amount of rain has produced the country's only temperate rain forests and some of the largest trees on earth. Although the Sitka spruce is the most characteristic tree of these rain forests, it is the Douglas fir, common throughout the Northwest and second only to the coast redwood of northern California in overall size, that's the most impressive, sometimes reaching 300 feet in height. Other common trees of the rain forest include western hemlocks, Alaska cedars, western red cedars, and big-leaf maples. These latter trees are often draped with thick mats of mosses.

More than a century of intensive logging has, however, left the region's forests of centuries-old trees shrunken to remnant groves scattered in often remote and rugged areas. How much exactly is still left is a matter of hot debate between the timber industry and environmentalists, and the battle to save the remaining old-growth forests continues, with both sides claiming victories and losses with each passing year. Among this region's most celebrated and controversial wild residents is the northern spotted owl, which, because of its large requirements for undisturbed old growth forest and its listing as a federally endangered species, brought logging of old-growth forests to a virtual halt over the past few years. Today concern is also focusing on the marbled murrelet, a small bird that feeds on the open ocean but nests exclusively in old-growth forests.

The Olympic Mountains, which rise to 7,965 feet at the top of Mount Olympus, are a rugged range capped with alpine meadows, glaciers, and ice fields. Although deer are the most common large mammals of these mountains, there is also a population of mountain goats in Olympic National Park. However, these goats are not native to this area and attempts are being made to remove them because of the damage they cause the fragile high-elevation meadows. This removal program has proven controversial and expensive, and currently a new plan to deal with the problem is under study. The Roosevelt elk, the largest commonly encountered land mammals in the Northwest, can be found here and throughout the western regions of Washington and Oregon. It was to protect these animals that the land now known as Olympic National Park was originally set aside.

Behind the coastal mountains lies a lowland area comprised of the Willamette Valley and the Puget Sound region. Because of the mild climate of this lowland region, these areas have become the region's most densely populated. The most striking feature of these lowlands is Puget Sound, a maze of waterways that was formed by glacial activity during the last Ice Age. The polar ice sheets that stretched southward into the region carved out long narrow valleys that were later flooded as the glaciers retreated.

Just north of Puget Sound, in the waters surrounding the San Juan Islands, live some of the Northwest's most celebrated residents—orca whales, also known as killer whales. Once maligned, these largest members of the porpoise family have become a symbol of the region. With the plight of captive orcas brought to the public attention by the films *Free Willy* and *Free Willy II*, orcas have gained even more attention. Bald eagles also flock to this area. Though they can be seen throughout the year in Puget Sound and throughout the San Juan Islands, they gather in large numbers in winter on the nearby Skagit River.

To the east of the Puget-Willamette lowlands rise the mountains of the 700-mile-long Cascade range, which stretches from northern California to southern British Columbia. The most prominent features of the Cascades are its volcanic peaks: Baker, Rainier, St. Helens, Adams, and Hood. The eruption of Mount St. Helens on May 18, 1980, reminded Northwesterners that this is still a volcanically active region, and the remains of ancient Mount Mazama, which erupted with great violence 7,700 years ago, are today preserved as Crater Lake National Park. Near the town of Bend, geologically recent volcanic activity is also visible in the form of cinder cones, lava flows, and craters. Much of this volcanic landscape is now preserved as Newberry National Volcanic Monument.

The same rainfall that gives the Olympic Peninsula its rain forests leaves the Cascades with frequently heavy snows and dozens of glaciers, among which are the largest glacier, the lowest elevation glacier, and the only advancing glacier in the 48 contiguous states. In 1972, Mount Rainier set a record when $93^{1}/_{2}$ feet of snow fell.

Among the wild residents of the Cascades are mountain goats that can sometimes be seen in the North Cascades, along the shores of Lake Chelan, and in Mount Rainier National Park. Among the high country's smaller but more visible and audible residents are picas and marmots. The former is a mouse-sized relative of the rabbit, while the latter is the largest member of the squirrel family. Both live in high meadows and rocky slopes and both can be recognized by their distinctive whistles. The pica's is small and squeaky, while the marmot's is high, loud, and shrill. In the remote northern section of North Cascades National Park there are even wolves and grizzly bears, though these large predators are almost never encountered. Cougars also roam the forests throughout the Northwest and are even more elusive than the grizzly and the wolf.

East of the Cascades, less than 200 miles from the rain-forest valleys of the Olympic Peninsula, the landscape becomes a desert. Together, the Columbia Plateau of Washington and the Great Basin of Oregon comprise a vast, dry, high desert region that stretches to the Rockies. The Columbia Plateau was formed by sheets of lava flowing over the land and covering more than 100,000 square miles. Through this desolate landscape flows the Columbia River, which, together with its tributary the Snake, forms the second-largest river drainage in the United States. During the last Ice Age, roughly 13,000 years ago, a glacier blocked the flow of the Columbia, forming a huge lake behind its ice dam. This vast prehistoric lake repeatedly burst its ice dam, sending massive and devastating walls of water flooding down the Columbia. These floodwaters were sometimes 1,000 feet high and carried with them ice and rocks, which scoured out the Columbia Gorge. Today the gorge's many waterfalls are the most evident signs of such floods. These same floodwaters also scoured the landscape of eastern Washington, leaving in their wake abandoned river channels known as coulees and channeled scablands. The most famous of these coulees is Grand Coulee, site of one of the largest dams on earth.

How to Speak Northwestern

All across Washington and Oregon there are dozens of linguistic landmines waiting to trip up visitors to the region—place names that aren't pronounced the way they're spelled or that simply are so strange that no one could ever figure out how to pronounce them without a little coaching. So we include here a Northwest primer of place names to help nonnatives speak like locals and thus blend into the Northwest landscape. Think of the following knowledge as verbal camouflage.

Deschutes River	Duh-*shoots Riv*-ur
Heceta	Huh-*see*-tuh
Kalaloch	Kuh-*lay*-lock
Lake Chelan	Layk Shuh-*lan*
Methow Valley	*Met*-ou *Val*-ee
Oregon	*Ore*-uh-gun
Puyallup	Pew-*al*-up
Skagit	*Skaj*-it
Skamania	Skuh-*may*-nee-uh
Skamokawa	Skuh-*mock*-uh-way
Sequim	Skwim
Siuslaw	Sigh-*oos*-law
Spokane	Spo-*kan*
The Dalles	The Dals
Toutle River	*Too*-tul *Riv*-ur
Umatilla	You-muh-*til*-uh
Wallowa Mountains	Wuh-*lou*-uh *Moun*-tuns
Willamette River	Wih-*la*-met *Riv*-ur
Willapa	*Wi*-luh-puh
Yachats	*Yah*-hots

This and the dozens of other dams on the Columbia and Snake rivers have become the focus of one of the region's current environmental battles. Though many of these dams have fish ladders to allow salmon to return upriver to spawn, salmon populations have been steadily dwindling for more than a century. Overfishing for salmon canneries in the late 19th century struck the first major blow to salmon populations, and the large dams, mostly built during the middle part of this century, created further barriers both to returning adults and to young salmon headed downstream to the Pacific. Among the obstacles faced by these young salmon are slower river flow in the reservoirs behind the dams, turbines that kill fish by the thousands, and irrigation canals that often confuse salmon into swimming out of the river and into farm fields. Compounding the problem has been the use of fish hatcheries to supplement wild salmon populations (hatchery fish tend to be less vigorous than wild salmon). A salmon recovery plan was recently adopted to attempt to save threatened runs of native salmon, but farmers, electricity producers,

Washington

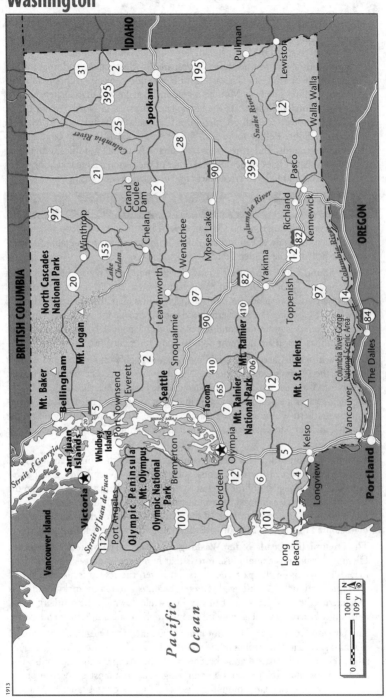

1913

shipping companies, and major users of hydroelectric power have continued to fight the requirements of the recovery plan, which includes lowering water levels in reservoirs to speed the downstream migration of young salmon.

South-central and southeastern Oregon are the most remote and unpopulated regions of the Northwest. This vast desert region does, however, support an abundance of wildlife. The Hart Mountain National Antelope Refuge shelters herds of pronghorn antelope, which are the fastest land mammal in North America. This refuge also protects a small population of California bighorn sheep. At Malheur National Wildlife Refuge more than 300 species of birds frequent large shallow lakes and wetlands, and at the Lower Klamath National Wildlife Refuge large numbers of bald eagles gather. Several other of the region's large lakes, including Summer Lake and Lake Abert, attract large populations of birds.

2   The Regions in Brief

The states of Washington and Oregon cover 154,893 square miles—roughly the same area as the state of California—and within this area is a geographical diversity unequaled in the United States.

Puget Sound   The Northwest's most densely populated region includes on its shores Seattle, Tacoma, Olympia, Bellingham, Everett, and Edmunds. The sound's maze of waterways extends for more than 100 miles. The area is characterized by hilly forested terrain. The southern sound is more heavily industrialized, while the northern sound is more rural and serves as a vacation area. The San Juan Islands and Whidbey Island are the most popular spots for excursions.

The Washington Cascades   Dividing the state roughly into eastern and western regions, the Washington Cascades are actually two very distinct mountain ranges. The North Cascades are jagged, glaciated granite peaks, while the southern Washington Cascades are primarily volcanic in origin. Mount St. Helens, an active volcano in southern Washington, last erupted in 1980. Also within this region are the North Cascades National Park, Mount Rainier National Park, and glacial Lake Chelan.

Eastern Washington   This area gets only a fraction of the rainfall characteristic of the western part of the state. Consequently, eastern Washington is a sparsely populated desert region of little interest to most tourists. Irrigation waters from the Columbia River have allowed the region to develop agriculturally. Spokane is the region's largest metropolitan area. In the southeast corner of the state lie the rolling Palouse Hills, whose rich soils are the most fertile wheat fields in the nation.

The Olympic Peninsula & the Washington Coast   The western slopes of the Olympic Mountains contain lush forests that have been almost completely decimated by logging in the past 100 years. However, the region is also the site of Olympic National Park. Rugged remote beaches separated by rocky headlands characterize the northern part of this region, while down on the southern coast, long sandy beaches prevail along with a concentration of beach resorts and towns.

The Oregon Coast   Stretching for nearly 300 miles, the Oregon coast is one of the most spectacular coastlines in the country. Backed by the Coast Range mountains, the coast alternates sandy beaches with rocky capes and headlands. The mountainous shoreline provides breathtaking vistas at almost every turn of the road. Haystack rocks, large monoliths just offshore, give the coast a drama and

Oregon

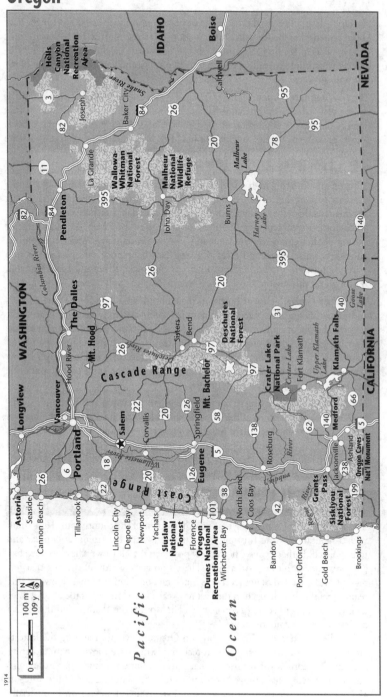

1914

beauty. Along the central coast, huge dunes, some as much as 500 feet high, have been preserved as the Oregon Dunes National Recreation Area. Small towns, some known as fishing ports and some as artists' communities, dot the coast. Unfortunately waters are generally too cold for swimming, and a cool breeze often blows even in summer.

The Willamette Valley   This is Oregon's most densely populated region, the home of Portland, Eugene, and Salem. The valley's farmland grows the greatest variety of crops of any region of the United States. Among these crops are hops, mint, grass seed, berries, and hazelnuts. The Willamette Valley is also a wine region, with vineyards cropping up along its entire length.

Central & Eastern Oregon   Large and sparsely populated, central and eastern Oregon are primarily high desert interspersed with small mountain ranges. In the western part of the region, Bend, Sunriver, and Sisters are developing as resort destinations that take advantage of the region's abundant sunshine, and the Mount Bachelor ski area provides the best skiing in the Northwest. In the northeast corner of the region rise the Blue and Wallowa mountains, which are remote, though popular, recreation areas. Carving North America's deepest gorge, and partially forming the border with Idaho, is the Snake River and Hells Canyon. Throughout this region, signs of the Oregon Trail can still be seen.

Columbia Gorge   East of Portland, the Columbia Gorge is one of the region's most breathtaking sites. Declared a national scenic area to preserve its beauty, the gorge is the site of numerous waterfalls, including Multnomah Falls, which are the fourth highest in the United States. Winds regularly blast through the gorge and have attracted sailboarding enthusiasts to the area. The town of Hood River is now one of the world's top sailboarding spots. Rising above the gorge on the south side is Mount Hood, the tallest peak in Oregon.

Southern Oregon   Lying midway between San Francisco and Portland, southern Oregon is best known as the site of Crater Lake National Park, which preserves the deepest lake in the United States. However, the region is also known for its many outdoor recreational opportunities, including near-legendary salmon and steelhead fishing on the Umpqua and Rogue rivers. The area is also known for cultural offerings, particularly in Ashland.

3   The Northwest Today

The Northwest has something that no other region of the country can claim—rain with a reputation—and this rain for many years kept the region unpopular and unpopulated. Perhaps you've heard how people in the Northwest have webbed feet and how they don't tan—they rust. There's no getting around the fact that few regions of the United States receive as much rain or cloudy weather. However, the region's rainfall has changed in the past few years. It no longer has the effect it once had. It's no longer keeping people away. The word is out that the Northwest is a beautiful place despite the rain.

For the past decade, Washington and Oregon have been among the fastest-growing states in the nation as high-tech industries have moved manufacturing here and Californians, fed up with that state's pollution, crime, congestion, and high cost of living, have moved north in search of a better quality of life. Oregon and Washington are today riding a boom that has fueled rapid growth, especially in the high-tech industries. Both Microsoft and Intel, two companies that dominate the computer industry, are headquartered in the Northwest, and many other smaller companies are locating here as well. This economic growth has, however, begun to undermine the very values that have allowed people living in the Northwest to ignore the weather. Urban sprawl, congested roads, and sky-rocketing housing costs are all changing the character of the Northwest. However, people in the two states are working hard to preserve the region's unique charac-ter and to keep cities such as Seattle and Portland as livable as they have always been. To see what it is that Northwesterners want preserved, it's only necessary to lift one's eyes to the far horizons. From almost anywhere in the two states it's possible to look up and see forests or mountains or sparkling waters.

Northwesterners don't let the weather stand between them and the outdoors. The temptation is too great to head for the hills, the river, the beach, the sound, or the islands, no matter what the weather. Consequently, life in Northwest cities tends to revolve less around cultural venues and other urban pastimes such as shopping, than around parks, gardens, waterfronts, and other outdoor spaces. Seattle has its lakes and Puget Sound; Portland its Forest Park, Rose Gardens, Japanese Gardens, and Waterfront Park; Eugene its riverside parks; and Spokane its Riverfront and Minto parks. These parks are where people find tranquillity, where summer festivals are held, where locals take their visiting friends and relatives.

This is not to say, however, that the region is a cultural wasteland. The Seattle Opera is one of the finest companies in the country, as is the Seattle Symphony, and Seattle has recently become a center for live theater. Portland, Tacoma, Olympia, and Eugene all have large, modern, and active performing arts centers. During the summer months numerous festivals take music, theater, and dance outdoors. Most impressive of these are the Oregon Shakespeare Festival and the Britt Festivals, both of which are staged in southern Oregon. However, there are also many other festivals featuring everything from chamber music to the grunge sound that first put Seattle on the alternative rock map several years ago. Even Hollywood has discovered the Northwest, and though the hit TV shows "Northern Exposure" and "Twin Peaks" are off the air now, film and television producers continue to head to the Northwest to shoot their productions. NBC's current hit "Frasier" brings a slice of Seattle life to TV viewers each week.

Coffee has been the region's biggest export of recent years. By now almost everyone has heard about the Seattle espresso scene that's slowly spreading to the rest of the country. Once an urban phenomenon, the demand for rich, strong espresso has spread to small towns throughout the region, and travelers exploring even the most remote parts of Washington or Oregon can find an espresso stand parked by the side of the road somewhere nearby.

This demand for only the best has also spread to the realm of malt beverages. Today the Northwest is the microbrewery capital of the country. Small breweries and brewpubs throughout Washington and Oregon are producing delicious and unique draft ales that range from light, fruit-flavored wheat beers to hearty, barleywine ales. Not to be left behind, the region's wineries are giving California a run for its money. Oregon pinot noirs are ranking up there with those from France, and chardonays, reislings, and many other varietals are getting good press.

Northwest politics has also been at the forefront of national news over the past few years. In 1992 the Northwest lost a long-standing member of Congress when Rep. Tom Foley, Speaker of the House, was voted out of office. That same year, Washington became one of the few states to choose a female senator when it elected Patty Murray. And Oregon Sen. Bob Packwood was the center of a scandal that has unfolded over the last couple of years. Packwood was first accused of sexual misconduct and then of tampering with evidence necessary to the Senate Ethics Committee's investigation of the misconduct charges. He resigned from the Senate in September 1995 after the committee recommended his expulsion. With the pronounced urban population growth over the past few years, politics has taken a very pronounced urban-rural split, with politicians in both states arguing that population centers such as Seattle and Portland are dictating the politics for rural regions that have little in common with the cities.

However, despite differences of opinions and politics, Washingtonians and Oregonians share a common interest in the outdoors, and it is this interest that dominates the character of the region. Nowhere else in the country is such a diverse natural beauty so close at hand, even for those who live in the cities. And if winters are long, gray, and rainy, well, you just put on a colorful rain jacket and head for the hills, mountains, rivers, or coast regardless.

4 History 101

Dateline

- **10,000 B.C.** Earliest known human inhabitation of the Northwest.
- **1542** Spanish exploratory ship reaches what is now the southern Oregon coast.
- **1579** Englishman Sir Francis Drake reaches the mouth of the Rogue River.
- **1602** Spain's Martín de Aguilar explores the coast of Oregon, probably as far as Coos Bay.
- **1774** Spanish explorer Juan Perez sails to 54° north latitude; Bruno de Heceta and Francisco de la Bodega y Quadra chart the Northwest coast.
- **1785** James Hanna becomes the first fur trader to ship pelts from the Northwest to China.
- **1805–6** Expedition led by Meriwether Lewis and William Clark crosses the continent and spends the winter at the mouth of the Columbia River.
- **1810** Americans attempt first settlement at the Columbia River's mouth.

continues

EARLY HISTORY Native Americans inhabiting the Northwest developed very distinct cultures depending on the food-gathering constraints of their territory. It's estimated that before the arrival of whites in the region, there were 125 Northwest tribes speaking 50 languages.

Between the 1780s, when white explorers and traders began frequenting the Northwest coast, and the 1830s, when the first settlers began arriving, the Native American population of the Northwest was reduced to perhaps a tenth of its historic numbers. It was not war that wiped out these people, but the white men's diseases—smallpox, measles, malaria, and influenza. The Native Americans had no resistance to these diseases and entire tribes were soon wiped out by fast-spreading epidemics.

THE AGE OF EXPLORATION Though a Spanish ship reached what is now southern Oregon in 1542, the Spanish had no interest in the gray and rainy coast. Nor did famed British buccaneer Sir Francis Drake, who in 1579 sailed his ship the *Golden Hind* as far north as the mouth of the Rogue River. Drake called off his explorations in the face of what he described as "thicke and stinking fogges."

Though the Spanish laid claim to all of North America's west coast, they had little interest in the lands north of Mexico. However, when the Spanish found out that Russian fur traders were establishing themselves in Alaska and along the North Pacific coast, Spain took a new interest in the Northwest. Several Spanish expeditions sailed north from Mexico to reassert the Spanish claim to the region. In 1775 Spanish explorers Bruno de Heceta and Francisco de la Bodega y Quadra charted much of the Northwest coast, and though they found the mouth of the Columbia River, they did not enter it.

Within a few years the Spanish found their claims to the region also being challenged by English traders. Capt. James Cook, on a voyage of discovery that began in 1776, spent time at Nootka Sound on Vancouver Island, where the native peoples were eager to trade furs. Though Cook was subsequently killed in Hawaii later in the same voyage, his crew discovered en route back to England that the Chinese would pay astronomical prices for Northwest furs, especially sea otter.

By 1785 the fur trade between the Northwest and China was underway, with the British now asserting a claim to the Pacific Northwest. The Spanish and English teetered on the brink of war, but a compromise was worked out and the Spanish agreed to allow continued English trade in the area.

The negotiations of this settlement took place in 1792 at Nootka Sound, with Capt. George Vancouver serving as English envoy. Before reaching Nootka Sound, Vancouver spent time exploring and mapping much of the Northwest. Though he passed the Columbia River off as unimportant, he sailed up the Strait of Juan de Fuca and discovered a large inland sea that he named Puget Sound, after one of his lieutenants. Vancouver's negotiations at Nootka failed to establish a firm British claim to the land, but with sea-otter populations decimated by several intense years of trading, interest in the Northwest was waning both in England and Spain.

Now a new player entered the Northwest arena of trade and exploration in the person of American trader Robert Gray. Risking a passage through treacherous sandbars, Gray sailed his ship, *Columbia Rediviva,* into the mouth of the long-speculated-upon Great River of the West, which he named Columbia's River after his ship. This discovery established the first American claim to the region.

When news of the Columbia's discovery reached the United States and England, both countries

- **1819** Spain cedes all lands above 42° north latitude.
- **1824–25** Russia gives up claims to land south of Alaska; Fort Vancouver founded by Hudson's Bay Company.
- **1840** First settlers move to what is now Oregon.
- **1843** First wagons cross the continent on the Oregon Trail.
- **1846** The 49th parallel is established as the boundary between American and British territories in the Northwest.
- **1847** Marcus and Narcissa Whitman and several other residents of their mission are massacred by the Cayuse.
- **1848** Oregon becomes first U.S. territory west of the Rockies.
- **1853** Washington becomes a U.S. territory.
- **1859** U.S. and Britain come to the brink of war over a pig killed on San Juan Island; Oregon becomes a state.
- **1860** Gold discovered in eastern Oregon.
- **1883** Northern Pacific Railroad connects Puget Sound with St. Paul, Minnesota.
- **1889** Washington becomes a state.
- **1897** Klondike gold rush begins.
- **1905** Lewis & Clark Exposition attracts worldwide attention to Oregon.
- **1916** William Boeing launches his first airplane on the waters of Seattle's Lake Union.
- **1940s** Kaiser shipyards in the Portland area become the world's foremost

continues

shipbuilders; Boeing airplane plants in Oregon turn out thousands of B-17s and B-29s.

- **1943** U.S. government builds top-secret plutonium-manufacturing plant in Hanford, Washington, which produces the nuclear material for the bomb dropped on Nagasaki; Japanese Americans are relocated to internment camps.

- **1945** Oregon becomes the only state to have civilian war casualties when six children are killed by a Japanese balloon bomb.

- **1962** Seattle's Century 21 world's fair gives the city its most identifiable structure—the Space Needle.

- **1980** Mount St. Helens erupts violently on May 18.

- **1980s** Microsoft becomes a world leader in the software field; the Northwest's timber industry suffers a severe economic downturn.

- **1994** Speaker of the U.S. House of Representatives Tom Foley of Washington voted out of office.

- **1995** Sen. Bob Packwood resigns after the Senate Ethics Committee recommends his expulsion for sexual misconduct.

began speculating on a northern water route across North America. Such a route, if it existed, would facilitate trade with the Northwest. In 1793 Scotsman Alexander MacKenzie made the first overland trip across North America north of New Spain. Crossing British Canada on foot, MacKenzie arrived somewhere north of Vancouver Island.

After reading MacKenzie's account of his journey, Thomas Jefferson decided that the United States needed to find a better route overland to the Northwest. To this end he commissioned Meriwether Lewis and William Clark to lead an expedition up the Missouri River in hopes of finding a single easy portage that would lead to the Columbia River. Beginning in 1804 the members of the Lewis and Clark expedition paddled up the Missouri, crossed the Rocky Mountains on foot, and then paddled down the Columbia River to its mouth. A French Canadian trapper and his Native American wife, Sacajawea, were enlisted as interpreters, and it was the presence of Sacajawea that helped the expedition gain acceptance among western tribes. After the very dismal, wet winter of 1805–06 spent at the mouth of the Columbia, the expedition headed back east. Discoveries made by the expedition added greatly to the scientific and geographical knowledge of the continent.

In 1819 the Spanish relinquished all claims north of the present California-Oregon state line, and the Russians gave up their claims to all lands south of Alaska. This left only the British and Americans dickering for control of the Northwest. **SETTLEMENT** Only six years after Lewis and Clark spent the winter at the mouth of the Columbia, employees of John Jacob Astor's Pacific Fur Company managed to establish themselves at a site they called Fort Astoria. The War of 1812 between the United States and Britain produced no firm decision about possession of the Northwest. The British still dominated the region, but American trade was tolerated.

With the decline of the sea-otter population, British fur traders turned to the beaver and headed inland up the Columbia River. For the next 30 years or so, fur-trading companies would be the sole authority in the Northwest. Fur-trading posts were established throughout the region, though most were on the eastern edge of the territory in the foothills of the Rocky Mountains. The powerful Hudson's Bay Company (HBC) eventually became the single fur-trading company in the Northwest.

In 1824 the HBC established its Northwest headquarters at Fort Vancouver, 100 miles up the Columbia near the mouth of the Willamette River. Between 1824 and 1846, when the 49th parallel was established as the boundary between British and American northwestern lands, Fort Vancouver was the most important settlement in the region.

By the 1830s the future of the Northwest had arrived in the form of American missionaries. The first was Jason Lee, who established his mission in the Willamette Valley near present-day Salem, Oregon. Two years later, in 1836, Marcus and Narcissa Whitman, along with Henry and Eliza Spaulding, made the overland trek to Fort Vancouver, then backtracked into what is now eastern Washington and Idaho, to establish two missions. This journey soon inspired other settlers to make the difficult overland crossing.

In 1840 a slow trickle of American settlers began crossing the continent, a 2,000-mile journey. Their destination was the Oregon country, which had been promoted as a veritable Eden where land was waiting to be claimed. In 1843 Marcus Whitman, after traveling east to plead with his superiors not to shut down his mission, headed back west, leading 900 settlers on the Oregon Trail. Before these settlers ever arrived, the small population of retired trappers, missionaries, and HBC employees who were living at Fort Vancouver and in nearby Oregon City had formed a provisional government in anticipation of the land-claim problems that would arise with the influx of settlers to the region.

Oregon City became, in 1844, the first incorporated town west of the Rocky Mountains. This outpost in the wilderness, a gateway to the fertile lands of the Willamette Valley, was the destination of the wagon trains that began traveling the Oregon Trail, each year bringing more and more settlers to the region. As the land in the Willamette Valley was claimed, settlers began fanning out to different regions of the Northwest so that during the late 1840s and early 1850s many new towns, including Seattle and Portland, were founded.

Many wagon trains stopped at the Whitman mission near present-day Walla Walla, and it was one of these groups of pioneers that brought the measles to the region. The Cayuse tribe, who lived at the Whitman mission, had no resistance to the disease, and soon the Cayuse population was decimated. Whitman and his family seemed immune to the disease. In retribution for Whitman's inability to cure the Native Americans of this horrible disease, several Cayuse attacked the mission and killed the Whitmans and several other whites who were staying there. Though the line between American and British land in the Northwest had been established at the 49th parallel (the current Canadian-American border) in 1846, Oregon was not given U.S. territorial status until 1848. It was the Whitman massacre and the subsequent demand for territorial status and U.S. military protection that brought about the establishment of the first U.S. territory west of the Rockies. However, Washington would not gain territorial status until 1853.

The establishment of the 49th parallel as the boundary between U.S. and British territories extended only as far as the main channel between the mainland and Vancouver Island, which was firmly in the hands of the British. However, because there was disagreement over where the main channel was, American and British troops jointly occupied San Juan Island. When, in 1859, a British pig rooting in an American soldier's potato patch was shot and killed, the two nations came to the brink of war. It took international arbitration to settle the disagreement, which was finally resolved by turning San Juan Island over to U.S. control. In that same year of 1859 Oregon gained statehood.

The discovery of gold in eastern Oregon in 1860 set the stage for one of the saddest chapters in Northwest history. With miners pouring into eastern Oregon and Washington, conflicts with Native Americans over land were inevitable. Since 1805, when Lewis and Clark had first passed this way, the Nez Percé tribes had been friendly to the white settlers. However, in 1877 a disputed treaty caused friction. Led by Chief Joseph, 700 Nez Percé, including 400 women and children, began a march from their homeland to their new reservation. Along the way, several angry young men, in revenge for the murder of an older member of the tribe, attacked a white settlement and killed several people. The U.S. Army took up pursuit of the Nez Percé, who fled across Idaho and Montana, only to be caught 40 miles from the Canadian border and sanctuary.

In 1883 the first transcontinental railroad linked the Northwest with the eastern United States. Tacoma was finally chosen by the Northern Pacific Railroad as the end of the tracks that extended from St. Paul, Minnesota. With the arrival of the railroads, the Northwest took a great leap forward in its development. No longer a remote wilderness, the region began to attract industry, and in 1889 Washington gained statehood.

INDUSTRIALIZATION & THE 20TH CENTURY   From the very beginning of white settlement in the Northwest, the region based its growth on an extractive economy. When, in 1848, gold was discovered in California, the Northwest benefited from the sudden demand for lumber and wheat. Even oysters were shipped from the Northwest to the tables of San Francisco restaurants. In 1897 another gold rush, this time in Alaska and the Klondike, brought sudden prosperity to Seattle, where merchants enjoyed a thriving business supplying hopeful miners with the tools of the trade.

Lumber and salmon were exploited ruthlessly. The history of the timber and salmon-fishing industries have run parallel for more than a century and have each led to similar results in the 1990s.

The trees in the Northwest grew to gigantic proportions. Nurtured on steady rains, such trees as Douglas fir, Sitka spruce, western red cedar, Port Orford cedar, and hemlock grew tall and straight, sometimes as tall as 300 feet. The first sawmill in the Northwest began operation near present-day Vancouver, Washington, in 1828. Between the 1850s and 1870s Northwest sawmills supplied the growing California market as well as a limited foreign market. When the transcontinental railroads arrived in the 1880s, a whole new market opened up and mills began shipping to the eastern states.

Sawmills developed a cut-and-run policy that leveled the forests. By the turn of the century the government had gained more control over public forests in an attempt to slow the decimation of forestlands, and sawmill owners were buying up huge tracts of land. At the outbreak of World War I, more than 20% of the forestland in the Northwest was owned by three companies—Weyerhauser, the Northern Pacific Railroad, and the Southern Pacific Railroad—and more than 50% of the workforce labored in the timber industry.

The timber industry has always been extremely susceptible to fluctuations in the economy and has experienced a roller-coaster ride of boom and bust throughout the 20th century. Boom times in the 1970s brought on record-breaking production that came to a screeching halt in the 1980s, first with a nationwide recession and then with the listing of the northern spotted owl as a threatened species. When the timber industry was born in the Northwest, there was a belief that the forests of the region were endless. However, by the latter half of this century, big lumber companies had realized that the forests were dwindling. The first tree farms were planted, but the large old trees continued to be cut. By the 1980s environmentalists, shocked by the vast clear-cuts, began trying to save the last old-growth trees. The battle between the timber industry and environmentalists is today the region's most heated debate.

Salmon were the mainstay of the Native Americans' diet for thousands of years before the first whites arrived, but within 10 years of the opening of the first salmon cannery in the Northwest, the fish population was decimated. In 1877 the first fish hatchery was developed to replenish dwindling runs of salmon, and that same year Washington canceled the salmon-fishing season. Salmon canning reached a peak on the Columbia River in 1895 and on Puget Sound in 1913. Later in the 20th century salmon runs would be further decimated by the construction of numerous dams on the Columbia and Snake rivers. Though fish ladders helped adult salmon make their journeys upstream, the young salmon heading downstream had no such help and a large percentage were killed by the turbines of hydroelectric dams. One solution to this problem has been barging and trucking young salmon downriver. Today the salmon population of the Northwest is so diminished that entire runs of salmon have been listed as threatened or endangered.

Manufacturing began gaining in importance during and after World War II. In 1916 William Boeing launched a small seaplane from the waters of Seattle's Lake Union and laid down the foundation for what would become the Seattle area's single largest employer: Boeing. The company became a major employer in Seattle when it began manufacturing B-17s and B-29s for the war effort. Likewise in the Portland area, the Kaiser Shipyards employed tens of thousands of people in the construction of warships. Though the postwar years saw the demise of the Kaiser facilities, Boeing has continued to be a major employer in the Puget Sound area. However, this has had its drawbacks for Seattle. The city's fortunes have been so closely linked to the aircraft manufacturer that any cutback in production at Boeing has a devastating ripple effect through the local economy. Recent years have seen a diversification into high-tech industries, with such major manufacturers as software giant Microsoft adding to the local economy.

5 Northwest Cuisine

The cuisine of the Northwest features such regional produce as salmon, oysters, halibut, raspberries, blackberries, apples, pears, and hazelnuts. A classic Northwest dish is raspberry chicken, which provocatively pairs meat and fruit, or oysters with a hazelnut crust.

Fresh seafood is a major element of regional cuisine. A look at the map will quickly show that there's a lot of saltwater in these parts. Salmon is king of Northwest fish and has been for thousands of years. It's prepared in seemingly endless ways, but the most traditional method is smoking over alderwood. You'll find such smoked salmon for sale at gourmet food shops, at better grocery stores, and in restaurants.

With plenty of clean cold waters in its bays and estuaries, the Northwest raises an astounding array of oysters. Stop in at an oyster bar and you'll find the succulent bivalves introduced by their first names—Kumamoto, Quilcene, Willapa Bay,

Yaquina Bay. Then there are the mussels and clams. Two local clams of particular note are the razor clam, which can be tough and chewy if not prepared properly, and the gargantuan geoduck (pronounced *gooey duck*), which generally only shows up minced in clam chowders. The Dungeness crab is the region's other great seafood offering. Though not as large as an Alaskan king crab, the Dungeness is usually big enough to make a meal for one person.

The Northwest's combination of climate and abundant irrigation waters has helped make this one of the nation's major fruit-growing regions. Washington state is known the world over for its apples, which are grown on the east side of the Cascades near Yakima, Wenatchee, and Chelan. Hood River in Oregon is also a big apple-growing region. Just a few miles east of Hood River, around the Dalles, cherries are supreme, with the blushing Rainier cherry a regional treat rarely seen outside the Northwest. Down in southern Oregon, near Grants Pass and Medford, are some of the largest pear orchards in the country. The Willamette Valley, south of Portland, has become the nation's center for the production of berries. Strawberries, raspberries, and numerous varieties of blackberries are grown. All these fruits show up in the summer months at farm stands all over the region. These stands make a drive through the Northwest in the summer a real treat. Pick-your-own farms are also fairly common throughout the Northwest.

One last Northwest food that we should mention is the wild mushroom. As you'd expect in such a rainy climate, mushrooms abound in this region. The most common wild mushrooms are morels, which are harvested in spring, and chanterelles, which are harvested in the autumn. We don't suggest heading out to the woods to pick your own unless you or a companion are experienced mushroom hunters. However, you will find wild mushrooms showing up on menus of better restaurants throughout the region, so by all means try to have some while you're here.

Both Washington and Oregon have thriving wine industries, which have for quite a few years been producing award-winning varietal wines. The Northwest is on the same latitude as the French wine regions of Burgundy and Bordeaux and produces similar wines. Though the wet autumn weather in western Oregon, where that state's wine grapes are grown, can adversely affect wines there, in Washington the vineyards are primarily on the dry east side of the Cascades, where irrigation is used to produce very reliable and consistent vintages. Wineries throughout the Northwest are open to the public for tastings and better restaurants also tend to stock plenty of local wines. Fruit-flavored wines and fruit-based distilled liqueurs are also produced in the Northwest. Whidbey Island's loganberry liqueur is one such drink.

The microbrewery business that's sweeping the country these days had its start in the Northwest, where such tiny local breweries as those of the McMennamin brothers in Portland and the Red Hook Brewery in the Seattle area started brewing rich, flavorful ales and beers the likes of which had not been brewed in the United States since before Prohibition. Today nearly every city in the region, and even some fairly small towns, boasts at least one microbrewery.

Coffee keeps the Northwest going through long gray winters—and even through hot sunny summers, for that matter. Coffee in the Northwest is not the standard bottomless cup of insipid black liquid that's passed off as coffee in the rest of the country. The coffee that has become a Northwest obsession is rich, dark, flavorful espresso, often served with a generous portion of steamed milk. This milky elixir goes by the name of latte and is served in coffee shops and from espresso carts. In

Seattle it's almost impossible to walk a block without passing an espresso purveyor of some sort.

6 Recommended Books

GENERAL   The single best introduction to the Northwest, both past and present, is Timothy Egan's *The Good Rain* (Vintage Departures, 1991), which uses a long-forgotten Northwest explorer as the springboard for an exploration of all the forces that have made the Northwest what it is today. *The Final Forest* by William Dietrich (Simon & Schuster, 1992) objectively addresses the conflicting views of the logging industry and environmentalists, who are locked in a battle for the last old-growth forests in the Northwest. In *Stepping Westward* (Henry Holt and Company, 1991), Sallie Tisdale blends memoir, travel, and history in an evocation of the landscapes and life of Washington, Oregon, and Idaho.

The Journals of Lewis and Clark (Mentor, 1964), compiled by Meriwether Lewis and William Clark during their 1804–06 journey across the continent, is a fascinating account of a difficult journey and includes a wealth of observations on Native Americans and North American flora and fauna. David Freeman Hawke's *Those Tremendous Mountains: The Story of the Lewis and Clark Expedition* (W. W. Norton & Company, 1980) is a more readable form of the journals and also has a considerable amount of background information.

For a complete history of the Northwest, try *The Pacific Northwest: An Interpretive History* by Carlos A. Schwantes (University of Nebraska Press, 1989) or *The Great Northwest: The Story of a Land and Its People* (America West Publishing, 1973).

The pioneer period is the subject of *Women's Diaries of the Westward Journey* (Schocken Books, 1992), a collection of writings of women pioneers moving west compiled by Lillian Schlissel. *The Well-traveled Casket: A Collection of Oregon Folklife* by Tom Nash and Twilo Scofield (University of Utah Press, 1992) captures the folk and folklore of the Northwest's African American, Hispanic, Chinese, Native American, and Basque immigrants who came here as farmers, miners, loggers, and fishermen.

FICTION   The Northwest has not inspired a great deal of fiction, though Tom Robbins, a Northwest resident, does manage to work a bit of the Northwest into most of his novels. Vince Kohler set his Eldon Larkin mysteries *Rainy North Woods* (St. Martin's Press, 1990) and *Rising Dog* (St. Martin's Press, 1992) in Oregon. Ernest Callenbach's *Ecotopia* (Bantam, 1975) is a novel of the near future in which the Northwest secedes from the United States to pursue its own environmentally conscious beliefs (unfortunately much has changed in the Northwest since the idealistic early 1970s when this novel was written). In *The River Why* (Sierra Club, 1983), David J. Duncan writes of the search for self along the rivers of Oregon. This could best be described as a sort of "Zen and the Art of Flyfishing."

Other novels set in the Northwest include Ken Kesey's *Sometimes a Great Notion* (Viking Penguin, 1977) and *One Flew Over the Cuckoo's Nest* (Viking Penguin, 1977). The former, in its portrayal of a logging family, is more evocative of the region. In 1936 H. L. Davis won the Pulitzer Prize for his novel *Honey in the Horn* (Larlin, 1975), a realistic portrayal of homesteading in the Northwest in the early 1900s. The life of a 19th-century mountain man is the subject of Don Berry's *Trask* (Comstock Editions, 1984).

TRAVEL   The outdoors is a way of life in the Northwest and enjoying it might require a specialized guidebook to get you to the best places. Depending on your interests, you might want to check out one of the following: *A Walking Guide to Oregon's Ancient Forests* by Wendell Wood (Oregon Natural Resources Council, 1991); *Ancient Forests of the Pacific Northwest* by the Wilderness Society and Elliot A. Norse (Island Press, 1990); *100 Hikes in the Oregon Cascades* by William L. Sullivan (Navillus Press, 1991); *100 Hikes in Oregon* by Rhonda and George Ostertag (The Mountaineers, 1992); *The Umbrella Guide to Bicycling the Oregon Coast* by Robin Cody (Umbrella Books, 1990); *Bicycling the Pacific Coast* by Tom Kirkendall and Vicky Spring (The Mountaineers, 1990); *A Waterfall Lover's Guide to the Northwest* by Gregory A. Plumb (The Mountaineers, 1989); and, last, *Garden Touring in the Pacific Northwest* by Jan Kowalczewski Whitner (Alaska Northwest Books, 1993).

Planning a Trip to Washington & Oregon

Before any trip, you need to do a bit of advance planning. When should I go? What is this trip going to cost me? Can I catch a festival during my visit? And where should I head to pursue my favorite sport? We'll answer these and other questions for you in this chapter.

1 Visitor Information & Money

SOURCES OF INFORMATION

For information on Washington, call the **Washington State Tourism Office,** 101 General Administration Building (P.O. Box 42500), Olympia, WA 98504-2500 (☎ **800/544-1800**). For information on Seattle and vicinity, contact the **Seattle–King County Convention & Visitors Bureau,** 520 Pike St., Suite 1300, Seattle, WA 98101 (☎ **206/461-5800**).

For information on Oregon, contact the **Oregon Tourism Division,** 775 Summer St. NE, Salem, OR 97310 (☎ **800/547-7842**), or the **Portland Oregon Visitor Association,** Three World Trade Center, 26 SW Salmon St., Portland, OR 97204 (☎ **503/222-2223** or 800/345-3214).

Also keep in mind that most cities and towns in Washington and Oregon have either a tourist office or chamber of commerce that can provide you with information. When approaching cities and towns, watch for signs along the highway directing you to these information centers. See the individual chapters for specific addresses.

CityNet keeps excellent hotlists of many city, and some regional, Websites. Log into **http://www.city.net/countries/united_states/washington** for cities in Washington, or substitute the word **"oregon"** for "washington" to get the Oregon page. For another hotlist of Washington resources, check out **City Web USA** at **http://www.scescape.com/cityweb/wash.html**. For Oregon regional Websites, try **Oregon Reference** at **http://www.Teleport.com/~samc/index1.html**.

You can also get travel information covering Washington and Oregon from the American Automobile Association (AAA) if you're a member.

To get information on outdoor recreation in national parks and national forests of Oregon and Washington, write or call the **National Park Service,** Outdoor Recreation Information Office, 915 Second Ave., Room 442, Seattle, WA 98174 (☎ **206/220-7450**). You could also contact the **U.S. Forest Service Recreational Information Office,** 800 NE Oregon St., Portland, OR 97232 (☎ **503/326-2877**).

For information on camping in Oregon state parks, contact the **Oregon Parks & Recreation Department,** Reservation/Information Center, 3554 SE 82nd Ave., Portland, OR 97266 (☎ **503/731-3411** or 800/452-5687). To find out more about camping opportunities in Washington, contact **Washington State Parks and Recreation,** 7150 Cleanwater Lane (P.O. Box 42650), Olympia, WA 98504-2650 (☎ **360/902-8563;** a toll-free number should be in service by early 1996).

For information on ferries, contact **Washington State Ferries,** Colman Dock, Seattle, WA 98501 (☎ **206/464-6400** or 800/843-3779 in Washington).

MONEY

What will a vacation in the Northwest cost? That depends on your tastes. If you drive an R.V. or carry a tent, you can get by very inexpensively and find a place to stay almost anywhere in the Northwest. On the other hand, you can easily spend a couple of hundred dollars a day on a room at one of the Northwest's resorts. However, if you want to stay in clean, modern motels at Interstate highway off-ramps, expect to pay $40 to $65 a night for a double room in most places. When it comes time to eat, you can get a great meal almost anywhere in the Northwest for under $25, but if you want to spend more, or less, that's also possible.

What Things Cost in Seattle	U.S. $
Taxi from the airport to the city center	27.00
Bus ride between any two downtown points	free
Local telephone call	.25
Double room at the Alexis Hotel (very expensive)	185.00
Double room at the Pacific Plaza Hotel (moderate)	74.00
Double room at the Kings Inn (inexpensive)	55.00
Lunch for one at the Queen City Grill (moderate)	12.00
Lunch for one at Emmett Watson's Oyster Bar (inexpensive)	7.00
Dinner for one, without wine, at Chez Shea (expensive)	27.00
Dinner for one, without wine, at Ivar's Salmon House (moderate)	19.00
Dinner for one, without wine, at the Wild Ginger Asian Restaurant (inexpensive)	14.00
Pint of beer	3.50
Glass of Coca-Cola	1.00
Cup of espresso (latte)	1.50
Roll of ASA 100 Kodacolor film, 36 exposures	5.25
Admission to the Seattle Art Museum	6.00
Movie ticket	6.50
Theater ticket to the Seattle Repertory Theater	13.50–34.00

Cities and towns throughout the Northwest have banks with automatic teller machines (Star, Plus, Interlink, Cirrus, and Excel networks are widely available; MasterCard and Visa may also be used), so you can get cash as you travel.

2 When to Go

Though gray skies and mild temperatures are what the Northwest is known for, the region is characterized by a range of climates almost unequaled in the United States for its diversity. For the most part, moist winds off the Pacific Ocean keep temperatures west of the Cascade Range mild year round. Although summers in the Willamette Valley and southern Oregon can see temperatures over 100° Fahrenheit, in the Puget Sound area you're likely to need a sweater or light jacket at night even in August. The Northwest rains that are so legendary fall primarily as light-but-almost-constant drizzle between October and early July. There are windows of sunshine during this period, but they usually last no more than a few days. There are also, unfortunately, occasional wet summers, so be prepared for wet weather whenever you plan to visit. Winters usually include one or two blasts of Arctic air that bring snow and freezing weather to the Seattle and Portland areas.

There are several exceptions to the mild and rainy climate of the Northwest. If you visit the coast, expect grayer, wetter weather than in the Seattle or Portland area. The Oregon coast can be quite cool in the summer and is often foggy or rainy throughout the year. The Olympic Peninsula in northwest Washington is the rainiest spot in the mainland United States, with rainfall reaching 140 inches per year.

On the other hand, regions east of the Cascades in both Washington and Oregon are characterized by lack of rain and temperature extremes. These high desert areas can be very cold in the winter and can get moderate amounts of snow in the foothill regions. In summer the weather can be blazing hot, though nights are often cool enough to require a sweater or light jacket.

In the Cascades, Olympics, and other smaller mountain ranges, snowfall is heavy in the winter and skiing is a popular sport.

Seattle's Average Monthly Temperatures & Rainfall

	Jan	Feb	Mar	Apr	May	June	July	Aug	Sept	Oct	Nov	Dec
Temp. (°F)	46	50	53	58	65	69	75	74	69	60	52	47
Temp. (°C)	8	10	11	15	18	21	24	23	21	16	11	9
Days of Rain	19	6	17	14	10	9	5	7	9	14	18	20

Portland's Average Monthly Temperatures & Rainfall

	Jan	Feb	Mar	Apr	May	June	July	Aug	Sept	Oct	Nov	Dec
Temp. (°F)	40	43	46	50	57	63	68	67	63	54	46	41
Temp. (°C)	4	6	8	10	14	17	20	20	17	12	8	5
Days of Rain	18	16	17	14	12	10	4	5	8	13	18	19

NORTHWEST CALENDAR OF EVENTS

February

- **Northwest Flower & Garden Show,** Washington State Convention Center, Seattle. The largest flower and garden show in the Northwest, with beautiful displays and hundreds of vendors. ☎ 206/789-5333. Mid- to late February.

✪ **Oregon Shakespeare Festival.** The repertory company features a dozen plays in three unique theaters: some by Shakespeare and others by classical and contemporary playwrights. Backstage tours, a museum, and lectures round out the festival.

> **Where:** Ashland, OR. **When:** February to October. **How:** Call the festival box office at 541/482-4331 for details and ticket information.

March

• **Whale Fest,** Westport, WA. Kickoff celebration for whale-watching season, when 20,000 gray whales migrate along the Washington coast from Baja California to the Bering Sea. ☎ 800/345-6223. Second week in March through the end of May.

April

• **Skagit Valley Tulip Festival,** Skagit Valley, WA. View a rainbow of blooming tulip fields. ☎ 800/4-TULIPS. First two weeks in April.

• **Hood River Blossom Festival,** Hood River, OR. Celebration of the blossoming of the orchards outside the town of Hood River. ☎ 541/386-2000. Third weekend in April.

• **Spring Barrel Tasting,** Yakima Valley, WA. Straight-from-the-barrel wine tasting of spring-release wines at Yakima Valley wineries. ☎ 509/575-1300. End of April.

• **Washington State Apple Blossom Festival,** Wenatchee, WA. Eleven days and 40 different events. ☎ 800/57-APPLE. End of April to early May.

May

• **Irrigation Festival,** Sequim, WA. The oldest continuous festival in Washington, with a grand parade, logging show, dancing, arts and crafts. ☎ 360/683-6197. Early May.

• **Mother's Day Rhododendron Show,** Crystal Springs Rhododendron Gardens, Portland, OR. ☎ 503/771-8386. Mother's Day.

• **Viking Fest,** Poulsbo, WA. Norwegian heritage on display in picturesque Poulsbo, with a parade and entertainment. ☎ 360/779-4848. Mid-May.

• **Spokane Lilac Festival,** Spokane, WA. A 55-year tradition celebrating the blooming of the lilacs. ☎ 509/326-3339. Third weekend in May.

• **Boatnik,** Grants Pass, OR. Boat race and picnic in the park. ☎ 541/474-2361. Memorial Day weekend.

✪ **Northwest Folklife Festival.** This is the largest folk-life festival in the country with dozens of national and regional folk musicians performing on numerous stages. In addition, craftspeople from all over the Northwest show and sell. Lots of good food and dancing, too.

> **Where:** Seattle Center, Seattle. **When:** Memorial Day weekend. **How:** Call 206/684-7300 for information.

June

• **Cannon Beach Sand Castle Festival,** Cannon Beach, OR. Artistic sand-sculpted creations appear along the beach. ☎ 503/436-2623. Early June.

• **Mural-in-a-Day,** Toppenish, WA. The small town of Toppenish has covered its blank walls with murals and each June one more is added in a day of intense painting. ☎ 509/865-3262. Early June.

✪ **Portland Rose Festival.** From its beginnings back in 1888, when the first rose show was held, the Rose Festival has blossomed into Portland's biggest celebration.

The festivities have now spread throughout Portland and the surrounding communities and include a rose show, floral parade, rose-queen contest, music festival, car races, footrace, boat races, and even an air show.

Where: Portland, OR. **When:** Most events take place during the first three weeks of June. **How:** Hotel rooms can be hard to come by; plan ahead. Contact the Portland Rose Festival Association, 220 NW Second Ave., Portland, OR 97209 (☎ 503/227-2681), for information on tickets to specific events.

○ **Britt Festivals.** Multi-arts festival that offers performances of world-class artists in jazz, classical, folk, country, dance, musical theater, and pop in a beautiful natural setting. Bring a blanket and have a picnic supper before the performance.

Where: Jacksonville, OR. **When:** June to September. **How:** Call 541/773-6077, or 800/88-BRITT, for details and ticket information.

• **Fort Vancouver Days,** Vancouver, WA. Riverside jazz concert, chili cookoff, and rodeo. ☎ 360/693-2430 or 360/693-1313. Late June to early July.

July

• **Fourth of July Fireworks,** Vancouver, WA. The biggest fireworks display west of the Mississippi. July 4.
• **World Championship Timber Carnival,** Albany, OR. Logging events, parade, food, and fireworks. ☎ 541/928-2391. Fourth of July weekend.
• **Oregon Country Fair,** Eugene, OR. Counterculture craft fair and festival for Deadheads young and old. ☎ 541/343-4298. Second weekend in July.
• **Da Vinci Days,** Corvallis, OR. Three-day celebration of science and technology with performances, art, interactive exhibits, children's activities, food, and wine. ☎ 541/757-6363. Mid-July.
• **Pacific Northwest Arts and Crafts Fair,** Bellevue, WA. Regional artists and craftspeople display at one of the largest shows of its kind in the country. ☎ 206/454-4900. Third week in July.
• **Salem Arts Festival,** Salem, OR. The largest juried art fair in Oregon, under the trees in Bush Park, with musical entertainment and food booths. ☎ 503/581-2228. Third weekend in July.

○ **Seafair.** The biggest event of the year, with festivities every day, including parades, hydroplane boat races, performances by the navy's Blue Angels, a Torchlight Parade, ethnic festivals, sporting events, and open houses on naval ships. This one really packs in the out-of-towners and sends Seattleites fleeing on summer vacations.

Where: Seattle. **When:** The third weekend in July to the first weekend in August. **How:** Call 206/728-0123 for details on events and tickets.

• **Chief Joseph Days,** Joseph, OR. Rodeo plus exhibits and demonstrations by local Native Americans. ☎ 541/432-1015. Last full weekend in July.
• **Oregon Brewers Festival,** Waterfront Park, Portland, OR. Microbreweries show off their suds. ☎ 503/778-5917. Last weekend in July.

August

• **Mount Hood Festival of Jazz,** Mount Hood Community College, Gresham, OR. For the serious jazz fan, this is the highlight of the summer. It features the greatest names in jazz. ☎ 503/232-3000. First full weekend of August.
• **Omak Stampede and World Famous Suicide Race,** Omak, WA. Rodeo and horse race down a cliff face. ☎ 800/225-OMAK or 509/826-1983. Early August.

- **Chief Seattle Days,** Suquamish, WA. Powwow with salmon bake, canoe races, dancing, and crafts. ☎ 360/598-3311. Mid-August.
- **Astoria Regatta,** Astoria, OR. See a fleet of boats in full sail in the historic harbor. ☎ 503/325-6311. Third weekend in August.
- **Washington State International Kite Festival,** Long Beach, WA. World-class competition between kite flyers. ☎ 800/451-2542. Third week in August.
- **Oregon State Fair,** Salem, OR. A typical agricultural state fair. ☎ 503/378-3247, or 800/833-0011 in Oregon. The 12 days prior to and including Labor Day.
- **Cascade Festival of Music,** Bend, OR. Classical and popular music in a park setting. ☎ 541/382-8381. August 24–31

September

- **Artquake,** Portland, OR. Radiating out from Pioneer Courthouse Square along Broadway, Artquake is Portland's grand festival of the arts. ☎ 503/227-2787. Labor Day weekend.

✪ **Bumbershoot,** Seattle. The second most popular festival in Seattle takes its name from the British term for umbrella. Lots of music and other events packs Seattle's youthful set into the Seattle Center and other venues. Plenty of arts and crafts are on display as well.

　　Where: Seattle. **When:** Labor Day weekend. **How:** Call 206/682-4386 for schedule.

- **Ellensburg Rodeo/Kittitas County Fair,** Ellensburg, WA. The state's biggest rodeo and fair. ☎ 509/962-7831. Labor Day weekend.
- **Mount Angel Oktoberfest,** Mount Angel, OR. Biergarten, Bavarian-style oompah bands, food booths. ☎ 503/845-6882. Mid-September.
- **Pendleton Round-Up and Happy Canyon Pageant,** Pendleton, OR. Rodeo, Native American pageant, country-music concert. ☎ 541/276-2553, or 800/43-RODEO. Mid-September.
- **Wooden Boat Festival,** Port Townsend, WA. Historic boats on display, demonstrations. ☎ 360/385-3628. Mid-September.
- **Eugene Celebration,** Eugene, OR. Street party celebrating the diversity of the community. Festivities include the crowning of a Slug Queen. ☎ 541/687-5215. Third weekend in September.
- **Western Washington Fair,** Puyallup, WA. One of the 10 largest fairs in the nation. ☎ 206/841-5045. Third week in September.
- **Annual Washington State Autumn Leaf Festival,** Leavenworth, WA. Bavarian costumes, food, music, and autumn foliage. ☎ 509/548-5807. Late September to early October.
- **International Kite Festival,** Lincoln City, OR. Kite carnival including the world's largest spinning wind sock and lighted night kite flights. ☎ 800/452-2151. Late September to early October.

October

- **Cranberry Festival,** Long Beach Peninsula, WA. Cranberry bog tours, arts and crafts. ☎ 800/451-2542. Mid-October.

November

- **Holiday Festival of Lights,** Ashland, OR. A thousand points of light decorate the town. ☎ 541/482-3486. Thanksgiving to New Year's Eve.

December
- **Festival of Trees,** Portland, OR. Extravagantly decorated Christmas trees are displayed among gingerbread houses and trains at the Oregon Convention Center. ☎ 503/235-7575. Early December.
- **Winter Solstice Renaissance Festival,** Oregon Museum of Science and Industry, Portland, OR. Renaissance costumes and festivities. ☎ 503/797-4000. Two weekends in mid-December.

3 The Active Vacation Planner

The abundance of outdoor recreational activities is one of the reasons people choose to live in the Northwest. With both mountains and beaches within an hour's drive of the major metropolitan areas, there are numerous choices for the active vacationer.

Outdoor enthusiasts with Web access will want to check out **GORP**'s resource listings for on-line information on area parks and activities from fishing to skiing to kayaking. Head for **http://www.gorp.com/gorp/location/wa/wa.htm** for Washington, or substitute **"or/or.html"** for "wa/wa.htm" to get to the Oregon hotlist.

ACTIVITIES A TO Z

BICYCLING/MOUNTAIN BIKING   The San Juan Islands, with their winding country roads and Puget Sound vistas, and the Oregon coast are the most popular bicycling locales in the Northwest.

Of the four main San Juan Islands (San Juan, Orcas, Lopez, and Shaw), Lopez has the easiest and Orcas the most challenging terrain for bikers. Here you can pedal for as many or as few days as you like.

It takes about a week to pedal the Oregon coast if you're in good shape and are traveling at a leisurely pace. During the summer months it's best to travel from north to south along the coast because of the prevailing winds. Also keep in mind that many state parks have designated hiker/biker campsites.

Other regions growing in popularity with cyclists include the wine country of Yamhill County, Oregon, other parts of the Willamette Valley, the Olympic Peninsula, and the Methow Valley. Seattle, Tacoma, Spokane, Yakima, Portland, and Eugene all have easy bicycle trails that are either in parks or connect parks.

The region's national forests provide miles of logging roads and single-track trails for mountain biking. Among the most popular mountain-biking areas are the Methow Valley, on the east side of the North Cascades in Washington, and the Bend area of central Oregon.

For information on bicycle routes in Washington, contact the **Bicycle Program, Washington State Department of Transportation,** 310 Maple Park Ave., Olympia, WA 98501 (☎ **360/705-7277**). You can get a free Oregon coast bicycle map, as well as other bicycle maps for the state of Oregon, by contacting the **Bikeway Program Manager,** Oregon Department of Transportation, Bicycle/Pedestrian Program, Transportation Building, Room 200, Salem, OR 97310 (☎ **503/ 378-3432**).

BIRDWATCHING   With a wide variety of habitats, Washington and Oregon offer many excellent birdwatching spots. Each winter in January, bald eagles flock

Following the Lewis & Clark Trail

Although they were not the first to explore the Northwest, Meriwether Lewis, William Clark, and their Corps of Discovery, sent westward by President Thomas Jefferson in 1804, were the first to chart an overland route from the Mississippi to the Pacific Ocean. Their expedition's purpose was partly to explore the Louisiana Purchase, which the United States had just acquired from France, and partly to determine whether there was an easy water route to the Oregon country. Through their observations and journal entries Lewis and Clark added immensely to the scientific knowledge of western North America.

Lewis and Clark left a legacy throughout the West as they named geographical landmarks and the many previously unknown plants and animals they encountered along their route. The prairie dog and the pronghorn antelope were first recorded by the two explorers. At least two species of birds have been named after Lewis and Clark: Clark's nutcracker and Lewis's woodpecker. In later years their names would be affixed to numerous features of the western landscape as well: Lewiston and Clarkston, towns on opposite sides of the Snake River at the Washington-Idaho state line; Lewis and Clark counties in Washington; the Lewis River. Other geographic features still bear the names Lewis and Clark assigned them in their journals: Beacon Rock, Washington; Hat Rock, Oregon; Pompeys Pillar, Montana; Council Bluffs, Iowa.

Today there are many locations in Washington and Oregon where you can learn more about the Corps of Discovery and the important role it played in the history of both the Northwest and the United States. Starting in the east, near the town of Clarkston, there is **Chief Timothy State Park,** with an interpretive

to the Skagit River, north of Seattle, to feast on salmon. Birders can observe from shore or on a guided raft trip. Migratory shorebirds make annual stops at Bowerman Basin in the Gray's Harbor Wildlife Refuge outside the town of Hoquiam. One of Washington's best birding excursions is a ride through the San Juan Islands on one of the Washington State Ferries. From these floating observation platforms, birders can spot bald eagles and numerous pelagic birds.

Malheur National Wildlife Refuge, in central Oregon, is that state's premier birdwatching area and attracts more than 300 species of birds over the course of the year. Nearby Summer Lake also offers good birdwatching, with migratory waterfowl and shorebirds most prevalent. There's also good birdwatching on Sauvie Island, outside Portland, where waterfowl and eagles are to be seen, and along the coast, where you can see tufted puffins, pigeon guillemots, and perhaps even a marbled murrelet. The Klamath Lakes region of south-central Oregon is well known for its large population of bald eagles.

CAMPING Public and private campgrounds abound all across Washington and Oregon, with those in Mount Rainier National Park and along the Oregon coast among the most popular. In Washington, Olympic National Park is also popular, and North Cascades National Park has campgrounds as well. Camping is on a first-come, first-served basis at all three national parks.

Washington also has 80 state parks with campgrounds. Moran State Park on Orcas Island and Deception Pass State Park are two of the most enjoyable campgrounds. For information on camping in Washington state parks, contact the

center that focuses on the expedition's interactions with this area's Native Americans. Farther west, at the confluence of the Snake and Columbia rivers, there's an interpretive center at **Sacajawea State Park,** named for the Shoshone woman who accompanied the expedition and acted as an interpreter. **Horsethief Lake State Park,** east of the Dalles on the Washington side of the Columbia, is the site of the expedition's portage around Celilo Falls; there's an interpretive sign here. Across the river, on the west side of the Dalles, a sign marks the **Rock Fort,** one of the few known campsites used by the explorers. Farther downstream, west of Hood River, there's information on the expedition at the **Bonneville Dam visitor center.** West of here stands **Beacon Rock,** a massive monolith named by Clark on November 2, 1805. Near Troutdale, at **Lewis and Clark State Park,** you can learn more about the many plants named by the two explorers. Continuing westward to the mouth of the Columbia River, you'll find two of the most important centers devoted to the Corps of Discovery. Outside Astoria, Oregon, stands the **Fort Clatsop National Memorial,** a reproduction of the fort in which the corps spent the winter of 1805–06. At this memorial, interpreters in period costume provide enlightening insights into what life was like at Fort Clatsop. Across the river in Washington, at **Fort Canby State Park,** the Lewis and Clark Interpretive Center provides much interesting background information on the explorers. Back in Oregon, in the town of **Seaside,** a rock cairn and sign mark the possible location of a camp where members of the expedition spent two months boiling sea water to make salt for the return trip eastward. Here in Seaside each July and August, there's also an outdoor stage production dramatizing the Lewis and Clark expedition.

Washington State Parks and Recreation Commission, 7150 Cleanwater Lane (P.O. Box 42650), Olympia, WA 98504-2650 (☎ 360/902-8500; there are plans to add a toll-free number, but it has not yet been established).

Throughout Oregon, campgrounds on lakes stay particularly busy. However, beach campgrounds and those at Crater Lake National Park are the most popular. During the summer months, campground reservations are almost a necessity at many state parks, especially those along the coast. For state park campground reservations and information, contact the **Oregon Parks & Recreation Department,** Reservation/Information Center, 3554 SE 82nd Ave., Portland, OR 97266 (☎ 503/731-3411 or 800/452-5687). Summer campsite reservations are taken beginning June 1.

CANOEING/KAYAKING   White-water kayakers in Washington head for such rivers as the Wenatchee around Leavenworth, the Methow near Winthrop, the Skagit and Skykomish rivers north of Seattle, and the White Salmon River near Trout Lake. On the Olympic Peninsula, the Queets, Hoh, and Elhwa rivers are the main kayaking rivers. One of the most popular canoeing lakes in Washington is Lake Ozette in Olympic National Park.

White-water kayaking is popular on many of the rivers that flow down out of the Cascade Range in Oregon, including the Deschutes, the Clackamas, the Mollala, and the Sandy. Down in southern Oregon, the North Umpqua and the Rogue provide plenty of white-water action. Canoeing is also popular on many of Oregon's lakes. A few favorite canoeing lakes include Crescent Lake,

Upper Klamath Lake (where there's a canoe trail), Waldo Lake and Crescent Lake southeast of Eugene, and the many lakes of the Cascade Lakes Loop southwest of Bend.

FISHING   For information on freshwater fishing in Washington, contact the **Department of Wildlife,** 600 Capitol Way N., Olympia, WA 98501 (☎ **206/ 753-5700**). For information on freshwater fishing in Oregon, contact the **Oregon Department of Fish and Wildlife** (☎ **503/229-5403**).

GOLFING   Although the rainy weather in western Washington puts a bit of a damper on golfing, the mild temperatures mean that it's possible to play year round. The state has only a handful of resorts with golf courses, but most larger cities have public courses.

Oregon has nearly 200 private and public golf courses, including several resort courses. The majority of courses are clustered in the Portland metropolitan area and in the Bend-Redmond area where numerous resorts are to be found.

GUEST RANCHES   Though this is the Northwest, it's still the West and cowboys and Indians are as much a part of life here as they are in the Southwest. You'll find several guest ranches around the region, including the Flying M Ranch in Yamhill, Oregon (see Chapter 13), and Minam Lodge, near Joseph, Oregon (see Chapter 15).

HANG GLIDING   Lakeview, in south-central Oregon near the California state line, is Oregon's premier hang-gliding location. Strong steady winds and high bluffs provide perfect conditions for experienced hang gliders.

HIKING & BACKPACKING   Washington and Oregon have an abundance of hiking trails, including the Pacific Crest Trail, which runs along the spine of the Cascades from Canada to the California line (and onward all the way to Mexico). Elsewhere in Washington, you'll find hikes along the beach, up rain-forest valleys, and through alpine meadows in Olympic National Park, through forests and the state's most beautiful meadows in Mount Rainier National Park (hikes from Sunrise and Paradise are the most spectacular), and through the state's most rugged scenery in North Cascades National Park. The Alpine Lakes region outside Leavenworth is breathtakingly beautiful, but so popular that permits are required. Another popular hike is to the top of Mount St. Helens. Lesser known are the hiking trails on Mount Adams in southern Washington. In the Columbia Gorge, the hike up Dog Mountain is strenuous but rewarding.

Oregon's thousands of miles of hiking trails are concentrated primarily in national forests, especially in wilderness areas, in the Cascade Range. Along the length of the Pacific Crest Trail in Oregon are such scenic hiking areas as the Mount Hood Wilderness, the Mount Jefferson Wilderness, the Three Sisters Wilderness, the Diamond Peak Wilderness, the Mount Thielsen Wilderness, and the Sky Lakes Wilderness. However, many state parks also have extensive hiking-trail systems.

The Oregon Coast Trail is a designated route that runs the length of the Oregon coast. In most places it travels along the beach, but in other places it climbs up and over capes and headlands through dense forests and windswept meadows. The longest stretches of the trail are along the southern coast in Samuel H. Boardman State Park. There's also a long beach stretch in the Oregon Dunes National Recreation Area.

Other coastal parks with popular hiking trails include Saddle Mountain State Park, Ecola State Park, Oswald West State Park, and Cape Lookout State Park. Silver Falls State Park, east of Salem, is also a popular hiking spot. The many trails of the Columbia Gorge National Scenic Area are also well trodden, with Eagle Creek Trail being a longtime favorite. For a quick hiking fix, Portlanders often head for the city's Forest Park. The trails leading out from Timberline Lodge on Mount Hood lead through forests and meadows at the treeline and are particularly busy on summer weekends.

MOUNTAINEERING   Mount Rainier, Mount Hood, and several other Cascades peaks offer challenging mountain climbing and rock climbing for both the novice and the expert. Both Mount Rainier and Mount Hood have guide services and mountaineering schools. See "Outfitters and Adventure Travel Operators," below, for details.

ROCK CLIMBING   Smith Rocks State Park, near Redmond in central Oregon, is a rock-climbing mecca of international renown. Some of the routes here are among the toughest in the world, and so numerous are the routes that an entire book has been written about these climbs. Many climbers claim that sport climbing got its American start here. In Washington, popular climbing spots include the countless peaks and crags of the North Cascades and the far more modest Peshastin Pinnacles near Leavenworth.

SCUBA DIVING   Though the waters of Puget Sound are cold, they are generally quite clear and harbor an astounding variety of life, including giant octopi. Consequently, the sound is popular with divers. There are underwater parks for scuba divers at Fort Worden, Kopachuck, Blake Island, Saltwater, and Tolmie. For more information, contact the **Washington Scuba Alliance,** 120 State Ave., Suite 18, Olympia, WA 98501-8212.

SEA KAYAKING   Sea kayaks differ from river kayaks in that they are much longer, more stable, and able to carry gear as well as a paddler or two. There are few places in the country that offer better sea kayaking than the waters of Puget Sound and around the San Juan Islands. Consequently, this sport is especially popular in the Seattle area. The protected waters of Puget Sound offer numerous spots for a paddle of anywhere from a few hours to a few days. There's even a water trail under development that will link camping spots throughout the sound. The San Juan Islands are by far the most popular sea kayaking spot in the region, and several tiny islands, accessible only by boat, are designated state campsites. In the Seattle area, Lake Union and Lake Washington are both popular kayaking spots. Willapa Bay, on the Washington coast, is another popular paddling spot.

SKIING   Washington and Oregon have more than two dozen ski areas spread across the two states, from Hurricane Ridge in the Olympic Mountains to Mount Spokane near the Idaho border and from Mount Baker Ski Area near the Canadian border to Ski Ashland near the California line. The most popular areas in Washington are Mount Baker Ski Area near Bellingham, Stevens Pass near Leavenworth, Alpental/Ski Acres/Snoqualmie/Hyak near Seattle, and Crystal Mountain just outside Mount Rainier National Park. Smaller and more remote ski areas include Mount Spokane and 48 Degrees North, both north of Spokane; Sitzmark, in central Washington near the Canadian border; White Pass, southeast of Mount Rainier National Park; Mission Ridge, near Wenatchee; Loup Loup, near Winthrop; Echo Valley, near Lake Chelan; Ski Bluewood, near Walla Walla; and Hurricane Ridge, in Olympic National Park. There's also heli-skiing available near Winthrop.

Ski areas in Oregon include Mount Hood Meadows, Mount Hood Ski Bowl, Timberline Ski Area, and Summit Ski Area, all of which are on Mount Hood outside Portland. Farther south, there are Hoodoo Ski Bowl, east of Salem, and Willamette Pass, east of Eugene. Outside of Bend is Mount Bachelor, the most popular ski area in the state. In the eastern part of the state, Anthony Lakes and Spout Springs provide a bit of powder skiing. Down in the south, Ski Ashland is the only option. There's also snow-cat skiing north of Crater Lake on Mount Bailey.

Many downhill ski areas in both states also offer groomed cross-country ski trails. The most popular cross-country areas in Washington include the Methow Valley (one of the largest trail systems in the country), Leavenworth, Ski Acres/Hyak, White Pass, Stevens Pass, and near Mount St. Helens and Mount Adams. In Oregon, cross-country skiers will find an abundance of trails up and down the Cascades. Teacup Lake, Trillium Basin, and Mount Hood Meadows, all on Mount Hood, offer good groomed trails. Near Mount Bachelor there are also plenty of groomed trails. Crater Lake is also a popular spot for cross-country skiing. Backcountry skiing is also popular in the Wallowa Mountains in eastern Oregon.

WINDSURFING   The Columbia River Gorge is one of the most renowned windsurfing spots in the world. Here, high winds and a strong current come together to produce radical sailing conditions. As the winds whip up the waves, skilled sailors rocket across the water and launch themselves skyward to perform aerial acrobatics. On calmer days and in spots where the wind isn't blowing so hard, there are also opportunities for novices to learn the basics. Summer is the best sailing season, and the town of Hood River is the center of the boarding scene with plenty of windsurfing schools and rental companies. The southern Oregon coast also has some popular spots, including Floras Lake just north of Port Orford and Pistol River beach south of Gold Beach. Windsurfing is also popular on Lake Union in Seattle and Vancouver Lake in Vancouver, Washington.

WHALE WATCHING   Orca whales, commonly called killer whales, are a symbol of the Northwest and are often seen in Puget Sound and around the San Juan Islands, especially during the summer. Dozens of companies offer whale-watching trips from the San Juans. You can also spot orcas from San Juan Island's Lime Kiln State Park. Out on the Washington coast, migrating gray whales can be seen March through May. In the town of Westport, there are both viewing areas and companies operating whale-watching excursions.

Depoe Bay, north of Newport, is not only the smallest harbor in the world, but it's also home port for several whale-watching boats that head out in the late winter and early spring to look for migrating gray whales. It's also possible to whale watch from shore, with Cape Lookout and Cape Meares offering the best vantages.

WHITE-WATER RAFTING   Plenty of rain and lots of mountains combine to produce dozens of good white-water–rafting rivers in both Washington and Oregon, depending on the time of year and water levels. In the Washington Cascades, some of the popular rafting rivers include the Wenatchee outside Leavenworth, the Methow near Winthrop, the Skagit and Skykomish rivers north of Seattle, and the White Salmon River near Trout Lake. On the Olympic Peninsula, the Queets, Hoh, and Elhwa rivers are the main rafting rivers. In Oregon, the Deschutes, which flows through central Oregon, and the Rogue, which is in southern Oregon and was featured in the movie *The River Wild,* are the two most popular rafting rivers. Other popular rafting rivers include the Clackamas outside Portland and the McKenzie outside Eugene. Out in the southeastern corner, the remote Owyhee River provides adventurers with still more white water. See the respective chapters for information on rafting companies operating on these rivers. Rates generally range from $45 to $75 for a day of rafting.

OUTFITTERS & ADVENTURE TRAVEL OPERATORS

BICYCLING   **Backroads,** 1516 Fifth St., Berkeley, CA 94710-1740 (☎ 510/527-1555 or 800/462-2848; fax 510/527-1444), offers guided trips in the San Juan Islands, the North Cascades, and on the Oregon coast and the Olympic Peninsula. Tour prices range from $698 to $1,248. **Bicycle Adventures,** P.O. Box 7875, Olympia, WA 98507 (☎ 206/786-0989 or 800/443-6060), offers trips in the San Juan Islands, the Oregon Cascades, the Columbia Gorge, and on the Oregon coast and Olympic Peninsula. Tour prices range from $598 to $1,548. **CycleWest,** 75 Bush St., Ashland, OR 97520 (☎ 541/482-1088), offers inn-to-inn bicycle vacations with tours to the San Juan Islands, the Oregon coast, and the towns of southern Oregon. **Oregon Bicycle Adventures,** P.O. Box 7566, Eugene, OR 97405 (☎ 541/686-4265 or 800/678-2252), offers trips in different parts of Oregon with tour prices ranging from $69 to $749.

MOUNTAINEERING   If you're interested in learning some mountain-climbing skills or want to hone your existing skills, you can do so on Mount Rainier or Mount Hood, and other Cascade peaks. **Rainier Mountaineering,** 535 Dock St., Suite 209, Tacoma, WA 98402 (☎ 206/627-6242 or 360/569-2227; fax 206/627-1280), which operates out of Paradise inside Mount Rainier National Park, offers one-day classes for $75, three-day summit climbs for $403, and five-day mountaineering seminars for $667. **Timberline Mountain Guides,** P.O. Box 23214, Portland, OR 97281 (☎ 503/636-7704; fax 503/636-0344), leads summit climbs on Mount Hood. It also offers snow-, ice-, and rock-climbing courses. A two-day Mount Hood mountaineering course with summit climb costs $220. Rates for other courses range from $75 for a day-long rock-climbing class at Smith Rock to $625 for a five-day mountaineering seminar.

SEA KAYAKING   If you'd like to explore Puget Sound in a sea kayak, contact the **Northwest Outdoor Center,** 2100 Westlake Ave. N., Seattle, WA 98109 (☎ 206/281-9694). This center rents kayaks and also offers various classes and guided trips. Day trips are $60, three-day trips are $200, and five-day trips are $350. **San Juan Kayak Expeditions,** P.O. Box 2041, Friday Harbor, WA 98250 (☎ 360/378-4436), and **Shearwater Adventures,** P.O. Box 787, Eastsound, WA 98245 (☎ 360/376-4699), also offer multiday kayak trips. Three-day trips range in price from around $220 to $290. **Sea Quest Expeditions/Zoetic Research,** P.O. Box 2424, Friday Harbor, WA 98250 (☎ 360/378-5767), is a nonprofit organization that sponsors educational sea-kayaking trips through the San Juans.

4 Educational & Volunteer Vacations

Older travelers who want to learn something from their trip to the Northwest or who simply prefer the company of like-minded older travelers should look into programs by **Elderhostel,** 75 Federal St., Boston, MA 02110 (☎ 617/426-7788).

To participate in an Elderhostel program, either you or your spouse must be 55 years old. In addition to one-week educational programs, Elderhostel offers short getaways with interesting themes.

The Nature Conservancy is a nonprofit organization dedicated to the global preservation of natural diversity, and to this end it operates educational field trips and work parties to their own nature preserves and those of other agencies. For information about field trips **in Oregon,** contact the Nature Conservancy, 1205 NW 25th Ave., Portland, OR 97210 (☎ **503/228-9561**). For field trips **in Washington,** contact the Nature Conservancy, 217 Pine St., Suite 1100, Seattle, WA 98101 (☎ **206/343-4344**).

If you enjoy the wilderness and want to get more involved in preserving it, consider a Sierra Club Service Trip. These trips are for the purpose of building, restoring, and maintaining hiking trails in wilderness areas. It's a lot of work, but it's also a lot of fun. For more information on Service Trips, contact the **Sierra Club Outing Department,** 730 Polk St., San Francisco, CA 94109 (☎ **415/923-5630;** fax 415/923-0636).

Earth Watch, 680 Mt. Auburn St., Watertown, MA 02172 (☎ **617/926-8200**), sends volunteers on scientific research projects. Contact it for a catalog listing trips and costs. Current projects include studies of orcas, chimpanzee communication, and Oregon caves.

Habitat for Humanity is an organization that enlists volunteers to help build homes for people who could not otherwise afford them. Contact the Northwest Regional Office of **Habitat for Humanity,** 1005 NW Galveston Ave., Bend, OR 97701 (☎ **503/383-4637**).

5 Travel Insurance

Before going out and spending money on various sorts of travel insurance, check your existing policies to see if they'll cover you while you're traveling. Make sure your health insurance will cover you when you're away from home. Some credit and charge cards offer automatic flight insurance when you purchase an airline ticket with that card. These policies insure against death or dismemberment in case of an airplane crash.

Also, check your credit/charge cards to see if any of them pick up the collision-damage waiver (CDW) when you rent a car. The CDW can run as much as $12 a day and can add 50% or more to the cost of renting a car. Check your automobile insurance policy, too; it might cover the CDW as well.

If you own a home or have renter's insurance, see if that policy covers off-premises theft and loss wherever it occurs.

If you're traveling on a tour or have prepaid a large chunk of your travel expenses, you might want to ask your travel agent about trip-cancellation insurance.

If, after checking all your existing insurance policies, you decide that you need additional insurance, a good travel agent can give you information on a variety of different options. **Teletrip Company (Mutual of Omaha),** at Mutual of Omaha Plaza, Floor 7, Teletrip, Omaha, NE 68175 (☎ **800/228-9792**), offers four different types of travel-insurance policies for one day to six months. These policies include medical, baggage, trip cancellation or interruption insurance, and flight insurance against death or dismemberment.

6 Tips for Special Travelers

FOR TRAVELERS WITH DISABILITIES Almost all hotels and motels in the Northwest, aside from bed-and-breakfast inns and older or historic lodges, offer disabled-accessible accommodations. However, when making reservations be sure to ask.

The public transit systems found in most Northwest cities have either disabled-accessible regular vehicles or offer special transportation services for the disabled.

Oregon lodgings that are disabled-accessible are listed in the *Oregon Traveler's Guide to Accommodations.* To get a copy of this magazine, contact the **Oregon Tourism Division,** 775 Summer St. NE, Salem, OR 97310 (☎ **800/547-7842**).

Oregon State Parks has a TDD (Telephone Device for the Deaf) information line for the deaf (☎ **800/735-2900**) that provides recreation and camping information. The **Oregon Paralyzed Veterans of America** (☎ **503/652-0241** or 800/ 333-0782) may be able to advise disabled visitors on accessibility in Oregon.

If you plan to visit any national parks or monuments, you can avail yourself of the **Golden Access Passport.** This lifetime pass is issued free to any U.S. citizen or permanent resident who has been medically certified as disabled or blind. The pass permits free entry into national parks and monuments and also provides a 50% discount on campgrounds and recreational activities provided by the federal government (but not those provided by private concessionaires).

Rick Crowder of the **Travelin' Talk** network, P.O. Box 3534, Clarksville, TN 37043-3534 (☎ **615/552-6670** Monday through Friday between noon and 5pm central time), organizes a network for disabled travelers. An eight-page newsletter is available for any contribution. A directory listing people and organizations around the world who are networked to provide the disabled traveler with first-hand information about a chosen destination is available for $35.

FOR GAY & LESBIAN TRAVELERS The *Seattle Gay News,* with offices at 1605 12th Ave., Suite 31, Seattle, WA 98122 (☎ **206/324-4297**), is the Seattle gay community's newspaper. For a guide to Seattle's gay-friendly businesses, get a copy of the *Greater Seattle Business Association (GSBA) Guide Directory,* available from 2033 Sixth Ave., Suite 804, Seattle, WA 98121 (☎ **206/ 443-4722**). Also in Seattle is the **Lesbian Resource Center,** 1808 Bellevue Ave., Suite 204 (☎ **206/322-3953**).

Gay men and women visiting Portland can pick up a copy of *Just Out,* a gay monthly newspaper. You can usually find copies at Powell's Books, 1005 W. Burnside St., or phone 503/236-1252 to find out where you can obtain a copy. They also publish a free resource guide called *The Just Out Pocket Book.*

FOR SENIORS When making airline reservations, always mention that you're a senior citizen. Many airlines offer discounts. You should also carry some sort of photo ID card (drivers license, passport, etc.) to avail yourself of senior-citizen discounts on attractions, hotels, motels, and public transportation, as well as another good deal—the Golden Age Passport, which is available for $10 to U.S. citizens and permanent residents age 62 and older. This federal government pass carries entrance privileges and a 50% discount on recreation fees at parks, forests, and other federal recreation areas. You can apply in person for this passport at a national park, forest, or other location where it's honored, and you must show reasonable proof of age.

If you're not already a member, the **American Association of Retired Persons (AARP),** 601 E St. NW, Washington, DC 20049 (☎ **800/424-3410**), is a good source of information for senior citizens. Membership is only $8 for two people.

If you'd like to do some studying while on vacation, consider Elderhostel (see "Educational and Volunteer Vacations," earlier in this chapter).

7　Getting There

BY PLANE　The region's two **main airports** are Seattle-Tacoma International Airport (Sea-Tac) and Portland International Airport. All the major car-rental companies have locations at both airports.

Seattle and Portland are served by the following **airlines:** Alaska Airlines (☎ 800/426-0333), America West (☎ 800/235-9292), American Airlines (☎ 800/433-7300), Continental (☎ 800/525-0280), Delta (☎ 800/221-1212), Horizon Air (☎ 800/547-9308), Northwest (☎ 800/225-2525), Southwest (☎ 800/435-9792), TWA (☎ 800/221-2000), United Airlines (☎ 800/241-6522), and USAir (☎ 800/428-4322).

BY CAR　The distance from Los Angeles to Seattle is 1,190 miles; from Salt Lake City, 835 miles; from Spokane, in the eastern part of Washington, 285 miles; and from Vancouver, B.C., 110 miles. Portland is 175 miles south of Seattle.

If you're driving up from California, I-5 runs up through the length of the state and continues up toward the Canadian border; it will take you through both Portland and Seattle. If you're coming from the east, I-90 runs from Montana and Idaho into Washington, eventually hitting Seattle. I-84 leads from southern Idaho up into Oregon, where it branches west and heads into Portland.

BY TRAIN　Seattle and Portland are served by **Amtrak** (☎ **800/872-7245**). Three trains serve the region: The *Coast Starlight* operates between Los Angeles and Seattle with stops in San Francisco and Portland, as well as at smaller towns and cities. The *Empire Builder* and the *Pioneer* connect the Northwest with Chicago. The former follows the northern route through North Dakota and Montana, while the latter follows the southern route through Colorado and Wyoming. At press time the round-trip fare between San Francisco and Portland was about $108.

BY BUS　**Greyhound Lines** buses (☎ **800/231-2222**) offer service to the Northwest from around the country. These buses operate primarily along the Interstate corridors (I-5, I-84, I-90, and I-82) and to a few other towns and cities on major highways. The fare between San Francisco and Seattle is $39 one way and $78 round-trip.

BY FERRY　The high-speed **Victoria Clipper** passenger ferries, Pier 69, 2701 Alaskan Way, Seattle, WA 98121 (☎ **206/448-5000** or 800/888-2535), operate between Seattle and Victoria, British Columbia. The trip aboard these speedy catamarans takes 2¹/₂ to 3 hours. The round-trip fare for adults is $69 to $89; for seniors, $69 to $79; and for children ages 1 to 11, $41.50 to $44.50. Round-trip tickets are substantially cheaper if purchased in advance. Bellingham, north of Seattle, is the port for Alaska ferries and cruise ships.

PACKAGE TOURS　**Gray Line of Seattle,** 720 S. Forest St., Seattle (☎ **800/426-7505**), offers two- to six-day bus tours that include Seattle, Mount St. Helens, Vancouver, and Victoria. Summer-season prices range from $300 for a three-day/two-night trip to $660 for a seven-day/six-night trip. **Alaska Sightseeing Cruise**

West, Fourth and Battery Building, Suite 700, Seattle (☎ **206/441-8687** or 800/426-7702), offers an eight-day cruise from Portland on the Columbia and Snake rivers, and four- to eight-day cruises from Seattle to British Columbia and the San Juan Islands. Fares range from $445 to $3,195.

8   Getting Around

BY CAR   A car is by far the best way to see the Northwest. There just isn't any other way to get to the more remote natural spectacles or to fully appreciate such regions as the Oregon coast or Olympic Peninsula.

Rentals   Seattle and Portland, the Northwest's two gateway cities, both have dozens of car-rental agencies, including branches at both cities' airports. Prices at rental agencies elsewhere in the state tend to be higher, so if at all possible, try to rent your car in one or the other of these two cities.

For the very best deal on a rental car, make your reservation at least one week in advance. It also pays to shop around and call the same companies a few times over the course of a couple of weeks. If you decide on the spur of the moment to rent a car, check to see whether there are any weekend or special rates available. If you're a member of a frequent-flyer program, be sure to mention it: You might get mileage credit for renting a car. Keep asking about special promotions and try different combinations of where to pick up and drop off your car—rental-car agencies, like airlines, don't tell you about the cheapest deals unless you ask, and they have a maze of different offerings and rates.

Major **car-rental companies** with offices in Portland and Seattle include Alamo (☎ 800/327-9633), Avis (☎ 800/331-1212), Budget (☎ 800/527-0700), Dollar (☎ 800/800-4000), Hertz (☎ 800/654-3131), National (☎ 800/227-7368), and Thrifty (☎ 800/367-2277).

Gasoline   The Northwest is a big region, so keep your gas tank as full as possible when traveling in the mountains or on the sparsely populated east side of the Cascades. There are no self-service gas stations in Oregon.

Maps   Maps are available at most highway tourist information centers, at the tourist information offices listed earlier in this chapter, and at gas stations throughout the region. For a free map of Washington call the **Washington State Tourism Office** (☎ **800/544-1800**). For a map of Oregon contact the **Oregon Tourism Division** (☎ **800/547-7842**). Members of the AAA can get detailed road maps of the Northwest by calling their local AAA office.

Driving Rules   A right turn on red is permitted after first coming to a complete stop. You may also turn left on a red light if you're in the far-left lane of a one-way street and are turning into another one-way street. Seat belts are required, as are car seats for children.

Breakdowns/Assistance   In the event of a breakdown, stay with your car, lift the hood, turn on your emergency flashers, and wait for a police patrol car. *Do not leave your vehicle.* If you're a member of the American Automobile Association and your car breaks down, call 800/AAA-HELP for 24-hour emergency road service.

BY PLANE   The Northwest is a large region, and if you're trying to see every corner of it in a short time, you may want to consider flying. **Airlines** operating

Oregon–Washington Driving Distances

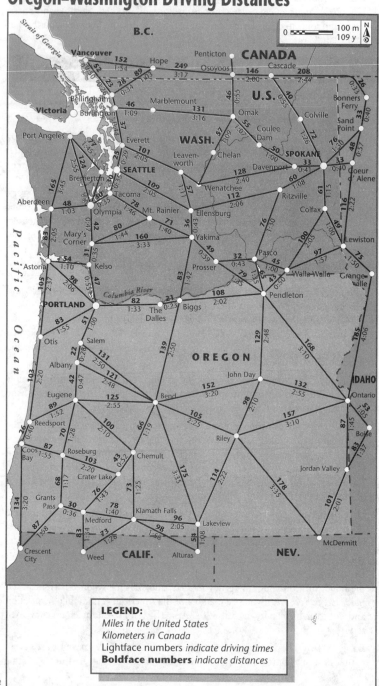

LEGEND:
Miles in the United States
Kilometers in Canada
Lightface numbers *indicate driving times*
Boldface numbers *indicate distances*

short hops between the major cities include Alaska Airlines (☎ 800/426-0333), America West (☎ 800/235-9292), Horizon Air (☎ 800/547-9308), Southwest (☎ 800/435-9792), and United Express (☎ 800/241-6522).

In addition to these major airlines, there are several small airlines that fly out **to the San Juan Islands.** Kenmore Air (☎ 206/364-6990, or 800/543-9595) has seaplane flights from Seattle, and Harbor Airlines (☎ 800/359-3220) flies between Sea-Tac International Airport in Seattle and Whidbey Island. West Isle Air (☎ 800/874-4434) flies to the San Juans from Bellingham and Anacortes.

BY TRAIN   Though there is **Amtrak** (☎ 800/872-7245) passenger rail service linking southern Oregon, Seattle, and Vancouver, B.C., and from Portland eastward along the Columbia River and north from there to Spokane, service is not very frequent. We don't recommend the train for getting around the region except perhaps for the run between Portland and Seattle, which takes about four hours and costs $25 one way (reservations are required).

BY FERRY   **Washington State Ferries** (☎ 206/464-6400 or 800/84-FERRY in Washington) operates the most extensive ferry network in the United States. There are ferries connecting Seattle to Vashon Island, Bremerton, Southworth, and Bainbridge Island; Tacoma to Vashon Island; Edmunds to Kingston; Mukilteo to Clinton; Keystone to Port Townsend; and Anacortes to San Juan, Orcas, Lopez, and Shaw Islands, and Sidney, B.C. (for Victoria).

There are also a number of smaller county or private ferries. The most important of these are the **Black Ball Transport** (☎ 360/457-4491 or 604/386-2202 in Victoria) and **Victoria Rapid Transit** (☎ 360/452-8088, 604/361-9144 in Victoria, or 800/633-1589 in Washington) ferries that operate between Port Angeles and Victoria, B.C. There's also passenger-ferry service between Seattle and Friday Harbor on San Juan Island, and between Seattle and Victoria, British Columbia, on the **Victoria Clipper** ferries (☎ 800/888-2535).

BY R.V.   An economical way to tour the Northwest is with a recreational vehicle. If you're considering renting an R.V., look under "Recreational Vehicles—Rent and Lease" in the yellow pages of the local phone book. They can be rented for a weekend, a week, or longer. In Portland, you might try **Cruise America Motorhome Rental,** 9245 SE 82nd Ave., Portland, OR 97266 (☎ 503/788-9627). In Seattle, try **AAA Recreational Vehicles, Inc.,** 12715 Aurora N., Seattle, WA 98133 (☎ 206/364-7857 or 800/458-7857). If you're going to be traveling in the peak season of summer, it's important to make reservations for your R.V. at least three months ahead of time.

9   Cruising the Columbia River

Paddlewheel steamboats played a crucial role in the settling of the Northwest, shuttling people and goods down the Columbia River before railroads came to the region. Today, the *Queen of the West,* a paddlewheel cruise ship operated by the American West Steamboat Company, 520 Pike St., Suite 1400, Seattle, WA 98101 (☎ 800/434-1232) is cruising the Columbia offering a luxury never before known in Columbia River paddlewheelers. Cruises range from 2 to 7 days and cover as much as 1,000 miles of river. Rates range from a minimum of $279 per person in a basic stateroom for a two-night cruise up to a maximum of $3,945 per person in the owner's suite for a seven-night cruise.

FAST FACTS: Washington & Oregon

AAA   If you're a member of the American Automobile Association and your car breaks down, call 800/AAA-HELP for 24-hour emergency road service.

American Express   In Seattle, their office is in the Plaza 600 Building at 600 Stewart St. (☎ 206/441-8622) and in Portland they're located at 1100 SW Sixth Ave. (☎ 503/226-2961). Both offices are open Monday through Friday from 9am to 5pm. Call the Seattle or Portland office for information on American Express services in other outlying towns. To report lost or stolen traveler's checks, call 800/221-7282.

Area Code   The telephone area code for Portland and the northwest part of Oregon is 503. Other parts of Oregon use the area code 541. The area code for Seattle and surrounding areas south to Tacoma, east to Kirkland, and north to Everett use the area code 206. Other parts of western Washington use area code 360, while east of the Washington Cascades the area code is 509.

Banks and ATM Networks   ATMs in Washington and Oregon generally use the following systems: Star, Plus, Interlink, Cirrus, and Excel networks. MasterCard and Visa may also be used.

Car Rentals   See "Getting Around," earlier in this chapter.

Climate   See "When to Go," earlier in this chapter.

Embassies and Consulates   See "Fast Facts: For the Foreign Traveler" in Chapter 4.

Emergencies   Call **911** for fire, police, and ambulance.

Information   See "Visitor Information & Money," earlier in this chapter, and individual city chapters for local information offices.

Liquor Laws   The legal drinking age in Washington and Oregon is 21. Bars can legally stay open until 2am.

Maps   See "Getting Around," earlier in this chapter.

Pets   Many hotels and motels in the Northwest accept small, well-behaved pets. However, there's often a small fee charged to allow them into guest rooms. Many places, in particular bed-and-breakfast inns, don't allow pets at all. On the other hand, many bed-and-breakfasts have their own pets, so if you have a dog or cat allergy, be sure to mention it when making a bed-and-breakfast reservation. Two good resources for dog owners are *Frommer's On the Road Again with Man's Best Friend: Northwest* and *Frommer's America on Wheels: Northwest* (both from Macmillan), which will steer you toward dog-friendly accommodations. Pets are usually restricted in national parks for their own safety, so call each park's ranger station to check before setting out.

Police   To reach the police, dial 911.

Taxes   The state of Washington makes up for its lack of an income tax with its sales tax of between 6% and 8.2%. Oregon is a shopper's paradise—there's no sales tax.

Time Zone   The Northwest is on Pacific standard time (PST) and observes daylight saving time from the last Sunday in October to the first Sunday in April, making it consistently three hours behind the East Coast.

Weather   In Seattle, call 206/526-6087; in Portland, call 503/236-7575.

For Foreign Visitors 4

This chapter will provide some specifics about getting to the United States as economically and effortlessly as possible, plus some helpful information about how things are done in the Northwest—from receiving mail to making a local or long-distance telephone call.

1 Preparing for Your Trip

ENTRY REQUIREMENTS

DOCUMENT REGULATIONS   Canadian citizens may enter the United States without visas; they need only proof of residence.

British subjects and citizens of New Zealand, Japan, and most western European countries traveling on valid passports may not need a visa for fewer than 90 days of holiday or business travel to the United States, providing that they hold a round-trip or return ticket and enter the country on an airline or cruise line participating in the visa waiver program. (Citizens of these visa-exempt countries who first enter the United States may then visit Mexico, Canada, Bermuda, and/or the Caribbean islands and then reenter the United States, by any mode of transportation, without needing a visa. Further information is available from any U.S. embassy or consulate.)

Citizens of countries other than those stipulated above, including citizens of Australia, must have two documents: (1) a valid passport, with an expiration date at least six months later than the scheduled end of the visit to the United States; and (2) a tourist visa, available without charge from the nearest U.S. consulate.

To obtain a visa, the traveler must submit a completed application form (either in person or by mail) with a $1^1/_2$-inch-square photo and demonstrate binding ties to a residence abroad. Usually you can obtain a visa at once or within 24 hours, but it may take longer during the summer rush from June to August. If you cannot go in person, contact the nearest U.S. embassy or consulate for directions on applying by mail. Your travel agent or airline office may also be able to provide you with visa applications and instructions. The U.S. consulate or embassy that issues your visa will determine whether you will be issued a multiple- or single-entry visa and any restrictions regarding the length of your stay.

MEDICAL REQUIREMENTS   No inoculations are needed to enter the United States unless you are coming from, or have stopped over in, areas known to be suffering from epidemics, especially of cholera or yellow fever.

If you have a disease requiring treatment with medications containing narcotics or drugs requiring a syringe, carry a valid signed prescription from your physician to allay any suspicions that you're smuggling drugs.

CUSTOMS REQUIREMENTS   Every adult visitor may bring in free of duty: 1 liter of wine or hard liquor; 200 cigarettes *or* 100 cigars (but no cigars from Cuba) *or* 3 pounds of smoking tobacco; and $100 worth of gifts. These exemptions are offered to travelers who spend at least 72 hours in the United States and who have not claimed them within the preceding six months. It is altogether forbidden to bring into the country foodstuffs (particularly cheese, fruit, cooked meats, and canned goods) and plants (vegetables, seeds, tropical plants, and so on). Foreign tourists may bring in or take out up to $10,000 in U.S. or foreign currency with no formalities; larger sums must be declared to Customs on entering or leaving.

INSURANCE

There is no national health-care system in the United States. Because the cost of medical care is extremely high, we strongly advise every traveler to secure health insurance coverage before setting out. You may want to take out a comprehensive travel policy that covers (for a relatively low premium) sickness or injury costs (medical, surgical, and hospital); loss or theft of your baggage; trip-cancellation costs; guarantee of bail in case you are arrested; and costs associated with accident, repatriation, or death. Such packages (for example, "Europe Assistance" in Europe) are sold by automobile clubs at attractive rates, as well as by insurance companies and travel agencies.

MONEY

CURRENCY & EXCHANGE   The U.S. monetary system has a decimal base: one American **dollar** ($1) = 100 **cents** (100¢).

Dollar bills commonly come in $1 (a "buck"), $5, $10, $20, $50, and $100 denominations (the last two are not welcome when paying for small purchases and are not accepted in taxis). There are also $2 bills (seldom encountered).

There are six denominations of coins: 1¢ (one cent, or a "penny"); 5¢ (five cents, or a "nickel"); 10¢ (ten cents, or a "dime"); 25¢ (twenty-five cents, or a "quarter"); 50¢ (fifty cents, or a "half dollar"); and the rare $1 piece.

Note: The foreign-exchange bureaus so common in Europe are rare in the United States, and nonexistent outside major cities. Try to avoid having to change foreign money, or traveler's checks not denominated in U.S. dollars, at a small-town bank, or even a branch bank in a big city. In fact, leave any currency other than U.S. dollars at home—it may prove more nuisance to you than it's worth.

TRAVELER'S CHECKS   Traveler's checks denominated in U.S. dollars are readily accepted at most hotels, motels, restaurants, and large stores, but the best place to change traveler's checks is at a bank. Do not bring traveler's checks denominated in other currencies.

CREDIT & CHARGE CARDS   The method of payment most widely used is credit and charge cards: Visa (BarclayCard in Britain), MasterCard (EuroCard in Europe, Access in Britain, Chargex in Canada), American Express, Diners Club, Discover, and Carte Blanche. You can save yourself trouble by using "plastic money" rather than cash or traveler's checks in most hotels, motels, restaurants, and retail stores (a growing number of food and liquor stores now accept credit/charge cards). You must have a credit or charge card to rent a car. It can also be used as proof of identity (it often carries more weight than a passport) or as a "cash card," enabling you to draw money from banks and automated-teller machines (ATMs) that accept it.

SAFETY

GENERAL   While tourist areas are generally safe, crime is on the increase everywhere, and U.S. urban areas tend to be less safe than those in Europe or Japan. Visitors should always stay alert. This is particularly true in large U.S. cities. It is wise to ask the city's or area's tourist office if you're in doubt about which neighborhoods are safe.

Remember that hotels are open to the public, and in a large hotel, security may not be able to screen everyone entering. Always lock your room door—don't assume that once inside your hotel you are automatically safe and no longer need be aware of your surroundings.

DRIVING   Safety while driving is particularly important. Question your rental agency about personal safety, or ask for a brochure of traveler safety tips when you pick up your car. Obtain from the agency written directions, or a map with the route marked in red, to show you how to get to your destination. If possible, arrive and depart during daylight hours.

Recently more and more crime has involved cars and drivers. If you drive off a highway into a doubtful neighborhood, leave the area as quickly as possible. If you have an accident, even on the highway, stay in your car with the doors locked until you assess the situation or until the police arrive. If you are bumped from behind on the street or are involved in a minor accident with no injuries, and the situation appears to be suspicious, motion to the other driver to follow you. *Never* get out of your car in such situations.

If you see someone on the road who indicates a need for help, *don't stop.* Take note of the location, drive on to a well-lit area, and telephone the police by dialing 911.

If someone attempts to rob you or steal your car, do *not* try to resist the thief/carjacker—report the incident to the police department immediately.

You may wish to contact the visitor information centers in either Seattle or Portland for a safety brochure. In Portland, contact the **Portland Oregon Visitors Association,** Three World Trade Center, 26 SW Salmon St., Portland, OR 97204-3299 (☎ **503/222-2223** or 800/345-3214); in Seattle, contact the **Seattle–King County Convention & Visitors Bureau,** 520 Pike St., Suite 1300, Seattle, WA 98101-9927 (☎ **206/461-5840**).

2   Getting To & Around the U.S.

GETTING TO THE U.S.

Travelers from overseas can take advantage of the **APEX (advance-purchase excursion)** fares offered by all the major international carriers.

From Canada, there are flights from Toronto to Seattle and Portland on Air Canada (☎ 800/268-7240 in Canada or 800/361-8620 in the U.S.), Northwest, and United. There are flights from Vancouver, B.C., to Seattle and Portland on Air Canada, Horizon, Northwest, and United.

Airlines traveling **from London** to Seattle and Portland are American, Delta, Northwest, TWA, and United. British Airways flies direct to Seattle from London. You can make reservations by calling the following numbers in Britain: American (☎ 0181/572-5555), British Airways (☎ 0345/222-111), Delta (☎ 0800/414-767), Northwest (☎ 01293/56-1000), TWA (☎ 0171/439-0707), United (☎ 0181/990-9900), and Virgin Atlantic (☎ 0293/747-747). **From Ireland,** you can also try Aer Lingus (☎ 01/844-4747 in Dublin or 061/415-556 in Shannon).

From New Zealand and Australia, there are flights to Los Angeles and San Francisco on Qantas (☎ toll free 008/177-767 in Australia) and to Los Angeles on Air New Zealand (☎ 0800/737-000 in Auckland or 3/379-5200 in Christchurch). Both airlines can book you through to a destination in Washington and Oregon on a connecting flight offered by a domestic airline. United flies direct to Seattle from New Zealand and Australia (☎ 02/237-8888 for the Sydney ticket office, 09/256-8481 in Auckland, New Zealand).

The visitor arriving by air, no matter what the port of entry, should cultivate patience and resignation before setting foot on U.S. soil. Getting through Immigration control may take as long as two hours on some days, especially summer weekends. Add the time it takes to clear Customs and you'll see that you should make very generous allowance for delay in planning connections between international and domestic flights—an average of two to three hours at least.

In contrast, travelers arriving by car or by rail from Canada will find border-crossing formalities streamlined to the vanishing point. And air travelers from Canada, Bermuda, and some places in the Caribbean can sometimes go through Customs and Immigration at the point of departure, which is much quicker and less painful.

GETTING AROUND THE U.S.

BY PLANE   Some large airlines (for example, American Airlines, Delta, Northwest, TWA, and United) offer travelers on their transatlantic and transpacific flights special discount tickets under the name **Visit USA,** allowing travel between any U.S. destinations at minimum rates. They are not on sale in the United States—they must be purchased before you leave your foreign point of departure. This system is the best, easiest, and fastest way to see the United States at low cost. You should obtain information well in advance from your travel agent or the office of the airline concerned, since the conditions attached to these discount tickets can be changed without advance notice.

BY TRAIN   Long-distance trains in the United States are operated by **Amtrak** (☎ 800/872-7245), the national rail passenger corporation. International visitors can buy a **USA Railpass,** good for 15 or 30 days of unlimited travel on Amtrak. The pass is available through many foreign travel agents. Prices in 1995 for a 15-day pass are $229 off-peak, $340 peak; a 30-day pass costs $339 off-peak, $425 peak (off-peak is August 31 to June 15). (With a foreign passport, you can also buy passes at some Amtrak offices in the United States, including locations in San Francisco, Los Angeles, Chicago, New York, Miami, Boston, and Washington, D.C.) Reservations are generally required and should be made for each part of your trip as early as possible. Amtrak also offers an **Air/Rail Travel Plan** that allows you to travel both by train and plane; for information call 800/321-8684.

Visitors should also be aware of the limitations of long-distance rail travel in the United States. With a few notable exceptions, service is rarely up to European standards: Delays are common, routes are limited and often infrequently served, and fares are rarely significantly lower than discount airfares. Thus cross-country train travel should be approached with caution.

BY BUS   The cheapest way to travel in the United States is by bus. **Greyhound** (☎ **800/231-2222**), the sole nationwide bus line, offers an **Ameripass** for unlimited travel. At press time, a seven-day pass was $179, a 15-day pass was $289, and a 30-day pass was $399. Bus travel in the United States can be both slow and uncomfortable, so this option is not for everyone.

BY CAR   The United States is a nation of cars and the most cost-effective, convenient, and comfortable way to travel through the country is by driving. The Interstate highway system connects cities and towns all over the country, and in addition to these high-speed, limited-access roadways, there is an extensive network of federal, state, and local highways and roads. Another convenience of traveling by car is the easy access to inexpensive motels at Interstate-highway off-ramps. Such motels are almost always less expensive than hotels and motels in downtown areas.

The American Automobile Association (AAA) can provide you with an **International Driving Permit** validating your foreign license. You may be able to join the AAA even if you're not a member of a reciprocal club. To inquire, call 800/ AAA-HELP. In addition, some automobile rental agencies now provide these services.

FAST FACTS: For the Foreign Traveler

Accommodations   It's always a good idea to make hotel reservations as soon as you know your trip dates. Reservations usually require a deposit of one night's payment. Hotels throughout the Northwest are particularly busy during the summer months and hotels book up in advance, especially on holiday weekends. If you don't have a reservation, it's best to look for a room in midafternoon. If you wait until later in the evening, you run the risk that hotels will already be filled. Major downtown hotels, which cater primarily to business travelers, commonly offer weekend discounts of as much as 50% to entice vacationers to fill up the empty hotel rooms. However, resorts and hotels near tourist attractions tend to have higher rates on weekends.

Automobile Organizations   Auto clubs will supply maps, suggested routes, guidebooks, accident and bail-bond insurance, and emergency road service. The major auto club in the United States, with 955 offices nationwide, is the **American Automobile Association (AAA).** Members of some foreign auto clubs have reciprocal arrangements with the AAA and enjoy its services at no charge. If you belong to an auto club in your home country, inquire about AAA reciprocity before you leave. The AAA can provide you with an **International Driving Permit** validating your foreign license. You may be able to join the AAA even if you're not a member of a reciprocal club. To inquire, call 800/AAA-HELP. In addition, some automobile rental agencies now provide these services, so you should inquire about their availability when you rent your car.

Automobile Rentals   To rent a car you need a major credit or charge card and a valid driver's license. Sometimes a passport or an international driver's license is also required if your driver's license is in a language other than English. You usually need to be at least 25, although some companies do rent to younger people but may add a daily surcharge. Be sure to return your car with the same amount of gasoline you started out with, as rental companies charge excessive prices for gas. Keep in mind that a separate motorcycle driver's license is required in most states. See "Getting Around" in Chapter 3 for specifics on auto rental in Washington and Oregon.

Business Hours   The following are general open hours; specific establishments may vary. **Banks:** Monday through Friday from 9am to 5pm (some are also open on Saturday from 9am to noon). There is also 24-hour access to banks through automatic-teller machines (ATMs). **Offices:** Monday through Friday from 9am to 5pm. **Stores:** Monday through Saturday from 10am to 6pm and on Sunday from noon to 5pm (malls usually stay open until 9pm Monday through Saturday). **Bars:** Nightly until 2am.

Climate   See "When to Go" in Chapter 3.

Currency   See "Preparing for Your Trip," earlier in this chapter.

Currency Exchange   You'll find currency-exchange services in major airports with international service. To exchange money **in Seattle,** go to American Express, 600 Stewart St. (☎ 206/441-8622), or Thomas Cook, 906 Third Ave. (☎ 206/623-6203). To exchange money **in Portland,** go to American Express, 1100 SW Sixth Ave. (☎ 503/226-2961), or Thomas Cook at Powell's Travel Store, 701 SW Sixth Ave. (☎ 503/222-2665). It's not convenient to change foreign currency outside of the major cities, so try to anticipate your needs.

Drinking Laws   The legal drinking age in both Washington and Oregon— as in most other states—is 21. The penalties for driving under the influence of alcohol are stiff.

Electricity   The United States uses 110–120 volts, 60 cycles, compared to 220–240 volts, 50 cycles, as in most of Europe. In addition to a 110-volt transformer, small appliances of non-American manufacture, such as hairdryers or shavers, will require a plug adapter with two flat, parallel pins.

Embassies & Consulates   All embassies are located in Washington, D.C.; some consulates are located in major cities, and most nations have a mission to the United Nations in New York City.

   Listed here are the embassies and consulates of the major English-speaking countries. If you're from another country, you can get the telephone number of your embassy by calling information in Washington, D.C. (☎ 202/555-1212).

   The local Canadian consulate is at 412 Plaza 600 Building, Sixth Avenue and Stewart Street, Seattle, WA 98101-1286 (☎ 206/443-1777).

   There's a British consulate in Seattle at 999 Third Ave., Suite 820, Seattle, WA 98104 (☎ 206/622-9255).

Emergencies   Call **911** to report a fire, call the police, or get an ambulance. This is a toll-free call (no coins are required at a public telephone).

   If you encounter traveler's problems, check the local telephone directory to find an office of the **Traveler's Aid Society,** a nationwide nonprofit social-service organization geared to helping travelers in difficult straits. Their services might include reuniting families separated while traveling, providing food and/or shelter to people stranded without cash, or even emotional counseling. If you're in trouble, seek them out.

Gasoline (Petrol)   One U.S. gallon equals 3.8 liters, while 1.2 U.S. gallons equals one Imperial gallon. You'll notice there are several grades (and price levels) of gasoline available at most gas stations. And you'll also notice that their names change from company to company. The unleaded ones with the highest octane rating are the most expensive (most rental cars take the least expensive "regular" unleaded); leaded gas is the least expensive, but only older cars can take this anymore, so check if you're not sure. In Oregon you are not allowed to pump your own gasoline, but in Washington, self-service gas stations are common and are less expensive than full-service stations.

Holidays   On the following legal national holidays, banks, government offices, post offices, and many stores, restaurants, and museums are closed: January 1 (New Year's Day), third Monday in January (Martin Luther King, Jr., Day), third Monday in February (Presidents Day/Washington's Birthday), last Monday in May (Memorial Day), July 4 (Independence Day), first Monday in September (Labor Day), second Monday in October (Columbus Day), November 11 (Veteran's Day/Armistice Day), last Thursday in November (Thanksgiving Day), and December 25 (Christmas). The Tuesday following the first Monday in November is Election Day, and is a legal holiday in presidential-election years (1996 is an election year).

Legal Aid   If you are stopped for a minor infraction (say, speeding on the highway), never attempt to pay the fine directly to the police officer; you may wind up arrested on the much more serious charge of attempted bribery. Pay fines by mail, or directly into the hands of the clerk of the court. If you're accused of a more serious offense, say and do nothing before consulting a lawyer. Under U.S. law, an arrested person is allowed one telephone call to a party of his or her choice. Call your embassy or consulate.

Mail   If you want to receive mail on your vacation and you aren't sure of your address, your mail can be sent to you, in your name, [c/o] **General Delivery** at the main post office of the city or region where you expect to be. The addressee must pick it up in person and produce proof of identity (driver's license, credit or charge card, passport, etc.).

If your mail is addressed to a U.S. destination, don't forget to add the five-figure **postal code,** or ZIP (Zone Improvement Plan) code, after the two-letter abbreviation of the state to which the mail is addressed (WA for Washington, OR for Oregon, CA for California, and so on).

Safety   See "Safety" in "Preparing for Your Trip," earlier in this chapter. Whenever you're traveling in an unfamiliar city or country, stay alert. Be aware of your immediate surroundings. Be particularly careful with cameras, purses, and wallets—all favorite targets of thieves and pickpockets. Seattle and Portland are both particularly prone to car break-ins, so never leave any valuables in your car. The entertainment districts of Seattle and Portland are both adjacent to areas frequented by homeless people. Don't travel alone in these areas late at night.

Taxes   In the United States there is no VAT (value-added tax) or other indirect tax at a national level. Every state, and each county and city in it, is allowed to levy its own local tax on purchases (including hotel and restaurant checks and airline tickets) and services. In Washington state, the sales tax rate is between 6% and 8.2%. In Portland and the rest of Oregon, there is no sales tax.

Telephone, Telegraph, and Fax   The telephone system in the United States is run by private corporations, so rates, especially for long-distance service and operator-assisted calls, can vary widely—even on calls made from public telephones. Local calls usually cost 25¢.

Generally, hotel surcharges on long-distance and local calls are astronomical. You're usually better off using a **public pay telephone.** Outside metropolitan areas, public telephones are more difficult to find. Stores and gas stations are your best bet.

Most **long-distance and international calls** can be dialed directly from any phone. For calls to Canada and other parts of the United States, dial 1 followed by the area code and the seven-digit number. For international calls, dial 011 followed by the country code, then the city code, and the telephone number of the person you wish to call.

For **reversed-charge or collect calls,** and for **person-to-person calls,** dial 0 (zero, *not* the letter "O") followed by the area code and number you want; an operator will then come on the line and you should specify what you want. If your operator-assisted call is international, ask for the overseas operator.

For **local directory assistance** ("information"), dial 411; for **long-distance information,** dial 1, then the appropriate area code and 555-1212.

Like the telephone system, **telegraph** and **telex** services are provided by private corporations like ITT, MCI, and above all, Western Union. You can bring your telegram in to the nearest Western Union office (there are hundreds across the country) or dictate it over the phone (a toll-free call: 800/325-6000). You can also telegraph money, or have it telegraphed to you, very quickly over the Western Union system.

If you need to send a fax, almost all shops that make photocopies offer fax service as well.

Time   The United States is divided into six time zones. From east to west these are eastern standard time (EST), central standard time (CST), mountain standard time (MST), Pacific standard time (PST), Alaska standard time (AST), and Hawaii standard time (HST). Always keep changing time zones in your mind if you are traveling (or even telephoning) long distances in the United States. For example, noon in Seattle (PST) is 1pm in Phoenix (MST), 2pm in Chicago (CST), 3pm in New York City (EST), 11am in Anchorage (AST), and 10am in Honolulu (HST). **Daylight saving time** is in effect from 2am on the first Sunday in April until 2am on the last Sunday in October except in Arizona, Hawaii, part of Indiana, and Puerto Rico.

Tipping   This is part of the American way of life, on the principle that you must expect to pay for any service you get (many service personnel receive little direct salary and must depend on tips for their income). Here are some rules of thumb:

In **hotels,** tip bellhops $1 per piece and tip the chamber staff $1 per day. Tip the doorman or concierge only if he or she has provided you with some specific service (for example, calling a cab for you or obtaining difficult-to-get theater tickets).

In **restaurants, bars, and nightclubs,** tip the service staff 15% of the check, tip bartenders 10% to 15%, tip checkroom attendants $1 per garment, and tip valet-parking attendants $1 per vehicle. Tip the doorman only if he has provided you with some specific service (such as calling a cab for you). Tipping is not expected in cafeterias and fast-food restaurants.

Tip **cab drivers** 15% of the fare.

As for **other service personnel,** tip redcaps at airports or railroad stations $1 per piece and tip hairdressers and barbers 15% to 20%.

Tipping ushers in cinemas, movies, and theaters and gas-station attendants is not expected.

Toilets Foreign visitors often complain that public toilets (or "restrooms") are hard to find in most U.S. cities. True, there are none on the streets, but the visitor can usually find one in a bar, restaurant, hotel, museum, department store, or service station—and it will probably be clean (although service-station restrooms sometimes leave much to be desired). The cleanliness and safety of toilets at public transportation depots is open to question. Some public places are equipped with pay toilets, which require you to insert one or more coins into a slot on the door before it will open.

5 Seattle

Don't look now, but it's all around. It's in your computer, on your radio, in your TV, on the big screen at your local movie theater, in your cup of coffee. "It," of course, is Seattle, a city propelled by geography, climate, and chance into the consciousness of the nation. Once a backwater with bad weather, Seattle has in the past few years surged into the national spotlight.

A few years ago, Seattle was voted "America's most livable city" and this praise, along with other accolades, prompted a massive influx (primarily of Californians) into the Seattle metropolitan area. About the same time that California refugees were discovering Seattle, the music industry decided that Seattle's guitar-driven grunge rock was the next big sound to succeed, a sound that would supplant the music of Athens and Minneapolis. The youth of America discovered Seattle and headed for the city by the sound (Puget, that is) with guitars in hand and dreams of Nirvana haunting their sleeping and waking hours.

Today, however, despite its grunge music and frequent movie appearances (Seattle has become a sort of Hollywood north), despite Microsoft and Boeing (the area's two most important employers), Seattle is best known as the coffee capital of America. To understand Seattle's coffee addiction it's necessary to study the city's geography and climate. Seattle lies at almost 50° north latitude, which means that winter days are short. The sun comes up around 7:30am and goes down as early as 4:30pm and is frequently hidden behind leaden skies. A strong stimulant is almost a necessity to get people out of bed and through the gray days of winter. Seattleites love to argue over which coffee bar in town serves the best coffee, and surprisingly, the answer isn't always Starbucks, despite this company's expansion across the country.

Seattle's popularity and rapid growth, though it has brought fine restaurants, a new art museum, rock-music fame, and national recognition of the city's arts scene, has not been entirely smooth. The streets and highways have been unable to handle the increased traffic load and commuting has become almost as nightmarish as down in California, from whence so many of the city's commuters once fled partly because of the traffic congestion. Despite congested roadways, the city in 1995 once again voted not to build a light-rail mass-transit system to alleviate congestion. Residents of the suburbs were unwilling to take on higher taxes in exchange for lighter traffic.

With roads growing ever more congested and the cost of living continuing to rise, Seattle may not be the Emerald City it once was, but it remains a city with a singularly spectacular setting. To stand in a park on Queen Anne Hill and gaze down at Puget Sound, the city skyline, and Mount Rainier in the distance is to understand why Seattleites love their city despite its flaws.

1 Orientation

ARRIVING

BY PLANE   Located 14 miles south of the city, **Seattle-Tacoma (Sea-Tac) International Airport** (☎ 206/431-4444) is connected to the city by I-5. Generally, allow 30 minutes for the trip between the airport and downtown (longer during rush hour). Major car-rental companies have facilities at the airport.

   Gray Line Airport Express (☎ 206/626-6088) provides service between the airport and downtown Seattle daily from 5am to midnight. The shuttle vans stop at several downtown hotels. Rates are $7 one way and $12 round-trip. **Shuttle Express** (☎ 206/622-1424 or 800/487-RIDE) provides 24-hour service between Sea-Tac and the Seattle area. The rates vary from $18 to $23. To leave the airport, just give them a call when you arrive. Push 48 on one of the courtesy phones outside the baggage-claim areas. You need to make a reservation to get to the airport.

   Metro Transit (☎ 206/553-3000) operates three buses between the airport and downtown. It's a good idea to call for the current schedule when you arrive in town. At this writing, no. 174 and no. 184 operate every 15 to 30 minutes around the clock; they make local stops, and the trip takes about an hour. Number 194, an express taking only 30 minutes, also departs every 30 minutes and operates between about 4:30am and 7:30pm Monday through Friday, and on Saturday from about 6:30am. The fare is $1.10 during off-peak hours and $1.60 during peak hours. Buses no. 174 and 184 operate to Ninth Avenue and Stewart Street. Number 194 operates to either Third Avenue and Union Street or the Convention Place Station of the Bus Tunnel, depending on the time of day.

   A taxi into downtown Seattle will cost you about $27. **Graytop Cab** (☎ 206/282-8222) has a special rate of $20 from Sea-Tac to downtown Seattle. There are usually plenty of taxis around the airport, but if not, call **Yellow Cab** (☎ 206/622-6500) or **Farwest Taxi** (☎ 206/622-1717). The flag-drop rate is $1.80; after that it's $1.80 per mile.

BY CAR   I-5, the Seattle Freeway, is the main north-south artery through Seattle, continuing south to Portland and north to the Canadian border. I-90 comes into Seattle from Spokane and ends just after 23rd Avenue. Washington Hwy. 99, the Alaskan Way Viaduct, is another major north-south highway through downtown Seattle; it passes through the waterfront section of the city.

BY TRAIN   If you arrive in Seattle on an Amtrak train, you'll find yourself at the **King Street Station** (☎ 206/382-4125), right across the parking lot from the Kingdome. The heart of downtown Seattle is only a few blocks north.

BY BUS   The **Greyhound Lines** bus station is at Eighth Avenue and Stewart Street (☎ 206/628-5508), which is slightly northeast of downtown Seattle.

BY SHIP   **Washington State Ferries** (☎ 206/464-6400, or 800/84-FERRY in Washington) dock at Pier 52. The **Victoria Clipper** ferries (☎ 206/448-5000 or 800/888-2535), which connect Victoria, British Columbia, with Seattle, dock at Pier 69.

VISITOR INFORMATION

Information on Seattle and the surrounding area is available by contacting the **Seattle–King County Convention & Visitors Bureau,** 520 Pike St., Suite 1300 (☎ 206/461-5840), or by stopping by the **information center** at the Washington State Convention & Trade Center, 800 Convention Place, Galleria Level, at the corner of Eighth Avenue and Pike Street (☎ 206/461-5840). The bureau is open Monday through Friday from 8:30am to 5pm. To find this information center, walk up Union Street until it goes into a tunnel under the convention center. You'll see the information center on your left as you enter the tunnel.

This same office operates another **Visitor Information Center** in the baggage-claim area at Sea-Tac Airport (☎ 206/433-5218), across from carousel no. 8. It's open daily from 9:30am to 7:30pm.

CITY LAYOUT

MAIN ARTERIES & STREETS   There are only three Interstate highways serving Seattle. **I-90** comes in from the east and ends downtown. I-405 bypasses the city completely, traveling up the east shore of Lake Washington through Bellevue. The main artery is **I-5,** which runs smack through the middle of Seattle. Take the James Street exit west if you're heading for the Pioneer Square area, take the Seneca Street exit for the Pike Place Market, or the Olive Way exit for Capitol Hill.

Downtown is roughly defined as extending from Yesler Way on the south to Denny Way on the north and from Elliott Bay on the west to Broadway on the east. Within this area most of the avenues are numbered, whereas the streets have names.

FINDING AN ADDRESS   After you become familiar with the streets and neighborhoods of Seattle, there's really only one important thing to remember in order to find an address: Pay attention to the compass point of the address. Downtown streets have no directional designation attached to them, but when you cross I-5 going east, most streets and avenues are designated "East." South of Yesler Way, which runs through Pioneer Square, streets are designated "South." West of Queen Anne Avenue, streets are designated "West." The University District is designated northeast ("NE"); the Ballard neighborhood, northwest ("NW").

Odd-numbered addresses are likely to be on the west and south sides of the street, whereas even-numbered addresses will be on the east and north sides of the street. Downtown, address numbers increase by 100 as you move away from Yesler Way going north or south and as you go east from the waterfront.

STREET MAPS   You can get a free map of the city from the Seattle–King County Convention & Visitors Bureau or at the Visitor Information Center in the baggage-claim area at Sea-Tac Airport. If you want to obtain a more detailed map of Seattle, stop by **Metsker Maps,** 702 First Ave. (☎ 206/623-8747). If you're a member of the **AAA,** you can get free maps of Seattle and Washington state either at an office near you or at the Seattle office, 330 Sixth Ave. N. (☎ 206/448-5353).

NEIGHBORHOODS IN BRIEF

Downtown   This is Seattle's main business district, roughly defined as the area from Pioneer Square in the south to just north of the Pike Place Market and from

Greater Seattle Orientation

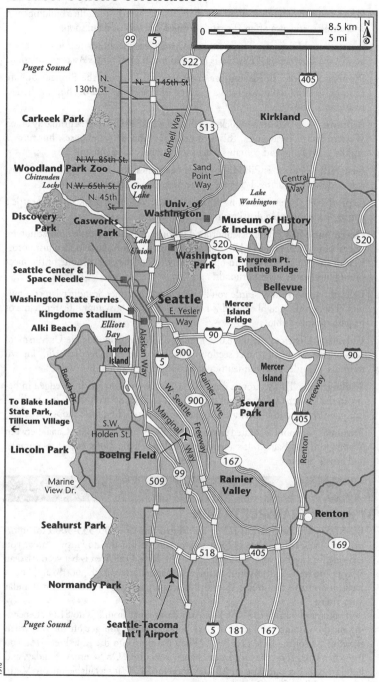

0   8.5 km
     5 mi

Puget Sound

Carkeek Park

N. 130th St.

N. 145th St.

Kirkland

Bothell Way

N.W. 85th St.

Woodland Park Zoo
Chittenden Locks

Sand Point Way

N.W. 65th St.

N. 45th St.

Green Lake

Discovery Park

Univ. of Washington

Lake Washington

Central Way

Gasworks Park

Lake Union

Museum of History & Industry

Washington Park

Evergreen Pt. Floating Bridge

Seattle Center & Space Needle

Bellevue

Washington State Ferries

Seattle

Kingdome Stadium

E. Yesler Way

Mercer Island Bridge

Alki Beach

Elliott Bay

Harbor Island

Alaskan Way

Mercer Island

Beach Dr.

To Blake Island State Park, Tillicum Village ←

W. Seattle Freeway

Rainier Ave.

Seward Park

S.W. Holden St.

Lincoln Park

Boeing Field

Marginal Way

Rainier Valley

Marine View Dr.

Seahurst Park

Renton

Renton Freeway

Normandy Park

Puget Sound

Seattle-Tacoma Int'l Airport

First Avenue to Seventh Avenue. It's characterized by high-rise office buildings and steep streets, and also offers the city's greatest diversity of retail shops.

International District The most immediately recognizable of Seattle's neighborhoods, the International District is home to much of the city's Asian population.

Pioneer Square Bordering the International District, the Pioneer Square Historic District is known for its restored old buildings full of shops, galleries, restaurants, and bars.

Belltown Located in the blocks north of the Pike Place Market primarily along Western and First avenues, this area once held mostly warehouses, but now is rapidly gentrifying and contains lots of restaurants and nightclubs.

First Hill Known as Pill Hill by most Seattleites, this hilly neighborhood just east of downtown across I-5 is the home of several hospitals.

Capitol Hill Centered along Broadway near Volunteer Park, this is Seattle's cutting-edge shopping district and gay community.

Queen Anne Hill This neighborhood is home to some of Seattle's oldest homes, several of which are now bed-and-breakfast inns. Queen Anne is located just northwest of the Seattle Center and offers great views of the city. It's one of the most prestigious Seattle neighborhoods.

Ballard In northwest Seattle you'll find Ballard, a former Scandinavian community. Though the neighborhood is now known for its busy nightlife, remnants of its past are still visible.

University District As the name implies, this area surrounds the University of Washington in the northeast section of the city. The "U" District, as it's known to locals, provides all the amenities of a college neighborhood.

Wallingford This section is one of Seattle's up-and-comers. It's wedged in between the University District and Ballard and is filling up with small, inexpensive-but-good restaurants. There are also quite a few interesting little shops.

Fremont Fremont is located north of the Lake Washington Ship Canal between Wallingford and Ballard. It's a neighborhood of eclectic shops, ethnic restaurants, and artists' studios.

2 Getting Around

BY PUBLIC TRANSPORTATION

BY BUS The best part of riding the **Metro bus** (☎ **206/553-3000** for information) in Seattle is that as long as you stay within the downtown area, you can ride for free between 4am and 9pm. The **Ride Free Area** is between Alaskan Way in the west, Sixth Avenue in the east, Battery Street in the north, and South Jackson Street in the south. Within this area are many of Seattle's most popular attractions.

If you travel outside the Ride Free Area, **fares** range from 85¢ to $1.60, depending on the distance and time of day. You pay when you get off the bus when traveling out of the Ride Free Area. When traveling into the Ride Free Area, you pay when you get on the bus. Exact change is required. On Saturday, Sunday, and holidays, you can purchase an **All Day Pass** for $1.70; it's available on any Metro bus or the Waterfront Streetcar.

Metro's **Bus Tunnel** is a sort of subway that allows buses to drive underneath downtown Seattle, thus avoiding traffic congestion. The tunnel extends from the International District in the south to the Convention Center in the north, with three stops in between. Commissioned artworks decorate each of the stations, making a trip through the tunnel more than just a way of getting from point A to point B. It's open Monday through Friday from 5am to 7pm and on Saturday from 10am to 6pm. When the Bus Tunnel is closed, buses operate on surface streets. Because the tunnel is within the Ride Free Area, there's no charge for riding through the tunnel.

BY MONORAIL   Seattle's monorail connects the Westlake Center, at Fifth Avenue and Pine Street, with the Seattle Center and covers the 1.2 miles in 90 seconds. The monorail leaves every 15 minutes daily from 9am to midnight during the summer; the rest of the year, Sunday through Thursday from 9am to 9pm, on Friday and Saturday until midnight. The one-way fare is 90¢ for adults, 70¢ for children 5 to 12, and 35¢ for seniors and the disabled.

BY WATERFRONT STREETCAR   Old-fashioned streetcars run along the waterfront from Pier 70 to the corner of Fifth Avenue South and South Jackson Street on the edge of the International District. The trolley operates Monday through Friday from around 7am to around 6:30pm, departing every 20 to 30 minutes; on Saturday, Sunday, and holidays, from just after 10am to almost 7pm, departing about every 20 minutes. The one-way fare is 85¢ in off-peak hours and $1.10 in peak hours. Metrobus transfers are available, and the streetcars are wheelchair accessible.

BY CAR

Before you venture into downtown Seattle by car, remember that traffic congestion is severe, parking is limited, and streets are almost all one way. You're better off to leave your car outside the downtown area.

RENTALS   All the major auto-rental companies have offices in Seattle, and there are also plenty of independent companies as well. Major rental-car companies include **Avis** (☎ 800/331-1212), at Sea-Tac Airport (☎ 206/433-5231) and 1919 Fifth Ave. (☎ 206/448-1700); **Budget Rent A Car** (☎ 800/527-0700), at Sea-Tac Airport (☎ 206/431-8800), downtown at Fourth Avenue and Columbia Street (☎ 206/682-8989), and at Westlake Avenue and Virginia Street (☎ 206/448-4859); **Dollar** (☎ 800/800-4000), at 15858 Pacific Hwy. S. (☎ 206/433-6777) and Seventh Avenue and Stewart Street (☎ 206/682-1316); **Hertz** (☎ 800/654-3131), at the Sea-Tac Marriott Hotel (☎ 206/433-5275), at the Sea-Tac Red Lion Hotel (☎ 206/246-0159), and at 722 Pike St. (☎ 206/682-5050); and **Thrifty** (☎ 800/367-2277), at 18836 Pacific Hwy. S. (☎ 206/246-7565) and at 801 Virginia St. (☎ 206/625-1133).

PARKING   On-street parking is extremely limited, rarely available near your destination, and very expensive. Downtown parking decks (either above or below ground) charge $7 to $16 per day. Many lots offer early-bird specials: if you park by a certain time in the morning (around 9 or 10am) you can park all day for $6 or $7. With the purchase of $20 or more, many downtown merchants offer Easy Streets tokens that can be used toward parking fees in many downtown lots. Look for the black-and-yellow signs. You'll also save money by parking up toward the Space Needle, where parking lots charge around $6 per day, and taking the monorail into downtown. If you don't mind a bit of a walk, try down at the south lot of the Kingdome, where all-day parking costs about $2 (the best deal in town).

DRIVING RULES   A right turn at a red light is permitted after coming to a full stop. A left turn at a red light is permissible from a one-way street onto another one-way street. If you park your car on a sloping street, be sure to turn your wheels to the curb—you may be ticketed if you don't. When parking on the street, be sure to check the time limit on parking meters. It ranges from 15 minutes to four hours. Also be sure to check whether or not you can park in a parking space during rush hour.

BY TAXI

Taxis can be difficult to hail on the street in Seattle, so it's best to call or wait at the taxi stands at the major hotels. **Yellow Cab** (☎ 206/622-6500) and **Farwest Taxi** (☎ 206/622-1717) charge $1.80 at flag-drop and $1.80 per mile after that. **Graytop Cab** (☎ 206/282-8222) charges $1.20 at flag-drop and $1.40 per mile.

BY FERRY

The **Washington State Ferries** (☎ 206/464-6400 or 800/84-FERRY in Washington) system connects Seattle with Bainbridge Island, Vashon Island, Bremerton, and Southworth. At press time, one-way fares from Seattle to Bremerton or Bainbridge Island were $5.90 for a car and driver, $3.50 for passengers, $1.75 for children and seniors. Fares for passengers are collected on westbound journeys only, though cars and drivers must pay in both directions.

ON FOOT

Seattle is a surprisingly compact city. You can easily walk from Pioneer Square to the Pike Place Market. Remember, though, that the city is also very hilly. When you head in from the waterfront, you'll be climbing a very steep hill. If you get tired of walking around downtown Seattle, remember that you can always catch a bus for free as long as you plan to stay within the Ride Free Area. Cross streets only at corners and only with the lights—jaywalking is a ticketable offense.

FAST FACTS: Seattle

American Express   In Seattle, the office is at Plaza 600, 600 Stewart St. (☎ 206/441-8622), open Monday through Friday from 9am to 5pm.

Area Code   The area code in Seattle is 206.

Babysitters   Check with your hotel first, or contact Best Sitters (☎ 206/682-2556).

Camera Repair   See "Photographic Needs," below.

Car Rentals   See "Getting Around," earlier in this chapter.

Climate   See "When to Go," in Chapter 3.

Dentist   Contact the Dentist Referral Service, in the Medical Dental Building, Fifth Avenue and Olive Way (☎ 206/448-CARE).

Doctor   Call the Medical Dental Building line (☎ 206/448-CARE).

Emergencies   For police, fire, or medical emergencies, phone **911**.

Eyeglass Repair   Try Davis Optical X-press, 314 Stewart St. (☎ 206/623-1758), which can replace your glasses in an hour.

Hospitals   One of the hospitals most convenient to downtown Seattle is the Virginia Mason Medical Center, 925 Seneca St. (☎ 206/583-6433 for emergencies or 206/624-1144 for information). There's also the Virginia Mason Fourth Avenue Clinic, 1221 Fourth Ave. (☎ 206/223-6490), which provides medical treatment for minor ailments without an appointment.

Hotlines   The *Seattle Times* Info Line at 206/464-2000 provides a wealth of information on topics that range from traffic reports to business news, from entertainment listings to the weather report and marine forecast. The local rape hotline is 206/632-7273.

Information   See "Visitor Information," earlier in this chapter.

Liquor Laws   The legal drinking age in Washington is 21.

Luggage Storage/Lockers   There's a luggage-storage facility at Amtrak's King Street Station. It costs $1.50 per day. The Greyhound Bus Station at 811 Stewart St. has luggage lockers.

Newspapers/Magazines   The *Seattle Post-Intelligencer* is Seattle's morning daily, and the *Seattle Times* is the evening daily. The arts and entertainment weekly for Seattle is the *Seattle Weekly*.

Pharmacies   Peterson's Pharmacy, 1629 Sixth Ave. (☎ 206/622-5860), and Pacific Drugs, 822 First Ave. (☎ 206/624-1454), are both conveniently located downtown.

Photographic Needs   Cameras West, 1908 Fourth Ave. (☎ 206/622-0066), is the largest-volume camera and video dealer in the Northwest. Best of all, it's right downtown and also offers one-hour film processing. It's open Monday through Saturday from 10am to 6pm and on Sunday from noon to 6pm.

Police   For police emergencies, phone **911.**

Post Office   The main post office is at Third Avenue and Union Street (☎ 206/442-6340). There are also convenient branches in Pioneer Square at 91 Jackson St. S. (☎ 206/623-1908) and on Broadway at 101 Broadway E. (☎ 206/324-2588). All stations are open Monday through Friday with varying hours; the Broadway station is open on Saturday from 9am to 1am as well.

Restrooms   There are public restrooms in the Pike Place Market and the Convention Center.

Safety   Although Seattle is rated as one of the safest cities in the United States, it has its share of crime. Take extra precautions with your wallet or purse when you're in the crush of people at the Pike Place Market—this is a favorite spot for pickpockets. Whenever possible, try to park your car in a garage, not on the street, at night. The Pioneer Square area, site of numerous bars and nightclubs, sees more than its share of late-night muggings.

Taxes   Seattle and King County have an 8.2% sales tax. The hotel-room tax of 7% in Seattle, when added to the sales tax, makes a total of 15.2%.

Taxis   See "Getting Around," earlier in this chapter.

Time Zone   Seattle is in the Pacific time (PST) zone, making it three hours behind the East Coast.

Transit Information For 24-hour information on Seattle's Metro bus system, call 206/553-3000. For information on the Washington State Ferries, phone 206/464-6400, or 800/84-FERRY; for Amtrak information, 800/872-7249; for the King Street Station (trains), 206/382-4125; and for the Greyhound Bus Station, 206/628-5508.

Weather Call 206/526-6087.

3 Accommodations

Seattle's largest concentrations of hotels are downtown and near the airport, with a few good hotels in the University District and over in the Bellevue/Kirkland area. If you don't mind the high prices, the downtown hotels are the most convenient for most visitors. However, if your budget won't allow for a first-class business hotel, you'll have to stay near the airport or elsewhere on the outskirts of the city.

In the following listings, "Very Expensive" hotels are those charging more than $125 per night for a double room; "Expensive" hotels are those charging $90 to $125 per night; "Moderate" hotels, $60 to $90; and "Inexpensive" hotels, less than $60. These rates do *not* include the state and local sales and room taxes, which add up to 15.2% (slightly less at airport hotels). Room rates are almost always considerably lower October to April, and downtown hotels usually offer substantially reduced rates on weekends. Parking rates are per day.

Almost all hotels in the Seattle area now offer no-smoking rooms, and, in fact, most B&Bs are exclusively no-smoking establishments. Most hotels also offer wheelchair-accessible rooms, and allow children to stay for free in their parents' room. Many hotels also offer special packages, especially on weekends and in the off-season. If you're looking to save money, be sure to ask about the availability of such packages—the reservations agent may not volunteer this information.

There are a number of fine bed-and-breakfast establishments in Seattle, and we have listed a few of our favorites in this chapter. In addition, the **Pacific Reservation Service,** 701 NW 60th St., Seattle, WA 98107 (☎ **206/784-0539;** fax 206/782-4036), offers many accommodations, mostly in bed-and-breakfast homes in the Seattle area. Rates range from $45 to $150 for a double, and a small booking fee may be charged. There's a $5 charge for a directory of their members.

DOWNTOWN
VERY EXPENSIVE

✪ Alexis Hotel & Arlington Suites
1007 First Ave. (at Madison St.), Seattle, WA 98104. ☎ **206/624-4844** or 800/426-7033 outside Washington. Fax 206/621-9009. 54 rms, 43 suites. A/C TV TEL. $185–$205 double; $220–$355 suite. Rates include continental breakfast and tips. AE, CB, DC, MC, V. Parking $15.

This elegant little hotel has an enviable location halfway between the Pike Place Market and Pioneer Square. Throughout the hotel there's a pleasant mix of the contemporary and the antique that gives the Alexis a very special atmosphere. Each room is furnished with antique tables, overstuffed chairs, and brass reading lamps. In your black-tiled bath, you'll find a marble counter, terrycloth robes, and a telephone. The nicest rooms are the fireplace suites, which have raised king-size beds, whirlpool baths, and wet bars. If you need more space and a kitchen, you can stay at the Alexis's adjacent Arlington Suites.

Dining/Entertainment: The hotel's main dining room, the Painted Table, serves highly creative meals (see "Dining," later in this chapter, for details). Just off the lobby is the Bookstore Bar, which serves light lunches as well as drinks.

Services: Concierge, room service, valet/laundry service, morning paper, evening turndown service, complimentary evening sherry, shoeshine service.

Facilities: Steamroom, privileges at two sports clubs.

⊖ The Edgewater

Pier 67, 2411 Alaskan Way, Seattle, WA 98121. ☎ **206/728-7000** or 800/624-0670. Fax 206/441-4119. 230 rms, 3 suites. A/C TV TEL. $119–$210 double; $300 suite. AE, CB, DC, DISC, MC, V. Parking $6.

Set back from Alaskan Way on Pier 67, the Edgewater is Seattle's only waterfront hotel and has the feel of a deluxe mountain lodge. A vaulted open-beamed ceiling and river-stone fireplace greet you as you enter the lobby, where a wall of window-paned glass looks out on ships and sailboats on Elliott Bay. The mountain-lodge theme continues in the rooms, which feature rustic furniture. Half the rooms have minibars and balconies over the water. Unfortunately, many rooms are quite small.

Dining/Entertainment: You'll find Northwest cuisine featured on the menu and a stunning view of the harbor from all the tables in the woodsy main dining room. In the pine-walled lounge there's live piano music in the evenings and a fireplace to warm you in winter.

Services: Concierge, room service, laundry/valet service, courtesy shuttle to downtown locations, access to a nearby health club.

✪ Four Seasons Olympic Hotel

411 University St., Seattle, WA 98101. ☎ **206/621-1700** or 800/332-3442, 800/821-8106 in Washington, 800/268-6282 in Canada. Fax 206/682-9633. 450 rms, 200 suites. A/C MINIBAR TV TEL. $225–$255 double; $245–$1,150 suite. AE, CB, DC, ER, JCB, MC, V. Parking $15.

Old-fashioned grandeur is what you'll find when you step through the doors of this Italian Renaissance palace. Gilt-and-crystal chandeliers hang from the high ceiling, ornate cornices and moldings grace the glowing hand-burnished oak walls and pillars, and at either end of the expansive lobby, curving stairways lead to the mezzanine. The guest rooms are all quite spacious and tastefully appointed with modern furnishings, and contain thoughtful extras like hairdryers and plush bathrobes.

Dining/Entertainment: The Georgian Room is the most elegant restaurant in Seattle. The menu combines creative Northwest and continental cuisine (see "Dining," later in this chapter, for details). Downstairs from the lobby is an English pub featuring fresh seafood, and a third restaurant is found in a spacious skylighted room.

Services: Concierge, room service (24-hour), same-day valet/laundry service, one-hour pressing, complimentary shoeshine, valet parking; massage available.

Facilities: Indoor pool, whirlpool spa, sauna, sundeck, health club, exclusive shopping arcade.

Hotel Vintage Park

1100 Fifth Ave., Seattle, WA 98101. ☎ **206/624-8000** or 800/624-4433. Fax 206/623-0568. 126 rms, 1 suite. A/C TV TEL. $185–$215 double; $370 suite. AE, CB, DC, DISC, JCB, MC, V. Valet parking $16.

Seattle Accommodations—Downtown

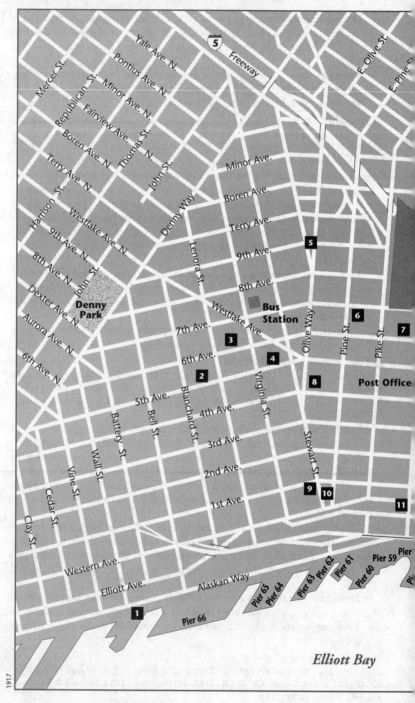

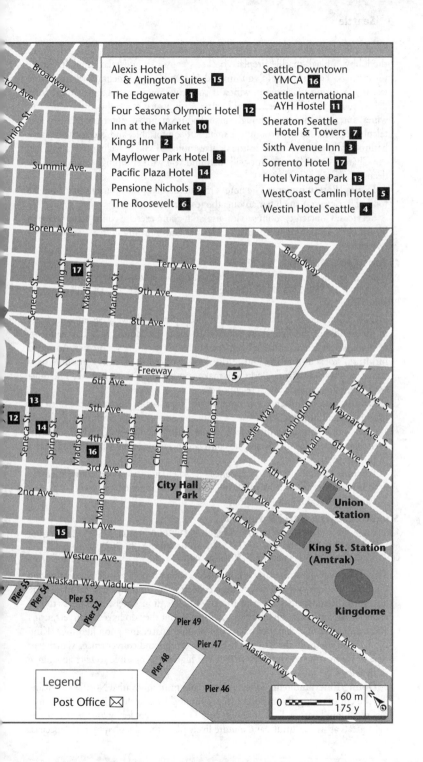

Alexis Hotel
& Arlington Suites **15**

The Edgewater **1**

Four Seasons Olympic Hotel **12**

Inn at the Market **10**

Kings Inn **2**

Mayflower Park Hotel **8**

Pacific Plaza Hotel **14**

Pensione Nichols **9**

The Roosevelt **6**

Seattle Downtown
YMCA **16**

Seattle International
AYH Hostel **11**

Sheraton Seattle
Hotel & Towers **7**

Sixth Avenue Inn **3**

Sorrento Hotel **17**

Hotel Vintage Park **13**

WestCoast Camlin Hotel **5**

Westin Hotel Seattle **4**

Legend

Post Office ⊠

Small and classically elegant—that's the best way to describe the Vintage Park. In the lobby, a black-marble fireplace beckons you to sit and relax amid Italianate furnishings. To further help you unwind, there are complimentary evening wine tastings featuring Washington wines. If you're willing to spend a little more for a deluxe room, you'll experience real luxury: A minibar is stocked with Washington wines, and the bathrooms, though small, feature granite counters, hairdryers, and telephones. The standard rooms are small but comfortable, and, surprisingly, have bathrooms larger than those in the deluxe rooms. If you're feeling like a splurge, the Château Ste. Michele suite will surround you with stunningly contemporary decor.

Dining/Entertainment: The hotel's restaurant serves Italian meals based on the food of Tuscany. A small bar adjoins the restaurant.

Services: Concierge, room service, use of in-room exercise equipment, access to health club, complimentary daily newspaper and morning coffee, valet/laundry service.

✪ Inn at the Market

86 Pine St., Seattle, WA 98101. ☎ **206/443-3600** or 800/446-4484. 65 rms, 9 suites. A/C MINIBAR TV TEL. $115–$190 double; $205–$245 suite. AE, CB, DC, DISC, MC, V. Parking $14.

French country decor is the theme of this inconspicuous but very elegant little hotel in the middle of the Pike Place Market. In the guest rooms, wide bay windows overlook Puget Sound and can be opened to let in refreshing sea breezes. Antiqued furniture, stocked minibars and refrigerators, coffeemakers with complimentary coffee, and well-lit writing desks will make you feel right at home here. The huge bathrooms are equipped with telephones.

Dining/Entertainment: The hotel's little bistro serves juices, simple-but-tasty breakfasts, and lunches, while Café Campagne offers French country–style meals and take-out. Campagne, the hotel's formal dining room, is an excellent southern French restaurant located across the courtyard from the lobby (see "Dining," later in this chapter).

Services: Limited room service, concierge, valet/laundry service, complimentary limousine service in downtown Seattle, privileges at athletic club.

Facilities: Health spa, hair salon.

Sheraton Seattle Hotel & Towers

1400 Sixth Ave., Seattle, WA 98101. ☎ **206/621-9000** or 800/325-3535. Fax 206/621-8441. 840 rms, 42 suites. A/C TV TEL. $168–$230 double; $195–$625 suite. AE, CB, DC, DISC, ER, JCB, MC, V. Valet parking $15; self-parking $13.

This 35-story tower is the largest hotel in Seattle, and you'll almost always find the building buzzing with activity. A large collection of contemporary art makes the Sheraton the most interesting of the city's convention hotels. The guest rooms are not as luxurious as the lobby would suggest, but they do have hairdryers, irons and ironing boards, plenty of bathroom counter space, and good lighting. "King rooms" and rooms in the Tower offer more comfort and convenience. Whichever type of room you stay in, make sure it's as high up as possible to take advantage of the views.

Dining/Entertainment: The very finest and most innovative Northwest cuisine has the critics raving about Fullers (see "Dining," later in this chapter). A less formal restaurant boasts a 27-foot dessert bar. There's a quiet lobby lounge that serves light meals as well as drinks and a more lively place that does happy hour specials.

Services: Concierge, room service (24-hour), valet/laundry service, tour desk, American Airlines desk.

Facilities: Indoor pool, whirlpool spa, sauna, exercise room, business center.

Westin Hotel Seattle

1900 Fifth Ave., Seattle, WA 98101. ☎ **206/728-1000** or 800/228-3000. Fax 206/728-2259. 822 rms, 43 suites. A/C MINIBAR TV TEL. $180–$205 double; from $225 suite. AE, CB, DC, DISC, JCB, MC, V. Valet parking $17; self-parking $13.

This high-rise hotel has the amenities to be expected, but service can be impersonal and the crowds overwhelming. The standard rooms are rather worn and feature dated furnishings, but the remodeled deluxe rooms with an Italianate decor are everything you'd expect. These latter rooms include work desks facing the window's view of Seattle and safes for your valuables. The rooms on the upper floors offer fine views of the city and Puget Sound.

Dining/Entertainment: The Palm Court is a glitzy restaurant serving Northwest cuisine, while Nikko is one of Seattle's finest Japanese restaurants. A casual café is done up to look as if it belongs in the Pike Place Market. The quiet lobby court and a more lively lounge provide two different ambiences in which to enjoy a drink.

Services: Concierge, room service (24-hour), one-day valet/laundry service.

Facilities: Indoor pool, exercise room, whirlpool spa, sauna, barber, beauty salon.

EXPENSIVE

Mayflower Park Hotel

405 Olive Way, Seattle, WA 98101. ☎ **206/623-8700** or 800/426-5100. Fax 206/382-6996. 173 rms, 22 suites. A/C TV TEL. $120–$150 double; from $165 suite. AE, CB, DC, DISC, MC, V. Parking $9.

Built in 1927, the Mayflower Park offers subdued elegance and is a great, convenient choice if you've come to shop. All the rooms have been remodeled in the past few years and most are furnished with an eclectic blend of contemporary Italian and traditional European furnishings and Chinese accent pieces. Some of the rooms have bathrooms that are old-fashioned, small, and lack counter space, but have large old tubs that are great for soaking. If you crave space, ask for one of the large corner rooms or a suite.

Dining/Entertainment: The hotel's restaurant features Northwest cuisine, while the lounge provides a cheerful spot for light lunches or drinks.

Services: Room service (24-hour), valet/laundry service, privileges at athletic club.

The Roosevelt

1531 Seventh Ave., Seattle, WA 98101. ☎ **206/621-1200** or 800/426-0670. Fax 206/233-0335. 151 rms, 12 suites. A/C TV TEL. $95–$170 double; $135–$220 suite. AE, DC, DISC, MC, V. Parking $9.75.

Though the Roosevelt hints at the elegance of times gone by, it's surprisingly expensive for what you get unless you stay in the off-season. In the guest rooms, there are king-size beds, couches, wet bars, and recessed lighting. The "queen rooms" are rather small, but the "king deluxe rooms" have good layouts. Most rooms have cramped bathrooms with little counter space. If you choose to pay for one of the suites, you can enjoy a whirlpool bath, honor bar, hairdryer, shoeshine machine, and terry-cloth robes.

Dining/Entertainment: The hotel's restaurant serves steaks, chicken, and salmon cooked over apple wood.

Services: Concierge, room service, valet/laundry service.

Facilities: Exercise room.

Ⓢ WestCoast Camlin Hotel

1619 Ninth Ave., Seattle, WA 98101. ☎ **206/682-0100** or 800/426-0670. 136 rms, 12 suites. TV TEL. $83–$114 double; $175 suite. AE, DC, DISC, MC, V. Parking $9.

Located a block from the Washington State Convention and Trade Center, the WestCoast Camlin has the feel of a classic European hotel. However, the high-ceilinged lobby, with its ornate trim and marble floors, often has a disquieting feeling of emptiness hanging over it. The guest rooms, though showing signs of wear, are still a good deal when you see the prices charged at nearby convention hotels. There are many different floor plans, so you may get a room that's quite spacious or one that just isn't big enough for today's traveler.

Dining/Entertainment: The top-floor restaurant and lounge serves a varied menu with an emphasis on fresh seafood. Great views!

Services: Room service, laundry service.

Facilities: Outdoor pool.

MODERATE

✪ The M.V. *Challenger*

1001 Fairview Ave. N. (Yale Street Landing, on Chandler's Cove at the south end of Lake Union), Seattle, WA 98109. ☎ **206/340-1201.** Fax 206/621-9208. 8 rms, 5 with bath. TEL. $75–$165 double. Rates include full breakfast. AE, CB, DC, MC, V. Free parking.

If you love ships and the sea and don't mind cramped quarters, don't pass up this opportunity to spend the night on board a restored and fully operational 45-year-old tugboat. You're welcome to visit the bridge for a great view of Lake Union and the Seattle skyline or delve into the mechanics of the tug's enormous diesel engine. A conversation pit with granite fireplace fills the cozy main cabin, and in each of the guest cabins you'll find lots of polished wood.

Pacific Plaza Hotel

400 Spring St., Seattle, WA 98104. ☎ **206/623-3900** or 800/426-1165. Fax 206/623-2059. 160 rms. A/C TV TEL. $70–$97 double. Rates include continental breakfast. AE, DC, DISC, MC, V. Parking $9.

Built in 1928, this old hotel was renovated a few years back and offers basic rooms and good value. The building is halfway between the Pike Place Market and Pioneer Square and just about the same distance to the waterfront. The rooms are small and sometimes cramped but they come with such amenities as ceiling fans and alarm clocks. Wingback chairs and cherrywood finishes on the furnishings give each guest room an elegant touch. The bathrooms are small and dated.

Dining/Entertainment: A Red Robin Restaurant serving gourmet hamburgers is on the lower level of the hotel.

Services: Valet/laundry services.

Pensione Nichols

1923 First Ave., Seattle, WA 98101. ☎ **206/441-7125** or 800/440-7125. 8 rms, none with bath; 2 suites. $85 double; $160 suite. Rates include full breakfast. AE, DISC, MC, V. No parking.

If you have ever traveled through Europe on a budget, you've probably stayed at B&Bs that started on the second or third floor of a building. This city-center B&B

is just such a lodging, and you'll find it up two flights of stairs. Located only a block from the Pike Place Market, Pensione Nichols is a touch expensive for what you get, though it's hard to beat the location. Only two of the guest rooms have windows (the two rooms facing the street), but all the rest have skylights. On the other hand, the two suites are huge and have full kitchens as well as large windows overlooking the bay. These also have the occasional antique, as does the inn's living room, which also overlooks the water.

⑤ Sixth Avenue Inn

2000 Sixth Ave., Seattle, WA 98121. ☎ **206/441-8300** or 800/648-6440. 166 rms. A/C TV TEL. $80–$99 double. Rates depend on season. Children 16 and under stay free in parents' room. AE, CB, MC, V. Free parking.

This is more than your standard moderately priced hotel. On a small shelf in each guest room is a selection of old hardcover books, and old photos of Seattle provide a glimpse into the city's past. Wicker furniture and large potted plants give the rooms the feeling of a tropical greenhouse, and there are even brass beds.

Dining/Entertainment: The hotel's restaurant serves steaks and seafood. In the lounge, warm dark-wood paneling and a fireplace are part of the cozy environment.

Services: Room service, valet/laundry service.

INEXPENSIVE

Kings Inn

2100 Fifth Ave., Seattle, WA 98121. ☎ **206/441-8833** or 800/546-4760. Fax 206/441-0730. 68 rms, 21 suites. A/C TV TEL. $55–$60 double; $65–70 suite. AE, CB, DC, DISC, MC, V. Free parking.

You'll find this economical motel in the shadow of the monorail just about midway between the Westlake Center and the Space Needle. The rooms are a bit small and show their age, but new carpets and wallpaper make them feel more comfortable. The suites have various sleeping arrangements that can fit several people. You just won't find an acceptable room in downtown for less than this. We suggest that finicky travelers ask to see a room here before committing.

Seattle Downtown YMCA

909 Fourth Ave., Seattle, WA 98104-1194. ☎ **206/382-5000.** 185 rms, 3 with bath. TEL. $39–$43 double ($1 discount to YMCA members). Weekly rates available. MC, V.

This YMCA welcomes men, women, and families, and has mostly rooms without private baths. If you want, you can get a room with a TV or just walk down the hall to the TV lounge. The rooms are basic and fairly clean. The best part of staying here is that you'll have full use of all the athletic facilities.

Seattle International AYH Hostel

84 Union St., Seattle, WA 98101-2084. ☎ **206/662-5443.** Fax 206/682-2179. 126 beds. $16.25 per person for members. JCB, MC, V. Walk down Post Alley, which runs through and under the Pike Place Market, to the corner of Union Street.

This conveniently located hostel is housed in the former Longshoreman's Hall, which was built in 1915. If you don't provide your own sheets, you can rent them for $2 for the duration of your stay. If you plan to stay for three nights or less, you need not be an AYH member, but you'll have to pay a $3 surcharge each night, which can later be applied toward membership. After your first three nights and any time between June and September, you must buy a membership for $25. There's a kitchen and self-service laundry.

NEAR SEA-TAC AIRPORT
EXPENSIVE

Holiday Inn, Sea-Tac Airport
17338 Pacific Hwy. S., Seattle, WA 98188. ☎ **206/248-1000** or 800/465-4329. Fax 206/242-7089. 260 rms. A/C TV TEL. $74–$134 double. AE, CB, DC, DISC, JCB, MC, V. Free parking.

Although the halls and elevators are getting a bit battered, this is still a good choice if you're looking for a full-service hotel. The best features here are the indoor pool and rooftop restaurant. The lobby is also quite attractive, with lots of slate and marble and a decor that gives the room the feeling of a small European hotel. The guest rooms, especially those with a single king-size bed, are designed with the business traveler in mind, but lack sufficient closet space or bathroom counter space for a stay of more than a night or two. Rooms on the higher floors offer good views (ask for a room on the Mount Rainier side of the hotel). The "King Leisure rooms" come with sofas, desks, king-size beds, and a bit more space than the standard rooms.

Dining/Entertainment: A rotating dining room on the 12th floor features a sweeping vista of the airport and the surrounding area, plus continental and American fare prepared with fresh local ingredients. The lobby lounge is a dark and lively place.

Services: Room service, courtesy airport shuttle, valet/laundry service.

Facilities: Indoor pool, exercise room, whirlpool spa, coin laundry.

✪ Seattle Marriott Hotel Seatac
3201 S. 176th St., Seattle, WA 98188. ☎ **206/241-2000** or 800/228-9290. 459 rms, 5 suites. A/C TV TEL. $104–$139 double; $195–$350 suite. AE, CB, DC, DISC, MC, V. Free parking.

You can't pick a better place to stay in the airport area. With its soaring atrium garden full of plants, a swimming pool, and two whirlpool tubs, this resort hotel may keep you so enthralled you won't want to leave. There are even waterfalls and totem poles for that Northwest outdoorsy feeling. Although all the rooms are relatively large and attractively decorated, the concierge-level rooms are particularly appealing. In the bathroom are scales and a hairdryer.

Dining/Entertainment: The hotel's restaurant, with stone pillars and rough-hewn beams, will have you thinking you're in the middle of the gold rush. The lobby lounge is a greenhouse that looks into the atrium.

Services: Concierge, room service, free airport shuttle, car-rental desk, valet/laundry service.

Facilities: Indoor pool, whirlpools, health club, sauna, games room.

MODERATE TO INEXPENSIVE

Among the better and more convenient chain motel choices are the following (see the Appendix for a list of toll-free telephone numbers for chain motels): **Motel 6 (Sea-Tac South),** 18900 47th Ave. S., Seattle, WA 98188 (☎ **206/241-1648**), charging $36 to $40; **Motel 6 (Sea-Tac Airport),** 16500 Pacific Hwy. S., Seattle, WA 98188 (☎ **206/246-4101**), charging $36 to $40 for a double; **Super 8 Motel,** 3100 S. 192nd St., Seattle, WA 98168 (☎ **206/433-8188**), charging $57 to $62 for a double; and **Travelodge Seattle Airport,** 2900 S. 192nd St., Seattle, WA 98188 (☎ **206/241-9292**), charging $39 to $70 double.

Hampton Inn Seattle–Airport

19445 International Blvd., Seattle, WA 98188. ☎ **206/878-1700** or 800/426-7866. Fax 206/824-0720. 131 rms, 1 suite. A/C TV TEL. $75–$77 double; $100 suite. Rates include continental breakfast. Rates lower in winter. AE, CB, DC, DISC, MC, V. Free parking.

You'll get much more at the Hampton Inn than you'd expect from a small hotel in this price range. All the rooms are attractively furnished with modern appointments. There's a free restaurant and airport shuttle, valet/laundry service, free local calls, an outdoor pool, and an exercise room.

FIRST & CAPITOL HILL
VERY EXPENSIVE

✪ Sorrento Hotel

900 Madison St., Seattle, WA 98104-9742. ☎ **206/622-6400** or 800/426-1265. Fax 206/343-6155. 76 rms, 42 suites. A/C MINIBAR TV TEL. $160–$180 double; $185–$1,000 suite. AE, DC, DISC, MC, V. Parking $12.

From the wrought-iron gates and palm trees of the courtyard entrance to the plush seating of the octagonal lobby, the Sorrento whispers style and grace, and the service here is as fine as you can expect anywhere in town. All rooms have remote-control TVs and stereos hidden inside large armoires, minibars and minirefrigerators, plush robes, and dual-line telephones. You even have a choice of down or fiber-filled pillows, and in colder months you'll slip into a bed that has been warmed with an old-fashioned hot-water bottle.

Dining/Entertainment: The Hunt Club, a dark and intimate restaurant, serves superb Northwest cuisine (see "Dining," later in this chapter). In the adjacent bar, dark-wood paneling continues the clublike atmosphere. Several nights a week a pianist provides musical atmosphere. Afternoon tea is also served.

Services: Concierge, room service, valet/laundry service, complimentary town-car service in downtown Seattle, morning paper.

Facilities: Fitness center.

MODERATE

Gaslight Inn

1727 15th Ave., Seattle, WA 98122. ☎ **206/325-3654.** 9 rms, 5 with bath; 3 suites. TV. $62–$118 double; $98–$118 suite. Rates include continental breakfast. AE, MC, V.

Anyone who's a fan of the arts-and-crafts movement will enjoy a stay at this 1906 vintage home. The common rooms are spacious and attractively decorated with a combination western and northwestern flare. A library filled with interesting books and magazines makes a comfortable spot for a bit of free time, or if it's cold out, take a seat by the fireplace. In summer, guests can swim in the backyard pool. The guest rooms continue the design themes of the common areas with lots of oak furnishings and heavy, peeled-log beds in some rooms. An annex has three suites.

⊛ Salisbury House

750 16th Ave. E., Seattle, WA 98112. ☎ **206/328-8682.** Fax 206/720-1019. 4 rms. $70–$105 double. Rates include full breakfast. AE, MC, V.

This grand old house on a tree-lined avenue has a wide porch that wraps around two sides. Inside there's plenty to admire as well. Two living rooms (one with a wood-burning fireplace) and a second-floor sun porch provide plenty of spots for relaxing and meeting other guests. The guest rooms all have queen-size beds with

Family-Friendly Hotels

Seattle Downtown YMCA *(see p. 75)*   This Y has a good downtown location, plenty of rooms, and economical rates that will please any family on a tight budget. However, the best feature of a stay here is the access to all the Y's athletic facilities.

Seattle Marriott Hotel Seatac *(see p. 76)*   With this hotel's huge jungly atrium containing a swimming pool and whirlpool spas, kids can play Tarzan and never leave the hotel. There's also a games room that will keep the young ones occupied for hours if need be.

down comforters, and one has a unique canopy bed hung with pink satin. One of the other rooms has a clawfoot tub in the bathroom. Breakfasts here might include fresh fruit, juice, a piece of quiche, fresh-baked muffins or bread, or maybe oatmeal pancakes. Cathryn and Mary Wiese, a mother and daughter, are the friendly innkeepers.

NORTH SEATTLE
MODERATE

⑤ Meany Tower Hotel
4507 Brooklyn Ave. NE, Seattle, WA 98105. ☎ **206/634-2000** or 800/648-6440. 155 rms. A/C TV TEL. $79–$90 double. AE, DC, MC, V. Free parking.

If you need to be near the university and want a view of downtown Seattle and the surrounding hills and water, book a room in this moderately priced high-rise hotel. There's no swimming pool but there is a fitness room, and the views are superb. Every room is a corner room. You'll also find an extremely large television in each room. The hotel's dining room features prime rib, steaks, and fresh seafood in an elegant atmosphere. Room service, valet/laundry service, and a complimentary newspaper are provided and there's an exercise room as well.

✪ University Inn
4140 Roosevelt Way NE, Seattle, WA 98105. ☎ **206/632-5055** or 800/733-3855. Fax 206/547-4937. 102 rms, 12 junior suites. A/C TV TEL. $86–$106 double; $104–$108 junior suite. Rates include continental breakfast. AE, DC, DISC, MC, V. Free parking.

Located within easy walking distance of the university, this hotel offers very attractive rooms, many of which have views of Lake Union. The standard rooms have only showers in their bathrooms, but compensate for this lack with small balconies. The deluxe rooms are more spacious and have double vanities. For even more room, opt for one of the junior suites, which have large windows, microwaves, refrigerators, coffeemakers, and bathroom telephones. Facilities include a heated outdoor pool, a whirlpool, and a tiny exercise room.

BELLEVUE & KIRKLAND
Bellevue and Kirkland, on the east side of Lake Washington and at the heart of the region's high-tech industrial growth, are two of Washington's fastest-growing cities. From here it's only 15 minutes to downtown Seattle if it isn't rush hour.

VERY EXPENSIVE

Hyatt Regency Bellevue

900 Bellevue Way NE, Bellevue, WA 98004. ☎ **206/462-1234** or 800/233-1234. Fax 206/
646-7567. 382 rms, 21 suites. A/C TV TEL. $175–$200 double; $185–$800 suite. AE, CB, DC,
DISC, JCB, MC, V. Valet parking $11; self-parking $7.

Located across from the Northwest's largest shopping mall and connected to a
smaller, more exclusive shopping center, this high-rise hotel is a sure bet for anyone who likes to shop. From the upper floors, west-facing rooms offer good views
of Lake Washington and the distant Seattle skyline. The decor in the public
areas is a mixture of traditional European styling and Asian art and antiques. The
guest rooms include marble-top desks and rattan chairs. In rooms on the Regency
Club floors, you'll get extra amenities, the best views, and access to a concierge
lounge.

Dining/Entertainment: The hotel's main dining room serves primarily Mediterranean cuisine. An adjacent lounge provides a quiet spot for a drink, while a
sports pub features plenty of televisions for monitoring the big game.

Services: Room service (24-hour), valet/laundry service, evening bed turndown.

Facilities: For $7 extra per day you can get a membership to the adjacent health
club.

✪ The Woodmark Hotel at Carillon Point

1200 Carillon Point, Kirkland, WA 98033. ☎ **206/822-3700** or 800/822-3700. 100 rms,
25 suites. A/C MINIBAR TV TEL. $155–$195 double; $225–$900 suite. AE, CB, DC, ER, JCB,
MC, V. Parking $8.

Set on the shores of Lake Washington, the Woodmark is the most luxurious
waterfront hotel in the Seattle area. In the lobby, the effect is of being in the
living room of a well-traveled friend, and a wide staircase curves past a wall of
glass that frames the lake. The guest rooms are no less impressive and are filled with
the sort of amenities appreciated by frequent travelers—a VCR, floor-to-ceiling
windows that open, terry-cloth robes, oversize towels, a TV and hairdryer in the
bathroom, a large work desk, two telephones, computer hookup, complimentary
coffee and a coffeemaker, and a stocked minibar. In addition there are views of the
lake from most rooms, so sit back and enjoy.

Dining/Entertainment: The restaurant serves a combination of Northwest and
continental cuisines at fairly high prices. Sunday brunch is lavish and delicious. The
quiet lounge adjacent to the dining room is evocative of a library.

Services: Concierge, room service, courtesy local shopping van, complimentary
newspaper, shoeshine service, laundry/valet service, complimentary late-night
snacks, video lending library, complimentary use of laptop computer, cellular
phone, pager.

Facilities: Exercise room, business center.

MODERATE

Best Western Bellevue Inn

11211 Main St., Bellevue, WA 98004. ☎ **206/455-5240** or 800/421-8193. Fax 206/
455-0654. 179 rms. $85–$100 double. AE, DC, DISC, JCB, MC, V. Free parking.

The Bellevue Inn is one of the few hotels in the Seattle area that captures the feel
of the Northwest in its design and landscaping. The sprawling two-story hotel is
roofed with cedar-shake shingles and lushly planted with rhododendrons, firs,

Seattle Accommodations—North & Northeast

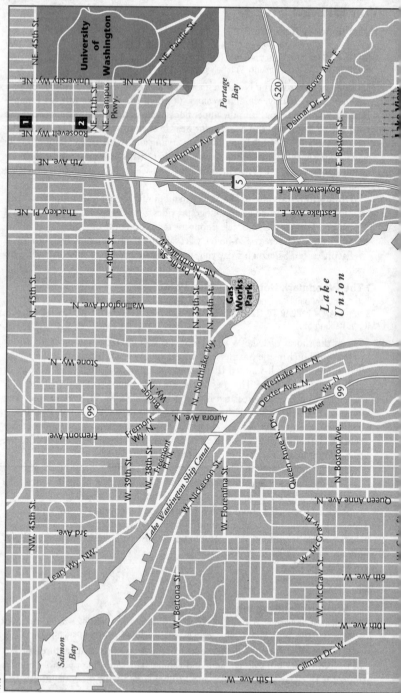

NE 45th St.

University of Washington

NE. Pacific St.

15th Ave. NE.

University Wy. NE.

NE. 41st St.

NE. Campus Pkwy.

NE. 40th St.

Portage Bay

520

Bover Ave. E.

Delmar Dr. E.

E. Boston St.

1

Roosevelt Wy. NE.

2

7th Ave. NE.

Fuhrman Ave. E.

5

Boylston Ave. E.

Eastlake Ave. E.

Lake Vie...

Thackery Pl. NE.

N. 45th St.

N. 40th St.

Pacific St.

NE. Northlake St.

N. 35th St.

N. 34th St.

Wallingford Ave. N.

Gas Works Park

Lake Union

Stone Wy. N.

N. Northlake Wy.

Westlake Ave. N.

Dexter Ave. N.

Dexter Wy. N.

99

66

Bridge Wy. N.

Aurora Ave. N.

Dexter

Fremont Wy. N.

Fremont Ave.

W. 39th St.

W. 38th St.

Fremont Pl. N.

Queen Anne N Dr.

N. Boston Ave.

Queen Anne Ave. N.

NW. 45th St.

3rd Ave.

Leary Wy. NW.

Lake Washington Ship Canal

W. Nickerson St.

W. Florentina St.

W. McGraw Pl.

6th Ave. W.

Salmon Bay

W. Bertona St.

W. McGraw St.

10th Ave. W.

Gilman Dr. W.

15th Ave. W.

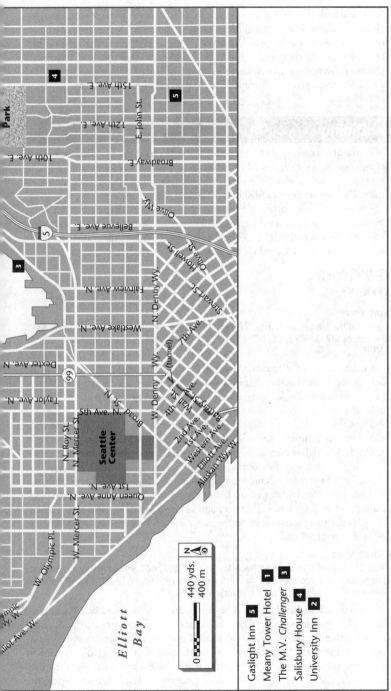

Elliott Bay

Park

10th Ave. E.
12th Ave. E.
15th Ave. E.
E. John St.
Broadway E.
Olive Wy.
Bellevue Ave. E.
Howell St.
Olive St.
Stewart St.
Fairview Ave. N.
Westlake Ave. N.
Dexter Ave. N.
Taylor Ave. N.
N. Denny Wy.
7th Ave.
(tunnel)
Wall St.
Battery St.
4th Ave.
2nd Ave.
1st Ave.
Western Ave.
Elliott Ave.
Alaskan Wy. W.
W. Denny Wy.
Broad St.
N. Roy St.
N. Mercer St.
5th Ave. N.
Queen Anne Ave. N.
1st Ave. N.
W. Mercer St.
W. Olympic Pl.
Elliott Ave. W.
W.

Seattle Center

N

0   440 yds.
0   400 m

Gaslight Inn **5**
Meany Tower Hotel **1**
The M.V. *Challenger* **3**
Salisbury House **4**
University Inn **2**

ferns, and azaleas. Try to get a poolside first-floor room. These rooms, though a bit dark, have sunken, rock-walled patios. The bathrooms have plenty of counter space, and there are built-in hairdryers. The hotel's restaurant serves a mix of American and continental dishes, with the occasional touch of Northwest creativity. Complimentary passes to local athletic club, free local van service, and a rental-car desk give are all available here, as are an outdoor pool, exercise room, and newsstand.

4 Dining

With the area's cosmopolitan population, Seattle's restaurants serve a wide range of cuisines. However, it should come as no surprise that seafood is emphasized in many restaurants. Views of the water, whether it be Puget Sound, Lake Union, or Lake Washington, are an added bonus at many restaurants.

For the following listings, a restaurant is considered **Expensive** if a meal, without wine or beer, would average $25 or more. **Moderate** restaurants serve complete dinners in the $15 to $25 range, and **Inexpensive** listings are those where you can get a complete meal for less than $15.

DOWNTOWN
EXPENSIVE

Campagne
In the Inn at the Market, 86 Pine St. ☎ **206/728-2800.** Reservations highly recommended. Main courses $14–$26. AE, CB, DC, MC, V. Daily 5:30–10pm (café dining until midnight). FRENCH.

On the far side of the fountain that bubbles in the courtyard of the Inn at the Market, the French country decor continues at the aptly named Campagne. Cheerful and unpretentious, Campagne is one of the most enjoyable French restaurants in Seattle.

The cuisine of Provence is the specialty of the house, and meals are consistently excellent. There are daily fresh-fish specials that feature whatever happens to be in season and of high quality at the nearby market. On one recent evening a subtly flavorful Provençal-style fish soup highlighted the best of the market. However, the entrée list definitely focuses on meats, and you might find such dishes as lamb loin encrusted with finely chopped truffles or a venison noisette with a cracked black pepper and madeira sauce. There are also lighter pasta dishes and even a token, though quite imaginative, pizza on the menu nightly. Desserts are the equal of any other dish on the menu.

✪ Chez Shea
94 Pike St., Suite 34, in the Pike Place Market. ☎ **206/467-9990.** Reservations highly recommended. Main courses $21; fixed-price four-course dinner $36. AE, MC, V. Tues–Sun 5:30–10pm (late-night menu until 1:30am). NORTHWEST.

It's hard to believe that there could be a quiet corner of the Pike Place Market, but here it is. Dark and intimate, Chez Shea is one of the finest restaurants in Seattle. A dozen candlelit tables, with views across Puget Sound to the Olympic Mountains, are the perfect setting for a romantic dinner. The ingredients used in preparing the meals here come from the market below and are always the freshest and the finest. Dinner is strictly fixed price on weekends, but on weeknights there are also à la carte dinners available. The menu changes to reflect the season and on a recent wintery night included filet of salmon seared with braised savoy cabbage, tarragon, and a red-butter sauce; and a succulent loin of lamb roasted in walnut crust with a pear-bourbon sauce. Though dessert is à la carte, you'll find it impossible to pass up. The adjoining Shea's Lounge serves lighter dishes along the same vein.

Elliott's

Pier 56, near Seneca St. ☎ **206/623-4340.** Reservations recommended. Main courses $13–$28. AE, DISC, JCB, MC, V. Sun–Thurs 11am–10pm, Fri–Sat 11am–11pm (later in summer). SEAFOOD.

Elliott's oyster bar is widely hailed as having the best selection of oysters in Seattle, with a new menu printed weekly that lists the available oysters. Overhead, the massive timbers of this former pier warehouse have been exposed, while down at floor level, etched and frosted glass and pale-aquamarine lighting offer a striking contrast. Seafood is everything here, and the preparations are primarily Mediterranean, southwestern, and pan-Pacific. You'll encounter such creations as pan-fried oysters with a whiskey, brown sugar, and Dijon mustard sauce and poached salmon with a wine, orange, and basil sauce. The selection of wine and microbrewery ale is chosen for its ability to complement the restaurant's various seafood offerings.

✪ Fuller's

In the Seattle Sheraton Hotel, 1400 Sixth Ave. ☎ **206/447-5544.** Reservations highly recommended. Main courses $17.25–$24.50; prix-fixe dinner $40. AE, CB, DC, DISC, JCB, MC, V. Mon–Fri 11:30am–2pm and 5:30–10pm, Sat 5:30–10pm. NORTHWEST.

Fuller's, named for the founder of the Seattle Art Museum, is dedicated to the culinary and visual arts of the Northwest. Each memorable dish is artfully designed as well as superbly prepared, and surrounding you in this elegant dining room are works of art by the Northwest's best artists.

Fuller's shows its imagination in dishes such as roast venison with pear-armagnac sauce and pan-seared kasu cod with soy-ginger vinaigrette. This latter dish is a house specialty and is made with a flavorful by-product of saké rice-wine brewing. Local fruits are also put to excellent use in the restaurant's desserts, which should be accompanied by the special coffee tray with shaved chocolate, cinnamon sticks, whipped cream, and other accompaniments. Lunch, with its lower prices, is especially popular. The wine list reflects the seasonal changes on the menu.

The Georgian Room

In the Four Seasons Olympic Hotel, 411 University St. ☎ **206/621-1700.** Reservations recommended. Main courses $19–$32. AE, CB, DC, V. Mon–Thurs 6:30–11am and 5:30–10pm, Fri 6:30–11am and 5:30–10:30pm, Sat 6:30am–noon and 5:30–10:30pm, Sun 7am–1pm. CONTINENTAL/NORTHWEST.

Nowhere in Seattle is there a more elegant restaurant. The soaring ceiling is decorated with intricate moldings and the huge windows are framed by luxurious draperies. On a small marble floor in the center of the room stands a baby grand piano on which a pianist plays soothing music. The excellent service will convince you that your table is the only one being served.

Veal, New York tenderloin with mushrooms, and aged Black Angus steak are signature dishes, while for more daring diners, a few touches of Northwest flair are a suitable introduction to that cuisine. Such dishes are mountain berry–spiced game hen with dried fruit and pear gravy, roast rack of Ellensburg lamb with a casserole of olives, and venison pepper steak. As you'd expect, the wine list is well suited to both the cuisine and the dining room.

Seattle Dining—Downtown

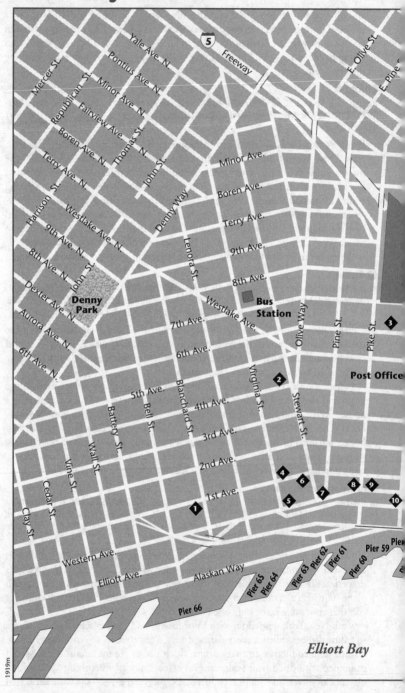

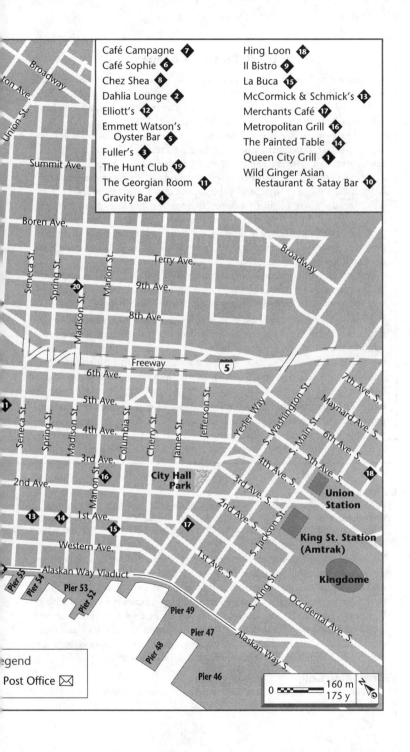

Café Campagne 7
Café Sophie 6
Chez Shea 8
Dahlia Lounge 2
Elliott's 12
Emmett Watson's
Oyster Bar 5
Fuller's 3
The Hunt Club 19
The Georgian Room 11
Gravity Bar 4

Hing Loon 18
Il Bistro 9
La Buca 15
McCormick & Schmick's 13
Merchants Café 17
Metropolitan Grill 16
The Painted Table 14
Queen City Grill 1
Wild Ginger Asian
Restaurant & Satay Bar 10

Broadway
ton Ave.
Union St.
Summit Ave.
Boren Ave.
Seneca St.
Spring St.
Marion St.
Terry Ave.
9th Ave.
Broadway
Madison St.
20
8th Ave.
Freeway
5
6th Ave.
5th Ave.
Madison St.
Columbia St.
Cherry St.
James St.
Jefferson St.
Yesler Way
S. Washington St.
Main St.
7th Ave. S.
Maynard Ave. S.
6th Ave. S.
4th Ave.
S. Main St.
4th Ave. S.
5th Ave. S.
18
3rd Ave.
3rd Ave. S.
Marion St.
16
City Hall
Park
2nd Ave. S.
Union
Station
2nd Ave.
Seneca St.
Spring St.
Madison St.
13 14 1st Ave.
15
17
S. Jackson St.
King St. Station
(Amtrak)
Western Ave.
1st Ave. S.
Kingdome
Pier 55
Alaskan Way Viaduct
S. King St.
Occidental Ave. S.
Pier 54
Pier 53
Pier 52
Alaskan Way S.
Pier 49
Pier 47
Pier 48
egend
Post Office ✉
Pier 46
0   160 m
     175 y
N

Life in the Espresso Lane

"I'll take a double half-caf tall skinny latte with a shot of hazelnut syrup; hold the foam." It may sound like a foreign language to you, but it doesn't take long to decipher the complexities of espresso. The following primer should soon have you speaking (and understanding) coffeespeak like a Seattle native.

There are two basic types of coffee beans—robustus and arabica. The former are the cheaper, lower-quality beans and are used primarily in standard American supermarket coffees. The latter are the higher-quality beans, with richer flavor, and are used for gourmet coffees and espresso. Flavor in either of these beans is determined in large part by the way the raw bean is roasted. Most regular coffees are given a light to medium roasting that produces a rougher, less complex flavor. A dark or espresso roast provides a dark oily-looking bean that produces a well-rounded, rich, deep flavor. Roasting coffee beans is an art that produces immense variations in flavors and causes educated coffee drinkers to develop loyalties to different coffee roasters.

But espresso isn't quite ubiquitous in every corner of the United States, so for those of you who are not yet cruising in the espresso lane, here are some important definitions and examples of how to order coffee Seattle style:

Espresso—a specially roasted and ground coffee that has hot water forced through it to make a small cup of dense, flavorful coffee. Straight espresso is definitely an acquired taste. Espresso developed in Italy, where today it's often drunk with a twist of lemon. European shots of espresso are smaller than American shots. Different coffeehouses serve different size shots, which means you might get more or less coffee flavor in your drink.

Latte—a shot of espresso topped off with steamed milk at roughly a three to one ratio. The correct term for this drink is *caffe latte*. This translates as coffee milk, but in the Northwest, folks just say "I'll have a latte," which really means "I'll have a milk." Oh well, so much for learning a second language.

Il Bistro

93-A Pike St. and First Ave. (inside the Pike Place Market). ☎ **206/682-3049.** Reservations recommended. Main courses $16–$26.50; pastas $10–$16. AE, CB, DC, MC, V. Mon–Thurs 11:30am–3pm and 5:30–10pm, Fri–Sat 11:30am–3pm and 5:30–11pm, Sun 5:30–10pm. (Bar, nightly until 2am.) ITALIAN.

You'll find Il Bistro to the left of the famous Pike Place Market sign. Il Bistro puts the region's bountiful ingredients to good use, including excellent local crops of wild and cultivated mushrooms. Watch for them on the menu—they're always a treat. The menu lists such mouth-watering starters as calamari sautéed with garlic vinegar, fresh basil, and white wine. Pastas can be a genuine revelation when served with the likes of shiitake mushrooms, hot pepper flakes, vodka, and tomato cream. Hundreds of loyal fans insist that the rack of lamb with wine sauce is the best in Seattle. Don't take their word for it—decide for yourself.

Metropolitan Grill

818 Second Ave. ☎ **206/624-3287.** Reservations recommended. Main courses $11–$30. AE, CB, DC, DISC, JCB, MC, V. Mon–Fri 11am–3:30pm and 5–11pm, Sat 5–11pm, Sun 5–10pm. STEAK.

Single—one shot of espresso. You say, "I'll have a single latte."

Double—two shots of espresso. You say, "I'll have a double latte."

Tall—a latte with extra milk. A tall usually comes with one shot of espresso, but you can also get two shots. You say, "I'll have a double tall latte."

Grande—a 16-ounce latte with two shots of espresso. This is pretty high-octane, so leave it to the pros until you've worked your way up the latte ladder.

Skinny—skimmed milk. You say, "I'll have a tall, skinny latte." You can also get lattes made with 2% milk or with whole milk.

Half-caf—a drink made with half decaffeinated coffee. You say, "I'll have a double tall, skinny, half-caf latte." They say, "Why bother?"

Foam—formed by steaming milk, this is the topping on a latte. Some people want it and some people don't.

Flavorings—sweet syrups with different flavors for giving your latte a bit more complexity. Sort of the wine cooler of the espresso lane. You can get everything from caramel to mango.

Cappuccino—espresso with hot milk and usually a sprinkling of cinnamon on top. A cappuccino's color is the same as that of a Capuchin monk's habit and thus the name.

Macchiato—an espresso with a dollop of foamed milk on top to keep the coffee hotter just a little bit longer.

Mocha—espresso, steamed milk, and chocolate. Slap some whipped cream on top and you've got the ultimate high-octane, high-calorie pick-me-up.

Americano—a single shot of espresso topped off with water to make an approximation of traditional American-style coffee but with more flavor.

Café au lait—regular brewed or drip-filter coffee mixed with hot or steamed milk. These don't have the intense flavor of a latte and aren't readily available in Seattle.

This reliable restaurant for aspiring financial whiz kids and their mentors is dedicated to meat eaters. Green-velvet booths, bar stools, and floral-design carpets are the keynote of the sophisticated atmosphere. Mirrored walls and a high ceiling trimmed with elegant plasterwork make the dining room feel larger than it actually is. Perfectly cooked steaks are the primary attraction, and if you're going to eat here, you might as well order one. They're considered the best steaks in Seattle by those in the know. A baked potato and a pile of crispy onion rings complete the perfect steak dinner.

MODERATE

✪ Café Campagne

1600 Post Alley. ☎ **206/728-CAFE.** Reservations not accepted. Main courses $8–$15. AE, MC, V. Mon–Sat 8am–10pm, Sun 8am–3pm (brunch). FRENCH.

This cozy little café is an offshoot of the Inn at the Market's popular Campagne, and though it's located in the heart of the Pike Place Market neighborhood, its turn-of-the-century Parisian atmosphere is a world away from the market madness. Glass cases just inside the door display roast chickens, salads, luscious tarts, and plenty of other delicacies. The menu changes with the season, but might include a hearty country-style pâté or baked marinated goat cheese on the appetizer menu, or a side dish of baby artichokes stewed in olive oil with lemon and garlic. Entrées include filling sandwiches such as the popular lamb burger with aïoli or roast pork tenderloin on focaccia with apricot mustard. The café also doubles as a wine bar and has a good selection of reasonably priced wines by the glass or by the bottle.

Café Sophie

1921 First Ave. ☎ 206/441-6139. Reservations highly recommended. Main courses $13–$20; desserts $5–$10. MC, V. Mon–Thurs 11:30am–2:30pm and 5:30–9:30pm, Fri–Sat 11:30am–2:30pm and 5:30–10:30pm (late-night menu until 1am). CONTINENTAL.

The Café Sophie hearkens back to the grand old days of supper clubs on the Continent. The grand salon with dark-green walls covered with mirrors and paintings is terribly romantic, while the library room overlooks the bay and is a good spot for viewing the moon or ferry lights. The menu pulls its gastronomic references from all over the world, but is primarily continental. On a recent evening, straightforward coq au vin shared the menu with pork Schnitzel with artichoke lemon aïoli. The extravagant desserts are main reason most people come here.

✪ Dahlia Lounge

1904 Fourth Ave. ☎ 206/682-4142. Reservations highly recommended. Main courses $12–$20. AE, DC, DISC, MC, V. Mon–Thurs 11:30am–2:30pm and 5:30–10pm, Fri 11:30am–2:30pm and 5:30–11pm, Sat 5:30–11pm, Sun 5–9pm. NORTHWEST.

The neon chef holding a flapping fish may suggest that this restaurant is little more than a roadside diner, but a glimpse inside at the stylish decor will change your mind. Chef Tom Douglas brings to the Dahlia all his culinary expertise and imagination, making it one of Seattle's finest restaurants. Mouth-watering and succulent Dungeness crab cakes, a bow to Douglas's Maryland roots, are the house specialty and should not be missed. Menu influences also extend to the far side of the Pacific Rim, from which the Dahlia special fried rice with grilled prawns, shiitake mushrooms, and daikon originates. The housemade gnocchi is dense and delicious, while the Tuscan bread salad is a meal in itself. The lunch menu features many of the same offerings at slightly lower prices.

La Buca

102 Cherry St. ☎ 206/343-9517. Reservations recommended. Main courses $12–$16. AE, DC, MC, V. Mon–Thurs 11:30am–2:30pm and 5–11pm, Fri 11:30am–2:30pm and 5pm–midnight, Sat 5pm–midnight, Sun 5–10pm. SOUTHERN ITALIAN.

Turn off Pioneer Square onto Cherry Street, walk down a flight of steps, and you'll be dining in the Seattle underground. Dark and cavernous with brick arches supporting the ceiling, La Buca is reminiscent of a huge wine cellar. The menu is primarily southern Italian, but goes far beyond spaghetti and meatballs. A housemade sausage is braised with red wine, garlic, peppers, and tomatoes, and served on a bed of polenta, while the saddle of lamb is served with fresh rosemary, figs, port, and Gorgonzola. Appetizers and first courses are equally creative and flavorful. Such dishes as pan-roasted quail with aromatic vegetables and fresh herbs, and polenta with pecorino cheese and a topping of lamb ragoût show off the mouthwatering fare that comes out of La Buca's kitchen.

⑤ McCormick & Schmick's

1103 First Ave. ☎ 206/623-5500. Reservations recommended. Main courses $10–$19.60; box lunches $6. AE, DC, DISC, MC, V. Mon–Fri 11:30am–11pm, Sat–Sun 5–11pm. SEAFOOD.

Force your way past the crowds of business suits at the bar and you'll find yourself in a classic fish house. From the polished brass to the sparkling leaded glass to the dark-wood paneling, everything about this restaurant shines. A recent menu included blackened Canadian lingcod with tomato-ginger chutney; yellowfin tuna with soy, wasabi, and ginger; and halibut stuffed with crab, shrimp, and brie cheese. From 3 to 6pm and 10pm to closing daily, you can get appetizers in the bar for only $1.95, and if you're in the mood for a downtown picnic, they also prepare box lunches. Weekdays between 5 and 6pm, a limited menu is available for between $5 and $6.

The Painted Table

In the Alexis Hotel, 92 Madison St. ☎ **206/624-3646.** Reservations recommended. Main courses $12–$20. AE, CB, DC, DISC, MC, V. Mon–Fri 6:30–10am, 11:30am–2pm, and 5:30–10pm; Sat–Sun 7am–noon and 5:30–10pm. NORTHWEST/FRENCH.

Artistically presented meals are *de rigueur* these days at expensive restaurants, but here at the Painted Table it isn't just the entrées that are works of art—it's the plates as well. Every table is set with colorful hand-painted plates done by West Coast ceramic artists. Should you take a fancy to your plate, you can take it home with you for about $65. If you're lucky you might run across smoked-duck tamales with mango salsa on the appetizer list. One comes wrapped in a banana leaf and the other in a corn husk. The pasta with tea-smoked duck, glazed turnips, roasted walnuts, and dried cherries is one of our favorite dishes, while herb-crusted lamb filet with grilled eggplant and fennel polenta is another winner. For dessert, try the espresso-flavored crème brûlée.

✪ Queen City Grill

2201 First Ave. ☎ **206/443-0975.** Reservations recommended. Main courses $8–$20. AE, DC, DISC, MC, V. Mon–Thurs 11:30am–4:30pm and 4:30–11pm, Fri 11:30am–4:30pm and 4:30pm–midnight, Sat 4:30pm–midnight, Sun 4:30–11pm. INTERNATIONAL.

Battered wooden floors and high-backed wooden booths give this restaurant a look of weathered age. The spare decor and sophisticated lighting underscore an exciting menu. Some people come here just for the crab cakes (with just the right amount of roasted pepper/garlic aïoli) but everything else is just as inspired. Seafood is the specialty of the house, so you might start off with tuna carpaccio accompanied by lime, ginger, and mustard sauce. There are always several daily seafood specials, and Dungeness crab cakes and Szechuan prawns are always on the menu. The wine list here contains over 500 labels from the Northwest and around the world.

Wild Ginger Asian Restaurant & Satay Bar

1400 Western Ave. ☎ **206/623-4450.** Main courses $7–$18. AE, DC, DISC, MC, V. Mon–Thurs 11:30am–3pm and 5–11pm, Fri 11:30am–3pm and 5pm–midnight, Sat 11:30am–3pm and 4:30pm–midnight, Sun 4:30–11pm. (Satay bar, nightly until 1am.) CHINESE/SOUTHEAST ASIAN.

With sushi bars becoming old hat these days, the satay bar may be a worthy replacement. Pull up a comfortable stool around the large grill and watch the cooks grill little skewers of anything from fresh produce to fish, pork, prawns, or lamb. Each skewer of grilled delicacies is served with a small cube of sticky rice and a dipping sauce. Order three or four satay sticks and you have a meal. You can also sit at a table and have a more traditional dinner. Try the pungent Malaysian geram assam—tiger prawns in a curry of tamarind, turmeric, candlenuts, chiles, and lemon. Accompany your meal with a pot of jasmine tea or a beer from China or

Thailand for a real Southeast Asian experience. As in Asia, the lunch menu leans toward noodle dishes.

INEXPENSIVE

Emmett Watson's Oyster Bar

1916 Pike Place No. 16. ☎ **206/448-7721.** Reservations not accepted. Soups $1.75–$6; main courses $3–$6. No credit cards. Mon–Thurs 11:30am–8pm, Fri–Sat 11:30am–9pm. In winter, also Sun 11:30am–5pm, and closes one hour earlier the other nights. SEAFOOD.

Tucked away in a rare quiet corner of the Pike Place Market (well, actually it's across the street in the market overflow area), Emmett Watson's looks like a fast-food place, but in fact the service here is infamously slow. The booths are tiny, so it's best to come on a sunny afternoon when you can sit in the courtyard. The restaurant is named for a famous Seattle newspaper columnist, and there are clippings and photos all over the walls. Oysters on the half shell are the raison d'être for this little place, but the fish dishes are often memorable as well. Check the chalkboard for specials.

Gravity Bar

113 Virginia St. ☎ **206/448-8826.** Meals $4–$7; juices $2–$4.75. MC, V. Mon–Thurs 11am–9pm, Fri 11am–10pm, Sat 10am–10pm, Sun 10am–8pm. NATURAL.

If you're young-at-heart and hip and concerned about the food you put into your body, this is the place to frequent in Seattle. Postmodern neo-industrial decor (lots of sheet metal on the walls, bar, and menus) is the antithesis of the wholesome juices and meals they serve here. The juice list includes all manner of unusual combinations, all with catchy names like the Martian Martini or the Seven-Year Spinach. Be there or be square.

There's also a location at 415 E. Broadway (☎ **206/325-7186**), open Monday through Thursday from 9am to 10pm, on Friday and Saturday from 9am to 11pm, and on Sunday from 9am to 9pm (later in summer).

☺ Hing Loon

628 S. Weller St. ☎ **206/682-2828.** Main courses $5.25–$9. Sun–Thurs 10am–midnight, Fri–Sat 10am–2am. CHINESE.

No atmosphere, bright fluorescent lighting, and big Formica-top tables—this is the sort of restaurant you'd walk by if you were aimlessly searching for a bite in the International District. Forget the rest, with the fancy decor, and take a seat in Hing Loon. Seafood is the house specialty and none is done better than the oysters with ginger and green onion on a sizzling platter. For a veggie dish, don't miss the eggplant in Szechuan sauce. If you're feeling really daring, try the cold jellyfish; it's not at all the way you'd imagine it to be. Be careful of the pork dishes, which tend to have Chinese-style pork that's 90% fat. The restaurant also makes all its own noodles.

Merchants Café

109 Yesler Way. ☎ **206/624-1515.** Main courses $7–$12. CB, DC, MC, V. Sun–Mon 10am–3pm, Tues–Thurs 10am–7pm (to 4pm in winter), Fri–Sat 10am–9pm. AMERICAN.

The Merchants Café is Seattle's oldest restaurant and looks every bit of its 100-plus years. A well-scuffed tile floor surrounds the bar, which came around the Horn in the 1800s. An old safe and gold scales are left over from the days when Seattle was the first taste of civilization for those returning from the Yukon gold fields. This may be the original Skid Row saloon, since Yesler Way was the original "skid

---

🎭 Family-Friendly Restaurants

Ivar's Salmon House *(see p. 97)*   This restaurant is built to resemble a Northwest coast Native American longhouse and is filled with artifacts that kids will find fascinating. If they get restless, they can go out to the floating patio and watch the boats passing by.

Ivar's Acres of Clams   (206/624-6853) You'll find this Ivar's seafood restaurant in an old warehouse on Pier 54 in downtown Seattle. It's convenient to the Seattle Aquarium and the Omnidome Film Experience Theater, two popular kids' attractions.

---

road" down which logs were skidded to the sawmill. Straightforward sandwiches and steaks are the mainstays of the menu, though a few more imaginative entrées also appear.

SEATTLE CENTER/LAKE UNION AREA/QUEEN ANNE
EXPENSIVE

Canlis
2576 Aurora Ave. N. ☎ **206/283-3313.** Reservations highly recommended. Jacket required for men. Main courses $19.50–$30. AE, DC, MC, V. Mon–Sat 5:30–10pm. AMERICAN/ CONTINENTAL.

This restaurant has enjoyed unflagging popularity for 40 years now. The reason? It could be the perfectly prepared steaks and seafoods, or it could be the excellent service by kimono-clad waitresses, or it could be the view across Lake Union from high on a hillside. A huge stone fireplace and stone columns lend a cool, dark air to the main dining room, while outside the tops of fir trees jut into your view of the lake far below. This is the perfect place to close a big deal or celebrate a very special occasion. The perfect meal? Filet mignon with the restaurant's legendary baked potato and a salad tossed at your table finished off with a Grand Marnier soufflé.

Kaspar's
19 W. Harrison St. ☎ **206/298-0123.** Reservations recommended. Main courses $13–$19; vintners dinners $55; chef's table dinners $50 for five courses, $75 for eight courses. AE, MC, V. Tues–Thurs 5–9:30pm, Fri–Sat 5–10pm. INTERNATIONAL/NORTHWEST.

Though Kaspar's has been around for years, the restaurant moved in 1994 to a new setting in the Lower Queen Anne neighborhood. The main dining room is elegant yet spare, with dramatic lighting illuminating the tables, while in the lounge there are long walls of glass that take in great summer sunsets. For the connoisseur and oenophile there are vintner's dinners, or, for the ultimate in personal service, try a chef's table dinner and dine in the kitchen with chef Kaspar Donier. For light meals, drinks, and desserts, there's the lounge. The menu here draws on worldwide influences and produces such dishes as an Asian antipasto plate that included a crab sushi roll, smoked ahi, and a vegetable spring roll. Pasta might be flavored with a fragrant and flavorful hazelnut-and-rosemary pesto, and mussels might be scented with lemon grass and curry. However, the scallops in spicy bacon sauce have become the restaurant's signature dish.

Pirosmani

2220 Queen Anne Ave. N. ☎ **206/285-3360.** Reservations recommended. Main courses $16–$22. AE, DC, MC, V. Tues–Thurs 5:30–10pm, Fri–Sat 5:30–10:30pm. GEORGIAN/ MEDITERRANEAN.

Named after the Republic of Georgia's most famous artist, Pirosmani is a small, informal restaurant in a Victorian home in the Queen Anne district. The chef pulls her uncommon gastronomic references from both Georgia and the sunny Mediterranean. You may whet your appetite with such dishes as juicy traditional Georgian pork and beef dumplings seasoned with mint, onion, green pepper, and paprika, or chicken breast stuffed with olives and bulgur, and wrapped in grape leaves. The detail and attention given to each dish—lamb, duck, rabbit, and fresh fish—makes each one distinctive, but we recommend the tuna wrapped in grape leaves with an unexpected tart and savory sauce containing pomegranate, walnuts, and roasted red peppers. Save room for one of the light and unusually flavored desserts.

✪ Ponti Seafood Grill

3014 Third Ave. N. ☎ **206/284-3000.** Reservations recommended. Main courses $14–$23.50; early dinner $13.95. AE, MC, V. Mon–Thurs 11:30am–2:30pm and 5:30–10pm, Fri–Sat 11:30am–2:30pm and 5:30–11pm, Sun 10am–2:30pm (brunch) and 5:30–10pm. SEAFOOD.

Situated at the south end of the Fremont Bridge and overlooking the Lake Washington Ship Canal, Ponti is one of Seattle's most elegant and sophisticated restaurants. The menu here has an international flavor, though it also offers some solidly northwestern creations. On a recent evening, the appetizers list included a decadent dish of smoked salmon served with a corn pancake, vodka crème fraîche, chives, and caviar. For a pleasing twist on a classic, try the Caesar salad with smoked prawns. The pasta menu always includes some highly creative dishes such as Dungeness crab ravioli with herbs and champagne buerre blanc, and the daily listing of fresh seafoods might include such tempting entrées as macadamia nut–crusted marlin with Chinese plum-wine sauce and pineapple salsa. Early dinners are served between 5 and 6pm.

MODERATE

Kamon on Lake Union

1177 Fairview Ave. N. ☎ **206/622-4665.** Reservations recommended. Main courses $11–$19. AE, JCB, MC, V. Mon–Thurs 11:30am–2:30pm and 5–9:30pm, Fri 11:30am–2:30pm and 5–10pm, Sat 5–10pm, Sun 5–9:30pm. JAPANESE/INTERNATIONAL.

Of the many big waterfront restaurants at the south end of Lake Union, Kamon is still our favorite. There are, of course, the views across the lake to the sunset sky and later the twinkling lights of the city, but there are also Asian-inspired dishes both traditional and contemporary. Sushi fans can take a seat at the long sushi bar, but, if it's summer, we'd much rather be sitting out on the deck. If you prefer a bit more lively entertainment with your meal, try a teppanyaki dinner and watch the chef cook your meal right at your table. Japanese, Chinese, Thai, and Indo-nesian dishes all show up on the menu, and for those with a more nouvelle leaning, there are such dishes as pasta with smoked scallops in a ginger-cream sauce, as well as raspberry teriyaki chicken.

✪ Serafina

2043 Eastlake Ave. E. ☎ **206/323-0807.** Reservations recommended. Main courses $10–$15; pastas $8–$13. MC, V. Mon–Thurs 11:30am–2pm and 5:30–10pm, Fri 11:30am–2pm and 5:30–11pm, Sat 5:30–11pm, Sun 5:30–10pm. ITALIAN/EUROPEAN.

The atmosphere at Serafina is rustic and serves to underscore the earthy Italian country dishes here. It's one of our favorite dining spots, with just a touch of sophistication in an oversize floral arrangement, a casual ambience in the stacked wine bottles and loaves of bread. In the summer there's dining in the romantic garden courtyard. For starters, try the antipasti or fresh mussels smoked in a leek, vermouth, and lime broth. Among the pastas you'll find are penne pasta with artichokes and spinach in a leek-and-Gorgonzola–cream sauce, and linguine with prawns in a spicy sauce of olives, tomatoes, anchovies, and capers. For a main dish, try a classic that will conjure up dreams of Italy—Italian sausages sautéed with grapes and onions and served with soft polenta. Nearly every evening there's jazz and Latin-influenced live music.

FIRST HILL, CAPITOL HILL & EAST SEATTLE

EXPENSIVE

✪ The Hunt Club

In the Sorrento Hotel, 900 Madison St. ☎ **206/343-6156.** Reservations recommended. Main courses $19–$26. AE, DC, MC, V. Mon–Thurs 7–10am, 11am–2:30pm, and 5:30–10pm; Fri 7–10am, 11am–2:30pm, and 5:30–11pm; Sat 7am–noon and 5:30–11pm; Sun 7am–noon and 5:30–10pm. CONTINENTAL.

The Hunt Club is dark, intimate, and well suited to business lunches and romantic celebration. Mahogany paneling lines the walls, and deep-rose upholstery adds rich splashes of color. If you need a little privacy, folding louvered doors can be pulled across to create your own dining area. You might start a meal with Dungeness crab risotto with wild mushrooms or butternut squash ravioli with rock shrimp. For a main dish, try the grilled King salmon with succotash or alderwood- and rosemary-smoked rack of lamb. For dessert there are usually confections such as crème brûlée, chocolate espresso silk tart, and raspberry roulade.

✪ Rover's

2808 E. Madison St. ☎ **206/325-7442.** Reservations required. Main courses $22.75–$26.95; five-course *menu dégustation* $44.50–$54.50. AE, DC, MC, V. Tues–Sat 5:30–11pm. NORTHWEST.

Tucked away in a quaint clapboard house behind a chic little shopping center is one of Seattle's most talked-about restaurants. Chef Thierry Rautureau received classic French training before falling in love with the Northwest and all the wonderful ingredients it has to offer. Voilà! Northwest cuisine with a French accent. Perennial appetizer favorites include warm foie-gras salad, sometimes served with wild greens and a balsamic-vinegar sauce, and vegetable flans with caramelized turnips and a red burgundy sauce. Among the main dishes, you'll likely encounter salmon or halibut, with pomme mousseline, an ocean salad, and one of Rautureau's imaginative sauces with dry vermouth; or roast squab with green lentils and a black-peppercorn sauce. In summer, don't miss the raspberry desserts—for that matter, don't pass up the desserts at any time of year.

Seattle Dining—North & Northeast

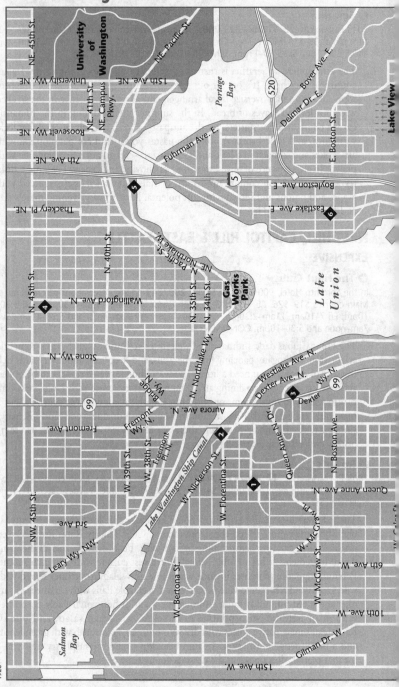

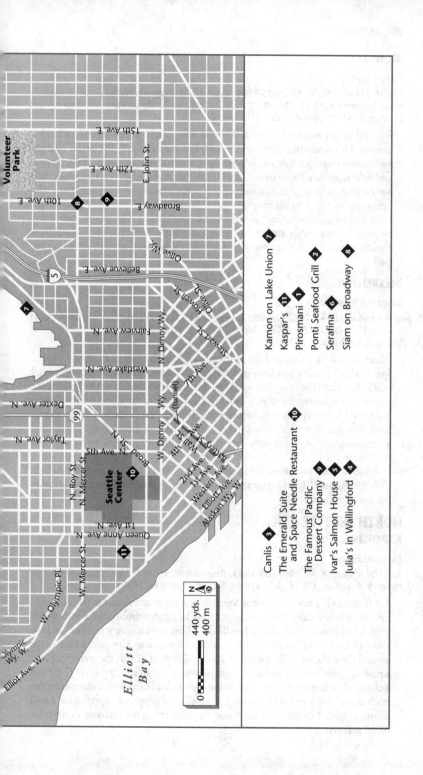

Volunteer Park

5

99

Elliott Bay

Seattle Center

Canlis 3

The Emerald Suite
and Space Needle Restaurant

The Famous Pacific
Dessert Company 9

Ivar's Salmon House 5

Julia's in Wallingford 4

Kamon on Lake Union 7

Kaspar's 11

Pirosmani 1

Ponti Seafood Grill 2

Serafina 6

Siam on Broadway 8

0   440 yds.
0   400 m

MODERATE

Café Flora

2901 E. Madison St. ☎ **206/325-9100.** Reservations accepted only for parties of eight or more. Main courses $7.25–$14. MC, V. Tues–Fri 11:30am–10pm, Sat 9am–2pm (brunch) and 5–10pm, Sun 9am–2pm (brunch). VEGETARIAN.

Big and bright and airy, this café will dispel any notions that vegetarian food is boring. This is meatless gourmet cooking and it's delicious. The menu changes weekly and might include a sauté of shiitake mushrooms, onions, peppers, carrots, and celery, seasoned with lemon grass, basil, ginger, lime, and coconut milk, and served with basamati rice and fruit chutney. A couple of unusual pizzas typically are on the menu. A recent artichoke-pesto pizza came with artichoke-heart pesto, fried Yukon gold potatoes, radicchio, and goat cheese. The dessert tray that's brought to your table always has plenty of temptations, such as a chocolate-mousse pie with whole strawberries inside. In the summer you can sit out on the patio.

INEXPENSIVE

Siam on Broadway

616 Broadway E. ☎ **206/324-0892.** Reservations recommended on weekends. Main courses $5.75–$8.25. AE, MC, V. Mon–Thurs 11:30am–10pm, Fri 11:30am–11pm, Sat 5–11pm, Sun 5–10pm. THAI.

All the way at the north end of the Broadway shopping district in trendy Capitol Hill is one of Seattle's best inexpensive Thai restaurants. Siam on Broadway is small and very casual. The tom yum soups, made with either shrimp or chicken, are the richest and creamiest we've ever had—and also some of the spiciest. If you prefer your food less fiery, let your server know (they mean it when they say super-hot). The pad thai is excellent, and the muu phad bai graplau (spicy meat and vegetables), one of our all-time favorites, was properly fragrant with chiles and basil leaves.

Another Siam restaurant is located on Lake Union at 1880 Fairview Ave. E. (☎ **206/323-8101**); it's larger and has the same good food, but that location has less personality.

NORTH SEATTLE
EXPENSIVE

Le Gourmand

425 NW Market St. ☎ **206/784-3463.** Reservations required. Three-course fixed-price dinner $18–$28. AE, CB, DC, MC, V. Wed–Sat 5:30–10pm. FRENCH/NORTHWEST.

Chefs Bruce Naftaly and Robin Sanders, former music students who came to Seattle to study voice, have converted this aging storefront into a memorable French restaurant. With only a handful of tables, service is very personal and the atmosphere is very inviting, with a woodland mural in airy colors that wraps around the walls, and silk bolsters as accents. On our last visit the menu included a pâté of rabbit liver flavored with cognac, port, and thyme for a starter. There was a choice of eight different entrées, but the roast rack of lamb with a sauce of home-made mustard flavored with roasted and pickled red peppers was perfect for a cold winter's night. A choice from the tempting pastry tray is not included in the price of the prix-fixe dinner.

Ray's Boathouse and Café
6049 Seaview Ave. NW. ☎ **206/789-3770.** Reservations recommended on weekends; not necessary upstairs. Main courses $11–$27 (slightly less upstairs); early dinners (5–6pm) $13. AE, CB, DC, MC, V. Mon–Thurs 11:30am–2pm and 5–10pm, Fri 11:30am–2pm and 5–10:30pm, Sat 4:30–10:30pm, Sun 4:30–10pm. SEAFOOD.

Upstairs at Ray's, where you'll find the lounge, the crowd of suntanned boating types can get pretty rowdy. The restaurant compensates by reducing the price of the food here. Downstairs, everything is quiet, cozy, and sophisticated. Luckily, everyone gets similar fine meals. As at other Seattle restaurants, fresh herbs are making bold appearances on the menu in dishes such as Manila clam fettuccine with peppered bacon and fresh herbs in garlic-lemon cream. There are many more delicious reasons why this is considered one of the best restaurants in Seattle. Grilled black cod in saké kasu with ginger is a bow to the Japanese influences that have crept into Northwest kitchens.

MODERATE

Ivar's Salmon House
401 NE Northlake Way. ☎ 206/632-0767. Reservations recommended. Main courses $10.45–$19; fish bar $4–$7. AE, MC, V. Main restaurant, Mon–Thurs 11:30am–2:30pm and 4:30–10pm, Fri 11:30am–2:30pm and 4:30–11pm, Sat 4–11pm, Sun 10am–2pm (brunch) and 4–10pm; fish bar, Sun–Thurs 11am–10pm, Fri–Sat 11am–11pm. SEAFOOD.

The Salmon House commands an excellent view of the Seattle skyline from the north end of Lake Union. Floating docks out back are like magnets for weekend boaters, who abandon their own galleys in favor of clam chowder and the restaurant's famous alder-smoked salmon. The theme here is Northwest Coast Indian, and the building even won an award from the Seattle Historical Society for its accuracy in creating a replica of a tribal longhouse. Kids, and adults, love this place.

CAFES, COFFEEHOUSES, DESSERTS & A TEA ROOM

Among our favorites are the following Seattle cafés: **Counter Intelligence,** 94 Pike St., in the Pike Place Market (☎ 206/622-6979), is a quiet place hidden away on the second floor of a building across Pike Street from the Pike Place Market information booth.

In an old house on a nondescript street, the **Green Room Café,** 4026 Stone Way N. (☎ 206/632-6420), is a warren of cozy little rooms decorated in a funky college style. The fireplace is great on a cold rainy night. Great desserts.

The very contemporary decor and artwork at **110 Espress + Panini Bar,** 110 Union St. (☎ 206/343-8733), plus good soups and sandwiches, make it a popular spot.

Fremont is Seattle's most eclectic neighborhood, and **Still Life in Fremont Coffeehouse,** 709 N. 35th St. (☎ 206/547-9850), reflects this eclecticism. It's big, always crowded, and serves good vegetarian meals.

Torrefazione, 320 Occidental Ave. S. (☎ 206/624-5773), and also at 622 Olive Way (☎ 206/624-1429), has the feel of a classic Italian caffè, with hand-painted Italian crockery and great pastries. The one in the Pioneer Square area has more atmosphere.

Zio Rico, 1415 Fourth Ave. (☎ 206/467-8616), is the most elegant café in Seattle, with big, comfortable easy chairs and lots of dark-wood paneling. It's a great place to sit and read the *Wall Street Journal.*

If coffee isn't your cup of tea, check out **The Crumpet Shop,** 1503 First Ave. (☎ 206/682-1598), a tea shop in the Pike Place Market. Crumpets are the specialty.

If you should suddenly be struck by an uncontrollable craving for tiramisù, velvet mousse cake, raspberry Linzer torte, chocolate-orange Victorian soufflé cake, hazelnut-praline cheesecake, or any other indecently hedonistic dessert, head for the hill—Capitol Hill, that is—and the **Famous Pacific Dessert Company,** 516 Broadway E. (☎ 206/328-1950). At any given time you can choose from among more than 30 calorific plates of instant gratification. Open Sunday through Thursday from noon to midnight and on Friday and Saturday from noon to 1am.

DINING WITH A VIEW

The Emerald Suite and Space Needle Restaurant
In the Seattle Center, 219 Fourth Ave. ☎ 206/443-2100. Reservations required. Main courses $22–$31; Sun brunch $16.50–$19.95. AE, CB, DC, MC, V. Mon–Sat 7–10:30am, 11am–3:30pm, and 4–10:45pm; Sun 8am–2:45pm (brunch) and 5–11pm. NORTHWEST.

There may not be a more difficult restaurant in Seattle to get into than the Emerald Suite at the Space Needle. With seating for only 50 people, the attractively decorated restaurant is cozy, elegant, and almost always booked solid. The Space Needle Restaurant offers the same views in a more casual setting. Both the views and the prices are some of the highest in the city, and this 500-foot-high dining room rotates, assuring you a new view with each course. Menus at both the Emerald Suite and the Space Needle Restaurant are almost identical.

QUICK BITES & BREAKFASTS
Macheezmo Mouse, 211 Broadway Ave. E. (☎ 206/325-0072), serves healthy Mexican fast food. They're also at 701 Fifth Ave./Columbia Center (☎ 206/382-1730), 425 Queen Anne Ave. N. (☎ 206/282-9904), and 1815 N. 45th St. (☎ 206/545-0153). **Marcos's Filipino Cuisine,** 4106 Brooklyn Ave. NE (☎ 206/633-5696), located a couple of blocks from the University of Washington, serves daily specials and large portions of Filipino food. The Belltown burger at the **Belltown Pub,** 2322 First Ave. (☎ 206/728-4311), just might be the best burger in Seattle. This neighborhood pub is located a few blocks north of the Pike Place Market. The **Triangle Café,** 3507 Fremont Place N. (☎ 206/632-0880), is located in the middle of the Fremont neighborhood. This local hang-out serves cheap and imaginative sandwiches.

Consider **Julia's in Wallingford,** 4401 Wallingford Ave. N. (☎ 206/633-1175), for eye-opening breakfasts such as avocado omelets with ranchero sauce, and bakery take-out. **The Surrogate Hostess,** 726 19th Ave. E. (☎ 206/328-0908), also has great breakfasts and is located in a neighborhood aways out from the Capitol Hill commercial area.

5 Attractions

THE TOP ATTRACTIONS

✪ Pike Place Market
Between Pike and Pine sts. at First Ave. ☎ 206/682-7453. Free admission. Mon–Sat 9am–6pm, Sun 11am–5pm. Take any downtown bus.

The Pike Place Market was founded in 1907 when housewives complained that middlemen were raising the price of produce too high. The market allowed shoppers to buy directly from farmers and fishermen, and thus save on their grocery bills. However, by the 1960s the market was no longer the popular spot it had once been. The site was being eyed for a major redevelopment project when a grassroots movement succeeded in saving the 7-acre market and having it declared a National Historic District. Today it's once again a bustling market, but the 100 or so farmers and fishmongers who sell here are only a small part of the attraction. More than 200 local craftspeople and artists can be found selling their creations at different times of year. Dozens of restaurants and hundreds of shops fill the market, and street performers serenade the milling crowds. There's an information booth almost directly below the large PIKE PLACE MARKET sign where you can pick up a market map. Watch for the flying fish and Rachel the giant pig.

Seattle Art Museum

100 University St. ☎ **206/654-3100.** Admission $6 adults, $4 seniors and students, free for children 12 and under, free to all on the first Tues of each month. Tues–Wed and Fri–Sun 10am–5pm, Thurs 10am–9pm; first Tues of each month until 7pm. Closed Jan 1, Thanksgiving, and Dec 25. Bus: 10, 12, 15, 18, 21, 22, 23, or any bus using the bus tunnel.

This is the city's premier museum, and out front, Jonathon Borofsky's *Hammering Man,* a giant black silhouette of a steel sculpture, toils unceasingly. Here you'll find one of the nation's premier collections of Northwest Coast Native American art and artifacts, and an equally large collection of African art. These displays juxtapose cultures rich in religious and decorative arts. On the top floor you'll find the museum's collection of European and American art, covering periods from the ancient Mediterranean to the medieval, Renaissance, and baroque periods in Europe. A large 18th-century collection and a smaller 19th-century exhibition lead up to a large 20th-century collection that includes a room devoted to Northwest contemporary art.

✪ Museum of Flight

9404 E. Marginal Way S. ☎ **206/764-5720.** Admission $6 adults, $3 children 6–15, free for children 5 and under, free for everyone the first Thurs of the month 5–9pm. Fri–Wed 10am–5pm, Thurs 10am–9pm. Closed Dec 25. Bus: 174. Take Exit 158 off I-5.

Right next door to Boeing Field, 10 miles south of Seattle, lies one of the world's best aviation museums. A six-story glass-and-steel building holds most of the collection. To start things off, there's a replica of the Wright brothers' first glider, and then the exhibits bring you right up to the present state of flight. Suspended in the Great Hall are 20 planes, including a DC-3 and the first air force F-5 supersonic fighter. You'll also see the Blackbird, the world's fastest jet; a rare World War II Corsair fighter, rescued from Lake Washington and restored to its original glory; and an exhibit on the U.S. space program featuring an Apollo command module. See "Attractions," later in this chapter, for information on a tour of the Boeing plant.

✪ Seattle Aquarium

Pier 59, Waterfront Park. ☎ **206/386-4320.** Admission $6.95 adults, $5.50 senior citizens, $4.50 children 6–18, $2.25 children 3–5. Labor Day–Memorial Day, daily 10am–5pm; Memorial Day–Labor Day, daily 10am–7pm. Bus: 15 or 18; then walk down Pike Place Hillclimb. Waterfront Trolley: Pike Place Market stop.

The Seattle Aquarium is a fascinating place to spend a few hours learning about marine and freshwater life in the Northwest. From the underwater viewing dome, you'll get a fish's-eye view of life beneath the waves, and the salmon ladder is particularly exciting in autumn when the salmon return to the aquarium to spawn.

❓ Did You Know?

- After the Great Seattle Fire of 1889, the city built on top of its ruins; there are still remains of old Seattle under the sidewalks and buildings of the Pioneer Square area.
- KJR radio became the second radio station in America when it broadcast over the airwaves in 1920.
- There used to be seven hills in Seattle, but now there are only six; Denny Hill was leveled by high-powered water hoses because it was just too steep.
- There are three floating bridges in the Seattle area (one of which nearly sank in 1990).
- Seattle's Freeway Park is built *on top of* I-5.
- It rains fewer inches per year in Seattle than it does in New York, Boston, or Washington, D.C.
- The term "skid row" is derived from Skid Road, a road down which logs are skidded to a lumber mill.
- The first Boeing airplane took off from Lake Union in 1916; today Boeing is the largest employer in the Seattle metropolitan area.
- The geoduck (pronounced *gooeyduck*) clam, harvested from the Puget Sound area, weighs more than 5 pounds.

There's a beautiful, large coral-reef tank and a telling exhibit on the pollution of Puget Sound shows the effect of human population expansion in the area. One of the aquarium's most popular exhibits is an interactive tidepool and discovery lab that re-creates Washington's wave-swept intertidal zone.

Seattle Asian Art Museum

Volunteer Park, 14th Ave. E. and E. Prospect St. ☎ **206/654-3100.** Admission $6 adults, $4 students and senior citizens, free for children 12 and under, free for everyone on the first Tues of each month. Ticket also valid at Seattle Art Museum if used within two days. Tues–Wed and Fri–Sun 10am–5pm, Thurs 10am–9pm; first Tues of each month until 7pm. Closed Jan 1, Thanksgiving, and Dec 25. Bus: 10.

Housed in the renovated art deco building that once served as the city's main art museum, the Asian art collection has an emphasis on Chinese and Japanese art but also includes pieces from Korea, Southeast Asia, South Asia, and the Himalayas. The Chinese terra-cotta funerary art, snuff bottles, and Japanese *înetsukesï* (belt decorations) are among the more notable collections. One room is devoted almost exclusively to Japanese screens and painting while another holds Japanese folk art. The central hall is devoted to the stone religious sculptures of South Asia. Special exhibits change every six months.

Pacific Science Center

200 Second Ave. N., in the Seattle Center. ☎ **206/443-2001** or 206/443-2880 for information. Admission $6 adults, $5 seniors and children 6–13, $3.50 children 2–5, free for children under 2. IMAX®, $2 as an add-on to the general-admission ticket, or $5.50 adults, $4.50 seniors and children 6–13, $3.50 children 2–5, free for children under 2. Laser show,

Seattle Attractions

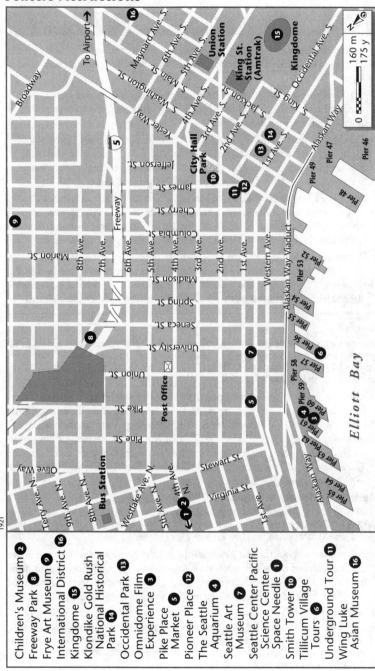

Children's Museum **2**
Freeway Park **8**
Frye Art Museum **9**
International District **16**
Kingdome **15**
Klondike Gold Rush National Historical Park **14**
Occidental Park **13**
Omnidome Film Experience **3**
Pike Place Market **5**
Pioneer Place **12**
The Seattle Aquarium **4**
Seattle Art Museum **7**
Seattle Center Pacific Science Center **1**
Space Needle **1**
Smith Tower **10**
Tillicum Village Tours **6**
Underground Tour **11**
Wing Luke Asian Museum **16**

1921

Frommer's Favorite Seattle Experiences

Riding the Ferry. For $3.50 you can ride across Puget Sound and back with a great view of the Seattle skyline and sometimes the Olympic Mountains and Mount Rainier.

Sea Kayaking on Lake Union. Seattle is the nation's sea-kayak capital—the waters all around the city are ideal for leisurely paddling. You can even pull up at waterfront restaurants for a meal.

Taking the Seattle Underground Tour. The humor is slightly off-color and the history isn't what you learned in grade school, but that's what makes this tour so much fun. Go beneath the sidewalks and old buildings of the Pioneer Square area to see what Seattle was like before the Great Fire of 1889.

Spending a Day at the Pike Place Market. There's no better place in Seattle to shop for fresh local and gourmet produce, fish, or meat. The displays are beautiful even if you don't buy. The market maze is also home to hundreds of craftspeople, vendors, and shops filled with all kinds of amazing goods.

Watching the Salmon Return to Spawn. At the Seattle Aquarium, a fish ladder allows salmon that were hatched there to return from the sea as adults and spawn right on the aquarium grounds. These graceful and powerful fish are an integral part of Northwest culture—it's always reassuring to see them return.

$6 for evening performances ($3 Tues), $2 for matinee performances as an add-on to the general-admission ticket only. June–Sept, daily 10am–6pm; Oct–May, Mon–Fri 10am–5pm, Sat–Sun 10am–6pm. Closed Dec 25. Bus: 1, 2, 3, 4, 6, 13, 15, 16, 18, 19, 24, or 33. Monorail: Seattle Center Station.

Although its exhibits are aimed primarily at children, the Pacific Science Center is fun for all ages. The primary goal of this sprawling complex at the Seattle Center is to teach kids about science and hopefully to instill in them a sense of curiosity about the scientific world. To that end there are dozens of fun hands-on exhibits addressing the biological sciences, technology, physics, and chemistry. There is an IMAX® theater and a planetarium that does laser shows. There are also special events, including a bubble festival.

Museum of History & Industry

2700 24th Ave. E. ☎ **206/324-1126.** Admission $5.50 adults, $3 seniors and children 6–12, $1 children 2–5, free for children under 2; on Tues by donation. Daily 10am–5pm. Closed Jan 1, Thanksgiving, and Dec 25. Bus: 25, 43, or 48.

You can learn about the history of Seattle and the Northwest in this museum at the north end of the Washington Park Arboretum. There's a Boeing mail plane from the 1920s and an exhibit on the 1889 fire that leveled Seattle. Re-created storefronts provide glimpses into the lives of Seattle's 19th-century citizenry.

Omnidome Film Experience

Pier 59, Waterfront Park. ☎ **206/622-1868** or 206/622-1869. Admission $6 adults, $5 seniors and children 13–18, $4 children 3–12, free for children 2 and under. Sun–Thurs 10am–9pm, Fri–Sat 10am–11pm. Bus: 15 or 18; then walk down Pike Place Hillclimb. Trolley: Pike Place Market stop.

The Omnidome, for those who have never experienced it, is a movie theater with a 180° screen that fills your peripheral vision and puts you right in the middle of the action. This huge wraparound theater is located adjacent to the Seattle Aquarium.

MORE ATTRACTIONS
MUSEUMS
Burke Museum

On the University of Washington campus, 17th Ave. NE and NE 45th St. ☎ **206/543-5590.** Admission by donation, $3 adults, $2 students and seniors, $1.50 children 6–18. Daily 10am– 5pm. Closed Jan 1, July 4, Thanksgiving, and Dec 25. Bus: 70, 71, 72, 73, or 74.

The Burke Museum features exhibits on the natural and cultural heritage of the Pacific Rim. It's noteworthy primarily for its Northwest Native American art collection. In front of the museum are replicas of totem poles carved in the 1870s and 1880s. Try to visit on a Saturday afternoon or a Sunday when parking is cheaper.

Frye Art Museum

704 Terry St. (on First Hill, at Cherry St.). ☎ **206/622-9250.** Free admission. Mon–Sat 10am–5pm, Sun noon–5pm. Closed Thanksgiving and Dec 25. Bus: 3, 4, or 12.

This museum focuses primarily on late 19th-century painters, with works by Thomas Hart Benton, Edward Hopper, Albert Bierstadt, Pablo Picasso, and Winslow Homer. The museum will be closed for renovation until around October 1996.

Klondike Gold Rush National Historical Park

117 S. Main St. ☎ **206/553-7220.** Free admission. Daily 9am–5pm. Closed Jan 1, Thanks-giving, and Dec 25. Bus: 15, 18, 21, 22, or 23. Waterfront Trolley: Occidental Park stop.

It isn't in the Klondike (which isn't even in the United States) and it isn't a park (it's a single room in an old store), but this is a fascinating little museum. Would-be miners heading for the Klondike goldfields in the 1890s made Seattle their outfitting center and transformed it into a prosperous city. When they struck it rich up north, they headed back to Seattle, the first outpost of civilization, and unloaded their gold, making Seattle doubly rich. Film buffs can catch a free screening of Charlie Chaplin's *Gold Rush* the first Sunday of each month at 3pm.

Wing Luke Asian Museum

407 Seventh Ave. S. ☎ **206/623-5124.** Admission $2.50 adults, $1.50 students and seniors, 75¢ children 5–12, free for children 4 and under, free for everyone on Thurs. Tues–Fri 11am– 4:30pm, Sat–Sun noon–4pm. Closed Jan 1, Easter, July 4, Veteran's Day, Thanksgiving, and Dec 24–25. Bus: 7 or 14.

In the heart of the International District, Asian American culture, art, and history are explored. The emphasis is on the life of Asian immigrants in the Northwest, and special exhibits are meant to help explain foreign customs to non-Asians. Asians, primarily Chinese and Japanese, played an integral role in settling the Northwest, and today the connection of this region with the far side of the Pacific is opening up many new economic and cultural doors.

Ye Olde Curiosity Shop

Pier 54, Alaskan Way. ☎ **206/682-5844.** Free admission. Mon–Thurs 9:30am–6pm, Fri– Sat 9am–9pm, Sun 9am–6pm.

It's a museum. It's a souvenir shop. It's weird! It's tacky! If you have a fascination with the bizarre—and we think everyone does—shoulder your way into this crowded shop and erstwhile museum. See Siamese-twin calves, a natural mummy, the Lord's Prayer on a grain of rice, a narwhal tusk, shrunken heads, and much,

much more of the weird stuff that fascinated you as a child. The collection of oddities was started in 1899 by Joe Standley, who developed a more-than-passing interest in strange curios.

NEIGHBORHOODS

INTERNATIONAL DISTRICT   Seattle's large and prosperous Asian neighborhood is called the International District rather than Chinatown because so many Asian nationalities call this area home. Running from Fifth Avenue South to Eighth Avenue South between South Main Street and South Lane Street, this has been the traditional Asian neighborhood for 100 years or more, and you can learn about the history of the neighborhood at the **Wing Luke Museum** (see above for details). There are of course lots of restaurants and import and food stores, including the huge Uwajimaya (see "Shopping," later in this chapter, for details). Both the **Nippon Kan Theatre,** 628 S. Washington St. (☎ 206/467-6807), and the **Northwest Asian American Theater,** 409 Seventh Ave. S. (☎ 206/340-1049), feature performances with an Asian flavor.

FREMONT DISTRICT   Extending from the north end of Fremont Bridge around the intersection of Fremont Avenue North and North 36th Street, this funky neighborhood calls itself the Republic of Fremont, and has as its motto "De Libertas Quirkas," which roughly translated means "free to be peculiar." At this crossroads business district, you'll find unusual outdoor art, the Fremont Sunday Market, several vintage clothing and furniture stores, a brew pub, and many more unexpected and unusual shops, galleries, and cafés. Among the public artworks in the neighborhood are *Waiting for the Interurban* (at the north end of the Fremont Bridge), the *Fremont Troll* (under the Aurora Bridge on North 36th Street), and *The Rocket at the Center of the Universe* (at the corner of Evanston Avenue North and North 35th Street).

TOTEM POLES

Totem poles are the quintessential symbol of the Northwest, and although this Native American art form actually comes from farther north, there are quite a few totem poles around Seattle. The ones in **Occidental Park,** at Occidental Avenue South and South Washington Street, were carved by local artist Duane Pasco. The tallest is 35-foot-high *The Sun and Raven,* which tells the story of how Raven brought light into the world. A block away, in the triangular park of **Pioneer Place,** you can see Seattle's most famous totem pole. Up near the Pike Place Market, at **Victor Steinbrueck Park,** which is at the intersection of Pike Place, Virginia Street, and Western Avenue, are two 50-foot-tall totem poles. To see the largest concentration of authentic totem poles, visit the University of Washington's **Burke Museum** (see above for details).

PANORAMAS

If you want to take home a drop-dead photo of the Seattle skyline at sunset, head up to **Highland Park,** on Queen Anne Hill. To reach the park, head north from the Seattle Center on Queen Anne Avenue North and turn left on West Highland Drive. When you reach the park, you'll immediately recognize the view—it's on the cover of virtually every Seattle tourist booklet available.

Space Needle

219 Fourth Ave. N., at the Seattle Center. ☎ **206/443-2100.** Admission $7 adults, $6.50 seniors. Bus: 1, 2, 3, 4, 6, 13, 15, 16, 18, 19, 24, or 33. Monorail: Seattle Center Station.

From a distance it resembles a flying saucer on top of a tripod, and when it was built it was meant to suggest future architectural trends. Erected for the 1962 World's Fair, the 605-foot-tall tower is the most popular tourist sight in Seattle. The views from the observation deck at 520 feet above ground level are stunning, and there are displays identifying more than 60 sites and activities in the Seattle area. High-powered telescopes let you zoom in on things. There's a lounge, and two very expensive restaurants. If you don't mind standing in line and paying quite a bit for an elevator ride, make this your first stop in Seattle so you can orient yourself.

Smith Tower
508 Second Ave. ☎ **206/682-9393.** Admission $2 adults, $1 children and seniors. Daily 10am–10pm. Bus: 15, 18, 21, 22, 23, 39, 70, 136, or 137.

Despite all the shiny glass skyscrapers crowding the Seattle skyline these days, you can't miss this one. It sits off all by itself, a tall white needle on the edge of the Pioneer Square District. At 42 stories, it was the tallest building west of the Mississippi for many years. There's an observation platform way up near the top. You should call ahead if you're going out of your way since the observation floor is sometimes closed because of special functions.

PARKS & GARDENS

Freeway Park
Sixth Ave. and Seneca St. Free admission. Daily dawn–dusk. Take any bus that goes to the downtown bus tunnel to the Convention Center stop.

What do you do when a noisy Interstate runs right through the middle of your fair city and you haven't got enough parks for all the sun worshippers and Frisbee throwers? Put a roof on the highway and build a park over all the rushing cars and trucks. Terraced gardens, waterfalls, grassy lawns—they're all here.

The Hiram M. Chittenden Locks
3015 NW 54th St. ☎ **206/783-7059.** Free admission. Park and locks, daily 7am–9pm. Visitor center, June–Sept, daily 10am–7pm; Oct–May, Thurs–Mon 11am–5pm. Closed Jan 1, Thanksgiving, and Dec 25. Bus: 17 or 46.

These locks connect Lake Washington and Lake Union to Puget Sound and allow boats to travel from the lakes onto open water. Mostly used by small boats, the locks are a popular spot for salmon watching. People watch salmon jumping up the cascades of a fish ladder as they return to spawn in the stream where they were born, and windows below the waterline give you an idea of what it's like to be a salmon. The best time of year to see the fish is July and August.

Japanese Gardens
In the Washington Park Arboretum, Lake Washington Blvd. E. (north of E. Madison St.). ☎ **206/684-4725.** Admission $2 adults; $1 seniors, the disabled, and children 6–18. Mar to the last Sat in Apr, daily 10am–6pm; last Sun in Apr to May, daily 10am–7pm; June–Aug, daily 10am–8pm; Sept to the fourth Sat in Oct, daily 10am–6pm; fourth Sun in Oct to Nov, daily 10am–4pm. Closed Dec–Feb. Bus: 11 or 84.

Situated on 3¹/₂ acres of land, the Japanese Gardens are a perfect little world unto themselves. Babbling brooks, a lake rimmed with Japanese irises and filled with colorful koi (Japanese carp), and a cherry orchard for spring color are peaceful any time of year. Unfortunately, noise from a nearby road can be distracting at times. A special Tea Garden encloses a Tea House, where, between April and October on the third Saturday of each month at 1:30pm, you can attend a traditional tea ceremony.

Volunteer Park

E. Prospect St. and 14th Ave. E. ☎ **206/684-4743.** Free admission. Park, daily dawn–dusk. Conservatory, May–Sept 15, daily 10am–7pm; Sept 16–Apr, daily 10am–4pm.

Volunteer Park is surrounded by the elegant mansions of Capitol Hill and is a popular spot for suntanning and playing Frisbee. A stately conservatory houses a large collection of tropical plants, including palm trees, orchids, and cacti. The Seattle Asian Art Museum (see above) is also here.

Washington Park Arboretum

2300 Arboretum Dr. E. ☎ **206/543-8800.** Free admission. Arboretum, daily dawn–dusk; visitor center, Mon–Fri 10am–4pm, Sat–Sun noon–4pm. Bus: 11, 43, 48, or 84.

Acres of trees and shrubs stretch from the far side of Capitol Hill all the way to the Montlake Cut, a canal connecting Lake Washington to Lake Union. Within the arboretum are quiet trails that are most beautiful in spring, when azaleas, cherry trees, rhododendrons, and dogwoods are all in flower. There are more than 5,000 varieties of plants in the 200-acre park. The north end, a marshland that's home to ducks and herons, is popular with kayakers and canoeists.

○ Woodland Park Zoo

5500 Phinney Ave. N. ☎ **206/684-4800.** Admission $7 adults, $5.25 seniors and the disabled, $4.50 children 6–17, $2.25 children 3–5; free for children 2 and under. Mar 15– Oct 14, daily 9:30am–6pm; Oct 15–Mar 14, 9:30am–4pm. Parking $3. Bus: 5.

This big, sprawling zoo in north Seattle has outstanding new exhibits focusing on such bioclimatic zones as Alaska, tropical Asia, the African savanna, and the tropical rain forest. The brown bear enclosure is an amazing reproduction of an Alaskan stream and hillside, and in the savanna, zebras gambol as antelopes and giraffes graze contentedly. An elephant forest provides plenty of space for the zoo's pachyderms. The tropical nocturnal house has fascinating exhibits that allow visitors to see nocturnal creatures when they're at their most active. Gorilla and orangutan habitats also are memorable. For the little ones, there's a farm-animals area.

ESPECIALLY FOR KIDS

In addition to the attractions below, kids will be interested in the **Seattle Aquarium,** the **Pacific Science Center,** and **Woodland Park Zoo** (all described earlier in this section). They may also enjoy the stage productions of the **Seattle Children's Theatre,** performed at the Charlotte Martin Theatre at Seattle Center, Second Avenue North and Thomas Street (☎ **206/441-3322**), and the **Northwest Puppet Center,** 9123 15th Ave. NE (☎ **206/523-2579**).

Enchanted Village & Wild Waves

36201 Enchanted Pkwy. S., Federal Way. ☎ **206/661-8000.** Admission $11–$18.50 adults, $9–$16.50 children 3–9, free for children 2 and under. Easter–late May, Sat–Sun 11am–5pm (Enchanted Village only); late May–June, Mon–Fri 9:30am–5pm, Sat–Sun 11am–6pm; mid June–Labor Day, daily 11am–7pm. Take I-5 south to Exit 142B, Puyallup.

The littlest kids can watch the clowns and ride on miniature trains, merry-go-rounds, and the like at Enchanted Village. The older kids, teenagers, and adults will want to spend the hot days of summer riding the wild waves, tubing down artificial streams, and swooshing down water slides.

Seattle Center

305 Harrison St. ☎ **206/684-7200.** Free admission; pay per ride or game. June 2–Labor Day, daily noon–midnight; Labor Day to mid-Mar, Sat–Sun noon–6pm; mid-Mar to June 1,

Seattle Center

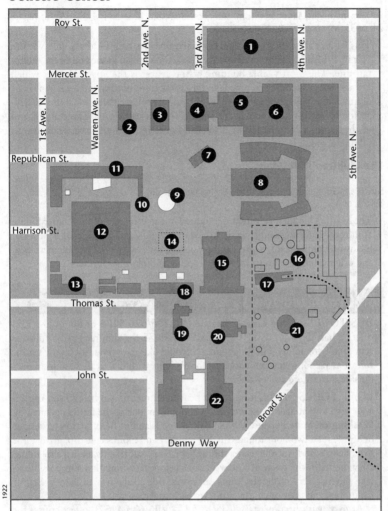

Roy St.

2nd Ave. N.

3rd Ave. N.

4th Ave. N.

Mercer St.

1st Ave. N.

Warren Ave. N.

5th Ave. N.

Republican St.

Harrison St.

Thomas St.

John St.

Broad St.

Denny Way

1922

Amusement Park Area **16**

Arena **6**

Bagley Wright Theatre **2**

Center House **15**

Coliseum **12**

Exhibition Hall **4**

Flag Pavilion **18**

Flag Plaza **14**

High School Memorial Stadium **8**

International Fountain **9**

Intiman Playhouse **3**

Mercer Street Parking Garage **1**

Monorail Terminal **17**

Mural Amphitheatre **20**

Northwest Crafts Center **10**

Northwest Rooms **11**

Opera House **5**

Pacific Arts Center **19**

Pacific Science Center **22**

Seattle Center Pavilions **13**

Space Needle **21**

Veterans Hall **7**

Fri 7pm–midnight, Sat noon–11pm, Sun noon–8pm. Bus: 1, 2, 3, 4, 6, 13, 15, 16, 18, 19, 24, or 33. Monorail: Seattle Center Station.

This 74-acre amusement park and cultural center was built for the Seattle World's Fair in 1962 and stands on the north edge of downtown at the end of the monorail line. The most visible building at the center is the Space Needle, which provides an outstanding panorama of the city from its observation deck. However, of much more interest to children are the rides (a roller coaster, log flume, merry-go-round, ferris wheel) and arcade games. This is Seattle's main festival site, and in the summer months hardly a weekend goes by without some celebration's filling the grounds.

The Children's Museum

Center House, in the Seattle Center. ☎ **206/298-2521.** Admission $3.50 per person. Tues–Sun 10am–5pm. Closed Jan 1, Thanksgiving, and Dec 25. Bus: 1, 2, 3, 4, 6, 13, 15, 16, 18, 19, 24, or 33.

The Seattle's Children's Museum is located in the basement of the Center House at the Seattle Center and recently tripled in size. The museum includes plenty of hands-on cultural exhibits, workshops, a time zone, a mountain wilderness area, and other exhibits to keeps kids busy learning and playing for hours.

6 Organized Tours

BUS TOURS   Gray Line of Seattle (☎ **206/626-5208** or 800/426-7532) offers a half-day tour at $19.50 for adults, $9.75 for children; and a full-day tour at $28 for adults, $14 for children. If you'd like an overview of Seattle's main tourist attractions, you can pack in a lot of sights with one of these tours. Tours outside the city are also available.

BOAT TOURS   In addition to the boat tours mentioned below, you can do your own low-budget cruise simply by hopping on one of the ferries operated by **Washington State Ferries.** Try the Bainbridge Island or Bremmerton ferries out of Seattle for a two-hour round-trip. For a longer and more scenic trip, drive north to Anacortes and ride the ferries through the San Juan Islands, perhaps spending a few hours in the town of Friday Harbor before returning. It's also possible to take the first ferry of the day from Anacortes, ride all the way to Sidney, British Columbia, and then catch the next ferry back to Anacortes.

Argosy, with headquarters at Pier 55 (☎ **206/623-4252**), offers cruises for $12.70 to $19.90 for adults, $5.80 to $10.65 for children 5 to 12. There's a Seattle harbor cruise (departs from Pier 55), a cruise through the Hiram Crittenden Locks to Lake Union (departs from Pier 57), and a cruise around Lake Washington (departs from downtown Kirkland).

A WALKING TOUR   If you have an appreciation of off-color humor and are curious about the seamier side of Seattle history, the **Underground Tour,** 610 First Ave. (☎ **206/682-4646**), will likely entertain and enlighten. The tours lead down below street level in the Pioneer Square area where vestiges of Seattle businesses built before the great fire of 1889 still remain. This is Seattle's most popular tour, offered daily at $5.50 for adults, $4.50 for seniors, $4 for students 13 to 17, and $2.50 for children 6 to 12.

OTHER TOURS   Great scenery and good food are the appeal of a scenic railway excursion on the *Spirit of Washington* **Dinner Train,** 625 S. Fourth St.,

Renton (☎ **206/227-RAIL** or 800/876-RAIL). Running from Renton, at the south end of Lake Washington, to the Columbia Winery near Woodinville, at the north end of the Lake, this train rolls past views of the lake and Mount Rainier. Along the way, you're fed lunch, dinner, or brunch. At the turn-around point, you can tour a winery and taste some wines. Trip prices run $57 to $69.

Northwest Native American culture comes alive at Tillicum Village, across Puget Sound from Seattle at Blake Island Marine State Park. Totem poles stand vigil outside a huge cedar longhouse fashioned after the traditional dwellings of the Northwest tribes. You'll enjoy a meal of alder-smoked salmon while watching traditional Northwest tribal masked dances. All around stand the carved and painted images of fanciful animals, and you can watch the park's resident woodcarver create more of these beautiful works of art. After the dinner and dances, you can explore the island. **Tillicum Village Tours** is headquartered at Pier 56 (☎ **206/443-1244**). Tour prices are $46.50 for adults, $43 for seniors, $30 for youths 13 to 19, $18.50 for children 6 to 12, $9.25 for children 4 and 5. Tours are offered daily May to October; in other months the schedule varies.

7 Outdoor Activities

BEACHES   **Alki Beach,** on Puget Sound, is the closest beach to downtown Seattle. It stretches for 2^1/$_2$ miles down the west side of the Alki Peninsula, which is the promontory you see across Elliott Bay from Seattle's waterfront. This is a busy beach, but the views across the sound to the Olympic Mountains can be stunning on a clear day.

For a less urban beach experience, head to northwest Seattle's **Golden Gardens Park,** which is on Seaview Avenue NW and has beaches backed by green lawns.

BICYCLING   **Gregg's Green Lake Cycle,** 7007 Woodlawn Ave. NE (☎ **206/523-1822**); **The Bicycle Center,** 4529 Sand Point Way NE (☎ **206/523-8300**); and **Sammamish Valley Cycle,** 8451 164th Ave. NE, Redmond (☎ **206/881-8442**)—all rent bikes by the hour, day, or week. Rates range from $4 to $7 per hour and $15 to $32 per day. These three shops are all convenient to the Burke-Gilman Trail or Sammamish River Trail. The former is a 12^1/$_2$-mile trail created from an old railway bed. The trail starts at Gasworks Park and continues to Kenmore Logboom Park at the north end of Lake Washington by way of the University of Washington. Serious riders can then connect to the Sammamish River Trail that leads to Lake Sammamish. There are lots of great picnicking spots along both trails.

GOLF   There are more than a dozen public golf courses in the Seattle area. The **Jackson Park Municipal Golf Course,** 1000 NE 135th St. (☎ **206/363-4747**); the **Jefferson Park Municipal Golf Course,** 4101 Beacon Ave. S. (☎ **206/762-4513**); and the **West Seattle Municipal Golf Course,** 4470 35th Ave. SW (☎ **206/935-5187**), are three of the most convenient courses. Greens fees are $19.50 if you're not a King County resident, $15 if you are.

HIKING   Within an easy drive of the city are three national parks, Mount St. Helens National Volcanic Monument, and numerous national forests, offering hikes of varying lengths and difficulty. See the following chapters for details on these parks.

HORSEBACK RIDING   At the south end of Lake Washington near the airport you can rent horses at **Aqua Barn Ranch,** 15227 SE Renton–Maple Valley Hwy.,

Renton (☎ 206/255-4618), which offers guided rides for $19.50 per hour; reservations are required.

IN-LINE SKATING   You can rent in-line skates at **Greg's Green Lake Cycle,** 7007 Woodlawn Ave. NE (☎ 206/523-1822), and **Seattle Ski & Skate,** 907 NE 45th St. (☎ 206/548-1000), for about $12 per day or $4 per hour. The trail around Green Lake and the Burke-Gilman Trail (see "Bicycling," above) are both good places for skating.

KAYAKING/CANOEING   The **Northwest Outdoor Center,** 2100 Westlake Ave. N. (☎ 206/281-9694), is located on Lake Union, and will rent you a sea kayak for $8 to $12 per hour. You can also opt for guided paddles lasting from a few hours to several days, and there are plenty of classes available for those who are interested. The **University of Washington Waterfront Activities Center,** on the university campus behind Husky Stadium (☎ 206/543-9433), is open to the public and rents canoes and rowboats for $4 per hour. Rentals are available February to October, daily from 10am to about an hour before sunset.

SAILBOARDING   Seattle's waters are ideal for beginning boardsailors—the winds are light and the water is flat. **Urban Surf,** 2100 N. Northlake Way (☎ 206/545-WIND), rents boards and will give you lessons if you need them. Rates are $35 per day for a board. Private lessons are $35 per hour, and a four-hour group class is $59.

SAILING   The **Center for Wooden Boats,** 1010 Valley St. (☎ 206/382-BOAT), a maritime museum that rents classic boats, is at Waterway 4 at the south end of Lake Union (open June to Labor Day, daily from 11am to 7pm; Labor Day to May, Wednesday through Monday from noon to 6pm). There are rowboats and large and small sailboats. Rates range from $6 to $15 per hour. Individual sailing instruction is also available.

SKIING   Both downhill and cross-country skiers will find a number of locations in the Seattle area to enjoy their sport.

Downhill   Four ski areas—**Alpental, Ski Acres, Snoqualmie,** and **Hyak** (☎ 206/232-8182, or 206/236-1600 for snow conditions)—are located less than 50 miles east of Seattle off I-90. These four ski areas offer more than 60 ski runs, rentals, and lessons. Adult lift ticket prices range from $14 to $16 for midweek night skiing to $29 for a weekend all-day pass.

The **Crystal Mountain Resort** (☎ 360/663-2265 for general information, or 206/634-3771 for snow conditions) is 76 miles southeast of Seattle off Wash. 410. Many Seattle skiers prefer this ski area over the Snoqualmie Pass ski areas. Lift ticket prices range from $16 for night skiing to $32 for a weekend all-day pass.

Stevens Pass (☎ 360/973-2441 for general information, or 206/634-1645 for snow conditions) is 78 miles east of Seattle on U.S. 2. A little more than half the runs here are for intermediate skiers. Adult lift ticket prices range from $10 for midweek night skiing to $31 for a weekend all-day pass.

Cross-Country   In the Snoqualmie Pass area, less than 50 miles east of Seattle on I-90, the **Ski Acres Cross-Country Center** (☎ 206/434-7669) offers rentals, instruction, and many miles of groomed trails, and even has lighted trails for night skiing. Trail fees are $5 to $9.

The **Stevens Pass Nordic Center** (☎ 360/973-2441 for general information, or 206/634-1645 for snow conditions) is 83 miles east of Seattle on U.S. 2 and is open Friday through Sunday and holidays. There are 50 miles (30km) of groomed trails here. Use of the trails costs $7.50 for adults and $6.50 for children.

When renting skis, be sure to get a Sno-Park permit. These are required in parking areas near ski trails. They are available at ski shops.

TENNIS **Seattle Parks and Recreation** (☎ 206/684-4077) operates dozens of outdoor tennis courts all over the city. The most convenient are in Volunteer Park, 15th Avenue East and East Prospect Street, and in Lower Woodland Park, West Green Lake Way North. If it happens to be raining and you had your heart set on playing tennis, there are indoor public courts at the **Seattle Tennis Center,** 2000 Martin Luther King, Jr., Way S. (☎ **206/684-4764**). Rates are $12 for singles and $16 for doubles for 1¼ hours.

8 Spectator Sports

Tickets for major sporting events can be purchased through **TicketMaster** at 206/628-0888 or **Pacific Northwest Ticket Service** at 206/232-0150.

BASEBALL The American League's **Seattle Mariners** (☎ 206/628-3555), led by star center fielder Ken Griffey, Jr., won their division in 1995 and finally turned Seattle into a baseball town. They play in the Kingdome from April to October. In 1995 Seattle residents narrowly voted down a proposal to build the team a new stadium, despite threats that the Mariners might depart. However, the state stepped in with a plan to raise funds to build the stadium, and the new plans were approved. Ticket prices range from $6 to $15, and are available at the Kingdome box office or by calling TicketMaster at 206/628-0888. Parking is next to impossible, so plan to leave your car behind.

BASKETBALL The NBA's **Seattle Supersonics** (☎ 206/281-5800) play in the Seattle Center Coliseum from November to May. They've become a strong team in recent years, though they haven't been able to perform in the playoffs. Games start at 7pm, and tickets are $7 to $60. Tickets are available through TicketMaster at 206/628-0888.

FOOTBALL The **Seattle Seahawks** NFL team (☎ 206/827-9777 for schedule and ticket information) plays in the Kingdome from September to December. Games are on Sunday at 1pm, and tickets, at $19 to $38, are very difficult to get. Parking in the Kingdome area is nearly impossible during games, so take the bus.

HOCKEY Members of the Western Hockey League, the **Seattle Thunderbirds Hockey Club** (☎ 206/728-9121) plays at the Seattle Center Arena and Coliseum September to March. For tickets, call 206/448-PUCK or Ticketmaster at 206/628-0888.

A MARATHON The **Seattle Marathon** takes place in November. There's a runners' hotline in Seattle with more information on this and other races in the area; call 206/524-RUNS.

9 Shopping

THE SHOPPING SCENE

SHOPPING AREAS The heart of Seattle's shopping district is at the corner of Pine Street and Westlake Avenue. Within one block of this intersection are two major department stores—Nordstrom and the Bon Marché—and a shopping mall.

If you're young at heart and possess a very personal idea of style, you head over to Broadway on Capitol Hill to do your shopping. Pioneer Square, Seattle's historic district, is filled with art galleries, antique shops, and other unusual stores. Seattle's most famous shopping area is the Pike Place Market, a produce market, but also much more. It's located at the foot of Pine Street overlooking the waterfront.

SHOPPING HOURS   Shops in Seattle are generally open Monday through Saturday from 9 or 10am to 5 or 6pm, with shorter hours on Sunday. The major department stores usually stay open later on Friday evening, and many shopping malls stay open until 9pm Monday through Saturday.

SHOPPING A TO Z
ANTIQUES

For an absolutely astonishing selection of antiques, head north of Seattle to the town of Snohomish (near Everett), where you'll find more than 150 antiques shops.

The Crane Gallery
1203-B Second Ave. ☎ **206/622-7185.**

Chinese, Japanese, and Korean antiquities are the focus of this shop, which prides itself in selling only the best pieces. Some Southeast Asian and Indian objects are also available.

Honeychurch Antiques
1008 James St. ☎ **206/622-1225.**

For high-quality Asian antiques—including Japanese woodblock prints, textiles, furniture, and ivory and wood carvings—few Seattle antiques stores can approach Honeychurch Antiques. Regular special exhibits give this shop the feel of a tiny museum.

Antique Malls & Flea Markets
Fremont Sunday Market
Fremont Ave. N. and N. 35th St. ☎ **206/282-5706.**

Crafts, imports, antiques, collectibles, fresh produce, and live music all combine to make this Seattle's second favorite public market (after the Pike Place Market). Open from the end of April through Christmas.

Pioneer Square Mall
602 First Ave. ☎ **206/624-1164.**

This underground antiques mall is in the heart of Pioneer Square and contains 80 shops selling all manner of antiques and collectibles.

ART GALLERIES

Pioneer Square also has Seattle's greatest concentration of art galleries. Wander around south of Yesler Way and you're likely to stumble upon a gallery showing the very latest contemporary art from the Northwest. There are also many antiques stores and galleries selling Native American art in the Pioneer Square area.

✪ The Legacy
1003 First Ave. ☎ **206/624-6350.**

On the Trail of Dale Chihuly

In the past few years, Northwest glass artist Dale Chihuly, one of the founders of the Pilchuck School for glass art north of Seattle, has been garnering nation-wide media attention for his fanciful and color-saturated contemporary glass art. From table-top vessels to massive window installations that capture and trans-form the sun, his creations in glass have a depth and richness of color that has captured the attention of collectors across the country. Sensuous forms include vases within bowls that are reminiscent of Technicolor birds' eggs in giant nests. His ikebana series, based on the traditional Japanese flower-arranging technique, are riotous conglomerations of color that twist and turn like so many cut flowers waving in the wind.

So where do you go to see the works of this master of molten glass? There's no one place in Seattle to see a collection of his work, but there are numerous **public displays around the city.** In the lobby of the Sheraton Seattle Hotel, 1400 Sixth Ave., there are works by Chihuly and other Northwest glass artists. The Stouffer Madison Hotel, 515 Madison St., also has a piece on display in the lobby. In the U.S. Bank Centre (formerly the Pacific First building), between Fourth and Fifth avenues on Pike Street, there's an extensive exhibit. The City Centre shopping arcade, 1420 Fifth Ave., has displays by numerous glass artists, including Chihuly. Up on the third floor of the Washington State Convention and Trade Center is a case with some smaller, but beautifully lighted, vases.

If you're willing to drive to Chihuly's hometown of Tacoma, 32 miles south of Seattle, you can see the largest museum exhibit of Chihuly's work at the **Tacoma Art Museum,** 1123 Pacific Ave. Just up the street from here, at Tacoma's restored **Union Station** (now the federal courthouse), some of the artist's larger pieces have been installed.

If after tracking down Chihuly's works you decide you must have some for yourself, stop in at the **Foster/White Gallery,** 311 Occidental Ave., which represents Chihuly here in Seattle.

The Legacy is Seattle's oldest and finest gallery of contemporary and historic Northwest coast Indian and Alaskan Eskimo art and artifacts. You'll find a large selection of masks, boxes, bowls, baskets, ivory artifacts, jewelry, prints, and books. For the serious collector.

Northwest Tribal Art

1417 First Ave. ☎ **206/467-9330.**

Located next to the Pike Place Market is one of Seattle's most important galleries selling Northwest coast Indian and Eskimo art.

Glass Art

✪ Foster/White Gallery

311 Occidental Ave. S. ☎ **206/622-2833.**

Seattle's largest fine-arts dealer represents the foremost contemporary artists of the Northwest, including glass artists from the Pilchuck School of Glass, which is renowned for its creative glass sculptures.

There's another Foster/White Gallery in Kirkland at 126 Central Way (☎ **206/ 822-2305**).

The Glass Eye
1902 Post Alley, in the Pike Place Market. ☎ **206/441-3221.**

The Glass Eye is one of Seattle's oldest art-glass galleries and specializes in hand-blown glass pieces containing ash from the 1980 eruption of Mount St. Helens.

Books

Elliott Bay Book Company
101 S. Main St. ☎ **206/624-6600.**

With heavy wooden fixtures, balconies, and an open staircase descending to the basement, this could very well be the most aesthetically pleasing bookstore in the Northwest. It's located just south of Pioneer Square, and has an excellent selection of books on Seattle and the Northwest.

Shorey's Book Store
1411 First Ave. ☎ **206/624-0221.**

In business since 1890, Shorey's will be happy to find you books from the year it opened (or any other year for that matter). Rare, antiquarian, and out-of-print books are a specialty.

Crafts

The Northwest seems to be a mecca for craftspeople, and one of the places to see what they're creating is at the Pike Place Market. Although there are quite a few permanent shops in the market that sell local crafts, you can meet the craftspeople themselves on the weekends when they set up tables on the main floor of the market.

✪ Fireworks Fine Crafts Gallery
210 First Ave. S. ☎ **206/682-8707.**

Playful, outrageous, bizarre, beautiful—these are just some of the terms that can be used to describe the eclectic collection of Northwest crafts here. Other stores are at the Westlake Center, 400 Pine St. (☎ **206/682-6462**), and 2016 Bellevue Sq. (☎ **206/688-0933**).

Northwest Gallery of Fine Woodworking
202 First Ave. ☎ **206/625-0542.**

This store is a showcase for some of the most amazing woodworking you'll ever see. Furniture, boxes, sculptures, vases, bowls, and much more are created by more than 35 Northwest artisans. A second shop is at 122 Central Way in Kirkland (☎ **206/889-1513**).

Department Stores

The Bon Marché
Third Ave. and Pine St. ☎ **206/344-2121.**

Seattle's only full-line department store, the Bon offers seven floors of merchandise. You'll find nearly anything you could possibly want at this store.

Nordstrom
1501 Fifth Ave. ☎ **206/628-2111.**

Nordstrom originated here in Seattle, and its customers are devotedly loyal. Prices are comparable to those at other department stores, but you get the best service available. There are very popular sales.

DISCOUNT STORES

J. Thompson
205 Pine St. ☎ **206/623-5780.**

This store sells designer women's clothing at 30% to 70% off retail. Styles are rather conservative.

The Rack
1601 Second Ave. ☎ **206/448-8522.**

Discounts similar to those at J. Thompson are available at the Rack, which sells clearance items from Nordstrom.

FASHION

Eddie Bauer
Fifth Ave. and Union St. ☎ **206/622-2766.**

Eddie Bauer got his start here in Seattle back in 1922 and today is one of the country's foremost purveyors of upscale outdoor fashions. A visit to this store is a must for anyone who dresses the Eddie Bauer look.

Northwest Pendleton
1313 Fourth Ave. ☎ **206/682-4430.**

For Northwesterners, and many other people all across the nation, Pendleton is and always will be *the* name in classic wool fashions. This store features tartan plaids and Indian-pattern separates, accessories, and blankets. Other stores are at the Southcenter Mall, Bellevue Square, and Tacoma Mall.

Weather or Not
In the Westlake Center, 400 Pine St. ☎ **206/682-3797.**

Seattle's inclement weather is legendary, and so it comes as no surprise that there's a store here devoted exclusively to weathering this climate. Weather or Not sells everything from umbrellas and raincoats to underwater paper, waterproof matches, and floating briefcases.

Children's Fashions

✪ Boston St.
101 Stewart St. ☎ **206/728-1490.**

With sizes 0 through 14, this store stocks fun play clothes as well as more dressy fashions for kids. There's lots of 100% cotton clothing, and prices are moderate. A second store is at 1815 N. 45th Ave. (☎ **206/634-0580**).

Men's Fashions

The Forum
95 Pine St. ☎ **206/624-4566.**

Located in the Pike Place Market neighborhood, the Forum features sophisticated fashions from the likes of Perry Ellis, Girbaud, and Robert Comstock.

Zebraclub
1901 First Ave. ☎ **206/448-7452.**

If you're young and hip and believe that clothes shopping should be an audio-visual experience, make the scene at Zebraclub, where rock videos playing on overhead monitors set the shopping tempo.

Women's Fashions

✪ Ardour
1115 First Ave. ☎ **206/292-0660.**

The fashions here are romantic without being fussy and are something of a cross between a Seattle and a Paris look. You can put together a very nice ensemble here, though it won't be cheap.

Baby & Co.
1936 First Ave. ☎ **206/448-4077.**

Claiming stores in Seattle and on Mars, this trendy store stocks up-to-the-minute Seattle fashions.

Local Brilliance
1535 First Ave. ☎ **206/343-5864.**

If you want to return from your trip to Seattle wearing a dress you know no one else at the office will have ever seen before, visit Local Brilliance. The shop carries a selection of fashions by Northwest fashion designers.

Ragazzi's Flying Shuttle
607 First Ave. ☎ **206/343-9762.**

Hand-woven fabrics and hand-painted silks are the specialties here. Of course such unique fashions require equally unique body decorations in the form of exquisite jewelry creations.

FOOD

✪ Pike Place Fish
86 Pike Place, in the Pike Place Market. ☎ **206/682-7181.**

All the seafood vendors in the Pike Place Market will pack your fresh salmon or Dungeness crab in an airline-approved container that will keep it fresh for up to 48 hours. Located just behind Rachel the life-size bronze pig, Pike Place Fish is famous for its flying fish. Pick out a big silvery salmon, ask them to filet it, and watch the show.

Port Chatham Smoked Seafood
1306 Fourth Ave., Rainier Sq. ☎ **206/623-4645.**

This store sells smoked sockeye, king salmon, rainbow trout, and oysters—all of which will keep without refrigeration until the package is opened. Other stores are at 632 NW 46th St. (☎ **206/783-8200**) and in the Bellevue Square Mall (☎ **206/453-2441**).

Starbuck's
In the Pike Place Market. ☎ **206/448-8762.**

Seattle has developed a reputation as a city of coffee-holics, and Starbuck's is a major supplier. This company has coffeehouses all over the city, but this is probably the most convenient if you're just visiting Seattle.

GIFTS/SOUVENIRS

The Pike Place Market is the Grand Central Terminal of Seattle souvenirs, with stiff competition from the Seattle Center and Pioneer Square.

Made in Washington

Post Alley at Pine St., in the Pike Place Market. ☎ **206/467-0788.**

You'll find a good selection of Washington state products in this shop. Other Made in Washington locations include the Westlake Center (☎ **206/623-9753**) and Bellevue Square, Bellevue (☎ **206/454-6907**).

MALLS/SHOPPING CENTERS

Bellevue Square

Bellevue Way and NE Eighth Ave., Bellevue. ☎ **206/454-2431.**

Over in Bellevue, on the east side of Lake Washington, you'll find one of the area's largest shopping malls, with more than 200 stores. The Bellevue Art Museum is also here.

Broadway Market

401 Broadway E. ☎ **206/322-1610.**

A trendy mall located in the stylish Capitol Hill neighborhood, the Broadway Market houses numerous small shops and restaurants with reasonable prices.

Century Square

191 Fourth Ave. and Pike St.

There are many fine stores in this upscale mall a block from the Westlake Center.

City Centre

Sixth Ave. and Union St.

This upscale downtown shopping center houses such stores as Barneys New York, Benetton, and Ann Taylor. Displays of art glass by Dale Chihuly and his contemporaries make City Centre worth a visit even if you're only window-shopping.

Rainier Square

1326 Fifth Ave.

Rainier Square is filled with 50 upscale shops and restaurants. Built on the bottom floors of several skyscrapers, the Rainier Square mall is a veritable maze.

Westlake Center

400 Pine St. ☎ **206/467-1600.**

This covered shopping mall is in the heart of the downtown shopping district and includes 80 specialty shops. The monorail terminal is on the second floor of the mall.

MARKETS

✪ Pike Place Market

Pike St. and First Ave. ☎ **206/682-7453.**

The Pike Place Market is one of Seattle's most famous landmarks and tourist attractions. See "The Top Attractions" under "Attractions," earlier in this chapter, for details.

Uwajimaya
519 Sixth Ave. S. ☎ **206/624-6248.**

Imagine your local supermarket with nothing *but* Asian foods, housewares, produce, and toys. That's Uwajimaya, Seattle's Asian supermarket in the heart of the International District.

RECREATIONAL GEAR

The North Face
1023 First Ave. ☎ **206/622-4111.**

The North Face is one of the country's best-known names in the field of outdoor gear, and here in its downtown shop you can choose from among a diverse selection.

REI
1525 11th Ave. ☎ **206/323-8333.**

Recreational Equipment, Incorporated (REI), was founded here in Seattle 1938 and today is the nation's largest co-op selling outdoor gear. There's an amazing selection of gear on the many floors of this store, which is located on Capitol Hill.

TOYS

✪ Archie McPhee Toy Store
3510 Stoneway N. ☎ **206/545-8344.**

You may already be familiar with this temple of the absurd through its mail-order catalog. Now imagine wandering through aisles and aisles full of goofy gags. Give yourself plenty of time and take a friend.

Magic Mouse
603 First Ave. ☎ **206/682-8097.**

Adults and children alike have a hard time pulling themselves away from this toy store. It's conveniently located on Pioneer Square and has a good selection of European toys.

WINES

Pike & Western Wine Merchants
1934 Pike Place, in the Pike Place Market. ☎ **206/441-1307.**

Visit this shop for an excellent selection of Northwest wines as well as French, Italian, and California wines. The extremely knowledgeable staff here will be happy to send you home with the very best wines available in Seattle.

10   Seattle After Dark

Seattle, once considered a cultural backwater, has been making a splash on the national performance scene for several years now with its world-class opera company, known for its Wagner productions, and its prolific theater scene. Fringe theaters have been springing up all over the city, and all manner of venues are staging theater productions and performance art these days. Grunge music, which launched itself on the nation's youth from alternative clubs in Seattle several years ago, continues to dominate the rock 'n' roll airwaves, despite the much-publicized death of Kurt Cobain, founding member of seminal grunge band

Nirvana. The Seattle Center and Pioneer Square are the city's focal points for evening entertainment, with the former area housing several theaters and the latter being home to numerous rock and jazz clubs.

TicketMaster Northwest (☎ **206/628-0888**), open Monday through Saturday from 8am to 9pm and on Sunday from 10am to 6pm, is the primary ticket sales company in Seattle and handles most theaters, large concert halls, and sporting events. For half-price, day-of-show tickets, contact **Ticket/Ticket** (☎ **206/324-2744**) at the Pike Place Market, First Avenue and Pike Street (open Tuesday through Sunday from noon to 6pm), or at the Broadway Market, 401 Broadway E. (open Tuesday through Sunday from 10am to 7pm).

To find out what's going on when you're in town, pick up a copy of the *Seattle Weekly* (75¢), which is Seattle's weekly arts-and-entertainment newspaper. You'll find it in bookstores, convenience stores, grocery stores, newsstands, and sidewalk boxes. In the "Tempo" section of the Friday *Seattle Times,* you'll also find a guide to the week's arts-and-entertainment offerings.

THE PERFORMING ARTS

From exquisitely staged productions of the Seattle Opera to the eclectic offerings of the Velvet Elvis Arts Lounge, Seattle today has one of the most diverse performing arts scenes in the country. The main venues for the performing arts in Seattle are clustered in the Seattle Center, but fringe theaters are now scattered all over the city in all manner of out-of-the-way spaces.

At the Seattle Center, in the shadow of the Space Needle, you'll find the **Seattle Opera House** (☎ **206/389-7676**), the **Bagley Wright Theater** (☎ **206/443-2222**), the **Intiman Playhouse** (☎ **206/626-0782**), the **Seattle Children's Theatre** (☎ **206/441-3322**), and **The Group** theater (☎ **206/441-1299**), as well as the Seattle Center Coliseum and Memorial Stadium.

The **Paramount Theater,** Pine Street and Ninth Avenue (☎ **206/682-1414**), which underwent a complete remodeling and modernization in 1995, is a popular venue for touring rock bands and stage companies. The **5th Avenue Theatre,** 1308 Fifth Ave. (☎ **206/625-1418**), first opened in 1926 as a vaudeville house, is the city's most beautiful theater and is a loose re-creation of the imperial throne room in Beijing's Forbidden City. In addition to staging productions by major touring shows, the theater now has its own resident musical theater company (tickets $19 to $45).

Several performing arts series bring a wide variety of productions to the city each year. These include the **Seattle International Music Festival** (☎ **206/233-0993**), a summer classical music series; the **University of Washington World Series** (☎ **206/543-4880**), which is actually several series that include world dance, world music, classical piano, and chamber music; and the **Seattle Fringe Theater Festival** (☎ **206/325-5446**), which is held each year in the spring and includes more than 300 theater performances.

OPERA & CLASSICAL MUSIC COMPANIES

In addition to the two major companies listed below, the **Northwest Chamber Orchestra** (☎ **206/343-0445**), which performs primarily in Kane Hall on the University of Washington campus, is worthy of note (tickets $13 to $19.50). Active for more than 20 seasons now, this company is a showcase for Northwest performers. The annual Bach Festival is the highlight of the season, which runs from September to April.

✪ Seattle Opera Association

Performing in the Seattle Opera House, Fourth Ave. N. and Mercer St. ☎ **206/389-7699.**
Tickets $28–$95.

The Seattle Opera is considered one of the finest opera companies in the country and is *the* Wagnerian opera company. The stagings of Wagner's four-opera *The Ring of the Nibelungen* are breathtaking spectacles that draw crowds from around the country. In addition to classical operas, the season usually includes a more contemporary musical (*Porgy and Bess* during the 1994–95 season).

Seattle Symphony Orchestra

Performing in the Seattle Opera House, Fourth Ave. N. and Mercer St. ☎ **206/443-4747.**
Tickets $8–$51.

Each year the Seattle Symphony Orchestra, under the baton of Gerard Schwarz, offers an amazingly diverse musical season that runs from September to May. There are evenings of classical, light classical, and pops, plus morning concerts, children's concerts, guest artists (the 1994–95 season included performances by Leontyne Price, the Labeque sisters, Pinchas Zukerman, and even Garrison Keilor), and much more.

THEATER COMPANIES

The **Intiman Theatre Company** (☎ 206/626-0782), which performs at the Intiman Playhouse, Seattle Center, 201 Mercer St. (tickets $16 to $34; $10 for standing room), is a favorite of Seattle theatergoers. This company's season starts in May and then picks up again in August. Past seasons have included the world première of the Pulitzer Prize–winner *The Kentucky Cycle* and an acclaimed production of Tony Kushner's award-winning epic *Angels in America.*

The **Seattle Repertory Theater** (☎ 206/443-2222), which has been around for more than 30 years and performs at the Bagley Wright Theater, Seattle Center, 155 Mercer St., is the city's other top theater company (tickets $10.50 to $34). The Rep season (October to May) picks up where the Intiman leaves off, giving Seattle excellent year-round professional theater. Productions range from classics to world premières to Broadway musicals.

Among the city's smaller theater companies, **A Contemporary Theater (ACT),** 100 W. Roy St. (☎ 206/285-5110), is known for staging more adventurous productions than other major theater companies in Seattle (tickets $13.50 to $26). The season runs from late April to mid-November.

Another reliable theater for new and unusual works is the **Empty Space Theatre,** 3509 Fremont Ave. N. (☎ 206/547-7500), which stages its plays between October and June (tickets $10 to $19). If you enjoy the new and unusual, the Empty Space will more than likely have something for you.

Even further out on the fringes are such spaces as the **Annex Theater,** 1916 Fourth Ave. (☎ 206/728-0933); the **Velvet Elvis Arts Lounge Theatre,** 107 Occidental Ave. (☎ 206/624-8477); and **The Weathered Wall,** 1921 Fifth Ave. (☎ 206/448-5688). Innovative puppet theater for children and adults is the domain of the **Northwest Puppet Center,** 9123 15th Ave. NE (☎ 206/523-2579).

DANCE COMPANIES

The **Pacific Northwest Ballet** (☎ 206/292-2787) which performs at the Seattle Opera House, Third Avenue North and Mercer Street, presents a wide range of classics, new works, and pieces choreographed by George Balanchine (tickets $11 to $65). If you happen to be in Seattle in December, try to get a ticket to this company's performance of *The Nutcracker*. In addition to the outstanding dancing, you'll enjoy sets and costumes by children's book author and illustrator Maurice Sendak.

For modern dance enthusiasts, **On the Boards** (☎ **206/325-7901**), which performs at the Washington Hall Performance Gallery, 153 14th Ave., provides innovative contemporary dance performances (tickets $5 to $16). The Northwest New Works Festival, which is held every spring, is one of the season's highlights.

THE CLUB & MUSIC SCENE
CABARET & COMEDY CLUBS

Cabaret de Paris

In the Crepe de Paris Restaurant, Rainier Sq., 1305 Fourth Ave., Suite 1015. ☎ **206/ 623-4111.** Cover $12 plus dinner off the menu.

Crepe de Paris is one of Seattle's oldest French restaurants, and though it fries up a mean crêpe, it's better known these days as the city's favorite cabaret. Thursday through Saturday nights, talented performers entertain with humor, music, and dance.

Comedy Underground

222 S. Main St. ☎ **206/628-0303.** Cover $3–$10.

This underground nightspot in the Pioneer Square area is dedicated to laughter, with local and nationally known comedians appearing.

Showbox Comedy & Supper Club

1426 First Ave. ☎ **206/628-5000.** Cover $6–$10 plus a two-drink minimum.

What's the difference between December and June in Seattle? Answer: June only has 30 days. Not all the jokes are about the weather in Seattle, but you can bet there'll be a few on any given night. The Showbox features nationally known comedians and also has a good restaurant.

FOLK, COUNTRY & ROCK

For the past few years, Seattle bands have been making rock 'n' roll headlines. If the Seattle sound is still riding the crest of the wave when you're in town, grab a copy of the *Seattle Weekly* and check the club listings for where the hot new bands are appearing. The **Pioneer Square area** is Seattle's main live-music neighborhood (almost everything but classical) and the clubs have banded together to make things easy on music fans. The **"Joint Cover" plan** lets you pay one admission to get into 10 or so clubs. The charge is $5 on weeknights and $7 on weekends. Participating clubs currently include the Fenix, Fenix Underground, Doc Maynard's, Central Café, Colourbox, the Bohemian Cafe, and a few other nightspots.

The Backstage

2208 NW Market St. ☎ **206/781-2805.** Cover $5–$20.

This is Seattle's top venue for contemporary music of all kinds and packs in the crowds most nights. The audience ranges from just-reached-drinking-age up to graying rock 'n' rollers.

Ballard Firehouse

5429 Russell St. ☎ **206/784-3516.** Cover $3—$20.

An eclectic assortment of musical styles finds its way onto the bandstand of this converted firehouse. You might catch one of your jazz favorites here.

Central Café

207 First Ave. ☎ **206/622-0209.** Cover $5–$7.

The crowd is young and the music is rock and R&B. You can catch both local and out-of-town bands here.

Crocodile

2200 Second Ave. ☎ **206/441-5611.** Cover $2–$7.

With its rambunctious decor, this Belltown establishment is a combination nightclub, bar, and restaurant. Grunge dominates the schedule, but folk and jazz sometimes show up.

Doc Maynard's

610 First Ave. ☎ **206/682-4649.** Cover $6–$12.

By day it's the starting point of the Underground Tour, but by night it's one of Seattle's most popular clubs for live rock 'n' roll. This place attracts all types of rock music lovers.

Fenix/Fenix Underground

315 and 323 Second Ave. ☎ **206/467-1111.** Cover Wed–Sun $5–$18.

Located in the heart of the Pioneer Square area, these two clubs are among the best in the area and book an eclectic blend of rock, reggae, and world-beat music by primarily regional acts.

✪ Kells

1916 Post Alley, in the Pike Place Market. ☎ **206/728-1916.** Cover Fri–Sat only, $3.

This friendly Irish pub has the look and feel of a casual Dublin pub. They pull a good Guinness stout and feature live traditional Irish music Wednesday through Saturday.

JAZZ & BLUES

✪ Dimitriou's Jazz Alley

2033 Sixth Ave. ☎ **206/441-9729.** Cover $10.50–$18.50.

This is *the* place for great jazz music in Seattle. Cool and sophisticated, Dimitriou's is reminiscent of New York jazz clubs. The club books only the very best performers.

New Orleans Creole Restaurant

114 First Ave. S. ☎ **206/622-2563.** Cover weeknights free, weekends $7.

If you like your food and your jazz hot, check out the New Orleans. Tuesday is Cajun night, but the rest of the week you can hear Dixieland, R&B, jazz, and blues.

DANCE CLUBS/DISCOS

Downunder

2407 First Ave. ☎ **206/728-4053.** Cover $5.

Located in the Belltown neighborhood north of the Pike Place Market, the Downunder is another underground club. Wild decor, light shows, and a high-energy music attract a Gen X crowd. Techno to grunge. Open Friday and Saturday from 9pm to 4am.

Iguana Cantina
2815 Alaskan Way. ☎ **206/728-7071.** Cover $3–$8.

Over on the waterfront is a cavernous place popular with Seattle's singles set. There's live Top 40 dance music most nights, and the restaurant has great views of Elliot Bay.

THE BAR SCENE
BREW PUBS

Big Time Brewery and Alehouse
4133 University Way NE. ☎ **206/545-4509.**

Located in the University District and decorated to look like a turn-of-the-century tavern complete with 100-year-old back bar and wooden refrigerator, the Big Time serves up seven of its own brews, which you can see being made on the premises.

✪ Pacific NW Brewing Co.
322 Occidental Ave. S. ☎ **206/621-7021.**

The Pioneer Square area is filled with bars and nightclubs, but if what you really want is a selection of microbrews, check out this brewpub. It usually has six of its own brews on tap, plus plenty of other popular local micros.

The Pub at the Hart Brewery
1201 First Ave. S. ☎ **206/682-8322.**

This pub is located south of the Kingdome and serves Thomas Kemper lagers and Pyramid ales and offers brewery tours, good pub food, and other special events.

The Trolleyman
3400 Phinney Ave. N. ☎ **206/548-8000.**

This is the taproom of the Red Hook Brewery, one of the Northwest's most celebrated microbreweries. It's located in a restored trolley barn on the Lake Washington Ship Canal. You can sample the ales brewed here, have a bite to eat, and tour the brewery.

BARS

FX Mcrory's Steak, Chop, and Oyster House
419 Occidental Ave. S. ☎ **206/623-4800.**

The clientele is upscale, and you're likely to see members of the Seahawks or the Supersonics at the bar. The original Leroy Neiman paintings on the walls lend an abundance of class to this sports bar. You'll also find Seattle's largest selection of bourbon and microbrew beers and ales.

McCormick & Schmick's
1103 First Ave. ☎ **206/623-5500.**

This place is very busy during happy hour as brokers wind down with a few stiff drinks. If you long to rub shoulders with the movers and shakers of Seattle, this is the place for you.

Sneakers
567 Occidental Ave. S. ☎ **206/625-1340.**

Located almost directly across the street from the Kingdome, Sneakers is a favorite of Seattle sports fans. The walls are covered with celebrity signatures and old sports photos.

THE GAY & LESBIAN SCENE
DANCE CLUBS/DISCOS

Neighbours

1509 Broadway. ☎ **206/324-5358.** No cover.

This has been the favorite disco of Capitol Hill's gay community for years, and recently the word has gotten out to straights that it's a fun dance club. Still, the clientele is primarily gay. The Friday and Saturday buffets are extremely popular.

✪ Re-Bar

1114 Howell St. ☎ **206/233-9873.** Cover $3–$10.

Each night there's a different theme, with the DJs spinning everything from world beat to funk and soul to theater performances. It's popular with straights and visiting celebrities as well. Thursday and Saturday nights attract the gayest crowds.

BARS

The Easy

916 E. Pike St. ☎ **206/323-8343.**

This Capitol Hill bar is popular with the lesbian singles crowd and doubles as a dance club.

Thumpers

1500 E. Madison St. ☎ **206/328-3800.**

Perched high on Capitol Hill with an excellent view of downtown Seattle, Thumpers is a classy bar done up with lots of oak.

Wildrose

1021 E. Pike St. ☎ **206/324-9210.**

This friendly restaurant/bar is another long-time favorite with the Capitol Hill lesbian community.

11 Side Trips from Seattle

ACROSS PUGET SOUND

Outlined here is a possible day trip that starts on one ferry and ends on another. The excursion takes in the quiet and picturesque bedroom community of Bainbridge Island, which is popular for its miles of waterfront, sound-and-mountain views, and rural feel. Continuing on, you can visit a Scandinavian town, a museum dedicated to undersea exploration, a mothballed destroyer, a Native American museum, and a town full of antiques malls. There's more here than you can easily do in one day, so pick and choose what interests you the most.

BAINBRIDGE ISLAND   Start the trip by taking the Bainbridge Island ferry from the ferry terminal at Pier 52 on the Seattle waterfront. For a current sailing schedule, contact **Washington State Ferries** (☎ 206/464-6400 or 800/84-FERRY). From on board, you can get a view of the Seattle skyline, and on a clear day, Mount Rainier to the southeast and the Olympic Mountains to the west.

Just up the hill from the Bainbridge Island ferry terminal is the island's main shopping district, where you'll find some interesting shops and restaurants. If you'd like to sample the local wine, drop in at the **Bainbridge Island Winery** (☎ 206/842-WINE), located a quarter mile up the hill from the ferry landing.

Down at the south end of the island, you'll find **Fort Ward State Park** on the quiet shore of Rich Passage. The **Bainbridge Island Historical Museum** (☎ 206/ 842-2773) is located in Strawberry Hill Park 1^1/$_2$ miles west of Wash. 305 on High School Road and is housed in a restored one-room schoolhouse built in 1908 (open Saturday and Sunday from 11am to 3pm). Garden enthusiasts will want to call ahead and make a reservation to visit the **Bloedel Reserve,** 7571 NE Dolphin Dr. (☎ 206/842-7631), which is 6 miles north of the ferry terminal off Wash. 305 (turn right on Agate Point Road). Expansive and elegant grounds are the ideal place for a quiet stroll amid plants from around the world. Nearby, at the northern tip of the island, you'll find **Fay Bainbridge State Park,** which offers camping and great views across the sound to the Seattle skyline.

SUQUAMISH   After crossing the Agate Passage Bridge to the mainland of the Kitsap Peninsula, take your first right and, as you approach the town of Suquamish, you'll see signs for the **grave of Chief Sealth,** for whom Seattle was named. To visit the site of the Old Man House, which was a large Native American longhouse, return to Wash. 305, continue west, turn left at the Suquamish Hardware building, and watch for the sign. **The Old Man House** itself is long gone, but you'll find an informative sign and a small park with picnic tables. Continuing a little farther on Wash. 305, you'll see signs for the **Suquamish Museum,** 15838 Sandy Hook Rd. (☎ 360/598-3311), on the Port Madison Indian Reservation. The museum houses a compelling history of Puget Sound's native people. It's open May to September, daily from 10am to 5pm; October to April, Friday through Sunday from 11am to 4pm. Admission is $2.50 for adults, $2 for seniors, and $1 for children.

POULSBO   Continuing north on Wash. 305, you next come to the small town of Poulsbo, which overlooks fjordlike Liberty Bay. Settled in the late 1880s by Scandinavians, Poulsbo was primarily a fishing, logging, and farming town until the town decided to play up its Scandinavian heritage. Shops in the Scandinavian-inspired downtown sell all manner of Viking and Scandinavian souvenirs. In May the annual Viking Fest celebrates traditional Scandinavian culture, as do the Midsommar Fest and Yule Log Festival. Between downtown and the waterfront, you'll find **Liberty Bay Park,** and at the south end of Front Street you'll find the **Marine Science Center,** 17771 Fjord Dr. NE (☎ 360/779-5549), which houses interpretive displays about Puget Sound. It's open Tuesday through Saturday from 10am to 4pm. Admission is $2 for adults, $1 for seniors and children 2 to 12, and $5 families; free for everyone on Tuesday. If you have a sweet tooth, don't miss **Sluys Poulsbo Bakery,** 18924 Front St. NE (☎ 360/697-BAKE), which bakes mounds of goodies, as well as stick-to-your-ribs breads.

If you enjoy microbrewery ales, head north of Poulsbo 2 miles to the **Thomas Kemper Brewery,** 22381 Foss Rd. NE (☎ 360/697-1446), which is also a good spot for lunch.

PORT GAMBLE   If you have time and enjoy visiting historic towns, continue north from Poulsbo on Wash. 3 to Port Gamble. This community was established in 1853 as a company town for the Pope and Talbot lumber mill, which today is the oldest operating lumber mill on the West Coast (although a closure has just been announced). Along the town's shady streets are many Victorian homes that were restored by Pope and Talbot. Stop by the **Port Gamble Country Store** (☎ 360/297-2623), which now houses the Port Gamble Historical Museum as well as the Of Sea & Shore Museum. The former is a collection of local memorabilia, while the latter exhibits seashells from around the world.

BREMMERTON　From Port Gamble, head south on Wash. 3 toward Bremmerton to begin an exploration of the area's naval history. Between Poulsbo and Silverdale, you'll be passing just east of the Bangor Navy Base, which is home port for a fleet of Trident nuclear submarines. The base is on the Hood Canal, a long narrow arm of Puget Sound. Near the town of Keyport, you can visit the **Naval Undersea Museum** (☎ 360/396-4148), 3 miles east of Wash. 3 on Wash. 308. It's open daily from 10am to 4pm (closed Tuesday from October to May); admission free. The museum explores all aspects of undersea exploration, with interactive exhibits, models, displays that include a deep-sea exploration and research craft, a Japanese kamikaze torpedo, and a deep-sea rescue vehicle.

Continuing south, you come to Bremmerton, which is home to the **Puget Sound Naval Shipyard,** where mothballed U.S. Navy ships have included the aircraft carriers USS *Nimitz* and USS *Midway* and the battleships USS *Missouri* and USS *New Jersey*. One mothballed destroyer, the USS *Turner Joy,* is now operated by the **Bremmerton Historic Ships Association** (☎ 360/792-2457) and is open to the public as a memorial to those who have served in the U.S. Navy and who have helped build the navy's ships. It's open in winter, Thursday through Monday from 11am to 4pm, and in summer, daily from 10am to 5pm; admission is $5 for adults, $4 for seniors and military personnel, $3 for children 5 to 12. The *Turner Joy* is docked about 150 yards east of the Washington State Ferries terminal. Nearby is the **Bremmerton Naval Museum,** 130 Washington Ave. (☎ 360/479-7447), which showcases naval history and the historic contributions of the Puget Sound Naval Shipyard. It's open Monday through Saturday from 10am to 5pm and on Sunday from 1 to 5pm (closed Monday from Labor Day to Memorial Day); admission is free.

PORT ORCHARD　At one time dozens of small ferries, known as the mosquito fleet, operated around Puget Sound. One of the last remaining private mosquito fleet ferries still operates between Bremmerton and Port Orchard. If you park your car on the waterfront in Bremmerton, you can step aboard the little passenger-only ferry and cross the bay to Port Orchard. In this little waterfront town, you'll find several antiques malls that can provide hours of interesting browsing.

BACK TO SEATTLE　To return to Seattle, take the foot ferry back to Bremmerton, pick up your car, and drive onto the car-ferry to Seattle. Fares back to Seattle are charged for vehicles and drivers only, not for passengers.

AN ALTERNATIVE EXCURSION　An alternative excursion for anyone who would like to spend more time on the water and less time driving is also possible. Start out by taking the Bremmerton ferry from Seattle. In Bremmerton, you can then take the **Kitsap Harbor Tours** (☎ 360/377-8924) fast ferry that goes to the Naval Undersea Museum and Poulsbo. This ferry operates four times a day during the summer months. After returning to Bremmerton, if you still have time, you can visit Port Orchard.

NORTH OF THE CITY

This driving excursion takes in the world's largest building, a town full of antiques stores, wineries, and a picturesque lakeshore community.

EVERETT   Roughly 30 miles north of Seattle on I-5 on the shore of Puget Sound is the city of Everett. Though for the most part it has become a bedroom community for Seattle commuters, it's also home to the region's single largest employer—**Boeing.** It is here in Everett that the aircraft manufacturer has its main assembly plant. This is the single largest building, by volume, in the world and easily holds several 747s. Free guided tours of the facility are held Monday through Friday between 9am and 1pm, and sometimes again later in the day. Children under 4 feet tall are not allowed, and the tours are first-come, first-served. For more information, contact the **Boeing Tour Center,** Wash. 526, Everett (☎ **206/ 342-4801**).

SNOHOMISH   A few miles east of Everett off U.S. 2, you can jump from the jet age to horse-and-buggy days in the historic town of Snohomish. Established in 1859 on the banks of the Snohomish River, this historic town was until 1897 the county seat. However, when the county seat was moved to Everett, Snohomish lost its regional importance and development slowed considerably. Today an abundance of turn-of-the-century buildings are the legacy of the town's early economic growth. By the 1960s these old homes began attracting people interested in restoring them to their original condition, and soon antiques shops began proliferating in historic downtown Snohomish. Today the town has **more than 300 antiques dealers.** Surrounding the town's commercial core of antiques stores are neighborhoods full of **restored Victorian homes.** Each year in September you can get a peek inside some of the town's most elegant homes on the annual **Historical Society Home Tour.** You can pick up a copy of a guide to the town's antiques stores and its historic homes by stopping by or contacting the **Snohomish Chamber of Commerce,** Waltz Building, Avenue B (P.O. Box 135), Snohomish, WA 98290 (☎ **360/568-2526**).

Right next door to the chamber of commerce building is the **Blackman Museum,** 118 Ave. B (☎ **360/568-5235**). This 1879 Queen Anne Victorian has been restored and filled with period furnishings. It's open in summer, daily from noon to 4pm; in other months, Wednesday through Sunday from noon to 4pm. Admission is $1 for adults and 50¢ for seniors and children. For another glimpse into the town's past, head over to **Pioneer Village,** a collection of restored cabins and other old buildings on Second Street. Each of the buildings is furnished with period antiques.

WOODINVILLE   Heading south from Snohomish to Woodinville brings you into Puget Sound's small winery region. Largest and most famous of the wineries in the area is **Chateau Ste. Michelle,** One Stimson Lane, Woodinville (☎ **206/ 488-4633**), which is located in an grand château on a historic estate that was established in 1912. An amphitheater on the grounds stages music performances throughout the summer. To reach the winery, head south from Woodinville on Wash. 202 and watch for signs.

Right across the road from Chateau Ste. Michelle, you'll find the **Columbia Winery,** 14030 NE 145th St. (☎ **206/488-2776**). Other wineries in the area include **French Creek Cellars,** 17721 132nd Ave. NE (☎ **206/486-1900**), which is just north of Woodinville, and the **Facelli Winery,** 12335 134th Court NE, Redmond (☎ **206/823-9466**), which is south of Chateau Ste. Michelle off NE 14th Street.

KIRKLAND   Finish your day with a walk around downtown Kirkland, which is along the Moss Bay waterfront. You can stroll along the waterfront and stop in at interesting shops and any of more than a dozen art galleries. There are also several decent restaurants in the area. We like the **Cafe Juanita,** 9702 NE 120th Place (☎ **206/823-1505**), an excellent Italian restaurant.

To get back to Seattle, take I-405 south to I-90.

EAST OF THE CITY

If you were a fan of David Lynch's "Twin Peaks" or of "Northern Exposure," you can visit some spots you'll likely recognize by heading east from Seattle to see where these shows were filmed. Even if you weren't a fan of either show, you'll likely enjoy a trip out this way for its mountain scenery and a chance to visit the most spectacular waterfall in the Seattle area.

Snoqualmie Falls, located 35 to 45 minutes east of downtown Seattle on I-90, plummet 270 feet into a pool of deep blue water. The falls are surrounded by a park owned by Puget Power, which operates a hydroelectric plant inside the rock wall behind the falls. The plant, built in 1898, was the world's first underground electric-generating facility. In the park you'll find two overlooks near the lip of the falls and a half-mile-long trail leading down to the base of the falls.

Nearby, off Exit 22 from I-90, you'll find one of the Northwest's best-loved farms—**The Herbfarm,** 32804 Issaquah–Fall City Rd. (☎ **206/784-2222**). Started in 1974 with a wheelbarrow full of potted herbs, the Herbfarm has since blossomed into a farm, country store, school, theme gardens, mail-order business, and the region's most famous restaurant (see below for details).

Anyone interested in seeing other "Twin Peaks" filming sites should stop by the **Salish Lodge** before heading into the town of North Bend to the **Mar-T Cafe** (☎ **206/888-1221**), where you can still get "damn good pie."

One of the best ways to see this area is from a rail car on the **Puget Sound & Snoqualmie Railroad** (☎ **206/746-4025**), which has historic depots in Snoqualmie and North Bend. The excursion trains operate on weekends between April and October, but be sure to call ahead for a current schedule; the fare is $6 for adults, $5 for seniors, $4 for children 3 to 12.

Continuing east on I-90 another 50 miles or so will bring you to the remote town of **Roslyn,** which was just a quietly decaying old coal-mining town until television turned it into Cicely, Alaska, for "Northern Exposure." Now the little town has become a major tourist attraction and popular day trip from Seattle. Crowds of visitors wander up and down the town's two-block-long main street hoping to catch a glimpse of someone they recognize from the TV show. Aside from dining at the **Roslyn Cafe,** Pennsylvania and Second streets (☎ **509/649-2763**), you can pay a visit to the **Roslyn Museum** next door to the café. About the only other activity in town is wandering through the town's 25 cemeteries, which are up the hill from the Roslyn Cafe. These cemeteries each contain the graves of different nationalities of miners who lived and died in Roslyn.

On your way back to Seattle, you may want to stop in **Issaquah,** at Gilman Village, an interesting collection of old homes that have been restored and turned into shops and restaurants. Take Exit 17.

WHERE TO STAY

Salish Lodge

37807 SE Fall City–Snoqualmie Rd. (P.O. Box 1109), Snoqualmie, WA 98065. ☎ **206/ 888-2556** or 800/826-6124. 91 rms, 4 suites. A/C TV TEL. $165–$295 double; $500–$575 suite. AE, CB, DC, DISC, MC, V.

Set at the top of 270-foot Snoqualmie Falls and only 35 minutes east of Seattle on I-90, Salish Lodge is a popular weekend getaway spot for folks from Seattle. With its country-lodge atmosphere, the Salish aims for casual comfort and hits the mark. The guest rooms are furnished with wicker and Shaker furnishings and have down comforters on the beds. With fireplaces and whirlpool baths in every room, this lodge is made for romantic weekend getaways. Anyone who was a fan of "Twin Peaks" should immediately recognize the hotel.

Dining/Entertainment: The lodge's country breakfast is a legendary feast that will likely keep you full right through to dinner, when you can dine on creative Northwest cuisine in the Salish Dining Room, which has one of the most extensive wine lists in the state. In the lounge, you can catch a glimpse of the falls through the window.

Services: Room service, valet/laundry service.

Facilities: Exercise room, hot tub, general store, volleyball/badminton court.

WHERE TO DINE

✪ The Herbfarm

32804 Issaquah–Fall City Rd. ☎ **206/784-2222.** Reservations required. Prix-fixe nine-course dinner $115; six-course lunch $60. AE, MC, V. Seatings Thurs–Sat only. Closed mid-Feb to Mar. NORTHWEST.

The Herbfarm, the most highly acclaimed restaurant in the Northwest, is housed in a quaint little cottage and has a Victorian country elegance that sets off the extraordinarily lavish meals. Throughout the year the menu changes every week or two, with different themes to match the seasons. Wild gathered vegetables, Northwest seafoods and meats, organic vegetables, wild mushrooms, and of course the generous use of fresh herbs are the ingredients from which the restaurant's chef creates his culinary extravaganzas. Dinners are paired with complimentary wines, often from northwestern wineries.

This restaurant is so incredibly popular that reservations are taken only twice a year (once in the spring and once in the fall). However, 25% of seats are held available for reservations made one week in advance. These seats can be reserved at 1pm each Friday.

6

The San Juan Islands & Puget Sound

When English explorer Capt. George Vancouver first sailed down the Strait of Juan de Fuca in 1792, he discovered a vast inland sea he named the Puget Sound. Just to the north of this sound, within a convolution of twisting channels, narrow straits, and elongated bays, lay an archipelago of islands, and rising to the east in a magnificent backdrop stood a range of snowcapped peaks. Several of the archipelago's islands—San Juan, Lopez, Fidalgo, and Guemes—had already been named by earlier Spanish explorers, but Vancouver's two months of exploring and charting the waters of the sound left Northwest maps with many new names, such as Deception Pass, Whidbey Island, Bellingham Bay, and Mount Baker.

More than 50 years later, in 1844, western Washington's first white settlers put down roots in the southern reaches of Puget Sound. They settled on the banks of the Deschutes River at Tumwater Falls, taking advantage of water power to run their mills. Ten years later, the community of Steilacoom became Washington's first incorporated town. Less than 40 years later, when the first transcontinental railroad reached the Northwest, Tacoma was chosen as the end of the line, thus sealing that city's fate as an industrial center. Six years after the railroad arrived Washington became a state, and Olympia was chosen to be the capital.

Over the century since statehood, Tacoma developed a less-than-complimentary reputation, Steilacoom lost regional importance, and historic Tumwater nearly disappeared in the sprawl of modern Olympia. Although southern Puget Sound is primarily urban and working-class, it does have a bit of historical significance and lots of beautiful views across the waters of Puget Sound to both the Olympic Mountains and Mount Rainier.

On the other hand, Washingtonians have made northern Puget Sound and the San Juan Islands their summer playground and weekend getaway. Shimmering waters, mountain vistas, and tranquil islands are the ingredients of the tonic that revives the weary souls of vacationing urbanites from the densely populated and industrialized southern Puget Sound. Though it's only 30 miles from Seattle to Whidbey Island and 85 to the San Juans, the distance is multiplied by the serenity that descends as you cross the sound by ferry and leave the mainland behind.

The San Juan Islands & Puget Sound

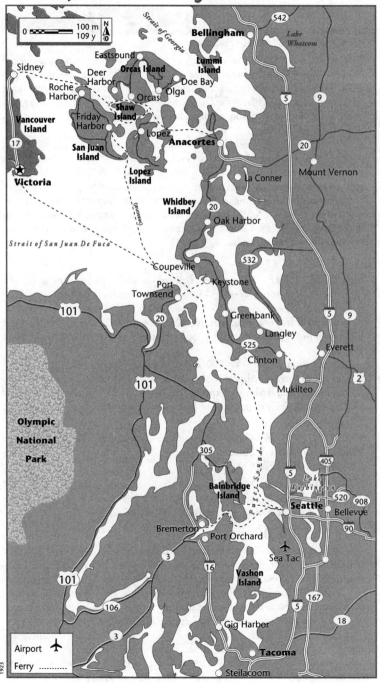

0   100 m
     109 y

Strait of Georgia

542

Lake Whatcom

Bellingham

Sidney

Eastsound

Orcas Island

Lummi Island

Deer Harbor

Doe Bay

Roche Harbor

Orcas

Olga

5

9

Shaw Island

Vancouver Island

Friday Harbor

San Juan Island

Lopez

Anacortes

17

La Conner

Mount Vernon

20

Lopez Island

Victoria

(seasonal)

Whidbey Island

20

Oak Harbor

Strait of San Juan De Fuca

Coupeville

532

101

Port Townsend

Keystone

5

9

20

Greenbank

Langley

101

525

Clinton

Everett

2

Mukilteo

Olympic National Park

305

Lake Washington

5

405

Bainbridge Island

520

908

Seattle

Bellevue

Bremerton

Port Orchard

90

Puget Sound

3

16

Sea Tac

101

Vashon Island

5

167

106

18

3

Gig Harbor

Airport ✈

Tacoma

Ferry ··········

Steilacoom

1923

1   Bellingham & Environs

90 miles N of Seattle, 60 miles S of Vancouver

Bellingham is a small but vibrant city, in large part because of the presence of Western Washington University, which is known for its extensive sculpture gardens. Still an active shipping port, Bellingham enjoys excellent views across Puget Sound to the San Juan Islands, and at Squalicum Harbor there's a large commercial and private boat marina and promenade that provides residents and visitors a chance to enjoy the bay.

Whatcom County, which extends from the coast to the top of 10,778-foot Mount Baker and beyond, is still, however, primarily a rural area. Near the coast farming predominates, and several nearby farm towns are worth visiting for a glimpse of local history and a chance to explore the countryside. Mount Baker itself is a popular downhill skiing area in winter, while in summer hiking trails lead through meadows and forest. South of the city the mountains dip down to the sea and a drive along scenic Chuckanut Drive provides glimpses of spectacular coastline and the San Juan Islands.

ESSENTIALS

GETTING THERE   **I-5** connects Bellingham with Seattle to the south and Vancouver to the north. **Wash. 542,** the North Cascades Scenic Highway, connects Bellingham with eastern Washington by way of Winthrop.

Bellingham International Airport, 4255 Mitchell Way, 5 miles northwest of downtown Bellingham, is served by Alaska Airlines, Horizon Airlines, and United Express.

The **Airporter Shuttle** (☎ **800/235-5247**) runs between Sea-Tac Airport in Seattle and Bellingham Airport (fare: $29 one way).

In summer, **Island Shuttle Express** (☎ **360/671-1137**) offers passenger ferry service between Bellingham and San Juan and Orcas islands (fares: $20 one way, $33 round-trip).

VISITOR INFORMATION   Contact the **Bellingham Whatcom County Visitors & Convention Bureau,** 904 Potter St., Bellingham, WA 98226 (☎ **360/ 671-3990** or 800/487-2032).

GETTING AROUND   If you need a taxi, contact **City Cab** (☎ **360/ 733-8294**). Public bus service around the Bellingham area is provided by the **Whatcom Transportation Authority** (☎ **360/676-7433**).

WHAT TO SEE & DO

The **Whatcom Museum of History and Art,** 121 Prospect St. (☎ **360/ 676-6981**) is a striking example of Victorian architecture. Inside you'll find reconstructions of old stores from the turn-of-the-century town. Special exhibits focus on Northwest artists and local history, while up on the third floor you'll find old toys, tools, and fashions. An adjacent building contains an excellent collection of Northwest coast Native American artifacts that are beautifully displayed. It's open Tuesday through Sunday from noon to 5pm. Admission is by donation; for special exhibits, $2 for adults and $1 for children 11 and under.

Two doors down from the Whatcom Museum is the **Children's Museum Northwest,** 227 Prospect St. (☎ **360/733-8769**), which, though small, offers lots of fun hands-on experiences for kids. It's open on Sunday, Tuesday, and

Wednesday from noon to 5pm, and Thursday through Saturday from 10am to 5pm; admission is $2.

Another major landmark in downtown Bellingham is the **Mount Baker Theatre,** 104 N. Commercial St. (☎ 360/734-6080). The theater's 110-foot-tall lighthouse tower is visible from all over the city, and though the exterior decor is quite subdued, inside you'll find an extravagant lobby designed to resemble a Spanish galleon. Movies and live performances alternate here.

If your interest is art, you shouldn't miss the **Western Washington University Outdoor Sculpture Collection,** off the Bill McDonald Parkway south of downtown. The collection of massive sculptures includes a piece by Isamu Noguchi. You can pick up a guide to the collection at the Visitor's Information Center or at the university's Western Gallery (☎ 360/650-3900), which features exhibits of contemporary art.

Though downtown Bellingham has a fair number of restaurants and a few galleries, the **Fairhaven district** is the most popular neighborhood in town. Fairhaven was once a separate town and many of its brick buildings, built between 1880 and 1900, have now been restored and house unusual shops and several good restaurants. Also in Fairhaven is the Bellingham Cruise Terminal, the southern terminal for ferries to Alaska.

Railroad buffs will want to know about the **Lake Whatcom Railway** (☎ 360/595-2218), which operates a historic steam-train excursion from the town of Wickersham southeast of Bellingham. The schedule varies from year to year, but there are usually weekend trips in July and August. Call for details.

CHUCKANUT DRIVE

Chuckanut Drive, a scenic 10-mile road, begins in Fairhaven and winds its way south through the Chuckanut Mountains, which rise from the shore of Chuckanut Bay. Though most of the way is through dense woods, there are pull-offs where you can gaze out to the San Juan Islands or up and down this rugged section of coastline. Chuckanut Drive is particularly popular at sunset and there are several very good restaurants along the way.

WHERE TO STAY

Chain motels in town include **Motel 6,** 3701 Byron St. (Exit 252 off I-5), Bellingham, WA 98225 (☎ 360/671-4494), charging $36 double; and **Best Western Lakeway Inn,** 714 Lakeway Dr. (Exit 253 off I-5), Bellingham, WA 98226 (☎ 360/671-1011), charging $69 to $105 double.

✪ Schnauzer Crossing

4421 Lakeway Dr., Bellingham, WA 98226. ☎ **360/733-0055** or 800/562-2808. Fax 360/734-2808. 3 rms. TEL. $110–$180 double. Rates include full breakfast. MC, V.

Located less than 4 miles from downtown, Schnauzer Crossing is set in a quiet neighborhood overlooking Lake Whatcom. The living room, with its Asian decor and wall of windows, looks out on the lake, huge old trees, green lawns, and a garden. There's a very private cottage with a private deck, gas fireplace, TV and VCR, and double whirlpool tub. In the equally appealing master suite you'll find a skylit bathroom with a double whirlpool tub, a king-size bed, a wood-burning fireplace, TV and VCR, and separate sitting room. And should you stay in the one room that doesn't have a private whirlpool tub, you can simply step outside to the hot tub in the Japanese garden.

NEARBY ACCOMMODATIONS IN BLAINE

The Inn at Semiahmoo

9565 Semiahmoo Pkwy., Blaine, WA 98230-9326. ☎ **360/371-2000**, or 800/822-4200 in the U.S., 800/631-4200 in Canada. 198 rms. A/C TV TEL. Summer, $150–$225 double; winter, $110–$155 double. AE, DC, DISC, MC, V.

Located at the end of a sandy spit, the Inn at Semiahmoo is nearly in Canada. Gables and gray shingles give the resort a timeless look, and throughout the classically styled interior of the main lodge are numerous lounges overlooking the water. Artwork abounds, with Native American and nautical themes prevailing. Not all guest rooms have views, but those that do have beds facing out the windows to the sea. We prefer the patio rooms on the ground floor, since these allow you to step out of your room and right onto the beach.

Dining/Entertainment: The main dining room overlooks the water and offers excellent meals and an extensive wine list. The menu is primarily continental. There are also weekend buffets, and an oyster bar and lounge where you can get light meals.

Services: Concierge, room service, San Juan Island cruises, bicycle rentals, spa programs.

Facilities: Golf course, indoor tennis courts, racquetball, squash, indoor/outdoor pool, whirlpools, sauna, steam room, exercise room, indoor track, marina, bike and running paths.

WHERE TO DINE

✪ Café Toulouse

114 W. Magnolia St. ☎ **360/733-8996.** Reservations recommended. Sandwiches, salads, and pastas $6–$8. MC, V. Mon–Fri 7am–7pm, Sat–Sun 8am–3pm. NORTHWEST.

This artistic café isn't very large, but in addition to the handful of tables in the main dining room, there are some café tables in the interior courtyard of the building. Toulouse made its name on breakfasts such as smoked-salmon omelets and lunches such as pork loin sandwiches with jalapeño jelly, but it also does great pasta dishes. At lunch there's usually a soup special. Desserts are works of art that are light enough not to weigh you down after a big meal.

Colophon Café & Deli

In Village Books, 1208 11th St. ☎ **360/647-0092.** Most items $3–$7. MC, V. Mon–Sat 9am–10pm, Sun 10am–8pm (longer hours in summer). SOUPS/SANDWICHES.

Northwesterners spend a lot of time in bookstores hiding from the rain, so, of necessity, bookstores often provide sustenance. Here at the Colophon, you can chill out with some ice cream in summer, warm up with an espresso in winter, or make a filling meal of the star attractions here—homemade soups. You'll always find African peanut soup, Mexican corn-and-bean soup, split-pea soup, and clam chowder on the menu.

Il Fiasco

1309 Commercial St. ☎ **360/676-9136.** Reservations highly recommended. Main courses $12–$23. AE, DC, MC, V. Mon–Fri 11:30am–2:30pm and 5:30–9:30pm, Sat–Sun 5:30–9:30pm. ITALIAN.

Named for those straw-covered bottles that chianti comes in, this restaurant mixes contemporary art and classic Italianate decor with innovative dishes. Service is extremely friendly and prompt, and there's an extensive list of Italian wines. You'll find such appetizers as fried calamari with garlic-artichoke sauce, and if pasta is your passion, we suggest roast duck and mushroom ravioli with sweet-peppercorn sauce. For an entrée, you'll have choices such as zinfandel-cured pork loin with roasted shallots and a berry-and-brandy glaze, or grilled seafood over saffron risotto with red- and yellow-pepper coulis. But save room for some white-chocolate espresso cheesecake.

⑤ La Belle Rose

Harbor Center, 1801 Roeder Ave., Suite 102. ☎ **360/733-8755.** Reservations highly recommended. Four-course dinner $15–$22. AE, MC, V. Wed–Sat 11am–2pm and 5:30–9pm, Sun 10am–2pm. Closed Mar. FRENCH/MEDITERRANEAN.

With only seven tables, La Belle Rose vies for the distinction of smallest restaurant in Bellingham, but its reputation is far-reaching. It's a one-woman show: The owner cooks, waits on table in a personable fashion, and travels the world for food inspiration. Among the dishes we sampled were a carrot soup topped with crème fraîche; linguini with scallops, prawns, and mussels in a tomato coulis with saffron and white wine; and a chicken breast with garlic aïoli, tomatoes, and capers. We also manged to squeeze in some chocolate decadence for dessert. La Belle Rose is one of the city's best restaurant values.

NEARBY DINING

Oyster Creek Inn

Chuckanut Dr. ☎ **360/766-6179.** Reservations recommended. Main courses $14.50–22.50. MC, V. Daily noon–9pm. SEAFOOD.

There may be better views on Chuckanut Drive, but because there's an oyster farm only a few feet downhill, you aren't going to find fresher bivalves. The Oyster Creek Inn is almost in Oyster Creek, and with walls of windows wrapping around the dining room there's a good view of the tumbling waters. The fried oyster poorboy with jalapeño tartar sauce is a tasty creation, and the creamy oyster stew is extremely satisfying on a rainy day. Sandwiches are pricey, but most are made with seafood.

EXPLORING AROUND BELLINGHAM

MOUNT BAKER

On a clear day it seems to loom close enough to touch, but on other days you'd never even know it was there. At 10,778 feet, Mount Baker dominates the eastern skyline and serves as a snowcapped backdrop for the northern Puget Sound area.

Mount Baker Ski Area (☎ 360/734-6771) is open for skiing from November to May. Lift tickets range from $18 to $27.50. The ski area is about 62 miles from Bellingham on Wash. 542. Heather Meadows, site of the ski area, lies between Mount Baker and Mount Shuksan, which is one of the most photographed mountains in the state.

Another 3 miles farther you come to aptly named **Artist Point,** where there are sweeping panoramas. En route to Mount Baker there are lots of places to stop, so you should leave yourself plenty of time for the trip. The best mountain viewpoints en route are at milepost 29, from Wells Creek Road, and from the Mount Baker Vista at the end of Glacier Creek Road.

Where to Dine

✪ Innisfree

9393 Mt. Baker Hwy., Deming. ☎ **360/599-2373.** Reservations recommended. Main courses $9–$16. AE, DISC, MC, V. Mon–Tues and Thurs–Fri 4–10pm, Sat 3–10pm, Sun 2–9pm (closed one additional day in winter). NORTHWEST.

Located 31 miles east of Bellingham, Innisfree serves seasonal, regional cuisine. This is one of the finest restaurants in the region and the owners, who have a self-sufficient philosophy, use fresh produce from their own 20-acre organic farm. The menu changes weekly, offering five entrées (both meat and vegetarian) and two soups. Though the dishes display a distinct Northwest flavor, recipes from all over the world show up. Candles and fresh flowers give the restaurant a casual elegance that allows both hikers down from the hills and well-dressed couples up from Bellingham to feel comfortable.

LYNDEN: A DUTCH THEME TOWN

Located on Wash. 539 off I-5, Lynden is a self-styled Dutch theme town. The most convincing pieces of Dutch architecture are the four-story windmill that houses the Dutch Village Inn and the adjacent Dutch Village Mall.

For a look at Lynden pioneer life back in the days when Dutch immigrants were settling in the surrounding rich farmlands, visit the **Lynden Pioneer Museum,** 217 Front St. (☎ **360/354-3675**). Among the museum's collections are restored buggies, wagons, carts, and horse-drawn vehicles. It's open April to October, Monday through Saturday from noon to 4pm; November to March, Thursday through Saturday from noon to 4pm.

A visit to Lynden isn't complete without a bit of Dutch food, and **Hollandia,** 655 Front St. in the Dutch Village Mall (☎ **360/354-4133**), is the spot to try it.

Where to Stay

Dutch Village Inn

655 Front St., Lynden, WA 98264. ☎ **360/354-4440.** 6 rms. $65–$95 double. Rates include full breakfast. MC, V.

Housed in the windmill that's the focus of Lynden's Dutch decor, this inn features rooms decorated according to the style of different provinces in the Netherlands. Our favorite room is the Friesland Room up on the windmill's top floor. There's a view of Mount Baker and valley farms outside of town.

LUMMI ISLAND: AN UNDISCOVERED GETAWAY

If the San Juan Islands have grown too crowded for you, consider a visit to another island that rightfully should be considered part of the San Juans. Lummi Island is not on the main ferry route through the San Juans, and so is often overlooked as a quiet island retreat for a weekend getaway. Instead it has its own little ferry that leaves hourly from north of Bellingham. Just about anything you can do in the San Juans, you can do on Lummi Island—except get stuck in crowds and traffic jams.

Where to Stay

✪ Loganita by the Sea

2825 W. Shore Dr., Lummi Island, WA 98262. ☎ **360/758-2651.** 2 rms, 3 suites, 1 cottage. $110 double; $145–$225 suite; $225 cottage. MC, V.

The breathtaking setting overlooking the Georgia Strait and several of the San Juan Islands would be enough to recommend any bed-and-breakfast in this location, but Loganita is far more than just a great location. Lawns and gardens full of flowers provide a picturesque foreground, and cut flowers fill the inn almost any time of year. The turn-of-the-century villa has windows seemingly everywhere, and through every one is that view. Romantic decor abounds and there's original Northwest and Canadian art throughout the house. Should you choose to stay in one of the suites or the carriage house cottage, you may find you have a private deck or fireplace.

The Willows Inn

2579 W. Shore Dr., Lummi Island, WA 98262. ☎ **360/758-2620.** 7 rms. $110–$290 double. Rates include full breakfast on weekends. AE, MC, V.

Located across the street from the water and with great views from the gardens, front deck, and living room, this inn is primarily a weekend getaway. Simple country styling prevails in the guest rooms, and if you're looking for solitude and space, you may want to splurge on the honeymoon cottage or guesthouse. Note that these are the only rooms available on weekdays and only come with breakfast on weekends. Friday and Saturday evenings gourmet dinners are also served at an additional $38 to $45 per person, including wine.

2   La Conner

70 miles N of Seattle, 10 miles E of Anacortes, 32 miles S of Bellingham

La Conner is named for Louisa A. (LA) Conner, who helped found the town in the 1870s. Dating back to a time when Puget Sound towns were connected by water and not by road, La Conner clings to the shore of Swinomish Channel; its waterfront was once busy with steamers that made the run to Seattle. The town reached a commercial peak around 1900 and continued as an important grain- and log-shipping port until the Depression. La Conner never recovered from the hard times of the 1930s, and when the highways bypassed the town it became a neglected backwater. The wooden false-fronted buildings built during the town's heyday were spared the waves of progress that swept over the Northwest during the latter half of this century, and today these quaint old buildings give the town its charm.

Beginning in the 1940s, La Conner's picturesque setting attracted several visual artists and writers. By the 1970s La Conner had become known as an artists' community (Tom Robbins wrote about the area in his novel *Another Roadside Attraction*), and tourism began to revive the economy. The mid-19th-century commercial buildings that line the La Conner waterfront have been restored and are today filled with art galleries, boutiques, antiques stores, and crafts shops. For most visitors shopping is the town's main attraction—and on summer weekends the crowds can be formidable.

Adding still more color to an already-vibrant little town are the commercial flower farms of the surrounding Skagit Valley. In the spring, tulips and daffodils carpet the surrounding farmlands with great swaths of red, yellow, and white. These wholesale flower farms have given rise to quite a few nurseries and garden stores in La Conner, so if gardening is your passion, don't miss this quaint little waterfront town.

ESSENTIALS

GETTING THERE   From I-5, take U.S. 20 west toward Anacortes. La Conner is south of U.S. 20 on La Conner–Whitney Road. Alternatively, take the Conway exit off I-5 and head west on Fir Island Road to Chilberg Road, which leads into La Conner.

The **Anacortes–Oak Harbor–Sea-Tac Airporter** (☎ 360/679-0600 or 800/ 235-5247, 800/448-8443 in Washington) makes a stop at the Farmhouse Inn, which is at the junction of Wash. 20 and La Conner–Whitney Road, north of La Conner (one-way fares: $23 for adults, $20 for seniors, $12 for children).

VISITOR INFORMATION   Contact the **La Conner Chamber of Commerce,** P.O. Box 1610, La Conner, WA 98257 (☎ 360/466-4778).

GETTING AROUND   If you need a **taxi,** call Rainbow Van Service (☎ 360/ 466-5324 or 800/733-5320).

SEEING THE SIGHTS

La Conner's biggest annual event is the annual **Skagit Valley Tulip Festival** (☎ 800/4-TULIPS), held each year in March and April. For a few short weeks at this time, the countryside around La Conner erupts with color as the tulip and daffodil fields burst into bloom in a floral display that rivals the legendary flower fields of the Netherlands. La Conner's flowers, which are grown for their bulbs, cover acres and acres of countryside outside town, and if you're here for the festival, stop by the **La Conner Chamber of Commerce** at Fourth and Morris streets (☎ 360/466-4778) for a scenic tour map of the flower fields.

Alternatively, just head out to **RoozenGaarde Flowers & Bulbs,** 1587 Beaver Marsh Rd. (☎ 360/424-8531 or 800/732-3266), which has a gift shop open daily March to May and Monday through Saturday in other months. Any time of year, you can visit the English country gardens of **La Conner Flats,** 1598 Best Rd. (☎ 360/466-3190), northeast of La Conner. Back in town, there's the **Tillinghast Seed Company,** at the corner of Morris and Maples streets as you enter town (☎ 360/466-3552). This is the oldest seed company in the Northwest and now includes a country store, nursery, gardening supply store, and florist. It's open daily.

A steep flight of stairs leads up a hill behind First Avenue, and atop this hill you'll find the **Skagit County Historical Museum,** 501 S. Fourth St. (☎ 360/ 466-3365), to brush up on your local history. Commercial and domestic life are chronicled with displays of antiques donated by local families. It's open Tuesday through Sunday from 11am to 5pm; admission is $2 for adults, $1 for children. The nearby **Gaches Mansion and Valley Museum of Northwest Art,** Second Street and Benton Avenue (☎ 360/466-4288 or 360/466-4446), will give you a glimpse of a classic La Conner home that now houses a collection of works by several Northwest artists, such as Morris Graves, Mark Tobey, and Guy Anderson, all of whom once worked in La Conner. It's open in summer Friday through Sunday from 1 to 5pm, in winter until 4pm; admission is $2. Two blocks down the street from the Gaches Mansion is the much less pretentious **Magnus Anderson Cabin,** built in 1869 by the area's first white settler. Beside the cabin is the **La Conner Town Hall,** which is housed in a triangular bank building that was built in 1886. Across the street from these two buildings is **Totem Pole Park,** which in addition to having a totem pole, has a dugout canoe carved by local Swinomish artisans, whose reservation is just across the Swinomish Channel.

Eight miles north of La Conner at the **Padilla Bay National Estuarine Research Reserve and Breazeale Interpretive Center,** 1043 Bayview-Edison Rd. (☎ **360/428-1558**), you can learn about the importance of estuaries. Interpretive exhibits explore life in Padilla Bay and its salt marshes. The reserve is open daily; the interpretive center, Wednesday through Sunday from 10am to 5pm. Admission is free.

Between November and June, **Viking Cruises,** in the Lime Dock Building, 109 N. First St. (☎ **360/466-2639**), offers various cruises to see wildlife, including birds and whales (tours run $15 to $65). From May to September, this company also does three-day/two-night cruises to the San Juan Islands.

Shopping is the most popular pastime in La Conner, and as you wander up and down First Street, stop in at the **Wood Merchant,** 709 S. First St. (☎ **360/ 466-4741**), which features handcrafted wooden furniture and accent pieces; and **Earthenworks,** 713 S. First St. (☎ **360/466-4422**), which features fine crafts in ceramic, glass, wood, and other media.

WHERE TO STAY
VERY EXPENSIVE

✪ The La Conner Channel Lodge

205 N. First St., La Conner, WA 98257. ☎ **360/466-1500.** 38 rms, 2 suites. TV TEL. $140–$188 double; $182–$222 suite. Rates include continental breakfast. AE, DISC, MC, V.

Luxurious accommodations, Northwest styling, and views of Swinomish Channel from all but seven of the rooms make this a truly memorable lodge. A flagstone entry, cedar-shake siding, and a river-rock fireplace in the lobby set the tone for the rest of the lodge. Most guest rooms are large and all have small balconies and gas fireplaces. Fir accents and a combination of slate flooring and carpeting give the rooms a natural richness. Nautical accent pieces, wooden venetian blinds, and wrought-iron bed frames tie the rooms to La Conner's seafaring past and add touches of Italianate styling. The elegant buffet breakfast is served on the mezzanine above the lobby. If you have your own boat, you can tie up at the hotel's dock.

MODERATE

⑤ The Heron in La Conner

117 Maple Ave. (P.O. Box 716), La Conner, WA 98257. ☎ **360/466-4626.** 10 rms, 2 suites. TV TEL. $69–$83 double; $101–$135 suite. Rates include continental breakfast. AE, MC, V.

Located on the edge of town, the Heron is a modern Victorian country inn that has the feel of a B&B despite its size. There's a stone fireplace in the parlor and a front porch, which, unfortunately, overlooks only the parking lot. However, out back you'll find a pleasant garden and a hot tub. The guest rooms are all individually decorated with modern furnishings that reflect Victorian times. A few, including the bridal suite with its double whirlpool tub, have views across the fields to Mount Baker.

Hotel Planter

715 First St. (P.O. Box 702), La Conner, WA 98257. ☎ **360/466-4710** or 800/488-5409. Fax 360/466-1320. 12 rms. TV TEL. $70–$110 double. Lower rates off-season. AE, MC, V.

If nothing will do for you but to be right downtown in a historic building, the Hotel Planter is the place for you. Built in 1907 and completely restored in 1989, the hotel is up a flight of stairs from a row of storefronts. The rooms in front can be a bit noisy, but they do offer nice views through large windows. High ceilings and overhead fans, pine armoires, and wicker chairs all add up to a classic feel for this historic inn. A garden courtyard behind the hotel features a gazebo with hot tub.

La Conner Country Inn

107 S. Second St., La Conner, WA 98257. ☎ **360/466-3101.** 30 rms. TV TEL. $81–$102 double; $130 suite. Rates include continental breakfast. AE, MC, V.

Under the same management as the La Conner Channel Lodge, the Country Inn is a much more casual, folksy sort of place. It's set back a block from the water but is still right in downtown, so it's very convenient for shopping. The exterior looks as if this were a mountain lodge, and in the cozy lobby there's a huge stone fireplace. Every guest room here has a fireplace and the styling is decidedly country cute. Some rooms have brass beds and most have rustic pine furniture. Tulip photos abound in both public areas and guest rooms.

✪ The Wild Iris

121 Maple Ave. (P.O. Box 696), La Conner, WA 98257. ☎ **360/466-1400.** 20 rms, 10 suites. TV TEL. $85–$100 double; $130 suite. Rates include full breakfast. AE, MC, V.

The Wild Iris is a modern Victorian inn on the edge of town, and directly behind the inn is a farm that hybridizes dahlias. Ask for a second-floor room with a view in late summer and you'll have not only dahlias out your window, but a view of Mount Baker as well. The inn was designed for romantic weekends, and many of the rooms have double whirlpool tubs. In some the whirlpool tub is in the room, while in others it's on the balcony. Breakfasts are large and are served buffet style. Dinners are also served on Friday and Saturday nights.

The White Swan Guest House

1388 Moore Rd., Mount Vernon, WA 98273. ☎ **360/445-6805.** 3 rms, none with bath; 1 cottage. $75 double; $125 cottage. Rates include continental breakfast. MC, V.

If you're here for the tulip blossoms or if you're a gardener, make this your first choice. Located out in the country, this restored Victorian farmhouse is set beneath ancient poplar trees and is surrounded by stunning perennial gardens. Of the guest rooms in the main house, we like the one with the turret, though all are comfortable enough. For more space and privacy, opt for the rustic little cottage set on the far side of the gardens.

WHERE TO DINE

In addition to the restaurants listed below, La Conner has several pleasant spots to have an espresso or cup of tea. These include the **Café Pojante,** at 610 First St. (☎ 360/466-4818), for espresso; and the tearoom at **The Rose and Thistle,** 606 E. Morris St. (☎ 360/466-3313), for afternoon tea.

Calico Cupboard

720 S. First St. ☎ **360/466-4451.** Reservations not accepted. Most items $4–$8. No credit cards. Summer, daily 7:30am–6pm; the rest of the year, daily 8am–5pm. BAKERY.

If you happen to arrive in La Conner early in the morning, the Calico Cupboard is *the* place for breakfast. It's down at the south end of the waterfront and serves absolutely stupendous baked goods such as fresh raspberry danishes and cinnamon rolls. The decor is a touch too country cute for our taste, so we usually grab a latte and a danish and head down to one of the public parks along the waterfront. If the weather forces you inside or if you're in the mood for a full breakfast, there are plenty of tables in the country kitchen–style dining rooms.

La Conner Seafood and Prime Rib House

614 S. First St. ☎ **360/466-4014.** Reservations recommended. Main courses $9–$20. AE, DC, DISC, MC, V. Sun–Thurs 11:30am–10pm, Fri–Sat 11:30am–11pm (closes an hour earlier off-season). SEAFOOD/PRIME RIB.

With a long menu of reliable choices at moderate prices, this is your best bet in La Conner for a waterfront meal. Though the spacious building looks as if it's a restored historic building, a few years back an arson fire burned the original building to the ground, so this is actually a very good reproduction. If you like oysters, we recommend Grandma Lou's oysters or the sautéed oysters. Both are prepared with vegetables and bacon and are topped with parmesan cheese. If you like spicy food, try the Cajun prime rib. The lunch menu is as long as the dinner menu and includes plenty of seafood salads and sandwiches. Try the crab or shrimp Louis salad.

✪ Palmer's

In the La Conner Country Inn, 205 E. Washington Ave. ☎ **360/466-4261.** Reservations recommended. Main courses $14–$21; pub entrées $6–12. AE, MC, V. Sun–Thurs 11:30am–3pm and 5–9:30pm, Fri–Sat 11:30am–3pm and 5–10pm. INTERNATIONAL.

La Conner's finest meals are to be had at Palmer's, a cozy little restaurant attached to the La Conner Country Inn. Try to arrive early enough to have a drink in the pub that's downstairs from the main dining room. Dark wood, tiny booths, and a worn wood floor yield an honest reproduction of a cramped 19th-century English pub. Upstairs, deep-green carpeting, white tablecloths, and green napkins provide an elegant contrast to the rustic, mountain-lodge styling of the main dining room. There are no shortcuts taken in the preparation of dishes at Palmer's and most ingredients originate right here in the Skagit Valley. For a starter, try the gravlax, a salmon filet cured with brandy and dill. The seafood Madras is a rich and creamy curry made with scallops and prawns and flavored with ginger, coconut, and curry. Many of the same dishes show up on the pub menu.

3 The San Juan Islands & Anacortes

Anacortes: 75 miles N of Seattle, 39 miles S of Bellingham, 92 miles S of Vancouver

On a late afternoon on a clear spring day, the sun slants low, suffusing the scene with a golden light. The fresh salt breeze and the low rumble of the ferry's engine lulls you into a half-waking state. All around you emerald green islands, the tops of glacier-carved mountains flooded at the end of the last Ice Age, rise from a shimmering sea. A bald eagle swoops from its perch on a twisted madrona tree. Off the port bow, two knifelike fins slice the water. You catch a glimpse of black and white—killer whales. As the engine slows, you glide toward a narrow wooden dock with a simple sign above it that reads SAN JUAN ISLAND. With a sigh of contentment, you step out onto the San Juan Islands and a slower pace of life.

There's something magical about traveling to the San Juans. Some people say it's the light, some say it's the sea air, some say it's the weather (it only rains one-third as much as it does in Seattle). Whatever it is that so entrances, the San Juans are indeed magical. They have become the favorite getaway of urban Washingtonians, and if you make time to visit these idyllic islands, we think you, too, will fall under their spell.

There is, however, one caveat. The San Juans have been discovered. In summer there can be waits of several hours to get on ferries if you're driving a car. One solution is to leave your car on the mainland and either come over on foot or with a bicycle. If you choose to come over on foot, you can rent a car or bicycle or use taxis to get around. Then again, you can just stay in one place and really relax. Along with crowded ferries come hotels, inns, and campgrounds that can get booked up months in advance and restaurants that can't seat you unless you have a reservation. If it's summer, don't come out here without a reservation expecting to find a place to stay. Outside the summer months it's a different story.

Below you'll find information on Anacortes, which is where the ferry terminal is located, and three of the four islands served by the ferries (in total, there are more than 170 San Juan Islands). Shaw Island, the fourth, has no accommodations other than a small campground at **Shaw Island County Park,** C/O General Delivery, Shaw Island, WA 98286 (☎ 360/468-2867). The island is primarily a retreat center for nuns and the home of a few hundred hardy souls who like the solitude of the island and want to keep it undeveloped. Shaw Island makes a good day trip from any of the other three islands.

If you want to explore some of the other 168 islands that are not served by the ferries, you'll need a boat. Sailboats and sea kayaks are the two most popular types of vessels for exploring the San Juans. Many of the islands are private property, but a few are or have on them state parks with campsites. Contact the **Washington State Parks Information Request Line** (☎ 360/902-8563) for information on these marine state parks.

ESSENTIALS

GETTING THERE   Washington State Ferries (☎ 206/464-6400, or 800/84-FERRY in Washington) operates ferries between the town of Anacortes and four of the San Juan Islands—Lopez, Shaw, Orcas, and San Juan. One ferry a day also connects the San Juans with Sidney Harbor, British Columbia. The fare for a vehicle and driver from Anacortes is $12.30 to Lopez, $14.70 to Shaw or Orcas, $16.80 to San Juan, and $29.70 to Sidney; the fare for passengers from Anacortes is $4.95 to any of the islands, $6.90 to Sidney. The fare for a vehicle and driver on all westbound interisland ferries is $7, and foot passengers ride free. (Except for service from Sidney, fares are not collected on eastbound ferries.) If you plan to explore the islands by car, you'll save some money by starting your tour on San Juan Island and making your way back east through the islands. During the summer there's a peak-season surcharge and you may have to wait several hours to get on a ferry.

During the summer, passenger-ferry service to Friday Harbor is also offered from Seattle on Victoria Clipper's **San Juan Explorer** (☎ 800/888-2535); the fare is $36 one way and $59 round-trip; the trip takes 4¹/₂ hours. Summer passenger service is also offered from Bellingham on **Island Shuttle Express** (☎ 360/671-1137), which leaves from the Bellingham Cruise Terminal, 335 Harris Ave. The fare is $20 one way, $33 round-trip, and the trip takes just over 2 hours.

Kenmore Air (☎ 206/364-6990 or 800/543-9595) operates small seaplanes between Seattle and the San Juans. Flights leave from the west side of Lake Union, north of downtown Seattle. The fare to Friday Harbor is $70 one way, $99 to $130 round-trip. **West Isle Air** (☎ 800/874-4434) flies to the San Juans from Bellingham and Anacortes, charging $27 one way to Friday Harbor from Anacortes, $35 from Bellingham.

The **Anacortes–Oak Harbor–Sea-Tac Airporter** (☎ 360/679-0600 or 800/235-5247, 800/448-8443 in Washington) takes passengers from Sea-Tac

International Airport in Seattle to the ferry terminal in Anacortes. The cost is $27 for adults, $24 for seniors, and $14 for children.

VISITOR INFORMATION   For more information on San Juan Island, contact the **San Juan Island Chamber of Commerce,** P.O. Box 98, Friday Harbor, WA 98250 (☎ **360/378-5240**). For more information on all the islands, contact the **San Juan Islands Visitor Information Service,** P.O. Box 65, Lopez, WA 98261 (☎ **360/468-3663**). For information on Anacortes, contact the **Anacortes Chamber of Commerce,** 819 Commercial Ave., Suite G, Anacortes, WA 98221 (☎ **360/293-3832**).

GETTING AROUND   Car rentals are available on San Juan and Orcas islands. On the former, contact **Friday Harbor Car Rental** (☎ 360/378-4351), and on the latter, contact **Orcas Island Taxi and Car Rental** (☎ 360/376-8294). For a taxi on San Juan, call **Primo Taxi** (☎ 360/378-3550); on Orcas, call **Orcas Island Taxi** (☎ 360/376-8294); on Lopez, call **Angie's Cab Courier** (☎ 360/ 468-2227).

ANACORTES

Founded in the 1850s by Amos Bowman, Anacortes was first known as Annie Curtis, Bowman's wife's name. However, over the years the spelling of the town's name changed so that it would sound more Spanish and more in keeping with other local Spanish names such as San Juan, Lopez, and Guemes. Today Anacortes is still a fairly quiet fishing and boat-building town, and is best known as the site of the ferry terminal for ferries to the San Juan Islands and Sidney, B.C. (near Victoria).

However, a restored downtown business district and residential neighborhoods full of old Victorian homes have made Anacortes a bit of a destination in itself. Not only is the town worth a wander through, but it also makes a good base for exploring Whidbey Island, La Conner, and the San Juans.

Anacortes made its early fortunes on lumbering and fishing, and today commercial fishing, as well as boatbuilding, are still important to the town's economy. This marine orientation has given the town its character, which can be seen in the many restored buildings along Commercial Avenue. Any walking tour of downtown should be sure to include a visit to the historic **sternwheeler *W. T. Preston,*** which sits on dry land in a little park at the corner of Seventh Street and R Avenue; it's open Friday through Sunday from 11am to 5pm. Right next door is the terminal for the **Anacortes Railroad,** a restored narrow-gauge train that makes a short run through town on summer weekends and holidays. **Murals** are a mainstay of the Northwest's historic towns, and here in Anacortes they take the shape of life-size cutouts of the town's forefathers and foremothers.

If you want to learn more about local history, stop by the **Anacortes Museum,** 1350 Eighth St. (☎ 360/293-1915), housed in a former Carnegie Library. It's open from 10am to 5pm, daily in summer and Monday through Friday the rest of the year; admission is free. Across the street from the museum is **Causland Memorial Park,** the town's most unusual attraction. Built in 1919 to honor servicemen who died in World War I, the park contains rock walls that were constructed as giant mosaics. It's a piece of folk art that reflects a much simpler era.

Nature lovers can head to **Washington Park,** just a short distance past the ferry terminal. The park contains not only a campground and several miles of hiking trails, but tranquil **Sunset Beach,** which looks out across Rosario Strait to the San Juan Islands. For even more spectacular views, head up to **Mount Erie Park** on the summit of 1,270-foot Mount Erie. From here, on a clear day you can see Mount Rainier, Mount Baker, and the Olympic Mountains.

WHERE TO STAY

Cap Sante Inn

906 Ninth St., Anacortes, WA 98221. ☎ **360/293-0602.** 34 rms. $48–60 double. AE, DC, DISC, MC, V.

If you'd like to be right downtown, try the Cap Sante, named for the cape that's just across the marina from the motel. The rooms are comfortable and they even have a few books on the desk in case you forgot yours. Several good restaurants are within walking distance.

Channel House

2902 Oakes Ave., Anacortes, WA 98221. ☎ **360/293-9382** or 800/238-4353. Fax 360/299-9208. 6 rms. $69–$95 double. AE, DISC, MC, V.

Located right on the busy road to the ferry landing, this restored 1902 Victorian home has good views across the water to the San Juan Islands. Our favorite room has a view of the water from both the bedroom and from the clawfoot tub in the bathroom. If you're a light sleeper, you might find that the rooms in the rose cottage are a bit quieter than those in the main house; these rooms also have whirlpool tubs. Out in the attractive gardens you'll find a hot tub overlooking the water.

⑤ Islands Motel

3401 Commercial Ave., Anacortes, WA 98221. ☎ **360/293-4644.** 32 rms. A/C TV TEL. Summer, $75 double; other months, $48–$58 double. Rates include full breakfast. AE, DC, DISC, MC, V.

Located right at the end of U.S. 20, the Islands may look just like any other aging strip motel from the street, but after you check in you'll find that there are some differences. First of all, this is a bed-and-breakfast motel, and the breakfast is not just a doughnut and a cup of weak coffee. Instead you get a traditional Dutch breakfast complete with ham and cheese. Some of the rooms have fireplaces, and all have tiled entries and bathrooms. You may even find a second telephone in the bathroom. On top of all this, there's a pool in the summer and the motel's La Petite restaurant, one of the best in town, serves delicious European dishes with an emphasis on Dutch cooking. Entrée prices range from $15 to $20.

✪ The Majestic Hotel

419 Commercial Ave., Anacortes, WA 98221. ☎ **360/293-3355.** Fax 360/293-5214. 23 rms. TV TEL. $89–$148 double; $189 minisuite. Rates include continental breakfast. AE, DISC, MC, V.

Step through the front door of this downtown hotel and you're in for a very pleasant surprise. A soaring ceiling over a lobby furnished with Victorian antiques sets the elegant tone for the rest of the hotel. Throughout the hotel you'll find beautiful and unusual works of art that hearken back to the turn of the century. Outside there's a little English garden, and up on the roof an observatory provides a splendid panorama of the city. The guest rooms are furnished with antiques and have tile bathrooms, coffee makers, ceiling fans, and old-fashioned radiators. Just off the lobby you'll find an opulent restaurant serving excellent Northwest cuisine, with main courses ranging from $14 to $20. Through another door you'll find the hotel's casually elegant lounge, a sort of Victorian pub complete with wicker furniture and marble bar. The Majestic gets our vote for most elegant hotel in the area.

WHERE TO DINE

The two best restaurants in town are both attached to lodgings. The **Courtyard Bistro** at the Majestic Hotel serves Northwest and continental cuisine, while **La Petite Restaurant** at the Islands Motel serves primarily Dutch cuisine. **La Vie En Rose,** 416¹/₂ Commercial Ave. (☎ 360/299-9546), is a great little French pastry shop. If you're looking for a microbrew and some pub grub, check out the **Anacortes Brewhouse,** 320 Commercial Ave. (☎ 360/293-2444).

SAN JUAN ISLAND

Though it's the last ferry stop in the islands, San Juan Island is the most populous and most tourist oriented. **Friday Harbor,** where the ferry docks, is the county seat for San Juan County and host to numerous shops, restaurants, motels, and bed-and-breakfast inns. With its well-protected, large marina, it's also a popular place for boaters to drop anchor.

EXPLORING THE ISLAND

If you arrived by car, you'll first want to find a parking space, which can be difficult in the summer. Once on foot, stroll around town admiring the simple wood-frame shop buildings built back at the turn of the century. At that time, Friday Harbor was referred to as the southernmost port in Alaska and was a busy harbor. Schooners and steamships hauled the island's fruit, livestock, and lime (for cement) off to more populous markets. Today these pursuits have all died off, but reminders of the island's rural roots linger on, and these memories have fueled the island's new economic breadwinner—tourism. If you're particularly interested in island history, stop by the **San Juan Historical Museum,** 405 Price St. (☎ 360/ 378-3949), where you can pick up a walking map to Friday Harbor's historic buildings. The museum is open May to September only, Wednesday through Saturday from 1 to 4:30pm; admission is by donation.

Another place you should visit while you're in town is the headquarters of the **San Juan National Historic Park** at the corner of Spring and First streets (☎ 360/378-2240). This park has its main sites at the north and south ends of the island and commemorates the San Juan Island Pig War, one of North America's most forgotten confrontations. Way back in 1859 San Juan Island nearly became the site of a battle between the British and the Americans. The two countries had not yet agreed upon the border between the United States and Canada when a British pig on San Juan Island decided to have dinner in an American garden. The owner of the garden didn't take too kindly to this and shot the pig. The Brits, rather than welcoming this succulent addition to their evening's repast, threatened redress. In less time than it takes to smoke a ham, both sides were calling in reinforcements. Luckily, this pigheadedness was defused and a more serious confrontation was avoided. San Juan Island National Historic Park commemorates the Pig War with two parks on different sides of the island. One is called American Camp and the other is called English Camp. At both camps, you can visit historic buildings that are much as they might have looked in 1859. The headquarters visitor center can fill you in on details before you head out to visit the two camps.

On the way north toward English Camp, you might stop in at **Giannangelo Farms,** 5500 Limestone Point Rd. (☎ **360/378-4218**), an organic herb farm and garden off Rouleau Road. You can stroll through the gardens and perhaps buy some herbs or herbed vinegar.

Another worthwhile side trip is up to the **Roche Harbor Resort.** The main building of this resort is the historic Hotel de Haro, an imposing whitewashed wooden building with verandas wrapping around its two floors. Stop and admire the old-fashioned marina and colorful gardens. The deck of the hotel's lounge is one of the most photographed spots in the San Juans. Roche Harbor was once the site of large limestone quarries that supplied lime to much of the West Coast. Today many of the quarries' old structures are still visible. Be sure to visit the unusual **mausoleum** that was erected by the founder of both the quarries and the Hotel de Haro.

Continuing south on what is now West Valley Road, you'll soon come to **English Camp.** Set amid shady trees and spacious lawns, the camp is the picture of British civility. There's even a formal garden surrounded by a white picket fence. You can look inside the reconstructed buildings and imagine the days when this was one of the most far-flung corners of the British Empire. If you're full of energy, hike up to the top of 650-foot **Mount Young** for a panorama of the island. An easier hike is out to the end of **Bel Point.**

As you head south on West Valley Road, watch for the Bay Road turnoff. This connects to the Westside Road, which leads down the island's west coast. Along this road, you'll find **San Juan County Park,** a great spot for a picnic. A little farther south you'll come to **Lime Kiln State Park,** the country's first whale-watching park.

At the far south end of the island is the windswept promontory on which stood the **American Camp** during the Pig War. There's a visitor information center here (open daily from 8am to 4pm) and a few reconstructed buildings. Before the American Camp was built here, this was the site of a Hudson's Bay Company farm. The meadows sweeping down to the sea were once grazed by sheep and cattle, but today you'll see only rabbits browsing amid the high grasses and wildflowers. There are several **hiking trails** along the bluffs and down to the sea. One trail leads through a dark forest of Douglas firs. At the end of the trail you'll find **Jackle's Lagoon,** which is a great spot for birdwatching. Keep your eyes peeled for bald eagles, which are relatively plentiful around here.

WHALE WATCHING

Whale watching is one of the most popular summer activities in the San Juans, and before you head out to spot some spouts, you might want to stop by the **Whale Museum,** 62 First St. N. (☎ **360/378-4710**). This is the only museum in the United States dedicated entirely to whales. Here you can see whale skeletons and models of whales and learn all about the area's pods of killer whales, also known as orcas. The museum is open daily from 10am to 5pm (11am to 4pm in winter); admission is $3 for adults, $2.50 for seniors, $1.50 for children 5 to 12.

When it's time to spot some live whales, you have two choices. You can take a whale-watching cruise or head over to **Lime Kiln State Park,** where a short trail leads down to a rocky coastline from which orca whales, minke whales, Dall's porpoises, and sea lions can sometimes be seen. The best months to see orcas are June to September, but it's possible to see them throughout the year. Four-hour whale-watching cruises are offered in the summer by **Western Prince Cruises**

The Truth About Killer Whales

Killer whales, once maligned as the wolves of the deep and dreaded as ruthless marauders of the sea, have been going through a change of image over the past few years. As more has been learned about these highly intelligent members of the porpoise family, an unofficial public-relations campaign has been waged to convince people that these are not killer whales, but orca whales. The more one learns about these intelligent, family-oriented animals, the more evident it becomes that past images of this whale have been misinformed.

Orcas can be found in every ocean, but one of their highest concentrations is in the waters stretching north from Puget Sound along the coast of British Columbia. This has become one of the most studied and most publicized populations of orcas in the world.

Orcas, which can grow to be 30 feet long and weigh almost 9,000 pounds, are the largest member of the porpoise family. In the wild, they can live for up to 80 years, with female orcas commonly living 20 to 30 years longer than males. Orcas are among the most family-oriented animals on earth, and related whales will often live together for their entire lives, sometimes with three generations present at the same time. These family groups frequently band together with other closely related groups into extended families known as pods. A community of orcas consists of several pods, and in this area these communities number around 100 individuals. There are three populations of orcas living in the waters off Vancouver Island, British Columbia. These are known as the northern and southern resident communities and the transient community. It's the southern resident community that whale watchers in the San Juan Islands are most likely to encounter.

As predators, orcas do live up to the name "killer," and have been known to attack other whales much larger than themselves. Some orcas off the coast of Argentina even swim up onto the shore, beaching themselves to attack resting sea lions, then thrashing and twisting their way back into the water. However, not all orcas feed on other marine mammals. Of the three communities in this area, only the transients feed on mammals. The two resident communities feed primarily on salmon, which are abundant in these waters.

Numerous excursion boats offer whale-watching tours from the San Juan Islands during the summer months, when the whales visit this area to feed on migrating salmon. It's also possible to see orcas from land at Lime Kiln State Park on San Juan Island, which is also where you'll find the Whale Museum, the nation's only museum dedicated exclusively to whales.

Those who have seen the movie *Free Willy* may be interested to know that Keiko, the orca that starred in that film, was moved in early 1996 from its inadequate home in Mexico to a new home in a specially constructed facility at the Oregon State University Hatfield Marine Science Center in Newport, Oregon.

(☎ **360/378-5315** or 800/757-6722), which leaves from the main dock in Friday Harbor; the cost is $43 for adults, $31 for children 4 to 17. Should you happen to see a whale on your travels through the San Juans, report the sighting to the **Whale Sighting Hotline** (☎ **800/562-8832**).

OTHER OUTDOOR ACTIVITIES

If you'd rather catch salmon yourself instead of watching whales catch them, contact **Buffalo Works Fishing,** Friday Harbor (☎ 360/378-4612), which also offers bottom-fishing trips. If sailing the islands is more your idea of the perfect day, contact the skipper of the **S.V. Chinook,** a 45-foot trimaran (☎ 360/979-3230 or 206/939-8351). Sea kayaking is very popular in the San Juans. You can take a multiday kayak tour with **San Juan Kayak Expeditions,** Friday Harbor (☎ 360/378-4436), or **Shearwater Adventures,** Eastsound (☎ 360/376-4699), which offers kayaking trips of varying lengths between April and October.

Believe it or not, scuba diving is also extremely popular in the San Juans. Though the water stays frigid year round, it's also exceedingly clear. If you're a diver and want to rent equipment or go on a guided dive, or if you want to take a diving class while you're here, contact **Emerald Seas Dive Center,** 2-A Spring St., Spring St. Landing, Friday Harbor (☎ 360/378-2772 or 800/342-1570).

Bicycling is another favorite sport of island visitors. Winding country roads are almost ideal for leisurely trips. If you didn't bring your own bike, you can rent one from **Island Bicycles,** 380 Argyle St., in Friday Harbor (☎ 360/378-4941), which charges $3 to $10 per hour and $15 to $50 per day.

Golfers will find nine holes at the **San Juan Golf Club** (☎ 360/378-2254).

WHERE TO STAY

Very Expensive

✪ Friday Harbor House

130 West St., Friday Harbor, WA 98250. ☎ **360/378-8455.** Fax 360/378-8453. 20 rms. TV TEL. $165–$185 double; $295 suite. Rates include continental breakfast. AE, DC, DISC, MC, V.

Simultaneously spare and luxurious, this hotel is the first wave of Seattle-type sophistication to hit the San Juan Islands. Neutral tones and contemporary furnishings, a big closet, fireplace, refrigerator, and coffeemaker add to the comfort of the room, but the most prominent feature is a whirlpool tub separated from the bedroom by only a drapery. Most rooms have decks or balconies. Only rooms at the front of the hotel have harbor views. The dining room here has a seasonal menu with an emphasis on Northwest cuisine (see "Where to Dine," below).

Expensive

Hillside House Bed & Breakfast

365 Carter Ave., Friday Harbor, WA 98250 ☎ **360/378-4730** or 800/232-4730. 4 rms. $80–$155 double. Lower rates off-season. AE, DISC, MC, V.

Located less than a mile from downtown Friday Harbor, this contemporary home is in a residential neighborhood, but sits up on top of a hill and consequently has good views. A large aviary is the focal point of the inn and contains some interesting large birds, including a pheasant. The Eagle's Nest, the inn's best room, is luckily free of eagles, but does have a bird's-eye view of the harbor. This room also has a whirlpool tub, balcony, and all of the top floor.

The Inn at Friday Harbor

410 Spring St., Friday Harbor, WA 98250. ☎ **360/378-4000** or 800/752-5752. Fax 360/378-5800. 72 rms. TV TEL. $95–$125 double. Lower rates Nov–Apr. AE, CB, DC, MC, V.

Located right in Friday Harbor, this motel-style lodging offers modern, comfortable rooms with no surprises. A few of the more expensive rooms do, however, have kitchenettes, which makes them a good deal for longer stays or for families. Facilities include an indoor pool, whirlpool, and exercise room. There's also a courtesy van for ferry and airport pickups.

This hotel also operates the nearby Inn at Friday Harbor Suites, where rates are only slightly higher for more spacious accommodations.

Moderate

© Duffy House Bed & Breakfast Inn

760 Pear Point Rd., Friday Harbor, WA 98250. ☎ **360/378-5604** or 800/972-2089. Fax 360/378-6535. 5 rms. $89–$95 double. MC, V.

Don't despair when you find yourself in a gravel pit as you try to find this B&B. Keep going and you'll come out the other side of the gravel pit to find a secluded point on the slopes of which stands this 1920s Tudor home. Surrounded by a small farm, the inn has a great view over the water. The guest rooms, which are done in a country decor, can be a bit cramped but are still comfortable enough. Our favorite room is the one with the view of the eagle's nest.

Lonesome Cove Resort

5810 Lonesome Cove Rd., Friday Harbor, WA 98250. ☎ **360/378-4477.** 6 cabins. $85 cabin for two. Minimum stay two nights Sept–May, five nights June–Aug. MC, V.

If you want to be alone, there's no better place on San Juan Island than Lonesome Cove. This is the sort of place your grandparents might have frequented on summer vacation 50 years ago. Forests hide the 6-acre property from the rest of the world, while lawns and orchards surround the waterfront cabins. Each of the rustic cabins has a large deck, stone fireplace, full kitchen, and its own barbecue. There's a quarter mile of private beach, a trout pond, friendly ducks, romantic sunsets, and more peace and solitude than you'll find anywhere else on the island. The two things you won't find here are telephones and TVs.

✪ Olympic Lights Bed and Breakfast

4531-A Cattle Point Rd., Friday Harbor, WA 98250. ☎ **360/378-3186.** 5 rms, 1 with bath. $70–$105 double. Rates include full breakfast. No credit cards.

Located at San Juan's dry southwestern tip, the Olympic Lights is a yellow Victorian farmhouse surrounded by windswept meadows. If you couldn't see Puget Sound from here, it would be easy to mistake the setting for the prairies of the Midwest. There are colorful gardens, an old barn, even some hens to lay the eggs for your breakfast. The ocean breezes, nearby beach, and friendliness of innkeepers Christian and Lea Andrade lend a special feel to this American classic. If you seek creature comforts, opt for the Garden Room, which has a king-size bed and private bathroom. However, our personal favorite is the Ra Room, which is named for the Egyptian sun god and features a bay window in front of which are arranged two wicker chairs. The view out the windows is enough to settle the most stressed-out soul.

✪ Roche Harbor Resort

P.O. Box 4001, Roche Harbor, WA 98250. ☎ **360/378-2155** or 800/451-8910. Fax 360/378-6809. 16 rms, none with bath; 3 suites; 20 condos; 9 cottages. TEL. $70–$80 double; $100–$125 suite for two; $138 condo for two; $125–$165 cottage for two. Lower rates mid-Sept to May. AE, MC, V.

Located at the north end of the island, the Roche Harbor Resort is steeped in island history. The historic Hotel de Haro, established in 1886, is the centerpiece of the resort. A brick driveway and manicured gardens provide the foreground for the shimmering white historic hotel. Porches overlooking the dock run the length of both floors of the hotel. While the rooms in the historic hotel are small and lack private bathrooms, the condominiums provide modern amenities and styling.

Dining/Entertainment: The dining room and lounge is across the gardens from the Hotel de Haro building. The restaurant serves continental and Northwest cuisine and has a view of the little harbor and the docks. The deck here is the picture of Victorian gentility, especially in the golden light of late afternoon.

Facilities: Outdoor pool, tennis court, marina, general store.

Wharfside Bed & Breakfast

Slip K-13, Port of Friday Harbor, Friday Harbor, WA 98250. ☎ **360/378-5661.** 2 rms, neither with bath. $80–$85 double. Rates include full breakfast. MC, V.

Formerly of Portland, Oregon, Betty and Clyde Rice decided to leave their city ways and opted for life on a 60-foot ketch-rigged motorsailer. Before long they turned the boat into a bed-and-breakfast with two spacious yet cozy cabins. The cabins are comfortably furnished (one has space for two children), and the skylit main saloon is decorated with antiques and memorabilia. Listening to the soothing sound of water lapping against the boat's hull, you'll get a peaceful night's sleep here, and a filling breakfast on the sunny deck in the summer is a great way to begin a day.

Camping

Lakedale Campground, 2627 Roche Harbor Rd., Friday Harbor, WA 98250 (☎ 360/378-2350 or 800/617-CAMP), is 4 miles north of Friday Harbor. With 82 acres, several lakes, and campsites for tents as well as R.V.s, this private campground makes an ideal spot for a family vacation.

Our personal favorite campground, though, is the **San Juan County Park,** 380 Westside Rd. N., Friday Harbor, WA 98250 (☎ **360/378-2992;** call as far in advance as possible for a reservation), which is set on the site of an old waterfront farm. The views are unbeatable. This is a great spot for bicyclists. If you're heading up here in summer, make reservations months in advance (as early as January).

WHERE TO DINE

Expensive

Duck Soup Inn

3090 Roche Harbor Rd. ☎ **360/378-4878.** Reservations highly recommended. Main courses $18–$25. MC, V. Summer, Wed–Sun 5:30–10pm; spring and fall, Fri–Sat 5:30–10pm. Closed Thanksgiving–Mar. INTERNATIONAL.

A few miles north of Friday Harbor you'll find the Duck Soup Inn, a barnlike restaurant beside a pond frequented by—you guessed it—ducks. Inside this quintessentially Northwest building you'll find lots of exposed wood and numerous (right again) Marx brothers posters. Wanna buy a duck? You'll find it on the menu, served as duck confit. However, you'll also find other such local favorites as applewood-smoked oysters. The menu changes frequently depending on the availability of fresh produce, but is always very creative.

Friday Harbor House Dining Room

In the Friday Harbor House, 130 West St. ☎ **360/378-8455.** Reservations recommended. Main courses $16–$29.50. AE, DC, DISC, MC, V. Daily 5:30–9pm. Closed Tues–Wed in winter. NORTHWEST.

This restaurant impresses with its striking contemporary decor and harbor views, and is the most sophisticated place for dining out on San Juan Island. The Northwest-style cuisine, such as broiled Ellensberg lamb with fresh mint purée, is nicely presented but somewhat overpriced, and the dining room tends to be rather noisy.

Moderate

Roberto Paolo

At the corner of First and A sts. ☎ **360/378-6333.** Reservations highly recommended. Main courses $9–$16.50. AE, MC, V. Tues–Sat 5:30–9pm. Closed Jan–Feb. SOUTHERN ITALIAN.

Located in an old house that sits a bit above street level, the restaurant has about a dozen tables jammed into a tiny room that luckily opens onto a deck for summer overflow. Coral walls and relaxed lighting contrast with the bustling waitresses who take your order. We recommend chopped clams, bay shrimp, and linguini; and our cod with anchovy, garlic, caper, and parsley sauce was delicious, accompanied by perfectly grilled summer squash.

✪ Springtree Eating Establishment and Farm

310 Spring St. ☎ **360/378-4848.** Reservations recommended for dinner, and also for lunch in summer. Main courses $13–$18. MC, V. Summer, daily 11am–2:30pm and 5–9pm; winter, Tues–Sat 11:30am–2pm and 5:30–8 or 8:30pm. NORTHWEST.

Tucked in behind a white picket fence and a beautiful weeping elm tree at the top of Spring Street, the Springtree restaurant is an island favorite. The menu changes daily here, and seafood takes the fore, with the crab cakes a specialty. You can get these tender patties as an appetizer or as an entrée, at lunch or at dinner. Lightly breaded pan-fried oysters and steamed mussels also make regular appearances, accompanied by whatever new sauce strikes the chef's fancy. There's an excellent selection of wines, and desserts often feature local fruits. This is one of our favorite places for lunch in the San Juans. The prices are very reasonable and the food is delicious yet health-conscious.

Inexpensive

If you'd rather be outside enjoying the island and don't want to spend extended time in a restaurant, inexpensive light meals, soups, sandwiches, baked goods, and espresso can all be had at the following places. **Katrina's,** 65 Nichols St. (☎ **360/ 378-7290**), is tucked away behind a store called Funk & Junk, and somehow manages to crowd in a lunch counter with three stools. **Madelyn's,** at the top of the ferry lanes (☎ 360/378-4545), is a bagel and sandwich shop. The **Garden Path Café,** at the top of the ferry lanes and across from Madelyn's (☎ 360/378-6255), is a comfortably casual space.

ORCAS ISLAND

Named for the whales and shaped like a horseshoe, Orcas Island has long been a popular summer-vacation spot. The island is a favorite of nature lovers of all kinds who come to enjoy the views of green rolling pastures, forested mountains, and fjordlike bays. **Eastsound** is the largest town on the island and has several interesting shops and good restaurants; other, smaller villages include Deer Harbor, West Sound, and Olga.

Moran State Park, which covers 5,175 acres of the island, is the largest park in the San Juans and the main destination of most visitors to the island. If the weather is clear, you'll find great views from the summit of Mount Constitution, which rises 2,409 feet above Puget Sound. There are also five lakes, 32 miles of hiking trails, and an environmental learning center. Fishing, hiking, boating, biking, and camping are all popular park activities. For campground reservations or more information, contact Moran State Park, Star Route, Box 22, Eastsound, WA 98245 (☎ **360/376-2326**).

Active visitors may want to rent a bicycle at **Dolphin Bay Bicycles** (☎ 360/ **376-4157**), located just to the right as you get off the ferry. Bikes rent for between $5 and $8 per hour or $20 per day. If you're exploring the island by mountain bike, you may want to take the unpaved Dolphin Bay Road to Eastsound. If you're on a street bike, take the Crow Valley Road.

The best way to see the Orcas coast is by sea kayak. Guided tours are offered by **Shearwater Adventures,** Eastsound (☎ 360/376-4699). They offer three-hour tours for $35. **Island Kayak Guides** (☎ 360/376-4755) operates out of Doe Bay Village and offers a variety of trips, including moonlight trips; rates range from $25 to $125. For longer tours, contact **Pacific Water Sports** (☎ 206/246-9385 in Seattle), which operates two- to five-day trips ranging in price from $195 to $595.

If you'd like to go out fishing or whale watching, try **Eclipse Charters** (☎ 360/ **376-4663** or 800/376-6566). Rates range from $45 per person for whale watching to $55 per person for fishing.

Golfers will find the nine-hole **Orcas Golf Club** (☎ 360/376-4400) near Eastsound on the Horseshoe Highway.

To learn a little about the history of Orcas Island, drop by the **Orcas Island Historical Museum,** on North Beach Road in Eastsound (☎ 360/376-4839); it's open Memorial Day to Labor Day only, Monday through Saturday from 1 to 4pm. A second historical museum, the **Crow Valley School Museum** is located 3 miles southwest of Eastsound on Crow Valley Road (☎ 360/376-4260), open Memorial Day to Labor Day only, Thursday through Saturday from 1 to 4pm.

Island shops worth visiting include **Darvill's Rare Print Shop,** Eastsound (☎ 360/376-2351), which sells antique prints and maps; **Darvill's Book Shop,** Eastsound (☎ 360/376-2135), which specializes in Northwest fiction, history, and guidebooks; **Orcas Island Pottery,** near Eastsound (☎ 360/376-2813), the oldest pottery studio in the Northwest; **The Right Place Pottery Shop** (☎ 360/ **376-4023**) and **The Naked Lamb Wool Shop** (☎ 360/376-4606), located on West Beach across from the West Beach Resort; the **Clarion** gallery, in an old cottage at 10 Prune Alley (☎ 360/376-6040); and **Shinola Jewelry,** Northbeach Road, Eastsound (☎ 360/376-4508).

WHERE TO STAY

Expensive

Eastsound Landmark Inn

Main St. (Rte. 1, Box A108), Eastsound, WA 98245. ☎ **360/376-2423.** 17 condos. TV TEL. May–Sept, $99.50–$130 condo for two; Sept–May, $69.50–$100 condo for two. Weekly rates available. AE, MC, V.

Situated on a rocky knoll and surrounded by Northwest-style gardens on the edge of Eastsound, these condominiums feel far removed from town. Ask for a view room and you'll wake up each morning to a fjordlike panorama down the length of the sound. There are both one- and two-bedroom accommodations here sleeping up to eight people. The condos are spacious and are all individually decorated and have fireplaces and balconies.

Rosario Resort & Spa

1 Rosario Way, Eastsound, WA 98245-2222. ☎ **360/376-2222** or 800/562-8820. 179 rms. $95–$150 double; $160–$220 suite. Lower rates midweek Sept–June. AE, DC, DISC, MC, V.

The 1904 Moran Mansion, an imposing white stucco building at the foot of a steep, forested hillside on the edge of Cascade Bay, is the centerpiece of the Rosario Resort. The mansion houses the resort's main dining room, lounge, spa, and library. Many of the rooms are a bit of a walk from the mansion up a steep hill. However, these rooms have fireplaces and good views. New owners are in the process of renovating most guest rooms and giving the resort a more contemporary look and feel.

Dining/Entertainment: The resort's restaurant provides water views and serves continental and Northwest cuisine, with dishes in the $12 to $18 range. The lounge is a casual little bar overlooking the water and has live piano music on weekend evenings. There are also evening pipe organ and piano recitals in the mansion's music room.

Services: Rental cars, massages, herbal wraps, skin-care services, aerobics classes.

Facilities: Three pools (one indoor and two outdoor), whirlpool, exercise room, beauty shop, tennis courts, marina.

✪ Spring Bay Inn

P.O. Box 97, Olga, WA 98279. ☎ **360/376-5531.** Fax 360/376-2193. 4 rms. $150–175 double. Rates include continental breakfast, brunch, and daily kayak tour. MC, V.

As one of the only waterfront B&Bs in the San Juans, this inn would deserve recommendation. However, innkeepers Sandy Playa and Carl Burger, both retired park rangers, make a stay here fun and educational, and the setting and inn itself are great for a romantic getaway. You can soak in the hot tub on the beach and watch the sunset, spot bald eagles from just outside the inn's front door, and best of all, go for a guided sea-kayak tour each morning. Before heading out on the water you're served a continental breakfast, and upon returning you get a filling brunch. The four guest rooms all have fireplaces, two have views from their tubs, and two have balconies.

✪ Turtleback Farm Inn

Rte. 1, Box 650, Eastsound, WA 98245. ☎ **360/376-4914.** 7 rms. Apr–Oct and weekends and holidays year round, $80–$160 double; Nov–Mar weekdays, $80–$110 double. Rates include full breakfast. Two-night minimum stay May–Oct, weekends, and holidays. MC, V.

Nowhere on Orcas will you find a more idyllic setting than at the Turtleback Farm Inn. This bright-green restored farmhouse overlooks 80 acres of farmland at the foot of Turtleback Mountain. Simply furnished with antiques, the guest rooms range from cozy to spacious, and each has its own special view. Our favorite room is the Meadow View Room, which has a private deck and clawfoot tub. You can spend your days wandering around the farm or you can just sit and breathe in the view. The day starts with a big farm breakfast served at valley-view tables set with bone china, silver, and linen. Finish your day with a nip of sherry by the fire, and you have the perfect Orcas Island country day.

Windsong Bed & Breakfast

P.O. Box 32, Orcas, WA 98280. ☎ **360/376-2500.** 4 rms. $115–$140 double. Rates include full breakfast. DISC, MC, V.

Housed in a converted 1917 schoolhouse not far from the ferry landing, this B&B offers large guest rooms, three of which have their own fireplaces. Owners Kim and Sam Haines have worked hard to turn this building into a comfortable inn and their hard work shows in the beautifully painted walls and other attractive touches. A large lawn surrounds the inn and deer can often be seen grazing here. Massages are available and there's a whirlpool for warm soaks.

The breakfasts, prepared by co-owner Sam Haines, are gourmet repasts that can include such dishes as reisling-poached pears and apples, crab cakes, and grape sorbet.

Moderate

Beach Haven Resort

Rte. 1, Box 12, Eastsound, WA 98245. ☎ **360/376-2288.** 11 cabins, 4 apts. $90–$95 double in an apt.; $110–$125 cabin for four to six. Minimum stay, seven nights in summer, three nights on May and Sept holidays, two nights the rest of the year. MC, V.

No TVs and no telephones! If this is your dream come true, read on; if the thought strikes fear in your heart, try someplace else. The Beach Haven is just what its name implies, and more. It's a forest haven as well. These little waterfront log cabins are fronted by a pebble beach and backed by a grove of old-growth trees. The setting is tranquil, the cabins rustic. Though the cabins date back 50 years, they have been taken care of and modernized a bit over the years. Still, don't expect first-class accommodations. Sheets and towels are provided, but there's no maid service. Each cabin does, however, have a kitchen.

Deer Harbor Resort & Marina

P.O. Box 200, Deer Harbor, WA 98243. ☎ **360/376-4420.** 12 rms, 10 cottages, 3 villas. TV. $99–$109 double; $129–$169 cottage; $229 villa. Lower rates off-season. AE, DISC, MC, V.

Located on the spectacular Deer Harbor inlet, this casual resort offers, in our opinion, the best views on the island. Set on an open hillside above the harbor, it looks across the water to a forested rock wall. At the mouth of the harbor are a few small islands. Add to this the marina and sailboats bobbing at anchor, and you have the quintessential island setting. The Deer Harbor is quiet even by Orcas standards. Our favorite accommodations are the restored 1935 cottages, each of which has its own deck (some with whirlpools), wood stove, and minirefrigerator. The view from the cottages is superb. Facilities at the resort include two hot tubs, an outdoor pool, and a restaurant.

ⓢ Orcas Hotel

P.O. Box 155, Orcas, WA 98280. ☎ **360/376-4300.** 12 rms, 2 with bath. $69–$95 double without bath, $125 double with half bath, $180 double with bath. Rates include full breakfast. AE, DISC, MC, V.

Located right at the Orcas ferry landing, this B&B is an ideal choice for anyone coming over without a car. On the other hand, the proximity of the ferry precludes the tranquil setting available at other island bed-and-breakfasts. Nonetheless, the Orcas is a beautiful old Victorian hotel and has been welcoming guests since 1904. The guest rooms vary in size, but all are carpeted and furnished with antiques and have down comforters or quilts on the beds. On the first floor of this three-story building you'll find a quiet lounge, bakery, café, and restaurant.

Inexpensive

✪ Doe Bay Village Resort

Star Rte., Box 86, Olga, WA 98279. ☎ **360/376-2291**. 24 cottages, 6 hostel beds, 30 campsites. $45–$92 double; $14.50 hostel bed; $12–$16 campsite. AE, DISC, MC, V.

Doe Bay is not for everyone. Let us say that up front. Formerly a New Age community, this funky collection of cottages and tiny cabins is now a sort of counterculture resort. The cottages are furnished in early Salvation Army and are generally clean. The dining room serves vegetarian meals, but many of the cottages also have their own kitchens. The folks who stay here tend to have similar interests—healthy foods, the outdoors, relaxation. You can't help but absorb a bit of the laid-back attitude when you check in here, especially after you check out the spring-fed hot tubs and sauna, which are available for an additional $3 per person. They're set on a big deck overlooking a picturesque little cove with a pebble beach. The tubs, sauna, and beach are clothing optional. For those on a really tight budget, there are campsites and even a hostel. Kayak tours operate from the resort, and massages are also available. If you'd just like to drop by for a few hours and soak in the tubs or sauna, you can do so for only $6. Because of the low rates, Doe Bay is very popular; reserve early, even in winter.

Camping

With 151 sites, **Moran State Park,** Star Route, Box 22, Eastsound, WA 98245 (☎ **360/376-2326**), is the most popular camping spot on the island (see above for park details). Reservations are recommended April to September and are accepted by mail beginning January 1. Additional campsites are available at the **Doe Bay Village Resort.** If you enjoy roughing it, there are hike-in or paddle-in sites at **Obstruction Pass State Park** at the south end of the east arm of the island. Keep in mind that there is no water available at this isolated and beautifully situated park.

WHERE TO DINE

For local ambience, soups, sandwiches, and café lattes served in large bowls, you can't beat **Roses Bakery Café** in Eastsound Square, Eastsound (☎ **360/ 376-4220**).

Expensive

Christina's

Horseshoe Hwy., Eastsound. ☎ **360/376-4904**. Reservations highly recommended. Main courses $14.50–$25. AE, CB, DC, MC. Wed–Mon 5:30–9pm (longer hours in summer); Sun brunch from 10am. NORTHWEST.

Located upstairs from the gas station on Main Street, Christina's has a beautiful view down the sound, just right for sunsets, and if the weather is pleasant, you can dine on the deck. The menu here is short, changes regularly, and features innovative cuisine prepared from local products. The entrées are a tad on the expensive side and not as interesting as the appetizers. You might find dishes such as a plump chicken sausage with chard and mustard, or crab dumpling with scallops and black-bean sauce for starters. The desserts can be uneven, but when they are good, they're heavenly. Christina's has a short but very well-chosen wine list.

Moderate
Bilbo's Festivo
N. Beach Rd., Eastsound. ☎ **360/376-4728.** Reservations highly recommended. Main courses $6–$16. MC, V. Summer, Mon–Fri 11:30am–2:30pm and 5–10pm, Sat–Sun 11:30am–2:30pm and 4:30–10pm; winter, shorter dinner hours. Closed lunch in winter. MEXICAN.

This old bungalow has been transformed into a southwestern hacienda with the addition of stucco, tiles, and some rounded concrete walls on the patio, and over the years Bilbo's has developed a reputation for its Mexican food and Southwest/ Northwest ambience. Entrées here can at times be lackluster, so you might want to stick to several rounds of appetizers accompanied by tart margaritas. Summers see the crowds lined up to get into the restaurant's patio where the barbecue grill stays fired up with mesquite.

La Famiglia Ristorante
A St. and Prune Alley. ☎ **360/376-2335.** Reservations recommended. Main courses $9–$17. AE, DISC, MC, V. Mon–Sat 11:30am–2:30pm and 5–9pm, Sun 5–9pm (longer dinner hours in summer). ITALIAN.

La Famiglia serves up fresh Italian fare with an emphasis on seafood dishes and pasta. The decor is simple, with a large deck for sunny days and big windows to let in the thin light on gray days. Start your meal with an unusual combination of herbed artichoke with fruit and cheese or perhaps some steamer clams with garlic bread. Be sure to ask about any oyster specials they might have. You'll find an excellent selection of California and Northwest wines here.

Ship Bay Oyster House
Horseshoe Hwy. ☎ **360/376-5886.** Reservations recommended. Main courses $13–$17. AE, MC, V. Summer, daily 5:30–10pm; winter, Tues–Sat 5:30–9pm. SEAFOOD.

About midway between Eastsound and the turnoff for the Rosario Resort you'll spot the Ship Bay. This old white house sits in a field high above the water. Should you arrive after dark and be tempted to walk over to the water, be aware that the restaurant's front yard ends in a sheer cliff. Inside, you'll find a traditional maritime decor and plenty of windows to let you gaze out to sea. Since this is an oyster house, you'd be remiss if you didn't have some bivalves with your meal. You can opt for oysters Fitzgerald, pan-fried yearling oysters, oyster shooters, and of course, fresh local oysters on the half shell. You can make a meal on oysters alone, but the entrée menu includes plenty of tempting dishes as well.

Inexpensive
✪ Café Olga
Horseshoe Hwy., Olga. ☎ **360/376-5098.** Reservations recommended. Main courses $5.75–$8; breakfast $2.75–$6.65. MC, V. Mar–Oct, daily 10am–6pm; Nov–Dec, daily 10am–5pm. Closed Jan–Feb. INTERNATIONAL.

Housed in an old strawberry-packing plant that dates back to the days when these islands were known for their fruit, Café Olga is the best place on the island for breakfast or lunch. Everything here is homemade, using fresh local produce whenever possible. The menu changes frequently but might include the likes of a torta made with Italian sausage or a chicken-and-cashew-salad sandwich. The soup du jour and a sandwich make for a very filling meal, and the blackberry pie is a special treat. This building also houses Orcas Island Artworks, a gallery representing more than 70 Orcas Island artists.

LOPEZ ISLAND

Of the three islands with accommodations, Lopez is the least developed. It's flatter (and less spectacular) than Orcas or San Juan, and consequently is the most popular with bicyclists who prefer easy grades over stunning panoramas. Lopez maintains more of its agricultural roots than either of the two previously mentioned islands, and likewise has fewer activities for tourists. If you just want to get away from it all and hole up with a good book for a few days, Lopez may be the place for you. Lopez Islanders are particularly friendly in that they wave to everyone they pass on the road. The custom has come to be known as the Lopez Wave.

If you aren't into the outdoors, you won't find much of anything to do on Lopez. Eight county parks and one state park provide plenty of access to the woods and water. Together these parks make it a breeze to tour the island by bicycle. You can rent bicycles from **Lopez Bicycle Works,** Fisherman Bay Road (☎ **360/ 468-2847**). If you'd like to have a guide to show you Lopez, Orcas, or the San Juan Islands, contact **Cycle San Juans,** Route 1, Lopez Island, WA 98261 (☎ **360/468-3251**), which offers tours starting at $35.

The first park off the ferry is **Odlin County Park,** Route 2, Lopez (☎ **360/ 468-2496**), which has 30 campsites along the water and also provides boating access and picnic tables. Athletic fields make this more of a community sports center than a natural area. A little farther south and over on the east side of the island you'll find **Spencer Spit State Park,** Route 2, Lopez (☎ **360/468-2251**), which has 35 campsites set amid tall fir trees. The forest meets the sea on a rocky beach that looks across a narrow channel to Frost Island. You can hike the trails through the forest or explore the beach.

Down at the south end of the island, you'll find the tiny **Shark Reef Sanctuary,** where a short trail leads through the forest to a rocky stretch of coast. Small islands offshore create strong currents that swirl past the rocks here. Seals and occasionally whales can be seen just offshore. This is our favorite picnic spot on the island.

If you want to explore the island's coastline by kayak, contact **Lopez Kayaks** (☎ **360/468-2847**), which charges $37.25 for a half-day trip.

Taste wine made from locally grown grapes at **Lopez Island Vineyards,** located about 2¹/₂ miles from the ferry landing toward Lopez Village on Fisherman Bay Road (☎ **360/468-3644**).

The island even has a nine-hole golf course—the **Lopez Golf Club** (☎ **360/ 468-2679**).

WHERE TO STAY

✪ The Inn at Swifts Bay

Rte. 2, Box 3402, Lopez Island, WA 98261. ☎ **360/468-3636.** Fax 360/468-3637. 2 rms, neither with bath; 3 suites; 1 luxury cabin. $75–$85 double; $125–$155 suite. Rates include full breakfast. AE, DISC, MC, V.

You'll find the Inn at Swifts Bay on the north end of Lopez Island, and though you can't actually see the bay from the inn, it's just a short walk down to the private beach. Innkeepers Robert Herrmann and Christopher Brandmeir do all they can to assure that their guests enjoy an idyllic stay on the island. A gourmet breakfast (one of the best we've ever had) in a cafélike setting starts the day, and after long hours of exploring the island, you can soak in the hot tub and then gather by the fire for a social hour. The decor is pleasantly cluttered in a comfortable way with a cozy living room and separate library. The premier rooms here are, of course, the suites, all of which have gas fireplaces and two of which have private entries and their own decks. These upstairs suites are large and private, just right for a special celebration.

The Islander Lopez Resort

Fisherman Bay Rd. (P.O. Box 197), Lopez Island, WA 98261. ☎ **360/468-2233** or 800/736-3434. 36 rms. TV. June–Sept, $80–$120 double; Oct–May, $55–$80 double. AE, MC, V.

Located about a mile from Lopez Village, the Islander Lopez may not look too impressive from the outside, but it's a very very comfortable lodging. All the rooms have great views of Fisherman Bay, and the more expensive rooms have coffeemakers, wet bars, microwaves, and refrigerators, and most rooms have balconies. The Islander offers such amenities as a full-service marina with kayak rentals, seasonal restaurant, lounge, outdoor pool, whirlpool, and adjacent bike-rental shop.

WHERE TO DINE

✪ Bay Café

Village Center, Lopez Village. ☎ **360/468-3700.** Reservations highly recommended. Main courses $12–$18. MC, V. Summer, Wed–Mon 5:30–9pm; the rest of the year, Wed–Sun 5:30–8:30pm. NORTHWEST.

Ask anyone on Lopez where to have dinner and you'll be sent to the Bay Café. Housed in an old waterfront building, the Bay Café is small and casual—no views here, just great food! The menu ranges the globe and changes frequently. The entrée list includes orange-rosemary grilled chicken with wild-rice risotto; wok-seared scallops mizutaki with stir-fried bok choy and noodles; chicken satay with curried noodles; or fettuccine with artichoke hearts, roasted garlic butter, sun-dried tomatoes, and feta cheese. Accompany your meal with a bottle of wine from Lopez Island Vineyard and you have the quintessential Lopez dinner.

⑤ Bucky's

Lopez Plaza, Lopez Village. ☎ **360/468-2595.** Reservations recommended in summer. Main courses $9.25–$15. AE, MC, V. Sun–Thurs 9am–9pm, Fri–Sat 9am–10pm (shorter hours in winter). AMERICAN.

This is where the locals hang out. It's small, with a laid-back island feeling and an outside deck. The food is consistently good—nothing fancy, just delicious. We had a black-and-blue burger with bleu cheese and Cajun spices, and it was a contender for "best burger." From the open grill the chef serves up succulent fish and chips and fettuccine Alfredo, and those wonderful Lopez Island mussels.

Gail's

Lopez Village. ☎ **360/468-2150.** Reservations recommended in summer. Main courses $12–$17; lunch $4–$8. DISC, MC, V. Summer, daily 11am–9pm; winter, daily 8am–2pm. SEAFOOD.

You'll find Gail's in the middle of Lopez Village with a big deck that looks out over Fisherman Bay. Mainstays of the menu include homemade baked goods, vegetable omelets, handmade pastas, soups, salads fresh from the garden, and dinner entrées such as Tiger shrimp in coconut-curry sauce. Choose a Northwest wine from the affordable wine list. We haven't run into any problem here personally, but we've heard that hours and food can be inconsistent.

4 Whidbey Island

30 miles N of Seattle, 40 miles S of Bellingham

At 45 miles in length, Whidbey Island is one of the largest islands in the continental United States, and, at only 30 miles from Seattle, it's a popular weekend getaway for Seattleites who come here seeking romance and relaxation. Shaped roughly like an elongated C, the island is a mix of farms, forests, bluffs, and beaches. Never more than a few miles wide, Whidbey offers views of the water at every turn of its winding country roads, which compel one to slow down and enjoy the scenery. Two historic towns, Langley and Coupeville, offer such urban amenities as excellent restaurants, unique shops, and art galleries—without sacrificing their village atmosphere. Charming bed-and-breakfast inns and one of the state's most luxurious small hotels pamper visitors to the island and provide the romantic surroundings that are so much a part of the Whidbey experience.

What is there to do on Whidbey? Next to nothing, and that's the island's main appeal. You don't have to do anything—you can just sit back and relax.

Lest you get the impression that Whidbey Island is heaven on earth, let us make you aware of the Whidbey Island Naval Air Station, which, with its thundering jets, has considerably altered the idyllic atmosphere of the island's northern half. Oak Harbor, the island's largest community is located just outside the base and is characterized by the sort of strip-mall sprawl that surrounds most military bases. For this reason, the island's bed-and-breakfast inns are located mostly in the island's southern half. It's partly because of what has happened to Oak Harbor that Ebey's Landing National Historic Reserve was created. When people who had moved to the island because of its tranquil atmosphere saw what was happening around Oak Harbor, they acted quickly to preserve some of the island's rural beauty, which is the very essence of Whidbey Island.

ESSENTIALS

GETTING THERE   From I-5, take Wash. 20 west at Burlington. The highway turns south before you reach Anacortes and crosses over the Deception Pass Bridge to reach the north end of Whidbey Island.

Washington State Ferries operate between Mukilteo and Clinton at the south end of the island (fares: $4.80 for a vehicle and driver, $2.30 for westbound passengers) and from Port Townsend to Keystone (fares: $7.10 for a vehicle and driver, $1.75 for passengers).

Harbor Airlines (☎ **360/675-6666** or 800/359-3220) has regular service between Oak Harbor Airport and Seattle, Olympia, Orcas Island, and San Juan Island. The fare from Seattle is $60 one way and $110 round-trip.

The **Anacortes–Oak Harbor–Sea-Tac Airporter** (☎ **360/679-0600** or 800/235-5247, 800/448-8443 in Washington) offers daily service from Sea-Tac International Airport. The one-way fare is $27 to $30 for adults, $24 to $26 for seniors, and $14 to $15 for children. Pickup points are at the Whidbey Island Naval Air Station, downtown Oak Harbor, and Skyline Marina in Anacortes.

VISITOR INFORMATION   Contact the **Central Whidbey Chamber of Commerce,** 5 S. Main St. (P.O. Box 152), Coupeville, WA 98239 (☎ **360/678-5434**).

GETTING AROUND   Car rentals are available from **Budget** in Oak Harbor. **Island Transit** (☎ **360/678-7771** or 360/321-6688) offers public bus service on Whidbey Island. However, buses don't operate on Sunday.

FESTIVALS   Each year in late April, Oak Harbor celebrates its Dutch heritage with the **Holland Happening Festival.**

EXPLORING THE ISLAND

If you're coming from the south and take the ferry from Mukilteo to Clinton, then the best place to start exploring Whidbey Island is in the village of **Langley,** which lies to the north of Clinton. To reach Langley, take Langley Road off Wash. 525. Langley is a compact little village with a mix of sophisticated shops, interesting art galleries, and good, moderately priced restaurants occupying the restored wooden commercial buildings along the waterfront. First Street Park, right in downtown Langley, provides access to a rocky beach and offers views of Saratoga Passage and the distant Cascades.

Coupeville, just a little bit north of the turnoff for the ferry to Port Townsend, is another little historic waterfront village. A concentration of Victorian homes on large lots gives the town a more spacious and open feel than Langley has. Coupeville was founded in 1852 by Capt. Thomas Coupe, and the captain's 1853 home is among those in town that have been restored. The quiet charm of yester-year is Coupeville's greatest appeal. Several Victorian homes have now become bed-and-breakfast inns and offer visitors a chance to immerse themselves in the village history. As in Langley, old wooden commercial buildings along Coupeville's waterfront are now home to some interesting shops and good restaurants.

The **Island County Historical Society Museum,** on the corner of Alexander and Front streets in Coupeville (☎ **360/678-3310**), is the best place to learn about the island's seafaring, farming, and military history. It's open daily from 10am to 5pm (closed Tuesday through Thursday in winter). Here in Coupeville you can also find out about the **Ebey's Landing National Historic Reserve,** which includes much of the land around town. The reserve, one of the first of its kind in the nation, was created "to preserve and protect a rural community which provides an unbroken historic record from the nineteenth century exploration and settlement of Puget Sound to the present time." There is no visitor center for the reserve, but there is an information kiosk near the dock in Coupeville and the adjacent museum has copies of an informative brochure about the reserve.

Oak Harbor, at the north end of the island, was settled by Dutch immigrants, and here, at City Beach Park, which has a swimming lagoon, you'll find a large Dutch windmill. As the largest town on the island, Oak Harbor lacks the charm of Langley and Coupeville.

Deception Pass State Park (☎ **360/675-2417**), at the northern tip of the island, is the most popular state park in Washington. What draws the crowds are miles of beaches, quiet coves, freshwater lakes, dark forests, hiking trails, camping, and the views of Deception Pass, the churning channel between Whidbey Island and Fidalgo Island. A high bridge connects these two large islands by way of a smaller island in the middle of Deception Pass, and overlooks at the bridge allow you to gaze down on the tidal waters that surge and swirl between the islands. In the middle of the island, you'll find **Fort Casey State Park** (☎ **360/678-4519** or 360/678-5632), a former military base 3 miles south of Coupeville. The fort was built in the 1890s to guard Puget Sound and still has its gun batteries. In addition to the fort, the park includes the 1897 Admiralty Head lighthouse, beaches, hiking trails, a campground, and an underwater reserve for scuba divers. A few miles north of this park is the smaller **Fort Ebey State Park** (☎ 360/ **678-4636** or 360/678-3195), another former military site built to protect the sound. There are excellent views of the Strait of Juan de Fuca, as well as a campground, hiking trails, a lake for swimming and fishing, and a scuba-diving area. Four miles northwest of Freeland, you'll find **South Whidbey State Park** (☎ **360/331-4559**), with its 2 miles of shoreline, hiking trails, and campground. Smaller parks on the island include **Rhododendron State Park,** 1 mile east of Coupeville, where June brings a spectacular floral display; **Keystone State Park,** near the Keystone Ferry landing for ferries to Port Townsend, which is an underwater park for scuba divers; and **Joseph Whidbey State Park,** west of Oak Harbor, which has great westerly views and a long sandy beach.

Urbanites come to Whidbey Island seeking rural idylls, and they find them in the vistas of rolling farmlands. A few farms are even open to the public. **Whidbeys Greenbank Berry Farm,** on Wonn Road in Greenbank (☎ **360/678-7700**), is the largest loganberry farm in the country and the producer of Whidbeys, a loganberry liqueur. A gourmet foods shop and tasting room (open daily from 10am to 5pm) and picnic tables make this a great spot for a picnic. **Hummingbird Farm,** 2041 N. Zylstra Rd. in Oak Harbor (☎ **360/679-5044** or 800/201-8335), is a herb and everlasting (dried-flower) farm with a display garden, shop, and fields of herbs and flowers. It's open Monday through Saturday from 9:30am to 5:30pm and on Sunday from 11am to 5pm.

If you'd like to get out on the waters surrounding Whidbey Island, you have a few options. **Penn's Cove Kayak Adventures,** on the Coupeville Wharf (☎ **360/ 678-3545**), offers kayak rentals for those who'd like to explore Penn Cove on their own. The rate is $15 per hour for a double kayak. The *Cutty Sark,* which is operated by Aeolian Ventures, 2072 W. Captain Whidbey Inn Rd. (☎ **360/ 678-4097**), offers scheduled day-sail cruises for $37.50 per person, or you can charter the boat for $60 an hour with a two-hour minimum.

The country roads of Whidbey Island are perfect for exploring by bicycle. If you didn't bring your own bike, you can rent one from **All Island Bicycle,** 302 Main St., Coupeville (☎ **360/678-3351**). Rental rates are $8 per hour and $19 per day.

WHERE TO STAY
IN LANGLEY

✪ The Inn at Langley
400 First St., Langley, WA 98260. ☎ **360/221-3033.** 24 rms. TV TEL. $165–$245 double. Rates include continental breakfast. AE, MC, V.

With its weathered cedar shingles, exposed beams, works of contemporary art, and colorful garden, this lodge evokes all the best of life in the Northwest. The inn's four floors jut out from a bluff overlooking Saratoga Passage, and with 180° views from every room, you'll have plenty of opportunities to spot orca whales and bald eagles from your window. The guest rooms have a Zen-like quality that soothes and relaxes. Pale-gray walls, original artwork, and big balconies with pillow-covered bench seats are luxurious enough, but it's the bathrooms that are the star attractions here. Each comes with an open shower and a two-person whirlpool tub that looks out over the water. Pull back an opaque sliding window and you also get a view of the room's fireplace.

The inn's restaurant serves a five-course prix-fixe dinner focusing on Northwest flavors every Friday and Saturday night for $45.

✪ Log Castle

3273 E. Saratoga Rd., Langley, WA 98260. ☎ **360/221-5483.** 4 rms. $90–$115 double. Rates include full breakfast. MC, V.

A mile and a half outside of Langley, on a hillside overlooking Saratoga Passage and distant Mount Baker, stands another of Whidbey Island's unique inns. Though it's not exactly a castle, this sprawling log home is certainly grand in concept and construction. Everywhere you look inside this fascinating home are logs—the walls, the beams, the tables, the shelves, the door handles. Of the four rooms, the two turret rooms are the most popular, and the third-story octagonal turret room is the inn's favorite. From the room's five picture windows there are superb views of water and hills.

IN COUPEVILLE

✪ The Captain Whidbey Inn

2072 W. Captain Whidbey Inn Rd., Coupeville, WA 98239. ☎ **360/678-4097** or 800/366-4097. 25 rms, 13 with bath; 2 suites; 4 cottages; 3 houses. $85–$95 double without bath, $125 double with bath; $145 suite; $150 cottage; $175–$195 house. Rates include continental breakfast. AE, DC, DISC, MC, V.

Three miles west of Coupeville off Madrona Way stands one of the Northwest's most unique inns. Shady, quiet grounds offer a tranquil setting that has revived flagging spirits for almost a century. Built in 1907 of small madrona logs, the historic inn is architecturally fascinating, a bit of American folk art. The rooms in the main building are small and lack private bathrooms, but they manage to capture the feel of the island's seafaring past. Suites, cottages, and even a few houses are available for those who need more room.

The inn's dining room overlooks Penn Cove and serves creative Northwest cuisine that often features the inn's own mussels. Entrée prices range from $9 to $15. An adjacent bar offers good views of the cove as well as unusual cocktails.

The Colonel Crockett Farm

1012 S. Fort Casey Rd., Coupeville, WA 98239. ☎ **360/678-3711.** 5 rms. $65–$95 double. Rates include full breakfast. MC, V.

Built in 1855, this stately farmhouse is surrounded by rolling meadows and looks out over Crockett Lake to Admiralty Bay. The views are some of the best on the island, and no other inn on Whidbey better captures the island's idyllic rural feel. A huge red barn with a stone foundation dwarfs the house itself. A wood-paneled library with slate fireplace and solarium with wicker furniture provide guests with plenty of comfortable places to relax when they aren't out exploring the island. The guest rooms are furnished with antiques. The Crockett Room, with its canopied four-poster bed and clawfoot tub, is our favorite.

⑤ The Coupeville Inn

200 NW Coveland St., Coupeville, WA 98239. ☎ **360/678-6668,** or 800/247-6162 in Washington and British Columbia. 24 rms. TV TEL. $53.50–$85 double. Rates include continental breakfast. AE, DISC, MC, V.

Located right in the heart of Coupeville's historic district, and designed to fit in with the surrounding historic architecture, this modern motel offers large, comfortable rooms overlooking Coupeville and Penn Cove. All the rooms have small balconies.

Fort Casey Inn

1124 S. Engle Rd., Coupeville, WA 98239. ☎ **360/678-8792.** 9 apts. $75–$110 apt for two. Rates include full breakfast. AE, MC, V.

Built in 1909 as officers' quarters for Fort Casey, this row of four Georgian revival houses now serves as a bed-and-breakfast inn offering spacious two-bedroom accommodations. Eagles, military memorabilia, and a red, white, and blue color scheme reflect the houses' history, and Fort Casey State Park and the beach are just a short walk away. The grand old homes are each divided into two apartments that have farm kitchens and spacious living rooms on the first floor and two bedrooms and a bathroom with clawfoot tub on the second floor. Big front porches overlook Crockett Lake.

WHERE TO DINE

Two of the island's best dining rooms are associated with hotels that have been described above. The **Country Kitchen** at the Inn at Langley serves what most people agree are the finest meals on the island. However, these five-course, prix-fixe dinners are only available on Friday and Saturday evenings. The **Captain Whidbey Inn** also serves excellent meals in its water-view dining room. See "Where to Stay," above for details.

IN LANGLEY

✪ Café Langley

113 First St. ☎ **360/221-3090.** Reservations recommended. Main courses $13.75–$17. AE, MC, V. Sun–Mon and Wed–Thurs 11:30am–2:30pm and 5–8pm, Tues 5–8pm, Fri–Sat 11:30am–2:30pm and 5–9pm. Closed Tues Nov–Apr. GREEK/MEDITERRANEAN.

This diminutive café, with its red-tile floors, frosted-glass room divider, and white stucco walls, conjures up sunnier climes with its flavorful dishes. Though many of the dishes are faithfully Greek, some of the most popular offerings display a Northwest flare. The Dungeness crab cakes are served with a Mediterranean concasse and the local Penn Cove mussels are steamed in olive oil, garlic, and saffron vermouth. These latter are available as either an appetizer or an entrée. Weekly specials add yet another dimension to the menu.

Star Bistro

201½ First St. ☎ **360/221-2627.** Reservations recommended. Main courses $7–$18. AE, MC, V. Mon–Thurs 11:30am–8:30pm, Fri–Sat 11:30am–10pm, Sun noon–8:30pm. NORTHWEST.

Up on the second floor of one of Langley's old commercial buildings is an outpost of urban chic. Big black-and-white floor tiles fairly shout the word "bistro," and bold splashes of color everywhere provide a counterpoint. Creamy pasta dishes, flavorful salads, creative sandwiches, and fresh seafoods are all reliable choices, and in addition there are nightly specials. On sunny days everyone heads out to the rooftop patio.

IN COUPEVILLE

Captain's Galley

10 Front St. ☎ **360/678-0241.** Reservations recommended summer evenings. Main courses $12.50–$16. MC, V. Mon–Fri 11am–10pm, Sat–Sun 8am–10pm. STEAK/SEAFOOD.

Whidbey Island is surprisingly short on waterfront restaurants, but the Captain's Galley should satisfy those who crave a view of the water with their meal. The menu leans toward the flavors of the Mediterranean, and the dishes are generally well prepared. A favorite is the prime rib with a crust of rosemary, garlic, cracked black pepper, and olive oil. The fresh catch of the day is often your best seafood choice, but we also like the sautéed prawns with garlic-cream sauce. We also can't resist having some local Penn Cove mussels when we stop here.

Christopher's
23 Front St. ☎ **360/678-5480.** Reservations recommended. Main courses $12.50–$16.50. AE, CB, DC, DISC, MC, V. Wed–Thurs and Sat–Sun 5–9pm, Fri 11:30am–2pm and 5–9pm. NORTHWEST.

Located in the back of a warehouselike building that now houses a small collection of shops, Christopher's offers some of the most imaginative cuisine on the island. The restaurant is divided into two dining rooms and a lounge area, and also has a wine room where you can peruse the racks. The favored dining room is done up to resemble a library in an old home, which is a bit of a surprise in such a setting. The menu ranges the world and you might find roast pork tenderloin with a raspberry-zinfandel-cream sauce or shrimp and feta cheese baked in filo.

Rosi's Garden Restaurant
606 N. Main St. ☎ **360/678-3989.** Reservations recommended. Main courses $12–$16. MC, V. Daily 5–10pm. NORTHWEST/ITALIAN.

Located a few blocks from the water, this little Victorian cottage dates back to 1906. On the front porch and inside the old house you'll find a few tables and a quiet setting for a romantic dinner. Local Penn Cove mussels here show up in a wine, garlic, cream, and basil broth that's creamy and fragrant and available as an appetizer or an entrée. Entrées include preparations of halibut, salmon, chicken, calimari, prime rib, and gnocchi.

5 Tacoma

32 miles S of Seattle, 31 miles N of Olympia, 93 miles S of Port Townsend

In 1883 Tacoma became the end of the line for the Northern Pacific Railroad and the city's fate as the industrial center of the Puget Sound area was sealed. Things have changed a bit since the city's waterfront was lined with smoke-belching lumber and paper mills, and Tacoma has almost broken free from its old image as a polluted blue-collar city. In recent years the city has reclaimed a major portion of its waterfront along Ruston Way and turned it into an attractive park lined with restaurants. Sure, you can still stand in downtown's Fireman's Park and look down on an industrial wasteland, but if you then turn around, you'll be facing a new, revitalized Tacoma where the arts are flourishing and historic buildings are being preserved and renovated. Despite the city's continuing makeover, it is Point Defiance Park, and all the park's many attractions, that remains the city's star feature.

ESSENTIALS

GETTING THERE   Tacoma is on I-5 at the junction of Wash. 16, which is the main route north through the Kitsap Peninsula to Port Townsend and the rest of the Olympic Peninsula. Wash. 7 from the Mount Rainier area leads into downtown Tacoma from the south.

Seattle-Tacoma International Airport is located 22 miles north of Tacoma. **Capital Airporter** (☎ **360/754-7113**) operates an airport shuttle service; the fare is $13 one way to downtown Tacoma.

Amtrak has service to Tacoma. The station is at 1001 Puyallup Ave.

VISITOR INFORMATION   Contact the **Tacoma–Pierce County Visitor & Convention Bureau,** 906 Broadway (P.O. Box 1754), Tacoma, WA 98401 (☎ **206/627-2836** or 800/272-2662), or the **Tacoma Visitor Information Center,** 440 E. 25th St., Tacoma, WA 98421 (☎ **206/272-7801**).

GETTING AROUND   See "Getting Around" in Chapter 5 on Seattle for information on renting cars at Sea-Tac International Airport. If you need a taxi, contact **Yellow Cab** (☎ **206/472-3303**). Public bus service is provided by **Pierce Transit** (☎ **206/581-8000**); the fare is 90¢, and most bus routes start at 10th and Commerce streets downtown.

WHAT TO SEE & DO
POINT DEFIANCE PARK

Point Defiance Park (☎ **206/591-3690**), on the north side of town at the end of Pearl Street, is Tacoma's center of activity and one of the largest urban parks in the country. In the park are many of the city's main attractions, including the Point Defiance Zoo and Aquarium, Fort Nisqually, Camp 6, and Never Never Land. Founded in 1888, the park represents Tacoma's farsightedness in preserving one of the region's scenic points of land. Winding through the wooded park is **Five Mile Drive,** which connects all the park's main attractions as well as the picnic areas, and hiking and biking trails. Also in the park are a rose garden, a Japanese garden, a rhododendron garden, and a native-plant garden. You can reach the park by following Ruston Way or Pearl Street north.

✪ Point Defiance Zoo and Aquarium
5400 N. Pearl St. ☎ **206/591-5337.** Admission $6.75 adults, $6.25 seniors, $5 children 5–17, $2.50 children 3–4. Memorial Day–Labor Day, daily 10am–7pm; Labor Day–Memorial Day, daily 10am–4pm. Closed the third Fri in July, Thanksgiving, and Dec 25.

This highly regarded zoo focuses on the wildlife of the Pacific Rim countries, and to that end you'll find animals from such far-flung locations as the Arctic tundra, Southeast Asia, and the Andes Mountains. The Rocky Shores exhibit features marine mammals, including beluga whales. The Jewels of the Sea exhibit sheds a new light on jellyfish. Other exhibits include a northern Pacific aquarium, a Northwest tidepool, and a tropical coral reef aquarium that's home to more than 40 sharks. At the farm zoo, kids can pet various animals.

Fort Nisqually Historic Site
5400 N. Pearl St. ☎ **206/591-5339.** Free admission. Memorial Day–Labor Day, daily 11am–7pm (museum, noon–6pm); Labor Day–Memorial Day, Wed–Sun 9am–5pm (museum, 1–4pm).

Fort Nisqually was a trading post founded in 1833 by the Hudson's Bay Company for the purpose of acquiring beaver pelts. However, it was established at a time when the fur trade was in decline and was soon moved to a new location and converted to a commercial farming business. This reconstruction, built in the 1930s, is based on the design of that second fort. Inside the stockade walls are two original buildings and several reconstructed buildings. Note that though the fort is open daily in summer, only the museum itself is open on Monday and Tuesday. Also, once a month there's a living-history day with interpreters dressed in period costumes.

Camp 6 Logging Museum

5400 N. Pearl St. ☎ **206/752-0047.** Museum, free; logging train rides, $2 adults, $1 seniors and children. Mid-Jan to Mar and Oct, Wed–Sun 10am–4pm; Apr–Memorial Day, Wed–Sun 10am–5pm; Memorial Day–Sept, Wed–Fri 10am–6pm, Sat–Sun 10am–7pm. Closed Nov–mid-Jan.

This museum focuses on the days of steam power in Washington logging history. Exhibits include plenty of steam equipment as well as old bunkhouses and a railcar camp. This latter was a rolling logging camp with bunkhouses built on railroad cars. On weekends in spring and summer, Camp 6 offers rides on an old logging train.

Never Never Land

5400 N. Pearl St. ☎ **206/591-5845.** Admission $2.25 adults, $1.75 seniors and children 13–17, $1.25 children 3–12. Mar and Sept, Sat–Sun 11am–5pm; Apr–May, daily 11am–5pm; June–Aug, daily 11am–6pm. Closed Oct–Feb.

The kids will love seeing life-size figures of famous fairy-tale characters such as Humpty Dumpty, the Big Bad Wolf, Mother Goose, Peter Rabbit, Little Red Riding Hood, Hansel and Gretel, and Goldilocks and the Three Bears. Best of all, the park is located amid deep, dark forests that are straight out of the Grimm brothers' fairy tales.

MUSEUMS

Tacoma Art Museum

1123 Pacific Ave. ☎ **206/272-4258.** Admission $3 adults, $2 seniors and students, $1 children 6–12, free for children 5 and under; free for everyone on Tues. Tues–Wed and Fri–Sat 10am–5pm, Thurs 10am–7pm (to 8pm on the third Thurs), Sun noon–5pm.

A small but far-reaching permanent collection features works by such artists as Degas, Renoir, Corot, Pissarro, Edward Hopper, and Roy Lichtenstein. However, the museum's greatest claim to fame is the Dale Chihuly Retrospective Gallery. Chihuly, a Northwest glass artist, is widely acclaimed as the nation's foremost creator of art glass. This is the only comprehensive public display of his works. Additionally, there are exhibits of Japanese woodblock prints, Chinese imperial robes, Native American arts, and a collection of Soviet art.

Washington State Historical Society Museum

1911 Pacific Ave. ☎ **206/593-2830.** Admission $7 adults, $5 students 13–17, $4 children 6–12, $3 children 3–5. Tues–Wed and Fri–Sat 10am–5pm, Thurs 10am–8pm, Sun 11am–5pm.

At press time this museum was closed while it moved into a new building. The museum is scheduled to open in the fall of 1996 with extensive new displays on the history of Washington. Many of the displays will be interactive.

Fort Lewis Military Museum

Fort Lewis, Bldg. 4320, Main St. (at Exit 120 off I-5). ☎ **206/967-7206.** Free admission. Wed–Sun noon–4pm.

The Fort Lewis Military Museum is housed in a chaletlike building built in 1918 as an inn for soldiers and visitors to the fort. Displays chronicle the history of Fort Lewis and the U.S. Army in the Northwest. An outdoor park features historic vehicles and heavy equipment.

The Children's Museum of Tacoma

925 Court C. ☎ **206/627-2436.** Admission $3 per person. Tues–Fri 10am–5pm, Sat 10am–4pm, Sun noon–4pm.

With hands-on exhibits, this downtown museum addresses topics of interest to children in the areas of science, the arts, and creative play. Exhibits tend to change every year or two.

W. W. Seymour Botanical Conservatory

In Wright Park, 316 S. G St. ☎ **206/591-5330.** Free admission. Daily 8am–4:20pm.

Constructed in 1908, this elegant Victorian conservatory is one of only three of its kind on the West Coast. More than 200 species of exotic plants are housed in the huge greenhouse, which is built of more than 12,000 panes of glass. The conservatory stands in Wright Park, which has more than 800 trees of 100 species and is a shady retreat from downtown's pavement.

OTHER TACOMA PARKS

Although Point Defiance Park is Tacoma's premier park, Tacoma's **Ruston Way Parks** rank a close second. Once jammed with smoking, decaying industrial buildings and piers, the Tacoma waterfront was an industrial area of national infamy. However, since the city of Tacoma reclaimed the shore of Commencement Bay and turned it into parkland, it has become one of the most attractive waterfront parks on Puget Sound. With grassy areas, a sandy beach, a public fishing pier, and a paved pathway, the waterfront is popular with strollers, cyclists, and in-line skaters.

Downtown at the corner of A Street and South Ninth Street you'll find the tiny **Fireman's Park,** which has the world's tallest totem poles as well as a view of the Port of Tacoma below. After gazing down on the port, if you want to have a closer look, stop by the **Port of Tacoma Observation Tower** off East 11th Street. Here you can watch as ships from around the world are loaded and unloaded.

HISTORIC DISTRICTS & BUILDINGS

Tacoma has quite a few historic buildings, the most noticeable of which is **Union Station** at 1717 Pacific Ave. Built in the beaux arts style as the terminal for the first transcontinental railroad to reach the Northwest, the imposing building is now home to the federal courts and is the future home of the Washington State Historical Society Museum. In the lobby of this building you'll find a glass installation by Dale Chihuly.

Stadium High School, at 111 N. E St., is a French château–style structure that was built as a hotel and later converted to a high school. The school is the centerpiece of the historic **Stadium District,** which is at the north end of Broadway and has more than 100 Victorian homes and many little shops and restaurants. At the south end of the Stadium District is the **Old City Hall Historic District,** which is the city's main antiques neighborhood. **Freighthouse Square,** near the Tacoma Dome at the corner of 25th and East D streets, is housed in the renovated Milwaukee Railroad freight house and is a public market along the lines of Seattle's Pike Place Market. The **Proctor district** is in Tacoma's north end, about midway between downtown and Point Defiance Park along Proctor Street. This neighborhood is filled with shops offering Northwest crafts. There are also several cafés in this neighborhood.

At the Tacoma Visitor Information Center or Tacoma Visitors Bureau you can pick up brochures on the city's historic buildings.

WHERE TO STAY

Tacoma suffers from a pronounced shortage of hotels. Aside from the Sheraton and a few bed-and-breakfast inns, your only options are chain motels along the Interstate. If you're interested in staying at a bed-and-breakfast, contact **A Greater Tacoma Bed-n-Breakfast Reservation Service** (☎ 206/759-4088).

In addition to the following accommodation, inexpensive chain motels in the Tacoma area include the following (see the Appendix for a list of toll-free telephone numbers): **Travelodge Tacoma,** 8820 S. Hosmer St., Tacoma, WA 98444 (☎ **206/539-1152**), charging $50 to $70 double; **Comfort Inn,** 5601 Pacific Hwy. E., Tacoma, WA 98424 (☎ **206/926-2301**), charging $51 to $65 double; and **Days Inn Tacoma Mall,** 6802 S. Tacoma Mall Blvd., Tacoma, WA 98409-9924 (☎ **206/475-5900**), charging $57 to $70 double.

Sheraton Tacoma Hotel

1320 Broadway Plaza, Tacoma, WA 98402. ☎ **206/572-3200** or 800/845-9466. Fax 206/591-4105. 319 rms, 11 suites. A/C TV TEL. $85–$133 double; $140–$400 suite. AE, CB, DC, DISC, ER, JCB, MC, V. Valet parking $8; self-parking $4.

This 26-story downtown high-rise is Tacoma's biggest and best hotel. Art deco styling and a skylit atrium lobby provide both grandeur and character. The guest rooms, unfortunately, are none too large, but are both comfortable and tastefully decorated. For more personal services such as evening turndown, morning newspaper, and a continental breakfast, opt for a room on one of the concierge floors.

Dining/Entertainment: Up on the 26th floor you'll find an Italian restaurant serving both northern and southern Italian dishes. Down on the mezzanine level there's a more casual café. There's a quiet lounge just off the lobby, while a second lounge provides a more lively atmosphere, with dancing to recorded music.

Services: Concierge, room service, valet/laundry service, access to exercise facilities at the adjacent YMCA.

Facilities: Whirlpool, shoeshine stand.

WHERE TO DINE

⑤ Antique Sandwich Company

5102 N. Pearl St. ☎ **206/752-4069.** Reservations not accepted. Sandwiches $3–$6.50. MC, V. Summer, daily 7am–8pm; winter, daily 7am–7pm (later on Tues all year). SANDWICHES/SALADS.

Located in Tacoma's Ruston neighborhood just a few blocks from Point Defiance, the Antique Sandwich Company serves basic sandwiches and salads at very reasonable rates. What makes the sandwich shop memorable is its uncontrived old-fashioned feel. Turkish rugs hang on the walls and there's an antique back bar behind the counter. A couch, piano, and small stage are signs of the sandwich shop's other life as a live-music venue. At lunch, this place is popular with both families and local office workers.

Boathouse Grill

In Point Defiance Park, 5910 N. Waterfront Dr. ☎ **206/756-7336.** Reservations not accepted. Main courses $7.25–$12. DISC, MC, V. Summer, Sun–Thurs 7am–9pm, Fri–Sat 7am–9:30pm; winter, daily 7am–9pm. SEAFOOD.

The Boathouse is a Tacoma institution. The first boathouse at Point Defiance was built in 1903, and after fires ravaged this building in 1974 and 1984, a completely new Boathouse was built in 1986. This current incarnation resembles the original and still has the same great view of Vashon Island and Gig Harbor. The menu has a lot of deep-fried seafood, but also includes such dishes as smoked salmon fettuccine, hot crab pasta salad, and a tortellini salad with smoked salmon, artichokes, and mushrooms.

Harbor Lights

2761 Ruston Way. ☎ **206/752-8600.** Reservations recommended. Main courses $11–$30; lunch $4.75–$9. AE, CB, DC, DISC, MC, V. Mon–Thurs 11am–11pm, Fri 11am–1am, Sat noon–1am, Sun 2–9pm. SEAFOOD.

The oldest restaurant on the Ruston Way waterfront, Harbor Lights has an air of faded elegance about it. The restaurant is quite a bit smaller than the newer dining establishments along this section of waterfront and lacks any outside dining, but the views are the same. A collection of autographed celebrity photos attests to the restaurant's popularity and position as a Tacoma institution. The menu is extensive and portions are large, but try to find room for the clam chowder, which is made from a 1919 family recipe. Though the crab dishes are a bit pricey, there's a good selection. There's also a long list of oyster preparations including one tasty dish that's prepared with oysters, bacon, and green peppers, all in a tomato sauce.

The Lobster Shop

4015 Ruston Way. ☎ **206/756-9040.** Reservations recommended. Main courses $12–$20. AE, CB, DC, DISC, MC, V. Mon–Thurs 4:30–9:30pm, Fri–Sat 4:30–10:30pm, Sun 9:30am–2pm (brunch) and 4:30–9pm. SEAFOOD.

This is the most upscale of the Ruston Way seafood places and offers outside seating and views, views, views. Starters include a respectable New England–style clam chowder (a rarity in the Northwest) and a good lobster bisque. But the appetizer not to miss is the hot Dungeness crab dip, made with crab, artichoke hearts, onions, and Parmesan. Dishes on the main menu are reliable continental standards, but the daily fresh sheet has more creative dishes. The crab cakes, here served with a red-currant sauce, and the cioppino are always good bets.

Pacific Rim

100 S. Ninth St. ☎ **206/627-1009.** Reservations recommended. Main courses $10–$17. CB, DC, DISC, MC, V. Mon–Thurs 11am–10pm, Fri–Sat 5pm–midnight. NORTHWEST.

Housed in a small historic building in downtown, Pacific Rim is Tacoma's purveyor of creative Northwest cuisine. The menu keeps up with the times, changing regularly, and prices are surprisingly reasonable for the sort of creativity you find here. Currently, sun-dried tomatoes, fresh fruit, and smoked salmon are making frequent appearances under different guises. There are always plenty of delicious and beautiful desserts available.

TACOMA AFTER DARK

Opened in 1983, the **Tacoma Dome,** 2727 E. D St. (☎ **206/272-3663**), is the world's largest wood-domed arena and, with seating for 23,000 people, is the site of concerts, sporting events, and other large exhibitions. Smaller productions take to the stages at the **Broadway Center for the Performing Arts,** 901 Broadway Plaza (☎ **206/591-5894**), which consists of two historic theaters. The **Pantages** is a renovated vaudeville theater built in 1918. Its terra-cotta facade is done in a neoclassical style. The **Rialto Theatre,** 310 S. Ninth St., is a classic Italianate movie palace, built the same year as the Pantages. Together these two theaters present a wide variety of nationally recognized theater, music, and dance. Local performing arts companies that appear at these two theaters include the **Tacoma Philharmonic,** the **Tacoma Symphony,** and the **Tacoma Opera** (tickets run $5 to $28).

Tacoma supports a lively theater scene that includes the **Tacoma Little Theatre,** 210 N. I St. (☎ 206/272-2481), which claims to be the oldest continuously performing theater west of the Mississippi and has been staging plays for more than 75 years (tickets are $8 to $10). The **Tacoma Actors Guild,** 901 Broadway Plaza (☎ 206/272-2145), is Tacoma's premier professional theater company and presents seven productions a year, including both well-known and more experimental plays. Performances are held in the Theatre on the Square right next door to the Pantages Theatre (tickets cost $15 to $26).

SIDE TRIPS FROM TACOMA
GIG HARBOR

Connecting Tacoma to the Kitsap Peninsula, the **Tacoma Narrows Bridge** is the fifth-largest suspension bridge in the world and was built to replace the original bridge, which was known as Gallopin' Gertie. This earlier bridge, which got its name from the way it undulated during high winds, lasted only four months after it was completed in 1940. During a not-uncommon wind storm, the bridge shook itself apart. Today's bridge, though it often experiences high winds, is far more stable.

On the bridge's far side you'll find the quaint waterfront town of Gig Harbor, with its interesting little shops, art galleries, seafood restaurants, and fleet of commercial fishing boats. Framing this picture of Puget Sound's past is the snowcapped bulk of Mount Rainier. On the waterfront you'll find **Rent-a-Boat,** 8827 N. Harborview Dr. (☎ 206/858-7341), where you can rent a sailboat, powerboat, pedal boat, or kayak. Rates range from $8 to $75 an hour for the various types of watercraft. Guided sea kayak trips are also available from **Northwest Passages** (☎ 206/851-7987). Tours cost between $20 and $60.

Where to Dine

Tides Tavern

2925 Harborview Dr. ☎ **206/858-3982.** Reservations not accepted. Meals $3.25–$13. AE, MC, V. Mon–Thurs 11am–10pm, Fri–Sat 11am–10:30pm, Sun 11am–9:30pm. AMERICAN.

Though this is basically just a tavern with an extensive menu, it's by far the most popular dining spot in town and is located over the water at the east end of town. The menu is basic tavern fare—burgers, sandwiches, and pizzas—but it's all tasty if not entirely memorable. On Friday and Saturday nights there's live music. Because this is a tavern, you must be 21 or older to eat here.

STEILACOOM

Steilacoom was founded in 1854 by a Maine sea captain and is Washington's oldest incorporated town. Once a bustling seaport, the quiet little community is today a National Historic District with 32 preserved historic buildings. Right in town, there's the **Nathaniel Orr Home** and **Pioneer Orchard,** which was built between 1854 and 1857 and contains original furnishings. It's open May to September only, on Sunday from 1 to 4pm; admission is $2. The **Steilacoom Town Hall and Museum,** 112 Main St. (☎ 206/584-4133), houses exhibits on the town's pioneer history. It's open March to October, Tuesday through Sunday from 1 to 4pm; in February, November, and December, on Sunday from 1 to 4pm (closed January). At the **Steilacoom Tribal Cultural Center,** 1515 Lafayette St. (☎ 206/584-6308), you'll find a museum with displays on the area's Steilacoom tribe. It's open Tuesday through Sunday from 10am to 4pm; admission is $2 for

adults and $1 for seniors and students. At **Bair Drug & Hardware Store** (☎ 206/
588-9668) you'll find an operating 1906 soda fountain; it's open Monday through
Friday from 9am to 4pm and on Saturday and Sunday from 8am to 4pm. To reach
Steilacoom, take I-5 south from Tacoma to Exit 127 and follow the signs.

Where to Dine

E. R. Rogers

1702 Commercial St. ☎ **206/582-0280.** Reservations recommended. Main courses
$14–$30. MC, V. Mon–Sat 5–10pm, Sun 10am–2pm (brunch) and 4:30–9:30pm.
CONTINENTAL/AMERICAN.

Located in a restored Victorian home that was built in 1891, E. R. Rogers has
an excellent view of Puget Sound. The setting and service are quite formal and the
menu leans to well-prepared familiar fare such as oysters Rockefeller, shrimp
scampi, and prime rib. However, there are also more adventurous dishes, including Drambuie chicken and smoked-salmon fettuccine. The Sunday brunch,
with its many fish dishes, is an area institution. This is one of the south sound's
favorite special occasion restaurants.

6 Olympia

60 miles S of Seattle, 100 miles N of Portland

Located at the southernmost end of Puget Sound, Olympia is the capital of
Washington. The city clings to the shores of Budd Inlet's twin bays and is further
divided by Capitol Lake, above which, on a high bluff, stands the capitol building. Despite the political importance of being the state capital, Olympia still
has the air of a small town. The downtown is compact and low-rise, and when
the legislature isn't in session the city can be downright ghostly. Keeping things
alive, however, are the ever-progressive students of the liberal-arts Evergreen State
College.

The Olympia area has a long history. It was near here, in what is now the city
of Tumwater, that the first American pioneers settled in 1844. A historic district
and historical park along the Deschutes River preserves a bit of this history. However, it's not history or politics that has given Olympia its greatest fame—it's
Olympia beer, a staple of the suds trade throughout the West. Tours of the brewery
in Tumwater are as popular as tours of the capitol building (call 360/754-5177 for
information; they're not available year round, though you can always stop by the
hospitality room and gift shop).

ESSENTIALS

GETTING THERE   Olympia is on I-5 at the junction with U.S. 101, which
leads north around the Olympic Peninsula. Connecting the city to the central
Washington coast and Aberdeen/Hoquiam is U.S. 12/Wash. 8.

The nearest airport with scheduled service is Seattle-Tacoma International
Airport, 54 miles north. **Capital Airporter** (☎ 360/754-7113) provides a shuttle
between the airport and Olympia. The one-way fare is $20.

VISITOR INFORMATION   Contact the **Olympia/Thurston County
Chamber of Commerce,** 521 Legion Way (P.O. Box 1427), Olympia, WA 98507
(☎ 360/357-3362 or 800/753-8474; fax 360/357-3376), or the **State Capitol
Visitor Information Center,** at 14th Avenue and Capitol Way (☎ 360/
586-3460).

GETTING AROUND   If you need a taxi, contact **Capitol City Taxi** (☎ 360/ 357-4949). Public bus service is provided by **Intercity Transit** (☎ 360/ 786-1881), which operates free downtown shuttle buses.

SEEING THE SIGHTS

Located at 14th Avenue and Capitol Way, and set amid a large and attractively landscaped campus known for its flowering cherry trees and rose gardens, the neoclassical **Washington State Capitol** building bears a surprising resemblance to the Capitol in that other Washington. At 267 feet tall, this is the tallest domed masonry state capitol in the country. Around its campus you'll see sculptures, the Tivoli fountain, and a conservatory. The capitol is open daily and the temple of justice, conservatory, and old capitol building are all open Monday through Friday. For more information contact the **Capitol Visitor Center** (☎ 360/ 586-TOUR).

Washington State Capitol Museum

211 W. 21st Ave. ☎ **360/753-2580**. Admission $2 adults, $1 children. Tues–Fri 10am–4pm, Sat–Sun noon–4pm.

This small museum houses exhibits on the history of Washington both during its territorial days and since statehood. Of particular interest are the exhibits on Northwest Native Americans. The building itself is a Spanish-style mansion that was built for a former mayor of Olympia.

Wolf Haven International

3111 Offut Lake Rd., Tenino. ☎ **800/448-9653**. Admission $5 adults, $2.50 children 5–12; Howl-ins, $6 adults, $4 children 5–12. May–Sept, daily 10am–4pm; Oct–Apr, Wed– Sun 10am–3pm. Howl-ins, May–Sept only, Fri–Sat 6:30–9:30pm.

Dedicated to the preservation of wolves and the education of the general public on the subject of wolves, Wolf Haven is a sanctuary for more than 40 wolves. On the hourly tours of the facility, you'll get to meet many of these canines. In summer, there are Friday- and Saturday-evening howl-ins that include a tour, a chance to howl with the wolves, and a bit of storytelling and folksinging around a bonfire.

PRESERVES, PARKS & GARDENS

Nisqually National Wildlife Refuge, located 10 miles north of Olympia, preserves the delta of the Nisqually River, which is a resting and wintering ground for large numbers of migratory birds. Seven miles of trails lead through the refuge. Some 13 miles south of town, near the town of Littlerock, you'll find the **Mima Mounds Natural Area Preserve,** which is an area of hundreds of small hills, each around 7 feet high. No one is sure how the mounds were formed, but their curious topography has produced much speculation over the years. The preserve is open daily from 9am to dusk.

On the north side of Olympia along the East Bay of Budd Inlet, you'll find several miles of hiking trails and nice water views at **Priest Point State Park,** on East Bay Drive. Another spot worth a visit is the **Yashiro Japanese Garden,** at the corner of Ninth Avenue and Plum Street, just off I-5 at Exit 105; it's open daily from 10am to 5pm.

WHERE TO STAY

In addition to the hotels listed below, Olympia has several inexpensive chain motels including the following (see the Appendix for a list of toll-free telephone numbers):

Super 8 Motel, 4615 Martin Way, Lacey, WA 98503 (☎ 360/459-8888), charging $51 to $55 double; and a **Motel 6,** 400 W. Lee St., Tumwater, WA 98501 (☎ 360/754-7320), charging $35 double.

✪ Harbinger Inn

1136 E. Bay Dr., Olympia, WA 98506. ☎ **360/754-0389.** 4 rms, 3 with bath. $55 double without bath, $100 double with bath. Rates include full breakfast. AE, MC, V.

Located only a short distance from downtown's shops and restaurants and overlooking Budd Inlet and a marina, the Harbinger Inn is a very elegant 1910 stone house. White pillars and a large balcony give the house an antebellum appearance that would be right at home in Mississippi. Three of the four rooms have bay views. The nicest of these is the Blue Heron Suite, which has views of the Olympics, antique furnishings, and a sitting room. In addition to a filling breakfast, there are tea and cookies in the afternoon. Pay close attention when first arriving—the driveway is easy to miss.

Holiday Inn Select–Olympia

2300 Evergreen Park Dr., Olympia, WA 98502. ☎ **360/943-4000** or 800/551-8500. 191 rms. A/C TV TEL. $87–$148 double. AE, CB, DC, DISC, MC, V.

A tranquil setting high on a bluff above Capitol Lake and a great view of the capitol dome itself make this hotel a great choice in Olympia. Though you're only a five-minute drive from downtown, you'll feel as if you're out in the country. The grounds display a Northwest landscaping style with plenty of big old fir trees shading the property. Most rooms have decks or patios.

Dining/Entertainment: The hotel has both a formal restaurant and a café, and there's pub fare in the lounge.

Facilities: Outdoor pool, whirlpool.

Ramada Inn Governor House

621 S. Capitol Way, Olympia, WA 98501. ☎ **360/352-7700** or 800/2-RAMADA. 122 rms, 2 suites. A/C TV TEL. $130–$140 double; $155–$175 suite. AE, CB, DC, DISC, MC, V.

Located right downtown, the Governor House is Olympia's only high-rise hotel. Within walking distance are the Budd Inlet marina and Percival Landing Waterfront Park, the capitol campus, and the Washington Center for the Performing Arts, which are several good reasons to stay here. If you happen to be here on government business you'll almost certainly want to make this your first choice. Request a room on a higher floor with a view of the bay or Sylvester Park.

Dining/Entertainment: The hotel has a casual restaurant serving three meals a day and an adjacent sports bar.

Services: Room service, valet service.

Facilities: Outdoor pool, whirlpool, sauna, exercise room.

WHERE TO DINE

Budd Bay Café

Percival Landing, 525 N. Columbia St. ☎ **360/357-6963.** Reservations recommended. Main courses $6.50–$25. AE, DC, MC, V. Mon–Sat 11am–10pm, Sun 10am–9pm (brunch 10am–1pm). SEAFOOD.

Duking it out with Genoa's for the titles of most popular waterfront restaurant and best Sunday brunch is the Budd Bay Café, which is right in downtown and is much easier to find. The restaurant is right on the 1¹/₂-mile-long Percival Landing Waterfront Park boardwalk and has great views up the inlet. The menu includes such standards as salmon in a white-wine sauce with garlic, butter, and herbs, but you'll also find a Mediterranean-style chicken with black olives and artichoke hearts in an ouzo-cream sauce. There are several good salads, including a hot seafood salad. Sandwiches and burgers are the main lunch fare, and the Sunday brunch is the best in town.

✪ Chattery Down

209 Fifth Ave. ☎ **360/352-8483.** Reservations recommended. Main courses $13–$18. MC, V. Mon–Wed 11am–3pm, Thurs–Fri 11am–3pm and 5:30–9pm, Sat 9:30am–3pm and 5:30–9pm. NORTHWEST/FRENCH.

This eclectically furnished little restaurant is attached to a shop that specializes in wild foods such as mushrooms, and consequently wild mushrooms make frequent appearances on the menu here at Chattery Down. On weekdays this is a very popular lunch spot for downtown office workers, and then Thursday through Saturday nights dinners are also served. A recent menu include chicken Wellington as well as salmon en croûte, which was topped with Dungeness crab and a wine sauce.

Falls Terrace

106 Deschutes Way, Tumwater. ☎ **360/943-7830.** Reservations recommended. Main courses $11–$28. AE, DC, DISC, MC, V. Mon–Fri 11am–9pm, Sat 11:30am–9pm, Sun 11:30am–8pm. CONTINENTAL.

With its view of Tumwater Falls, the Falls Terrace restaurant is the Olympia area's traditional special-occasion restaurant. The menu is solidly continental with escargots bourguignons, sole amandine, crab au gratin, and bouillabaisse, but there are also forays into other cuisines. Several mesquite-grilled dishes are available, and you'll also find some Cajun dishes. The discount early dinners served between 4 and 5:45pm are a great deal.

Gardener's Seafood & Pasta

111 W. Thurston St. ☎ **360/786-8466.** Reservations recommended. Main courses $11–$19. AE, MC, V. Tues–Sat 5–9pm. SEAFOOD.

Located across the street from the Olympia Farmers' Market, Gardeners is a cavernous place. The restaurant makes good use of Puget Sound's bounty of seafoods and you'll find such dishes as cioppino, Dungeness crab casserole, and hot seafood salad on the menu. Among the pastas, we like the cannelloni stuffed with chicken, veal, spinach, mozzarella, Parmesan, and ricotta.

✪ Urban Onion

116 Legion Way. ☎ **360/943-9242.** Reservations recommended on weekends. Main courses $5.50–$13. AE, MC, V. Mon–Thurs 7:30am–10pm, Fri–Sat 7:30am–11pm, Sun 8am–9pm. INTERNATIONAL/VEGETARIAN.

As the site of ultra-progressive Evergreen State College, Olympia has more than its fair share of vegetarians, and for years this has been one of their top choices in town. However, the Urban Onion isn't strictly a vegetarian place. There are also burgers, chicken dishes (Mexican, Szechuan, or sautéed with vegetables), and a couple of seafood dishes. Most of the same dishes are available at lunch or dinner, with prices slightly lower at lunch. Meals are always reliable.

OLYMPIA AFTER DARK

Located downtown, the state-of-the-art **Washington Center for the Performing Arts,** 512 Washington St. SE (☎ 360/753-8586), hosts performances by regional, national, and international performers. The season always features plenty of theater, music, and dance. Various local performing arts companies call this center home. Tickets run $5 to $30.

The Washington Cascades

The population growth and urban sprawl in the Puget Sound area are turning that region into one long Pugetopolis stretching for 100 miles from Everett to Olympia. But if you turn your eyes to the east on a clear day, you'll be gazing at mountain wilderness. Dominating the eastern skyline of northern Puget Sound are volcanic Mount Baker and the North Cascades. In the southern regions of the sound, Mount Rainier, another dormant volcano, looms grandly on the horizon. It's the easy accessibility of these mountains that helps make the cities of Puget Sound so livable. With two national parks, a half-dozen major ski areas, dozens of lakes (including the third-deepest lake in the United States), a Bavarian village, and a false-fronted Wild West frontier town, these mountains offer a diversity of recreational and sightseeing activities.

Cloaked in places by dark forests of old-growth trees and stripped bare by logging clear-cuts in others, the Washington Cascades are a patchwork quilt of narrow valleys, rolling foothills, and rugged peaks. Lakes of the deepest blue are cradled beneath emerald forests. Glaciers carve their way inexorably from peaks that experience some of the heaviest snowfalls in the nation. It's possible to drive or hike almost to the edge of several of these glaciers and listen to their cracking and rumbling as gravity pulls at their centuries of ice. The Cascades, with their countless waterfalls, have also earned their name, sending white water cascading down from the heights.

Whatever the season, in good weather and bad, active Washingtonians head for the hills whenever they get the chance. In spring they come for the wildflowers, in summer for the hiking, in autumn for the leaf change, and in winter for the skiing.

1 Leavenworth: Washington's Own Bavarian Village

108 miles E of Everett, 22 miles W of Wenatchee, 58 miles SW of Chelan

You're out for a Sunday drive through the mountains, just enjoying the views, maybe doing a bit of hiking or cross-country skiing, when you come around a bend and find yourself in the Bavarian Alps. Folks in lederhosen and dirndls are dancing in the streets, a polka band is playing the old oompah-pah, and all the buildings look like alpine chalets. Have you just entered the Twilight Zone? No, it's just Leavenworth, Washington's Bavarian village.

Many an unsuspecting traveler has had just this experience, but if you're reading this, you'll be prepared for the sight of a Bavarian village transported to the middle of the Washington Cascades. Whether you think it's the most romantic town in the state, a great place to go shopping, or just a tacky tourist trap, there's no denying that Leavenworth makes an impression.

ACCOMMODATIONS IN INDEX, EN ROUTE FROM SEATTLE

The Bush House Country Inn

300 Fifth St., Index, WA 98256. ☎ **360/793-2312** or 800/428-BUSH. Fax 360/793-3673. 11 rms, none with bath. $59–$80 double. MC, V.

Purchased recently by a member of the famous Nordstrom department-store family, this historic lodge is a quiet and out-of-the-way spot for a weekend retreat. The main attractions in the area are all outdoor activities, including hiking, white-water kayaking, and downhill skiing. Antique furniture reflects the inn's heritage, but the overabundance of stuffed animals don't quite seem the style of the folks who frequent this neck of the woods. However, if you enjoy the quaint, country-inn look, you'll definitely enjoy this lodge. There are attractive gardens and great views. The dining room offers a good assortment of moderately priced meal options and there's a popular Sunday brunch.

ESSENTIALS

GETTING THERE   From I-5, take U.S. 2 from Everett, or, if you're coming from the south, take I-405 to Bothell and then head northeast to Monroe, where you pick up U.S. 2 heading east. From U.S. 97 in the central part of the state, head west on U.S. 2.

VISITOR INFORMATION   Contact the **Leavenworth Chamber of Commerce** (☎ **509/548-5807**); you'll find them in the clock tower.

GETTING AROUND   The Link bus system is free and services the Leavenworth, Lake Chelan, and Wenatchee areas.

FESTIVALS   During the annual **Maifest** (early May) and **Autumn Leaf Festival** (late September) Leavenworth rolls out the barrel and takes to the streets and parks with polka bands, Bavarian dancing, and plenty of craft vendors.

EXPLORING THE TOWN

Leavenworth's main attraction is the town itself. Thirty years ago this was just another mountain town struggling to get by on a limited economy. Sure the valley was beautiful, but beauty wasn't enough to bring in the bucks. A few years after a motel with alpine architecture opened in town, Leavenworth decided to give itself a complete makeover. Today nearly every commercial building in town, from the gas station to the Safeway, looks as if it had been built by Bavarian gnomes. What may come as a surprise is that they did a good job! Stroll around town and you'll convince yourself that you've just had the world's cheapest trip to the Alps. People here even speak German!

Any time of year the town's most popular tourist activity seems to be shopping for genuine Bavarian souvenirs in the many gift shops, and you'll find cuckoo clocks, Hummel figurines, imported lace, and nutcrackers.

If you tire of Bavarian *gemütlichkeit*, head over to the nearby town of **Cashmere**, which has adopted an Early American theme in an attempt to cash in on

The Washington Cascades

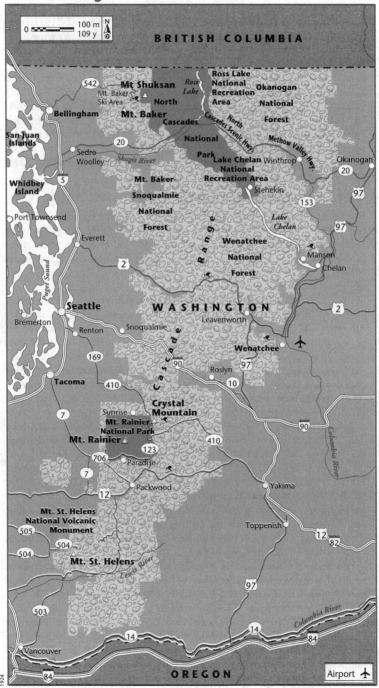

0 ———— 100 m
109 y
N

BRITISH COLUMBIA

542
Mt. Shuksan
Mt. Baker Ski Area
North
Ross Lake
Ross Lake National Recreation Area
Okanogan
Bellingham
Mt. Baker
Cascades
National Forest
National
Cascades Scenic Hwy.
North
Methow Valley Hwy.
San Juan Islands
20
Sedro Woolley
Skagit River
Lake Chelan National Recreation Area
Winthrop
Okanogan
5
Mt. Baker-
Stehekin
20
Whidbey Island
Snoqualmie
153
97
Port Townsend
National
Lake Chelan
97
Everett
Forest
Wenatchee
Manson
National
Chelan
Forest
Range
Puget Sound
Seattle
WASHINGTON
Bremerton
Snoqualmie
Leavenworth
2
Renton
Cascade
Wenatchee
169
90
Roslyn
97
Tacoma
410
10
90
7
Crystal Mountain
Columbia River
Sunrise
Mt. Rainier National Park
Mt. Rainier
123
410
706
Paradise
7
Packwood
Yakima
12
Mt. St. Helens National Volcanic Monument
505
Toppenish
504
504
12
82
Mt. St. Helens
Lewis River
503
97
Columbia River
14
14
84
Vancouver
84
OREGON
Airport ✈

1924

Leavenworth's popularity. The town's main attraction is the **Aplets & Cotlets Candy Factory and Country Store,** 117 Mission St. (☎ **509/782-2191**), where you tour the kitchens where these unusual fruit-and-nut confections are made. It's open May to December, Monday through Friday from 8am to 5:30pm and Saturday and Sunday from 10am to 4pm; January to April, Monday through Friday from 8 to 11am and noon to 5pm. Also worth a visit in Cashmere are the **Chelan County Museum and Pioneer Village,** 600 Cottage Ave. (☎ **509/782-3230**). Nearly 20 old log buildings have been assembled here and filled with period antiques. Inside the main museum building you'll find exhibits on the early Native American cultures of the region, pioneer history, and natural history. It's open April to October, Monday through Saturday from 9:30am to 5pm and on Sunday from 1 to 5pm; call for winter hours. Admission is $3 for adults, $2 for students and seniors, $1 for children 5 to 12.

SPORTS & OUTDOOR ACTIVITIES

If your interests tend toward hiking rather than Hummel figurines, you'll still find plenty to do around Leavenworth. Leavenworth is on the valley floor at the confluence of the Wenatchee and Icicle rivers and rising all around are steep, forested mountainsides. Spring through fall, there is rafting, hiking, mountain biking, and horseback riding, and in winter, there is downhill and cross-country skiing and snowmobiling.

April to July is **rafting** season on the Wenatchee River. If you're interested, contact All Rivers Adventure (☎ 509/782-2254 or 800/74-FLOAT) or Alpine Adventures (☎ 509/548-4159 or 800/926-RAFT). A day trip costs about $65 per person. If you'd like to go **horseback riding,** contact Eagle Creek Ranch (☎ 509/548-7798 or 800/221-7433). They offer everything from hour-long rides to overnight pack trips, and sleigh rides in the winter. Enchanted Mountain Tours offers **dog-sledding tours;** a one-hour ride costs about $55 per person. In the summer, try a **carriage ride** around town offered by Carriage Services of Leavenworth (☎ 509/548-6825 or 800/200-3354).

Mountain bikes can be rented at Der Sportsmann, 837 Front St. (☎ 509/548-5623), and the Leavenworth Ski & Sports Center, U.S. 2 and Icicle Road (☎ 509/548-7864). You can also put your bike on the free Link bus and go as far as Lake Chelan or Stevens Pass to start biking. For information on nearby **hiking trails,** contact the Leavenworth Ranger Station, 600 Sherbourne St. (☎ 509/782-1413). **Lake Wenatchee,** 25 miles north of town, is a year-round recreation area with hiking and cross-country ski trails, horseback riding, canoe rentals, windsurfing, swimming, fishing, mountain biking, camping, and snowmobiling. Golfers can play nine holes at the **Kahler Glen Golf Course,** 20890 Kahler Dr. (☎ 509/763-3785).

Leavenworth maintains about 30 miles (50km) of **cross-country ski trails** in winter. There are even $1\frac{1}{4}$ miles (2km) of lighted trails for night skiing. There is also beginner-level downhill skiing available at **Leavenworth Ski Hill** (☎ 509/548-5115), a mile outside of town. For more serious downhill skiing, there is **Stevens Pass** (☎ 360/973-2441), 40 miles west of town. Lift tickets range in price from $15 to $31. Also nearby is **Mission Ridge** ski area (☎ 509/663-7631 or 800/374-1693 for a snow report), located 35 miles southeast near Wenatchee. Mission Ridge is known for its powder snow, a rarity in the Cascades, and its sunny weather. Lift ticket prices are similar to those at Stevens Pass. Cross-country skis can be rented at Leavenworth Ski & Sports Center and Der Sportsmann (see above for addresses and phone numbers).

WHERE TO STAY
EXPENSIVE

✪ Run of the River Bed & Breakfast
9308 E. Leavenworth Rd., Leavenworth, WA 98826. ☎ **509/548-7171** or 800/288-6491. 6 rms. $90–$140 double. AE, DISC, MC, V.

Rustic yet contemporary, this log house on 2 acres outside of town is one of the Northwest's most tranquil bed-and-breakfast inns. The view out the windows over the Icicle River is as soul-satisfying as they come. You can almost feel the weight of your cares fall from your shoulders as you drive through the alpine rock garden that lines the driveway. Step through the front door and you enter a house full of bare wood, hand-hewn log furniture, and exposed stones (in both the fireplaces and entry floor). This extensive use of natural materials gives the inn a timeless mountain-lodge atmosphere that's complemented by contemporary architecture. Upstairs, the guest rooms have lofts that are great spaces for a bit of quiet reading, but for a quiet moment the log porch swings just can't be beat. Novice birdwatchers will appreciate the binoculars in every room.

MODERATE

✪ Abendblume Inn
12570 Ranger Rd., Leavenworth, WA 98826. ☎ **509/548-4059** or 800/669-7634. 6 rms. $70–$145 double. Rates include full breakfast. AE, DISC, MC, V.

This alpine chalet, built by owners Renee and Randy Sexauer after traveling through the Alps studying houses and inns, is a luxurious and romantic B&B overlooking Leavenworth and the valley. An eye for detail is apparent throughout the inn, from the hand-carved front door to the custom-made German-style breakfast-room chairs to the wrought-iron stair railing. In the living room, the fireplace is a popular gathering spot in winter, and a baby grand piano is available for musical guests.

Although there are a couple of smaller rooms, the large rooms with balconies overlooking the valley are the best. In these you'll find fireplaces, VCRs, and wonderfully luxurious beds and linens, but it's the bathrooms that are the real attractions. Our favorite has a triangular tub for two, elegant bottles of bubble bath, tubside candles, plush terry robes and towels, two sinks, and heated marble floors. Nowhere in Leavenworth is there a more romantic room. Buffet breakfasts include enough variety to keep everyone happy, but everyone always clamors for the little pancakes.

⑤ Blackbird Lodge
305 Eighth St., Leavenworth, WA 98826. ☎ **509/548-5800** or 800/446-0240. 15 rms. A/C TV TEL. $69–$105 double. Rates include continental breakfast. AE, DISC, MC, V.

Located right in downtown Leavenworth overlooking the Icicle River, this new hotel offers the convenience of being within walking distance of all the town's shops and restaurants but with the feel of a country inn. The guest rooms are large, but otherwise are standard motel-style rooms. However, the lobby, with its slate floor and dark, woodsy decor, set this lodge apart from other moderately priced lodgings in town.

Enzian Motor Inn

590 U.S. 2, Leavenworth, WA 98826. ☎ **509/548-5269,** or 800/223-8511 in Washington. 104 rms, 7 suites. A/C TV TEL. $88–$132 double; $152–$167 suite. Rates include continental breakfast. AE, CB, DC, DISC, MC, V.

Located on the highway just outside downtown Leavenworth, the Enzian offers both convenience and amenities. Of course, it has an alpine exterior, complete with half-timbering, steep roofs, and turrets, and inside you'll find an attractive lobby with a high ceiling and stone fireplace. To continue the Bavarian theme, the guest rooms are decorated with reproduction antique furniture imported from Germany. If you're feeling like a splurge, the tower suite is richly appointed with burgundy carpets, a heavy carved-wood canopy bed, and a double whirlpool tub in the sitting room.

Services: Complimentary use of cross-country ski equipment.

Facilities: Large indoor swimming pool, outdoor swimming pool, hot tubs, exercise room, racquetball, basketball, table tennis.

Haus Rohrback Pension

12882 Ranger Rd., Leavenworth, WA 98826. ☎ **509/548-7024** or 800/548-4477. 9 rms, 4 with bath; 3 suites. A/C. $65–$80 double without bath, $85–$95 double with bath; $150–$160 suite. Rates include full breakfast. AE, DISC, MC, V.

Located a mile out of town on a hillside overlooking the valley and mountains, the Haus Rohrbach is a copy of a lodge near Innsbruck, Austria. The big chalet has balconies stretching across the front on all three floors, and in the living room there's a wood stove to keep you cozy on winter nights. The decor is simple to the point of being rustic—with a Bavarian flare, of course. One suite, in the main lodge, is a bilevel unit with a private balcony, while the other two are housed in a separate building and have cathedral ceilings. All the suites have gas fireplaces and double whirlpool tubs.

Directly behind the inn are miles of hiking trails and mountain-biking roads, but if you aren't feeling that active, you can spend the afternoon by the swimming pool (in summer) or soaking in the hot tub.

Hotel Pension Anna

926 Commercial St., Leavenworth, WA 98826. ☎ **509/548-6273** or 800/509-ANNA. 12 rms, 3 suites. A/C. $75–$85 double; $140–$165 suite. Rates include full breakfast. AE, DISC, MC, V.

Though the guest rooms in the Pension Anna's main building are attractively appointed with pine furniture, including a four-poster bed in the honeymoon suite, the annex building contains the inn's two most outstanding rooms. The annex is a renovated church built in 1913, and the Old Chapel Suite even has the baptismal font in its foyer. This suite is a grand accommodation that includes part of the old choir loft, which is now a sleeping loft. Ceilings 20 feet high give the room an expansive feel, and in the bedroom you'll find an ornately carved headboard framed by draperies that reach to the ceiling. Though considerably smaller, the Parish Nook Room has an ornate king-size bed, marble-top bedside stands, and the original arched windows. Only slightly more expensive than a regular room, the Parish Nook is the inn's best deal.

INEXPENSIVE

⑤ Mrs. Anderson's Lodging House

917 Commercial St., Leavenworth, WA 98826. ☎ **509/548-6173** or 800/253-8990. 9 rms, 7 with bath. TV. $46–$51 double without bath, $58–$73 double with bath. Rates include continental breakfast. AE, DISC, MC, V.

Housed in the oldest wooden building in Leavenworth, Mrs. Anderson's is a former boarding house that's now an attractive bed-and-breakfast inn. The decor is simple, and a few of the rooms have mountain views out the windows, with the best view from Room 5. There's a long front porch and two parlors if you want to just sit and relax or play a game, and some rooms have their own balconies. With economical rates and cozy rooms, this makes an excellent budget choice.

WHERE TO DINE

In addition to the restaurants listed below, the Danish Bakery, 731 Front St. (☎ **509/548-7514**), does a wonderful burnt-cream Danish pastry, and of course, German chocolate and Black Forest cakes.

MODERATE

Edel Haus Inn

320 Ninth St. ☎ **509/548-4412.** Reservations recommended. Main courses $9–$18. DISC, MC, V. Mon–Fri 11:30am–2:30pm and 5–8:30pm, Sat–Sun 10am–2pm and 5–8:30pm. INTERNATIONAL.

This restaurant, a simple small house on the river at the center of town, offers many choices if you want to get away from Bavarian cuisine (although they do serve Schnitzel and bratwurst dinners). Chicken is done here in a variety of ways and served with pasta; and the pasta dishes (sometimes lemon linguine or corn-jalapeño fettuccine) come dressed with combinations such as roasted eggplant, pine nuts, and sun-dried tomatoes, or mushrooms, corn, and jicama in a spicy cilantro cream. You'll find steak au poive and grilled salmon here, too.

✪ Reiner's Gasthaus

829 Front St. ☎ **509/548-5111.** Reservations not accepted. Full dinner $11–$16.50. MC, V. Daily 11am–9pm. GERMAN.

No visit to town would be complete without a bite of German potato salad, some sauerkraut, and perhaps a Schnitzel or some Sauerbraten. So when you've worked up a suitably large appetite, climb the stairs to Reiner's Gasthaus, a quintessentially German establishment. If you have any doubts as to the authenticity of this restaurant, they'll quickly be dispelled by the German waitresses. On Saturday you'll often find live music. In addition to a couple of different Schnitzels, you'll also find Hungarian goulash and lemon-seasoned boneless trout on the menu. Lunches include a variety of wursts.

INEXPENSIVE

Andreas Keller

829 Front St. ☎ **509/548-6000.** Reservations recommended. Full dinner $7–$11. MC, V. Daily 11am–9pm. GERMAN.

Down in a cellar *(keller)* opposite the gazebo on Front Street, you'll find another of Leavenworth's true German experiences. From the waitresses shouting across the restaurant in German to the accordionist who plays on the weekends, everything about this place is Bavarian. Take a seat and you'll be surrounded by *gemütlichkeit*. Rotisseried chicken and wursts are the staple here.

The Leavenworth Brewery Restaurant & Pub

636 Front St. ☎ **509/548-4545.** Main courses $6–$13. MC, V. Sun–Thurs 11am–10pm, Fri–Sat 11am–midnight. PUB.

Upstairs from the brewery, the restaurant is a cozy and friendly place frequented by visitors as well as locals. We couldn't resist a German meal, so we tried the Bavarian dinner, which was big enough for two to split and included some delicious beer bread. But there are many other items on the menu, such as hamburgers, salads, and a house specialty, chicken fajitas. The brewery keeps eight of its beers on tap, and makes a dynamite root-beer float with its own root beer.

WENATCHEE: A STOP ON THE DRIVE FROM LEAVENWORTH TO LAKE CHELAN

As U.S. 2 continues east from Leavenworth, you quickly leave the mountains behind, and the valley fills with orchards that are irrigated with water from both the Wenatchee River and the Columbia River. The combination of warm, sunny days and abundant water have made Wenatchee the apple capital of the world. Apples are the single largest agricultural industry in Washington, and more than 50% of the apples sold in the United States come from central Washington. At the **Washington Apple Commission Visitor Center,** 2900 Euclid Ave. (☎ **509/ 663-9600** or 509/662-3090), located on the northern outskirts of town just off U.S. 97, you can learn all about apples and how they're grown and stored. It's open May to December, Monday through Friday from 8am to 5pm, on Saturday from 9am to 5pm, and on Sunday from 11am to 5pm; January to April, Monday through Friday from 8am to 5pm. Admission is free. The city celebrates its crop each year with the **Washington State Apple Blossom Festival,** which includes three weeks of festivities in late April and early May. For more information on the festival and the Wenatchee area, contact the **Wenatchee Area Visitor & Convention Bureau,** 2 S. Chelan Ave., Wenatchee, WA 98801 (☎ **509/662-4774** or 800/57-APPLE).

More apple-industry displays are part of the focus of the **North Central Washington Museum,** 127 S. Mission St. (☎ **509/664-5989**), but there are also interesting exhibits on the first transpacific flight and local Native American cultures. It's open Monday through Friday from 10am to 4pm and on Saturday and Sunday from 1 to 4pm; closed weekends in January. Admission is $2 for adults, $1 for children 6 to 12. Model-railroading buffs will enjoy the HO-scale Great Northern Railroad. This museum also hosts concerts, lectures, and traveling exhibitions, and a 1919 Wurlitzer organ is often played during concerts and as accompaniment to classic silent films.

Though it's only a dozen or so miles from the lush forests of the Cascades, Wenatchee is on the edge of central Washington's high desert. To bring a bit of the mountains' greenery into the desert, Herman Ohme and his family spent 60 years creating **Ohme Gardens,** 3327 Ohme Rd. (☎ **509/662-5785**), a lush alpine garden covering 9 cliff-top acres north of Wenatchee. It's open Memorial Day to Labor Day, daily from 9am to 7pm, closing an hour earlier the rest of the year. Admission is $5 for adults, $3 for children 7 to 17. The gardens wind along the top of a rocky outcropping that overlooks the Wenatchee Valley, Columbia River, and Cascade peaks. Rock gardens, meadows, fern grottos, and waterfalls give the gardens a very naturalistic feel similar to that of a Japanese garden.

With 15 acres of beautifully landscaped grounds, the nearby **Rocky Reach Dam,** on U.S. 97, is a popular picnicking spot. You can take a tour of the dam and watch salmon as they climb the fish ladder. Viewing windows even give you a fish's-eye view of the salmon.

WHERE TO STAY

Westcoast Wenatchee Center Hotel

201 N. Wenatchee Ave., Wenatchee, WA 98801. ☎ **509/662-1234** or 800/426-0670. Fax 509/662-0782. 147 rms, 4 suites. A/C TV TEL. $59–$95 double; $200 suite. AE, CB, DC, DISC, MC, V.

Because of its central location and the abundance of sunshine, Wenatchee has made a business of hosting small conventions. With the convention center across a skybridge from the lobby, the Westcoast Wenatchee caters almost exclusively to convention business, but it's also the city's most comfortable hotel. A rooftop dining room and lounge provide the best view in town and moderately priced meals, and room service is available. Facilities include an indoor/outdoor pool, whirlpool, and exercise room.

WHERE TO DINE

John Horan House Restaurant

2 Horan Rd. ☎ **509/663-0018.** Reservations recommended. Main courses $13–$23. AE, DISC, MC, V. Mon–Fri 11:30am–2pm and 5–10pm, Sat 5–10pm, Sun 9:30am–2pm (brunch). Cross the Wenatchee River bridge from downtown, take your first right, the next right, and then, at the end of the road, turn right a third time; at the end of this road, turn left into the restaurant driveway. CONTINENTAL.

Though it's a bit hard to find, and is in a rather unlikely spot surrounded by industrial complexes, the Horan House is well worth searching out. Secluded in its own little apple orchard, the 1899 Victorian farmhouse is a world apart. Several dining rooms and a patio provide various options for whatever your mood. The menu includes many standards as well as the currently popular flavors of the Mediterranean regions. Since this is apple country, you may want to opt for the chicken breast Calvados, made with sautéed apples, sparkling cider, cream, and brandy. The burnt-cream dessert is a house specialty.

2 Lake Chelan

166 miles E of Seattle, 37 miles N of Wenatchee, 59 miles S of Winthrop

A rare land-locked fjord, formed when a glacier-carved valley flooded, Lake Chelan is 1,500 feet deep, 55 miles long, and less than 2 miles wide in most places. It's the third-deepest lake in the United States (reaching 400 feet below sea level) and the longest natural lake in Washington. Only the southern 25 miles of the lake are accessible by road, yet at the northern end, the community of Stehekin (reachable only by boat, plane, or on foot) has managed to avoid becoming a ghost town for more than 100 years. Plenty of summer sunshine, clear water, and blue skies have made the lake the number one destination in eastern Washington—the towns of Chelan and Manson have the feel of beach towns despite the rugged mountain views all around. Apple orchards cover the foothills at the southern end of the lake, but beyond the end of the road, the forest takes over.

ESSENTIALS

GETTING THERE   Chelan is on U.S. 97, the main north-south highway in central Washington. From Seattle, take U.S. 2 to Wenatchee and then head north.

VISITOR INFORMATION   Contact the **Lake Chelan Chamber of Commerce,** 102 E. Johnson St., Chelan (☎ **509/682-3503** or 800/4-CHELAN).

GETTING AROUND   The Link bus system is free and services the Lake Chelan, Leavenworth, and Wenatchee areas.

CRUISES, SPORTS & OTHER THINGS TO DO

If you have time for only one thing, it should be an all-day boat ride up Lake Chelan to Stehekin at the northern end of the lake. The **Lake Chelan Boat Company,** South Shore Road (☎ **509/682-2224**), operates the two-passenger ferries— *Lady of the Lake II* and the faster *Lady Express*—that make the trip from Chelan to Stehekin. The *Lady of the Lake II* takes about eight hours for the round-trip and charges $21 per person, while the *Lady Express* takes about five hours and charges $39 for the same route. Unless you plan to stay overnight, you won't have more than 90 minutes to look around Stehekin unless you book a combination ticket that allows you to go up on the *Lady Express,* spend three hours in Stehekin, and return on the *Lady of the Lake II.* This combination ticket is only available in summer. The trip encompasses some of the most spectacular scenery in the Northwest as you travel from gentle rolling foothills to deep into the rugged North Cascades mountains. Wildlife, including deer, mountain goats, and even bears, are frequently seen from the boats.

If your destination is Stehekin and you want to get there in a hurry, you can make the trip by floatplane on **Chelan Airways** (☎ **509/682-5555**), which leaves from the dock next to the ferries. The fare is $80 round-trip. This company also offers flightseeing trips for between $50 and $100.

Opportunities for aquatic activities abound at Lake Chelan. Good places to swim include **Lakeside Park** on the South Shore Road, **Don Morse Memorial Park** on the edge of downtown Chelan, and at **Manson Bay Park** in Manson. **Lake Chelan State Park** (☎ **509/687-3710**) and **25-Mile Creek State Park** (☎ **509/687-3610**), both on South Shore Road, offer swimming, picnicking, and camping.

You can rent a jet ski from **Chelan Boat Rentals,** 1210 W. Woodin Ave. (☎ **509/682-4444**). Rates range from $40 an hour to $150 per day. If you've got the kids along, you'll find it impossible not to spend some time at **Slidewaters** water-slide park, 102 Waterslide Dr. (☎ **509/682-5751**), which has nine water slides, an inner-tube river ride, a 60-person hot tub, and a swimming pool. Admission is $10.95 for adults, $7.95 for children.

Beyond the end of the road lie thousands of acres of unspoiled forests and miles of **hiking and mountain-biking trails.** Access to the trails is from roadside trailheads or from flag stops along the route of the *Lady of the Lake II.* Many trails also begin in the Stehekin area. For more information on hiking and biking opportunities, contact the **Chelan Ranger Station,** 428 W. Woodin Ave., Chelan (☎ **509/682-2576**), or the **Lake Chelan National Recreational Area,** Stehekin (☎ **509/682-4404**). Horseback riding is available in Stehekin with **Cascade Corrals** at Stehekin Valley Ranch (☎ **509/682-4677**). A 2¹/₂-hour ride costs $32.

Bigfoot: Lost Primate or Tabloid Hoax?

On a recent summer day, we were talking to the ranger at the North Cascades National Park information center when another visitor began asking about bears in the area.

"I was hiking yesterday and spotted these bear scratches way up on the side of a tree. The paws must have been huge," he explained.

According to the ranger, this wasn't too surprising. The North Cascades have plenty of black bears and even a few grizzly bears roaming around.

"But then, what do you make of these?" the man asked, pulling several long black hairs from a small plastic bag. "They were caught in the scratch marks."

With hardly a glance, the ranger passed them off. "Probably horse hairs."

"But these were way too high off the ground to be from a horse," he explained.

The ranger was a little slow on the uptake, but we immediately caught the drift of where the man with the mysterious hairs was headed. "Oh, you think it may have been a bigfoot?" we asked.

"Well, yeah, maybe. These hairs were awfully high up to be from a horse, and I've seen bigfoot tracks out this way before."

We're sure a chemical analysis could have told us what kind of hairs they were, but maybe it was more appealing to just theorize about what they might be. The legend of bigfoot is firmly entrenched in the Northwest, and though there aren't too many people around who have seen one of its footprints, the reports have been steady enough over the years to keep the belief alive.

Variously described over the years as being anywhere from under 5 feet tall to over 8 feet tall, most bigfoots share the common trait of being hairy and very shy of humans. In a few instances they have displayed aggresive behavior toward humans, but for the most part they have simply been curious about human activities. More frequent than actual sightings have been discoveries of bigfoot tracks, and it was just such tracks, found north of the Klamath River in California, that prompted a reporter for the *Humboldt Times* newspaper to coin the term "bigfoot" in 1958. This beast's other common name, Sasquatch, is derived from a Native American name used in the Fraser River valley of British Columbia.

Though bigfoot reports have come from all over the country, and all over the world for that matter, the region from northern California to southern British Columbia has produced by far the most incidents. Since the first settlers began arriving in this region, there have been hundreds of reports of giant footprints and handprints, as well as actual sightings of these large apelike creatures.

Among the most famous reports are that of "Jacko," a wild man captured in British Columbia in 1884. However, after the first newspaper report of this curious beast, there were no more reports. The single most famous sighting was that of two Sasquatch hunters who, in 1967, spotted a bigfoot and managed to film it on their movie camera.

If you'd like to do a bit of searching for Sasquatch, you should pick up a copy of the *Field Guide to Sasquatch* by David George Gordon (Sasquatch Books, 1992). This little book details the history of bigfoot in the Northwest and cites various sightings over the years. It even gives tips on how to recognize Sasquatch footprints and what to do if you should have a bigfoot encounter.

The Lake Chelan area also offers both **cross-country and downhill skiing** possibilities. The former at Bear Mountain Ranch (☎ 509/682-5444), which is just west of Chelan and has 30 miles (50km) of groomed trails, and the latter at Echo Valley (☎ 509/687-3167), a small ski area just north of Chelan. For golfers, there's the **Lake Chelan Municipal Golf Course,** 1501 Golf Course Dr. (☎ 509/682-5421). Stehekin is also a great spot for cross-country skiing.

Lake Chelan history is on display at the **Chelan Museum,** 204 E. Woodin Ave. (☎ 509/682-5644), open June 1 to October 1. Two other historic buildings worth a visit are the old **Log Church** and the **Campbell House Restaurant,** both on East Woodin Avenue. Just outside town you can view **Chelan Falls,** where the waters of Lake Chelan cascade down to the Columbia River.

WHERE TO STAY
IN CHELAN

Campbell's Resort on Lake Chelan
104 W. Woodin Ave., Chelan, WA 98816. ☎ **509/682-2561** or 800/553-8225. Fax 509/682-2177. 148 rms, 7 cottages, 4 suites. A/C TV TEL. Summer, $104–$156 room or cottage for one to four people; $156–$276 suite. Lower rates off-season. AE, CB, DISC, MC, V.

The first Campbell Hotel opened in 1901 and has remained Chelan's most popular lodging. Located on the banks of the lake right in downtown Chelan, Campbell's is now a small convention hotel, which unfortunately gives it a rather crowded, busy, and impersonal appearance. Many of the guest rooms, though updated, have an older feel about them, as does the entire resort, which, because of the acres of surrounding parking lots, lacks visual appeal. For newer rooms, you'll have to spend quite a bit extra. Fortunately, every room here has a lake view, and many, including several of the cottages, have a kitchen or kitchenette.

Dining/Entertainment: The Campbell House Restaurant is located in the original 1901 Campbell Hotel, and offers the most elegant dining on the lake, albeit without a view of the lake. There's a lounge adjacent to the restaurant and another lakeside deck lounge.

Facilities: 1,200-foot beach, two outdoor swimming pools, indoor and outdoor hot tubs, boat docks.

Darnell's Resort Motel
901 Spader Bay Rd., Chelan, WA 98816. ☎ **509/682-2015.** 40 units. A/C TV TEL. Summer, $140–$180 one- or two-bedroom unit; $295 penthouse. Lower rates off-season. AE, DISC, MC, V.

Located just a couple of blocks from downtown Chelan, Darnell's is set back from the road and surrounded by wide green lawns. This combination of proximity and attractive landscaping makes this our top choice in Chelan itself. Families make up the bulk of the guests here, and when you see the wealth of activities available at no extra cost, you'll understand why. However, couples, too, will enjoy the numerous amenities. Rooms vary from a humongous so-called penthouse suite to one- and two-bedroom units, which have kitchens, decks, and views of the lake. These rooms sleep up to six people.

Services: Complimentary use of rowboats, canoes, pedalboats, bicycles.

Facilities: Outdoor swimming pool, hot tub, sauna, tennis courts, nine-hole pitch-and-putt course, children's play area, boat launch and docks, shuffleboard, volleyball, badminton.

○ Kelly's Resort

Rte. 1, Chelan, WA 98816. ☎ **509/687-3220.** 9 cottages, 4 apts. Summer, $80–$110 cottage or apt for two. The rest of the year, $54–$75 cottage or apt for two. MC, V.

Located 14 miles from Chelan on the South Shore Road, this small family-cottage resort has been in business for more than 40 years. Set on a steep hillside, Kelley's includes nine cabins in the trees across the road, but for the great views, you can't beat the four apartments built right on the water. Two of these apartments have fireplaces. Facilities include a sandy sunbathing area, swimming area, playground, volleyball court, a boat dock, cozy lobby with a fireplace, a Ping-Pong table, and a general store.

Westview Resort Motel

2312 W. Woodin Ave. (Rte. 1), Chelan, WA 98816. ☎ **509/682-4396** or 800/468-2781. 20 rms, 2 cabins, 3 suites. TV TEL. Summer, $98 double; $135–$155 cabin or suite. Off-season, $48 double; $78 cabin or suite. AE, CB, DC, DISC, MC, V.

With lake views from every room, an outdoor pool, a whirlpool, and a public park with a beach adjacent, this comfortable motel on the south shore of the lake is a good choice, especially for families. The guest accommodations range from standard motel rooms to cabins that feature complete kitchens. Some of the rooms have VCRs, and all have coffeemakers, microwaves, refrigerators, and balconies or patios.

IN MANSON

⑤ Mountain View Lodge

25 Wapato Point Pkwy., Manson, WA 98831. ☎ **509/687-9505** or 800/967-8105. 30 rms, 6 suites. A/C TV TEL. Summer, $61–$89 double; $73–105 suite. Off-season, $42–$54 double; $53–$76 suite. AE, DISC, MC, V.

This family-oriented motel is in one of Lake Chelan's best neighborhoods and offers mountain views from the rooms (unfortunately, however, you can't see the lake). The guest rooms are large and have small refrigerators and plenty of counter space. Clean, simple, and comfortable, the rooms here are quite a bit less expensive than comparable rooms in Chelan, which makes the Mountain View very popular—book early. For recreational activities, you'll find a 24-hour outdoor swimming pool and hot tub, and a volleyball court. There are several restaurants within walking distance.

IN STEHEKIN

If you're heading up to Stehekin and plan to do your own cooking during your stay, bring your own food. Only limited groceries are available in Stehekin.

⑤ North Cascades Lodge

P.O. Box 457, Chelan, WA 98816. ☎ **509/682-4494.** 28 units. $69–$85 unit for two. MC, V.

Located right at Stehekin Landing, the North Cascades Lodge is shaded by tall conifers and overlooks the lake. A variety of accommodations range from basic rooms with no lake view to spacious apartments. The studio apartments, which have kitchens, are the best deal and all have lake views. The lodge's restaurant serves three meals a day but is only open from May 1 to October 15. Boat and bicycle rentals are available, and after a long day of pedaling, paddling, hiking, or riding you'll appreciate the hot tub.

✪ Silver Bay Lodging & Resort

P.O. Box 85, Stehekin, WA 98852. ☎ **509/682-2212.** 2 rms, 2 cabins. $85–$150 double or cabin for two. Additional person $20 extra. Lower rates off-season. Minimum stay two nights (five nights for cabins in summer). No credit cards.

Situated right on the banks of both the lake and the Stehekin River, Silver Bay offers both bed-and-breakfast rooms and self-catering cabins. The views are superb, and should you stay in the master suite, you'll find antiques, a soaking tub, and decks with a view of the river. Breakfast is included if you stay in one of the two rooms, but if you plan to stay in a cabin you'll need to bring your own food to cook. Bicycles and canoes are available to guests free of charge, and there's an outdoor hot tub for soaking away your aches and pains. A nearby restaurant serves meals year round and in winter there are groomed cross-country ski trails.

Stehekin Valley Ranch

P.O. Box 36, Stehekin, WA 98852. ☎ **509/682-4677.** 12 cabins. $55 per adult, $45 per child 7–12, $30 per child 4–6, $15 per child 3 and under. Rates include all meals and transportation in lower valley. $5 off if you bring sleeping bag or sheets. No credit cards.

If you're a camper at heart, then the "cabins" at the Stehekin Valley Ranch should be just fine. With canvas roofs, screen windows, and no electricity or plumbing, the cabins are little more than permanent tents. Bathroom facilities are in the nearby main building. Activities available at additional cost include horseback riding, river rafting, and mountain biking.

WHERE TO DINE
IN CHELAN

The most elegant restaurant in the area is the **Campbell House Restaurant,** part of Campbell's Resort. See "Where to Stay," above, for details.

Goochi's

104 E. Woodin Ave. ☎ **509/682-2436.** Reservations recommended. Main courses $9.50–$21. AE, MC, V. Daily 11am–9pm (longer hours in summer). INTERNATIONAL.

Despite its cavernous proportions, this popular restaurant and tavern can be packed to overflowing in summer, so be prepared for a wait. Eclectic in both decor and menu, Goochi's offers up everything from basic burgers to steak-and-prawn combos. Fire-eaters won't want to miss the fire pasta, a combination of chicken, linguine, cream, and chiles. To accompany any dish, there are more than two dozen microbrewery ales on tap in the summer. A long list of appetizers offers plenty to snack on if you just happen to be whiling away a few hours here. We like the Louisiana black-bean chili and tortilla chips. Late nights see live or recorded rock music as well as a weekly comedy night in summer, making this the number-one nightspot in town.

IN MANSON

El Vaquero

75 Wapato Way. ☎ **509/687-3179.** Main courses $7.75–$12. MC, V. Daily 11am–9pm (longer hours in summer). MEXICAN.

Manson is surrounded by apple orchards in which Mexican migrant workers do most of the work, so it should come as no surprise that the tiny town has an excellent Mexican restaurant. It's gaily decorated inside with a few serapes and sombreros strewn about the walls and Mexican music playing on the stereo. One whiff of the aromas wafting from the kitchen will tell you that this is down-home cooking. The Mexican barbacoa and the carne asada are two winners worth a taste. For dessert, don't pass up the sopapillas.

3 Winthrop & the North Cascades Scenic Highway

193 or 243 miles E of Seattle, 53 miles N of Chelan

Driving into Winthrop, you may think you've driven onto a movie set. A covered wooden sidewalk lines the town's main street. Over there's the trading post, and there's the blacksmith shop. If it's a Saturday in summer, you might even see a shootout. But where are the cameras?

No, this isn't a Hollywood set—this is the real Winthrop. It was cut off from humanity for so many years that it just never developed past the pioneer stage.

Well, that's not *exactly* true. Winthrop needed a way to stop a few of the cars that started crossing the North Cascades when the scenic highway opened in 1972. Someone suggested that they cash in on their Wild West heritage and put up some old-fashioned cow-town false fronts. This rewriting of history worked and now Winthrop gets plenty of cars to stop. In fact it has become a destination in its own right, known for its cross-country skiing in winter and mountain biking, hiking, and horseback riding in summer.

Winthrop and the Methow River valley in which it is located actually do have a Wild West history. Until 1883 there were no white settlers in this picturesque valley. The only inhabitants were Native Americans who annually migrated into the valley to harvest camas bulbs and fish for salmon. The Native Americans felt it was just too cold to live in the Methow Valley, but when the first white settlers showed up, they refused to listen to the Native Americans' weather reports and built their drafty log cabins anyway. Gold was discovered in the late 1800s and fueled a short-lived boom, but it was agriculture in the form of apples that kept the valley alive until the advent of tourism in the 1970s.

Why an Old West theme town? Possibly because Owen Wister, author of *The Virginian,* a western novel that became a popular television series, was inspired to write his novel after visiting his former Harvard University roommate, who ran a trading post in Winthrop.

ESSENTIALS

GETTING THERE   In summer you can take Wash. 20, the North Cascades Scenic Highway, from I-5 at Burlington. However, in winter this road is closed and it's necessary to cross from north of Seattle on U.S. 2 to Wenatchee and then drive north on U.S. 97. to Wash. 153 at Pateros. If you're coming from north-central or eastern Washington, head east on Wash. 20 at Okanogan.

VISITOR INFORMATION   Contact the **Winthrop Chamber of Commerce** (☎ **509/996-2125**). For information on the North Cascades Scenic Highway, contact **North Cascades National Park,** 2105 Wash. 20, Sedro Woolley, WA 98284 (☎ **360/856-5700**), which operates an information center, in conjunction with the U.S. Forest Service, in Sedro Woolley.

EXPLORING THE TOWN & ENJOYING THE GREAT OUTDOORS

Though Winthrop is primarily a base for skiers, hikers, and mountain bikers, it does have quite a few interesting shops, including a blacksmith's shop. If you're interested in the town's history, visit the **Shafer Historical Museum** (☎ **509/996-2712**), which consists of a collection of historic buildings from around the area. It's open in May, Saturday and Sunday from 10am to 5pm; and June to September, daily from 10am to 5pm; admission is by donation. To find the museum, go up Bridge Street from the junction of Wash. 20 and Riverside Drive and turn right on Castle Avenue.

With its sunshine and winter snows, the Methow Valley is legendary in the Northwest for its **cross-country skiing.** Ski trails abound in the area and you can pick up maps and rent equipment at Winthrop Mountain Sports (☎ 509/996-2886) or Sun Mountain Ski (☎ 509/996-2211 or 800/572-0493), located at Sun Mountain Lodge, which is where some of the most popular ski routes start.

If you've graduated from day trips and are interested in **hut-to-hut ski touring** through the North Cascades, contact Rendezvous Outfitters (☎ 509/996-2148). Downhill skiers in search of virgin powder can, if they can afford it, do some **heli-skiing** with North Cascade Heli-Skiing (☎ 800/494-HELI). A day of skiing that includes 10,000 vertical feet of slopes will cost $450 per person. A far tamer experience is the small **ski hill** at Loup Loup, 20 minutes east of Twisp on Wash. 20 (no phone), open Wednesday and Friday through Sunday. You can also go **dog-sledding** with Malamute Express (☎ 509/997-6402), which offers day trips along the Twisp River.

May to August is **white-water rafting** season on the Methow River. If you're interested, contact Osprey River Adventures (☎ 509/997-4116 or 800/997-4116). Trips are $50 to $60 per person. Summer is also **mountain biking** season, and most of the cross-country ski trails become biking trails. Mountain bike rentals are available from Winthrop Mountain Sports (☎ 509/996-2886) for $5 an hour or $20 a day.

Hikers will find miles of trails, including the **Pacific Crest Trail,** within a few miles of Winthrop. For information, contact the **Okanogan National Forest,** Winthrop Ranger District, Winthrop, WA 98862 (☎ **509/996-2266**), or the **North Cascades National Park,** Skagit and Wilderness District Office, Marblemount, WA 98267 (☎ **360/873-4590**).

If you've come to Winthrop because you're a cowboy at heart, you'll probably be interested in doing some **horseback riding.** Early Winters Outfitting (☎ 509/996-2659 or 800/843-7951) in Mazama offers rides ranging from an hour ($15) to overnight ($125). North Cascade Outfitters (☎ 509/997-1015) in Twisp also offers day and overnight trips.

WHERE TO STAY
IN WINTHROP
Expensive

✪ Sun Mountain Lodge

P.O. Box 1000, Winthrop, WA 98862. ☎ **509/996-2211** or 800/572-0493. 87 rms, 12 cabins. Summer, $125–$185 double; $130–$260 cabins. Winter, $89–$155 double; $94–$215 cabins. Spring/fall, $49–$100 double; $54–$240 cabins. AE, MC, V.

If you're looking for resort luxuries and proximity to hiking, cross-country skiing, and mountain-biking trails, the Sun Mountain Lodge should be your first choice in the region. Perched on a mountaintop with grand views of the Methow Valley and the North Cascades, this luxurious lodge captures the spirit of the West in both its breathtaking setting and its rustic design. In the lobby, flagstone floors, stone fireplaces, and wagon-wheel tables all combine in a classically western style. Most guest rooms feature rustic western furnishings and views of the surrounding mountains. The rooms in the Gardiner wing have balconies and slightly better views than those in the main lodge. If seclusion is what you're after, opt for one of the less luxurious cabins down on Patterson Lake.

Dining/Entertainment: The inn's dining room is vertiginously balanced on the edge of a mountainside with nothing but mountain air between you and the valley floor far below. A superb menu that focuses on Northwest cuisine makes this the region's best restaurant. Prices range from $18 to $25 for entrees.

Services: Concierge, ski rentals and ski school, horseback and sleigh rides, guided hikes, boat rentals, mountain-bike rentals, ice-skate rentals.

Facilities: Outdoor heated pool, two whirlpools, tennis courts, exercise room, ski shop, children's playground, ice-skating pond, lawn games.

Moderate/Inexpensive

⑤ Hotel Rio Vista

P.O. Box 815, Winthrop, WA 98862. ☎ **509/996-3535.** 16 rms. A/C TV TEL. $65–$80 double. MC, V.

As with all the other buildings in downtown Winthrop, the Rio Vista looks as if it had been built for a Hollywood western movie set. Behind the false front you'll find modern rooms with pine furnishings and an understated country decor. Step out onto your balcony and you'll have a view of the confluence of the Chewuch and Methow rivers. Guests often see deer, bald eagles, and many other species of birds. A hot tub overlooks the river.

The Virginian

808 N. Cascades Hwy. (Wash. 20), Winthrop, WA 98862. ☎ **509/996-2535** or 800/ 854-2834. 40 rms, 7 cabins. A/C TV. $55–$85 double; $75 cabin. AE, DISC, MC, V.

Located just east of downtown Winthrop, the Virginian is a collection of small cabins and motel rooms on the banks of the Methow River. Though the cabins are quaint, they don't have river views. The deluxe rooms overlooking the river are our favorite rooms. These have high ceilings, balconies, and lots of space. The rooms and cabins are all lined with cedar, which not only gives them a rustic feel but also makes them smell like a sauna. A heated swimming pool, hot tub, horseshoe pit, and volleyball court provide recreational options. The Virginian Restaurant is one of the best in town, and the Bicycle Bar is a fun place to hang out, especially if you're into cycling.

⑤ WolfRidge Resort

Wolf Creek Rd., Winthrop, WA 98862. ☎ **509/996-2828,** or 800/237-2388 in the Northwest. 12 rms, 6 suites, 6 town houses. TV TEL. $59–$69 double; $93 suite for two; $139 town house for two. MC, V. Head south out of Winthrop, cross the bridge, and turn right on Twin Lakes Road; after 1 1/2 miles, turn right onto Wolf Creek Road and drive for 4 miles to the lodge (the road turns to gravel after 3 miles).

Set at the edge of a pasture on both the Methow River and the cross-country ski trails, this lodge is a great choice in winter or summer. Accommodations are in modern log buildings, and many of the rooms have log-beam ceilings. The town houses and suites are big enough for families, and the smaller rooms are fine for couples. The lodge has an outdoor pool, indoor whirlpool, a recreation room with a pool table, and a children's playground.

IN MAZAMA

The Mazama Country Inn

42 Lost River Rd., Mazama, WA 98833. ☎ **509/996-2681,** or 800/843-7951 in Washington. Fax 509/996-2646. 14 rms. Summer, $70–$80 double. Winter (including all meals), $165–$175 double. MC, V.

Set on the flat valley floor but surrounded by rugged towering peaks and tall pine trees, this modern mountain lodge is secluded and peaceful and offers an escape from the crowds in Winthrop. If you're out here to get some exercise, be it hiking, mountain biking, cross-country skiing, or horseback riding, the Mazama Country Inn makes an excellent base of operations. After a hard day of having fun, you can come back and soak in the hot tub and have dinner in the rustic dining room with its massive freestanding fireplace and high ceiling. The guest rooms are of medium size and simply furnished, but modern and clean.

WHERE TO DINE

The best meals in the area are to be had at the dining room of the **Sun Mountain Lodge,** where you'll also enjoy one of the most spectacular views in the state. See "Where to Stay," above, for details.

IN WINTHROP

The Duck Brand

Wash. 20. ☎ **509/996-2192.** Reservations recommended in summer. Main courses $9.25–$15. AE, MC, V. Daily 7am–9pm. MEXICAN.

Located across the street from the gas station and partially hidden by trees, the Duck Brand is a casual restaurant with a big deck that's a great spot for a meal on a warm summer day. Be sure to notice the stream that runs under the deck. In cold or rainy weather, you can grab a table in the small dining room and order a plate of fajitas or ribs or any of the standard Mexican dishes, with a microbrew to wash it down. Just inside the front door on the left, you'll find a bakery case with muffins and cinnamon rolls that you can take with you for a trailside snack.

The Virginian Restaurant

808 N. Cascades Hwy. (Wash. 20). ☎ **509/996-2536.** Reservations recommended. Main courses $8.50–$15.75. AE, DISC, MC, V. Daily 7:30am–9pm. INTERNATIONAL.

With a name like the Virginian, you'd expect something very rustic, with a Wild West theme—but that's just not the case here. It's a very tastefully decorated dining room with knotty-pine paneling, antiques, lots of potted plants, and soft lighting. The adjacent Bicycle Bar is a cozy place with bicycles and cycling paraphernalia hanging from the walls and ceiling. There's a good selection of pastas, and a tasty chicken with mushrooms, green olives, artichokes, and green onions in a sherry wine sauce. Hummus and stir-fried pork are representative of the restaurant's international offerings.

Winthrop Brewing Company

155 Riverside Ave. ☎ **509/996-3183.** Main courses $7–$8. DISC, MC, V. Wed–Thurs and Sun 3:30–11pm, Fri–Sat 3:30pm–midnight. PUB.

In downtown Winthrop, this place is a popular local watering hole. It's quite jolly and friendly and you don't know who might be sitting next to you. We were fortunate to be here on St. Paddy's Day and had large dinners of corned beef, cabbage, and green mashed potatoes, but there's also chili with sausage and pale

ale, and Grandpa Clems's filling stew with brown ale. On weekends you might find a music jam going on.

THE NORTH CASCADES SCENIC HIGHWAY

Though numerous attempts were made over the years to build a road through the craggy, glacier-sculpted North Cascade mountains, it was not until 1972 that Wash. 20 finally connected Winthrop with the Skagit Valley and the communities of northern Puget Sound. Today the road is known as the North Cascades Scenic Highway, and it's one of the most breathtakingly beautiful stretches of road anywhere in the United States.

Unfortunately, because of heavy winter snows and avalanches, the road is only open from April to November (depending on the weather). The scenic highway begins just west of Winthrop, and along its length you'll find more than a dozen campgrounds. Backpackers can head off on hundreds of miles of trails through wilderness areas, national forest, national park, and national recreation areas. For information on camping and backpacking, contact the **Okanogan National Forest** or **North Cascades National Park** (see "Exploring the Town & Enjoying the Great Outdoors," above, for addresses and phone numbers) or **Mount Baker–Snoqualmie National Forest,** Mount Baker Ranger District, Sedro Woolley, WA 98284 (☎ **360/856-5700**).

The first place to stop along the highway is about 20 miles from Winthrop at **Washington Pass Overlook** (5,447 feet in elevation). On a clear day you can see the vistas of the North Cascades, dominated here by the granite peak of Liberty Bell Mountain.

It's another 5 miles to **Rainy Pass,** where the **Pacific Crest Trail** crosses the highway. This is a great place to get out for a bit of hiking. The **Rainy Lake Trail** is a mile-long paved trail that leads to a beautiful little lake. From Rainy Pass, you descend for the next 30 miles with **North Cascades National Park** to the south.

At the **Whistler Basin Overlook,** you have a superb view of rugged Whistler Mountain and the lush meadows at its base. If you're up for a longer hike, stop at Canyon Creek and walk to Rowley's Chasm, a 200-foot-deep cleft in a rocky hillside. The chasm is 1.8 miles up **Canyon Creek Trail.**

At the **Ross Lake Overlook,** the dammed waters of the Skagit River come into view. **Ross Lake National Recreation Area** and the lake extend for 24 miles to the north, with the lake extending 1 1/2 miles into Canada. The only access to the lake is by trail or water. (See "Where to Stay," below, for information on a floating lodge on the waters of Lake Ross.)

Farther down the road, you come to the **Diablo Lake Overlook.** High above the turquoise lake you can see glaciated Colonial and Pyramid peaks. Glacier-fed waters carrying suspended particles of silt are responsible for the amazing color of Diablo Lake. Continue down into the quaint company town at the base of Diablo Dam, which provides power for Seattle. Here you can take a 4 1/2-hour **boat tour of Diablo Lake** that is operated by Seattle City Light Skagit Tours (☎ **206/684-3030** or 206/233-2709). The tours start with a trip up an incline railway to the top of 389-foot-tall Diablo Dam. From there you board a boat for the 5-mile cruise to Ross Lake Dam, where you get a tour of the powerhouse. Finishing up your tour is a chicken dinner. Tours cost $24.50 for adults, $22 for seniors, $12.50 for children 6 to 11. There are also 1 1/2-hour tours of **Diablo Dam,** for $5, that don't include the boat ride or dinner. Tours are offered Thursday through Monday during the summer and fall, and reservations are recommended.

Below Diablo Dam, the highway parallels the Skagit River, and you soon come to **Gorge Creek Falls and Gorge Dam.** Just past these you enter the Seattle City Light company town of Newhalem. Marblemount, the next town you come to, is the headquarters for **North Cascades National Park,** and you can pick up more information on the park, as well as get permits for overnight backpacking trips.

Below Marblemount, you enter a section of the Skagit River that's a wintering ground for hundreds of **bald eagles** that congregate here to feast on dying salmon. January and February are the best months for eagle watching. There are numerous pullouts at the prime eagle-watching sites, but it's more fun to spot them from a raft floating slowly down the river (no white water here). Companies offering **eagle-watching float trips** include Alpine Whitewater (☎ 800/926-RAFT), which charges about $70 for a three-hour trip, and Downstream River Runners (☎ 800/234-4644), which offers a similar trip.

Just west of Rockport, you can visit **Rockport State Park** and take a hike through a stand of old-growth Douglas firs, some of which are more than 300 years old. West of the town of Concrete, which was named for the concrete it produced, you'll come to the turnoff for **Baker Lake,** a 9-mile-long reservoir that's a favorite of boaters and anglers. There are numerous campgrounds along the lake, and the end of the road is the trailhead for Mounts Baker and Shuksan.

WHERE TO STAY

In Ross Lake

Ross Lake Resort

Rockport, WA 98283. ☎ 360/386-4437. 13 cabins. $54–$104 cabin for two. MC, V. Drive to Diablo Dam on Wash. 20, then take a tugboat to the end of Diablo Lake where a truck carries you around the Ross Dam to the lodge; or hike in on a 2-mile trail from Milepost 134 on Wash. 20.

There may not be another lodging of this sort anywhere in the United States. All 13 of the resort's cabins are built on logs floating in Ross Lake. If you're looking to get away from it all, this place comes pretty close—there's not even a road to the resort. There's no grocery store or restaurant here, so be sure to bring enough food for your stay. What do you do once you get here? Rent a boat and go fishing, rent a kayak or canoe, do some hiking, or simply sit and relax.

In Rockport

Clark's Skagit River Cabins

5675 Wash. 20, Rockport, WA 98283. ☎ 360/873-2250. 23 cabins. TV. $47–$97 cabin for two. DISC, MC, V.

The first thing you notice when you turn into the driveway to Clark's Skagit River Cabins is the rabbits. They're everywhere—hundreds of them in all shapes and sizes, contentedly munching the lawns or just sitting quietly. Today the bunnies are one of the main attractions at Clark's, but it's the theme cabins that keep people coming back. Western, nautical, Victorian, Native American, Adirondack, hacienda, and mill are the current choices of interior decor in these cabins. There are also other cabins that are equally comfortable, but the decor in the theme cabins is what makes Clark's just a bit different. These cabins are especially popular in winter when folks flock to the area to watch the bald eagles that congregate on the Skagit River.

4 Mount Rainier National Park

Paradise: 110 miles SE of Seattle, 70 miles SE of Tacoma, 150 miles NE of Portland, 85 miles NW of Yakima

At 14,410 feet high, Mount Rainier is the highest point in Washington, and to the sun-starved residents of Seattle the dormant volcano is a giant weather gauge. When the skies clear over Puget Sound, "The Mountain is out" is a phrase often heard around the city. And when the Mountain is out, all eyes turn to admire its broad slopes, which remain snow-covered throughout the year. The region's infamous moisture-laden air has made Mount Rainier one of the snowiest spots in the country, and in 1972, the mountain set a record when $93^1/_2$ feet of snow fell in one year. Such record snowfalls have created numerous glaciers on the mountain's flanks, and one of these, the Carbon Glacier, is the lowest-elevation glacier in the continental United States.

Snow and glaciers notwithstanding, Rainier has a heart of fire. Steam vents at the mountain's summit are evidence that, though this volcanic peak has been dormant for more than 150 years, it could erupt again at any time. However, scientists believe that Rainier's volcanic activity occurs in 3,000-year cycles—and luckily we have another 500 years to go before there's another big eruption.

Known to Native Americans as Tahoma, Mount Rainier received its current name in 1792 when British explorer Capt. George Vancouver named the mountain for a friend who never visited the region. The first ascent to the mountain's summit was made in 1870 by Gen. Hazard Stevens and Philemon Van Trump, and it was 14 years later that James Longmire built the first hotel on the flanks of Mount Rainier. In 1889 Mount Rainier became the fifth national park. Today the park covers 235,612 acres and is visited by more than two million people a year.

ESSENTIALS

GETTING THERE   If you're coming from Seattle and your destination is Paradise, head for the southwest (Nisqually) park entrance. Take I-5 south to Exit 127 and then head west on Wash. 512. Take the Wash. 7 exit and head south toward Elbe. At Elbe, continue east on Wash. 706.

If you're coming from Seattle and are heading for the northeast (White River) park entrance en route to Sunrise or Crystal Mountain, take I-90 to I-405 south. At Renton, take Wash. 169 south to Enumclaw, where you pick up Wash. 410 heading east.

Note that in winter only the roads from the Nisqually entrance to Paradise and from the Stevens Canyon (southeast) entrance to the Ohanapecosh Visitor Center are kept open.

From Portland, head north on I-5 to Exit 68 and then take U.S. 12 east to the town of Morton. From Morton, head north on Wash. 7 to Elbe and then turn east on Wash. 706, which will bring you to the Nisqually (southwest) park entrance.

From May to October, **Grayline of Seattle** (☎ **800/426-7532**) operates one bus daily between Seattle and Mount Rainier; the fare is $19.50 each way.

VISITOR INFORMATION   Contact **Mount Rainier National Park,** Tahoma Woods, Star Route, Ashford, WA 98304 (☎ **206/569-2211**).

PARK ADMISSION   The park entrance fee is $5 per vehicle and $3 per person for pedestrians or cyclists. Another option, if you plan to visit several national parks in a single year, is the Golden Eagle Passport, an annual pass good at all national parks and recreation areas. The pass costs $25 and is available at all national park visitor centers. If you're over 62, you can get a Golden Age Passport for $10, and if you have a disability, you can get a free Golden Access Passport.

SEEING THE HIGHLIGHTS

Just past the Nisqually (southwest) entrance, the park's main entrance, you'll come to **Longmire,** site of the National Park Inn, the Longmire Museum (with exhibits on the park's natural and human history), a hiker-information center that issues backcountry permits, and a ski-touring center where you can rent cross-country skis in winter.

The road then continues climbing to **Paradise** (elevation 5,400 feet), the aptly named mountainside aerie from which you get a breathtaking close-up view of the mountain. Paradise is the park's most popular destination, so expect crowds. During July and August the meadows here are ablaze with wildflowers. The circular **Henry M. Jackson Memorial Visitor Center** (☎ **360/569-2211,** ext. 2328) provides 360° panoramic views, and includes exhibits on the flora, fauna, and geology of the park, as well as a display on mountain climbing. The visitor center is open daily from early May to mid-October and on weekends and holidays from mid-October to early May. A 1.2-mile walk from the visitor center will bring you to a spot from which you can look down on the Nisqually Glacier. It's not unusual to find plenty of snow at Paradise as late as July, and it was here that the world-record snowfall of 1972 was recorded.

In the summer months you can continue beyond Paradise to the **Ohanapecosh Visitor Center** (☎ **360/569-2211,** ext. 2352), which is open weekends from late May to mid-June and daily from mid-June to early October. Nearby, you can walk through the **Grove of the Patriarchs,** a forest of old-growth trees, some of which are more than 1,000 years old.

Continuing around the mountain, you'll come to the turnoff for **Sunrise.** At 6,400 feet, Sunrise is the highest spot accessible by car. A beautiful old log lodge serves as the **Sunrise Visitor Center** (☎ **360/569-2211,** ext. 2357). From here you get a superb view of Mount Rainier and **Emmons Glacier,** which is the largest glacier in the 48 contiguous states.

If you want to avoid the crowds and see a bit of dense old-growth forest, or do a bit of uncrowded hiking, head for the park's **Carbon River entrance** in the northwest corner. This is the least visited region of the park because it only offers views to those willing to hike several miles uphill. Carbon River has another distinction as well. It's formed by melt water from the Carbon Glacier, a glacier that descends lower than any other glacier in the continental United States.

SPORTS & OUTDOOR ACTIVITIES

If, after a long day of exercising, you'd like to soak in a hot tub or get a massage, contact the little woodland spa called **Wellspring** (☎ 360/569-2514). You'll find Wellspring in Ashford not far from the Nisqually park entrance. An hour in the hot tub costs $10 per person, while an hour massage costs $45.

HIKING & BACKPACKING   Hikers have more than 240 miles of trails to explore within the park.

Although Paradise sees a lot of visitors, it also offers many excellent day hikes. The 5-mile **Skyline Trail** is the highest trail at Paradise and climbs above the treeline. Along the way there are views of Mount Adams, Mount St. Helens, and the Nisqually Glacier. The **Lakes Trail,** of similar length, heads downhill to the Reflection Lakes.

At Sunrise there are numerous trails of varying lengths. Among these, the 5-mile **Burroughs Mountain Trail** and the 5.6-mile **Mount Fremont Trail** are both very rewarding—the latter even offers a chance to see mountain goats. The **Summerland Trail,** which starts 3 miles from the White River park entrance (the road to Sunrise), is another very popular day hike. This trail starts in forest and climbs up into meadows with a great view of the mountain.

If you'd like to do a hike with a llama, contact the **Llama Tree Ranch** (☎ **206/ 491-LAMA**), which offers "lunch with a llama," a four- to five-hour hike in Gifford Pinchot National Forest just outside the park, for $35. Longer trips are also available.

The 95-mile-long **Wonderland Trail,** which circles the mountain, is the quintessential Mount Rainier backpacking trip. This trail takes 10 days to two weeks to complete and offers up spectacular scenery. However, there are also many shorter overnight hikes. Before heading out on any overnight backpacking trip, you'll need to pick up a permit at the Longmire Hiker Information Center, the White River Hiker Information Center, or the Carbon River Ranger Station.

For the less adventurous, there are naturalist-led programs and walks throughout the spring, summer, and fall. Check the park newspaper for schedules.

MOUNTAINEERING   Climbers will know of Mount Rainier's reputation as a training ground for making attempts on higher peaks, such as Mount Everest. If you're interested in taking a mountain-climbing class, contact **Rainier Mountaineering, Inc.,** 535 Dock St., Tacoma, WA 98402 (☎ **360/569-2227** in summer or 206/627-6242 in winter).

HORSEBACK RIDING   If you'd like to do some horseback riding, head 19 miles east of Chinook Pass on Wash. 410 to Bumping River Road where you'll find **Susee's Skyline Packers** (☎ **206/472-5558**), which offers rides of various lengths for $16 to $86.

WINTER SPORTS   In winter miles of trails are open to **cross-country skiing,** but there is limited access because of road closures. At Longmire, you'll find a ski touring and rental shop (☎ 360/569-2411). There are also **guided snowshoe walks** at Paradise.

Outside the park, near the town of Packwood, you can ski cross-country from hut to hut on an 88-mile trail system. For more information, contact the **Mount Tahoma Trails Association,** P.O. Box 206, Ashford, WA 98304 (☎ **360/569-2451**).

Just outside the northeast corner of the park, you'll find the **Crystal Mountain ski area;** see Chapter 5 for details. You'll also find downhill and cross-country skiing less than 20 miles from the southeast corner of the park on U.S. 12 at the small **White Pass ski area** (☎ **509/453-8731,** or 509/672-3100 for a ski report). You can ski downhill or cross-country, and rental equipment is available. Lift rates range from $13 for an adult half-day midweek ticket to $29 for a full-day weekend ticket.

A NEARBY WILDLIFE PARK

Northwest Trek Wildlife Park

11610 Trek Dr. E., Eatonville. ☎ **360/832-6116** or 800/433-TREK. Admission $7.85 adults, $7 seniors, $5.50 children 5–17, $3.50 children 3–4. Mar–July 3 and Labor Day–Oct, daily 9:30am–5pm; July 4–Labor Day, daily 8:30am–6pm; Nov–Feb, Fri–Sun 9:30am–dusk.

The animals of North America are the focus of Northwest Trek, a 635-acre wildlife park 35 miles south of Tacoma off Wash. 161. Bison roam, elk bellow, and moose munch contentedly knee-deep in a lake. Visitors are driven through the park in a tram accompanied by a naturalist and learn about the lives of the animals they see along the route. In separate areas, you can see a grizzly bear, a wolf, and such wild cats as cougars, lynx, and bobcats.

WHERE TO STAY
INSIDE THE PARK

⑤ National Park Inn

P.O. Box 108, Ashford, WA 98304. ☎ **360/569-2275.** 25 rms, 18 with bath. $60 double without bath, $84–$110 double with bath. AE, CB, DC, DISC, MC, V.

Located in Longmire in the southwest corner of the park, this rustic lodge was opened in 1920 and fully renovated in 1990. With only 25 rooms and open all year, the National Park Inn makes a great little getaway or base for exploring the mountain. The inn's front veranda has a view of Mount Rainier, and inside there's a guest lounge with a river-rock fireplace that's perfect for winter-night relaxing. The guest rooms vary in size, but come with rustic furniture, new carpeting, and coffeemakers. In winter this lodge is popular with cross-country skiers; rentals are available. The inn's restaurant has a limited menu that nevertheless manages to have something for everyone. There's also a small bar.

✪ Paradise Inn

P.O. Box 108, Ashford, WA 98304. ☎ **360/569-2275.** 126 rms, 95 with bath; 2 suites. $64 double without bath, $90–$116 double with bath; $123 suite. AE, CB, DC, DISC, MC, V. Closed early Oct to mid-May.

Built in 1917 high on the flanks of Mount Rainier in an area aptly known as Paradise, this rustic lodge offers breathtaking views of the mountain and the nearby Nisqually Glacier. Miles of trails and meadows make this the perfect spot for some relatively easy alpine exploring. Cedar-shake siding, huge exposed beams, cathedral ceilings, and a gigantic stone fireplace all add up to a quintessential mountain retreat. A warm and cozy atmosphere prevails. The guest rooms vary in size and amenities, so be sure to specify which type you'd like.

The inn's large dining room serves three meals a day, and the Sunday brunch, served from 11am to 2:30pm, is legendary. There's also a lounge and a snack bar.

OUTSIDE THE PARK
Expensive

Alta Crystal Resort

68317 Wash. 410 E., Greenwater, WA 98022. ☎ **360/663-2500.** 25 chalets. $79–$159 chalet for one to four. AE, MC, V.

This is the closest lodging to the northeast park entrance and the Sunrise area. Though this condominium resort with wooded grounds is most popular in winter when skiers flock to Crystal Mountain's slopes (just minutes away), there's also plenty to do in summer, with an outdoor pool and nearby hiking trails.

Accommodations are in one-bedroom and loft chalets. The former sleep up to four people and the latter have bed space for up to eight people. No matter what size condo you choose, you'll find a full kitchen and fireplace. The loft chalets also have two bathrooms and skylights.

Moderate
Alexander's Country Inn

37515 Wash. 706 E., Ashford, WA 98304. ☎ **360/569-2300** or 800/654-7615. 12 rms, 8 with bath; 2 suites. $75 double without bath, $89 double with bath; $125 suite. Rates include full breakfast. Lower rates Nov–Apr. MC, V.

This large bed-and-breakfast inn is located just outside the park's southwest entrance in a building that dates back to 1912 when it was first opened as an inn. Though the exterior is uninspiring, much care has been taken in restoring the interior. Up a flight of stairs, there's a big lounge for guests. You can sit by the fire on a cold night before heading off to your room. By far the best room in the house is the tower suite, which is in a turret and has plenty of windows looking out on the woods. After a hard day of playing on the mountain, there's no better place to relax than in the hot tub overlooking the inn's trout pond.

On the first floor you'll find the inn's acclaimed restaurant. The menu displays a Northwest creativity that's a welcome change from most mountain menus of steaks and burgers. Entrees are in the $14 to $18 range.

The Hobo Inn

P.O. Box 921, Elbe, WA 98330. ☎ **360/569-2500.** 8 rms. May–Oct, $70–$85 double. Oct–May, $50–$60 double. MC, V.

If you're a railroad buff, you won't want to pass up this opportunity to spend the night in a remodeled caboose. Each of the eight cabooses is a little bit different (one even has its own private hot tub). Though the oldest of the cars dates back to 1916, they have all been outfitted with comfortable beds and bathrooms. Some have bay windows while others have cupolas.

For the total railroad experience, you can dine in the adjacent Mount Rainier Dining Co. dining car restaurant and go for a ride on the Mount Rainier Scenic Railroad.

ⓈNisqually Lodge

31609 Wash. 706, Ashford, WA 98304. ☎ **360/569-8804.** 24 rms. A/C TV TEL. May–Oct, $67–$77 double. Oct–May, $50–$60 double. Rates include continental breakfast. AE, DC, MC, V.

Located just outside Ashford and very close to the park entrance, the Nisqually Lodge offers convenience and a chaletlike atmosphere. Stone pillars, exposed beams, and cedar siding create a quintessential mountain-lodge appeal from the outside, and inside the high-ceilinged lobby you'll find a large fireplace. Best of all, you don't have to pay a fortune for these pleasant surroundings. The guest rooms are basic motel style—clean and comfortable, but with no frills. A hot tub will warm you on cold nights.

Inexpensive
Hotel Packwood

102 Main St., Packwood, WA 98361. ☎ **360/494-5431.** 9 rms, 2 with bath. TV. $25–$30 double without bath, $38 double with bath. No credit cards.

Two stories tall with a wraparound porch and weathered siding, this renovated 1912 hotel looks like a classic mountain lodge even though it's right in the middle of this small town. The tiny rooms are for those who aren't finicky. Most guests here spend their days tripsing around on park trails and come back to the hotel thoroughly exhausted. Though the hotel lacks character, there are iron bed frames in some rooms, a fireplace in the lobby, and a hot tub. Packwood is about 10 miles from the southeast entrance to the park.

CAMPGROUNDS

There are five campgrounds within the park, all of which are available on a first-come, first-served basis and stay full throughout the summer. Arrive early. The fees range from $6 to $10 per campsite per night. No electrical or water hookups are available. The **White River Campground** is close to Sunrise, which is one of the most spectacular spots in the park. Only the **Sunshine Point Campground** (☎ **360/569-2211,** ext. 3314) is open year round. There are also numerous National Forest Service campgrounds along Wash. 410 east of the park.

WHERE TO DINE

The best place to dine near the Ashford entrance to the park is at **Alexander's Country Inn** (see "Outside the Park" under "Where to Stay," above, for details).

In the park there are dining rooms at the Paradise Inn and the National Park Inn. There are also snack bars at the Henry M. Jackson Memorial Visitor Center, at Paradise, and at Sunrise Lodge.

Mt. Rainier Railroad Dining Co.

Elbe. ☎ **360/569-2505.** Reservations recommended. Main courses $10–$17. MC, V. Mon–Fri 8am–8pm, Sat–Sun 6am–9pm. AMERICAN.

You can't miss this unusual restaurant in Elbe—just watch for all the cabooses of the adjacent Hobo Inn. Meals are basic, with steaks and fried seafoods the staples of the dinner menu, but the surroundings make this place worth a stop. You'll be dining in an old railroad dining car. Your car won't go anywhere while you dine, but you'll get a sense of being on a rail journey.

If you'd like to actually go somewhere while you dine in a rail car, you can, for $55 per person, take the Cascadian Dinner Train, which is operated by these same folks. The dinner train leaves from the nearby town of Morton and spends four hours riding the rails while diners enjoy a prime-rib dinner. Phone 360/569-2588 for reservations.

5 Mount St. Helens National Volcanic Monument

Coldwater Ridge Visitor Center: 90 miles N of Portland, 168 miles S of Seattle

Named in 1792 by Capt. George Vancouver for his friend Baron St. Helens, Mount St. Helens was once considered the most perfect of the Cascade peaks, a snow-covered cone rising above lush forests. However, on May 18, 1980, all that changed when Mount St. Helens erupted with a violent explosion previously unknown in modern times.

The eruption blew out the side of the volcano and removed the top 1,300 feet of the peak, causing the largest landslide in history. This blast is estimated to have traveled at up to 650 miles per hour, with air temperatures of up to 800° Fahrenheit. The eruption also sent more than 540 million tons of ash nearly 16 miles into the atmosphere. This massive volume of ash rained down on an area of 22,000 square miles and could be measured as far away as Denver.

Today the area surrounding the volcano is designated the Mount St. Helens National Volcanic Monument. The best place to start an exploration of the monument is at the **Visitor Center** (☎ **360/274-2100**), located at Silver Lake, 5 miles east of Castle Rock on Wash. 504; it's open daily from 9am to 6pm in summer,

9am to 5pm in winter. The visitor center houses extensive exhibits on the eruption and its effects on the region.

Before even reaching this center, you can stop and watch a 25-minute, 70mm film about the eruption at the **Mount St. Helens Cinedome Theater** (☎ **360/ 274-8000**), located at Exit 49 off I-5; tickets cost $5 for adults and $4 for seniors and children.

For a closer look at the crater, continue to the **Coldwater Ridge Visitor Center,** at milepost 47 on Wash. 504, only 8 miles from the crater. This center features interpretive displays on the events leading up to the eruption and the subsequent slow regeneration of life around the volcano; hours are the same as at the main center. Here at Coldwater Ridge you'll also find a picnic area, an interpretive trail, a restaurant, and a boat launch at Coldwater Lake.

On the road up to the Coldwater Ridge Visitor Center, you'll pass the **Hoffstadt Bluffs Visitor Center** at milepost 27 (open daily from 9am to 8pm; shorter hours in winter), which has a snack bar and is the takeoff site for helicopter flights over Mount St. Helens ($69).

A few miles farther, just past milepost 33, you'll come to the **Forest Learning Center,** open May to October only, daily from 10am to 7pm. It's primarily a pro-motional center for the timber industry but does show a short but fascinating video about the eruption in a theater designed to resemble an ash-covered landscape. There are also displays on how forests destroyed by the blast have been replanted. Outside the center you can look down on a herd of elk that live in the Toutle River Valley far below.

Though these two centers can give you an idea of the power of the explosion that blew off this mountain's top, you need to drive around to the monument's east side for a close-up view of how the eruption affected the surrounding lands. Here that you'll see the forest that was blown down by the eruption. For the best views, take U.S. 12 east from Exit 68 off I-5. In Randle, head south on Forest Road 25 and then take Local Route 26. The **Woods Creek Information Center,** on Route 25 just before the junction with Route 26, has information on this part of the monument. Route 26 travels through mile after mile of blown-down trees, and though the sight of the thousands of trees that were felled by a single blast is quite bleak, it reminds us of the awesome power of nature. More than a decade after the eruption, life is slowly returning to this devastated forest.

At Meta Lake, Route 26 joins Route 99, which continues to the **Windy Ridge Viewpoint,** where visitors get their closest look at the volcano. Below Windy Ridge lies **Spirit Lake,** which was once one of the most popular summer vacation spots in the Washington Cascades. Today the lake is desolate and lifeless.

For more information before you go, contact **Mount St. Helens National Volcanic Monument,** 42218 NE Yale Bridge Rd., Amboy, WA 98601 (☎ **360/ 750-3900**).

HIKING & CLIMBING

If you're an experienced hiker in good physical condition, you may want to con-sider climbing to the top of Mount St. Helens. It's an 8- to 10-hour, 10-mile hike and can require an ice axe. The trailhead is on the south side of the monument and permits are required between May 15 and October 31. Because this is a very popular climb, you should request a permit in advance (summer weekends book up months in advance). However, you can also try your luck at getting an unre-served permit on the day of your climb. These are issued at Jack's Restaurant and store on Wash. 503, 5 miles west of Cougar. To request a climbing permit, phone 360/750-3920.

On the south side of the monument you can explore the **Ape Cave,** a lava tube that was formed 1,900 years ago when lava poured from the volcano. When the lava finally stopped flowing, it left a 2-mile-long cave that's the longest continuous lava tube in the Americas. At the Apes Headquarters (open daily from late May to September), you can rent a lantern for exploring the cave on your own or join a regular ranger-led exploration of the cave.

Hikers who aren't making the climb to the summit will find many other hiking trails within the monument, some in blast zones and some in forests that were left undamaged by the eruption. Ask at any visitor center for trail information.

UNIQUE WAYS TO SEE THE MOUNTAIN

If you'd like a bird's-eye view of the volcano, you can take a **helicopter flight** from the Hoffstadt Bluffs Visitor Center ($69 per person) or go up in a **small plane** with C&C Aviation (☎ 503/760-6969 or 800/516-6969), which flies out of the Evergreen Airport in Vancouver, Washington ($50 per person). **Mountain-bike tours** just outside the monument are offered by Volcano View Mountain Bike Tours (☎ 360/274-4341). **Mount St. Helens Adventure Tours** (☎ 360/ 274-6542) offers a variety of personalized tours including van tours, cross-country ski tours, mountain-bike tours, horse tours, and others.

CAMPING & ACCOMMODATIONS

In addition to the motel listed below, you'll find 11 campgrounds near the monument. **Sequest State Park,** on Wash. 504, is the closest to Coldwater Ridge, and **Iron Creek Campground** is the closest to Windy Ridge. If you'd like to spend the night at a camp inside the blast zone, **Mount St. Helens Adventure Tours,** 980 Schaffran Rd., Castle Rock (☎ 360/274-6542; fax 360/274-8437), offers a tent-and-breakfast tour that includes a night in a large tent, plus dinner and breakfast for $75 per person.

Timberland Inn & Suites

1271 Mt. St. Helens Way, Castle Rock, WA 98611. ☎ **360/274-6002.** Fax 360/274-6335. 40 rms and suites. A/C TV TEL. $66–$98 double or suite. AE, DC, DISC, MC, V.

This newer motel is right off I-5 at Exit 49 and is adjacent to the Cinedome Theatre. The guest rooms are for the most part standard-issue motel rooms, but the suites have separate sitting areas. Some suites also have whirlpool tubs.

The Olympic Peninsula &
the Washington Coast

8

The Olympic Peninsula, located in the northwesternmost corner of Washington, is a rugged and remote region that was one of the last places in the continental United States to be explored. Its nearly impenetrable rain-soaked forests and steep, glacier-carved mountains effectively restricted settlement to the peninsula's coastal regions for many years. However, long before the first white settlers arrived various Native American tribes had called the peninsula home. The Makah, Quinault, Hoh, Elwha, and Skokomish tribes all inhabited different regions of the peninsula, but they, too, stayed close to the coast, where they could harvest the plentiful mollusks, fish, and whales.

When the white settlers arrived, they took one look at the 300-foot-tall trees that grew on the Olympic Peninsula and started sharpening their axes. Though the settlers began chopping away at the edges of the region's vast rain forests, the supply of trees seemed to be endless. However, by the 1980s the end was in sight for the trees that had not been preserved in the Olympic National Park, a vast reserve that covers the center of the peninsula. U.S. 101 was, and still is, surrounded by clear-cut forests for much of its length, a fact that takes many first-time visitors by surprise. The past two decades saw the virgin forests of the peninsula disappearing at an alarming rate that sent environmentalists scrambling for some way to stop the cutting before there were no more of the grand, old-growth trees that had so amazed the first settlers. The northern spotted owl, which is dependent on old-growth forests for its survival, proved to be just what was needed. With the listing of the owl as a federally threatened species (one step below endangered), the cutting of old-growth forests on public land came to a screeching halt.

Dozens of stately Victorian homes (many of which are now bed-and-breakfast inns) and a restored historic district filled with shops and restaurants have made the town of Port Townsend, in the northeast corner of the peninsula, one of the most popular destinations in Washington. Likewise, at the southern end of the Washington coast, the narrow Long Beach Peninsula provides Washington with its greatest concentration of beach resorts.

1 Port Townsend: A Restored Victorian Seaport

60 miles NW of Seattle, 48 miles E of Port Angeles, 40 miles S of Anacortes

Named by English explorer Capt. George Vancouver in 1792, Port Townsend did not attract its first settlers until 1851. By the 1880s the town had become an important shipping port and was expected to grow into one of the most important cities on the West Coast. Port Townsend felt that it was the logical end of the line for the transcontinental railroad that was pushing westward in the 1880s. Based on the certainty of a railroad connection, a real-estate and development boom struck Port Townsend. Merchants and investors erected mercantile palaces along Water Street and elaborate Victorian homes on the bluff above the wharf district. However, the railroad never arrived. Seattle got the rails and Port Townsend got the shaft. With its importance as a shipping port usurped by Seattle and Tacoma, Port Townsend slipped into quiet obscurity. Progress passed it by and its elegant homes and commercial buildings were left to slowly fade away. However, in 1976 the waterfront district and bluff-top residential neighborhood were declared a National Historic District and the town began a slow revival. Today the streets of Port Townsend are once again crowded with people. The waterfront district is filled with boutiques, galleries, and other unusual shops, and many of the Victorian homes atop the bluff have become bed-and-breakfast inns.

ESSENTIALS

GETTING THERE Port Townsend is on Wash. 20, off U.S. 101 in the northeast corner of the Olympic Peninsula.

There are flights to Port Townsend's Jefferson County International Airport from Seattle and the San Juan Islands on **Port Townsend Airways** (☎ 360/385-6554 or 800/385-6554).

Washington State Ferries (☎ 800/84-FERRY) operates a ferry between Port Townsend and Keystone on Whidbey Island. The crossing takes 30 minutes and costs $5.90 to $7.10 for a vehicle and driver and $1.75 for passengers.

VISITOR INFORMATION Contact the **Port Townsend Chamber of Commerce Visitors Information Center,** 2437 E. Sims Way, Port Townsend, WA 98368 (☎ 360/385-2722).

GETTING AROUND If you need a taxi, call **Peninsula Taxi** (☎ 360/385-1872).

FESTIVALS Port Townsend festivals include the **Hot Jazz Port Townsend** festival, the third weekend in February; the **Wooden Boat Festival,** the largest of its kind in the United States, in early September; the **Kinetic Sculpture Race,** using outrageous human-powered vehicles, the first Sunday in October; and the **Historic Homes Tours,** on the first weekend in May and the third weekend in September.

EXPLORING THE TOWN

Few places in America have such a collection of restored Victorian homes and commercial buildings—the most popular activity in town is to simply walk or drive the historic districts. **Water Street** is the main shopping district and a stroll here will likely turn up a few shops, boutiques, or galleries that interest almost anyone.

The Olympic Peninsula & the Washington Coast

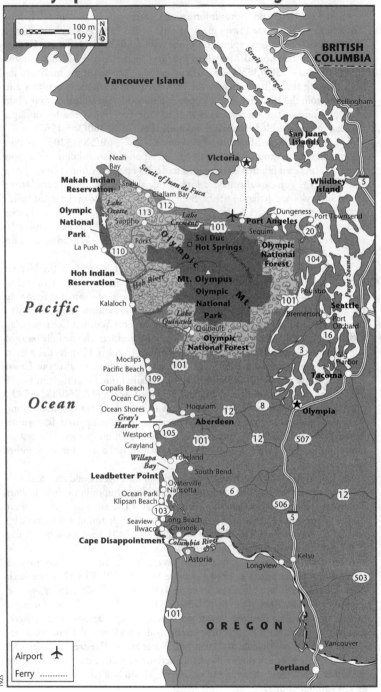

0 — 100 m / 109 y

BRITISH COLUMBIA

Vancouver Island

Strait of Georgia

Bellingham

San Juan Islands

Victoria

Whidbey Island

5

Neah Bay

Makah Indian Reservation

Sekiu

Strait of Juan de Fuca

Clallam Bay

Lake Ozette

113   112

Olympic National Park

Sappho

Lake Crescent

101

Port Angeles

Dungeness   Port Townsend

Sequim

20

Forks

Sol Duc Hot Springs

Olympic

Olympic National Forest

104

La Push

110

Hoh Indian Reservation

Hoh River

Mt. Olympus

Mts

101

Poulsbo

Seattle

Kalaloch

Olympic National Park

Bremerton   Port Orchard

Lake Quinault

Puget Sound

Pacific

Quinault

Olympic National Forest

16

Gig Harbor

Moclips

Pacific Beach

109

3

Tacoma

Copalis Beach

Ocean City

Ocean Shores

Hoquiam

12   8

Olympia

Ocean

Gray's Harbor

Aberdeen

Westport

105

Grayland

101   12

507

Willapa Bay

Tokeland

Leadbetter Point

South Bend

6

Oysterville

Nahcotta

Ocean Park

Klipsan Beach

103

506

5

12

Seaview

Ilwaco

Long Beach

Chinook

4

Cape Disappointment

Columbia River

Kelso

Astoria

Longview

503

OREGON

101

Vancouver

Airport ✈

Ferry ·········

Portland

1925

At the Port Townsend Visitor Information Center, you can pick up a **"Historic Tour Map"** that lists the town's many historic homes and commercial buildings. Before starting out on an exploration of the town, stop by the **Jefferson County Historical Museum and Maritime Library,** at the corner of Madison and Water streets (☎ **360/385-1003**), where you can learn about the history of the area. Among the collections here are regional Native American artifacts and antiques from the Victorian era. It's open Monday through Saturday from 11am to 4pm. You can also get an overview of historic Port Townsend by joining a walking tour by **Guided Historical Sidewalk Tours** (☎ **360/385-1967**).

The **Ann Starrett Mansion,** 744 Clay St. (☎ **360/385-3205**), is Port Townsend's most astoundingly ornate Queen Anne Victorian home and is now a bed-and-breakfast inn that offers guided tours. It's open daily from noon to 3pm; tours cost $3. You can also have a look inside the **Rothschild House,** at the corner of Taylor and Jefferson streets. Built in 1868, this is one of the oldest buildings in town and displays a very sober architecture as compared to other houses in town. It's open April to October 15, daily from 11am to 4pm; and October 16 to November, on Saturday and Sunday from 11am to 4pm. Admission is $2 for adults and $1 for children.

The **Fort Worden State Park Conference Center** is north of the historic district and can be reached by turning onto Kearney Street at the south end of town, or by turning onto Monroe Street at the north end of town, and following the signs. This former military installation was built at the turn of the century to guard the mouth of Puget Sound. You can visit the **Fort Worden Commanding Officer's House** (☎ **360/385-0854**), a Victorian-era officer's home fully restored and filled with period antiques. It's open April to October 15 only, daily from 10am to 5pm; admission is $1. The 360-acre park also contains the **Coast Artillery Museum** (☎ **360/385-0373**), open daily from 11am to 5pm for $1 admission; the **Port Townsend Marine Science Center** (☎ **360/385-5582**), open Tuesday through Sunday from noon to 6pm for $1 admission; along with with beaches, an underwater park for scuba divers, campgrounds, a **youth hostel** (☎ **360/385-0655**), picnic areas, a Rhododendron Garden, two restaurants, and the **Centrum** (☎ **360/385-3102**), which is the site of many summer concerts.

Sea kayaking is a favorite recreational activity in the Puget Sound area, and each year over the Labor Day weekend the Sea Kayaking Symposium is held in Port Townsend. This symposium also coincides with the annual Wooden Boat Festival. Any time of year you can try your hand at paddling a sea kayak by contacting **Kayak Port Townsend** (☎ **360/385-6240**), which offers half-day ($38) and full-day tours ($68) on nearby waters.

After dark, you can catch live music (everything from jazz to country to classical to rock) at **Lanza's,** 1020 Lawrence St. (☎ **360/385-6221**); the **Back Alley Tavern,** one block off Water Street on Tyler Street (☎ **360/385-2914**); and the **Public House,** 1038 Water St. (☎ **360/385-9708**). If you're lucky, you might catch a performance by Port Townsend's own **Flying Karamazov Brothers,** though they spend most of their time on the road. Check with the Visitors Information Center for a schedule of events. The **Water Street Theatre,** 926 Water St. (☎ **360/385-2422**), is a dinner theater located in the Water Street Deli. Plays are performed throughout the year and tickets are $25 to $28 with dinner and $12 to $14 without dinner.

WHERE TO STAY

○ Ann Starrett Mansion

744 Clay St., Port Townsend, WA 98368. ☎ **360/385-3205** or 800/321-0644, ext. 48. 11 rms, 10 with bath. $70–$225 double. Rates include full breakfast. AE, DISC, MC, V.

The Starrett is about being pampered amid Victorian elegance. Built in 1889 for $6,000 as a wedding present for Ann Starrett, this Victorian jewel box is by far the most elegant and ornate bed-and-breakfast in Port Townsend. A three-story turret towers over the front door of this rose- and teal-green mansion. Inside, you enter a museum of the Victorian era. Every room is exquisitely furnished in period antiques. In fact, if you aren't staying here, you can still have a look during one of the afternoon house tours ($3). Breakfast is an extravaganza that can last all morning and will certainly have you considering skipping lunch.

⑤ F. W. Hastings House/Old Consulate Inn

313 Walker St., Port Townsend, WA 98368. ☎ **360/385-6753** or 800/300-6753. Fax 360/385-2097. 8 rms. $59–$155 double. Rates include full breakfast. AE, MC, V.

Though not quite as elaborate as the Starrett Mansion, the Old Consulate Inn is another example of the sort of Victorian excess that's so wonderfully appealing today. The attention to detail and quality craftsmanship both in the construction and the restoration of this elegant mansion are evident wherever you look. However, despite its heritage, the Old Consulate avoids being a museum; it's just a comfortable yet elegant place to stay. For entertainment, you'll find a grand piano, a billiard table, and VCR, as well as stunning views out most of the windows. A multicourse breakfast is meant to be lingered over, so don't make any early-morning appointments. Afternoon tea, evening cordials, and a hot tub add to the experience here.

Fort Worden

At the Fort Worden State Park Conference Center, 200 Battery Way, Port Townsend, WA 98368. ☎ **360/385-4730.** 25 houses. $65–$210 house for up to 12 people. No credit cards.

The former officers' quarters at Fort Worden are now available on a nightly rental basis, and so popular are they that you should make reservations a year to the day in advance. Each of the old houses that comprise these rental properties has been renovated and many are refurbished with reproductions of antique furniture. There are also fully equipped kitchens in all the units. Many of the buildings, mostly large old clapboard houses with huge front porches, face the former parade ground. The units range in size from one to six bedrooms. Family reunions are particularly popular here.

Harborside Inn

330 Benedict St., Port Townsend, WA 98368. ☎ **360/385-7909** or 800/942-5960. 63 rms. A/C TV TEL. $64–$130 double. Rates include continental breakfast. AE, MC, V.

This modern motel is south of Port Townsend's historic district and overlooks the town's main marina. The guest rooms all have balconies that let you enjoy the view of the harbor and Admiralty Inlet. Facilities include an outdoor pool and hot tub, and if you're interested in fishing, you can arrange a charter right across the street.

James House

1238 Washington St., Port Townsend, WA 98368. ☎ **360/385-1238** or 800/385-1238. 8 rooms (6 with bath), 4 suites. $65–$75 double without bath, $95–$150 suite or double with bath. Rates include full breakfast. MC, V.

With an eclectic blend of antique and new furnishings, this grand Victorian from 1889 sits atop the bluff overlooking Admiralty Inlet. The entry hall features a parquet floor, and in the two parlors you'll find fireplaces that are the perfect gathering spot on a cool evening. The views from the upper front rooms are some of the best in town. You can even see Mount Rainier on a clear day. Our favorite rooms are the attic rooms, one of which has a brass bed and a futon couch. Another of these rooms has a beautiful sleigh bed and arched windows. If you prefer a bit more space, opt for the bridal suite or one of the garden suites.

⑤ Manresa Castle

Seventh and Sheridan sts., Port Townsend, WA 98368. ☎ **360/385-5750** or 800/732-1281. Fax 360/385-5883. 32 rms, 8 suites. $65–$75 double; $85–$175 tower suite. Rates include continental breakfast. DISC, MC, V.

Built in 1892 by a wealthy baker, this reproduction of a medieval castle later became a Jesuit retreat and school. Today Manresa Castle is, by far, Port Townsend's most elegant accommodation and also its best deal. A traditional elegance pervades the hotel's lounge and dining room (which happens to be the best restaurant in town), so try to have at least one meal and a drink here. The guest rooms have a genuine, vintage appeal that manages to avoid the contrived feeling that so often sneaks into bed-and-breakfast room decor. The best deal in the hotel is the tower suite during the off-season. For $105 a night you'll get a huge room with sweeping views from its circular seating area.

Palace Hotel

1004 Water St., Port Townsend, WA 98368. ☎ **360/385-0773** or 800/962-0741. 15 rms, 12 with bath. TV. $55 double without bath, $69–$119 double with bath. Rates include continental breakfast. AE, DISC, MC, V.

Located in the heart of the historic district, the Palace Hotel occupies a building that once served as a bordello. Today Madame Marie's suite is the best room in the house. It's a big corner room that even has a kitchenette. Most of the other rooms are named for former working girls. Miss Kitty's room is as nice as the madame's and includes a cast-iron wood stove and the best views at the Palace. The Crow's Nest room is another interesting room and features a sleeping loft, nautical theme, and wood stove. *Be forewarned:* The hotel is up a steep flight of stairs from the street and some rooms are up on the third floor. The bathroom shared by three rooms has a big clawfoot tub, so you aren't doing too badly if you take one of these rooms.

✪ Ravenscroft Inn

533 Quincy St., Port Townsend, WA 98368. ☎ **360/385-2784.** Fax 360/385-6724. 8 rms. $67–$165 double. Lower rates off-season. Rates include breakfast. AE, DISC, MC, V.

If a morning piano concert and lavish gourmet breakfast sound like the perfect way to start the day, then you'll want to book a room at this three-story B&B. Built in 1987 but designed in keeping with Port Townsend's historic homes, the inn offers rooms with distinctively different moods. The Mount Rainier Room, with its gorgeous views and whirlpool tub for two, is a perennial favorite, as is the Fireside Room, which has a fireplace, veranda, and canopy bed. Two other rooms also open onto a veranda, and some rooms on the upper levels have good views of the mountains and water. Pretty gardens surround the house, and there are a couple of Adirondack chairs on the lower veranda.

WHERE TO DINE

One place on nearly everyone's itinerary during a visit to Port Townsend is **Elevated Ice Cream,** 627 Water St. (☎ **360/385-1156**), which is open daily and scoops up the best ice cream in town.

EXPENSIVE

Manresa Castle Dining Room

Manresa Castle, Seventh and Sheridan sts. ☎ **360/385-5750.** Reservations recommended. Main courses $9.75–$24. MC, V. May–Oct, daily 5–9pm; Nov–Apr, Wed–Sat 5–9pm. CONTINENTAL.

Despite the number of restaurants in Port Townsend, few live up to the romantic Victorian atmosphere that pervades the town. If you're searching for a very special place for dinner while you're in town, Manresa Castle is your best bet. Arrive early and enjoy a drink in the elegant lounge before taking your table in the sumptuous dining room. If you're very lucky you might even get the table for two in the dining room's diminutive turret.

Start your meal with the oysters Château Manresa or some artichoke pâté. In summer, you'll appreciate the gazpacho sabrosa, especially delicious when made with tiny bay shrimp. Whatever size your appetite, you'll find an entrée to satisfy you. Stuffed baked quail and bouillabaisse Manresa are lighter offerings; heartier appetites will more likely be attracted by such dishes as spicy Dungeness crab cakes with lemongrass aïoli or salmon in a wine-and-saffron broth. Desserts are tempting enough to warrant ordering a light dinner.

MODERATE

Blackberries

In the Fort Worden State Park Conference Center. ☎ **360/385-9950.** Reservations accepted only for large parties. Main courses $10–$17. MC, V. Mon–Sat 5–9pm, Sun 9am–2pm. NORTHWEST.

Located near the historic officers' quarters at Fort Worden (on the right after the Centrum), Blackberries is a simple place with vintage appeal. The menu, however, is anything but old-fashioned. Imaginative Northwest cuisine at very reasonable prices make this place a definite winner. Locally grown ingredients are used as much as possible, and a few vegetarian dishes are always available. A recent menu included roast duckling with a blackberry-orange sauce, beefalo-burgundy ragoût, and a unique salmon-halibut braid with salal berry buerre rouge. The Sunday brunch is very popular with weekend visitors, especially in summer. All the profits from this restaurant assist community-action programs.

Café Piccolo

9793 Wash. 20. ☎ **360/385-1403.** Reservations recommended. Main courses $12–$15. MC, V. Mon–Fri noon–2:30pm and 5:30–9pm, Sat–Sun 5:30–9pm. ITALIAN.

Located on the highway south of town, this restaurant is popular both with couples out for a romantic evening and families who appreciate the children's play area out front. A creative menu features modern Italian cuisine rich with the flavors of fresh herbs and olive oil. We find the appetizer of roast eggplant with goat cheese, sun-dried tomatoes, garlic, and artichoke hearts absolutely irresistible. The kitchen excels in its preparation of seafood dishes such as angel-hair pasta with mussels, prawns, and bay scallops in a basil-cream sauce and Sicilian fisherman stew made with prawns, mussels, clams, scallops, fish, and plenty of garlic and herbs.

⊗ Silverwater Café

237 Taylor St. ☎ **360/385-6448.** Reservations accepted only for six or more. Main courses $8–$13.50. MC, V. Daily 11:30am–3pm and 5–9pm. CONTINENTAL.

Works by local artists, lots of plants, and New Age music on the stereo set the tone for this casually chic restaurant. Though the menu focuses on continental dishes, it includes preparations from around the world. You can start your meal with an artichoke-and-Parmesan pâté and then move on to amaretto chicken, beef bourguignon, or cioppino. The oysters in a bleu cheese sauce are a favorite of ours.

INEXPENSIVE

The Fountain Café

920 Washington St. ☎ **360/385-1364.** Reservations not accepted. Main courses $8.75–$12. AE, MC, V. Sun–Thurs 11:30am–3pm and 4–9pm, Fri–Sat to 10pm. INTERNATIONAL.

Housed in a narrow clapboard building, this funky little place is easy to miss. Eclectic hand-painted tablecloths decorate the half dozen or so tables and there are a few stools at the counter. Pasta dishes are the mainstay here, and the menu changes regularly. On one recent visit, there was a garlicky oyster stew, a spicy ginger chicken, Philippino-style prawns, and Greek pasta. The wide range of flavors assure that everyone in even a large party will find something to their liking.

⊗ Khu Larb Thai

225 Adams St. ☎ **360/385-5023.** Reservations suggested. Main courses $6.25–$8.50. MC, V. Sun–Thurs 11am–9pm, Fri–Sat 11am–10pm. THAI.

Located just half a block off busy Water Street, Khu Larb seems a world removed from Port Townsend's sometimes-overdone Victorian decor. Thai easy-listening music plays on the stereo and you're surrounded by cheap souvenirs from Thailand. However, don't let this lack of atmosphere put you off. One taste of any dish on the menu and you'll be convinced that this is great Thai food. Particularly memorable is the tom kha gai, a sour-and-spicy soup with a coconut-milk base. The steamed clams with ginger are another excellent dish, and even the pad thai is quite good. If you're feeling adventurous, try the black rice pudding for dessert.

The Salal Café

634 Water St. ☎ **360/385-6532.** Reservations not accepted. Most items $2.50–$7.50. MC, V. Wed–Mon 7am–2pm. NATURAL FOODS.

Once upon a time Port Townsend was a counterculture capital, a mecca for folks with alternative lifestyles. Today this isn't so much the case, but some of the restaurants from that time still linger on. Though most of the dishes on the menu at the Salal Café are vegetarian standards—tofu Stroganoff, miso soup, bean burgers, granola—you'll also find ham-and-cheese omelets and burgers. The Salal is best known for its breakfasts and stays packed all morning. Late risers will be glad to know that you'll still find blintzes, crêpes, and omelets on the lunch menu.

DRIVING ON TO PORT ANGELES VIA SEQUIM & DUNGENESS

Located in the rain shadow of the Olympic Mountains, Sequim (pronounced *Skwim*) is an anomaly that has attracted a great deal of attention in recent years. The rain shadow makes this one of the driest regions for miles around and, consequently, sodden, moss-laden Northwesterners have taken to retiring here in droves. They bask in their personal microclimate of sunshine and warmth while the rains descend on the rest of the region.

The nearby town of Dungeness is set at the foot of Dungeness Spit, which, at 7 miles in length, is the longest sand spit in the world. The spit is protected as the **Dungeness National Wildlife Refuge,** and near its base you'll find the **Dungeness Recreation Area,** which has a campground, picnic area, and trail leading out to the spit. More camping and water access are available at **Sequim Bay State Park,** about 4 miles east of Sequim. It's from the town of Dungeness that the Northwest's favorite crab takes its name.

While in the area, don't miss an opportunity to visit the **Museum & Arts Center** in the Sequim-Dungeness Valley, 175 W. Cedar St., Sequim (☎ **360/683-8110**), which houses a pair of mastodon tusks that were found near here in 1977. The mastodon had been killed by human hunters, and the discovery helped establish the presence of humans in this area 12,000 years ago. The museum also has an exhibit on the much more recent culture of the region's Clallam native peoples. The museum is open daily from 9am to 4pm; admission is free.

If you've got the kids with you, Sequim's **Olympic Game Farm,** 1423 Ward Rd. (☎ **360/683-4295**), is a must. As actors in Walt Disney films, the animals here have become international celebrities. More than 80 theater and television features have been made with animals from this farm. Among the animals are Siberian tigers, jaguars, lions, grizzly bears, polar bears, and many others. There are drive-through and walking tours as well as a petting farm. The farm is open daily from 9am; admission is $6 to $8 for adults and $5 to $6 for children and seniors.

If you'd like to taste some local wine, stop by the **Lost Mountain Winery,** 3174 Lost Mountain Rd. (☎ **360/683-5229**), or the **Neuharth Winery,** 148 Still Rd. (☎ **360/683-9652**). Another interesting place to visit is the **Cedarbrook Herb Farm,** 1345 Sequim Ave. S. (☎ **360/683-7733**), where you can buy herb plants as well as herb vinegars, potpourris, everlasting flowers, and the like.

WHERE TO DINE

The Three Crabs
11 Three Crabs Rd., Dungeness. ☎ **360/683-4264.** Reservations recommended. Main courses $6–$14. DISC, MC, V. Mon–Sat 11:30am–10pm, Sun 11:30am–9pm. Closed one hour earlier in winter. SEAFOOD.

Just as the Dungeness crab is a Northwest staple, so, too, is the Three Crabs an Olympic institution. Folks drive from miles around to enjoy the fresh seafood and sunset views at this friendly restaurant. For more than 35 years the Three Crabs has been serving up the local crustacean. You can order your crabs as a cocktail, a sandwich, cracked, and as crab Louie salad. Clams and oysters also come from the local waters and are equally good.

2 Olympic National Park & Surrounding Areas

Port Angeles park entrance: 48 miles W of Port Townsend, 55 miles E of Forks

Though much of the Olympic Peninsula was designated a National Forest Preserve in 1897, and in 1909 became a national monument, it was not until 1938 that the heart of the peninsula—the jagged, snowcapped Olympic Mountains—became Olympic National Park. The park is unique in the contiguous United States for its temperate rain forests, found in the valleys of the Hoh, Queets, Bogachiel, Clearwater, and Quinault rivers. In these valleys, rainfall can exceed 140 inches per year, trees grow more than 200 feet tall, and mosses hang from every limb. Trails lead from these valleys (and other points around the peninsula) into the interior of the park, providing access to hundreds of miles of hiking trails. In fact trails are the only access to most of the park, which has fewer than a dozen roads, none of which leads more than a few miles into the preserve. Within a few short miles of the park's rain forests, the Olympic Mountains rise up to the 7,965-foot peak of Mount Olympus and produce an alpine zone where no trees can grow at all. Together, elevation and heavy rainfall combine to form 60 glaciers within the park. It is these glaciers that have carved the Olympic Mountains into the jagged peaks that mesmerize visitors and beckon to hikers and climbers. Rugged and spectacular sections of the coast have also been preserved as part of the national park, and the offshore waters are designated as the Olympic Coast National Marine Sanctuary.

One of the main reasons the park was created was to protect the Roosevelt elk, which was named for President Theodore Roosevelt (who was responsible for the area becoming a national monument). These elk live in large herds and were once a mainstay in the diet of Northwest Native Americans. Deer, however, are more frequently spotted than elk, especially in high alpine meadows.

ESSENTIALS

GETTING THERE   U.S. 101 circles Olympic National Park, with main park entrances south of Port Angeles, at Lake Crescent, and at the Hoh River.

Fairchild International Airport in Port Angeles is served by Horizon Airlines. Rental cars are available in Port Angeles from Budget Rent A Car.

There is **bus service** to Port Angeles on Port Angeles–Seattle Bus Lines (☎ 360/681-7705 or 800/764-2287), as well as through Olympic Bus Lines (☎ 360/452-3858). Jefferson Transit (☎ 360/385-4777) has service from Port Townsend to Sequim, where you can transfer to service on Clallam Transit (☎ 360/452-4511 or 800/858-3747), which operates from Sequim on around the peninsula to Lake Crescent, Neah Bay, and La Push. There is service to Lake Quinault from Olympia and Aberdeen on Grays Harbor Transit (☎ 360/ 532-2770 or 800/562-9730).

Two **ferries,** one for foot passengers only and the other for vehicles and foot passengers, connect Port Angeles and Victoria, British Columbia. The ferry terminal for both ferries is at the corner of Laurel and Railroad streets. **Victoria Rapid Transit** (☎ **360/452-8088,** 604/361-9144 in Victoria, or 800/633-1589 in Washington) is the faster of the two ferries and carries foot passengers only. This ferry operates only between May and October. The crossing takes one hour and charges $20 round-trip for adults, $10 for children 5 to 11. The **Black Ball Transport** (☎ **360/457-4491** or 604/386-2202 in Victoria) ferry operates year round except for two weeks in late January and early February and carries vehicles as well as walk-on passengers. The crossing takes slightly more than $1^{1}/_{2}$ hours. The one-way fares are $6.50 for adults, $3.25 for children 5 to 11; $26 for a car, van, camper, or motor home and driver. Note that Black Ball Transport does not accept personal checks or credit/charge cards.

VISITOR INFORMATION   Contact the **Olympic Park Visitor Center,** 3002 Mount Angeles Rd., Port Angeles, WA 98362 (☎ **360/452-0330**). For more information on the Port Angeles area, contact the **Port Angeles Visitor Center,** 121 E. Railroad Ave., Port Angeles, WA 98362 (☎ **360/452-2363**). For more information on the rest of the northern Olympic Peninsula, contact the **North Olympic Peninsula Visitor and Convention Bureau,** P.O. Box 670, Port Angeles, WA 98362 (☎ **360/452-8552**, or 800/942-4042).

PARK ADMISSION   Park admission is $5 per vehicle and $3 per pedestrian or cyclist.

TOURS   If you'd like to see the park on a guided tour, contact **Olympic Van Tours** (☎ **360/452-3858**), which offers tours to Hurricane Ridge, the Hoh River rain forest, and ocean beaches. Tours cost $12.75 to $45.

SEEING THE HIGHLIGHTS

Port Angeles is the headquarters for the park, and it's here that you'll find the **Olympic Park Visitor Center,** 3002 Mount Angles Rd. (☎ **360/452-0330**), which is on the south edge of town on the road that leads up to Hurricane Ridge. In addition to having lots of information, maps, and books about the park, this center has exhibits on the park's flora and fauna, old-growth forests, and whaling by local Native Americans. It's open daily from 9am to 4pm, with longer hours in summer.

From the visitor center, continue another 17 miles on this road to **Hurricane Ridge,** which offers, on a clear day, the most breathtaking views in the park. In summer the surrounding subalpine meadows are carpeted with wildflowers. Several hiking trails lead into the park from here, and in winter Hurricane Ridge is a popular cross-country skiing area. A rope tow provides downhill skiing for beginners. The Hurricane Ridge Visitor Center has exhibits on alpine plants and wildlife.

West of Port Angeles on U.S. 101 lies **Lake Crescent,** a glacier-carved lake surrounded by steep forested mountains that give the lake the feel of a fjord. This is one of the most beautiful lakes in the state and has long been a popular destination. Between late May and early October, you can cruise the lake on the **paddlewheeler** *Storm King* (☎ **360/452-4520**), which has its ticket office at the Shadow Mountain General Store, milepost 233 on U.S. 101. The fare is $15 for adults, $14 for seniors, $10 for children 6 to 17. Near the east end of the lake, you'll find an **information center** and the 1-mile trail to 90-foot-tall Marymere Falls. At the west end, you'll find the **Fairholm General Store** (☎ **360/ 928-3020**), which has rowboats, canoes, and motorboats for rent.

Continuing west from Lake Crescent, watch for the turnoff to **Sol Duc Hot Springs.** For 14 miles the road follows the Soleduck River, passing the Salmon Cascades along the way. Sol Duc Hot Springs were for centuries considered healing waters by the local Native Americans, and after white settlers arrived in the area the springs became a popular resort. In addition to the hot swimming pool and soaking tubs, you'll find cabins, a campground, a restaurant, and a snack bar. The springs are open daily from May to September, and on Saturday and Sunday from April to October; admission is $5.90 for adults and $4.90 for seniors. A 6-mile loop trail leads to **Sol Duc Falls,** which are among the most photographed falls in the park.

Continuing west on U.S. 101 from the junction with the road to Sol Duc Hot Springs brings you to the crossroads of Sappho. Heading north at Sappho will bring you to Wash. 112, which is an alternative route from Port Angeles. About 40 miles west, Wash. 112 brings you to the community of **Neah Bay** on the Makah Indian Reservation. The reservation land includes Cape Flattery, which is the northwesternmost point of land in the contiguous United States. Just off the cape lies Tatoosh Island, site of one of the oldest lighthouses in Washington. Neah Bay is a busy commercial and sport-fishing port, and is also home to the impressive **Makah Museum** (☎ **360/645-2711**), which displays artifacts from a

Native American village that was inundated by a mud slide 500 years ago. This is the most perfectly preserved collection of Native American artifacts in the Northwest, and as part of the exhibit there are reproductions of canoes the Makah once used for hunting whales. There's also a longhouse that shows the traditional lifestyle of the Makah people. Each year in late August, **Makah Days** are celebrated with canoe races, Indian dancing, a salmon bake, and other events. The museum is open June to September 15, daily from 10am to 5pm, and September 16 to May, Wednesday through Sunday from 10am to 5pm; admission is $4 for adults, $3 for students and seniors.

A turnoff 16 miles east of Neah Bay leads south to **Ozette Lake,** where there are boat ramps, a campground, and, stretching north and south, miles of beaches that are only accessible on foot. A 3.3-mile trail on a raised boardwalk leads from the Ozette Lake trailhead to **Cape Alava,** which, along with Cape Blanco in Oregon, claims to be the westernmost point in the contiguous United States. The large rocks just offshore here are known as haystack rocks and are common all along the rocky western coast of the Olympic Peninsula, which is characterized by a rugged coastline. Aside from five coastal Native American reservations, almost all this northern coastline is preserved as part of the national park.

Returning back to U.S. 101, you soon come to the lumber town of **Forks.** This town has been at the heart of the controversy over protecting the northern spotted owl and has been suffering high unemployment for a decade or more. The **Forks Timber Museum,** south of town on U.S. 101 (☎ **360/374-9663**), chronicles the history of logging in this region, but it also has displays on Native American culture and pioneer days. It's open April to October only, daily from 11am to 4pm; admission is by donation.

The first place where you can actually drive right to the Pacific Ocean is just west of Forks. At the end of a spur road you come to the Quileute Indian Reservation and the community of **La Push.** Right in town there's a beach at the mouth of the Quileute River; however, before you reach La Push, you'll see signs for **Third Beach** and **Second Beach,** which are two of the prettiest beaches on the peninsula. Third Beach is a 1.6-mile walk and Second Beach is just over half a mile from the trailhead. **Rialto Beach,** just north of La Push, is another great beach; it's reached from a turnoff east of La Push. From here you can walk north for 24 miles to Cape Alava.

This region's most notable feature is its rain and consequent **rain forests.** The rainiest spots are in westward-facing Bogachiel, Hoh, Queets, and Quinault river valleys. However, only the **Hoh and Bogachiel valleys** are easily accessible. All the rain here has produced some of the largest trees on earth. Sitka spruce, western red cedar, Douglas fir, and western hemlock grow to monster proportions in this rain-drenched climate. There are several easily accessible short trails along this coast that will take you through groves of old-growth trees. Among these are the **Ancient Groves Trail** at Soleduck, the **Hall of Mosses Trail** in the Hoh Valley, and a short **trail near the Lake Quinault Lodge.**

Roughly 8 miles south of Forks is the turnoff for the Hoh River valley. It's 17 miles up this side road to the **Hoh Visitor Center** (☎ **360/374-6925**), campground, and trailheads. This valley receives an average of 140 inches of rain per year, making it the wettest region in the continental United States. At the visitor center you can learn all about the natural forces that cause this tremendous rainfall. To see the effect of so much rain on the landscape, walk the three-quarter-mile **Hall of Mosses Trail** where the trees, primarily Sitka spruce, western red cedar, and western hemlock, tower 200 feet tall. Here you'll see big-leaf maple trees with limbs draped in thick carpets of mosses. If you're up for a longer walk, try the **Spruce Nature Trail.** If you've come with a backpack, there's no better way to see the park and all its habitats than by hiking the **Hoh River Trail,** which is 17 miles long and leads past Blue Glacier to Glacier Meadows on the flanks of Mount Olympus.

Continuing south on U.S. 101, but before crossing the Hoh River, you'll come to a secondary road that heads west from the Hoh Oxbow campground. From the end of the road it's a hike of less than a mile to a rocky beach at the **mouth of the Hoh River.** You're likely to see sea lions or harbor seals feeding just offshore here, and to the north are several haystack rocks that are nesting sites for numerous sea birds. Primitive camping is permitted on this beach, and from here hikers can continue hiking for 17 miles north along a pristine wilderness of rugged headlands and secluded beaches.

U.S. 101 finally reaches the coast at **Ruby Beach.** This beach gets its name from its pink sand, which is comprised of tiny grains of garnet. For another 17 miles or so the highway parallels the wave-swept coastline. Along this stretch of highway there are pulloffs and short trails down to six beaches that have only numbers for names. At low tide, the northern beaches offer lots of tide pools to be explored. Near the south end of this stretch of road, you'll find Kalaloch Lodge, which has a gas station, and the **Kalaloch Information Station,** which is only open during the summer.

Shortly beyond Kalaloch the highway turns inland again passing through the community of **Queets** on the river of the same name. The Queets River valley is another rainy valley, and if you'd like to do a bit of hiking away from the crowds, head up the gravel road to the Queets campground, from which a hiking trail leads up the valley. A little more than 2 miles up this trail is one of the world's largest Douglas firs.

A long stretch of clear-cuts and tree farms, mostly on the Quinault Indian Reservation, will bring you to **Quinault Lake.** Surrounded by forested mountains, this deep lake offers boating and freshwater fishing opportunities, as well as more rain forests to explore. This is also a good area in which to spot **Roosevelt elk.**

SPORTS & OUTDOOR ACTIVITIES

With its rugged beaches, rain-forest valleys, alpine meadows, and mountain-top glaciers, the park offers an amazing variety of **hiking** opportunities. Among the most popular hikes are those along the coast between La Push and Oil City and from Rialto Beach north to Lake Ozette and onward to Shi Shi Beach. Day hikes and overnight and longer backpacking trips are all possible in these areas, though you'll need a special advance-reservation permit to overnight along the **Ozette Loop Trail** (for a reservation, call 360/452-0300). For most other overnight hikes you can pick up a permit at the trailhead, though there are a few exceptions in the high country. If in doubt, check with a park ranger before heading out to a trailhead for a backpacking trip. Other noteworthy hikes include the **trails in the Hoh and Quinault River valleys,** both of which are rain-forest valleys. For **alpine hikes,** head up to Hurricane Ridge or Deer Park.

There are also many trails outside the boundaries of the park. For information, contact the **Olympic National Forest,** 1835 Black Lake Blvd. SW, Olympia, WA 98502-5623 (☎ **360/956-2300**).

If you'd rather have a llama carry your gear, contact **Wooley Packer Llama Co.,** 5763 Upper Hoh Rd., Forks (☎ 360/374-9288).

If you want to do a one-way backpacking trip, you can arrange a shuttle through **Olympic Van Tours** (☎ 360/452-3858).

The steep mountains and plentiful rains of the Olympic Peninsula are the source of some great white-water rafting on the Elwha, Queets, and Hoh rivers. If you'd like to dig in a paddle, contact **Olympic Raft & Guide Service,** 239521 U.S. 101 W., Port Angeles, WA 98363 (☎ 360/452-1443). Rates start at $35.

If you're interested in exploring the region on a bike, you can rent one at **Pedal 'n' Paddle,** 120 E. Front St., Port Angeles (☎ 360/457-1240), which can recommend good rides and also offers bicycle tours. This same company also offers sea-kayak tours.

The town of Sekiu, on Clallam Bay, is a popular spot for both sport fishing and scuba diving. If you're interested in heading out on open water to do a bit of salmon or deep-sea fishing, contact **Herb's Charters** (☎ 360/963-2346) or **Olson's Charters** (☎ 360/963-2311). Divers will want to stop in at the **Sekiu Dive Shop** (☎ 360/963-2281), on the main road through town.

The rivers of the Olympic Peninsula are well known for their fighting salmon and trout, and in Lakes Crescent and Ozette you can fish for such elusive species as Beardslee and Crescenti trout. The **Four Seasons Guide Service** (☎ 360/327-3380) will take you fishing for steelhead, salmon, and trout on the region's rivers; rates are $180 per day for one person, $220 for two people.

The **Olympic Park Institute,** 111 Barnes Point Rd., Port Angeles (☎ 360/928-3720), which is located in the Rosemary Inn on Lake Crescent, offers a wide array of summer field seminars ranging from classes in Asian landscape painting to multiday backpacking trips.

NEARBY ATTRACTIONS

While in the Port Angeles area, you may want to check out the **Clallam County Historical Society Museum,** Fourth and Lincoln streets (☎ 360/417-2364). It's open Monday through Friday from 10am to 4pm, and also on Saturday in summer; admission is by donation. The **Port Angeles Fine Art Center,** Lauridsen Road (☎ 360/457-3532), is the town's only other museum and hosts changing exhibits of contemporary art. The art center is on attractively landscaped grounds and has a nice view. It's open Thursday through Sunday from 11am to 5pm; admission is free.

If you'd like to get a close-up look at some of the peninsula's aquatic inhabitants, stop by the **Arthur D. Feiro Marine Lab,** Port Angeles City Pier (☎ 360/452-3940). In the lab's tanks, you may spot a wolf eel or octopus, and there's a touch tank where you can reach in and pick up a starfish or sea cucumber. It's open in summer, Tuesday through Saturday from 10am to 5pm; in winter, on Saturday and Sunday from noon to 4pm. Admission is $1 for adults, 50¢ for seniors and children 6 to 12.

WHERE TO STAY

Beyond Port Angeles, accommodations are few and far between, and those places worth recommending tend to be very popular. Try to have room reservations before heading west from Port Angeles.

IN PORT ANGELES

As the biggest town on the northern Olympic Peninsula and a base of operations for families exploring Olympic National Park, Port Angeles abounds in budget hotels. You'll find dozens along the section of U.S. 101 east of downtown.

✪ Domaine Madeleine

146 Wildflower Lane, Port Angeles, WA 98362. ☎ **360/457-4174.** Fax 360/457-3037. 4 rms. TV TEL. $125–$165 double. Rates include full breakfast. MC, V.

Located 7 miles east of Port Angeles, this B&B is set at the back of a small pasture and has a very secluded feel. Combine this with the waterfront setting and you have a fabulous weekend hideaway—you may not even bother exploring the park. The guest rooms are in several different buildings that are surrounded by colorful gardens, and all have views that take in the Strait of Juan de Fuca and the mountains beyond. There are also fireplaces and VCRs in the rooms, and three have their own whirlpool tubs. The breakfasts are superb.

Red Lion Bayshore Inn

221 N. Lincoln St., Port Angeles, WA 98362. ☎ **360/452-9215** or 800/733-5466. Fax 206/452-4734. 187 rms, 3 suites. A/C TV TEL. $95–$125 double; $140 suite. Lower rates off-season. AE, CB, DC, DISC, MC, V.

If you're on your way to or from Victoria, there's no more convenient hotel than the Red Lion. Located on the waterfront, it's only steps from the ferry terminal. Most rooms have balconies and large bathrooms, and the more expensive rooms overlook the Strait of Juan de Fuca. There's a seafood restaurant adjacent to the hotel. Laundry/valet service is available, and an outdoor pool and hot tub provide recreational options.

The Tudor Inn

1108 S. Oak St., Port Angeles, WA 98362. ☎ **360/452-3138.** 5 rms, 2 with bath. Summer, $85–$125 double. The rest of the year, $75–$115 double. No credit cards.

Located in a quiet residential neighborhood 13 blocks from the waterfront, this 1910 Tudor home is surrounded by a large yard and pretty gardens. Innkeepers Jane and Jerry Glass spent 10 years living in Europe and have furnished their home with European antiques. On the ground floor you'll find a lounge and library, both with fireplaces that get a lot of use. Upstairs there are five rooms furnished with antiques. Our personal favorite is the Asian-theme room, though there are others with good views of the Olympic Mountains that make them equally appealing.

ON THE NORTH SIDE OF THE PARK

✪ Lake Crescent Lodge

416 Lake Crescent Rd., Port Angeles, WA 98363-8672. ☎ **360/928-3211.** 52 rms and cabins, 48 with bath. $67 double without bath; $88–$99 double with bath; $99–$130 cottage. AE, CB, DC, MC, V.

Twenty miles west of Port Angeles on the south shore of picturesque Lake Crescent stands this historic lodge. Wood paneling, hardwood floors, a stone fireplace, and a sun room make the lobby a popular spot for just sitting and relaxing. The guest rooms in this main lodge building are the oldest and all have shared bathrooms. We like these rooms best, even though they're a bit small. If you'd like more modern accommodations, there are a number of standard motel-style rooms. If you have your family or some friends along, we recommend reserving a cottage.

Those with fireplaces are the most comfortable (and are also the only rooms available between October 31 and late April), but the others are nice as well. All but the main lodge rooms have views of either the lake or the mountains.

With a view across the lake, the Lodge Dining Room serves a limited menu of continental cuisine with an emphasis on local seafood. Prices are moderate. A lobby lounge provides a quiet place for an evening drink. Rowboat rentals are available.

⊙ Log Cabin Resort

3183 E. Beach Rd., Port Angeles, WA 98362. ☎ **360/928-3325.** Fax 360/928-3245. 4 rms; 24 cabins, 8 with bath; 1 chalet. $42 cabin for two without bath, $67–$80 cabin for two with bath; $95 double; $109 chalet. MC, V. Closed Oct–May.

This log-cabin resort on the sunny north shore of Lake Crescent first opened in 1895 and still has buildings that date back to the 1920s. The least expensive accommodations here are rustic one-room log cabins in which you provide the bedding and share a bathroom a short walk away (basically this is camping without the tent). More comfortable are the 1928 cabins with private bathrooms, some of which also have kitchenettes (you provide the cooking and eating utensils). The lodge rooms and a chalet offer the greatest comfort and best views. The lodge dining room overlooks the lake and specializes in local seafood. The resort also has a general store and R.V. sites.

Sol Duc Hot Springs Resort

Sol Duc Rd., U.S. 101 (P.O. Box 2169), Port Angeles, WA 98362. ☎ **360/327-3583.** 32 cabins. $78–$88 cabin for two. AE, DISC, MC, V. Closed Oct to mid-May.

The Sol Duc Hot Springs have for years been a popular family vacation spot. Campers, day trippers, and resort guests all spend the day soaking and playing in the hot-water swimming pools. The grounds of the resort are grassy and open, but the forest is kept just at arm's reach. The cabins are done in modern motel style and are comfortable if not spacious. There's an excellent restaurant here, as well as a poolside deli, espresso bar, and grocery store. Three hot springs–fed swimming pools are the focal point at Sol Duc, and the pools are open to the public for a small fee. Massages are available.

ON THE WEST SIDE OF THE PARK

The town of Forks has several inexpensive motels and is a good place to look for cheap lodgings if you happen to be out this way without a reservation.

✪ Kalaloch Lodge

157151 U.S. 101, Forks, WA 98331. ☎ **360/962-2271.** Fax 360/962-2271. 18 rms, 40 cabins. $56–$80 double; $99–150 cabin for two. Lower rates weekdays Nov–May. AE, MC, V.

When you arrive at Kalaloch Lodge (pronounced Kah-*lay*-loch) you have an immediate sense of having arrived at the edge of the continent. The rustic, cedar-shingled lodge and its cluster of cabins perch on a grassy bluff. Below, the Pacific Ocean thunders against a sandy beach where huge driftwood logs are scattered like so many twigs. The breathtaking setting makes this one of the most popular lodges on the coast, and it's advisable to book rooms at least four months in advance. The rooms in the old lodge are the least expensive, but the ocean-view bluff cabins are the most in demand. The log cabins across the street from the bluff cabins don't have the knockout views. For comfort you can't beat the motel-like rooms in the Sea Crest House.

A casual coffee shop serves breakfast and lunch while a more formal dining room serves dinner with an emphasis on salmon dishes. Dinner entrée prices range from $10 to $17. The dining room features a curved wall of windows overlooking a pond. The lodge also has a general store and gas station.

✪ Lake Quinault Lodge

P.O. Box 7, Quinault, WA 98575. ☎ **360/288-2900,** or 800/562-6672 in Washington and Oregon. 92 rms, 6 suites. June–Oct, $92–$125 double; $170–220 suite. Oct–June, $52–$110 double; $100–$180 suite. AE, MC, V.

Located on the shore of Lake Quinault in the southwest corner of the park, this imposing grande dame of the Olympic Peninsula wears an ageless tranquillity. Huge old firs and cedars shade the rustic lodge, and Adirondack chairs on the deck command a view of the lawn.

The accommodations range from small rooms in the main lodge to modern rooms with wicker furniture and little balconies to rooms with fireplaces. The annex rooms are the least attractive, but they do have huge bathtubs. None of the rooms has a TV or telephone.

Dining/Entertainment: The dining room here is a large dark place as befits such a lodge, and the menu reflects the bounties of the Olympic Peninsula, with seafood a specialty. A lounge provides big-screen TV for those who just can't give up the big game or music videos.

Services: Rain-forest tours.

Facilities: Indoor pool, whirlpool, croquet, badminton, canoe and paddle-boat rentals.

⑤ Manitou Lodge

Kilmer Rd. (P.O. Box 600), Forks, WA 98331. ☎ **360/374-6295.** 7 rms. $60–$75 double. Rates include full breakfast. MC, V. Take Wash. 110 west from north of Forks; turn right on Spur 110 and then right on Kilmer Road.

This secluded B&B is set on 10 private acres and is only minutes from some of the most beautiful and remote beaches in the Northwest. The best room in the house is the Sacajawea, which has a marble fireplace and king-size bed. A separate cabin houses two of the rooms. Guests tend to gravitate to the comfortable living room, where a huge stone fireplace is the center of attention. Fires help chase away the chill and the damp of this neck of the woods. Breakfasts are hearty and sometimes include huckleberry-apple-walnut pancakes. There's also a Native American art gallery on the premises.

Miller Tree Inn

654 E. Division St. (P.O. Box 953), Forks, WA 98331. ☎ **360/374-6806.** 6 rms, 2 with bath. $45–$55 double without bath, $65–$70 double with bath. Rates include full breakfast. MC, V.

Located just a few blocks east of downtown Forks, this large B&B is on the edge of the country and is surrounded by large old trees and pastures. There's nothing fussy or pretentious about this place—it's just a comfortable, friendly inn that caters primarily to outdoors enthusiasts and, during the winter months, anglers.

CAMPING

If you plan to camp, you can find out about the region's numerous campgrounds by contacting the Olympic National Park or Olympic National Forest (see "Visitor Information" under "Essentials," and "Sports & Outdoor Activities," above, for the addresses and phone numbers).

There are 16 campgrounds within the national park. Campground fees range from $8 to $10 per night. Among these, the **Deer Park campground,** in the park's high country south of Port Angeles, is one of the most spectacular. If you want to say you've camped in the wettest campground in the contiguous United States, head for the **Hoh River valley.** The campground at **Sol Duc Hot Springs** is one of the most popular in the park for obvious reasons. At the west end of Lake Crescent, you'll find the **Fairholm Campground.** **Bogachiel State Park,** on the banks of the Bogachiel River, is another area option. There are also national park and private campgrounds along the shores of **Lake Quinault.**

North of the park, on the shore of the Strait of Juan de Fuca, there are two county parks with campgrounds. **Salt Creek County Park** is 13 miles west of Port Angeles on Wash. 112 and **Pillar Point County Park** is another 22 miles farther west on this same road.

Some of the best camping is along this coast's many beaches, which, however, do not have established campgrounds. Several beaches are within 3 miles or so of the nearest road, while others require several days' walk to reach.

Olympic Mountaineering, 221 S. Peabody St., Port Angeles (☎ **360/ 452-0240**), is a good place buy or rent camping equipment.

WHERE TO DINE

The choices below are all in Port Angeles. If you're hit with a craving for something sweet while in town, check out **Bonny's Bakery,** 502 E. First St. (☎ **360/ 457-3585**), housed in an old church. Both French pastries and American favorites are baked here.

Outside of Port Angeles, the restaurant choices become exceedingly slim. Your best choices are the dining rooms at the lodges listed above.

C'est Si Bon

23 Cedar Park Rd. ☎ **360/452-8888.** Reservations recommended. Main courses $19–$24. AE, CB, MC, V. Tues–Sun 5–11pm. FRENCH.

Located 4 miles south of town just off U.S. 101, C'est Si Bon is painted a striking combination of turquoise, pink, and purple that gives the restaurant a sort of happy elegance. Inside, the nontraditional paint job gives way to more classic decor—reproductions of European works of art, crystal chandeliers, and old musical instruments used as wall decorations. Most tables have a view of the restaurant's pretty garden. The menu is limited, which just about assures that each dish has been perfected, and the service is very French. Among the rich and flavorful dishes, there are a few surprising sauces. The beef tenderloin comes in a red-currant sauce and the duck breast comes with a berry sauce. Desserts are limited to a mousse au chocolat and a crème caramel.

The Coffee House Restaurant

118 E. First St. ☎ **360/452-1459.** Main courses $9–$13. MC, V. Sun–Mon 8am–4pm, Tues–Sat 8am–8pm. INTERNATIONAL.

Before you can take a seat in this casual café in downtown Port Angeles, you'll have to walk past the pastry case, which should clue you in to not eating too much before it's time for dessert. Though the menu here draws on the cuisines of the world, the emphasis is on Mediterranean and Middle Eastern. There's a modest selection of wines and, of course, espresso.

Downriggers

115 E. Railroad Ave. ☎ **360/452-2700.** Reservations recommended. Main courses $10–$26. DISC, MC, V. Mon–Thurs 11:30am–9pm, Fri–Sat 11:30am–10pm, Sun 4–9pm. SEAFOOD.

At the back of the Landing Mall on the second level you'll find this large, casual restaurant, which is very convenient to the ferry landing. Walls of glass provide views of the ferries (so you don't miss yours) and take in some great sunsets. A long menu nearly guarantees that you'll find something you like. The appetizer menu includes quite a bit of good seafood. The salmon Wellington and a fettuccine made with smoked salmon, prawns, and scallops are just a couple of interesting main dishes.

DRIVING ON TOWARD LONG BEACH VIA ABERDEEN & HOQUIAM

Lake Quinault marks the southern boundary of Olympic National Park. However, if you continue south on U.S. 101 another 16 miles to the town of **Humptulips,** there's a small road that will take you back to another spectacular section of the coast. High bluffs, haystack rocks, secluded beaches, and dark forests characterize the section of coast between Taholah on the Quinault Indian Reservation and Ocean City. Along this stretch of coast, which is commonly referred to as the North Beach area, there is **beach access** at Pacific Beach, Griffiths-Priday, and Ocean City state parks and **camping** at Pacific Beach and Ocean City.

At **Ocean City,** Wash. 109 heads east toward the port cities of **Aberdeen and Hoquiam.** Together these two cities comprise the largest urban area on the Washington coast. If you're at all interested in the history of this region, there are several places there worth visiting. If you like elegant old homes, don't miss **Hoquiam's Castle,** 515 Chenault Ave., Hoquiam (☎ **360/533-2005**). This stately Victorian mansion was built in 1897 by a local timber baron and is an amazing assimilation of turrets and gables, balconies and bay windows. Restored in 1973, the "castle," as it came to be known by locals, is furnished with period antiques. It's open mid-June to Labor Day, daily from 11am to 5pm; the rest of the year, on Saturday and Sunday from 11am to 5pm. Admission is $4 for adults, $1 for children 15 and under. The **Polson Museum,** 1611 Riverside Ave., Hoquiam (☎ **360/533-5862**), contains rooms full of antique furnishings and houses various collections including dolls, vintage clothing, Native American artifacts, and logging memorabilia. It's open in summer, Wednesday through Sunday from 11am to 4pm; in other months, on Saturday and Sunday from noon to 4pm. Admission is $2 for adults, 50¢ for children. The **Aberdeen Museum of History,** 111 E. Third St. (☎ **360/533-1976**), has similar displays and is open the same hours; admission is free. If maritime history is your interest, stop by the **Gray's Harbor Historical Seaport,** 813 E. Heron St. (☎ **360/532-8611**), where you can occasionally tour the *Lady Washington,* a replica of one of the ships Capt. Robert Gray sailed when he first explored the Northwest coast. The *Lady Washington* isn't always in port, but when it is, sailing excursions are available.

If you're a birdwatcher and you happen to be here in late April or early May, be sure to visit Bowerman Basin in the **Gray's Harbor National Wildlife Refuge,** which is adjacent to the Aberdeen/Hoquiam Airport. For a few short weeks in spring, the area becomes a resting place for tens of thousands of Arctic-bound shorebirds. For more information, contact the refuge headquarters (☎ **360/532-6237**).

WHERE TO STAY

If you can't get a room at any of the hotels listed below, contact the **Ocean Shores Reservations Bureau** (☎ **360/289-2430** or 800/562-8612). The listings below are in the order you'll pass them on the drive.

⑤ Ocean Crest Resort

Sunset Beach, Moclips, WA 98562. ☎ **360/276-4465** or 800/684-VIEW. 45 units. TV TEL. $54–118 unit for two. Lower rates Oct–Feb. AE, DISC, MC, V.

The Ocean Crest enjoys a very enviable position—you won't find a more spectacular location anywhere on the Washington coast. Perched high on a forested bluff, the hotel seems poised to go plummeting into the ocean below. The complex also straddles a forested ravine, and a wooden staircase winds down through the ravine to the beach.

The accommodations vary from small studios with no view to up to two-bedroom apartments with full kitchens and fireplaces. My vote for best rooms goes to the large third-floor ocean-view studios. These have cathedral ceilings, fireplaces, and balconies.

The hotel's restaurant has one of the best views at the resort, and is decorated in a Northwest motif. Steaks and seafood are the staples of the menu. The adjacent lounge is a great spot for a sunset drink. Facilities here include an indoor pool, whirlpool, sauna, exercise room, aerobics room, and playground, and massages are available.

The Sandpiper

P.O. Box A, Pacific Beach, WA 98571. ☎ **360/276-4580.** 17 suites. $55–$90 suite for two. Minimum stay two or three nights. MC, V.

Set into a steep slope and towered over by big firs, the buildings of the Sandpiper fit comfortably into this Northwest landscape. Their cedar shingles, weathered wood, and pierlike pilings all give the hotel a very beachy feel. What immediately grabs your attention is the dizzying view from the upper rooms, all of which are large suites. Far below you the ocean waves crash on the beach, and the distant roar lulls you to sleep at night. All the suites have kitchens, and all but one have fireplaces, so there's no need to leave this idyllic spot. What you won't find in any of the suites are TVs or phones, a big selling point at the Sandpiper—this is a place to relax. Barbecues and a playground also help make this a great spot for families.

✪ Iron Springs Ocean Beach Resort

P.O. Box 207, Copalis Beach, WA 98535. ☎ **360/276-4230.** Fax 206/276-4365. 28 cottages and apts. $60–$96 cottage or apt for two, $72–$124 cottage or apt for four. Three-night minimum stay in summer. AE, DISC, MC, V.

It's hard to imagine a more picture-perfect little cove than the one on which this rustic resort is set. Steep wooded hills surround the tiny cove, and at the mouth, a sandy beach begins. This is an isolated and little-developed stretch of beach, so even in summer you won't be bothered by crowds. The area is also very popular with razor-clam diggers. If you have a shovel and the tides are right, you, too, may be able to dig your dinner.

The cottages here are scattered through the woods on a bluff overlooking the ocean and vary quite a bit in design, decor, and size. However, they're all modestly comfortable and have fireplaces and complete kitchens. Facilities include an indoor pool, hiking trail, playground, and art gallery.

Lytle House

509 Chenault St., Hoquiam, WA 98550. ☎ **360/533-2320** or 800/667-2320. 8 rms (all with shared bath), 2 suites. $75 double, $95–$105 suite. Rates include full breakfast. AE, MC, V.

If a tour of Hoquiam's Castle had you wishing you could stay there, walk right next door and ring the bell on the Lytle House. Equally grand, this Victorian painted lady was built by the brother of the man who built Hoquiam's Castle. Equally elegant, the Lytle House offers antique-filled rooms, bathrooms with clawfoot tubs and heated towel racks, and a full breakfast, as well as afternoon tea. There are no fewer than four parlors where you can sit and relax with other guests, read a book, or even watch a classic movie on the VCR. Our favorite room is the Balcony Suite, which has, of course, a private balcony, as well as a private bathroom and separate clawfoot tub in the room. If you'd like to be able to look out your window at Hoquiam's Castle, opt for the Castle Room.

WHERE TO DINE

Billy's

322 E. Heron St., Aberdeen. ☎ **360/533-7144.** Reservations not accepted. Main courses $6–$13. AE, MC, V. Sun–Thurs 11am–11pm, Fri–Sat 11am–midnight. AMERICAN.

Named for an infamous local thug, Billy's evokes Aberdeen's rowdier days as a lawless, Wild West timber town. There's a bar down the length of the room, a pressed-tin ceiling, and old paintings and prints to give this bar and grill just the right dance-hall atmosphere. The menu features everything from burgers to fresh oysters to T-bone steak.

Levee Street Restaurant

709 Levee St., Hoquiam. ☎ **360/532-1959.** Reservations recommended. Main courses $10–$20. AE, DISC, MC, V. Tues–Sat 4:30–9:30pm. CONTINENTAL.

Perched out over the river, the Levee is the antithesis of what you'd expect in a working port town like Hoquiam. The restaurant is tastefully decorated in subdued colors, and a big picture window takes in a view of the lazy river rolling by. Meals are traditional continental fare such as coq au vin, steak Diane, and bouillabaisse Provençale, and portions are both generous and well prepared. It's definitely a light in the wilderness.

✪ Parma

116 W. Heron St., Aberdeen. ☎ **360/532-3166.** Reservations recommended. Main courses $9–$16. AE, DISC, MC, V. Tues–Thurs 4:30–9:30pm, Fri 11am–2:30pm and 4:30–10pm, Sat 4:30–10pm. ITALIAN.

This friendly little place is located in downtown Aberdeen and serves excellent northern and southern Italian dishes. Vol au vent (puff pasty filled with little raviolis) and veal strips sautéed in cognac are just two of the specialties here. There are also interesting daily specials, but surprisingly little seafood.

3 The South Beach Area

67 miles W of Olympia, 67 miles S of Lake Quinault, 92 miles N of Long Beach

The South Beach area, on the central Washington coast, is so named because it occupies the south side of Gray's Harbor. The 18-mile stretch of flat beach is bordered on the south by Willapa Bay, across which lies the Long Beach Peninsula.

Considering how convenient these beaches are to both Olympia and Seattle, they're surprisingly undeveloped. However, they're not nearly as spectacular as the beaches to the north on the Olympic Peninsula.

ESSENTIALS

GETTING THERE   The South Beach area is 20 miles west of Aberdeen on Wash. 105. U.S. 12 connects Aberdeen with Olympia to the east, and U.S. 101 connects Aberdeen with Forks and Port Angeles to the north and Long Beach and Astoria to the south.

VISITOR INFORMATION   Contact the **Westport/Grayland Chamber of Commerce,** P.O. Box 306-D, Westport, WA 98595 (☎ **360/268-9422** or 800/ 345-6223).

FISHING, CLAMMING, WHALE WATCHING & OTHER THINGS TO DO

Charter fishing, clamming, and whale watching are the big attractions here, and most of the activity centers around the marina at Westport. Boats head out daily in summer in search of salmon, tuna, and bottom fish. If you'd like to try your luck at reeling in a big one, try **Bran Lee Charters** (☎ 360/268-9177 or 800/562-0163 in Washington) or **Deep Sea Charters** (☎ 360/268-9300 or 800/562-0151). Rates are between $50 and $70 for a day of fishing.

Crabbing and clamming are two other favorite area activities. For **crabbing,** you'll need an inexpensive crab trap and some bacon or chicken necks for bait. Find a spot on Westport's 1,000-foot-long pier, toss your trap over the side, and sit back and wait for the crabs to come to you—it's that easy. **Clamming** is a bit harder. You'll need a license, a shovel, and a tide table. With all three in hand, head out to the beach at low tide and start looking for clam holes. When you spot one, dig fast. Good luck!

Each year between February and May, gray whales migrating to the calving grounds off Baja California, Mexico, pass by the Washington coast. The whales sometimes come so close to the mouth of Gray's Harbor that they can be seen from the observation tower at the marina in Westport. However, for a closer look, you might want to head out on a whale-watching boat trip. Contact **Neptune Whale Watch Cruises** (☎ **360/268-0124** or 800/422-0425) or **Westport Charters** (☎ 360/268-9120 or 800/562-0157) in Westport if you're interested. Rates are around $23 for adults and $14 for children.

If you aren't here during the whale-watching season, you can at least have a look at a couple of whale skeletons at the **Westport Maritime Museum,** 2202 Westhaven Dr., Westport (☎ **360/268-0078**). Housed in a 1939 Coast Guard station, the museum contains Coast Guard exhibits, displays on early pioneer life in the area, and, in a glass-enclosed building outside, the skeletons of a minke whale, a gray whale, and part of a blue whale.

The 18 miles between Westport and Tokeland is called the South Beach, and there are plenty of places to access the sand and surf. Four state parks provide the best facilities and easiest access. **Twin Harbors State Park** (☎ **360/268-9717**) is 2 miles south of Westport and is the largest of the four, with more than 3 miles of beach. **Grayland Beach State Park** (☎ **360/268-9717**) is just south of the town of Grayland and has less than a mile of beach. Both of these parks have nature trails, picnic areas, and campgrounds. Just outside the marina area of

Westport is **Westhaven State Park** and just west of town is **Westport Light State Park.** These latter two parks are day-use areas only.

WHERE TO STAY

Château Westport Motel

710 Hancock St., Westport, WA 98595. ☎ **360/268-9101** or 800/255-9101. Fax 360/268-1646. 108 rms. TV TEL. $65–$214 double. Rates include continental breakfast. Lower rates Oct–May. AE, CB, DC, DISC, MC, V.

Though the use of *château* and *motel* in the same name may seem like a contradiction in terms, this is indeed a pleasant lodging. Attractively landscaped grounds and a location right on the beach make this a good place to park yourself for a few days of hanging out or exploring the region. Some rooms have their own fireplaces while others have kitchens, so you can pick your priority. An indoor swimming pool and hot tub make this a good choice any time of year.

✪ Tokeland Hotel

100 Hotel Rd., Tokeland, WA 98590. ☎ **360/267-7006.** 18 rms, none with bath. $65–$85 double. Rates include full breakfast. DISC, MC, V.

Located on the north shore of Willapa Bay, the Tokeland Hotel has been welcoming guests, though not continuously, since 1889. This area was once a popular summer resort, but when the steamers quit running from South Bend the hotel became too inaccessible. Today the Tokeland still feels remote. Lawns surround the inn, and beyond these lies the water. The first floor is taken up by a large open lobby and dining room, off which is a small library with a fireplace. Antique furnishings lend an air of authenticity to the inn. The rooms are arranged on either side of a long hall and have painted wood floors. The shared bathrooms all have clawfoot tubs.

The inn's moderately priced dining room is the most popular restaurant for miles around and is particularly noteworthy for its Sunday dinner, which includes a delicious cranberry pot roast.

WHERE TO DINE

Constantin's

321 E. Dock St., Westport. ☎ **360/268-0550.** Reservations recommended. Main courses $13–$20. AE, DISC, MC, V. Mon and Wed–Sat 5–9pm, Sun 5–8pm. CONTINENTAL.

Located only half a block from the marina, Constantin's started out as a Greek restaurant, but when Greek didn't go over so well with the locals, the owner switched to a menu he calls European. However, there are still plenty of Greek dishes and daily specials available, and in my book these are still the meals to choose.

✪ The Dunes Restaurant

793 Dunes Rd., Grayland. ☎ **360/267-1441.** Reservations recommended. Main courses $10–$23; sandwiches $4–$18. AE, CB, DC, DISC, MC, V. Daily 11am–9pm (from 9am on summer weekdays). SEAFOOD/STEAK.

Watch for the sign on the south side of Grayland. It will lead you down a potholed gravel road to what seems to be an old shack amid the dunes. The weatherbeaten old building, with its steamy greenhouse for an entry, has been around for years and looks it. Inside, the floors are bare and well sanded by the many folks who have come in off the beach. Good old home-cooking, beach style, is the specialty here.

Watch Your Step: Banana Slugs Crossing

If you happen to be a gardener who lives where summers are humid, you probably curse slugs, which can do immense damage to a vegetable patch. Now, imagine that those slimy little slugs chomping on your tomatoes are not an inch long but rather a foot long! Sound like a late-night monster movie? Think again. And if you go out in the woods today, be sure to watch your step.

The banana slug (*Ariolimax columbianus*), which can grow to be a foot in length and live for up to five years, is the only slug native to the Pacific Northwest. Taking its name from its yellowish color and elongated shape, this slug makes its way through the region's lowland forests, dining on plants, mushrooms, and decaying vegetable matter. Though slugs may seem to wander aimlessly, they have two eyes on the ends of long stalks and two olfactory organs on short stalks. The eyes detect light and dark and help them find cool dark places to sleep away the day, while the olfactory organs are used to locate food. A slug eats by shredding organic matter with its tongue, which is covered with thousands of tiny teeth and is known as a radula.

Aside from their disgusting appearance and annoying habit of devouring gardens, slugs get a bad rap for sliming anyone unlucky enough to grab one accidentally. Slug slime, if you take the time to study it instead of just rubbing your fingers furiously to remove it, is amazing stuff. It's at once both as slippery as soap and as sticky as glue. It's this unusual combination of properties that allows slugs to use their slime as a sort of instant highway on which to travel. Secreting the slime from their chin like so much drool, they stick the slime to the surface of whatever they're crawling on and then just slide along on this instant road. Do you think slugs are slow? Think again. One of these babies can do 0.007 miles per hour (3 to 4 inches per minute) on the straightaway as the muscles along its foot constrict in waves to move the slug forward. Slug slime may also

---

There's lots of simply prepared seafood in large portions, but remember to save room for some blackberry pie or cranberry upside-down cake.

DRIVING ON TO LONG BEACH

Though it's only about 5 miles across the mouth of Willapa Bay to the northern tip of the Long Beach Peninsula, it's about 85 miles around to the town of Long Beach by road. Along the way you'll be skirting the shores of Willapa Bay. There aren't too many towns on this bay, which is why it's such a great place to raise oysters. Punctuating the miles of unspoiled scenery are oyster docks and processing plants.

In the town of **South Bend** oystering reaches its zenith. South Bend claims to be the oyster capital of the world and holds the annual **Oyster Stampede** festival each year in late May. The best place to chow down on oysters is at **Boondocks Restaurant,** between the highway and the bay in South Bend (☎ 360/875-5155). Boondocks is open Monday through Saturday from 8am to 9pm and on Sunday from 8am to 8pm, and serves oysters just about any way you'd like.

South Bend's other claim to fame is its county **courthouse.** Though South Bend is the county seat today, back in 1892 it took a possibly rigged vote and force of arms to wrest the title of country seat from Oysterville, across the bay on the Long

serve as a defense mechanism. Slugs lack the protective shell of their close relatives the snails, but they can defend themselves by secreting copious amounts of slime, which renders them unpalatable to predators such as shrews, beetles, crows, and garter snakes.

It's hard to believe that something as soft and slow moving as a slug could ever be a threat to anything, but slugs are real scrappers. Catch one on a bad day, and if you happen to be another slug you could be in for trouble. That same serrated tongue that shreds lettuce so efficiently can also be used as a weapon against other slugs. If you start checking slugs closely, you're likely to find a few with old battle scars on their backs.

So now that you know a little more about slugs, you're probably wondering how slugs do it, right? Where *do* baby slugs come from? In fact, slugs come from wherever they want—you see, slugs are hermaphroditic. That's right, it only takes one to tango if you happen to be a slug. However, if two slugs should chance to meet on a dark night, well, sometimes the chemistry is just right. Let this last bit of information sink in and you'll soon realize that every one of those slugs out in your garden is going to lay eggs! Now that's a nightmare.

And how did banana slugs get their name? No one is quite sure whether it's because they so closely resemble bananas, right down to the brown spots, or because when stepped on, they have an effect similar to that of a banana peel. Either way, the name is quite appropriate.

Slugs are so much a part of Northwest culture and humor that they've been the subject of cartoons, humorous books, even a tongue-in-cheek cookbook. In Eugene, Oregon, there's even an annual festival held each September that crowns a slug queen. In gift shops all over the region, you'll find slug refrigerator magnets, so you can take a little bit of the Northwest home with you when you leave.

Beach Peninsula. Construction of the new courthouse began 18 years later, and upon completion the imposing structure was dubbed a "gilded palace of extravagance." The majestic courthouse, seeming quite out of place in such a quiet backwater, stands on a hill overlooking the town. The copper dome is lined inside with stained glass, and there are murals decorating the interior walls. It's definitely worth a look.

4 The Long Beach Peninsula

110 miles NW of Portland, 180 miles SW of Seattle, 80 miles W of Longview/Kelso

For more than 100 years folks have been flocking to these sandy shores to frolic in the sun, fly kites, and chow down on the local oysters and razor clams— and today the Long Beach Peninsula, a long narrow strip of low forest and sand dunes, is Washington's most developed stretch of beach. There are dozens of resorts, motels, rental cabins, vacation homes, and campgrounds up and down the peninsula.

Each of the peninsula's towns has its own distinct personality. In Seaview, there are restored Victorian homes and bed-and-breakfast inns. In Long Beach, go-kart tracks and family amusements hold sway. Klipsan Beach and Ocean Park are quiet retirement communities, while Nahcotta is still an active oystering port. Last and least is the tiny community of Oysterville, which is a National Historic District.

With 28 uninterrupted miles of sand, the Long Beach Peninsula claims to be the world's longest beach (though lately they have modified the claim—the world's longest beach that's open to vehicles). With this much beach, it isn't surprising that the spring and summer razor-clamming season is one of the most popular times of year. The razor-clamming season is strictly regulated, with specific dates, times, and areas for clamming. Beaches are often closed to clamming because of "red tides," which cause shellfish to store large quantities of a toxin that causes amnesic shellfish poisoning. Always check at a local store or motel to find out about restrictions.

Bivalves aren't the only seafoods that attract folks to the south coast. In Ilwaco, south of Long Beach, and in Westport, at the mouth of Gray's Harbor, are large fleets of charter fishing boats that can take you out in search of salmon, tuna, or bottom fish.

ESSENTIALS

GETTING THERE   The Long Beach Peninsula begins just off U.S. 101 in southwest Washington. U.S. 101 leads north to Aberdeen and south to Astoria, Oregon. Wash. 4 leads to Long Beach from Longview.

The Astoria Airport, across the Columbia River in Oregon, is served by Alaska Airlines.

VISITOR INFORMATION   Contact the **Long Beach Peninsula Visitor's Bureau,** P.O. Box 562, Long Beach, WA 98631 (☎ **360/642-2400** or 800/ 451-2542), which operates a visitor center at the intersection of U.S. 101 and Pacific Avenue in Seaview.

GETTING AROUND   The **Pacific Transit System** (☎ **360/642-9418**) operates public buses that serve the area from Astoria in the south to Aberdeen in the north. If you need a taxi, call **Seaside Cab Company** (☎ **360/738-5252**).

FESTIVALS   Annual events in Long Beach include the **Ragtime Rhodie Dixieland Jazz Festival** in April; the **Sandsations** sand-sculptures tournament in July; the **Washington State International Kite Festival** in August; and the **Water Music Festival** (chamber music) in October.

EXPLORING THE COAST: KITE FLYING, BIRDWATCHING, DIGGING FOR CLAMS & SEEING THE SIGHTS

Active vacations are the norm here on the Long Beach Peninsula, and there are plenty of activities to keep you busy. However, one activity you won't be doing much of is swimming in the ocean. Though it gets warm enough in the summer to lie on the beach, the waters here never warm up very much. Add to this unpredictable currents, rip tides, undertows, and heavy surf and you have a soup that's just not safe for swimming.

Instead of swimming, the beach's number-one activity is **kite flying.** Strong winds blow year round across the Long Beach Peninsula, and with it's 28 miles of beach, you won't have to worry about kite-eating trees. If you're a kite flyer, or even if you're not, you may want to stop by the **World Kite Museum and Hall of Fame,** Third Street NW, Long Beach (☎ **360/642-4020**), where you can see displays on kites of the world. It's open daily from 11am to 5pm in summer, on

Saturday and Sunday only in other months; admission is $1 for adults, 50¢ for children.

Another very popular Long Beach activity is beachcombing. The most sought after treasures are hand-blown glass fishing floats used by Japanese fishermen.

Long Beach is one of the few beaches on the West Coast that still allows vehicular traffic, so if you're of a mind to go for a drive on the beach, feel free. Just remember that the beach is a state highway and a 25-m.p.h. speed limit is enforced. There are beach access roads up and down the peninsula, and once you're on the beach, be sure you stay above the clam beds (sand nearest to the low-tide area) and below the dry sand.

If you've ever dreamed about riding a horse down the beach, you can make your dream come true here in Long Beach. You'll find **rental stables** by the boardwalk at 10th Street in Long Beach.

If you'd just like to get away from the crowds and find a piece of isolated shoreline to call your own, head to Leadbetter Point at the peninsula's northern tip. Here you'll find both **Leadbetter Point State Park Natural Area** and a portion of the **Willapa National Wildlife Refuge.** This area is well known for its variety of birds. More than 100 species have been sited here, including the snowy plover, which nests at the point. Because the plovers nest on the sand, a portion of the point is closed to all visitors from April to September. During these months you can still hike the trails, use the beach, and explore the marshes.

Anchoring the south end of the peninsula is forested **Fort Canby State Park** (☎ **360/642-3078**), at the mouth of the Columbia River; it's open from dawn to dusk, and admission is free. The park is a former military installation used to guard the river mouth, and many of the bunkers and batteries are still visible. Also within the boundaries of the park are the North Head and Cape Disappointment lighthouses. The latter was built in 1856 and is the oldest lighthouse on the West Coast. The park is also home to the **Lewis and Clark Interpretive Center,** which chronicles the 1805–06 journey of the two explorers; it's open daily from 10am to 5pm and admission is free. Cape Disappointment, here in the park, was the end of the westward trail for Lewis and Clark. Also within the park are several picnic areas, hiking trails, a campground, and **Waikiki Beach,** the prettiest little beach between here and Moclips. This tiny cove backed by steep cliffs is named for several Hawaiian sailors who lost their lives near here.

In the past 300 years more than 2,000 vessels and 700 lives have been lost in the treacherous waters at the mouth of the Columbia River, and consequently, the U.S. Coast Guard has its National Motor Life Boat School here. Lifeboat drills can be observed from observation platforms on the North Jetty. This jetty, completed in 1917, was built to improve the channel across the Columbia Bar. A side effect of the 2-mile-long jetty was the creation of a much wider beach to the north. This widening of the beach accounts for Long Beach's current distance from the waves.

Long Island, in the middle of Willapa Bay, is part of the Willapa National Wildlife Refuge, which has its headquarters about 9 miles up U.S. 101 from Seaview. The island is known for its grove of huge old red cedars and is popular with sea kayakers. There are a few campsites and some hiking trails.

To learn more about the history of the area, stop by the **Ilwaco Heritage Museum,** 115 SE Lake St. (☎ **360/642-3446**). This modern museum houses displays on the history of southwest Washington with exhibits on Native American culture, exploration and development of the region, and a working model of the Columbia River estuary.

Nine miles east of Ilwaco, Wash. 103 follows the shore of the Columbia to the Astoria-Megler Bridge, a 4¹/₂-mile-long span that connects Washington with Oregon. Shortly before you reach the bridge, you'll come to **Fort Columbia State Park** (☎ **360/642-3078** or 360/777-8755), another former military base that guarded the mouth of the river from 1896 until the end of World War II. The park's wooded bluff has some picnic tables and a few short hiking trails past the old bunkers. The views from here are breathtaking. Today the 1903-vintage buildings have been restored and house historical displays and a youth hostel (open April to September).

Up toward the north end of the peninsula, you'll find another history buffs' playground at the village of **Oysterville.** This old oystering community is a National Historic District. Old homes with spacious lawns cling to the edge of the marsh. In the days of the California gold rush, Oysterville was shipping tons of oysters to San Francisco, where people were willing to pay as much as $50 a plate for fresh oysters. Today Oysterville is a sleepy little community of restored homes and a white clapboard church that has occasional music or storytelling performances. Back down at **Seaview,** you'll find quite a few restored Victorian cottages.

The Long Beach Peninsula is not just a vacation destination. It's also an active agricultural and aquacultural region. Cranberries and oysters are the two crops that are harvested along the peninsula, and if you take a drive down almost any side road north of Long Beach, you'll drive past acres of **cranberry bogs.** The peninsula's other crop is **oysters.** Willapa Bay, the bay formed by the Long Beach Peninsula, is one of the cleanest bays in the country and consequently is perfect for raising oysters.

Because all the oysters are privately owned, you can't collect any. However, you can **dig for razor clams,** in season, up and down the peninsula. These long, narrow clams are best harvested on a low, or minus, tide, when it's easy to spot the holes made by the clams. All you'll need to go clamming is a clamming license, a clam shovel (available at hardware stores throughout the area), and a tide table. Keep in mind that there are seasons, hours, and limits for clamming, so check with a local before heading out.

At Ilwaco, you'll find charter boats that will take you out fishing for salmon, halibut, sturgeon, or bottom fish. Try **Pacific Salmon Charters** (☎ **360/642-3466** or 800/831-2695), or **Coho Charters** (☎ **360/642-3333**).

WHERE TO STAY
IN SEAVIEW

✪ Shelburne Country Inn

4415 Pacific Hwy., Seaview, WA 98644. ☎ **360/642-2442.** Fax 206/642-8904. 13 rms, 2 suites. $95–$135 double; $165 suite. Rates include full breakfast. AE, MC, V.

Though it isn't exactly in the country, the Shelburne Inn might as well be surrounded by acres of pastures and woods. At least that's the feeling you get the moment you walk through the door. Traffic noises disappear and a pale light, filtered by walls of stained-glass windows that were salvaged from a church in England, suffuses the entry. To your right is the inn's Shoalwater Restaurant, one of the two best restaurants on the peninsula, and to your left is the Heron and Beaver Pub, which serves delicious food as well as a good pint of Northwest microbrew.

Push through the second door and you enter another world entirely. Dark fir-paneled walls, a big oak table, and a fire crackling on the hearth all extend a classic country welcome. Most guest rooms are on the second floor, but there are a couple of suites on the ground floor. These overlook the gardens and have their own decks. Other rooms vary in size and decor, and those that are on the street side of the inn have stained-glass or frosted windows to screen your view and perpetuate the country feel of the inn.

IN LONG BEACH

Chautauqua Lodge

P.O. Box 757, Long Beach, WA 98631. ☎ **360/642-4401** or 800/869-8401. 180 rms. TV TEL. June 15–Sept 15, $49–$155 double. Sept 16–June 14, $35–$95 double. AE, DC, DISC, MC, V.

If you want to spend top dollar, and prefer resort amenities over the friendliness of a bed-and-breakfast inn, the Chautauqua is for you. Though the setting, in the wide grass strip between town and the beach, leaves a bit to be desired, this motel-style resort is about as close to the water as you can get in Long Beach. Cedar shingles and stone walls give the otherwise ordinary buildings a bit of style. The more expensive rooms are those with views, and there are also rooms with kitchenettes.

The restaurant features seafoods and steaks, and in the adjacent lounge you can sometimes catch a bit of live music while you sit by the fire. Facilities include an indoor pool, whirlpool, sauna, and games rooms.

IN KLIPSAN BEACH

Klipsan Beach Cottages

22617 Pacific Hwy., Ocean Park, WA 98640. ☎ **360/665-4888.** 9 cottages. Summer, $80–$150 cottage for two. Lower rates off-season. MC, V.

Set under the trees on the edge of the dunes that lead to the beach, these renovated beach cottages capture the less hectic spirit of turn-of-the-century seaside vacations. You can sit in your comfortable one-, two-, or three-bedroom cottage and gaze out over the dunes at glorious sunsets. The cottages have fireplaces and kitchenettes.

IN OCEAN PARK

Sunset View Resort

P.O. Box 399, Ocean Park, WA 98640. ☎ **360/665-4494** or 800/272-9199. 52 rms. TV TEL. June–Sept, $59–$154 double. Oct–May, $44–$108 double. AE, CB, DC, DISC, MC, V.

About midway up the peninsula, you'll find this attractive motel set back in the woods a bit on the far side of a little bridge. Tall fir trees and attractive gardens surround the resort, and out back, dunes stretch for 100 yards to the beach. Many of the rooms come equipped with kitchens, which makes this a good choice for families; some rooms also have fireplaces and balconies. Though there isn't a pool here, you'll find a sauna, a whirlpool, a volleyball court, horseshoes, a playground, and a picnic area.

IN NAHCOTTA

⑤ Moby Dick Hotel

Sandridge Rd. and Bay Ave., Nahcotta, WA 98637. ☎ **360/665-4543.** Fax 360/665-6887. 10 rms, 5 with bath. $55–$75 double without bath; $60–$80 double with bath. Rates include full breakfast. MC, V.

Though it looks a bit like a big yellow bunker from the outside, the Moby Dick is actually a very comfortable bed-and-breakfast inn. Built as a hotel back in 1930, the year before the train stopped running, the hotel quickly fell on hard times. Today it's a casual place that captures the spirit of small historic hotels. The location, up at the north end of the peninsula, is removed from the beach strip of Seaview and Long Beach, and is convenient to Leadbetter Park and its wild dunes and beaches. You'll also be within walking distance from the Ark Restaurant (see below). Low rates, friendly atmosphere, and a tranquil setting make this a great choice.

✪ Our House in Nahcotta

P.O. Box 33, Nahcotta, WA 98637. ☎ **360/665-6667.** 2 suites. $85 suite for two. Rates include full breakfast. MC, V. In Nahcotta, turn west on 268th Street and then right onto Dell Road.

This romantic little shingle-sided cottage, a cross between a forest cottage and a beach bungalow, is set at the end of a quiet lane and is surrounded by colorful gardens. The setting is light-years away from the bustle of Long Beach, which makes this a great spot for a relaxing weekend getaway, and you can even walk to the Ark, one of the best restaurants in the area. Part of the inn used to be the Nahcotta Schoolhouse, but it has since been added onto and updated. Today the house wears a Victorian look both inside and out. Breakfasts are served in the rooms.

IN ILWACO

Chick-a-Dee Inn at Ilwaco

120 Williams St. NE, Ilwaco, WA 98624. ☎ **360/642-8686.** Fax 360/642-8642. 12 rms. $75–$150 double. Rates include full breakfast. MC, V.

Built on a hill on the outskirts of tiny Ilwaco, this inn is a former Presbyterian church. Though the church itself now serves as a theater and dining room (open to guests only), an attached building, which once served as Sunday school and minister's home, now houses the inn's guest rooms. The decor is simple, with plenty of nautical decor. A 1940s Cadillac is available for chauffeur-driven picnics. Ilwaco makes a good base for exploring both the Long Beach Peninsula and Astoria.

WHERE TO DINE
IN SEAVIEW

✪ The Shoalwater Restaurant and the Heron and Beaver Pub

In the Shelburne Country Inn, Wash. 103 and 45th St. ☎ **360/642-4142.** Reservations highly recommended. Main courses $15–$24; pub entrées $7–$9. AE, CB, DC, DISC, MC, V. Restaurant, daily 5–9pm (to 9pm in summer). Pub, daily 11:30am–2:30pm and 5–9 or 10pm. NORTHWEST.

Not only is the Shoalwater one of the best restaurants on the Long Beach Peninsula, it's one of the best restaurants in the Northwest. Stained-glass windows salvaged from a church in England suffuse the elegant dining room with a soft light, while oak furnishings and deep forest-green wallpaper evoke the Victorian era during which the Shelburne Inn was built. The menu changes frequently but you can be sure you'll find creative dishes perfectly prepared with the freshest Northwest ingredients. Since this is cranberry country, you might want to start your meal with an appetizer of pâté with cranberry chutney and garlic crème fraîche.

Across the entry from the Shoalwater, you'll find the more casual Heron and Beaver Pub, which serves equally creative but lighter fare. Prices are considerably lower than they are at the Shoalwater, and both lunch and dinner are served.

IN LONG BEACH

If you're struck with an espresso craving while in Long Beach, head for **Pastimes Coffee & Collectibles,** Oceanic Building, South Fifth Street and Pacific Avenue (☎ **360/642-8303**), where you can do a little shopping while you sip a tall skinny half-caf latte and enjoy a pastry, salad, or sandwich. Should you be a chess player, you can sign up for a game.

Crab Pot Seafoods

1917 Pacific Ave. S. ☎ **360/642-2524.** Reservations not accepted. Meals $4–$19. MC, V. Summer, daily noon–9pm; the rest of the year, Fri–Tues noon–7pm. SEAFOOD.

As the name implies, crab is the specialty of the house here, but all the inexpensive seafood is fresh and flavorful. The aging building looks a bit like a gas station, but out front is a crab pot instead of gas pumps. The crab pots are kept busy throughout the day boiling up pounds and pounds of Dungeness crabs. The front half of the building is a seafood market where you can grab a crab to go. Around the side you'll find the small dining room, which is as casual as the building would suggest. Take-out orders are also available.

The Lightship Restaurant

In the Nendels Inn, 409 SW 10th St. ☎ **360/642-3252.** Reservations recommended. Main courses $11–$15. AE, DC, DISC, MC, V. Mon–Thurs 11am–9pm, Fri 11am–10pm, Sat 8:30am–10pm, Sun 8:30am–9pm. STEAK/SEAFOOD.

If you want to dine in Long Beach with a view of the ocean, this is your only option. Luckily the meals are almost as good as the view. The Lightship is a casual family place with windows on three sides so you can gaze up and down the beach while you dine. Sunsets, which come quite late in the summer, are the perfect backdrop to dinner. The Dungeness crab with vodka-lemon-pepper cocktail sauce is a great way to start a meal, as is the Northwest clam chowder. The entrée salads are large and, when accompanied by a couple of rolls, make a filling meal. A simple plate of pan-fried oysters with homemade tartar sauce is as satisfying as any dish on the menu. The one drawback is that service can be slow.

My Mom's Pie Kitchen

S. 12th St. and Pacific Ave. ☎ **360/642-2342.** Reservations recommended. Meals $3–$8. MC, V. Tues–Sun 11am–4pm. SANDWICHES/SALADS.

The name itself is enough to get most people to take a chance and step through the door of this aging mobile home, and the lace curtains, early Americana, and very traditional decor inside quickly set people at ease. Though you can get soups, salads, and sandwiches, what lured you in was the promise of pies, and there they sit in a glass display case just inside the door. You'll know the moment you see these pies that they're the real McCoy—flaky and oozing fruit filling from every pore. After you've had your slice, you might want to put in an order for a whole pie to go.

IN NAHCOTTA

☺ The Ark Restaurant & Bakery

Peninsula Rd. ☎ **360/665-4133.** Reservations highly recommended. Main courses $9–$18. DC, DISC, MC, V. Tues–Thurs 5–10pm, Fri–Sat 11am–2:30pm and 5–10pm, Sun 11am–9pm. Closed Jan–Mar 1. NORTHWEST.

Located at the north end of the Long Beach Peninsula in what's called "little old Nahcotta," the Ark is a gustatory sanctuary in the wilderness. Set at the foot of a working dock and surrounded by oyster canneries and the remains of many years of oyster shucking, the Ark has its own oyster beds, as well as its own herb and edible-flower garden and bakery. You can be sure that whatever you order here will be absolutely fresh, and that's exactly what has kept the Ark afloat since 1981. Though it's possible to order dishes that didn't originate in the surrounding waters, there seems no reason to bother—not when you can have crab cakes with corn relish and red-pepper coulis or grilled sea scallops with mandela sauce and papaya salad for a starter. Follow that with the Ark's all-you-can-eat oyster feed and you might just be in seafood heaven. However, it's hard to pass up the salmon Louise, which is made with chanterelles, lime, cilantro, sherry, and cream. If you have a sweet tooth, you might want to opt for one of the light meals so you can save room for dessert.

IN CHINOOK

Sanctuary Restaurant

U.S. 101 and Hazel St. ☎ **360/777-8380.** Reservations highly recommended. Main courses $10–$18.50. AE, CB, DC, MC, V. Wed–Sat 5–9pm, Sun 5–7pm (in summer, also Sun brunch 10am–2pm). CONTINENTAL/SCANDINAVIAN.

Built in 1906, the Sanctuary was once the Methodist Episcopal Church of Chinook. In 1983 the church was converted into a restaurant, and people have been flocking to the doors ever since. The church has changed very little since its days as a house of worship. Pews are used for bench seating at the tables, though if you manage to get a table on the altar, you may wind up in the minister's thronelike chair. The menu includes such staples as pan-fried oysters, as well as such imaginative dishes as marinated shrimp and chicken with ginger, garlic, cranberries, spices, and madeira. However, the Scandinavian dishes are the real specialty here.

9

Central & Eastern Washington

For many people who live on the wet west side of the Cascades, life in the Northwest would be impossible if it were not for the sunny east side of the mountains. Eastern Washington is in the rain shadow of the Cascades and, with many areas receiving less than 10 inches of rain per year, is considered a high desert. Along with the lack of rain comes plenty of sunshine—an average of 300 days per year. Statistics like these prove irresistible to folks from Puget Sound, who regularly head over to the Yakima Valley to dry out.

Though there's little rainfall, rivers such as the Columbia, which meanders through much of this region, have provided, with the assistance of several dams (including the huge Grand Coulee Dam), sufficient irrigation water to make the region a major agricultural area. Apples, pears, cherries, wine grapes (and wine), wheat, and potatoes have become the staple crops of a land that once grew little more than sagebrush and bunchgrass. The Columbia River was also responsible thousands of years ago for creating the region's most fascinating geological wonders—a dry waterfall that was once four times larger than Niagara Falls and abandoned riverbeds known as coulees.

Down in the southeastern corner of the state, near the college and wheat-farming town of Walla Walla, the desert gives way to the Blue Mountains. It was near here that the region's first white settlers, Marcus and Narcissa Whitman, set up a mission in order to convert Native Americans to Christianity. They would later be massacred by Cayuse native tribespeople angered by the Whitmans' inability to cure a measles epidemic. To the north of Walla Walla lie the Palouse Hills, a scenic region of rolling hills that are now blanketed with the most productive wheat farms in the United States.

Though Yakima attracts sunseekers from the western part of the state, it is Spokane, situated at the far eastern end of the state only a few miles from Idaho, that's the region's largest city. With its proximity to forests and mountains and its setting on the banks of the Spokane River, it appeals to those who value outdoor activities. The city's far easterly location, however, makes it seem less a part of the Northwest and more a part of the Rocky Mountain states. Thus it forms an eastern gateway both to Washington and to the Northwest.

1 Yakima & the Wine Country

150 miles SE of Seattle, 92 miles NW of Richland, 195 miles SW of Spokane

Located only three hours from Seattle, Yakima is in another world—the sunny side of the Cascades, which receives only about 8 inches of rain a year. Despite this lack of rainfall, the area has become one of Washington's main apple-growing regions. Hops, used in making beer, is another important crop in the Yakima Valley, but grapes have been bringing the valley international attention in recent years. On a visit to Yakima, you can sample the area's bounties at fruit stands, wineries, and even a microbrewery.

All the land around Yakima was once the homeland of the Yakama people. The first white settlers, Catholic missionaries, arrived in 1847 and set up their mission south of present-day Yakima, and by the 1850s growing hostilities between settlers and Native Americans had led to the establishment of Fort Simcoe, 38 miles west of Yakima. In 1880, when residents of Yakima City refused to sell land to the Northern Pacific Railroad, the railroad built North Yakima 4 miles away and proceeded to move 50 buildings from Yakima City to the new townsite, which grew into the Yakima of today.

ESSENTIALS

GETTING THERE   Yakima is on I-82 at the junction with U.S. 12, which connects to I-5 south of Centralia. U.S. 97 connects to I-84 east of the Dalles, Oregon.

The Yakima Municipal Airport, on the southern outskirts of town, is served by Horizon Airlines and United Express.

VISITOR INFORMATION   Contact the **Yakima Valley Visitors & Convention Bureau,** 10 N. Eighth St., Yakima, WA 98901 (☎ **509/575-1300**).

GETTING AROUND   If you need a taxi, contact **Diamond Cab** (☎ **509/453-3113**). Public bus service in the Yakima area is provided by **Yakima Transit** (☎ **509/575-6175**). For getting around downtown Yakima, there are free buses.

FESTIVALS   The annual **Spring Barrel Tasting** in late April is Yakima's biggest wine festival. During this festival, the previous year's vintages are tasted before being bottled.

A WINE COUNTRY TOUR

Located on the same latitude as France's main wine regions, the **Yakima Valley** receives around 300 days of sunshine a year. Combine these factors with rich volcanic soil and you have a near-perfect grape-growing climate. The only thing missing here is rain. Central Washington is virtually a desert, but irrigation long ago overcame this minor inconvenience and today the area is producing award-winning chardonnay, riesling, Chenin blanc, sauvignon blanc, Semillon, gewürztraminer, cabernet sauvignon, merlot, Lemberger, and muscat wines. You can get a guide and map of the region's wine country from the Yakima Valley Visitors & Convention Bureau or the **Yakima Valley Wine Growers Association,** P.O. Box 39, Grandview, WA 98930. However, even without a map, signs throughout the valley point the way to various vineyards and wineries, and you can just choose to wander the backroads between Zillah and Benton City, dropping

Central & Eastern Washington

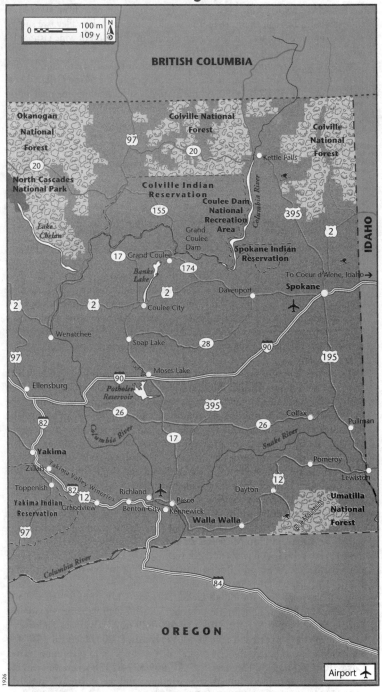

in at whichever winery strikes your fancy. Most wineries are open from 10 or 11am to 5pm daily. Though there are more than 20 wineries in the valley, we suggest picking no more than four or five to visit during an afternoon of wine tasting. It's also advisable to have a designated driver.

If you don't have time for a wine-country tour or would like to sample a few local wines before heading out to the vineyards, stop by the **Wine Cellar,** 15 W. Yakima Ave. (☎ 509/248-3590), in the Yesterday's Village shopping mall, or the **Thurston Wolfe Winery,** 27 N. Front St. (☎ 509/452-0335), both in Yakima's historic district.

Actual wine country starts about 20 miles southeast of Yakima near the town of **Zillah.** The first winery you come to is the **Staton Hills Winery,** 71 Gangl Rd. (☎ 509/877-2112), which is just off I-82 at Exit 40 and has a panoramic view of the valley and Mount Adams.

Because so many wineries have picnic areas and panoramas, you might want to pick up ingredients for your own picnic. In **Donald,** there's the **Donald Fruit and Mercantile,** 4461 Yakima Valley Hwy. (☎ 509/877-3115), which is housed in a restored 1911 general store and sells local and Northwest gourmet foods.

Before or after visiting wineries around Zillah, you might want to drive into the town of **Toppenish.** Toppenish was just a quiet little cow town until someone got the great idea of enlivening a few town walls with historical murals. Today there are more than 40 **murals** depicting aspects of Toppenish history. You'll see these murals on walls all over town, and if you stop in at almost any store in town you can pick up a map to the murals. Though some murals have taken as much as a month to paint, each year on the first Saturday in June Toppenish gets a mural-in-a-day. On this day crowds descend on the town to watch a new mural created in just one day.

Toppenish is within the boundaries of the Yakama Indian Reservation, which operates the **Yakama Indian Nation Cultural Center** on U.S. 97 (☎ 509/865-2800), just outside town. This large building, designed to resemble the traditional Yakama winter lodge, contains a museum, library, gift shop, and restaurant serving salmon, buffalo, and fry bread. Though the exhibits in the museum are by no means comprehensive and are rather poorly designed, they do manage to communicate the history and culture of the Yakama people. The Yakama are well known for their beadwork and you'll find pieces for sale in the gift shop. The center is open daily from 9am to 5pm; admission is $4 for adults, $2.75 for seniors and students.

At the **Toppenish Historical Museum,** 1 S. Elm St. (☎ 509/865-4510), you can see more Native American artifacts and a collection of antique barbed wire, and at the **American Hop Museum,** 22 S. B St. (☎ 509/865-HOPS), you can learn all about this beer ingredient. Each year over the Fourth of July weekend the **Toppenish Pow Wow and Rodeo** brings crowds of people to town to watch broncobusters and Native American dances.

In Zillah, you'll find the **Zillah Oakes Winery,** 1001 Vintage Valley Pkwy. (☎ 509/829-6990), right by the freeway. Other Zillah wineries include the **Bonair Winery,** 500 S. Bonair Rd. (☎ 509/829-6027), with its Tudor-style home surrounded by vineyards; the **Hyatt Vineyards,** 2020 Gilbert Rd. (☎ 509/829-6333), which has great views of the valley and is a good place for a picnic; **vey Run Wines,** 1500 Vintage Rd. (☎ 509/829-6235), where you can ob- the cellar operations through large windows; and the **Portteus Vineyards,** ighland Dr. (☎ 509/829-6970), which has a stupendous view. While in

Zillah, don't miss the opportunity to see the **Teapot Dome gas station,** a national historic building built in 1922 in the shape of a giant teapot to call attention to a scandal in the administration of President Warren G. Harding. You'll find the teapot on the south side of I-82. If you aren't planning on having a picnic, then consider having lunch at **El Ranchito,** 1319 E. First Ave. (☎ 509/829-5880), a near-legendary tortilla factory and restaurant with a very authentic Mexican feel.

Get back on I-82 and take Exit 54 to get to **Horizon's Edge Winery,** 4530 E. Zillah Dr. (☎ 509/829-6401), which takes its name from the tasting-room view of the valley and mountains, and the **Eaton Hill Winery,** 530 Gurley Rd. (☎ 509/854-2508), which is housed in the restored Rinehold Cannery building. Continuing on I-82 to Exit 58 and then heading south past the town of Granger will bring you to the **Stewart Vineyards,** 1711 Cherry Hill Rd. (☎ 509/854-1882), which sits atop Cherry Hill.

Getting back on the Interstate and continuing to Exit 67 and the town of Sunnyside, you'll find the **Washington Hills Cellars,** 111 E. Lincoln Ave. (☎ 509/839-9463), housed in a historic Carnation building. At Exit 69, you'll find the **Tucker Cellars,** 70 Ray Rd. (☎ 509/837-8701), which has an adjacent produce market. At Exit 73, near Grandview, is the **Château Ste. Michelle,** 205 W. Fifth St. (☎ 509/882-3928), which was Washington's pioneer winery and, with several impressive tasting rooms around the state, is also the most popular. Here in Grandview is where they produce their red wines—cabernet sauvignon, merlot, and port.

At Exit 80, you can stop in at **Chukar Cherries,** 320 Wine Country Rd. (☎ 509/786-2055), and sample dried cherries and lots of other dried fruits and candies. Nearby is the **Yakima River Winery** (☎ 509/786-2805), which is on North River Road across the river from Prosser. At this same exit, but on the opposite side of the Interstate, you'll find **Pontin del Roza** (☎ 509/786-4449) near the junction of Hinzerling and McCreadie roads. Prosser wineries include the **Hinzerling Winery,** 1520 Sheridan Rd. (☎ 509/786-2163), the oldest family-owned winery in the valley; **Chinook Wines,** Wine Country Road (☎ 509/786-2725), which has a pretty garden that's perfect for an afternoon picnic; and the **Hogue Cellars,** Wine Country Road (☎ 509/786-4557).

At Exit 96, near Benton City, you'll find the **Seth Ryan Winery,** Sunset Road (☎ 509/588-6780), which is one of the newest wineries in the valley; the **Oakwood Cellars,** De Moss Road (☎ 509/588-5332), with its 100-year-old European oak wine barrel; the **Kiona Vineyards,** off Sunset Road (☎ 509/588-6716); and **Blackwood Canyon,** near the junction of Sunset Road and Frontage Road (☎ 509/588-6249). From Benton City, it's 70 miles back to Yakima.

MUSEUMS & OTHER ATTRACTIONS

Local history is chronicled at the **Yakima Valley Museum,** 2105 Tieton Dr. (☎ 509/248-0747), where a collection of restored horse-drawn vehicles is on display. There are also displays on the Yakama peoples and former Supreme Court justice and environmentalist William O. Douglas, who was a Yakima resident. The museum is open Tuesday through Friday from 10am to 5pm and on Saturday and Sunday from noon to 5pm; admission is $2.50 for adults, $1.25 for seniors. The museum also operates the **Gilbert House,** an 1898 Victorian farmhouse, at 2109 W. Yakima Ave.

In Union Gap, the **Central Washington Agricultural Museum,** 4508 Main St. (☎ **509/457-8735**), displays more than 1,000 pieces of antique farm machinery and hand tools. The admission-free museum is open daily from dawn to dark. More local history is on view a few miles west of Union Gap in **Ahtanum,** where the first Catholic mission in the region was established in 1847. Though the mission was burned down during the Indian wars, a church built in 1867 is still standing. **Fort Simcoe,** 27 miles west of Toppenish in the Cascade foothills, was established in 1856 because of conflicts between Native Americans and settlers. Today the fort is a state park that preserves surprisingly elegant quarters that were used for only a few years before becoming a Native American school. It's open daily from April to October; in other months, on weekends only.

Front Avenue was the heart of early Yakima and over the past few years the area has been restored and now houses two unusual shopping areas—**Yesterday's Village,** in the old Fruit Exchange Building, and **Track 29,** a collection of old rail cars and old-fashioned buildings. Several good restaurants, a brew pub, and a wine shop can be found in this area.

On weekends and holidays from May to October you can ride **vintage electric trolleys** between Yakima and the nearby town of Selah. The trolleys depart from the corner of Third Avenue and West Pine Street and the round-trip takes less than two hours. The fare is $4 for adults, $3.50 for seniors, and $2.50 for children.

About 4 miles west of Yakima on U.S. 12, you can see **Native American pictographs** that were painted hundreds of years ago. In the winter months, if you continue west on this road for another 17 miles, you'll come to the **Oak Creek Game Management Preserve,** where you can see elk, and occasionally bighorn sheep, at a winter feeding station operated by the State of Washington Game Department.

OUTDOOR ACTIVITIES

Extending for 10 miles between Union Gap and Selah Gap, the **Yakima Greenway** follows the banks of the **Yakima River,** with a paved path along 5 miles of the greenway. The easiest place to access the path is at Sherman Park on Nob Hill Boulevard. In summer, **kayaking, rafting, and tubing** are popular on this section of the river, and the **birdwatching** is good year round.

If you'd like to see another scenic stretch of the river, head north to Selah and then take Wash. 821 north through the **Yakima River Canyon.** The river has been around for longer than the surrounding hills, which have risen at the same time the river is slicing through them. You can rent rafts, kayaks, and bikes from **Richie's River Rentals** (☎ **509/453-2112**), which also offers a shuttle service.

Golfers will enjoy playing a round at the **Apple Tree Golf Course,** 8804 Occidental Ave. (☎ **509/966-5877**), where the green on the 17th hole is an apple-shaped island! If you're a fan of horse racing, you can play the ponies at **Yakima Meadows,** Central Washington State Fairgrounds (☎ **509/248-3920**). The season runs from November to March with races starting at noon on Wednesday and Friday through Sunday.

WHERE TO STAY

For a list of bed-and-breakfast inns in wine country, contact the **Yakima Valley Wine Growers Association,** P.O. Box 39, Grandview, WA 98930.

ⓢ Best Western Rio Mirada

1603 Terrace Heights Dr., Yakima, WA 98901. ☎ **509/457-4444** or 800/521-3050. Fax 509/453-7593. 97 rms. A/C TV TEL. $58–$68 double. AE, MC, V.

Located east of I-82 on the banks of the Yakima River, the Rio Mirada is Yakima's most pleasant and popular budget accommodation. As such it regularly books up on weekends. The rooms are spacious, and most rooms have refrigerators. Balconies overlook the river. Walkers will be pleased to find a 5-mile walking-and-biking path running past the motel. There's a courtesy airport shuttle. Facilities include an outdoor pool, an indoor whirlpool, and an exercise room.

✪ Birchfield Manor

2018 Birchfield Rd., Yakima, WA 98901. ☎ **509/452-1960.** 11 rms. $70–$100 double. AE, DC, MC, V.

Located 2¹/₂ miles east of Yakima, Birchfield Manor is surrounded by pastures and is well known for its elegant dinners. Upstairs from the dining room in the 1910 Victorian farmhouse and in a new building constructed to resemble a vintage home, you'll find antique-filled guest rooms, most of which have good views out over the countryside. Breakfasts here are nearly as legendary as the dinners and are a great start for a day of wine touring.

Cavanaugh's at Yakima Center

607 E. Yakima Ave., Yakima, WA 98901. ☎ **509/248-5900** or 800/THE-INNS. Fax 509/575-8975. 152 rms. A/C TV TEL. $55–$95 double. AE, CB, DC, DISC, MC, V.

Because of its sunshine and central location, Yakima is a popular spot for small conventions, and this is the more attractive and most convenient of its convention hotels. The convention center and tourist information office are right across the parking lot. The rooms are of average size, though if you opt for a corporate room, you'll enjoy a few more amenities. We like the first-floor poolside rooms, which have patios within steps of the pool.

The hotel's restaurant is open for three meals a day and serves reasonably priced dishes. The wine list emphasizes local wines. For evening entertainment, there's live or recorded Top-40 dance music in the lounge. Room service is available and there are two outdoor pools.

The 37 House

4002 Englewood Ave., Yakima, WA 98908. ☎ **509/965-5537.** 4 rms, 1 suite. $67–$90 double; $140 suite. Rates include full breakfast. AE, MC, V.

Located on a hill on the western outskirts of the city, the 37 House is a large stone-faced colonial home built in 1937 (thus the name), and though it's on a busy road, the spacious gardens surrounding the house are more than sufficient to buffer the traffic noises. Built by an early fruit-growing family, the inn still contains much of the original furniture and some original wallpaper as well. A grand entry hall with hardwood floors divides the living room and den from the dining room, and up a curving staircase are the guest rooms. The rooms are tastefully decorated with a mix of modern and antique furnishings. Down in the basement you'll find a large recreation room that includes a pool table. Gourmet lunches at reasonable rates are served in the inn's downstairs common areas.

WHERE TO DINE

Birchfield Manor

2018 Birchfield Rd. ☎ **509/452-1960.** Reservations required. Prix-fixe three-course dinner $20–$28. AE, MC, V. Seatings Thurs–Fri at 7pm, Sat at 6 and 8:45pm. CONTINENTAL.

Out in the flat farmland to the east of Yakima, you'll find a grand old home surrounded by shade trees. This is Birchfield Manor, which doubles as a bed-and-breakfast and Yakima's best restaurant. The first floor of the old home has become the restaurant's dining room and looks as if a wealthy family had cleared out the regular furniture and brought in a few extra tables for a holiday dinner with family and friends. The prix-fixe menu changes with the season and includes a choice of six or seven entrées. The house specialty is salmon in puff pastry with a chardonnay sauce. The dinner includes fresh-baked bread, an appetizer, and salad.

⑤ Deli de Pasta

7 N. Front St. ☎ **509/453-0571.** Reservations recommended. Complete meals $9–$15. AE, MC, V. Mon–Sat 11:30am–9pm (to 10pm Fri–Sat in summer). ITALIAN.

It's small and inconspicuous, but Deli de Pasta has made a big impression on Yakima. All the pastas and sauces are made fresh on the premises and the menu lets you mix and match the two. You can combine black-pepper fettuccine with a creamy lemon sauce or herb linguine with pesto or rotelli with white clam sauce or whatever. However, it's the smoked-salmon ravioli with a basil-cream sauce that has been the restaurant's biggest hit.

⑤ Gasparetti's

1013 N. First St. ☎ **509/248-0628.** Reservations recommended. Main courses $9.50–$24.50. AE, DISC, MC, V. Tues–Fri 11:30am–2:30pm and 5:45–10:30pm, Sat 5:45–10:30pm. ITALIAN/INTERNATIONAL.

Though this restaurant is very nondescript from the outside, the owners have done much to create a feeling of elegance inside. The menu changes every other week and, though primarily Italian in flavor, often includes inspiration from around the globe. The rack of lamb, a regular on the menu, comes with different sauces at different times of year. A fine selection of local wines complements the menu offerings, and the extensive dessert list is, in itself, worth the visit.

Greystone Restaurant

5 N. Front St. ☎ **509/248-9801.** Reservations recommended. Main courses $12–$25. AE, MC, V. Tues–Sat 6–10pm. CONTINENTAL.

Located in Yakima's restored Front Street district, Greystone takes its name from the stone walls inside and outside the building. A high pressed-tin ceiling, an old mirrored side bar with marble counter, and antiques help capture the feel of Yakima's past. Consider starting your meal with some of Greystone's liver pâté, marinated in cognac and served with homemade pickles. If you prefer lighter fare, there are excellent salads, including the house specialty, made with chicken, fresh greens, tomatoes, capers, olives, and homemade pasta in a lemon, herb, and mayonnaise dressing. Lamb, steak, and pork tenderloin are mainstays of the menu and come with flavorful sauces such as ruby port and red peppercorn.

Santiago's

111 E. Yakima Ave. ☎ **509/453-1644.** Reservations recommended. Complete dinners $4.50–$11. MC, V. Mon–Fri 11am–2pm and 5–9pm, Sat noon–2pm and 5–9pm, Sun 5–9pm. Closed Sun in winter. MEXICAN.

Santiago's is the most upscale of Yakima's many Mexican restaurants and has been in business for more than a decade. Over the years, the restaurant's salsa has developed quite a following and comes to your table in a tiny carafe. Meals here are huge, so restrain yourself when ordering.

Dining in Nearby Grandview

Dykstra House Restaurant

114 Birch Ave. ☎ **509/882-2082.** Reservations required for Sat dinner. Main courses $12–$17. AE, DC, DISC, MC, V. Tues–Thurs 9:30am–4:30pm, Fri 9:30am–4:30pm and 6–9pm, Sat 11am–2pm and 6–9pm. ITALIAN/CONTINENTAL.

This eclectic eatery is primarily a lunch spot, but on weekends the owner, who is also the chef, cooks Italian on Friday night and a more imaginative menu on Saturday night. The menu changes every week, but a recent Saturday night included a locally inspired chicken breast with cherry sauce. Lunches are equally unpredictable—you never know what might show up on the menu, which makes a meal here all the more fun. You'll find Grandview toward the east end of the wine country, which makes this a good spot for lunch or dinner during a winery tour.

YAKIMA AFTER DARK

If you're looking for a convivial place to hoist a pint of microbrew ale, **Grant's Pub,** 32 N. Front St. (☎ **509/575-2922**), housed in half of Yakima's restored train station, is the place. Grant's serves up half a dozen of its own microbrews. On weekends there's live jazz and blues.

For more formal entertainment, including performances by the Yakima Symphony Orchestra, there's the **Capitol Theatre,** 19 S. Third St. (☎ 509/575-6267), which was built in 1920 and was the largest vaudeville theater in the Northwest at the time. A hand-painted mural on the inside of the theater's dome and ornate plasterwork make this a classic.

A SIDE TRIP TO ELLENSBURG: A GLIMPSE OF THE WILD WEST

The Wild West lives on in Ellensburg, which lies just east of the last Cascade foothills on the edge of cattle- and sheep-ranching country. It's an easy stop as you drive between Yakima and Seattle.

An attractive downtown historic district is full of buildings dating back to 1889, the year in which most of the town's commercial buildings were destroyed in a fire on the Fourth of July. Had it not been for this fire, the city would likely have become the state capital. But with only one commercial building, how could the government set up business in Ellensburg? Instead of becoming the capital, the town became the site of a state college that's now Central Washington University.

The annual Ellensburg Rodeo, held each year on Labor Day weekend, is the town's biggest event and is one of the top 10 rodeos in the United States. For more information, contact the **Ellensburg Rodeo and Kittitas County Fair** (☎ 509/962-7831 or 800/637-2444).

The western art of Ellensburg native John Clymer is displayed at the **Clymer Art Museum,** 416 N. Pearl St. (☎ 509/962-6416). A member of the prestigious Cowboy Artists of America, Clymer is best known for producing more than 80 *Saturday Evening Post* covers. The museum is open Monday through Friday from 10am to 5pm and on Saturday and Sunday from noon to 5pm; admission is $2 for adults, $1 for seniors and children.

Some 4¹/₂ miles southeast of town you'll find **Olmstead Place State Park** (☎ 509/925-1943), a heritage site that preserves a pioneer homestead of the 1870s. Northwest of Ellensburg at Exit 101 off I-90, in the town of Thorp, is the **Thorp Mill** (☎ 509/964-9640), an 1880s gristmill that now houses a museum; it's open on weekends from May 15 to October 15.

It's partly because of the rodeo and John Clymer that Ellensburg likes to see itself as a western town. However, the city has much more of a college town feel, with a youthful population and a cosmopolitan atmosphere that's much more urban than cowboy. For a look at some unique local art, walk down to **Dick & Jane's Spot** at 101 N. Pearl St. Their house and yard are decorated with hundreds of colorful objects. Other amusing artworks are the **cowboy sculpture** at Fifth Avenue and Pearl Street, and *The Ellensburg Bull* in the downtown historic district.

One other peculiar attraction well worth checking out are the **"Chimposiums"** at the university's Chimpanzee and Human Communication Institute, Nicholson Boulevard and D Street (☎ **509/963-2244**). At these programs, visitors learn about the university's primate communication project and get to observe several chimpanzees that have learned to use American Sign Language. Reservations are recommended; the programs, held on Saturday and Sunday, cost $10 for adults and $7.50 for students.

WHERE TO DINE

If you're in need of some espresso, pull up a saddle at the Cowboy Espresso Bar inside **Jaguar's,** 423 N. Pearl St. (☎ **509/962-2125**), which is a western-clothing store.

Giovanni's on Pearl

402 N. Pearl St. ☎ **509/962-2260.** Reservations recommended. Main courses $8–$14.75. AE, DISC, MC, V. Tues–Thurs 11am–8:30pm, Fri–Sat 11am–9:30pm. ITALIAN.

With its exposed-brick interior walls and elegant lavender armchairs, Giovanni's has a definite urban cachet. However, its location in historic downtown Ellensburg and the occasional country antiques around the dining room and lounge link the restaurant to the region's more rural roots. The menu is mostly straightforward Italian fare, but there are the occasional dishes highlighting local produce. The regionally renowned Ellensburg lamb shows up as kebabs and as rack of lamb. There's a short but appropriate wine list of local and imported wines.

✪ Valley Café

107 W. Third St. ☎ **509/925-3050.** Main courses $6–$16. AE, DC, MC, V. Mon–Thurs 11am–9pm, Fri 11am–10pm, Sat–Sun 9am–10pm. INTERNATIONAL.

Though this vintage café is unmarked, just look for the shining black glass facade. Inside you'll find a classic 1920s diner straight out of an Edward Hopper painting. Take a seat in one of the wooden booths and you'll swear you've stepped back in time. The menu features such dishes as blackened salmon, chicken with spicy peanut sauce, and tortellini. At lunch, meals are likely to range the globe and might include chimichangas or a chicken Dijon sandwich. Right next door there's the affiliated Valley Take-Out, an espresso bar that also serves pastries, sandwiches, and deli salads.

2 Walla Walla & the Palouse

50 miles E of Richland/Pasco/Kennewick, 155 miles S of Spokane, 39 miles NE of Pendleton

Despite the area's regional historic importance, it is onions made Walla Walla famous. The Walla Walla onion is a big sweet variety similar to the Vidalia onion of Georgia. At produce stands all over the valley you'll find big bags of these sweet onions for sale in early summer. There's even a **Walla Walla Sweet Onion Festival** held at harvest time.

Today Walla Walla is a quiet college town filled with stately old homes and large shade trees. Though the downtown is not very lively, three schools of higher learning—Walla Walla College, Whitman College, and Walla Walla Community College—give the town a rather cultured atmosphere.

ESSENTIALS

GETTING THERE   From I-82 west of Richland, take I-182 to Pasco and continue south and then west on U.S. 12. From Pendleton, Oregon, and I-84, take Ore. 11 north. From Spokane, take U.S. 195 south to Colfax, continuing south on Wash. 26 and then Wash. 127. In Dodge, you pick up U.S. 12 and continue south to Walla Walla.

VISITOR INFORMATION   Contact the **Walla Walla Area Chamber of Commerce,** 29 E. Sumach St., Walla Walla, WA 99362 (☎ **509/525-0850**).

EXPLORING THE HISTORIC SITES

The **Whitman Mission National Historic Site,** 7 miles west of Walla Walla just off U.S. 12 (☎ **509/522-6360**), is dedicated to a tragic page in Northwest history. Missionaries Marcus and Narcissa Whitman arrived in this area in 1836 and were some of the very first settlers to travel overland to the Northwest. Although the Whitmans had come here to convert the local Native Americans, Marcus Whitman was also a doctor and often treated the Cayuse people. During the mid-1840s a wagon train brought a measles epidemic to the area, and the Cayuse, who had no resistance to the disease, began dying. Though Whitman was able to save his own family, most of the Cayuse who contracted the disease died from it. The Cayuse had a tradition of killing medicine men who could not cure an illness, and on November 29, 1847, several Cayuse attacked and killed the Whitmans and 11 other residents of the mission. The massacre at the Whitman mission prompted a war on the Cayuse and a demand for territorial status for what was at that time the Oregon country. In 1848, in response to pleas brought about by the Whitman massacre, Oregon became the first territory west of the Rocky Mountains.

Today nothing remains of the mission, but a trail leads through the mission site and the locations of buildings are outlined with concrete. An interpretive center provides historical background on the mission and includes numerous artifacts from the days when the Whitmans worked with the Cayuse. The site is open daily: in summer from 8am to 6pm and in winter from 8am to 4:30pm; the park is open until dusk. Admission is $2.

In town, you'll find the **Fort Walla Walla Complex,** Myra Road (☎ **509/525-7703**). The museum is a collection of pioneer-era buildings, including log cabins, a one-room schoolhouse, an old railway station, and several other buildings. It's open April to September, Tuesday through Sunday from 10am to 5pm; and in October, on Saturday and Sunday from 10am to 5pm. Admission is $2.50 for adults and $1 for children. In addition to the displays on pioneer life, there's a large collection of horse-era farming equipment.

For a glimpse inside one of the town's elegant mansions, visit the **Kirkman House Museum,** 214 N. Colville St. (☎ **509/529-4373**), a brick Victorian home that's open Monday through Friday from 1 to 3pm. Also worth a visit is the **Carnegie Art Center,** 109 S. Palouse St. (☎ **509/525-4270**), which is housed in a former Carnegie library and includes a gallery and gift shop featuring Northwest artists and craftspeople.

ENJOYING THE OUTDOORS

Though the land immediately surrounding Walla Walla is rolling farm country, less than 20 miles to the east, the **Blue Mountains** rise to more than 6,000 feet. Hiking, mountain biking, fishing, and hunting are all popular in these little-visited mountains. For more information, contact the **Walla Walla Ranger District,** 1415 W. Rose St., Walla Walla, WA 99362 (☎ **509/522-6290**). In winter, skiers head for **Ski Bluewood** (☎ **509/382-4725** or 509/529-9685), 21¹/₂ miles south of Dayton. Adult lift ticket prices range from $17 for a half day to $23 for a full day.

WHERE TO STAY

In addition to the bed-and-breakfast inn listed below, you'll find a few inexpensive chain motels in Walla Walla. These include the following (see the Appendix for toll-free telephone numbers): **Comfort Inn Walla Walla,** 520 N. Second St., Walla Walla, WA 99362 (☎ **509/525-2522**), charging $63 to $97 double; and the **Super 8 Motel,** North Wilbur Avenue and Eastgate Street, Walla Walla, WA 99362 (☎ **509/525-8800**), charging $47 to $51 double.

✪ Green Gables Inn

922 Bonsella St., Walla Walla, WA 99362. ☎ **509/525-5501.** 5 rms, 1 carriage house. A/C TV. $75–$100 double; $160 carriage house for four. Rates include full breakfast. AE, DISC, MC, V.

This massive 1909 Arts and Crafts–style B&B takes up half the small block it sits on. Two sitting rooms downstairs are furnished with antiques (the owner was quite a collector) and have fireplaces at each end that make it quite cozy on a chill evening. Appetizing breakfasts are served in the large dining room. Some guest rooms are furnished with mahogany antiques and clawfoot tubs. The carriage house easily sleeps four and has 1¹/₂ baths and a living room.

WHERE TO DINE

The Addition

16 S. Colville St. ☎ **509/529-7336.** Reservations recommended. Main courses $9–$26. MC, V. Mon–Fri 11am–9pm, Sat 5:30–9pm. MEDITERRANEAN/INTERNATIONAL.

Just off Main Street, in a block that's mostly car-repair shops and the like, you'll find Walla Walla's most upscale restaurant. However, don't expect stuffy surroundings. The Addition's dining rooms consist of a patio, a screened porch, a large casual dining room, and two slightly more formal parlor dining rooms. The menu here changes weekly, and when we last visited some dishes that attracted our interest were the breast of duck Grand Marnier, the rack of lamb in a spicy ginger sauce, and red-pepper scampi. The Addition is also a catering company, so it should come as no surprise that they do a great job on desserts such as raspberry-cream pie and a variety of cheesecakes.

Jacobi's Café

416 N. Second Ave. ☎ **509/525-2677.** Main courses $5.50–$11.25. AE, DISC, MC, V. Sun–Thurs 6am–9pm, Fri–Sat 6am–11pm. ITALIAN.

Housed in Walla Walla's renovated railroad depot, Jacobi's is a casual Italian deli and pizza parlor. The obligatory railroad theme is carried so far as to include a restored dining car attached to the main dining room and a train whistle that's enough to cause diners to leap from their seats and reach for their luggage.

During the summer there's patio dining. If you need a cappuccino fix, there's an espresso bar. The menu includes several frittattas, and a variety of fettuccine dishes. However, it's the pizzas that seem to be most popular. Plenty of local wines are available, and a deli case near the door is full of rich desserts.

Pastime Café
215 W. Main St. ☎ **509/525-0873.** Main courses $6.45–$14.50. No credit cards. Mon–Sat 5:30am–midnight. ITALIAN.

This old-time diner turned Italian restaurant is one of the most reliable dining spots in Walla Walla. From the neon sign and green tile facade out front to the pink vinyl booths and neon wall clock inside, this place fairly screams "vintage diner." A separate dining room looks even older, as if it might date back to the days of Fort Walla Walla. The food is good old-fashioned American-Italian diner fare, with lots of spaghetti and ravioli as well as steaks, fried chicken, and even liver and onions. A full bar is one of the restaurant's popular features.

THE PALOUSE: A SLICE OF SMALL-TOWN RURAL WASHINGTON

Between Walla Walla and Spokane lie the rolling Palouse Hills, some of the most productive wheat country in the nation. However, before the advent of large irrigation projects the scant annual rainfall made farming the rich soils a dicey proposition. Prior to the settlement of the region by whites, the Native American peoples had discovered that the Palouse, as it's known, offered ideal grazing land for horses, which had reached the Northwest sometime after the Spanish conquered the southern regions of North America. By the time Lewis and Clark passed through the Palouse, the local Native Americans had become well known for their horses, which they had bred for their stamina and sure-footedness. Today these native-bred horses are known as Appaloosas for the Palouse Hills from which they came.

Throughout the Palouse, small towns that have long been out of the mainstream of Northwest development are nestled along creek banks at the base of hills. The roads wind through endless zebra-striped hills covered with wheat. The zebra stripes are alternating sections of land left untilled to reduce erosion on the steep hills.

Among the many little towns along the route from Walla Walla to Spokane, **Dayton** is by far the prettiest. Its old-fashioned small-town American feel is as genuine as it gets. Dayton was once one of the most important towns in this region and you'll find a historic railway depot that's now a museum (open Tuesday through Saturday from 11am to 6pm), the oldest courthouse in Washington, and 88 registered historic homes. About 36 miles northwest of Dayton, you'll find **Palouse Falls State Park.** The spectacular falls here cascade 198 feet into a rock-walled canyon.

Pomeroy, with its historic county courthouse, old flour mill, small historical museum, and turn-of-the-century buildings is another town worth a closer look. **Pullman** is the largest town in the region and is the home of Washington State University. The university's **Museum of Art,** Stadium Way (☎ **509/335-1910**), is worth a visit. It's open Monday and Wednesday through Friday from 10am to 4pm, on Tuesday from 10am to 10pm, and on Saturday and Sunday from 1 to 5pm; admission is free.

In **Colfax** you can take a look at the largest chainsaw sculpture in the world. It's called the **Codger Pole,** and it depicts the members of two football teams who got together in 1988 to replay their 1938 game. Some 18 miles north of Colfax, **Kamiak Butte County Park** provides the ideal vantage point for surveying the vast Palouse. Nearby is **Steptoe Butte State Park,** which offers good views of the surrounding landscape.

WHERE TO DINE IN DAYTON

✪ Patit Creek Restaurant

725 Dayton Ave. ☎ **509/382-2625.** Reservations recommended. Main courses $14–$20. MC, V. Tues–Thurs 11:30am–1:30pm and 4:30–8pm, Fri 11:30am–1:30pm and 4:30–8:30pm, Sat 4:30–8:30pm. FRENCH.

This little green cottage beside the road on the north side of Dayton is alone worth the trip to this small Palouse town. There's a pretty perennial garden out front and colorful windsocks to let you know you're at the right place. Stained-glass front windows hide the passing traffic from diners and allow guests to immerse themselves in the enjoyment of the food. Though lunches include everything from burgers to veal picatta, all at reasonable prices, dinners are on a very different level. You might start a meal with duck mousse pâté or baked Danish herb cheese in phyllo pastry. The entrée menu includes such dishes as filet mignon poivre verte with green peppercorns, cognac, and cream; and lamb chops Provençal with a reduction of cognac, garlic, and Provençal herbs. If you're anywhere in the region, try to schedule a dinner at this surprising little restaurant.

3 Spokane

284 miles E of Seattle, 195 miles NE of Yakima, 155 miles N of Walla Walla

Until the 1974 World's Fair focused the eyes of the nation on Spokane and its renovated waterfront and downtown area, the city was little more than an eastern gateway to the Pacific Northwest. Today, however, Spokane is the second-largest city in Washington, the largest city between Seattle and Minneapolis, and a center for both commercial and cultural pursuits.

For thousands of years Native Americans lived along the Spokane River, and it was at the Spokane Falls that the Spokan-ee tribe congregated each year to catch salmon. When the first explorers and fur traders arrived in 1807, it was near these falls that they chose to establish a trading post where they could barter with the Native Americans for beaver pelts. Spokan House (the original spelling had no letter *e*), established in 1810 downriver from the Spokane Falls, became the first settlement in the area, but it was not until 1872 that a settlement was established at the falls themselves. When the Northern Pacific Railroad arrived in 1881, the town of Spokan Falls became the most important town in the region. However, in the summer of 1889 the city's downtown commercial district was destroyed by fire. Within two years the city had fully recovered from the fire and also changed the spelling of its name.

ESSENTIALS

GETTING THERE Spokane is on I-90, Washington's east-west Interstate. U.S. 2 is an alternative route from western Washington. U.S. 395 is the main route from Canada south to Spokane. U.S. 195 connects to Lewiston, Idaho.

Spokane International Airport is located 10 miles west of downtown and is served by Alaska Airlines, Delta, Horizon, Northwest, Southwest, United, and United Express.

Amtrak passenger trains provide service to Spokane. The station is at 221 W. First Ave. (☎ **509/624-5144**).

VISITOR INFORMATION   Contact the **Spokane Convention & Visitors Bureau,** 926 W. Sprague Ave., Suite 180, Spokane, WA 99204 (☎ **509/ 747-3230,** or 800/248-3230).

GETTING AROUND   Rental cars are available from Avis, Budget, Dollar, National, and Thrifty. If you need a taxi, contact **Inland Taxi** (☎ **509/ 326-8294**). Public bus service is provided by the **Spokane Transit System** (☎ **509/328-7433**); the fare is 75¢.

FESTIVALS   The city's biggest annual event is the **Lilac Festival,** which is held each year in the third week of May.

WHAT TO SEE & DO

Spokane has made it very easy for visitors to get a sense of what the city is all about by mapping out a **Spokane City Drive** that takes in all the city's highlights. The well-signed route meanders through Spokane and passes by all the city attractions listed below. The drive also takes in some great vistas from the hills to the south of the city.

RIVERFRONT PARK

Created for the 1974 World's Fair Expo and set on island in the middle of the Spokane River, 100-acre **Riverfront Park** (☎ **509/625-6600**) is the city's pride and joy. The land on which the park stands was once a maze of railroad tracks and depots, and the polluted river was nearly inaccessible to the public. The creation of the park helped rejuvenate downtown Spokane, and today crowds flock here to enjoy everything from summertime concerts to ice skating in the winter. Activities for both adults and children abound in the park. The restored 1909 **Looff Carrousel,** with its hand-carved horses, is one of the most beautiful in the country. More contemporary entertainment is offered at the **IMAX Theatre,** where 70mm films are shown on screens five stories high; tickets cost $5 to $7.50 for adults, $4.50 to $6.25 for seniors, and $4 to $5 for children. A family fun center includes kiddie rides, miniature golf, and arcade games. Throughout the summer there are lunchtime and evening concerts, special events, and a weekend arts-and-crafts market.

Serving as a spectacular backdrop for the park is the Spokane River, which here cascades over the **Spokane Falls.** The best view of the falls is from the **Gondola Skyride** that swings out over the falls; rides cost $3 for adults, $2.40 for senior citizens, and $1.80 for children.

MORE ATTRACTIONS

Cheney Cowles Museum and Campbell House

W. 2316 First Ave. ☎ **509/456-3931.** Admission $3 adults, $2 seniors and children (half price on Wed). Tues and Thurs–Sat 10am–5pm, Wed 10am–9pm, Sun 1–5pm.

Though it's not very large, the Cheney Cowles Museum does an outstanding job of presenting the history of the Spokane area. Beginning with a display on Plateau

Native American culture and artifacts, the museum moves through the fur-trading and pioneer years. In addition to the historical displays, there's a fine-arts gallery in the museum. Adjacent to the museum is the historic Campbell House, a restored 1898 Tudor-style home.

Crosbyana Room

In the Crosby Student Center of Gonzaga University, E. 502 Boone Ave. ☎ **509/328-4220.** Free admission. Mon–Fri 7:30am–midnight, Sat–Sun 11am–midnight (shorter hours June–Aug).

Though Bing Crosby made his name in Los Angeles, he got his start here in Spokane, where he spent most of his youth. When young Bing's aspirations soared beyond the bounds of Spokane, he set his sights on the big city. The members of his band who chose to stay safely at home must have long regretted their decision. All of Crosby's gold records and plenty of other memorabilia are on view.

Spokane House Interpretive Center

Wash. 291, Nine Mile Falls. ☎ **509/466-4747.**

Fur trappers and traders first arrived in the Spokane area between 1807 and 1810. On the banks of the Spokane River they erected the Spokan House trading post. Here at the sight of the post, an interpretive center relates this early pioneer history. Even before the arrival of the white traders, this area was a fishing ground for the Spokan-ee people. A nearby trail leads to some Native American pictographs. You'll find the center about 10 miles north of Spokane on Wash. 291.

Manito Park

4 W. 21st Ave. ☎ **509/625-6622.** Free admission. Daily 8am–dusk. Japanese Garden closed Nov–Mar.

Among the rocks and pine forest of this park are several gardens that are among the most beautiful in the Northwest. Foremost of these is the classically propor-tioned Duncan Garden, a formal garden patterned after those of 17th-century Europe. The adjacent Gaiser Conservatory brims with exotic tropical plants. The perennial garden and rose garden are at their exuberant peaks in June and should not be missed. A separate Japanese Garden is a tranquil spot for contemplation.

Cat Tales Endangered Species Conservation Park

17020 N. Newport Hwy., Mead. ☎ **509/238-4126.** Suggested donation $3 adults, $2 children. May–Sept, Wed–Sun 10am–6pm; Oct–Apr, Wed–Sun 10am–4pm.

Primarily a breeding center for endangered species, Cat Tales is home to more than two dozen wild cats from around the world. Tours of the facility emphasize the need for captive breeding of endangered species.

Walk in the Wild Zoo

E. 12600 Euclid St. ☎ **509/924-7221.** Admission $3.75 adults, $3.25 seniors and students, $2.25 children. Summer, daily 10am–7pm; winter, daily 10am–4pm.

With 240 acres, this zoo 10 miles east of downtown is home to more than 200 animals from five continents. The setting makes excellent use of the natural surroundings, and a petting zoo thrills the young ones.

WINE TOURING

In the Spokane area there are several wineries that you can visit. Right downtown are **Caterina,** 905 N. Washington St. (☎ **509/328-5069**), and the **Knipprath Cellars,** 163 S. Lincoln St. (☎ **509/624-9132**). **Arbor Crest Wine Cellars,** 4705 N. Fruithill Rd. (☎ **509/927-9894**), is housed in the historic Cliff House atop a bluff overlooking the Spokane River. To reach Arbor Crest, take the Argonne North exit. The **Worden Winery,** 7271 W. 45th Ave. (☎ **509/455-7835**), has its tasting room in a log cabin. You'll find the winery off I-90 at Exit 276. The **Latah Creek Wine Cellars,** E. 13030 Indiana Ave. (☎ **509/926-0164**), is housed in a Spanish mission–style building reminiscent of wineries in the Napa Valley. To reach this winery, take Exit 289 off I-90.

OUTDOOR ACTIVITIES

Walkers, joggers, and cyclists will want to get in some exercise on the **Spokane River Centennial Trail.** The paved trail starts at the Spokan House historic site west of the city and parallels the river for 39 miles to the Idaho state line. Bicycle rentals are available at Riverfront Park.

Riverside State Park (☎ **509/456-3964**), which follows the meandering Spokane River on the west edge of the city, has hiking trails, picnic areas, and campgrounds.

Birdwatchers will want to visit the **Turnbull National Wildlife Refuge** (☎ **509/235-4723**), located south of the town of Cheney off Cheney-Plaza Road. The 17,000-acre refuge is a resting ground for migratory waterfowl and contains hiking trails and observation blinds.

For a great view of the region, head northwest 30 miles to **Mount Spokane State Park** (☎ **509/456-4169**), where you can drive to the top of the mountain.

Golf courses in Spokane include **Downriver Golf Course,** N. 3225 Columbia Circle (☎ **509/327-5269**); **Esmeralda Municipal Golf Course,** E. 3933 Courtland Ave. (☎ **509/487-6291**); and **Indian Canyon Municipal Golf Course,** W. 4304 West Dr. (☎ **509/747-5353**).

If you'd like to do a bit of wagering on the ponies, head to Spokane's **Playfair Race Course,** Main Avenue and Altamont Street (☎ **509/534-0505**). If you'd rather ride a horse than watch one race, you can try **Indian Canyon Stables,** Indian Canyon Park (☎ **509/624-4646**).

Within 90 miles of Spokane are several excellent downhill ski areas. These include **49 Degrees North Ski Area,** 52 miles north on U.S. 395 (☎ **509/935-6649**); **Silver Mountain Ski Area,** 70 miles east on I-90 (☎ **208/783-1111**); and **Schweitzer, Inc.,** located 75 miles north of Spokane (☎ **800/831-8810**). Cross-country skiers will find trails at **Mount Spokane State Park** (☎ **509/456-4169**).

SHOPPING

Twelve blocks in downtown Spokane are connected by a series of covered pedestrian bridges that form the **Skywalk System.** This is a bit like having an enclosed shopping mall in the heart of downtown. Stores and buildings connected by the Skywalk System include Nordstrom and Bon Marché department stores, the Spokane Pendleton shop, numerous specialty shops, and two large parking garages.

Two renovated downtown buildings, the **Bennet Block** on the corner of Main Avenue and Stevens Street, and the **Old City Hall,** at the corner of Spokane Falls Boulevard and Wall Street, now house specialty shops and restaurants. Just across Riverfront Park from downtown you'll find the **Flour Mill** at W. 621 Mallon St. This is yet another renovated building that has been turned into a shopping center. Housed in an old mill that was built beside Spokane Falls, the Flour Mill, has, in addition to its many interesting shops and restaurants, displays on the mill and Spokane history.

WHERE TO STAY
EXPENSIVE

✪ Cavanaugh's Inn at the Park

W. 303 N. River Dr., Spokane, WA 99201. ☎ **509/326-8000** or 800/THE-INNS. Fax 509/325-7329. 402 rms, 25 suites. A/C TV TEL. $90–$134 double; $185–$850 suite. AE, CB, DC, DISC, ER, MC, V.

There is no more conveniently located hotel in Spokane. In addition to the fun to be had in the adjacent park, the hotel offers a resortlike pool and a sunny atrium lobby. A wide variety of rooms accommodate all types of travelers. Anyone wishing a bit more luxury than the standard rooms afford may want to opt for the executive rooms, which come with balconies overlooking the pool or the river, a stocked minibar and snack basket, and a TV in the bathroom.

Dining/Entertainment: You have a choice of continental cuisine overlooking the river or less expensive meals in an atrium café. The lounge on the seventh floor provides drinks with a view, and in a second lounge, the dance crowd gathers for recorded Top 40 music.

Services: Concierge, room service, airport shuttle.

Facilities: Outdoor pool (with a water slide, island bar, and waterfall), indoor lap pool, exercise room, sauna, whirlpools; putting green, tennis court, and playground at the nearby Cavanaugh's River Inn.

Sheraton-Spokane Hotel

N. 322 Spokane Falls Court, Spokane, WA 99201. ☎ **509/455-9600** or 800/848-9600. Fax 509/455-6285. 370 rms, 66 suites. A/C TV TEL. $89–$118 double; $130–$475 suite. AE, CB, DC, DISC, MC, V.

If you're here to attend a convention, the Sheraton should probably be your first choice. The convention center is right across the parking lot, and this high-rise hotel offers almost every amenity you could want under one roof. The guest rooms all offer views of the city, river, and nearby mountains. In your room you'll find a coffee maker, hairdryer, and a moderate amount of bathroom counter space. Most rooms are fairly spacious, and all have modern furnishings.

Dining/Entertainment: Just off the lobby is the hotel's formal dining room, which offers a combination of Northwest and Mediterranean cuisines. The Lobby Café serves simple meals amid casual surroundings. When it comes time to relax with a drink you'll have plenty of choices: There's a tropical-theme bar, a dance lounge, and up on the 15th floor, a lounge for drinks with a view.

Services: Room service, valet/laundry service, airport shuttle.

Facilities: Indoor pool, beauty salon.

Westcoast Ridpath

W. 515 Sprague Ave., Spokane, WA 99204-0367. ☎ **509/838-2711** or 800/426-0670. 350 rms, 35 suites. A/C TV TEL. $95–$115 double; $130–$160 suite. AE, CB, DC, DISC, ER, JCB, MC, V.

Popular with conventions because of its size, the Ridpath seems to have invested its renovation dollars in its travertine-walled lobby that sports an Asian accent. The hotel consists of a high-rise and an adjacent motel that were both renovated and thoroughly updated. This latter wing holds the more spacious executive rooms and also overlooks the pool. The rooms in the older high-rise wing tend to be a bit small, and their older tiled bathrooms lack counter space. However, for convenience and value, it's hard to beat the Ridpath.

Dining/Entertainment: Ankeny's, up on the top floor, provides decent meals and great views of the city, while down in the lobby is the more casual Silver Grill.

Services: Concierge, room service, airport shuttle.

Facilities: Outdoor pool.

MODERATE

⑤ Cavanaugh's River Inn

N. 700 Division St., Spokane, WA 99202. ☎ **509/326-5577** or 800/THE-INNS. Fax 509/326-1120. 242 rms, 2 suites. A/C TV TEL. $75–$94 double; $130–$160 suite. AE, CB, DC, DISC, MC, V.

Only slightly less convenient than Cavanaugh's Inn at the Park, this low-rise hotel sprawls along the bank of the Spokane River. Spacious lawns, stained-wood buildings, and attractive landscaping give the hotel a very Northwest feel. In the room you'll find modern furnishings, big bathrooms, and plenty of closet space. Some rooms feature a colonial American decor. Most rooms have a river view, and many first-floor rooms have poolside patios.

Dining/Entertainment: Ripples on the River is a casually elegant dining room overlooking the river and the hotel's lawns. The adjacent lounge features a marble dance floor and live Top 40 and country dance bands.

Services: Room service, airport shuttle.

Facilities: Outdoor and indoor pools, whirlpools, saunas, tennis court, volleyball court, putting green, children's playground, beauty salon.

✪ The Fotheringham House

2128 W. Second Ave., Spokane, WA 99204. ☎ **509/838-1891.** 3 rms, 1 with bath. $70–$75 double. Rates include full breakfast. MC, V.

Located in the historic Browne's Addition neighborhood, this pretty, blue Queen Anne Victorian home is right across the street from Patsy Clark's Mansion, Spokane's most elegant restaurant. Most of the furnishings are period antiques, and in the large shared bathroom you'll find the original clawfoot bathtub.

Hampton Inn Spokane

2010 S. Assembly Rd., Spokane, WA 99204. ☎ **509/747-1100** or 800/HAMPTON. Fax 509/747-8722. 131 rms, 11 suites. A/C TV TEL. $73–$93 double; $155–$195 suite. Rates include continental breakfast. Children 17 and under stay free in parents' room. AE, DC, DISC, MC, V.

Located midway between the airport and downtown (there's a free airport shuttle), the Hampton Inn is a good choice for families or business travelers. Families will like the fact that there's no charge for the third or fourth guest in a room and children under 18 stay free. Business travelers will find computer jacks in every room. The guest rooms are large and comfortable. A casual deli serves simple lunches and dinners, and you'll find an indoor pool, whirlpool, and exercise room.

INEXPENSIVE

Suntree Inn

S. 211 Division St., Spokane, WA 99204. ☎ **509/838-6630** or 800/888-6630. 80 rms. A/C TV TEL. $58–$60 double. Rates include continental breakfast. AE, DC, DISC, MC, V.

Though it looks rather stark from the outside and is on a busy intersection, this budget motel offers clean, modern rooms with plenty of room. There's a hot tub for relaxing, and videos are available for rental. You'll find the motel only two blocks from I-90 at Exit 281. The heart of downtown is only a few blocks away.

⑤ Shilo Inn

E. 923 Third Ave., Spokane, WA 99202. ☎ **509/535-9000** or 800/222-2244. 105 rms. A/C TV TEL. $54–$61 double. AE, CB, DC, DISC, MC, V.

Though it's about a mile or so from the heart of downtown Spokane, the Shilo Inn is still convenient, and its economical rates and many amenities make it an excellent value. The guest rooms are fairly standard, but are quite clean and furnished with modern appointments and comfortable beds. The City Lights restaurant on the fifth floor serves reasonably priced meals and the adjacent lounge has happy-hour specials. A solarium houses an indoor pool and hot tub. A sauna and exercise room round out the facilities.

WHERE TO DINE
EXPENSIVE

○ Patsy Clark's Mansion

W. 2208 Second St. ☎ **509/838-8300**. Reservations recommended. Main courses $13–$19. AE, CB, DC, DISC, MC, V. Mon–Thurs 11am–1pm and 5–8:30pm, Fri–Sat 11am–1pm and 5–9:30pm, Sun 10am–1:30pm (brunch) and 5–8:30pm. NORTHWEST.

Built in 1895 as the grandest mansion in Spokane, Patsy Clark's is still just that. There are 26 rooms, each with a different style, nine fireplaces, and Tiffany stained-glass windows and lamps. The menu changes frequently, but might include such creative and complexly flavored dishes as cilantro-lime prawns with Yucatán butter sauce, huckleberry-glazed chicken breast, or duck with an amaretto sauce. Patsy Clark's tends to attract a very well-heeled clientele, so we suggest dressing for dinner or lunch.

Upstairs Downstairs

N. 216 Howard St. ☎ **509/747-9830**. Reservations recommended. Main courses $10–$16. AE, MC, V. Mon–Tues 11:30am–3pm, Wed–Thurs 11:30am–3pm and 5–9pm, Fri–Sat 11:30am–3pm and 5–10pm. Go up the stairs (or the glass elevator) at the back of the renovated Bennet Block building. CONTINENTAL/INTERNATIONAL.

This well-hidden restaurant has a combination rustic lodge and romantic French country inn atmosphere and is popular with downtown businesspeople. The lunch menu focuses on a few entrées and light meals, and salads such as mango-chutney curried-chicken salad and sandwiches such as an egg salad made with ripe olives, spinach, and basil and served on French bread. At dinner, more substantial though equally creative dishes are available. You might start your meal with figs wrapped in prosciutto or thyme-roasted garlic with ricotta cheese, roasted tomatoes, olives, and almonds. Sole seasoned with garlic and saffron aïoli or lamb chops with Dijon mustard and herbs are just two examples of dinner entrées you might find on the menu.

MODERATE

⑤ Cannon Street Grill

144 S. Cannon St. ☎ **509/456-8660**. Reservations recommended on weekends. Main courses $11–$17. MC, V. Sun–Tues 8am–3pm, Wed–Thurs 8am–9pm, Fri–Sat 8am–10pm. NORTHWEST/FRENCH.

Located in the Browne's Addition neighborhood around the corner from the Elk soda fountain, this neighborhood restaurant has a bistro ambience—pink napkins, dark-green wainscoting, candles on the tables, and the soft croon of Bing Crosby.

The chef here has a special touch for any meal of the day. For breakfast, try the raspberry pancakes; at lunch, his pesto-and-eggplant sandwich won our applause. His talents really shine at dinner, when he offers such dishes as crab and shrimp cakes with lemon aïoli or crispy duck with huckleberry–port wine sauce.

Fugazzi

1 N. Post St. ☎ **509/624-1133.** Reservations recommended. Main courses $9–$14. DISC, MC, V. Wed–Sun 9:30am–4:30pm. INTERNATIONAL.

In this sophisticated and airy space you can sample café fare such as grilled focaccia with fontina cheese, prosciutto, artichoke, and olives, or prawns with mango and red-lime sauce over linguine. The restored pre-1900s storefront also has small tables outside on the street, and to further the bistro atmosphere, a long list of beers, wines, and coffees. Scones, pastries, and crusty breads are available from the bakery.

Milford's Fish House and Oyster Bar

N. 719 Monroe St. ☎ **509/326-7251.** Reservations recommended. Main courses $12–$20. MC, V. Sun–Mon 4–9pm, Tues–Sat 5–10pm. SEAFOOD.

Over on the north side of the river near the Spokane County Courthouse, you'll find Spokane's best seafood restaurant. Milford's manages to look as if it's been around since the Great Fire of 1889. You can sidle up to the bar and peruse the day's oyster menu, or take a seat at one of the tables set with red-and-white table-cloths. You might indulge in a shrimp-and-scallop pie with a spicy cream sauce or perhaps trout with shrimp and a chardonnay-dill sauce. A good selection of wines is available by the glass.

INEXPENSIVE

Coyote Café

W. 702 Third Ave. ☎ **509/747-8800.** Main courses $6–$11. MC, V. Mon 11:30am–9pm, Tues–Thurs 11:30am–10pm, Fri 11:30am–11pm, Sat noon–11pm, Sun noon–9pm. TEX-MEX.

This unmistakably southwestern building on busy Third Avenue houses a cross between an urban diner and a Route 66 roadhouse. Coyotes and stacked tomato cans add color and kitsch to this popular place. The fajitas are the most popular item on the menu, but there are all the standard Mexican dishes as well. The spit-roasted coyote chicken is another good bet. Wash it all down with a north-western boysenberry margarita.

✪ The Elk

1931 W. Pacific Ave. ☎ **509/456-0454.** Sandwiches/salads $4.25–$7.25. No credit cards. Mon–Fri 7am–9pm, Sat 8am–9pm, Sun 9am–3pm. BAKERY/SANDWICHES.

The Elk has been around since the early 1900s when it was the Elk Drug Company, supplying medicines and soda fountain treats to the local inhabitants. Today it has been restored, complete with the original soda fountain, vintage advertising, and pharmaceutical paraphernalia. Not only do they serve malts, phosphates, and green rivers (a brilliant green soda), but also sandwiches, soups, and salads that appeal to contemporary tastes.

River View Thai Restaurant

In the Flour Mill, W. 621 Mallon St. ☎ **509/325-8370.** Main courses $4.50–$8.50. MC, V. Mon–Fri 11:30am–2:30pm and 5–9pm, Sat noon–9pm, Sun 5–8:30pm. THAI.

Downstairs in the renovated Flour Mill that rises above Spokane Falls, you'll find the city's best Thai restaurant. The menu lists more than 50 dishes, most of which will be familiar to fans of Thai cuisine. In addition to the Thai dishes, there are also a few Vietnamese and Laotian offerings.

⑤ Rock City Café

W. 505 Riverside Ave. ☎ **509/455-4400.** Reservations recommended. Main courses $5–$14. AE, CB, DC, MC, V. Sun–Thurs 11:15am–10pm, Fri–Sat 11:15am–11pm. MEDITERRANEAN/INTERNATIONAL.

The Rock City Grill, an outpost of contemporary urban chic, has taken up the challenge of satisfying jaded palates. Though Mediterranean flavors predominate on this inexpensive eatery's menu, entrées also include the likes of wood-oven roasted prawns and bistecca with brandy-cream sauce. The restaurant's creative pizzas are baked in the wood-fired oven. If you're in the mood for an espresso and a pastry, you won't do much better anywhere in town.

SPOKANE AFTER DARK

To find out what's going on around Spokane, pick up a copy of *The Inlander,* a free weekly arts-and entertainment newspaper. You'll find copies in restaurants, record stores, and bookstores.

As one of the largest cities in Washington, Spokane has a lively and varied performing arts scene. The **Spokane Opera House,** W. 334 Spokane Falls Blvd. (☎ 509/353-6500 or 509/325-7320), a modern performance hall adjacent to Riverfront Park in downtown Spokane, is the city's largest performance hall, and hosts the Spokane Symphony and many touring companies. Smaller shows usually get staged at the **Metropolitan Performing Arts Center,** W. 901 Sprague Ave. (☎ 509/455-6500), which is known to residents simply as "The Met." This hall hosts everything from rock bands to chamber music ensembles.

For classical music, the city turns to the **Spokane Symphony** (☎ 509/624-1200), which does both classical and pops concerts (tickets run $11 to $24), and **Allegro—Baroque and Beyond** (☎ 509/455-6865), which focuses on the music of the baroque (tickets are $8 to $15).

The city's theater scene includes the **Spokane Interplayers Ensemble,** S. 174 Howard St. (☎ 509/455-PLAY), a professional theater company (tickets cost $10 to $13); and the **Spokane Civic Theatre,** N. 1020 Howard St. (☎ 509/325-2507), a community theater company (tickets go for $9 to $15).

If you've just had a hard afternoon of having fun at Riverside Park and you need a cold ale to cool you off, just head across the street to the **Fort Spokane Brewery,** W. 401 Spokane Falls Blvd. (☎ 509/838-3809), which serves up four different brews.

A SIDE TRIP TO IDAHO

Lake Coeur d'Alene, Idaho, lies 30 miles east of Spokane and is the summer destination of choice for the city's vacationers. The lake sits at an elevation of 2,128 feet above sea level and is 25 miles long, with 135 miles of shoreline. The best way to appreciate this beautiful mountain lake is on one of the cruises offered by **Lake Coeur d'Alene Cruises** (☎ 208/765-4000). Cruise boats operate between May and October, and adult fares range from $9.75 for a 1 1/2-hour tour to $24.75 for a 2-hour dinner cruise. There's also a 6-hour cruise on the **St. Joe River,** the highest navigable river in the world.

4 The Grand Coulee Dam Area

85 miles W of Spokane, 92 miles NE of Wenatchee

The Grand Coulee Dam was the largest man-made structure in the world when construction was completed in 1941. The 5,223-foot-long dam turned the Columbia River into 150-mile-long Roosevelt Lake and was used to fill the formerly dry Grand Coulee with a reservoir 27 miles long. Grand Coulee is a geologic anomaly left over from the last Ice Age when a huge lake was formed on an upstream tributary of the Columbia River when a glacier dammed the river. When the lake overflowed its banks, the river waters flooded across central Washington, carving out deep valleys as they rushed southward to meet up with the river again. With the end of the Ice Age, the rivers returned to their original channels and the temporary flood channels were left high and dry. Early French explorers called these dry channels *coulées,* and the largest of them all was Grand Coulee, which is 50 miles long, between 2 and 5 miles wide, and 1,000 feet deep. The dam is built across the Columbia River at the northern end of Grand Coulee, which has been filled once again with water pumped from Roosevelt Lake. The waters of both Roosevelt Lake and Grand Coulee's Banks Lake have been used to irrigate the arid lands of eastern Washington, turning this region into productive farmlands. Since the dam began operation, its abundance of inexpensive electrical energy has attracted aluminum-smelting plants and other industries to the area.

ESSENTIALS

GETTING THERE   The towns of Grand Coulee and Coulee Dam are at the junction of Wash. 155, which runs south to Coulee City and north to Omak, and Wash. 174, which runs west to Wash. 17 and east to U.S. 2.

VISITOR INFORMATION   Contact the **Grand Coulee Dam Area Chamber of Commerce,** P.O. Box 760, Grand Coulee, WA 99133-0760 (☎ **509/633-3074**).

WHAT TO SEE & DO

You can learn the history of the dam by stopping in at the **Grand Coulee Dam Visitor Arrival Center,** which is open daily. There are guided and self-guided tours of the dam. Every night during the summer, the **world's largest laser-light show** is projected onto the face of the dam. The accompanying narration is broadcast over the AM radio and tells the history of Grand Coulee and the dam. Between Memorial Day and July 31, the show starts at 10pm; in August, at 9:30pm; and in September, at 8:30pm. There are also guided and self-guided tours of the dam daily between 10am and 6pm.

Lake Roosevelt, with its 600 miles of shoreline, provides ample opportunities for water sports and fishing and comprises the **Coulee Dam National Recreation Area,** P.O. Box 37, Coulee Dam, WA 99116 (☎ **509/633-0881**). Along the shores of the lake are more than 30 campgrounds. About 22 miles north of Davenport, at the confluence of the Spokane and Columbia rivers, stands **Fort Spokane,** which was built in 1880. Four of the original buildings are still standing. An 1892 brick guardhouse here is the recreation area's main visitor center.

Some 30 miles down the Grand Coulee, just south of Coulee City on Wash. 17, you can have a look at a natural wonder that's as impressive as the dam. **Dry Falls** are the remains of a waterfall created by the same flood of water that scoured out the Grand Coulee. At their peak flow, the waters cascading 400 feet over Dry Falls stretched 3¹/₂ miles wide—making this the largest waterfall of all time. An interpretive center stands beside the highway at the Dry Falls Overlook, and if you're interested in going to the base of the falls, continue south 2 miles to **Sun Lakes State Park,** which has a road leading back to the falls.

Ten miles south of Coulee City on Pinto Ridge Road are the impressive Summer Falls at **Summer Falls State Park.**

Another 20 miles or so will bring you to **Soap Lake,** an alkaline lake named for the soap suds that gather on its shores. For centuries the lake has attracted people who believe the waters have medicinal properties. Once a busy health spa, Soap Lake today is a quiet little town. However, it does have a couple of good lodges where you can soak in the lake's waters. A public town beach also provides access to the lake.

WHERE TO STAY

In addition to the hotels listed below, you can also stay on a houseboat and cruise up and down Lake Roosevelt. Houseboats are available from **Lake Roosevelt Resorts & Marinas,** P.O. Box 340, Kettle Falls, WA 99141 (☎ **509/738-6121** or 800/635-7585). Boats sleep 10 to 12 people and rates range from $795 for three days and two nights in the spring or fall up to $2,125 for a week in the summer.

IN COULEE DAM

Coulee House

110 Roosevelt Way, Coulee Dam, WA 99116. ☎ **509/633-1101.** 61 rms. A/C TV TEL. $46–$94 double. AE, CB, DC, DISC, MC, V.

If you want to catch the laser-light show, you should plan to spend the night in Coulee Dam and this should be your first choice. The rooms are modest but clean, and you'll find an outdoor pool, whirlpool, and exercise room on the premises.

IN SOAP LAKE

✪ The Notaras Lodge

P.O. Box 987, Soap Lake, WA 98851. ☎ **509/246-0462.** 20 rms. TV TEL. $45–$125 double. MC, V.

A modern log building only steps from the lake offers the most interesting lodgings in Soap Lake. Each room at the lodge is decorated differently and many commemorate local and national celebrities. Unusual woodworking, log beds, Native American artifacts, and western trappings are all part of the fantasy world at the Notaras Lodge. Eight rooms have whirlpool tubs, and all the rooms have lake water piped into them so you can soak in the therapeutic waters.

Portland 10

Portland may not be as lively as Seattle, but in its own laid-back way it has a lot to offer. However, to truly appreciate this city you'll have to cultivate an appreciation for Portland's subtle charms. A stroll through the Japanese Gardens on a misty May morning; a latte on the bricks at Pioneer Courthouse Square as the Weather Machine sculpture goes through its motions; an evening spent perusing the acres of volumes at Powell's City of Books; shopping for crafts at the Saturday Market; a summer festival on the banks of the Willamette River; a quick trip to the beach or Mount Hood—these are the quintessential Portland experiences. Of course, the city has museums, but, with the exception of the Museum of Science and Industry, they're small compared to those in Seattle. Sure, there are theaters for live stage shows, but not in the overwhelming numbers to be found in Seattle.

However, Portland seems to be a city on the verge. Restaurants and nightclubs are proliferating as never before, and the Trailblazers, the city's NBA basketball team, have just gotten a new coliseum. In hopes of alleviating traffic congestion, the city is extending its modern light-rail system into the western suburbs, and companies such as Nike and Intel are feeding the local economy. Attracted by the city's quality of life, more and more people are moving to Portland from all over the country.

Consequently, Portland today is growing quickly, though so far with a deliberation that has not compromised the city's values and unique characteristics. Whether this controlled and intelligent growth can continue remains to be seen. However, for now Portland remains a city both cosmopolitan and accessible, with a subtle appeal and a laid-back attitude that's refreshing in this high-speed, high-stress age.

1 Orientation

ARRIVING

BY PLANE **Portland International Airport** (☎ 503/335-1234) is located 10 miles northeast of downtown Portland. A taxi from the airport to downtown will cost you around $23.

All the major car-rental companies have locations at the airport, so it's easy to fly in and rent a car. See "Getting Around," later in this chapter, for details.

Many Portland hotels provide courtesy shuttle service to and from the airport, so be sure to check at your hotel when you make a reservation. Another way to get into town if you haven't rented a car at the airport is to take the **Raz Transportation Downtown Shuttle** (☎ 503/246-3301), located outside the baggage-claim area, which will take you directly to your hotel for $8.50. It operates every 30 minutes from 5am to 11pm daily.

Tri-Met public **bus no. 12** (Sandy Boulevard) leaves the airport approximately every 15 minutes from about 5:30am to 11:50pm for downtown Portland. The trip takes about 40 minutes and costs $1. The bus between downtown and the airport operates between about 5am and 12:30am and leaves from SW Sixth Avenue and Main Street.

BY CAR   Driving from airport to downtown takes about 20 minutes by way of I-205 to I-84, and the route is well signed. Portland's major Interstates and smaller highways are **I-5** (north to south), **I-84** (east), **I-405** (circles around the west and south of downtown Portland), **I-205** (bypasses the city to the east), and **U.S. 26** (west).

BY TRAIN   Amtrak trains use the historic **Union Station** at 800 NW Sixth Ave., in northwest Portland near downtown (☎ **503/273-4866,** or 800/872-7245 for Amtrak reservations).

BY BUS   The **Greyhound bus station,** at 550 NW Sixth Ave., is also in northwest Portland near downtown (☎ **503/243-2357** or 800/231-2222).

VISITOR INFORMATION

The walk-in office for the **Portland Oregon Visitors Association Information Center** is at Two World Trade Center, 25 SW Salmon St. in downtown Portland (☎ **503/222-2223** or 800/345-3214). The mailing address is Three World Trade Center, 26 SW Salmon St., Portland, OR 97204-3299. There's also an **information booth** by the baggage-claim area at the Portland airport.

If you happen to see two people walking down a Portland street wearing matching kelly-green hats and jackets, they're probably members of the Portland Guide service. They'll be happy to answer any question you have about Portland.

CITY LAYOUT

Portland is located in northwestern Oregon at the confluence of the Columbia River and the Willamette River. Circling the city to the west are the West Hills, which rise to more than 1,000 feet. Some 90 miles west of the West Hills is the Pacific Ocean and the spectacular Oregon coast. To the east are rolling hills that extend to the Cascade Mountains, about 50 miles away. The most prominent peak in this section of the Cascades is Mount Hood (11,235 feet), a dormant volcanic peak that looms over the city on clear days. From many parts of the city it's also possible to see Mount St. Helens, another volcano, which blew its top in 1980.

MAIN ARTERIES & STREETS   I-84 **(Banfield Freeway or Expressway)** comes into Portland from the east. East of the city is I-205, which bypasses downtown Portland but runs past the airport. **I-5 (East Bank Freeway)** runs through on a north-south axis, passing along the east bank of the Willamette River directly across from downtown. **I-405 (Stadium Freeway and Foothills Freeway)** circles around the west and south sides of downtown. **U.S. 26 (Sunset Highway)** leaves downtown heading west toward Beaverton and the coast. **Ore. 217 (Beaverton-Tigard Highway)** runs south from U.S. 26 in Beaverton.

The most important street to remember in Portland is **Burnside Street.** This is the dividing line between north and south Portland. Dividing the city from east to west is the **Willamette River,** which is crossed by eight bridges in the downtown area. All these bridges are named: from north to south they are Fremont, Broadway, Steel, Burnside, Morrison, Hawthorne, Marquam, and Ross Island. In addition to these bridges there are others farther from the downtown area.

For the sake of convenience we'll define downtown Portland as the area within the **Fareless Square.** This is the area in which you can ride for free on the city's public buses and MAX light-rail system. Fareless Square is that area bounded by I-405 on the west and south, by Hoyt Street on the north, and by the Willamette River on the east.

FINDING AN ADDRESS   Finding an address in Portland can be easy if you keep a number of things in mind. Every address in Portland, and even extending for miles out from the city, includes a map quadrant—Northeast (NE), Southwest (SW), etc. The dividing line between east and west is the Willamette River; between north and south it's Burnside Street. Any downtown address will carry a Southwest (SW) or Northwest (NW) prefix. An exception to this rule is the area known as North Portland. Streets here have a "North" designation. This is the area across the Willamette River from downtown going toward Jantzen Beach.

Avenues run north-south and streets run east-west. Street names continue on both sides of the Willamette River. Consequently, there's a Southwest Yamhill Street and a Southeast Yamhill Street. In northwest Portland the street names are alphabetical from Burnside to Wilson. Front Avenue is the road nearest the Willamette River on the west side, and Water Avenue is the nearest on the east side. After these, the numbered avenues begin. On the west side you'll also find Broadway and Park Avenue between Sixth Avenue and Ninth Avenue. With each block, the addresses increase by 100, beginning at the Willamette River for avenues and at Burnside Street for streets. Odd numbers are generally on the west and north sides of the streets and even numbers on the east and south sides.

Here's an example. You want to go to 1327 SW Ninth Ave. Because it's in the 1300 block, you'll find it 13 blocks south of Burnside Street, and because it's an odd number, on the west side of the street.

Getting *to* the address is a different story since streets in downtown Portland are mostly one way. Front Avenue is two way, but then First, Third, Fifth, Broadway, Ninth, and Eleventh are one way southbound. Alternating streets are one way northbound.

STREET MAPS   Stop by the **Portland Oregon Visitors Association,** Two World Trade Center, 25 SW Salmon St., or write to them at Three World Trade Center, 26 SW Salmon St., Portland, OR 97204-3299 (☎ **503/222-2223** or 800/345-3214), for a free map of the city. **Powell's "City of Books,"** 1005 W. Burnside St. (☎ **503/228-4651**, or 800/878-7323), has an excellent free map of downtown that also includes a walking-tour route and information on many of the sights you'll pass along the way. Members of the **American Automobile Association** can get a free map of the city at the AAA office at 600 SW Market St. (☎ **503/222-6734**).

NEIGHBORHOODS IN BRIEF

Downtown   This term usually refers to the business-and-shopping district south of Burnside Street and north of Jackson Street between the Willamette River and 13th Avenue. You'll find the major department stores, dozens of restaurants, most of the city's performing-arts venues, and almost all the best hotels in this area.

Chinatown   Portland has had a Chinatown almost since the city's earliest days. It's entered through the colorful Chinatown Gate at West Burnside Street and Fourth Avenue. Although there are a few nightclubs in the area, this is not a good place to wander late at night.

Skidmore District   Also known as Old Town, this is Portland's original commercial core, and centers around Southwest Ankeny Street and Southwest First Avenue. Many of the restored buildings have become retail stores, but despite the presence of the Saturday Market, the neighborhood has never become a popular shopping district, mostly because of its welfare hotels, missions, street people, and drug dealing.

Northwest   Centered along Northwest 23rd and Northwest 21st avenues at the foot of the West Hills, this is an old residential neighborhood that has been taken over by upscale shops, espresso bars, and restaurants and is currently Portland's most fashionable neighborhood.

Irvington   Though not as attractive as Northwest, Irvington, which centers around Broadway in northeast Portland, is almost as trendy. For several blocks along this avenue, you'll find unusual boutiques, import stores, and lots of excellent-but-inexpensive restaurants.

Hollywood District   This section of northeast Portland centers around the busy commercial activities of Sandy Boulevard near 42nd Avenue. The district came into being in the early years of this century; the name comes from a landmark movie theater. Throughout this neighborhood are craftsman-style houses and vernacular architecture of the period.

Pearl District   This neighborhood of galleries, artists' lofts, cafés, breweries, and shops is bounded by the Park blocks, Lovejoy Street, I-405, and Burnside Street. Crowds flock here on the first Thursday of the month, when the galleries and other businesses are open late.

Sellwood   This is Portland's antiques district, full of restored Victorian houses.

Hawthorne District   This enclave of southeast Portland is full of eclectic boutiques, moderately priced restaurants, and hip young college students from nearby Reed College.

2 Getting Around

BY PUBLIC TRANSPORTATION

FREE RIDES   Portland is committed to keeping its downtown uncongested, and to this end it has invested a great deal in its public transportation system. The single greatest innovation and best reason to ride the Tri-Met public buses and MAX light-rail system is that they're free within an area known as the **Fareless Square.** That's right, free! There are 300 blocks of downtown included in the Fareless Square, and as long as you stay within the boundaries you don't have to pay a cent. This applies to both the buses and the MAX light-rail trolleys. Fareless Square covers the area between I-405 on the south and west, Hoyt Street on the north, and the Willamette River on the east.

BY BUS

Tri-Met buses operate daily over an extensive network. You can pick up the **"Tri-Met Guide,"** which lists all the bus routes with times, or individual route maps and time schedules at the **Tri-Met Customer Assistance Office,** behind and beneath the waterfall fountain at Pioneer Courthouse Square (☎ **503/238-7433**). It's open Monday through Friday from 9am to 5pm.

Outside the Fareless Square, **fares** on Tri-Met buses are $1 or $1.30, depending on how far you travel. Seniors 65 years and older pay 50¢ with valid proof of age. You can also make free transfers between the bus and the MAX light-rail system. A day ticket costing $3.50 is good for travel to all zones and is valid on both buses and MAX. Day passes can be purchased from any bus driver.

BY MAX

The **Metropolitan Area Express (MAX)** is Portland's aboveground light-rail system, which now connects downtown Portland with the suburb of Gresham, 15 miles to the east. MAX is basically a modern trolley, and, in fact, there are vintage trolley cars that operate certain times of the day. You can ride the MAX for free if you stay within the boundaries of the Fareless Square, which includes all the downtown area. However, be sure to buy your ticket before you get on the MAX if you're traveling out of the Fareless Square. **Fares** are the same as on buses. There are ticket-vending machines at all MAX stops that tell you how much to pay for your destination. These machines also give change. The MAX driver cannot sell tickets. There are ticket inspectors who randomly check tickets—if you don't have one, you can be fined up to $300.

BY CAR

Although downtown Portland is so compact that you can easily get around on foot or by hopping a free trolley or bus, to see outlying attractions it's best to have a car.

RENTALS   You'll find all the major car-rental companies represented in Portland, and there are also many independent and smaller car-rental agencies listed in the *Portland Yellow Pages*. At Portland International Airport, across the street from the baggage-claim area in the short-term parking garage, you'll find the following companies: **Avis** (☎ 503/249-4950 or 800/831-2847), with an office downtown at 330 SW Washington St. (☎ 503/227-0220) and in Beaverton at 11135 SW Canyon Rd. (☎ 503/526-0614); **Budget** (☎ 503/249-6500 or 800/527-0700), with offices downtown at 2033 SW Fourth Ave., on the east side at 2323 NE Columbia Blvd., and in Beaverton at 10835 SW Canyon Rd.; **Dollar** (☎ 503/249-4792 or 800/800-4000), with an office downtown at NW Broadway and NW Davis Street (☎ 503/228-3540); **Hertz** (☎ 503/249-8216 or 800/654-3131), with an office downtown at 1009 SW Sixth Ave. (☎ 503/249-5727); and **National** (☎ 503/249-4900 or 800/227-7368).

Outside the airport is **Thrifty,** 10800 NE Holman St. (☎ 503/254-6563 or 800/367-2277), which also has an office downtown at 632 SW Pine St. (☎ 503/227-6587).

PARKING   Parking meter time limits range from 15 minutes to six hours or more. You don't have to feed the meters after 6pm or on Sunday.

The best parking deals in town are at **Smart Park** garages, which charge 75¢ per hour or $3 all day on the weekends. You'll find Smart Park garages at First

Avenue and Jefferson Street; Fourth Avenue and Yamhill Street; Tenth Avenue and Yamhill Street; Third Avenue and Alder Street; O'Bryant Square; and Front Avenue and Davis Street.

If you're going shopping, look for a red-and-green sign that says 2 HR FREE PARK DOWNTOWN at pay parking lots and garages. Spend $15 or more at any participating merchant and you get two hours of free parking. Don't forget to have the merchant validate your parking stub. Rates in public lots range from about $1 to about $2.75 per hour.

DRIVING RULES   You may turn right on a red light after a full stop, and if you're in the far-left lane of a one-way street you may turn left into the adjacent left lane at a red light after a full stop.

BY TAXI

Because Portland is fairly compact, getting around by taxi can be economical. Although there are almost always taxis waiting in line at major hotels, you won't find them cruising the streets—you'll have to phone for one. **Broadway Cab** (☎ **503/227-1234**) and **Radio Cab** (☎ **503/227-1212**) both offer 24-hour radio-dispatched service and accept American Express, Discover, MasterCard, and Visa credit and charge cards. Fares are $2 for the first mile and $1.50 for each additional mile.

BY BICYCLE

Bicycles are a popular way of getting around Portland. The traffic is not very heavy and drivers are accustomed to sharing the road with bicyclists. You can pick up a copy of a bike map of the city of Portland at most bike shops and at the centrally located **Bike Gallery,** 821 SW 11th Ave. (☎ **503/222-3821**).

ON FOOT

City blocks in Portland are about half the size of most city blocks, and the entire downtown area covers only about 13 blocks by 26 blocks. This makes Portland a very easy city to explore on foot. The city has been very active in encouraging people to get out of their cars and onto the sidewalks downtown. The sidewalks are wide and there are many small parks with benches for resting, fountains for cooling off, and works of art to soothe the soul.

FAST FACTS: Portland

American Express   The American Express Travel Service Office is at 1100 SW Sixth Ave. (☎ 503/226-2961), open Monday through Friday from 9am to 5pm.

Area Code   The area code for the Portland metropolitan area is 503. For the rest of Oregon it's 541.

Babysitters   Call Wee-Ba-Bee Child Care (☎ 503/786-3837) if your hotel doesn't offer babysitting services.

Camera Repair   Call Advance Camera Repair, 8124 SW Beaverton-Hillsdale Hwy., Beaverton (☎ 503/292-6996) or Associated Camera Repair, 3401 NE Sandy Blvd. (☎ 503/232-5625).

Car Rentals   See "Getting Around," earlier in this chapter.

Dentist   Contact the Multnomah Dental Society for a referral at 503/223-4738.

Doctor   Contact the Multnomah County Doctor Referral Service at 503/222-0156.

Emergencies   In case of medical, police, or fire emergency, phone **911.**

Eyeglass Repair   See Binyon's Eyeworld Downtown at 803 SW Morrison St. (☎ 503/226-6688).

Hospitals   Three area hospitals are the Legacy Good Samaritan, 1015 NW 22nd Ave. (☎ 503/229-7711); St. Vincent Hospital, 9205 SW Barnes Rd. (☎ 503/291-2115), off U.S. 26 (Sunset Highway) before Ore. 217; and the Oregon Health Sciences University Hospital, 3181 SW Sam Jackson Park Rd. (☎ 503/494-8311), just southwest of the city center.

Hotlines   AIDS, 503/223-2437; battered women, 503/235-5333; child abuse, 503/731-3100; alcohol-and-drug help line, 503/232-8083; rape, 503/235-5333; suicide prevention, 503/223-6161.

Information   See "Orientation," earlier in this chapter.

Liquor Laws   The legal drinking age in Oregon is 21. Bars can stay open until 2am.

Newspapers/Magazines   Portland's morning daily newspaper is *The Oregonian.* For arts and entertainment information and listings, consult the "Arts & Entertainment" section of the Friday *Oregonian* or pick up a free copy of *Willamette Week* at Powell's Books and other stores. The *Portland Guide* is a weekly tourism guide available at hotels.

Police   To reach the police, call 911.

Post Offices   The main post office, at 715 NW Hoyt St. (☎ 503/294-2300), is open Monday through Friday from 7:30am to 6:30pm and on Saturday from 8:30am to 5pm.

Radio   KOPB-FM (91.5) is the local National Public Radio station.

Restrooms   There are public restrooms underneath the Starbucks coffee shop in Pioneer Courthouse Square.

Safety   Because of its small size and emphasis on keeping the downtown alive and growing, Portland is still a relatively safe city, and in fact strolling the downtown streets at night is a popular pastime. Take extra precautions, however, if you venture into the entertainment district along West Burnside Street or Chinatown at night. Parts of northeast Portland are controlled by street gangs, so before visiting anyplace in this area, get very detailed directions so that you don't get lost. If you plan to go hiking in Forest Park, don't leave anything valuable in your car. This holds true in the Old Town district as well.

Taxes   Portland is a shopper's paradise—there's no sales tax. However, there is a 9% tax on hotel rooms within the city of Portland. Outside the city the room tax varies.

Taxis   See "Getting Around," earlier in this chapter.

Time Zone   Portland is in the Pacific time (PST) zone, making it three hours behind the East Coast.

Weather   Call 503/236-7575.

3   Accommodations

In the following listings, **Very Expensive** hotels are those charging more than $120 per night for a double room; **Expensive** hotels charge $90 to $120; **Moderate** hotels, $60 to $90; and **Inexpensive** hotels charge less than $60. These rates do *not* include the hotel-room tax of 9%. A few of the hotels include breakfast in their rates, and this has been noted in the listing. Others offer complimentary breakfast only on certain deluxe floors. If you're planning to visit during the busy summer months, make your reservations as far in advance as possible and be sure to ask if there are any special rates available. Almost all large hotels offer weekend discounts of as much as 50%. In fact, you might even be able to get a discount simply by asking for one. Who knows—if the hotel isn't busy, you might just be able to negotiate.

For information on B&Bs in Portland, contact **Northwest Bed & Breakfast Travel Unlimited,** 610 SW Broadway, Portland, OR 97205 (☎ **503/243-7616;** fax 503/243-7672), which represents more than 75 B&Bs in the Portland and Seattle areas, and B&Bs and unhosted homes throughout Oregon, Washington, British Columbia, and parts of California. Rates for B&Bs average $45 to $85 for double rooms. For information on other B&Bs in the Portland area, call the **Portland Oregon Visitors Association** (☎ **800/345-3214**) for a brochure put out by Metro Innkeepers.

DOWNTOWN
VERY EXPENSIVE

The Benson Hotel

309 SW Broadway, Portland, OR 97205. ☎ **503/228-2000** or 800/426-0670. Fax 503/226-4603. 287 rms, 46 junior suites, 7 suites. A/C TV TEL. $170–$210 double; $275–$600 suite. AE, CB, DC, DISC, ER, JCB, MC, V. Valet parking $12.

With its mansard roof and French baroque lobby, the Benson, built in 1912, exudes old-world sophistication and elegance. In the lobby, crystal chandeliers hang from the ornate plasterwork ceiling and walnut paneling frames a marble fireplace. The guest rooms are housed in two towers above the lobby. All rooms are done in classic French Second Empire furnishings that include a large desk and an armoire that hides the television. The "deluxe kings" are particularly roomy and come with seven pillows per bed. The baths, unfortunately, have very little counter space.

Dining/Entertainment: Down in the vaults below the lobby, the London Grill, one of Portland's best restaurants, serves superb continental cuisine. A Trader Vic's serves up its trademark Polynesian fare and colossal cocktails. The Lobby Court has a bar and also serves a buffet lunch Monday through Friday.

Services: Concierge, room service (24-hour), valet parking, in-room voice mail and computer modems, valet/laundry service.

Facilities: Weight room, gift shop.

Governor Hotel

SW 10th Ave. and Alder St., Portland, OR 97205. ☎ **503/224-3400** or 800/554-3456. Fax 503/241-2122. 100 rms, 28 suites. A/C MINIBAR TV TEL. $175–$195 double; $195–$500 suite. AE, CB, DC, JCB, MC, V. Valet parking $10.

Throughout the hotel you'll spot references to Lewis and Clark, but it's the wall mural in the lobby that most captures the attention. The guest rooms feature an

Asian influence, including painted porcelain lamps and black-and-gold lacquered tables. Rooms vary considerably in size. The least expensive are rather small; however, they're still very comfortable. The suites are spacious, and some have huge patios overlooking the city.

Dining/Entertainment: A grand, old-fashioned restaurant with burnished-wood columns and slowly turning overhead fans is just off the lobby. The menu features grilled steak and seafood. Between the lobby and the restaurant, you'll find the Dome Room, notable for its stunning stained-glass dome skylight.

Services: Concierge, room service (24-hour), personal computer and fax machines available, complimentary morning newspaper and coffee, overnight shoeshine, valet/laundry service.

Facilities: Business center, hearing-impaired accommodations. The Princeton Athletic Club, down in the lower level of the hotel, includes a lap pool, indoor running track, whirlpool spa, steam rooms, sauna, and exercise room.

✪ The Heathman Hotel

SW Broadway at Salmon St., Portland, OR 97205. ☎ **503/241-4100** or 800/551-0011. Fax 503/790-7110. 151 rms, 40 suites. A/C TV TEL. $175–$200 double; $190–$325 suite. AE, CB, DC, MC, V. Parking $12.

Understated luxury and sophistication have made the Heathman, originally opened in 1927, the finest hotel in Portland, and original art gives the hotel a museum quality. The lobby opens onto the Tea Court, where a fireplace, a grand piano, and the original eucalyptus paneling create a warm atmosphere. Every guest room is decorated with its own original works of art, matching bedspreads and Roman shades, torchère lamps, and rattan bedsteads. In the bath are plush terry-cloth robes and large towels.

Dining/Entertainment: The Heathman Restaurant is one of the finest in Portland. The menu emphasizes fresh local produce, seafood, and game. B. Moloch/Heathman Bakery & Pub, a second restaurant, is located two blocks away. Both restaurants have cozy bars. (See "Dining," later in this chapter, for details on both restaurants.) In the Mezzanine Bar there's live jazz several nights a week for most of the year, and afternoon tea is served daily in the Lobby Lounge.

Services: Concierge, room service (24-hour), valet parking, valet/laundry service, complimentary newspaper, international business services, waterproof running map.

Facilities: Privileges at nearby athletic club, on-site fitness suite.

✪ Hotel Vintage Plaza

422 SW Broadway, Portland, OR 97205. ☎ **503/228-1212** or 800/243-0555. Fax 503/228-3598. 107 rms, 31 suites. A/C MINIBAR TV TEL. $160 double; $165–$205 suite. Rates include continental breakfast. AE, CB, DC, DISC, MC, V. Valet parking $12.

This deluxe hotel sports Italianate decor and a wine theme that plays up the budding Oregon wine industry. In the small lobby there's a fireplace flanked by bookshelves, and soaring up from the other side of the lobby is a 10-story atrium. Standard rooms have much to recommend them, with Roman window shades and old Italian architectural prints that continue the romanesque theme. The bathrooms, with their pink granite counters, gold-tone designer faucets, and taffeta shower curtain and walls, are the classiest in town. The starlight rooms are, however, truly extraordinary. Though small, they have greenhouse-style wall-into-ceiling windows that provide very romantic views. The two-level suites, some with Japanese soaking tubs and one with a spiral staircase, are equally stunning.

Portland Accommodations

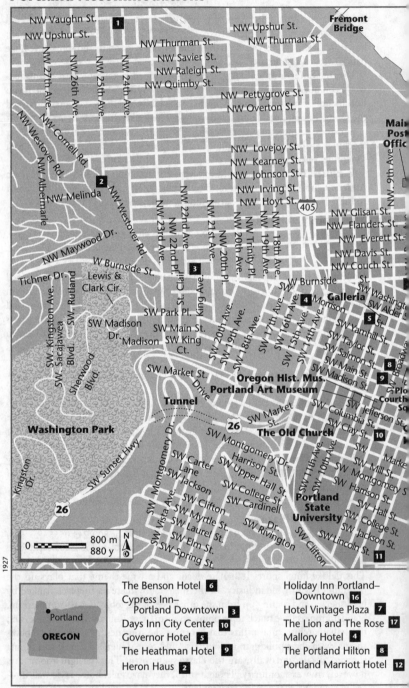

The Benson Hotel **6**

Cypress Inn–
  Portland Downtown **3**

Days Inn City Center **10**

Governor Hotel **5**

The Heathman Hotel **9**

Heron Haus **2**

Holiday Inn Portland–
  Downtown **16**

Hotel Vintage Plaza **7**

The Lion and The Rose **17**

Mallory Hotel **4**

The Portland Hilton **8**

Portland Marriott Hotel **12**

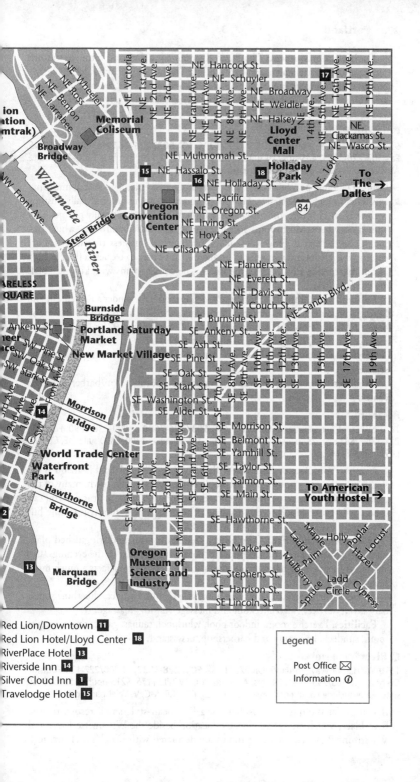

Red Lion/Downtown **11**
Red Lion Hotel/Lloyd Center **18**
RiverPlace Hotel **13**
Riverside Inn **14**
Silver Cloud Inn **1**
Travelodge Hotel **15**

Legend

Post Office ⊠
Information ⊘

Dining/Entertainment: The Pazzo Ristorante is a dark and intimate trattoria serving northern Italian cuisine (see "Dining," later in this chapter, for details).

Services: Complimentary evening wine, shoeshine service, morning newspaper and complimentary coffee, valet/laundry service, turndown service.

Facilities: Executive gym, business center.

Portland Hilton

921 SW Sixth Ave., Portland, OR 97204-1296. ☎ **503/226-1611** or 800/HILTONS. Fax 503/220-2565. 455 rms, 16 suites. A/C TV TEL. $150–$200 double; $300–$900 suite. AE, CB, DC, DISC, JCB, MC, V. Valet parking $16.

Centrally located near businesses, the performing-arts center, and several museums, this modern high-rise attracts tour groups and conventions and is usually bustling with activity. However, other than the Hilton name, you don't really get much for your money here. Most rooms are rather small, as are the bathrooms, which lack much counter space. However, for the overworked business traveler there are comfortable chairs and two phones in the rooms. Be sure to request a floor as high as possible to take advantage of the views. The corner rooms with king-size beds are our favorites.

Dining/Entertainment: From its 23rd-floor aerie, Alexander's Restaurant and Lounge offers a striking panorama of Portland, the Willamette River, and snow-covered Mount Hood. At lobby level is the informal Bistro 921 restaurant, with regional cuisine. There's a casual bar just off the lobby.

Services: Concierge, room service, laundry/valet service, overnight shoeshine service.

Facilities: Fitness center, heated indoor pool, beauty salon/barber, business center.

Portland Marriott

1401 SW Front Ave., Portland, OR 97201. ☎ **503/226-7600** or 800/228-9290. Fax 503/221-1789. 503 rms, 28 suites. A/C TV TEL. $109–$160 double; $300–$350 suite. AE, CB, DC, DISC, ER, JCB, MC, V. Valet parking $12.

Just across Front Avenue from the Willamette River, the Portland Marriott is the flashiest of the city's hotels. It boasts some of the best views in town; many of the rooms here have small balconies overlooking the river, and on a clear day you can even spot Mount Hood in the distance. The decor in the rooms is simple but attractive.

Dining/Entertainment: The hotel's restaurant is an undistinguished place serving traditional fare, and the popular sports bar gets noisy in the evenings. On weekends there's dancing to recorded music. The lobby bar attracts a much more sedate crowd.

Services: Room service, concierge floor, valet/laundry service, shoeshine stand, babysitting service, video checkout and message viewing, massage.

Facilities: Exercise room, indoor pool, whirlpool, saunas, games room, weight room, sundeck, hair salon and barbershop, newsstand.

✪ RiverPlace Hotel

1510 SW Harbor Way, Portland, OR 97201. ☎ **503/228-3233,** or 800/227-1333 outside Oregon. Fax 503/295-6161. 84 rms, 47 suites. A/C TV TEL. $175–$215 double; $205–$600 suite. Rates include continental breakfast. AE, CB, DC, JCB, MC, V. Valet parking $10.

If you prefer the quiet atmosphere of a European-style small resort, try the RiverPlace, which enjoys an enviable location beside the Willamette River and Waterfront Park. The spacious rooms are decorated with wingback chairs, teak tables, writing desks, and lacquered armoires. More than half the rooms here are suites, and some come with wood-burning fireplaces and whirlpool baths. All rooms come with wet bars and large windows you can open to let in cool breezes off the river.

Dining/Entertainment: The Esplanade Restaurant overlooks the river and serves Northwest and continental fare. For al fresco dining there's the casual Patio. Just off the lobby is a comfortable bar with live piano music and a crackling fire in cool weather.

Services: Concierge, room service (24-hour), turn-down service, complimentary shoeshine, valet/laundry service, complimentary morning paper, running map.

Facilities: Whirlpool, sauna, privileges at athletic club, in-room computer and fax connections, voice mail.

EXPENSIVE

Red Lion Hotel/Downtown

310 SW Lincoln St., Portland, OR 97201. ☎ **503/221-0450** or 800/547-8010. Fax 503/226-6260. 235 rms, 3 suites. A/C TV TEL. $114–$120 double; $225–$325 suite. AE, CB, DC, DISC, ER, JCB, MC, V. Free parking.

Situated on a shady tree-lined street on the southern edge of downtown Portland, this low-rise hotel offers comfort and a convenient location. The design and landscaping of the hotel reflect the Northwest, and in the courtyard surrounding the swimming pool are lush plantings of evergreens and other shrubs. Red Lion Inns are noted for the spaciousness of their guest rooms, and this one is no exception. Large windows let in lots of light, and all rooms come with king- or queen-size beds. Courtyard rooms are slightly more expensive.

Dining/Entertainment: The hotel's restaurant offers a wide variety of well-prepared meals, with the focus on fresh local seafood. A disco features live music Thursday through Saturday.

Services: Room service, complimentary airport shuttle, valet/laundry service.
Facilities: Outdoor pool.

Riverside Inn

50 SW Morrison Ave., Portland, OR 97204. ☎ **503/221-0711** or 800/648-6440. Fax 503/274-0312. 139 rms. A/C TV TEL. $95 double. AE, CB, DC, DISC, MC, V. Free parking.

Overlooking Waterfront Park and located on the MAX light-rail line, the Riverside has many unexpected features. As the name implies, you're only steps from the Willamette River, but you're also close to businesses, fine restaurants, and shopping. Colorful fine-art posters enliven the walls of the small lobby. The rooms, many with excellent views of the river and Morrison Bridge, feature a small library of hardbound books and modern furnishings.

Dining/Entertainment: A restaurant with large windows looking out over Waterfront Park and the river serves seafood, steaks, pastas, and sandwiches.

Services: Room service, valet/laundry service, complimentary newspaper, use of fitness club.

MODERATE

Cypress Inn–Portland Downtown

809 SW King St., Portland, OR 97205. ☎ **503/226-6288** or 800/225-4205. Fax 503/274-0038. 82 rms. A/C TV TEL. $63–$89 double. Rates include continental breakfast. AE, DC, DISC, MC, V. Free parking.

Family-Friendly Hotels

Red Lion Inn/Lloyd Center *(see p. 273)*   Let the kids loose in the huge Lloyd Center shopping mall across the street and they'll be content for hours—there's even an ice-skating rink in the mall.

Portland Marriott *(see p. 270)*   The games room and indoor pool are popular with kids, and just across the street is 2-mile-long Tom McCall Waterfront Park, which runs along the Willamette River.

Though the standard rooms here are rather cramped, for just a few dollars more you can get a much larger room, which may even have a kitchenette. The motel sits a little bit up into the hills west of downtown and has some good views over the city. Another plus here is that you're within walking distance of both the Northwest shopping-and-restaurant district and Washington Park, which is home to the Japanese Garden and the Rose Test Gardens. Be sure to avail yourself of the free local phone calls and the courtesy airport shuttle.

Days Inn City Center
1414 SW Sixth Ave., Portland, OR 97201. ☎ **503/221-1611** or 800/899-0248. 173 rms. A/C TV TEL. $71–$76 double. AE, CB, DC, MC, V. Free parking.

Located in the heart of downtown Portland, this hotel is an excellent choice for budget-minded business travelers and family vacationers. You'll find a small library of old hardbound books in every room, and in addition there are brass beds and framed old photos of Portland and famous people. Each room has a large picture window to let in lots of sunlight. With its brass rails and wood trim, the hotel's restaurant is popular with the business set for lunch. Room service, valet/laundry service, and complimentary newspapers are available, as is an outdoor pool.

❂ Mallory Hotel
729 SW 15th Ave., Portland, OR 97205-1994. ☎ **503/223-6311** or 800/228-8657. Fax 503/223-0522. 140 rms, 13 suites. A/C TV TEL. $60–$100 double; $90–$100 suite. AE, CB, DC, MC, V. Free parking.

The Mallory has long been a favorite of Portland visitors who want the convenience of a downtown lodging but aren't on a bottomless expense account. This is an older hotel, and though the lobby, with its ornate gilt-plasterwork trim and crystal chandeliers, has a certain classic grandeur, it also has that faded feel you might expect from a hotel in a Bogart movie. The guest rooms are not as luxurious as the lobby might suggest, but they are comfortable and clean. With room rates this low, you might want to go for one of the king-size suites. These accommodations are about as big as they come, with a walk-in closet, refrigerator, and sofa bed. All rooms have new carpets, drapes, and furniture. The dining room continues the grand design of the lobby. Heavy drapes hang from the windows and faux-marble pillars lend just the right air of imperial grandeur. Free local calls and valet/laundry service are available.

NORTHWEST PORTLAND
EXPENSIVE

❂ Heron Haus
2545 NW Westover Rd., Portland, OR 97210. ☎ **503/274-1846.** Fax 503/243-1075. 5 rms. TV TEL. $125–$250 double. Rates include continental breakfast. MC, V. Free parking.

Located a short walk from the bustling Northwest shopping-and-dining district, the Heron Haus B&B offers outstanding accommodations, spectacular views, and tranquil surroundings. There's even a small swimming pool with a sun deck. Surprisingly, the house still features some of the original plumbing, including one shower that has seven shower heads. In another room there's a modern whirlpool spa that affords excellent views of the city.

MODERATE

Silver Cloud Inn

2426 NW Vaughn St., Portland, OR 97210-2540. ☎ **503/242-2400** or 800/205-6939. Fax 503/242-1770. 67 rms, 14 minisuites. A/C TV TEL. $60–$70 double, $70–$89 minisuite. Rates include continental breakfast. AE, DC, DISC, MC, V.

This newer hotel is located just north of Portland's trendy Northwest neighborhood, and though it faces the edge of the city's industrial area, it's still a very attractive and comfortable place. Reasonable rates are the main draw here, but the hotel is also within a five-minute drive of half a dozen of the city's best restaurants. The standard rooms have refrigerators, while the minisuites come with refrigerators, wet bars, microwave ovens, and a separate seating area. The most expensive rooms are the "king rooms" with whirlpool tubs. Local phone calls are free, and facilities include a fitness room and a whirlpool. Try to get a room away from Vaughn Street.

NORTHEAST PORTLAND/SOUTHEAST PORTLAND
VERY EXPENSIVE

Red Lion Inn/Lloyd Center

1000 NE Multnomah St., Portland, OR 97232. ☎ **503/281-6111** or 800/547-8010. Fax 503/284-8553. 476 rms, 10 suites. A/C TV TEL. $139–$164 double; $435–$535 suite. Lower rates off-season. AE, CB, DC, DISC, ER, JCB, MC, V. Parking $6.

In the busy lobby of this modern high-rise, glass elevators shuttle up and down through the skylighted ceiling. Spreading out in different directions are hallways leading to the restaurants, gift shops, a swimming pool, and an elegant lounge. The Red Lion's rooms are spacious and some have balconies. The views from the higher floors are stunning—on a clear day you can see Mount Hood, Mount St. Helens, and even Mount Rainier.

Dining/Entertainment: Local seafood and steaks are the specialties in the main restaurant and there's also a Mexican restaurant as well as a coffee shop. A quiet lounge sometimes has live piano music.

Services: Concierge, room service, complimentary airport shuttle, valet/laundry service.

Facilities: Heated outdoor pool, exercise room.

EXPENSIVE

○ The Lion and the Rose

1810 NE 15th Ave., Portland, OR 97212. ☎ **503/287-9245** or 800/955-1647. Fax 503/287-9247. 7 rms, 5 with bath. TEL. $80–$120 double without bath, $105–$120 double with bath. Rates include full breakfast. AE, MC, V.

Set up a flight of stairs from the street, this imposing B&B looms over its corner like a castle. Though the inn is in a fairly quiet residential neighborhood, it's only one block off Northeast Broadway, and within four blocks are half a dozen excellent restaurants, eclectic boutiques, and a huge shopping mall. The living room and dining room are beautifully decorated with period antiques, including an ornate pump organ. The guest rooms each have a distinctively different decor ranging from the bright colors and turret sitting area of the Lavonna Room to the deep greens of the Starina Room, which features an imposing Edwardian bed and armoire. The Garden Room and the shared bathroom have clawfoot tubs, but some rooms have cramped, though attractive, bathrooms. Breakfasts are sumptuous affairs that are meant to be lingered over.

MODERATE

ⓢ Holiday Inn Portland–Downtown

1021 NE Grand Ave., Portland, OR 97232. ☎ **503/235-2100** or 800/HOLIDAY. Fax 503/238-0132. 166 rms, 6 suites. A/C TV TEL. $65–$95 double; $125–$250 suite. AE, CB, DC, DISC, MC, V. Free parking.

This hotel is located across the street from the Oregon Convention Center and is a popular choice with conventioneers. Because Portland's MAX light-rail system stops one block from the hotel, this is also a convenient location if you want to go downtown. You'll find all the rooms attractively furnished in modern decor with a hint of Asia. Large tables, writing desks, two phones, and comfortable armchairs allow guests to spread out. Upper floors have good views. The hotel's top-floor restaurant provides great views. You can dine on fresh Northwest cuisine or just have a drink in the lounge or on the outdoor terrace. Room service and valet/laundry service are available, as are a sauna and fitness center.

Travelodge Hotel

1441 NE Second Ave., Portland, OR 97232. ☎ **503/233-2401** or 800/255-3050. Fax 503/238-7016. 237 rms, 1 suite. A/C TV TEL. $65–$89 double; $200–$250 suite. Additional person $5 extra. AE, CB, DC, DISC, MC, V. Free parking.

Convenient to both the city center and the Convention Center, the Travelodge offers excellent views from its modern 10-story building. The small lobby and the guest rooms all have large windows, and you'll find a coffee maker in every room. There's also an executive club floor offering additional security, hairdryers, and free local phone calls. The hotel's restaurant serves seafood and steaks. For cocktails and conversation there's an adjacent lounge. Room service, complimentary airport shuttle, valet/laundry service, and free jogging maps are available, as are an outdoor pool and an exercise room.

INEXPENSIVE

ⓢ Ho-Jo Inn

3939 NE Hancock St., Portland, OR 97212. ☎ **503/288-6891.** Fax 503/288-1995. 48 rms. A/C TV TEL. $52–$56 double. AE, CB, DC, DISC, MC, V. Free parking.

Located in the Hollywood District of northeast Portland about halfway between the airport and downtown, the Ho-Jo Inn is an excellent choice in the budget-accommodation range. Some rooms are exceptionally large and were renovated a few years ago. Attractive modern furniture and comfortable beds will make your stay here enjoyable. Take a stroll around the neighborhood and you'll see why they call this the Hollywood District—the same style of southern California architecture prevails.

Portland AYH Hostel

3031 SE Hawthorne Blvd., Portland, OR 97214. ☎ **503/236-3380.** 36–50 beds. $12 per person for members, $14 for nonmembers. MC, V. Bus: 14 from downtown or 12 from the airport and then 14.

Housed in an old house on a busy street, this hostel is small and has primarily dormitory beds. The common room is small, but a large wraparound porch (that sometimes doubles as a dormitory) makes up for the lack of space inside. There's a large kitchen where guests can prepare their own meals and a grocery store is a short walk away. Membership is $10 per year for youths under 17, $25 for adults, and $15 for senior citizens over 55.

NEAR THE AIRPORT
EXPENSIVE

Shilo Inn Suites Hotel

11707 NE Airport Way, Portland, OR 97220-1075. ☎ **503/252-7500** or 800/222-2244. Fax 503/254-0794. 200 suites. A/C TV TEL. $112–$139 suite for two. Rates include continental breakfast. AE, DC, DISC, MC, V. Head straight out of the airport, drive under the I-205 overpass, and watch for the hotel ahead on the left.

If you want to stay near the airport and want the space and facilities of a deluxe hotel, this is one of your best bets. All the rooms here are large and have lots of amenities. There are roomy closets with mirrored doors, plenty of bathroom counter space, and three TVs (including one in the bathroom). Other amenities include hairdryers, VCRs, and double sinks. The main drawback here is that this is a convention hotel and is often very crowded.

Dining/Entertainment: The hotel's dining room serves surprisingly creative dishes amid casual surroundings, and there's an adjacent piano lounge.

Services: Room service, complimentary airport shuttle, valet service.

Facilities: Indoor pool, whirlpool, exercise room.

MODERATE

In addition to the hotel below, you'll also find a **Super 8 Motel** at 11011 NE Homan St. (☎ **503/253-1427**), just off Airport Way after you go under the I-205 overpass. This motel charges a surprisingly high $57 a night for a double.

Courtyard by Marriott

11550 NE Airport Way, Portland, OR 97220. ☎ **503/252-3200** or 800/321-2211. Fax 503/252-8921. 150 rms, 10 suites. A/C TV TEL. $54–$83 double; $100–$110 suite. AE, DC, DISC, MC, V. Head straight out of the airport, go under the I-205 overpass, and the hotel is ahead on the right.

Despite the name, this modern six-story hotel has no courtyard. What is does have is an elegant little lobby featuring lots of marble and modest but comfortable guest rooms. If you need some extra room, opt for one of the suites, which come with microwave ovens, wet bars, and small refrigerators. Ask for a room away from the road if you're a light sleeper. There's a comfortable lounge off the lobby as well as a moderately priced dining room. This is one of the most convenient hotels to the airport, and offers complimentary shuttle service. Other amenities include room service, a tiny outdoor pool, a whirlpool, and a fitness room.

4 Dining

Over the past couple of years the Portland restaurant scene has been hopping. Good new restaurants seem to be opening weekly, and many of these are locating in the Northwest neighborhood, especially along Northwest 21st Avenue. If you want a wide selection of great restaurants to choose from, stroll along this street and see what strikes your fancy.

Portland Dining

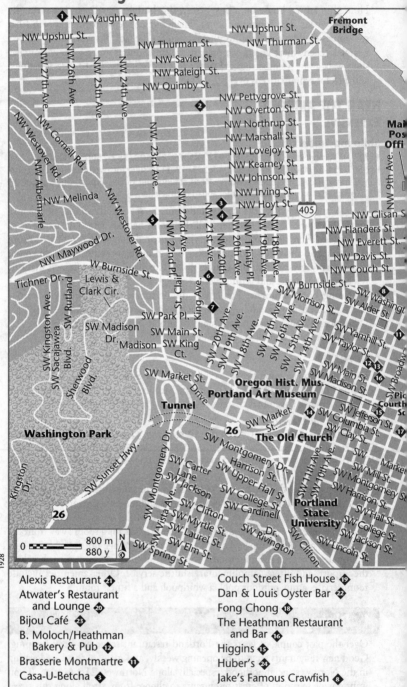

Alexis Restaurant ㉑	Couch Street Fish House ⑲
Atwater's Restaurant and Lounge ⑳	Dan & Louis Oyster Bar ㉒
Bijou Café ㉓	Fong Chong ⑱
B. Moloch/Heathman Bakery & Pub ⑫	The Heathman Restaurant and Bar ⑯
Brasserie Montmartre ⑪	Higgins ⑮
Casa-U-Betcha ❸	Huber's ㉔
	Jake's Famous Crawfish ❽

1928

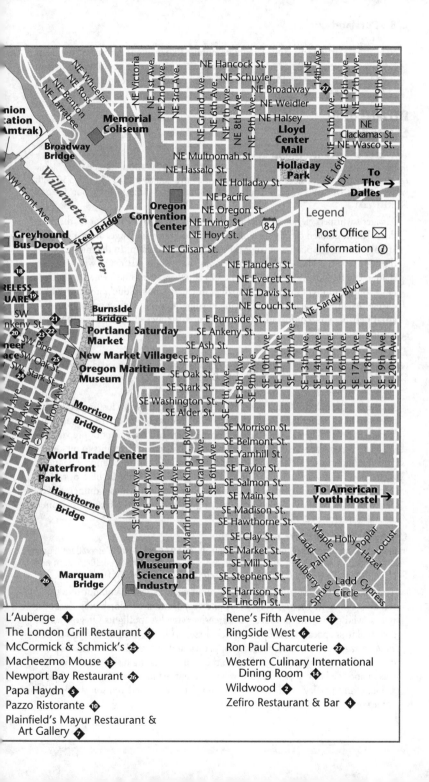

L'Auberge ①
The London Grill Restaurant ⑨
McCormick & Schmick's ㉕
Macheezmo Mouse ⑬
Newport Bay Restaurant ㉖
Papa Haydn ⑤
Pazzo Ristorante ⑩
Plainfield's Mayur Restaurant & Art Gallery ⑦

Rene's Fifth Avenue ⑰
RingSide West ⑥
Ron Paul Charcuterie ㉗
Western Culinary International Dining Room ⑭
Wildwood ②
Zefiro Restaurant & Bar ④

For these listings we considered a restaurant **Expensive** if a meal with wine or beer would average $25 or more. **Moderate** restaurants serve complete dinners in the $15 to $25 range, and **Inexpensive** listings are those where you can get a complete meal for less than $15.

DOWNTOWN
EXPENSIVE

Atwater's Restaurant and Lounge
In the U.S. Bancorp Tower, 111 SW Fifth Ave. ☎ **503/275-3600.** Reservations highly recommended. Main courses $18–$25; fixed-price five-course meal $35 ($47–$50 with wine). AE, CB, DC, MC, V. Mon–Thurs 5:30–9:30pm, Fri–Sat 5:30–10pm, Sun 5–9pm. NORTHWEST.

Atwater's whispers elegance from the moment you step off the elevator on the 30th floor. Richly colored carpets on a blond hardwood floor and large, dramatic flower arrangements add splashes of color throughout the restaurant. In the middle of the dining room is a glass-enclosed wine room that would put many wineshops to shame. Pacific Northwest cuisine is the specialty here, with unexpected and delectable combinations of ingredients. Roasted rosemary-smoked duck breast with bleu cheese, Asian pear salad, and port-wine vinaigrette is one such combination. For an appetizer, you could indulge in the seared pepper-encrusted salmon with mango-papaya relish.

Couch Street Fish House
NW Third Ave. and Couch St. ☎ **503/223-6173.** Reservations recommended. Main courses $14–$24; sunset dinners $13. AE, CB, DC, DISC, MC, V. Mon–Thurs 5–10pm, Fri–Sat 5–11pm. SEAFOOD.

Located in the heart of Old Town, this restaurant occupies two historic buildings, one of which is merely a parking lot behind the facade of an 1883 Italianate Victorian hotel. The succulent seafood entrées here run the gamut of preparation styles from pan-fried oysters coated with a crust of Oregon hazelnuts to mesquite-grilled salmon to such classics as lobster thermidor and shrimp scampi. The menu focuses on fresh seafood, but meat eaters are also served with the likes of rack of lamb and filet mignon with shiitake-mushroom glaze. The sunset dinner, served between 5 and 6pm, is a good deal, offering lighter fare and a chance to sample several tastes for $12.95.

✪ The Heathman Restaurant and Bar
In the Heathman Hotel, SW Broadway at Salmon St. ☎ **503/241-4100.** Reservations highly recommended. Main courses $9.50–$25. AE, CB, DC, MC, V. Mon–Sat 6:30am–2pm and 5–11pm, Sun 6:30am–3pm (brunch) and 5–11pm. NORTHWEST/FRENCH.

The menu in this elegant hotel dining room changes seasonally, but one thing remains constant: the ingredients are the very freshest of Northwest seafoods, meats, wild game, and produce. An extensive wine list spotlights Oregon wines, and local fruit appears in many of the rich desserts. On the walls are Andy Warhol's *Endangered Species*—rhino, zebra, lion, panda, and others. Both the adventurous diner and the traditionalist will find on the menu appealing dishes that reflect the season and the bounty of the Northwest. A recent menu offered red snapper with a potato-and-parsley crust, wild-mushroom fettuccine, and venison wrapped in applewood-smoked bacon.

Jake's Famous Crawfish

401 SW 12th St. ☎ **503/226-1419.** Reservations recommended. Main courses $11–$27. AE, DC, DISC, MC, V. Mon–Thurs 11:30am–11pm, Fri 11:30am–midnight, Sat 5pm–midnight, Sun 5–10pm. SEAFOOD.

Jake's has been serving up crayfish since 1909. The back bar here came all the way around Cape Horn in 1880, and much of the rest of the restaurant's decor looks just as old and well-worn. The noise level after work, when local businesspeople pack the bar, can be high, and the wait for a table can be long if you don't have a reservation. However, don't let these obstacles dissuade you from visiting this Portland institution. An extensive wine list and 15 to 20 daily specials make this one of Portland's most popular restaurants. Of course, crayfish prepared several different ways is always on the menu.

The London Grill Restaurant

In the Benson Hotel, 309 SW Broadway. ☎ **503/228-2000.** Reservations highly recommended. Main courses $18.75–$23; Sun champagne brunch $19.50. AE, CB, DC, DISC, ER, JCB, MC, V. Mon–Sat 6:30am–2pm and 5–10pm, Sun 9:30am–1:30pm (brunch) and 5–10pm. CONTINENTAL.

Modeled after the original London Grill, which was a favorite with Elizabeth I, this restaurant has the feel of an elegant wine cellar. Service by casually attired waiters is impeccable, and both breakfast and lunch are popular with business executives. The menu uses many of the Northwest's finest fresh fruits and vegetables in dishes such as stuffed quail and a venison chop with wild mushrooms, and yellow-fin tuna with sweet peppers and fried ginger. The Sunday champagne brunch is the most elegant in the city.

RingSide West

2165 W. Burnside St. ☎ **503/223-1513.** Reservations recommended. Main courses $12–$37. AE, DC, DISC, MC, V. Mon–Sat 5pm–midnight, Sun 4–11:30pm. STEAK.

Stop a Portlander on the street and ask where to get the best steak in town and you'll invariably be steered to RingSide. Though boxing is the main theme of the restaurant, the name delivers a two-fisted pun as well, referring to the incomparable onion rings that should be an integral part of any meal here. Have your rings with a side order of one of their perfectly cooked steaks for a knockout meal.

There's a RingSide East at 14021 NE Glisan St. (☎ **503/255-0750**).

MODERATE

✪ Alexis Restaurant

215 W. Burnside St. ☎ **503/224-8577.** Reservations recommended. Main courses $9–$14. AE, CB, DC, DISC, MC, V. Mon–Thurs 11:30am–2pm and 5–10pm, Fri 11:30am–2pm and 5–11pm, Sat 5–11pm, Sun 4:30–9pm. GREEK.

Alexis is a classic Greek *taverna*, and the crowds keep it packed as much for the great food as for the fun atmosphere that includes belly dancing on weekends. The menu has all your Greek favorites on it, but there's no need to read beyond the appetizer section. The not-to-be-missed appetizer list includes saganaki (pan-fried cheese flamed with ouzo), kalamarakia (perfectly fried squid), octopus, and the tart-and-creamy avgolemono soup. Accompany these with Alexis's own fresh breads, and wash it all down with a bottle of Greek wine for a meal beyond compare.

Ⓢ B. Moloch/Heathman Bakery & Pub

901 SW Salmon St. ☎ **503/227-5700.** Reservations not accepted. Main courses $8–$13.25. AE, DC, DISC, MC, V. Mon–Thurs 7am–10:30pm, Fri 7am–11:30pm, Sat 8am–11:30pm, Sun 8am–10:30pm. NORTHWEST.

At B. Moloch, corporate climbers and bicycle messengers rub shoulders, quaff microbrews, and chow down on creative wood-oven pizzas. The atmosphere is bright and noisy amid an industrial decor softened by colorful images of salmon. Gourmet pizzas are the mainstay here, with such appetizing combos as smoked salmon, rock shrimp, roasted peppers, onions, feta cheese, capers, and olive paste. In addition to pizzas, there are sandwiches, pasta dishes, great salads, and daily specials. Our personal favorites are the small plates such as grilled goat cheese, smoked tomatoes, and roasted garlic. Next door to the restaurant, on the other side of a wall of glass, is a microbrewery.

Brasserie Montmartre

626 SW Park Ave. ☎ **503/224-5552.** Reservations highly recommended. Main courses $9–$17.50. AE, CB, DC, MC, V. Mon–Thurs 11:30am–2am, Fri 11:30am–3am, Sat 10am–3am, Sun 10am–2am. (Bistro menu daily 2pm–closing.) NORTHWEST/FRENCH.

Though the menu lacks the creativity of other Northwest and French restaurants in Portland, the Bra (as it's known here in town) is hardly the stodgy and expensive place its full name implies. There's nightly jazz music, and Tuesday through Saturday nights a magician performs. On every table you'll find a paper tablecloth and a container of crayons. This playfulness is balanced out by formal dining rooms. Massive white pillars, black-and-white tile floors, velvet banquettes, and silk lampshades lend an air of *fin de siècle* Paris. You might start your meal with a pâté, then have a cup of onion soup with three cheeses, move on to salmon with lingonberry-and-ginger butter, and finish off with one of the divinely decadent pastries. The wine list is neither too extensive nor too expensive.

Ⓢ Dan & Louis Oyster Bar

208 SW Ankeny St. ☎ **503/227-5906.** Reservations recommended. Main courses $6–$13. AE, CB, DC, MC, V. Sun–Thurs 11am–10pm, Fri–Sat 11am–11pm. SEAFOOD.

Dan & Louis has been serving up succulent oysters since 1907, and these days the oysters come from Dan and Louis's own oyster farm on Yaquina Bay, Oregon. Half the fun of eating here is enjoying the old-fashioned surroundings. The front counter is stacked high with candies and cigars, and the walls are covered with founder Louis Wachsmuth's own collection of old and unusual plates. Louis began his restaurant business serving only two items—oyster stew and oyster cocktails. These two are still on the menu, and as good today as they were 85 years ago. The entrées are simple, no-nonsense seafood dishes—mostly fried—and the prices are great.

Ⓢ Higgins

1239 SW Broadway. ☎ **503/222-9070.** Reservations highly recommended. Main courses $13.25–$18.50. AE, DC, MC, V. Mon–Fri 11:30am–2pm and 5–10:30pm, Sat–Sun 5–10:30pm. NORTHWEST/MEDITERRANEAN.

Higgins, located just up Broadway from the Heathman Hotel, where chef Greg Higgins first made a name for himself, strikes a balance between contemporary and classic in both its decor and its cuisine. Details such as a wood-paneled dining area, waiters in long white aprons, and copper pots hanging on the wall of the open kitchen give the restaurant its classic ambience, but the menu explores more contemporary culinary horizons. The duck-liver flan with green peppercorns and walnut crackers was a light and creamy twist on a classic pâté, while oysters on the half shell were served with a spicy smoked-chile mignonette. Entrées usually include such dishes as grilled sausage made from chicken, sun-dried tomatoes, and rosemary, and served with fettuccine, greens, and mustard-Romano/cream sauce.

Huber's

411 SW Third Ave. ☎ **503/228-5686.** Reservations recommended, but not accepted Fri evenings. Main courses $6.50–$15. AE, DC, DISC, MC, V. Mon–Thurs 11am–10pm, Fri 11am–11pm, Sat 4–11pm. CONTINENTAL.

Portland's oldest restaurant first opened its doors to the public in 1879, though it didn't move to its present location until 1911. You'll find this very traditional old restaurant tucked inside the Oregon Pioneer Building and down a quiet hallway, where you'll come to a surprising little room with vaulted stained-glass ceiling, Philippine mahogany paneling, and the original brass cash register. The house specialty has been turkey since the day the first Huber's opened, so there really isn't any question of what to order. Lunch prices are much lower, with the turkey sandwich the star of the hour.

⑤ McCormick & Schmick's

235 SW First Ave. ☎ **503/224-7522.** Reservations highly recommended. Main courses $9–$20; bar meals $1.95; lunch $6–$12. AE, DC, MC, V. Mon–Thurs 11:30am–3pm and 5–10pm, Fri 11:30am–3pm and 5–11pm, Sat 5–11pm, Sun 5–10pm. (Bar meals, Mon–Sat 1:30–6:30pm and 9:30pm–close.) SEAFOOD.

The oysters go by their first names—Olympia, Royal Miyagi, and Quilcene—and the daily fresh menu sheet might list 25 different types of seafood. If you aren't interested in live oysters as an appetizer, there are plenty of cooked seafoods to start you out. Some outstanding entrées on a recent visit included grilled rainbow trout with apple-smoked bacon and currant chutney, and Cajun catfish with black beans and corn relish. The extensive wine list features quite a few excellent Oregon wines, and more than 30 single-malt scotches are available. There's an $8.25 dinner menu daily from 5 to 6:15pm and 9:30pm until closing.

Newport Bay Restaurant

0425 SW Montgomery St. ☎ **503/227-3474.** Reservations recommended. Main courses $10–$19; lunch and light main courses $5.25–$10. AE, CB, DC, DISC, MC, V. Mon–Thurs 11am–10pm, Fri–Sat 11am–11pm, Sun 11am–3pm (brunch) and 3–10pm (in summer, open one hour longer and Sun brunch 10am–3pm). SEAFOOD.

Though there are Newport Bay restaurants all over Portland, this one has the best location—floating on the Willamette River. Located in the marina at Portland's beautiful RiverPlace shopping-and-dining complex, the Newport Bay provides excellent views of the river and the city skyline, especially from the deck. Inside, the atmosphere is cheery and the service is efficient. Nearly everything on the menu has some sort of seafood in it—even the quiche, salads, and pastas. Entrées are mostly straightforward and well prepared—nothing too fancy.

✪ Pazzo Ristorante

In the Hotel Vintage Plaza, 627 SW Washington St. (at Broadway). ☎ **503/228-1515.** Reservations highly recommended. Main courses $8–$17. AE, CB, DC, DISC, MC, V. Mon–Thurs 7am–10pm, Fri 7am–11pm, Sat 8am–11pm, Sun 8am–10pm. NORTHERN ITALIAN.

The atmosphere in Pazzo is not nearly as rarefied as in the adjacent hotel lobby, and, in fact, if you take a seat at Pazzo's bar, you'll practically be ducking hanging hams, sausages, and garlic braids. Rustic decor and the stereotypical red-and-white-checked tablecloth speak of an Italian country *ristorante*. If you're a fan of garlic,

ⓜ Family-Friendly Restaurants

Aztec Willie, Joey Rose Taqueria   Located at 1501 NE Broadway (☎ 503/ 280-8900), the restaurant has a glass-enclosed play area overseen by a huge Mayan-like head. They serve Mexican food from a walk-up counter.

Brasserie Montmartre *(see p. 280)*   Though it's more of an adult restaurant, there are paper tablecloths and crayons to keep kids occupied and even a strolling magician most evenings.

Dan & Louis Oyster Bar *(see p. 280)*   You'll think you're eating in the hold of an old sailing ship, and all the fascinating stuff on the walls will keep kids entertained.

Old Wives Tales   Located at 1300 E. Burnside St. (☎ 503/238-0470), Old Wives Tales is just about the best place in Portland to eat if you've got small children. There are children's menus at all meals and in the back of the restaurant is a playroom.

this is the place for you, although there are also plenty of dishes without it. You can start your meal with a rosemary-crust pizzetta topped with roasted garlic and cambazola cheese (baked in the wood-burning oven), and then move on to a Caesar salad with plenty of anchovies, garlic, Parmesan, and croutons. Grilled duck breast with braised red cabbage, truffled celery root purée and dried fig sauce, and smoked-salmon-filled ravioli with asparagus and lemon-cream sauce are both delicious departures from the garlicky dishes.

Plainfield's Mayur Restaurant & Art Gallery
852 SW 21st Ave. ☎ **503/223-2995.** Reservations recommended. Main courses $8.50–$18. AE, DISC, MC, V. Daily 5:30–10pm. INDIAN.

Located in an elegant old Portland home, this is the city's premier Indian restaurant. The atmosphere is refined, with bone china and European crystal, and the service is informative and gracious. In addition to the three floors of dining rooms inside, there's a patio out back, an art gallery, and a tandoori show kitchen where you can watch the cooks bake bread and tandoori chicken. Every dish on the menu is perfectly spiced and redolent of the complex flavors and aromas of Indian cuisine. Be sure to ask them to go easy on the chile peppers if you can't handle spicy food. The dessert list is also an unexpected and pleasant surprise. Save room! The wine list here is one of the finest in the city.

ⓢ Western Culinary International Dining Room
1316 SW 13th Ave. ☎ **503/223-2245** or 800/666-0312. Reservations required. Five-course lunch $7.95; six-course dinner $14–$18; Thurs buffet $14.95. MC, V. Tues–Fri 11:30am–1pm and 6–8pm. CONTINENTAL.

If you happen to be a frugal gourmet whose palate is more sophisticated than your wallet can afford, you'll want to schedule a meal here. The dining room serves five- to six-course gourmet meals prepared by advanced students at prices even a budget traveler can afford. For each course you have a choice of two to five offerings. A sample dinner menu might begin with veloute Andalouse, followed by pâté of rabbit, a pear sorbet, grilled chicken breast with blackberry-balsamic sauce, Chinese salad with smoked salmon, and chocolate-mousse cake. Remember, that's all for less than $20! The five-course lunch for is an even better deal.

INEXPENSIVE
Bijou Café
132 SW Third Ave. ☎ **503/222-3187.** Reservations not accepted. Meals $2.75–$6.25. No credit cards. Daily 7am–3pm. INTERNATIONAL/NATURAL.

Although open only for breakfast and lunch, the Bijou is still one of the most popular restaurants in Portland, and the lines can be long, especially on the weekends. The folks here take both food and health seriously. They'll let you know where the eggs come from, and they'll even serve you a bowl of steamed brown rice for breakfast if you're interested. However, the real hits here are the hash browns and the muffins.

Fong Chong
301 NW Fourth Ave. ☎ **503/220-0235.** Reservations not accepted. Main courses $4–$10; dim sum meals under $10. MC, V. Mon–Thurs 10:30am–9pm, Fri–Sun 10:30am–10pm. (Dim sum, daily 11am–3pm.) CHINESE.

This popular Chinese restaurant is in a grocery store, but don't worry, you won't be eating between the aisles—the restaurant occupies its own room. Although most of the food here is above average, the dim sum is the best in the city. Flag down a passing cart and point to the most appetizing-looking little dishes. At the end of the meal, your bill is calculated by the number of plates on your table.

Macheezmo Mouse
723 SW Salmon St. ☎ **503/228-3491.** Complete dinner $4–$7. MC, V. Mon–Sat 11am–10pm, Sun noon–10pm. MEXICAN/HEALTHY.

Known for both its healthful fast food and its unusual contemporary art, Macheezmo Mouse is for those who want convenience but also care about their health. The menu is primarily Mexican and lists the calorie count for each meal. Most dishes have also been approved by the American Heart Association.

There are other locations at 811 NW 23rd Ave. (☎ 503/274-0500), 3553 SE Hawthorne Blvd. (☎ 503/232-6588), 1200 NE Broadway (☎ 503/249-0002), and in Pioneer Place (☎ 503/248-0917).

ⓢ Rene's Fifth Avenue
1300 SW Fifth Ave. ☎ **503/241-0712.** Reservations recommended. Lunch $6–$9. MC, V. Mon–Fri 11:30am–2:30pm. CONTINENTAL.

Comfortable and elegant, this 21st-floor lunch spot in the First Interstate Tower is always crowded. Local businesspeople flock here as much for the great view as for the food. The menu, though short, is varied and includes daily specials and plenty of seafood. When we last visited, we had blackened salmon with a lemon sauce, pasta salad, soup, and a splendid view of the Northwest hills, for $7.95!

NORTHWEST PORTLAND
EXPENSIVE

L'Auberge
2601 NW Vaughn St. ☎ **503/223-3302.** Reservations recommended. Main courses $8.50–$19.75; four-course fixed-price dinner $34.50–$36. AE, CB, DC, DISC, MC, V. Sun–Thurs 5pm–midnight, Fri–Sat 5pm–1am. NORTHWEST/FRENCH.

Located at the edge of the industrial district, this little country cottage consistently offers some of the best French-accented Northwest cuisine in Portland. The restaurant is divided into the main dining room, where a more formal atmosphere reigns, and the lounge and deck area. On Sunday nights the French flavor is forsaken in favor of succulent ribs and burgers, and a movie is shown in the bar. The fixed-price dinners usually offer a couple of entrée choices, such as rack of lamb with port-garlic sauce or duck breast with green peppercorns in lime demiglace. You can top this off with a delectable morsel from the desert tray. The wine list is extensive.

Papa Haydn

701 NW 23rd Ave. ☎ **503/228-7317.** Reservations not accepted. Main courses $15–$24; desserts $4–$5. AE, MC, V. Tues–Thurs 11:30am–11pm, Fri–Sat 11:30am–midnight, Sun 10am–3pm (brunch). ITALIAN.

Say the words "Papa Haydn" to Portlanders and blissful smiles will light up their faces as the praises spill forth. What is it about this bistro that produces such raves? Desserts! Though Papa Haydn is a respectable Italian restaurant, it's legendary for its desserts. At last count the menu included 25 decadent delicacies such as lemon-chiffon torte, raspberry gâteau, black velvet, Georgian peanut butter–mousse torte, and boccone dolce. Expect a line at the door (that's the price you pay for a Papa Haydn symphony).

There's another location at 5829 SE Milwaukee Ave. (☎ **503/232-9440**).

✪ Wildwood

1221 NW 21st Ave. ☎ **503/248-WOOD.** Reservations highly recommended. Main courses $13.50–$22. AE, MC, V. Mon–Thurs 11:30am–2:30pm and 5:30–10pm, Fri–Sat 11:30am–2:30pm and 5:30–10:30pm, Sun 10am–2pm (brunch) and 5–8:30pm. MEDITERRANEAN.

With an elegant and spare interior decor and a menu that changes daily, it isn't surprising that Wildwood is a hit with urban sophisticates. Booths, a meal counter, a bar area, and a patio appeal to celebratory groups, businesspeople, couples, and solo diners. The short menu relies primarily on the subtle flavors of the Mediterranean, which often seem both exotic and familiar at the same time. Recently the appetizers list included fennel-cured salmon with a cucumber-and-red-onion salad as well as a couple of pizzas, one of which had a cornmeal-and-sage crust and was topped with Cheddar cheese, walnuts, and bacon. Entrées included grilled salmon with tangerine, blood orange, and grilled red onion; and roast lamb with a white-bean purée.

✪ Zefiro Restaurant & Bar

500 NW 21st Ave. ☎ **503/226-3394.** Reservations highly recommended. Main courses $14–$17.50. AE, DC, MC, V. Mon–Thurs 11:30am–2:30pm and 6–10:30pm, Fri 11:30am–2:30pm and 5:30–11pm, Sat 5:30–11pm. MEDITERRANEAN.

Simple black chairs, mustard-colored walls, and tiny halogen lamps hanging from the ceiling give this restaurant a minimalist urban chic that allows the outstanding creativity of chef Christopher Israel to take the fore. The menu at this ever-popular restaurant can only be categorized as Mediterranean, with old-style French and Italian predominating. However, Moroccan, Greek, Spanish, and even Asian influences creep in. Roast mahimahi with a herb salsa verde made from tarragon, parsley, thyme, oregano, capers, garlic, lemon, and olive oil was a recent entrée that captured all the fragrance of a Mediterranean herb garden in one dish. For dessert, a lemon tartlet rounded out the meal with its tangy citrus flavor.

MODERATE

Casa-U-Betcha

612 NW 21st Ave. ☎ **503/222-4833.** Reservations recommended. Main courses $8.50–$12.25. AE, MC, V. Daily 5–10pm. MEXICAN.

If you like your restaurant to be a work of art, slide into one of the colorful booths at this trendy nouvelle Mexican restaurant where garishly painted tables, strings of chile-pepper lights, and neo-industrial cacti create a real scene. We find the appetizers menu so fascinating that we usually just make a meal of a couple of these and skip the combo dinners and other Mexican entrées. Our favorite appetizer is the Mexican sushi made with tortillas, smoked salmon, black beans, guacamole, and wasabi. The ginger-jalapeño dipping sauce that comes with it is a real knockout. The bar serves about 20 different kinds of tequilas, and when it's crowded, the restaurant can get noisy.

There's another location at 1700 NE Broadway (☎ **503/282-4554**).

SOUTHEAST PORTLAND
EXPENSIVE

✪ Genoa

2832 SE Belmont St. ☎ **503/238-1464.** Reservations required. Fixed-price dinner $40 for four courses, $48 for seven courses. AE, CB, DC, DISC, MC, V. Mon–Sat 5:30–9:30pm (four-course dinner available 5:30–6pm only). NORTHERN ITALIAN.

Without a doubt, this is the best Italian restaurant in Portland, and with only 10 tables it's also one of the smallest. Everything is made fresh in the kitchen, from the breads to the luscious desserts temptingly displayed just inside the front door. The fixed-price menu changes every couple of weeks, but a typical dinner might start with bruschetta and a shellfish stew followed by a soup of creamy wild mushrooms. The pasta course might be fresh wide noodles in a spicy tomato sauce, followed by a salad of Belgian endive, roasted walnuts, and Gorgonzola. There's always a choice of main courses such as pork tenderloin marinated with gin, juniper berries, coriander, and rosemary and then grilled with pancetta bacon, chicken livers, and fresh sage, all served over polenta with a veal demi-glaze and flamed marsala. This is an ideal setting for a romantic dinner.

MODERATE

Bread & Ink Café

3610 SE Hawthorne St. ☎ **503/239-4756.** Reservations recommended. Main courses $5.25–$14.50; Sun brunch $11.50. AE, DISC, MC, V. Mon–Thurs 7am–10pm, Fri 7am–11pm, Sat 8am–noon and 5–11pm, Sun 9am–2pm (brunch) and 5–9pm. NORTHWEST.

This is a casual neighborhood café, bright and airy, with pen-and-ink artwork on the walls. Every meal here is carefully and imaginatively prepared using fresh Northwest ingredients. The last time we visited, we had an unusual appetizer—chicken liver pâté, seasoned with apples, sage, juniper berries, and dry vermouth. Desserts are a mainstay of Bread & Ink's loyal patrons, so don't pass them by. The Yiddish Sunday brunch is one of the most filling brunches in the city, as are the everyday breakfasts. Put your name on the waiting list on a small table at the front of the restaurant and you'll get seated sooner.

✪ Il Piatto

2348 SE Ankeny St. ☎ **503/236-4997.** Reservations highly recommended Thurs–Sat. Main courses $6.25–$8.50 at lunch, $7–$13 at dinner. MC, V. Mon 5:30–10pm, Tues–Thurs 11:30am–2:30pm and 5:30–10pm, Fri 11:30am–2:30pm and 5:30–11pm, Sat 5:30–11pm, Sun 9:30am–2:30pm (brunch) and 5:30–10pm. NORTHERN ITALIAN.

Il Piatto is a small neighborhood restaurant with a relaxed atmosphere; antiqued walls, dried flowers, and overstuffed chairs in the lounge area provide a comfortable place for sipping coffee or waiting for your table. For starters, crusty bread appears with oven-dried tomato pesto. We chose risotta de gamberi—arborio rice with sautéed prawns, mussels, and leeks, with a low-key taste of saffron that was intriguing. The marinated rabbit has also gotten rave reviews. Italian desserts such as tiramisù made with cornmeal cake are all made here in the kitchen by the pastry chef. Il Piatto is open throughout the day for coffee and pastry.

✪ Indigine

3725 SE Division St. ☎ **503/238-1470.** Reservations recommended on weekends. Main courses $10–$14; three-course dinner $16–$20; Sat-night Indian feast $26. MC, V. Tues–Sat 5:30–10pm, Sun 9am–2pm (brunch). INDIAN/INTERNATIONAL.

At Indigine you can delight your tastebuds with tantalizing flavors you may never have encountered before. The menu here is eclectic, with Indian, Mexican, French, and American offerings during the week and an extravagant Indian feast on Saturday evenings. During the week you can sample some of Indigine's flavorful Indian cuisine by ordering the vegetarian sampler. On the other hand the seafood enchilada perfectly mixes cheeses with shrimp and scallops so fresh you can almost smell the salt air. When the irresistible appetizer tray comes around, keep in mind that dinner portions are large enough for two people, and you'll want to be sure to save room for one of the luscious desserts such as ginger cheesecake.

✪ Santé

3000 SE Division St. ☎ **503/233-4340.** Reservations recommended. Main courses $11–$15. MC, V. Mon–Thurs 5–9pm, Fri 5–10pm, Sat 9am–3pm (brunch) and 5–10pm, Sun 9am–3pm (brunch) and 5–9pm. NORTHWEST/INTERNATIONAL.

Though cafés and casual eateries frequently show up in Portland grocery stores, this is the first upscale restaurant in a supermarket. Located in the Nature's Northwest natural-foods grocery, Santé serves highly imaginative Northwest and international dishes that are delicious, healthful, and often organically grown. Although there are plenty of vegetarian dishes on the menu, this is not specifically a vegetarian restaurant. The menu changes daily and on a recent evening included such appetizers as lentil cakes with mole sauce and pear salsa and such entrées as pan-roasted chicken with a maple-pecan sauce. On weekends Santé does a brisk brunch business serving the likes of teriyaki fish and eggs, organic buckwheat pancakes, and Jamaican jerk burgers.

✪ Westmoreland Bistro and Wines

7015 SE Milwaukee Ave. ☎ **503/236-6457.** Reservations highly recommended. Main courses $14–$16. MC, V. Tues–Sat 11am–4pm and 5–8:30pm. NORTHWEST.

Westmoreland Bistro and Wines is easy to miss. It's small, it's nondescript, and it's located in a neighborhood that, though attractive, is not one of the city's busiest. Caprial Pence, who helped put the Northwest on the national restaurant map, is the chef here, and even though this is a strong contender for best restaurant in Portland, it's a very casual place. The menu changes monthly and is limited to four or five main dishes and as many appetizers. About half the restaurant is given over to a superb selection of wine and a wine bar. Entrées combine perfectly cooked meats and fishes such as roast pork loin or lightly breaded oysters, with vibrant sauces such as cranberry-shallot compôte or sweet red-pepper pesto. Desserts, such as chocolate-almond-ricotta cake, are rich without being overly sweet.

INEXPENSIVE

Ⓢ Esparza's Tex-Mex Café

2725 SE Ankeny St. ☎ **503/234-7909.** Reservations not accepted. Main courses $5.25–$10.
MC, V. Tues–Sat 11:30am–10pm (in summer, Fri–Sat until 10:30pm). TEX-MEX.

With red-eyed cowskulls on the walls and marionettes, model planes, and stuffed iguanas and armadillos hanging from the ceiling, the decor here can only be described as Tex-clectic, an epithet that is equally appropriate when applied to the menu. Sure there are enchiladas and tamales and tacos, but they might be filled with buffalo, smoked salmon, or even calf brains. Rest assured, you can also get standard ingredients such as chicken and beef. Main courses come with some of the best rice and beans we've ever had. The nopalitos (fried cactus) are worth a try, and the margaritas just might be the best in Portland.

NORTHEAST PORTLAND
EXPENSIVE

L'Etoile

4627 NE Fremont St. ☎ **503/281-4869.** Reservations recommended. Main courses $17–$24. MC, V. Tues–Sat 5–9:30pm. FRENCH.

With its *fin de siècle* decor, intimate Parisian bar, and Edith Piaf on the stereo, L'Etoile is quintessentially French. The dishes here revel in the richness of classic French cuisine, from the crusty bread to the escargots (here simmered with garlic, tomatoes, walnuts, and bacon) to the roast quail with rosemary stuffing. Main courses might include venison with a chestnut, fennel, walnut, and onion compôte or duck breast with tangerines and cranberries. The dessert list includes plenty of rich chocolate desserts, but we're always tempted by the more unusual, such as a pumpkin tart with praline ice cream. There's a good selection of domestic and French wines, including plenty of dessert wines.

MODERATE

✪ Ron Paul Charcuterie

1441 NE Broadway. ☎ **503/284-5347.** Reservations not accepted. Main courses $5.75–$14.25; sandwiches $5.25–$7.75. AE, MC, V. Mon–Thurs 8am–10:30pm, Fri 8am–midnight, Sat 9am–midnight, Sun 9am–4pm. MEDITERRANEAN/DELI.

This is a casual deli-style place in an upwardly mobile neighborhood in northeast Portland. Light streams through the walls of glass illuminating long cases full of tempting pasta-and-vegetable salads, cheeses, quiches, pizzas, sandwich fixings, and, most tempting of all, decadent desserts. After 5pm there are specials, such as lamb in phyllo with goat cheese and mint or spring vegetable ravioli with asparagus, snow peas, and a red-pepper coulis. Both locations serve brunch on Saturday and Sunday, and have extensive selections of Northwest wines.

There's another location at 6141 SW Macadam Ave. (☎ **503/977-0313**).

CAFES & QUICK BITES

There are many cafés in the Portland area, and here's just a quick mention of several interesting ones. **The Pied Cow,** 3244 SE Belmont St. (☎ **503/230-4866**), is a café in a Victorian house opulently decorated in bohemian chic. **Torrefazione Italia,** 838 NW 23rd Ave. (☎ **503/228-2528**), is the classical

Northwest/Italian interpretation of a place to sip an espresso. The **Brazen Bean,** 2075 NW Glisan St. (☎ **503/294-0636**), is a café with a Victorian theme, open late nights.

The Merchant of Venice, 1432 NE Broadway (☎ **503/284-4558**), serves outstanding and very inexpensive pizza and sandwiches. For homemade soups, breads, and salads—and yummy berry pie sometimes—try the **Kitchen Table Café,** 400 SE 12th St. (☎ **503/230-6977**), which has a homey colorful setting. **Marsee Baking,** 1323 NW 23rd Ave. (☎ **503/295-4000**), supplies Portlanders with lovely cakes, tarts, panini (Italian sandwiches), and other baked wonders. For late-night noshing, there's **Garbanzos,** NW 21st Avenue and NW Lovejoy Street (☎ **503/227-4196**), for falafels and other Middle Eastern sandwiches, or you could try **Montage,** 301 SE Morrison St. (☎ **503/234-1324**), which serves Cajun food in an industrial-hip setting.

5 Attractions

THE TOP ATTRACTIONS

✪ Japanese Garden Society of Oregon

Off Kingston Ave. in Washington Park. ☎ **503/223-1321.** Admission $5 adults, $2.50 students and seniors, free for children 5 and under. Apr–May and Sept, daily 10am–6pm; June–Aug, daily 9am–8pm; Oct–Mar, daily 10am–4pm. Closed Jan 1, Thanksgiving, and Dec 25. Bus: 63.

What makes this garden so special is not only the design, plantings, and tranquility, but the view. From the Japanese-style wooden house in the center of the garden, you can, on a clear day, see over Portland to Mount Hood, a perfectly shaped volcanic peak reminiscent of Mount Fuji. It almost seems as if it were placed there just for the sake of this garden.

✪ International Rose Test Garden

400 SW Kingston Ave. in Washington Park. ☎ **503/823-3636.** Free admission. Daily dawn–dusk. Bus: 63.

Covering $4^{1}/_{2}$ acres of hillsides in the West Hills above downtown Portland, these are the largest and oldest rose test gardens in the United States. The gardens were established in 1917 by the American Rose Society, which itself was founded in Portland. You'll see here some familiar roses, new hybrids, a separate garden of miniature roses, and a Shakespearean Garden. After this, you'll certainly understand why Portland is known as the City of Roses and why the annual Rose Festival (held in June) is the biggest celebration of the year in Portland.

✪ Metro Washington Park Zoo

4001 SW Canyon Rd., in Washington Park. ☎ **503/226-1561.** Admission $5.50 adults, $4 seniors, $3.50 children 3–11, free for children 2 and under; free second Tues of each month 3pm–closing. Memorial Day–Labor Day, daily 9:30am–6pm; Labor Day–Memorial Day, daily 9:30am–4pm. Bus: 63.

This zoo has been successfully breeding elephants for many years and has the largest breeding herd in captivity. The African exhibit includes a simulated rain forest, and zebras, rhinos, giraffes, hippos, and other animals in one of the most lifelike habitats we've ever seen in a zoo. Equally impressive is the Alaskan-tundra exhibit, with grizzly bears, wolves, and musk oxen. For the younger set there's a children's petting zoo filled with farm animals. The Washington Park and Zoo Railway travels between the zoo and the International Rose Test Garden and

Japanese Gardens. In the summer there are concerts on Wednesday and Thursday night from 7 to 9pm.

Portland Saturday Market

Underneath the Burnside Bridge between SW First Ave. and SW Ankeny St. ☎ **503/222-6072**. Free admission. Mar–Christmas Eve, Sat 10am–5pm, Sun 11am–4:30pm. Bus: Any downtown bus. MAX: Skidmore Fountain Station.

The Saturday Market (which is held on both Saturday and Sunday) is arguably Portland's single most important and best-loved event. Every Saturday and Sunday nearly 300 artists and craftspeople sell their crafts and creations here. You'll also find flowers, fresh produce, ethnic and unusual foods, and lots of free entertainment. This is the single best place in Portland to shop for one-of-a-kind gifts. On Sunday, on-street parking is free.

Portland Art Museum

1219 SW Park Ave. ☎ **503/226-2811**. Admission $5 adults, $3.50 seniors, $2.50 children 6–18, free for children 5 and under; seniors free Thurs; free for everyone 4–9pm on the first Thurs of each month. Tues–Sat 11am–5pm, Sun 1–5pm (first Thurs of each month 11am–9pm). Any downtown bus. MAX: Library Station.

Although this small museum has a respectable collection of European, Asian, and American art, it's the Northwest coast Native American exhibit that requires a special visit. Particularly fascinating are the transformation masks. Worn during ritual dances, the masks are transformed from one face into a completely different visage by pulling several strings. A totem pole and many other woodcarvings show the amazing creative imagination of the Northwest tribes. There are also exhibits of regional contemporary art, Asian antiquities, primitive African art from Cameroon, and a large hall for temporary exhibits. On Wednesday nights (except in summer), the Museum After Hours program presents live music.

Oregon Museum of Science and Industry (OMSI)

1945 SE Water Ave. ☎ **503/797-4000** or 800/955-6674. Admission $7 adults, $6 seniors, $4.50 children 3–17; OMNIMAX, Sky Theater and light shows cost extra, although discounted combination tickets are available. Sat–Wed 9:30am–5:30pm (to 7pm in summer), Thurs–Fri 9:30am–9pm. Closed Dec 25. Bus: 63.

The impressive OMSI building on the east bank of the Willamette River has six huge halls, and kids and adults find the exhibits both fun and fascinating. Two of the most exciting exhibits allow visitors to touch a tornado or ride an earthquake.

❓ Did You Know?

- Measuring 24 inches in diameter, Mill Ends Park is the world's smallest dedicated park.
- The Portland Building was the first postmodern office building in the U.S.
- Portland is the only city in America with an extinct volcano within its city limits—Mount Tabor.
- Portland has been called the most polite city in the U.S.
- The statue of *Portlandia* in front of the Portland Building is the second-largest hammered bronze statue in the U.S., second only to the Statue of Liberty.
- Matt Groenig, creator of "The Simpsons," got his start in Portland.

Portland Attractions

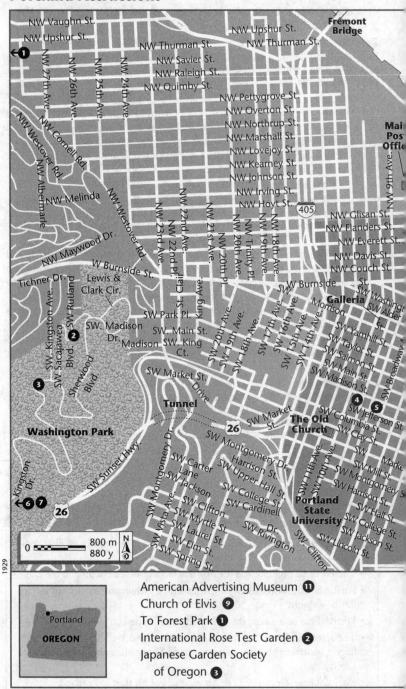

NW Vaughn St.
NW Upshur St.
NW Upshur St.
NW Thurman St.
NW Thurman St.
Fremont Bridge
NW Savier St.
NW Raleigh St.
NW Quimby St.
NW 27th Ave.
NW 26th Ave.
NW 25th Ave.
NW 24th Ave.
NW Pettygrove St.
NW Overton St.
NW Northrup St.
NW Cornell Rd.
NW Westover Rd.
NW Marshall St.
Main Post Office
NW 9th Ave.
NW Albermarle
NW Lovejoy St.
NW Kearney St.
NW Johnson St.
NW Irving St.
NW Melinda
NW Hoyt St.
405
NW Glisan St.
NW Flanders St.
NW Everett St.
NW Davis St.
NW Couch St.
NW Maywood Dr.
NW Westover Rd.
NW 22nd Ave.
NW 22nd Pl.
NW 23rd Ave.
NW 21st Ave.
NW 20th Pl.
NW 20th Ave.
NW 19th Ave.
NW Trinity Pl.
NW 18th Ave.
Tichner Dr.
W Burnside St.
Lewis & Clark Cir.
W Burnside
SW Washington
Galleria
SW Alder
SW Park Pl.
SW Kingston Ave.
SW Rutland
SW Sacajawea Blvd.
SW. Madison Dr.
Madison
SW. Main St.
SW. King Ct.
Clair St.
King Ave.
SW 20th Ave.
SW 19th Ave.
SW 18th Ave.
SW 17th Ave.
SW 16th Ave.
SW 15th Ave.
SW 14th Ave.
SW Morrison
SW Yamhill St.
SW Taylor St.
SW Salmon St.
SW Main St.
SW Madison St.
SW Broadway A
Sherwood Blvd.
SW Market St.
Washington Park
Kingston Dr.
Tunnel
26
SW Market Drive
SW Market St.
The Old Church
SW Columbia St.
SW Clay St.
SW Jefferson St.
SW
SW Mill St.
SW Market
SW Montgomery Dr.
SW Montgomery
SW Harrison St.
SW Hall St.
SW College St.
SW Jackson St.
SW Lincoln St.
SW Montgomery Dr.
Harrison St.
SW Upper Hall St.
SW Carter Lane
SW College St.
SW Cardinell
Portland State University
SW Sunset Hwy.
SW Montgomery Dr.
SW Jackson
SW Clifton
SW Myrtle St.
SW Laurel St.
SW Elm St.
SW Spring St.
SW Vista Ave.
SW Rivington Dr.
SW. Clifton
26
26

0 ____ 800 m
880 y
N

American Advertising Museum ⑪
Church of Elvis ⑨
To Forest Park ①
International Rose Test Garden ②
Japanese Garden Society
of Oregon ③

Portland
OREGON

1929

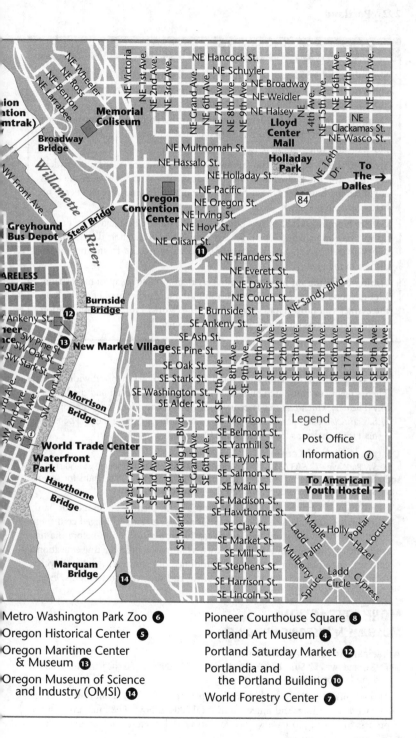

NE Wheeler
NE Ross
NE Benton
NE Larrabee

NE Victoria
NE 1st Ave.
NE 2nd Ave.
NE 3rd Ave.

NE Hancock St.
NE Schuyler
NE Broadway
NE Weidler
NE Halsey

NE Grand Ave.
NE 6th Ave.
NE 7th Ave.
NE 8th Ave.
NE 9th Ave.

NE 16th Ave.
NE 17th Ave.
NE 19th Ave.

NE 14th Ave.
NE 15th Ave.

ion
ation
mtrak)

Memorial Coliseum

Broadway Bridge

NW Front Ave.

Lloyd Center Mall

NE Clackamas St.
NE Wasco St.

NE Multnomah St.
NE Hassalo St.
NE Holladay St.

Holladay Park

NE 16th Dr.

To The Dalles →

Willamette

Steel Bridge

Oregon Convention Center

NE Pacific
NE Oregon St.
NE Irving St.
NE Hoyt St.

(84)

Greyhound Bus Depot

River

NE Glisan St.

11

NE Flanders St.
NE Everett St.
NE Davis St.
NE Couch St.

NE Sandy Blvd.

ARELESS
QUARE

Burnside Bridge

E Burnside St.
SE Ankeny St.
SE Ash St.

Ankeny St. **12**
SW Pine St
ace
SW Oak St.
SW Stark St.

13 **New Market Village**

SE Pine St

SE Oak St.
SE Stark St.
SE Washington St.
SE Alder St.

SE 7th Ave.
SE 8th Ave.
SE 9th Ave.
SE 10th Ave.
SE 11th Ave.
SE 12th Ave.
SE 13th Ave.
SE 14th Ave.
SE 15th Ave.
SE 16th Ave.
SE 17th Ave.
SE 18th Ave.
SE 19th Ave.
SE 20th Ave.

rd Ave.
SW 2nd Ave.
SW 1st Ave.

Morrison Bridge

SE Morrison St.
SE Belmont St.
SE Yamhill St.
SE Taylor St.
SE Salmon St.
SE Main St.
SE Madison St.
SE Hawthorne St.

Legend

Post Office
Information *(i)*

(i)

World Trade Center
Waterfront Park

Hawthorne Bridge

SE Water Ave.
SE 1st Ave.
SE 2nd Ave.
SE 3rd Ave.
SE Martin Luther King Jr. Blvd.
SE Grand Ave.
SE 6th Ave.

To American Youth Hostel →

SE Clay St.
SE Market St.
SE Mill St.
SE Stephens St.
SE Harrison St.
SE Lincoln St.

Marquam Bridge

14

Maple Holly Poplar
Ladd Palm Hazel Locust
Mulberry Spruce Ladd Circle Cypress

Metro Washington Park Zoo **6**
Oregon Historical Center **5**
Oregon Maritime Center & Museum **13**
Oregon Museum of Science and Industry (OMSI) **14**

Pioneer Courthouse Square **8**
Portland Art Museum **4**
Portland Saturday Market **12**
Portlandia and the Portland Building **10**
World Forestry Center **7**

Frommer's Favorite Portland Experiences

Shopping and Food Sampling at the Saturday Market. This large arts-and-crafts market is an outdoor showcase of the best of the Northwest's creative artisans. Food stalls sell delicious and unusual meals.

Quaffing a Brew at the Mission Theater. At this combination movie theater and brewpub you can taste Portland's best beers while watching recently released movies—and you don't have to pay to see the film.

Strolling the Grounds of the Japanese Garden. Portland's Japanese Gardens are the best in the United States. They're at their peak in June when the irises are in bloom, but they're beautiful and tranquil at any time of year. There's no better place in the city to relax.

Gallery Hopping. On the first Thursday of every month, Portlanders get dressed up and visit art galleries. Openings can include live music, hors d'oeuvres, and wine, as well as art. Special shuttle buses carry people from one gallery district to the next.

Hiking & Skiing on Mount Hood. Less than an hour away from Portland, Mount Hood offers year-round skiing and hiking. Timberline Lodge, high on the extinct volcano's slopes, was built by the Works Project Administration during the Depression; it's a testament to craftsmanship.

This is a hands-on museum and everyone is urged to get involved with displays. There's plenty of pure entertainment at an OMNIMAX theater and the Murdock Sky Theater, which features laser-light shows and astronomy presentations. The U.S.S. *Blueback* submarine is docked here and tours are given daily. There's also a small train that runs from here to the Oaks Park amusement park.

Oregon Historical Center

1200 SW Park Ave. ☎ **503/222-1741.** Admission $4.50 adults and seniors, $1.50 students and children 5–18, free for members and children 4 and under; free Thurs for seniors. Mon–Sat 10am–5pm, Sun noon–5pm. Any downtown bus. MAX: Library Station.

The Oregon Territory was a land of promise and plenty. Thousands of hardy individuals set out along the Oregon Trail to cross a vast and rugged country to reach the fertile valleys of Oregon's rivers. Oregon history from before the first white men arrived to well into this century is chronicled in fascinating educational exhibits, incorporating parts of old buildings, old snow skis, dolls, bicycles, fashions, Native American artifacts, nautical and surveying instruments, even a covered wagon.

MORE ATTRACTIONS
MUSEUMS & HISTORIC BUILDINGS

American Advertising Museum

524 NE Grand Ave. ☎ **503/226-0000.** Admission $3 adults, $1.50 children 11 and under. Wed–Sun 11am–5pm. Bus: 6.

At this unusual museum you'll learn (and perhaps reminisce) about historic advertisements, celebrities, and jingles from the 1700s to now. The museum is in the process of moving to its new location on Grand Avenue, and should have its permanent collection in place sometime in 1996. Until then, traveling exhibits will be showcased and hours of operation may be irregular, so call before you visit.

Pittock Mansion

3229 NW Pittock Dr. ☎ **503/823-3624.** Admission $4 adults, $3.50 seniors, $1.50 children 6–18. Daily noon–4pm. Closed the first three weeks of Jan, three days in late Nov, and most major holidays. Bus: 20 to Burnside and Barnes, then a half-mile walk.

Once slated to be torn down to make way for new housing, this grand château overlooking the city has been fully restored and furnished with 18th- and 19th-century antiques, much as it might have been when it was built in 1914. Designed in a French Renaissance style, the mansion featured many innovations when it was built, including multiple showerheads in the baths. Lunch and afternoon tea are available in the Gate Lodge (☎ **503/823-3627**), and reservations are recommended.

Where's the Art?/The Church of Elvis

720 SW Ankeny St. ☎ **503/226-3671.** Admission by donation. Irregular hours; call. Any downtown bus.

This is Portland's most bizarre attraction: a video psychic and the church of Elvis. The "museum" is full of kitschy contraptions bearing the visage of the King and other pop culture characters. Care to have Elvis hear your confession? No problem. Great fun if you're a fan of Elvis, tabloids, or the unusual.

World Forestry Center

4033 SW Canyon Rd. ☎ **503/228-1367.** Admission $3 adults, $2 seniors and children 6–18, free for children 5 and under; free for everyone the second Sun of the month. Summer, daily 9am–5pm; winter, daily 10am–5pm. Closed Dec 25. Bus: 63.

This center serves as an educational facility teaching visitors about the importance of our forest resources. Here you'll find exhibits on forests of the world and old-growth trees. In the summer there's a vintage carousel on the grounds.

Oregon Maritime Center & Museum

113 SW Front Ave. ☎ **503/224-7724.** Admission $4 adults, $3 seniors, $2 students, free for children 7 and under. Summer, Wed–Sun 11am–4pm; winter, Fri–Sun 11am–4pm. Any downtown bus. MAX: Skidmore Fountain Station.

On display here, you'll find models of ships that once plied the Columbia and Willamette rivers, early navigation instruments, and maritime memorabilia. The historic stern-wheeler *Portland,* moored across Waterfront Park from the museum, is also open to the public.

OUTDOOR ART/PLAZAS/ARCHITECTURAL HIGHLIGHTS

Pioneer Courthouse Square, which is bounded by Broadway, Sixth Avenue, Yamhill Street, and Morrison Street, is the heart of downtown Portland and acts as an outdoor stage for everything from flower displays to protest rallies. However, not too many years ago this beautiful brick-paved square was nothing but a parking lot. The parking lot itself had been created by the controversial razing in 1951 of what had been the most elegant hotel in the city. Today the square, with its tumbling waterfall fountain and free-standing columns, is Portland's favorite gathering spot—especially at noon when the "Weather Machine," a mechanical sculpture, predicts the weather for the upcoming 24 hours. Keep your eyes on the square's brick pavement for some surprising names.

A few blocks away at 1120 SW Fifth Ave. stands ***Portlandia,*** which is the symbol of the city. This hammered bronze statue is reminiscent of a Greek goddess, and is the second-largest such statue in the country (the largest is the

The City of Books

Though Seattle claims the largest library system in the country, Portland has **Powell's "City of Books,"** 1005 W. Burnside St. (☎ **503/228-4651**), the bookstore to end all bookstores. Covering an entire city block three floors deep, Powell's sells more than three million volumes each year. Though there are arguments over whether the "City of Books" is the biggest bookstore in the country, most people agree that Powell's has more titles on its shelves than any other bookstore in the United States. Suffice it to say, there's no denying that Powell's is a contender for the bragging rights of being the biggest bookstore in the country.

Powell's has its origins in two used-book stores, one in Chicago and one in Portland, both of which opened in the early 1970s. The Chicago store was opened by current store owner Michael Powell, while the Portland store was opened by Walter Powell, Michael's father. In 1979 Michael joined his father in Portland and together they began building the store into what it is today.

The "City of Books" shelves all its books, new and used, hardback or paperback, together. With roughly three-quarters of a million new and used books on the shelves at any given time, the store had to give up trying to keep a computer inventory of what's in stock. This can be extremely frustrating if you're looking for an old or out-of-print title, but the staff is good about searching the shelves for you, and if they don't have what you're looking for, they can try tracking down a copy. The upside of not being able to go straight to the book you're looking for is that you end up browsing.

Browsing is what Powell's is really all about. Before you even get through the front door, you can browse the display of bizarre book titles in the front window—titles such as *What Sign Is Your Pet?*, *Euclid's Outline of Sex*, *Moby Dick: A Hindu Avatar*, *The Mysterious You*, and *It's a Gas: A Study of Flatulence* reflect the store's literary sense of humor.

Once inside you can pick up a store map that will direct you to color-coded rooms containing different collections of books. In the Gold Room, you'll find

---

Statue of Liberty). This classically designed figure perches above the entrance to the Portland Building, considered the first postmodern structure in the country.

PARKS

Crystal Springs Rhododendron Garden

SE 28th Ave. ☎ **503/777-1734**. Admission Mar 1–Labor Day, Thurs–Mon from 10am–6pm, $2 free other months, days, and hours). Daily dawn–dusk. Bus: 19.

Eight months out of the year this is a tranquil garden, with a waterfall and ducks to feed. But when the rhododendrons and azaleas bloom from March to June, it becomes a spectacular mass of blazing color. The Rhododendron Show and Plant Sale is held here on Mother's Day weekend.

Forest Park

Bounded by W. Burnside St., Newberry Rd., St. Helens Rd., and Skyline Rd. ☎ **503/823-4492**. Free admission. Daily dawn–dusk. Bus: 15, 17, 20, or 63.

With 4,800 acres of wilderness, this is the largest forested city park in the United States. There are 50 miles of trails and old fire roads for hiking and jogging. More than 100 species of birds call these forests home, making this a birdwatchers' paradise.

science fiction and children's books; in the Rose Room, you'll find books on ornithology, civil aviation, Christian theology, and metaphysics among other subjects; in the Orange Room, there are books on art history, antiques, film, drama, and music. Serious book collectors won't want to miss a visit to the Rare Book Room, where you could—if you wished—buy a copy of a copy of the writings of Cicero published by the Aldine Press in 1570. The most expensive book ever sold here was a Fourth Folio Shakespeare with archival repairs for $6,000.

It's so easy to forget the time while browsing at Powell's that many customers miss meals and end up in the store's in-house café. The Anne Hughes Coffee Room serves espresso and pastries and is always packed with folks perusing books they've pulled from the shelves. This is also where Powell's keeps its extensive magazine rack. So don't fret if you forgot to pack a lunch for your Powell's outing.

But wait, did we hear you say, "This store isn't so big"? We guess we forgot to mention that the "City of Books" outgrew this space and had to open a few satellite stores. There's **Powell's Technical Bookstore,** 33 NW Park St. (☎ 503/228-3906); **Powell's Books for Cooks,** 3739 SE Hawthorne Blvd. (☎ 503/235-3802); **Powell's Travel Store,** Pioneer Courthouse Square, SW Sixth Avenue and Yamhill Street (☎ 503/228-1108); **Powell's Books for Kids,** Cascade Plaza, 8775 SW Cascade Ave., Beaverton (☎ 503/671-0671); **Powell's Books for Health,** at Emanuel Hospital, 501 N. Graham St. (☎ 503/280-3988); **Powell's at PDX,** Portland International Airport (☎ 503/249-1950); and a couple of others.

One warning: Before stepping through Powell's door, check your watch. If you haven't got at least an hour of free time, you enter at your own risk. Getting lost in the miles of aisles at Powell's has caused many a bibliophile to miss an appointment. Be prepared!

A SPECIAL RIDE FOR THE TRAIN & TROLLEY BUFF

Willamette Shore Trolley
311 N. State St., Lake Oswego. ☎ **503/222-2226.** Round-trip $5 adults, $3 children 11 and under. Mar–Dec, Fri–Sun and hols.

A fully restored trolley dating from the early part of this century operates on a 7-mile line connecting Portland with the prestigious suburb of Lake Oswego. The trip takes 45 minutes each way. It's especially fun at Christmastime when there are lots of holiday lights to see—but make reservations.

ESPECIALLY FOR KIDS

The **Oregon Museum of Science and Industry** is primarily geared for kids, with lots of hands-on exhibits, including a NASA training room, a full computer lab, a chicken hatchery, and laser shows in its planetarium (see "The Top Attractions," above). At the **World Forestry Center** there's a carousel operating during the summer months (see "More Attractions," above). The **Metro Washington Park Zoo** is particularly known for its elephant-breeding program. From inside the zoo, it's possible to take a small train through Washington Park to the Rose Gardens (see "The Top Atttractions," above).

In addition to these, there are a couple of other attractions in Portland geared to kids.

Portland Children's Museum

3037 SW Second Ave. ☎ **503/823-2227**. Admission $3.50 adults and children; free for infants under 1. Daily 9am–5pm. Closed some national holidays. Bus: 1, 12, 40, 41, 43, or 45.

Visitors can shop in a kid-size grocery store, play waiter or diner in a restaurant, or pretend to be a doctor in a medical center. Clayshop is usually open for families who want to build with clay. In "H2 Oh!" kids can blow giant bubbles and pump water. The Children's Cultural Center presents a child's view of such environments as an African or Native American village complete with artifacts and hands-on activities. There's plenty to entertain kids at this big little museum.

Oaks Park

At the east end of Sellwood Bridge. ☎ **503/233-5777**. Free admission; all activities are on individual tickets. Mar–June 18, Sat–Sun noon–5pm; June 19–Labor Day, Tues–Thurs noon–9pm, Fri–Sat noon–10pm, Sun noon–7pm. Closed mid-Oct–Mar.

What would summer be like without the screams of happy thrillseekers risking their lives on a roller coaster? Beneath the shady oaks for which this amusement park is named, you'll find plenty of wild rides, waterfront picnic sites, miniature golf, music, and the largest roller-skating rink in the Northwest.

6 Organized Tours

BUS TOURS   Gray Line (☎ 503/285-9834) offers several half-day and full-day city sightseeing tours. But the trip we most recommend is the full-day Mount Hood loop—if you aren't doing the driving, you can enjoy the scenery more. Other tours offered are an excursion to the Columbia Gorge that includes a ride on a stern-wheeler, and a northern Oregon coast tour. Tour prices run $18 to $38 for adults, $9 to $19 for children.

BOAT TOURS   A trip up the Columbia River, with its towering cliffs, is a spectacular and memorable excursion. The **Columbia Gorge Stern-Wheeler** (☎ 503/223-3928) cruises the Columbia River between mid-June and mid-October and the Willamette River between October and mid-June. It includes stops at the Cascade Locks and Bonneville Dam. Call for information on lunch, dinner, and dance cruises. Prices for a two-hour cruise are $11.95 for adults and $5.95 for children; on other tours, prices vary.

Rose City Riverboat Cruises (☎ 503/234-6665) offers modern catamaran power yacht cruises on the Willamette River between mid-April and October. Dinner, moonlight, Sunday brunch, Portland Harbor, and historical river tours are also available. Tickets cost $9 to $27 for adults, less for children and seniors.

OTHER TOURS   The **John Palmer House** (☎ 503/284-5893), a restored Victorian bed-and-breakfast, offers horse-drawn carriage tours. Rides cost $65 for up to four people.

If you'd like to learn more about downtown Portland and the city's history, contact **Apple Tours** (☎ 503/638-4076 or 800/939-6326) for a walking tour of the area. Tour prices are $15 for adults, $13 for seniors, and $5 for children.

Ecotours of Oregon, 1906 SW Iowa St. (☎ 503/245-1428), offers tours to the Columbia River Gorge, Mount Hood, Mount St. Helens, the Oregon coast, ancient forests, and places to whale-watch or experience Native American culture, at a cost of $45 to $60 per person.

For an in-depth winery tour of the Willamette Valley, call **Grape Escape** (☎ **503/282-4262**). An all-day tour includes three wineries, an elegant picnic lunch, and pickup and drop-off at your hotel for $60 per person.

For dinner during a picturesque train ride, contact the *Spirit of Oregon Dinner Train* (☎ **503/324-1919**). The train ride, which begins 25 miles west of Portland, takes passengers up to the summit of the Coast Range. Two separate 4$1/2$-hour rides are available, one for dinner ($75) and one for Sunday brunch ($60).

If you'd like to explore this part of the Northwest's great outdoors, **The Wild Side** (☎ **503/354-3112**) offers mountain-biking trips, as well as fishing, hiking, and cross-country skiing trips, priced at $45 to $125.

7 Outdoor Activities

BEACHES   There are a couple of freshwater beaches on the **Columbia River** within 45 minutes of Portland. **Rooster Rock State Park,** just off I-84 east of Portland, includes several miles of sandy beach, as does **Sauvie Island,** off Oregon 30 northwest of Portland. You'll need to obtain a parking permit for Sauvie Island; it's available at the convenience store located just after you cross the bridge onto the island. Both beaches include sections that are clothing optional.

BIKING   You'll notice many bicyclists on Portland streets. If you want to get rolling with everyone else, head over to **Fat Tire Farm,** 2714 NW Thurman St. (☎ **503/222-3276**), to rent a mountain bike for $30 a day. In nearby **Forest Park,** the Leif Erikson trail is a stretch of road that goes on for miles and is popular with bicyclists and runners.

At **Agape Cycle & Fitness,** 2314 SE Division St. (☎ **503/230-0317**), you can rent road or mountain bikes for about $20 per day. Once you have your bike you can head for **Waterfront Park,** where there's a 2-mile bike path. The **Terwilliger Path** starts at the south end of Portland State University and travels for 10 miles up into the hills to Tryon Creek State Park, with great views up at the top. Stop by a bike shop to pick up a copy of the "Getting There" map.

GOLF   There are plenty of public courses around the area, and greens fees for nonresidents are only $19 for 18 holes on a weekday and $21 on weekends and holidays. Public golf courses operated by the Portland Bureau of Parks and Recreation include **Eastmoreland Golf Course,** 2425 SE Bybee Blvd. (☎ **503/775-2900**); **Heron Lakes Golf Course,** 3500 N. Victory Blvd. (☎ **503/ 289-1818**); **Rose City Golf Course,** 2200 NE 71st Ave. (☎ **503/253-4744**); and **Double Eagle Golf Center,** Progress Downs Golf Course, 8200 SW Scholls Ferry Rd., Beaverton (☎ **503/646-5166**).

HIKING   The hiking opportunities in the Portland area are almost unlimited. For short hikes you don't even have to leave the city. Bordered by West Burnside Street on the south, Newberry Road on the north, St. Helens Road on the east, and Skyline Road on the west, **Forest Park** is the largest forested city park in the country. You'll find more than 50 miles of trails through this urban wilderness.

ICE-SKATING   The **Lloyd Center Ice Pavilion** at the Lloyd Center mall (☎ **503/288-6073**) has skate rentals and a fairly good skating surface.

IN-LINE SKATING   **Waterfront Park** is a popular and fairly level place for skating. In-line skates can be rented at the nearby **Sports Works,** 421 SW Second Ave. (☎ **503/227-5323**), for about $20 a day, which includes all safety gear.

SEA KAYAKING   You can rent a sea kayak at **Ebb & Flow Paddlesports,** 0604 SW Nebraska St. (☎ **503/245-1756**), and cart it a couple of blocks to where you can paddle on the Willamette River. Rental for a double is $26 for half a day.

SKIING   Portland has several ski resorts, all within about an hour's drive, on the slopes of Mount Hood. One of them even boasts skiing all summer. **Timberline Ski Area** (☎ **503/231-7979** in Portland, 503/272-3311 outside Portland, or 503/222-2211 for a snow report) is the highest ski area on Mount Hood and has one slope that's open all the way through summer. This is the site of the historic Timberline Lodge, which was built during the Depression by the WPA. Adult lift-ticket prices range from $10 for night skiing to $28 for a weekend all-day pass. Call for hours of operation. **Mount Hood Meadows** (☎ **503/337-2222**, or 503/227-7669 for a snow report) is the largest ski resort on Mount Hood, with more than 2,000 skiable acres, 2,777 vertical feet, and a wide variety of terrains. Lift-ticket prices range from $14 for night skiing to $37 for a weekend all-day pass. Call for hours of operation. **Mt. Hood SkiBowl** (☎ **503/272-3206**, or 503/222-2695 for a snow report) is the closest ski area to Portland and, with 1,500 vertical feet, has more expert slopes than any other ski area on the mountain. SkiBowl also claims to be the largest lighted ski area in the United States. Adult lift-ticket prices range from $13 for midweek night skiing to $28 for a weekend all-day pass. Call for hours of operation.

There are also plenty of **cross-country ski trails** in the area. You can rent equipment in Sandy or Government Camp (two towns that lie along Ore. 26 east of the city) and find out about the best cross-country trails for your skill level. Before heading out cross-country skiing, be sure you pick up a Sno-Park permit. These cost $3 for one day and are available at convenience stores and ski shops in Sandy and Government Camp.

TENNIS   Portland Parks and Recreation operates more than 120 tennis courts, both indoor and out, all over the city. Outdoor courts are generally free and available on a first-come, first-served basis. Our personal favorites are those in **Washington Park** just behind the Rose Garden. Some of these courts can be reserved by contacting the **Portland Tennis Center,** 324 NE 12th Ave. (☎ **503/823-3189**); rates are $2 per hour. If the weather isn't cooperating, head for the Portland Tennis Center, which has indoor courts and charges $11 to $12.50 per person per hour for singles matches and $15 to $17 per person per hour for doubles.

WHITE-WATER RAFTING   The Cascade Mountains produce some of the best white-water rafting in the country and the **Deschutes River, White Salmon River,** and **Clackamas River** offer plenty of opportunities to shoot the rapids from early spring to early fall. **River Drifters,** 13570 NW Lakeview Dr. (☎ **503/645-6264**, or 800/972-0430), leads trips on these rivers for $65 (with lunch included). **Carrol White-Water Rafting,** in Maupin, OR (☎ **503/395-2404**), and **Ewings' Whitewater,** in Maupin, OR (☎ **800/538-7238**), offer similar trips on the Deschutes and other rivers. A four-hour trip costs $75 and includes a barbecue lunch. Longer trips are also possible.

8 Spectator Sports

Tickets for certain of the sporting events listed below can be purchased through **GI Joe's/Ticketmaster** (☎ **503/224-4400**).

AUTO RACING   **Portland International Raceway,** 1940 N. Victory Blvd. (☎ **503/285-6635**), operated by Portland Parks and Recreation, is the site of various types of car races. February to October are the busiest months here. Admission is $5.50 to $75.

BASEBALL   The **Portland Rockies Baseball Club** plays AAA baseball at the Civic Stadium, at Southwest 20th Avenue and Morrison Street (☎ **503/223-2837**). Box office hours are Monday through Friday from 9am to 5pm and from 9am the day of the game. Admission is $5 to $6 for adults and $4 for children 14 and under.

BASKETBALL   The **Portland Trail Blazers,** one of the hottest NBA teams in recent years, pound the boards at the Rose Garden, at the Broadway exit off I-5 (☎ **503/231-8000**), between fall and spring. Call for current schedule and ticket information. Tickets run from about $15 to about $70.

GREYHOUND RACING   The race season at the **Multnomah Greyhound Track,** Northeast 223rd Avenue in Wood Village (☎ **503/667-7700**), runs from April to September. Post time is at 7:30pm Wednesday through Saturday, with Saturday and Sunday matinees at 1pm. In July and August there are also Tuesday-night races. Admission is $1 to $3.50.

HORSE RACING   At **Portland Meadows,** 1001 N. Schmeer Rd. (☎ **503/285-9144**), the race season runs from October to April, with post time at 6pm on Friday and 12:30pm on Saturday and Sunday. Admission is $2 to $3.

ICE HOCKEY   The **Portland Winter Hawks,** a junior-league hockey team, carves up the ice at Memorial Coliseum, 1401 N. Wheeler St. (☎ **503/238-6366**), from October to March. Call for schedule and ticket information. Admission is $8.75 to $12.75.

MARATHONS   The **Portland Marathon** is held sometime in late September or early October. For further information, call 503/226-1111.

9 Shopping

Perhaps the single most important fact about shopping in Portland, and all of Oregon for that matter, is that there's **no sales tax.** The price on the tag is the price you pay. If you come from a state with a high sales tax, you might want to save your shopping for your visit to Portland.

THE SHOPPING SCENE

Over the past few years Portland has managed to preserve and restore a good deal of its historic architecture, and many of these late 19th-century and early 20th-century buildings have been turned into unusual and attractive shopping centers. **New Market Village** (50 SW Second Ave.), **Morgan's Alley** (515 SW Broadway), and **Skidmore Fountain Square** (28 SW First Ave.) are all examples of how Portland has preserved its historic buildings and kept its downtown area filled with happy shoppers.

Portland's most happening **shopping areas,** along with downtown Portland, are the Northwest neighborhood along Northwest 23rd Avenue, beginning at West Burnside Street; Northeast Broadway around Northeast 15th Avenue; and Southeast Hawthorne Street around Southeast 32nd Avenue. In these neighborhoods you'll find antiques stores, boutiques, card shops, design studios, ethnic restaurants, florists, galleries, home-furnishings stores, interior decorators, pubs, and all the other necessities of bohemian neighborhoods gone upscale.

SHOPPING A TO Z
ANTIQUES

Old Sellwood Antique Row, at the east end of Sellwood Bridge on Southeast 13th Street, with its old Victorian homes and turn-of-the-century architecture, is Portland's main antiques district. You'll find 13 blocks with more than 30 antiques dealers and restaurants.

ART GALLERIES

If you're in the market for art, try to arrange your visit to coincide with the first Thursday of a month. On these days, galleries in downtown Portland schedule coordinated gallery openings in the evenings. As an added bonus, the **Portland Art Museum,** 1219 SW Park Ave. (☎ **503/226-2811**), offers free admission from 4pm on these nights.

An art-gallery guide listing more than 50 Portland galleries is available at the **Portland Oregon Visitors Association,** Two World Trade Center, 25 SW Salmon St.(tel. **503/222-2223**, or 800/345-3214).

Gango Gallery
205 SW First Ave. ☎ **503/222-3850.**

Gango offers a juried selection from over 50 contemporary regional and national artists, both established and emerging, in a variety of media.

The Laura Russo Gallery
805 NW 21st Ave. ☎ **503/226-2754.**

The focus here is on Northwest contemporary artists. Young emerging artists as well as the estates of well-known artists are showcased.

Quartersaw Gallery
528 NW 12th Ave. ☎ **503/223-2264.**

With an emphasis on figurative and expressionistic landscape, Quartersaw is a showcase for progressive Northwest art.

✪ Quintana Galleries–Old Town
139 NW Second Ave. ☎ **503/223-1729.**

Virtually a small museum of Native American arts, this store sells everything from pottery and masks to contemporary paintings and sculpture. The jewelry selection is outstanding. Northwest coast Native American and Eskimo art offerings can be found at their second gallery, at 818 SW First Ave. (☎ **503/223-4202**).

BOOKS

✪ Powell's "City of Books"
1005 W. Burnside St. ☎ **503/228-4651** or 800/878-7323.

This is one of the largest bookstores on the West Coast selling new and used books. You'll find nearly a million books in this massive store. The store is open Monday through Saturday from 9am to 11pm and on Sunday from 9am to 9pm.

If you're looking for a technical book, try **Powell's Technical Books,** 33 NW Park St. (☎ **503/228-3906**), a block away.

Powell's Travel Store

701 SW Sixth Ave. ☎ **503/228-1108.**

Located beneath Pioneer Courthouse Square at the corner of Southwest Sixth Avenue and Yamhill Street, this travel bookstore has plenty of books and maps on Portland, the Northwest, and every other part of the world.

CRAFTS

For the largest selection of local crafts, visit the **Saturday Market** (see "The Top Attractions" under "Attractions," earlier in this chapter, for complete details).

Contemporary Crafts Gallery

3934 SW Corbett Ave. ☎ **503/223-2654.**

In business since 1937, this is the nation's oldest nonprofit art gallery showing exclusively artwork in clay, glass, fiber, metal, and wood. The majority of the gallery is taken up by glass and ceramic pieces, with several cabinets full of designer jewelry.

Hoffman Gallery

8245 SW Barnes Rd. ☎ **503/297-5544.**

The Hoffman Gallery is located on the campus of the Oregon School of Arts and Crafts, which has been one of the nation's foremost crafts education centers since 1906. The gallery's gift shop has an outstanding selection of handcrafted items.

✪ The Real Mother Goose

901 SW Yamhill St. ☎ **503/223-9510**.

This store showcases only the very finest contemporary American crafts, including imaginative ceramics, colorful art glass, intricate jewelry, exquisite wooden furniture, handmade fashions, and sculptural works. Other locations include Washington Square, Tigard (☎ **503/620-2243**), and the Portland Airport, Main Terminal (☎ **503/284-9929**).

DEPARTMENT STORES

Meier & Frank

621 SW Fifth Ave. ☎ **503/223-0512.**

Meier & Frank has been doing business here for more than 100 years. The store is open daily, with Friday usually the late night. Other locations include 1100 Lloyd Center (☎ **503/281-4797**) and 9300 SW Washington Square Rd. in Tigard (☎ **503/620-3311**).

Nordstrom

701 SW Broadway. ☎ **503/224-6666.**

Directly across the street from Pioneer Courthouse Square, Nordstrom is a top-of-the-line department store that originated in the Northwest and takes great pride in its personal service and friendliness.

FASHION

Nike Town
930 SW Sixth Ave. ☎ **503/221-6453.**

This super-glitzy showcase for Nike products sports George Segal–style plaster statues of athletes, videos, and jerseys and running shoes worn by sports personalities. A true shopping experience.

Norm Thompson
327 SW Morrison St. ☎ **503/243-2680.**

Known throughout the rest of the country from its mail-order catalogs featuring classic outdoor clothing, Norm Thompson is a mainstay of the well-to-do in Portland. A second store is at the Portland International Airport (☎ **503/249-0170**).

The Portland Pendleton Shop
SW Fifth Ave. (between Salmon and Taylor sts.). ☎ **503/242-0037.**

This company's fine wool fashions for men and women define the country-club look in the Northwest and in many other parts of the country. Pleated skirts and tweed jackets are *de rigueur*, as are colorful wool blankets.

Men's

Mario's
In the Galleria, 921 SW Morrison St. ☎ **503/227-3477.**

Located inside the Galleria, Mario's sells stylish European men's fashions straight off the pages of *GQ* and *M*. If you long to be European but your birth certificate says otherwise, here you can at least adopt the look.

Women's

Byrkit
2006 NE Broadway. ☎ **503/282-3773.**

Byrkit specializes in natural fabric clothing of cotton, silk, rayon, and linen for women. The contemporary designs, including dresses, jumpers, and separates, are built for comfort but include a lot of style.

Changes
927 SW Yamhill St. ☎ **503/223-3737.**

Located next door to the Real Mother Goose gallery, this shop specializes in handmade clothing, including hand-woven scarves, jackets, and shawls, hand-painted silks, and other wearable art.

✪ The Eye of Ra
5331 SW Macadam Ave. ☎ **503/224-4292.**

Women with sophisticated tastes in ethnic fashions will want to visit this shop in the Water Tower at John's Landing shopping center. Silks and rayons predominate and there's plenty of ethnic jewelry to accompany any ensemble. Ethnic furniture and home decor are also for sale.

Mario's for Women
811 SW Morrison St. ☎ **503/241-8111.**

Flip through the pages of a European edition of *Vogue* magazine and you'll get an idea of the fashions you can find at the women's version of fashionable Mario's.

GIFTS/SOUVENIRS

For unique handmade souvenirs of your trip to Portland, your best bet is the **Saturday Market** (see "The Top Attractions" under "Attractions," earlier in this chapter, for complete details).

Made in Oregon
In the Galleria, 921 SW Morrison St. ☎ **503/241-3630** or 800/828-9673.

Your one-stop shop for all manner of made-in-Oregon gifts, food products, and clothing, this is the place to visit for salmon, filberts, jams and jellies, Pendleton woolens, and Oregon wines. If you forgot to pick up a salmon or any of their other popular products while you were in town, give them a call on their toll-free number.

Other Portland area branches can be found in the Portland Airport's Main Terminal (☎ 503/282-7827); in Lloyd Center at Southeast Multnomah Street and Southeast Broadway (☎ 503/282-7636); at Clackamas Town Center, 12000 SE 82nd Ave. (☎ 503/659-3155); in Old Town at 10 NW First Ave. (☎ 503/273-8354), and at Washington Square, off Ore. 217, in Tigard (☎ 503/620-4670). All branches are open daily, though hours vary from store to store.

JEWELRY

✪ Twist
30 NW 23rd Place. ☎ **503/224-0334.**

Twist showcases handmade jewelry from artists around the United States, from Thomas Mann techno-romantic jewelry to imaginative charm bracelets to hand-sculpted earrings. Surely you will find a piece you'll want to wear every day. They also carry furniture, housewares, and pottery. Another store is located in the Pioneer Place mall (☎ **503/222-3137**).

MALLS/SHOPPING CENTERS

The Galleria
921 SW Morrison St. ☎ **503/228-2748.**

Located in the heart of downtown Portland, the Galleria is a three-story atrium shopping mall with more than 50 specialty shops and restaurants, including a Made in Oregon store where you can stock up on Oregon-made gifts. Parking validation is available for adjacent parking garage.

Jantzen Beach Center
1405 Jantzen Beach Center. ☎ **503/289-5555.**

There are four major department stores and more than 80 other shops here. You'll also find the REI co-op recreational equipment store here. This mall has long been popular with residents of Washington state who come to shop where there's no sales tax.

Lloyd Center
Bounded by SE Multnomah St., SE Broadway, SE 16th Ave., and SE Ninth Ave. ☎ **503/282-2511.**

There are now more than 165 shops here, including a Nordstrom and a Meier & Frank. A food court, ice-skating rink, and eight-screen cinema complete the mall's facilities.

✪ New Market Village
50 SW Second Ave. ☎ **503/228-2392.**

Housed in a brick building built in 1872, this small shopping center is listed in the National Register of Historic Places. You'll find it directly across the street from the Skidmore Fountain and the Saturday Market.

✪ Pioneer Place
700 SW Fifth Ave. ☎ **503/228-5800.**

Located only a block from Pioneer Courthouse Square, Portland's newest downtown shopping center is also its most upscale. Along with a Saks Fifth Avenue, you'll also find Portland's branch of the Nature Company and the city's only Godiva chocolatier here.

The Water Tower at John's Landing
5331 SW Macadam Ave. ☎ **503/228-9431.**

Hardwood floors, huge overhead beams, and a courtyard paved with Belgian cobblestones from Portland's first paved streets give this shopping center plenty of character. There are about 40 specialty shops and restaurants here.

A Market

✪ Portland Saturday Market
Underneath the Burnside Bridge between SW First Ave. and SW Ankeny St. ☎ **503/ 222-6072.** MAX: Skidmore Fountain Station.

Every Saturday and Sunday nearly 300 artists and craftspeople sell their exquisite crafts and creations here. You'll also find ethnic foods and lots of free entertainment. This is the single best place in Portland to shop for one-of-a-kind gifts. On Sunday on-street parking is free. The market is open from March to Christmas Eve on Saturday from 10am to 5pm and on Sunday from 11am to 4:30pm.

TOYS

✪ Finnegan's Toys & Gifts
922 SW Yamhill St. ☎ **503/221-0306.**

Your inner child will be kicking and screaming in the aisles if you don't buy that silly little toy you never got when you were young.

WINES

An excellent selection of Oregon wines can be found at any **Made in Oregon** shop. They're located in the Lloyd Center shopping center, the Galleria, Washington Square, and Portland Airport. See "Gifts/Souvenirs," above, for details.

Great Wine Buys
1515 NE Broadway. ☎ **503/287-2897.**

Oenophiles will want to stop in at this wineshop and stock up before heading home. This is one of the best wineshops in Portland. The staff is helpful, and on Friday and Saturday there are wine tastings.

10 Portland After Dark

Portland is the Northwest's second cultural center. Its symphony, ballet, and opera are all well regarded, and the many theater companies offer classic and contemporary plays. In summer, festivals move the city's cultural activities outdoors.

To find out what's going on during your visit, pick up a copy of the *Willamette Week,* Portland's weekly arts-and-entertainment newspaper. You can also check the Friday A & E section and Sunday editions of *The Oregonian*, the city's daily newspaper.

Many of the theaters and performance halls in Portland offer discounts for students and seniors, and you can often save money by buying your ticket on the day of a performance or within half an hour of curtain time.

Tickets for many of the venues listed below can be purchased through **GI Joe's/ Ticketmaster** (☎ **503/224-4400**) or **Fastixx** at Fred Meyer (☎ **503/224-8499**).

THE PERFORMING ARTS

The **Portland Center for the Performing Arts,** 1111 SW Broadway (☎ **503/ 248-4496**), is comprised of four theaters in three different buildings. These include the **Arlene Schnitzer Concert Hall,** Southwest Broadway and Southwest Main Street, an immaculately restored movie palace; the **Intermediate and Winningstad theaters** in the New Theatre Building, across the street from Schnitzer Hall; and the **Portland Civic Auditorium,** Southwest Third Avenue and Southwest Clay Street, the largest of the four.

Between these theaters, the center plays host to the **Oregon Symphony** (☎ **503/228-1353** or 800/228-7343), the **Oregon Ballet Theatre** (☎ **503/ 222-5538**), the **Portland Opera** (☎ **503/241-1802**), the **Portland Center Stage** (☎ **503/274-6588**), and touring companies.

The **Portland Repertory Theater,** World Trade Center, 25 SW Salmon St. (☎ **503/224-4491**), is the city's oldest Equity theater and offers consistently excellent productions, which have such a reputation that it's almost impossible to get individual tickets to performances. When they're available, tickets run $20 to $28.

If you're a fan of the Bard, check the schedule of the **Tygres Heart Shakespeare Co.,** 710 SW Madison St., Suite 506 (☎ **503/222-9220**), which does only works by Shakespeare. Tickets are $7.50 to $25.

THE CLUB & MUSIC SCENE
NIGHTCLUBS/COMEDY

Darcelle XV
208 NW Third Ave. ☎ **503/222-5338.** Cover $8. Reservations recommended Fri–Sat.

This is a campy Portland institution with a female-impersonator show that has been a huge hit for years. Shows are Wednesday through Saturday at 8:30 and 10:30pm.

Harvey's Comedy Club
436 NW 6th Ave. ☎ **503/241-0338.** Cover $6 Sun–Thurs, $8 Fri–Sat.

There were these three comedians, see, and one of them was nationally known . . . not a joke, but what you'll find at Harvey's every night except Monday. The club is entirely no-smoking and a full dinner menu is available. Shows are Sunday through Thursday at 8pm and on Friday and Saturday at 8 and 10:30pm.

FOLK/ROCK/JAZZ/BLUES

Aladdin Theater
30178 SE Milwaukee Ave. ☎ **503/233-1994.** Tickets $10–$20.

This former movie theater now serves as one of Portland's main venues for touring performers from a very diverse musical spectrum.

Portland's Brewing up a Microstorm

Though espresso is the drink that drives Portland, educated beer drinkers head to the city's dozens of brewpubs when they want to relax over a flavorful pint of ale. No other city in America has such a concentration of brewpubs, and it was here that the microbrewery business really got its start back in the mid-1980s. Today brewpubs continue to proliferate here in Munich on the Willamette with cozy neighborhood pubs vying for business with big, polished establishments.

There are four basic ingredients in beer: malt, hops, yeast, and water. The first of these, malt, is made from grains, primarily barley and wheat, which are roasted to convert their carbohydrates into the sugar needed to grow yeast. The amount of roasting the grains receive during the malting process will determine the color and flavor of the final product (the darker the malt, the darker and more flavorful the beer or ale). Yeast, in turn, converts the malt's sugar into alcohol. There are many different strains of yeast that all lend different flavors to beers. The hops are added to give beer its characteristic bitterness (the more "hoppy" the beer or ale, the more bitter it becomes). The Northwest happens to be the nation's only commercial hop-growing region, with 75% grown in Washington and 25% grown in Oregon and Idaho. With these four basic ingredients it's possible to produce an amazingly wide variety of beers and ales. Throw in a bit of extra flavoring such as raspberry or blueberry (two popular ingredients among Northwest microbreweries) and you'll have some of the region's most popular beers.

Pilsners are the most common beers in America and are made from pale malt with a lot of hops added to give them their characteristic bitter flavor. Lagers are made in much the same way as pilsners but are cold-fermented, which gives them a distinctive flavor. Ales, which are the most common brews served at microbreweries, are made using a warm fermentation process and usually more and darker malt than is used in lagers and pilsners. Porters (also known as stouts) get their characteristic dark coloring and flavor from the use of dark, even charred, malt.

A bit out from the city, but close to I-84 in nearby Troutdale, there's the McMenamin brothers' sprawling **Edgefield** brewery complex, 2126 SW Halsey St. (☎ **800/669-8610**), which includes a brewery and brewpub, a restaurant and bar, a winery, a bed-and-breakfast inn, and a hostel, all housed on the grounds of the completely renovated former Multnomah County poor farm. Another McMenamin's brewpub, the **Cornelious Pass Roadhouse,** east of Portland off Ore. 26 (Sunset Highway) in the town of Hillsboro, is housed in yet another historic building, this time an old two-story farmhouse. Also on the grounds is a hexagonal barn that's one of the only such structures in the state.

If you prefer a more urban, though no less historic, setting in which to down a pint, try the **Bridgeport Brewery & Brew Pub,** 1313 NW Marshall St. (☎ **503/241-7179**), which is housed in the oldest commercial building in the

Bojangles's

2229 SE Hawthorne Blvd. ☎ **503/233-1201.** Cover $5–$10.

This is currently Portland's most popular blues club, and books local bands as well as acts with a national following.

city and was the first brewpub to open in Portland. This is one of the few brewpubs in Portland that serves cask-conditioned "real" ales.

If you're an outdoors type interested in kayaking, mountain biking, skiing, and similar sports, you may want to pay a visit to the **Nor'wester Public House,** 66 SE Morrison St. (☎ **503/232-9771**), where you'll likely be drinking with likeminded individuals who enjoy ales and beers with flavor and body. The weizen berry beer is a favorite here.

If you prefer a lighter flavor in your beer, try *weizen* (wheat) beer, which is also served unfiltered as *hefeweizen*. The Widmer Brewing Company is Portland's undisputed king of hefeweizen. You can sample their suds at almost any pub in town, but you owe it to yourself to check out either their **Gasthaus,** 929 N. Russel St. (☎ **503/281-3333**), which is located adjacent to their main brewery, or their smaller microbrewery at the **B. Moloch/Heathman Bakery & Pub,** 901 SW Salmon St. (☎ **503/227-5700**), which is one of the most popular pubs in Portland, largely because of its excellent, inexpensive meals and lively, contemporary setting.

Microbrews are becoming big business (so big in fact that "microbrewery" is beginning to lose its meaning) and just as wineries in the Napa Valley have become more and more glitzy, so, too, have brewpubs. With huge copper fermenting vats proudly displayed in the window and polished to a high sheen, the Portland Brewing Company's **Brewhouse Tap Room & Grill,** 2730 NW 31st Ave. (☎ **503/228-5269**), is by far the city's most ostentatious, though certainly not largest, brewpub. Running a close second is the new **Rock Bottom Brewery,** 206 SW Morrison St. (☎ **503/796-2739**), in downtown Portland. This is an outpost of a small brewing empire that started out in Boulder, the West's other brewing capital. This place is a bit corporate, but is popular with the after-work crowd from downtown offices.

Everybody knows that beer goes with pizzas and burgers, but in Portland microbrews also go with movies. Three McMenamin brothers brewpubs are also movie theaters showing recent releases. The **Mission Theater & Pub,** 1624 NW Glisan St. (☎ **503/223-4031**), the **Bagdad Theater & Pub,** 3702 SE Hawthorne Blvd. (☎ **503/230-0895**), and the **Power Station, Pub and Theater,** 2126 SW Halsey St., Troutdale (☎ **800/669-8610**), may not be the best places to catch a movie (it's hard for some people to stop talking and sightlines aren't the greatest), but ticket prices are low.

So no matter what vision you have of the ideal brewpub, you're likely to find your dream come true here in Portland. Whether you're wearing bike shorts or a three-piece suit, there's a pub in Portland where you can get a handcrafted beer, maybe a light meal, and enjoy the convivial atmosphere that only a pub can provide. And, if you're like me, half the fun will lie in finding your personal favorite.

Brasserie Montmartre

626 SW Park Ave. ☎ **503/224-5552.** No cover.

There's live jazz nightly from 8:30pm at this French restaurant. Both food and music are popular with a primarily middle-aged clientele that likes to dress up.

Key Largo

31 NW First Ave. ☎ **503/223-9919.** Cover $3–$8 (higher for national acts).

A tropical atmosphere prevails at this spacious club. Rock, reggae, blues, and jazz performers all find their way to Key Largo's stage. Local R&B bands are a mainstay, and occasionally a nationally known act shows up.

✪ La Luna

215 SE Ninth Ave. ☎ **503/241-5862.** Cover $6.50–$18.

The stage at La Luna is in a cavernous room with a ceiling so high that the cigarette smoke doesn't get too bad. Here you can catch a wide range of lesser-known national acts for a reasonable price.

Parchman Farm

1204 SE Clay St. ☎ **503/235-7831.** Cover $2 after 9pm.

If you're into jazz, Parchman Farm is where you hang out in Portland. This club features live music nightly starting between 8 and 9:30pm.

Roseland Theater

8 NW Sixth Ave. ☎ **503/224-7469.** Cover $5–$15.

The Roseland Theater is only a couple of blocks from Key Largo, and the same diversity of popular musical styles prevails.

DANCE CLUBS/DISCOS

Embers Avenue

110 NW Broadway. ☎ **503/222-3082.** Cover $3 Thurs–Sat.

Though this is still primarily a gay disco, straights have also discovered its great dance music. Lots of flashing lights and sweaty bodies until the early morning. There are drag shows seven nights a week.

Panorama

341 SW Tenth Ave. ☎ **503/221-7262.** Cover $3 Fri–Sat.

Panorama is a large dance club playing currently popular dance music. The scene here is primarily gay, but a lot of straight people come here too. Open Friday, Saturday, and Sunday.

✪ Rock n' Rodeo

220 SE Spokane St. ☎ **503/235-2417.** Cover $5 after 8:30pm.

If you're a fan of western dancing (or you just want to learn), join the fun at Rock n' Rodeo where a one-hour lesson costs only $1. As the evening progresses, this place becomes a swirl of cowboy boots, skirts, and tight jeans.

THE BAR & BREW PUB SCENE

✪ Atwater's

111 SW Fifth Ave. ☎ **503/275-3600.**

Located on the 30th floor of the U.S. BanCorp building, this bar has the best view in Portland. Thursday through Saturday evenings there's live jazz.

Bridgeport Brewery & Brew Pub

1313 NW Marshall St. ☎ **503/241-7179.**

Portland's oldest microbrewery was founded in 1984 and is housed in the city's oldest industrial building. Windows behind the bar let you watch the brewers. It has four to seven of its brews on tap on any given night, and great pizza.

Champions
In the Portland Marriott, 1401 SW Front Ave. ☎ **503/274-2470.**

If sports is your forte, this is the bar for you. However, there's also a small dance floor here with dancing to the DJ's Top 40 tunes Thursday through Saturday.

Dublin Pub
6821 Beaverton-Hillsdale Hwy. ☎ **503/297-2889.**

Located west of downtown toward the suburb of Beaverton, this pub has 102 beers on tap, which is the Northwest's largest selection.

✪ Hillsdale Brewery & Public House
1505 SW Sunset Blvd. ☎ **503/246-3938.**

This was the cornerstone of the McMenamin brothers' microbrewery empire, which now includes more than 20 pubs in the greater Portland metropolitan area. These pubs craft flavorful and unusual ales.

Other McMenamin pubs include the **Cornelius Pass Roadhouse,** Sunset Highway and Cornelius Pass Road, Hillsboro (☎ **503/640-6174**), in an old farmhouse; the **Blue Moon Tavern,** 432 NW 21st St. (☎ **503/223-3184**), on a fashionable street in northwest Portland; and the **Ram's Head,** 2282 NW Hoyt St. (☎ **503/221-0098**), between 21st and 22nd avenues.

11 Side Trips from Portland

VANCOUVER, WASHINGTON

Because Vancouver, Washington, is part of the Portland metropolitan area, and because it bears the same name as both a large island and a city in Canada, it's often overlooked by visitors to the Northwest. However, the city has several historic sites and other attractions that make it a good day-long excursion from Portland. The first three attractions listed here are all in the 1-square-mile **Central Park,** which is located just east of I-5 (take the East Mill Plain Boulevard exit just after you cross the bridge into Washington).

It was here that much of the Northwest's important early pioneer history unfolded at the Hudson's Bay Company's (HBC) Fort Vancouver. The HBC, a British company, came to the Northwest in search of furs, and for most of the first half of the 19th century was the only authority in this remote region. Fur trappers, mountain men, missionaries, explorers, and settlers all made Fort Vancouver their first stop in Oregon. Today the **Fort Vancouver National Historic Site,** 1501 E. Evergreen Blvd. (☎ **360/696-7655**), houses several reconstructed buildings that are furnished as they might have been in the middle of the 19th century. It's open daily from 9am to 5pm (to 4pm in winter); admission is $1.

After the British gave up Fort Vancouver, it became the site of the Vancouver Barracks U.S. military post, and stately homes were built for the officers of the post. These buildings are now preserved as the Officers' Row National Historic District. You can stroll along admiring the well-kept homes, and then stop in at the **Grant House Folk Art Center** (☎ **360/694-5252**), which is named for President Ulysses S. Grant, who was stationed here as quartermaster in the 1850s. It's open Tuesday through Sunday from 10am to 5pm. This building was the first commanding officer's quarters. In addition to the art center, there's a café that serves good lunches. Farther along Officers' Row you'll find the **George C. Marshall House** (☎ **360/693-3103**), a Victorian-style building that replaced the Grant House as the commanding officer's quarters; it's open Monday through

Friday from 10am to 5pm. You'll find the tree-shaded row of 21 homes just north of Fort Vancouver.

A very different piece of history is preserved at the nearby **Pearson Air Museum,** 1105 E. Fifth St. (☎ **360/694-7026**). Established in 1905, this is the oldest operating airfield in the United States. Dozens of vintage aircraft, including several World War I–era biplanes and the plane that made the first transpacific flight, are on display in a large hangar. The museum is open Wednesday through Sunday from noon to 5pm; admission is $2 for adults and $1 for children.

In the town of Washougal, 16 miles east of Vancouver on Wash. 14, you can visit the **Pendleton Woolen Mills and Outlet Shop,** 217th St., Washougal (☎ **360/835-2131**), and see how the famous wool blankets and classic wool fashions are made. The shop is open Monday through Saturday from 8am to 4pm; free mill tours are given Monday through Friday at 9, 10, and 11am, and 1:30pm.

Railroading buffs may want to drive north 10 miles to the town of Battle Ground and take a ride on the diesel-powered **Lewis River Excursion Train,** which has its depot at 1000 E. Main St. in Battle Ground (☎ **360/687-2626,** or 503/227-2626 in Portland). The two-hour excursions run from Battle Ground to Moulton Falls County Park, where there's a 20-minute stop for passengers to view the falls. Call for the schedule; tickets for regular excursions are $10 for adults and $5 for children. There are also dinner train excursions.

Some 23 miles north of Vanouver in the town of Woodland are the **Hulda Klager Lilac Gardens,** 115 S. Pekin Rd. (☎ **360/225-8996**). Between late April and Mother's Day each year, these gardens burst into color and the fragrance of lilacs hangs in the air. They're open daily from dawn to dusk; admission is $1.

Ten miles east of Woodland off Northeast Cedar Creek Road, you'll find the **Cedar Creek Grist Mill,** Grist Mill Road (☎ **360/225-9552**), the only remaining 19th-century grist mill in Washington. Built in 1876, the grist mill was restored over a 10-year period, and in 1989 once again became functional. It's open on Saturday from 1 to 4pm and on Sunday from 2 to 4pm; admission is by donation.

OREGON CITY & THE END OF THE OREGON TRAIL

When the first white settlers began crossing the Oregon Trail in the early 1840s, their destination was Oregon City and the fertile Willamette Valley. At the time Portland had yet to be founded and Oregon City, set beside powerful Willamette Falls, was the largest town in Oregon. However, with the development of Portland and the shifting of the capital to Salem, Oregon City began to lose its importance. Today this is primarily an industrial town, though one steeped in Oregon history and well worth a visit.

To get to Oregon City from Portland, take I-5 south to I-205 east or head south from downtown Portland on Southwest Riverside Drive and drive through the wealthy suburbs of Lake Oswego and West Linn. Once in Oregon City, your first stop should be just south of town at the **Willamette Falls overlook** on Ore. 99E. Though the falls have been much changed by industry over the years, they're still an impressive sight.

Oregon City is divided into upper and lower sections by a steep bluff. The nation's only **free municipal elevator** connects the two halves of the city and affords a great view from its observation area at the top of the bluff. You'll find the 100-foot-tall elevator at the corner of Seventh Street and Railroad Avenue. Service is available from 6am to 8pm daily. It's in the upper section of town that you'll find the town's many historic homes.

Oregon City's most famous citizen was retired Hudson's Bay Company chief factor John McLoughlin, who helped found Oregon City in 1829. By the 1840s immigrants were pouring into Oregon, and McLoughlin provided food, seeds, and tools to many. Upon his retirement in 1846 McLoughlin moved to Oregon City where he built what was at that time the most luxurious home in Oregon. Today the **McLoughlin House,** 713 Center St. (☎ **503/656-5146**), is a National Historic Site and is open to the public Tuesday through Saturday from 10am to 4pm and on Sunday from 1 to 4pm. Admission is $3 for adults, $2.50 for seniors, and $1 for children. The house is furnished as it would have been in McLoughlin's days and includes many original pieces.

Several other Oregon City historic homes are also open to the public. The **Clackamas County Historical Museum,** 211 Tumwater Dr. (☎ **503/655-5574**), houses collections of historic memorabilia and old photos from this area. It's open Monday through Friday from 10am to 4pm and on Saturday and Sunday from 1 to 5pm; admission is $3 for adults, $2 for seniors, and $1.50 for children. The **Stevens Crawford House,** 603 Sixth St. (☎ **503/655-2866**), is a foursquare-style home and is furnished with late 19th-century antiques. It's open Tuesday through Friday from 10am to 4pm and on Saturday and Sunday from 1 to 4pm (in summer, also on Monday from 1 to 4pm). Admission is $3 for adults, $2 for seniors, and $1.50 for children. The **Ermatinger House,** on the corner of Sixth and John Adams streets (☎ **503/657-8316**), is the town's oldest home. It's open Wednesday through Sunday from 10am to 4pm; admission is $1.50 for adults and 75¢ for children.

The story of the settlers who traveled the Oregon Trail is told at the **End of the Oregon Trail Interpretive Center,** 1726 Washington St. (☎ **503/657-9336**), which is designed to resemble three giant covered wagons. It's open Monday through Saturday from 9am to 6pm and on Sunday from 10am to 5:30pm; admission is $4.50 for adults, $2.50 for seniors and children 5 to 12. There are guided tours every 45 minutes.

Each summer the history of the Oregon Trail comes alive in Oregon City with the staging of the *Oregon Trail Pageant.* Performances are held in an amphitheater on the Clackamas Community College campus, located a few miles southeast of downtown Oregon City. Performances are held Tuesday through Saturday evenings at 7:15pm; ticket prices are $8 for adults, $7 for seniors, and $4 for children.

Another interesting chapter in Oregon pioneer history is preserved 13 miles south of Oregon City in the town of **Aurora,** which was founded in 1855 as a Christian communal society. Similar in many ways to such more famous communal experiments as the Amana Colony and the Shaker communities, the Aurora Colony lasted slightly more than 20 years. Today Aurora is a National Historic District and the large old homes of the community's founders have been restored. Many of the old commercial buildings now house **antiques stores,** which are the main reason most people visit Aurora. At the **Old Aurora Colony Museum** (☎ **503/678-5754**) you can learn about the history of Aurora. The museum is open March to December, Wednesday through Saturday from 10am to 4:30pm (June to August, also on Tuesday from 10am to 4:30pm and on Sunday from 1 to 4:30pm); in January and February, Thursday through Sunday from 1 to 4:30pm. Admission is $2.50 for adults and $1 for children.

On your way back to Portland, consider taking the **Canby ferry,** which is one of the last remaining ferries on the Willamette River. To take the ferry, head 4 miles north on Oreg. 99E to Canby and watch for the ferry signs.

11

The Columbia Gorge & Mount Hood

The Columbia Gorge, which begins a few miles east of Portland and extends for nearly 70 miles to The Dalles, is a giant bridge that cuts through the Cascade Range and connects the rain-soaked west-side forests with the desert-dry sagebrush scrublands of central Oregon. This change in climate is caused by moist air condensing into snow and rain as it passes over the crest of the Cascades. Most of the air's moisture falls on the western slopes, so that the eastern slopes and the land stretching for hundreds of miles beyond lie in what's called a rain shadow. Perhaps nowhere else on earth can you so easily witness this rain-shadow effect. It's so pronounced that as you come around a bend on I-84 just east of Hood River, you can see dry grasslands to the east and dense forests of moisture-loving Douglas fir over your shoulder to the west. In between the two extremes lies a community of plants that's unique to the Columbia Gorge. Springtime in the gorge sees colorful displays of wildflowers, many of which exist only here.

The Columbia River is second only to the Mississippi in the volume of water it carries to the sea, but more than just water flows through the Columbia Gorge. As the only break over the entire length of the Cascade Range the gorge acts as a massive natural wind tunnel. During the summer the sun bakes the lands east of the Cascades, causing the air over these lands to rise. Cool air from the west side then rushes up the river, whipping through Hood River with near gale force at times. These winds, blowing against the downriver flow of water, set up ideal conditions for sailboarding. The reliability of these winds, and the waves they kick up, has turned Hood River, once an ailing lumber town, into the Aspen of sailboarding.

The Columbia River is older than the hills. It's older than the mountains, too. And it's the river's great age that accounts for why the waters cut a gorge through the Cascades. The mountains have actually risen up *around* the river. Though the river's geologic history dates back 40 million years or so, it was a series of recent events—geologically speaking—that gave the Columbia Gorge its very distinctive appearance. About 15,000 years ago, toward the end of the last Ice Age, huge dams of ice far upstream burst and sent floodwaters racing down the Columbia. As the floodwaters swept through the Columbia Gorge, they were as much as 1,200 feet high. Ice and rock carried by the floodwaters helped the river to scour out the sides of the once gently sloping gorge, leaving behind the steep-walled gorge that we know today. The waterfalls that attract so many oohs and aahs are the most dramatic evidence of these great floods. As early as 1915 a scenic highway was built through the gorge and in 1986 much of the area was designated the **Columbia Gorge National Scenic Area** to preserve its spectacular and unique natural beauty.

Looming over the gorge are two snowcapped sentinels—Mount Adams and Mount Hood. Though Adams, at 12,307 feet in elevation, is not the tallest mountain in the Cascade Range (that distinction goes to Mount Rainier), its great bulk makes it the most massive. However, because it's the least accessible, it's also the least visited of the major Cascade peaks. Looking much more delicate, Mount Hood stands only 11,235 feet in elevation, which is still enough to make it the highest point in Oregon. As home to five ski areas and a historic mountain lodge built during the Great Depression by the WPA, Mount Hood is a four-season mountain playground for residents of the Portland metropolitan area.

For centuries the Columbia River has been an important route from the maritime Northwest into the dry interior. Lewis and Clark canoed down the river in 1805 and pioneers followed the Oregon Trail to its shores at The Dalles. It was here at The Dalles that many pioneers transferred their wagons to boats for the dangerous journey downriver to Oregon City. The set of rapids known as The Dalles and the waterfalls of the Cascades were the two most dangerous sections of the Columbia Gorge, so towns arose at these two points to transport goods and people around the treacherous waters. Locks and a canal helped circumvent these two sections of white water, but today the rapids of the Columbia lie flooded beneath the waters behind the Bonneville and The Dalles dams. Though the ease of navigating the river today has dimmed the importance of the Cascade Locks and The Dalles, these two river towns are still steeped in the history of the Columbia River Gorge.

1 The Columbia Gorge National Scenic Area

Though I-84 is the fastest road to Hood River, you shouldn't rush through the Columbia Gorge. With its many natural and man-made wonders, the gorge is well worth a leisurely day's explorations.

ESSENTIALS

GETTING THERE   I-84 and the Historic Columbia River Highway both pass through the gorge on the Oregon side of the Columbia. Wash. 14 runs through on the Washington side of the river.

VISITOR INFORMATION   Contact the **Columbia River Gorge National Scenic Area,** USDA Forest Service, 902 Wasco Ave., Suite 200, Hood River, OR 97031 (☎ **541/386-2333**).

LEARNING ABOUT THE GORGE & ITS HISTORY

✪ Columbia Gorge Interpretive Center

990 SW Rock Creek Dr., Stevenson. ☎ **509/427-8211.** Admission $5 adults, $4 seniors and students, $3 children 6–12, free for children 4 and under. Memorial Day–Labor Day, daily 10am–7pm; Labor Day–Memorial Day, daily 10am–5pm.

This new museum focuses on the Gorge's early Native American inhabitants and the development of the area by white settlers. Exhibits contain historical photographs by Edward Curtis and other photos that illustrate the story of portage companies and paddlewheelers. Period quotations and explanations of gorge history put the museum's many artifacts in their proper context. A relic here that you can't miss is a 37-foot-high replica of a 19th-century fishwheel, which gives an understanding of how salmon runs have been threatened in the past as well as in the present. Displays also frankly discuss other problems that the coming of civilization brought to this area. A slide program tells the history of the formation of the gorge, and when the volcanoes erupt, the floor in the theater actually shakes from the intensity of the low-volume sound track. When it's not cloudy, the center has an awesome view of the south side of the gorge.

A DRIVING TOUR

The **Historic Columbia River Highway,** which begins 16 miles east of downtown Portland at the second Troutdale exit off I-84, opened in 1915. It was a marvel of engineering when it was built. However, this man-made marvel is dwarfed by the spectacular vistas that present themselves whenever the scenic road emerges from the dark forest.

The first astounding view of the gorge comes at the **Portland Women's Forum State Park** viewpoint. This is also likely to be your first encounter with the legendary Columbia Gorge winds. To learn more about the historic highway and how it was built, stop at the **Vista House,** 733 feet above the river on **Crown Point.** Inside this historic 1916 building, there are informative displays, including old photos. However, most visitors can't tear their eyes away from the view long enough to concentrate on any of the exhibits. Some 30 miles of breathtaking views spread out in front of you as you gaze up and down the Columbia River. A side road near here leads 14 miles to the top of Larch Mountain.

From Crown Point, the historic highway drops down into the gorge and passes several picturesque **waterfalls**—Latourelle Falls, Shepherd's Dell Falls, Bridalveil Falls, Mist Falls, and Wahkeena Falls—that are either right beside the road or a short walk away. If you're interested in a longer hike, there are trails linking several of the falls, as well as other trails that lead south toward Mount Hood. However, **Multnomah Falls** is the largest and the most famous waterfall along this highway. At 620 feet from the lip to the lower pool, it's the tallest waterfall in Oregon and the fourth tallest in the United States. An arched bridge stands directly in front of the falls and is a favorite of photographers. A steep paved trail leads from the foot of the falls up to the top, from which other trails lead off into the **Mount Hood National Forest.** The historic Multnomah Falls Lodge has a restaurant, snack bar, and gift shop.

East of Multnomah Falls, the scenic highway passes by **Oneonta Gorge,** a narrow rift in the cliffs. Through this tiny gorge flows a stream that serves as a pathway for anyone interested in exploring upstream to **Oneonta Falls.** Continuing east, you'll pass **Horsetail Falls** shortly before the historic highway merges with I-84. Just after the two highways merge, you come to the exit for **Bonneville Lock and Dam** (☎ **541/374-8820**). The **Bradford Island Visitors Center** has exhibits on the history of this dam, which was built in 1927. One of the most important features of the dam is its fish ladder, which allows adult salmon to return upriver to spawn. Underwater windows let visitors see fish as they pass through the ladder. Visit the adjacent fish hatchery to see how trout, salmon, and sturgeon are raised before being released into the river.

The Columbia Gorge & Mount Hood

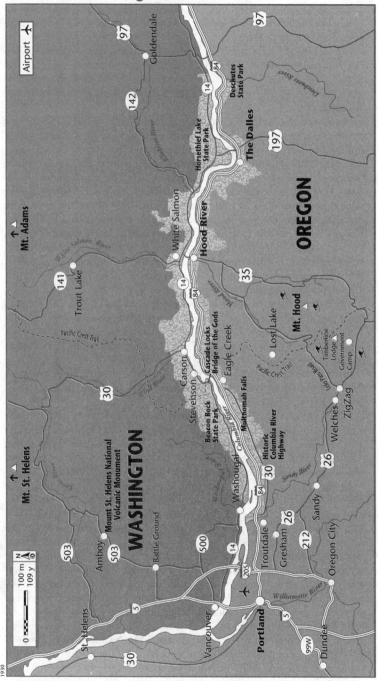

Beyond the dam is Eagle Creek, probably the single best area in the gorge for a hike. The **Eagle Creek Trail** leads past several waterfalls. You'll also find a campground and picnic area here.

Not far beyond Eagle Creek is the **Bridge of the Gods,** which connects Oregon and Washington at the site where, according to a Native American legend, a natural bridge used by the gods once stood. Geologists believe that the legend may have some basis in fact. There is evidence that a massive rockslide may have once blocked the river.

Just beyond the Bridge of the Gods is **Cascade Locks.** It was at this site that cascades once turned the otherwise-placid Columbia River into a raging torrent that required boats to be portaged around the cascades. In 1896 the Cascade Locks were built, allowing steamships to pass unhindered past the cascades. When the locks were opened, they made traveling between The Dalles and Portland much easier. However, the completion of the Columbia River Scenic Highway in 1915 made the trip even easier by land. With the construction of the Bonneville Lock and Dam, the cascades were flooded and the locks became superfluous. There are two small museums here at the locks. The **Cascade Locks Historical Museum,** Marine Park (☎ 541/374-8535), which is housed in the old lock-tender's house, includes displays of Native American artifacts and pioneer memorabilia, as well as the Northwest's first steam engine. It's open June to October, daily from 11am to 6pm, plus May weekends from noon to 5pm.

The **Port of Cascade Locks Visitors Center,** which has displays on river travel in the past, is also the ticket office for the stern-wheeler *Columbia Gorge* (☎ 503/223-3928 or 541/374-8427), which makes regular trips on the river all summer, priced at $11.95 for adults and $5.95 for children; dinner, lunch, breakfast, brunch, and other special cruises run $18.95 to $49.95.

Between the Cascade Locks and Hood River, you can do a bit of hiking on the **Lewis and Clark Trail** or at **Viento State Park,** which also has a sailboard-launching area.

Should you decide not to take the historic highway and stay on I-84, you may want to stop at **Rooster Rock State Park,** especially if it's a hot summer day. This park has a long sandy beach, and in a remote section of the park there's even a clothing-optional beach. From I-84 there's also easy access to Multnomah Falls, which is the main attraction of the Historic Columbia River Highway.

Another driving option is to cross to the Washington side of the Columbia River and take Wash. 14 east from Vancouver. This latter highway actually provides the most spectacular views of both the Columbia Gorge and Mount Hood. If you should decide to take this route, be sure to stop at **Beacon Rock,** an 800-foot-tall monolith that has a trail leading to its summit. At one time there was talk of blasting the rock apart to build jetties at the mouth of the river. Luckily, another source of rock was used and this amazing landmark continues to guard the Columbia. If you want to make better time, you can cross back to Oregon on the Bridge of the Gods. Continuing on the Washington side of the river, you'll come to Stevenson, site of the above-mentioned Columbia Gorge Interpretive Center.

Beyond Stevenson, you come to the town of Carson, where you can avail yourself of the therapeutic waters of the **Carson Hot Springs Resort** (☎ 509/427-8292), located just north of town. It's open daily from 8:30am to 7pm; the charge is $8 for a soak, $32 for an hour's massage. The resort has been in business since 1897 and looks every bit of its age. However, it's just this old-fashioned appeal that keeps people coming back year after year to soak in the springs (separate men's and women's soaking tubs) and have a massage. There are also some very basic hotel rooms and cabins available. If you're looking for natural hot springs, the folks here can give you directions to some that are nearby.

WHERE TO STAY

✪ Edgefield Bed & Breakfast Resort

2126 SW Halsey St., Troutdale, OR 97060. ☎ **503/669-8610** or 800/669-8610. 103 rms (3 with bath), 24 hostel beds. $65–105 double; $18 hostel bed. Rates include full breakfast. AE, DISC, MC, V.

B&Bs don't usually have 100 rooms, but this is no ordinary inn. This flagship of the McMenamin microbrewery empire is the former county poor farm. Today, after extensive remodeling, the property includes not only tastefully decorated guest rooms with antique furnishings, but a brewery, pub, restaurant, movie theater, winery, wine-tasting room, meeting facilities, extensive gardens, and a hostel. With so much in one spot, this makes a great base for exploring the area.

✪ Skamania Lodge

P.O. Box 189, Stevenson, WA 98648. ☎ **509/427-7700** or 800/221-7117. 195 rms, 6 suites. A/C TV TEL. $95–$160 double; $185–$585 suite. Lower rates in winter. AE, CB, DC, DISC, MC, V. Free parking. Take I-84 to Cascade Locks, cross the Bridge of the Gods, and continue east to Stevenson on Wash. 14.

Skamania Lodge is the first new luxury hotel to open in the gorge since 1915 and its placement on the Washington side of the river gives it the most spectacular vistas of any hotel in the area. This is a full-service resort and conference hotel catering almost exclusively to groups and consequently it can feel too crowded for a romantic getaway. Still, the interior decor is classically rustic with lots of rock and natural wood. In the cathedral-ceilinged lobby, huge windows take in the best view on the property. Big wicker chairs are set by the stone fireplace, so you can curl up with a book on a cold winter night. If you should opt for a fireplace room, you won't have to leave your bed to enjoy a fire. The river-view guest rooms are only slightly more expensive than the forest-view rooms, which look out over the huge parking lot as well as the forest. Throughout the hotel Northwest Native American art and artifacts are on display. Some of the most interesting are the rubbings of local petroglyphs.

Dining/Entertainment: Though the wood floors and stone walls can make the restaurant noisy, the casual Northwest cuisine is excellent (and the view of the Gorge is amazing). Such interesting dishes as toasted filbert cakes and fruit-wood roasted salmon have shown up recently. Dinner entrée prices range from $11 to $19.50. Adjacent to the dining room is a lounge with a large freestanding stone fireplace.

Services: Concierge, room service.

Facilities: 18-hole golf course, tennis courts, swimming pool, whirlpool, exercise facility, nature trails, volleyball court.

WHERE TO DINE

The area's best spot for a meal is the dining room of the **Skamania Lodge.**

Royal Chinook Inn

2605 NE Corbett Hill Rd., Corbett. ☎ **503/695-3237.** Main courses $13.25–$16. AE, MC, V. Wed–Sun 4–9:30pm. Take Exit 22 off I-84. SEAFOOD.

This joint has character and a nautical theme; it's the kind of place you'd like to bring your parents. The sign out front says FAMOUS FOR SMOKED SALMON and with good reason—someone here really knows how to smoke salmon. It was excellent—not too dry, and served as a dinner with a baked potato and smoked-salmon chowder. (Well, the potato was a little dry, but we remedied that with a dollop of sour cream.) The grilled salmon was simply seasoned and perfectly grilled. The secret is the salmon itself—it's not farm-raised fish, which tends to have a bland taste, but wild Alaskan King salmon.

2   Hood River: The Sailboarding Capital of the Northwest

62 miles E of Portland, 20 miles W of The Dalles, 32 miles N of Government Camp

They used to curse the winds in Hood River. In summer, the hot air rising over the desert to the east sucks cool air up the Columbia River Gorge from the Pacific. The winds are incessant and gusts can whip the river into a tumult of whitecaps.

But things change. Today Hood River prays for wind. Hood River, you see, is the sailboarding capital of America. People come from all over the world to catch the wind as it roars through the gorge. In early summer the boardheads, as they're known, roll into town in their gorgemobiles, the 1990s equivalent of surfers' woodies. They flock to riverside parks on both the Oregon and Washington sides of the Columbia, unfurl their sails, zip up their wetsuits, and launch themselves into the melee of thousands of other like-minded souls shooting back and forth across a mile of windswept water. And the talk on shore is of air time. High waves whipped up by gale-force winds provide perfect launching pads for rocketing skyward. Get enough air time and you might even be able to do a flip or a 360° turn.

If you're into sailboarding, don't plan on going anywhere else while you're in the Northwest. Even if you're not into this fast-paced sport, you'll certainly get a vicarious thrill from watching the boardheads going for air time. Hood River is pretty much a one-trick town, so if you're not a boardhead, you won't find much to do here. However, there are a couple of excellent old hotels (one of legendary status), several bed-and-breakfast inns, and a few memorable restaurants. Hood River has been completely transformed in the past decade from sleepy old timber town into an international mecca. Virtually every old home in town has been restored of late.

ESSENTIALS

GETTING THERE   Hood River is on I-84 at the junction with Ore. 35, which leads south to connect with U.S. 26 near the town of Government Camp.

Amtrak offers passenger rail service to Hood River. The station is at Cascade Avenue and First Street.

VISITOR INFORMATION   Contact the **Hood River County Visitors Council,** Port Marina Park, Hood River, OR 97031 (☎ **541/386-2000** or 800/ 366-3530).

FESTIVALS   The **Hood River Valley Blossom Festival** is held in mid-April. August brings the **Hood River Apple Jam music festival** and **Gravenstein Apple Fair,** and mid-October is time for the **Hood River Valley Harvest Fest.**

OUTDOOR ACTIVITIES: SAILBOARDING & MORE

Sailboarding gave Hood River, an ailing lumber town, a new lease on life. If you're here to ride the wind or just want to watch others as they race back and forth across the river, head to the **Columbia Gorge Sailpark** at Hood River Marina. Another good spot in the area is **Mayer State Park,** several miles east of town off I-84. Across the river in Washington, try the **Hood Vista Sailpark,** just west of the Hood River Bridge; the **fish hatchery,** west of the mouth of the White Salmon River; and **Swell City,** a park about 3 miles west of the bridge. You'll find several sailboarding shops in downtown Hood River where you can rent a board, take lessons, or buy a new, smaller sail.

When there isn't enough wind for sailing, there's still the option to go **rafting** on the White Salmon River just across the bridge from Hood River. Companies offering raft trips on this river include **Phil Zoller's Guide Service,** 1244 Wash. 141 (☎ **509/493-2641**), **and White Water Adventure,** 38 Northwestern Lake (☎ **800/366-2004**). The river-rafting season runs from March to October and a half-day trip will cost around $45 per person.

If you're interested in **horseback riding,** contact **Fir Mountain Ranch,** 4051 Fir Mountain Rd. (☎ **541/354-2753**), located about 9 miles south of Hood River. It charges $20 for an hour's horseback ride.

Hikers have their choice of trails in Mount Hood National Forest (try up at **Timberline**), the Columbia Gorge (try **Eagle Creek** or at any of the waterfalls along the Historic Columbia River Highway), or cross the river and head up Wash. 141 to **Mount Adams.** At 12,276 feet in elevation, Mount Adams is the second-highest peak in Washington. Its summit is popular with mountain climbers, but at lower elevations there are excellent trails for hikers and backpackers. The favorite summer spot for a hike is **Bird Creek Meadows** on the Yakama Indian Reservation north of the town of Trout Lake. These meadows are ablaze with wildflowers in July. Eight miles west of Trout Lake, you can explore several **ice caves.** The caves were formed by lava flows centuries ago. For more information on hiking on Mount Adams, contact the **Gifford Pinchot National Forest,** Mt. Adams Ranger District, 2455 Wash. 141, Trout Lake, WA 98650 (☎ **509/395-2501**).

OTHER THINGS TO SEE & DO

Any time of year, but especially during fruit-blossom time, the **Mount Hood Scenic Railroad** (☎ **541/386-3556**) offers a great way to see the Hood River valley and its acres of orchards. The diesel locomotives depart from the historic 1911 Hood River depot and pull restored Pullman coaches on four-hour excursions. Fares are $21.95 for adults, $18.95 for seniors, $13.95 for children 2 to 11. This is still a working railroad line, and along the way your train may stop to pick up a carload of lumber or fruit.

Hood River is Oregon's top apple- and pear-growing region. April (blossom time) and September and October (harvest season) are great times to visit. In the fall, fruit stands pop up along the roads around town, but any time of year you can stop in at the **River Bend Country Store,** 2363 Tucker Rd. (☎ **541/386-8766** or 800/755-7568), and stock up on seasonal and organic produce and other homemade specialties. You'll find the store 5 miles south of Hood River off Ore. 35.

In addition to pears and apples, the Hood River valley also grows quite a few acres of wine grapes. You can visit several wineries and taste the local fruit of the vine. Area wineries include **Flerchinger Vineyards,** 4200 Post Canyon Rd. (☎ 541/386-2882); and **Hood River Vineyards,** 4693 Westwood Dr. (☎ 541/386-3772). Across the river, you can visit the **Charles Hooper Family Winery,** Spring Creek Road North Fork (☎ 509/493-2324), in Husum, and the **Mont Elise Vineyards,** 315 W. Steuben Rd (☎ 509/493-3001), in Bingen.

If you're interested in learning about Hood River's history, stop in at the **Hood River County Museum,** Port Marina Park (☎ 541/386-6772), which has exhibits on Native American beads, baskets, and artifacts from this area. There are also plenty of displays on pioneer life. The museum is open April to August, Wednesday through Saturday from 10am to 4pm and on Sunday from noon to 4pm; and in September and October, Wednesday through Sunday from noon to 4pm. Admission is free.

WHERE TO STAY

Best Western Hood River Inn

1108 E. Marina Way, Hood River, OR 97031. ☎ **541/386-2200** or 800/828-7873. Fax 503/386-8905. 150 rms. A/C TV TEL. June–Sept, $83–$105 double; $145–$165 suite. Oct–May, $49–$81 double; $105–$135 suite. AE, DC, DISC, MC, V.

If you prefer comfort and predictability, this convention hotel is your best bet in Hood River, with amenities such as room service, and outdoor swimming pool, an exercise club ($5 per day), and a private dock and beach. It's the only area hotel right on the water.

The Riverside Grill serves dependable meals with a bit of Northwest imagination and a great view across the river. A diner-style coffee shop provides casual meals. The lounge has live Top 40 dance music on summer weekends.

✪ Columbia Gorge Hotel

4000 Westcliff Dr., Hood River, OR 97031. ☎ **541/386-5566** or 800/345-1921. Fax 503/386-3359. 42 rms. TV TEL. $150–$215 double. Rates include five-course breakfast. AE, DC, DISC, MC, V.

Located just west of Hood River off I-84, the Columbia Gorge has distinctive yellow-stucco walls and red-tile roofs. This 1921-vintage hotel would be right at home in Beverly Hills, and the hotel gardens could hold their own in Victoria, British Columbia. The hotel is perched more than 200 feet above the river on a steep cliff, and the stream that meanders through the gardens cascades over the precipice. With such a setting it's almost impossible to notice anything but the views. The guest rooms are all a little different, with a mixture of antique and classic furnishings including canopy and brass beds. Unfortunately, many of the rooms are rather cramped, as are the bathrooms, most of which have older fixtures and some exposed pipes. Windows also don't do justice to the vistas.

Dining/Entertainment: The Columbia River Court Dining Room is best known for its five-course farm breakfast. If you aren't staying at the hotel, breakfast will run you a whopping $22.95. Evening meals feature Northwest cuisine, with entrées ranging from $18 to $28.

Services: Limited room service, complimentary newspaper, turndown service with rose and chocolate.

ⓈHood River Hotel

102 Oak St., Hood River, OR 97031. ☎ **541/386-1900.** Fax 503/386-6090. 32 rms, 9 suites. TV TEL. $69–$95 double; $125–$145 suite. AE, DC, DISC, MC, V.

Though the location isn't as nice, the atmosphere of the Hood River Hotel is very similar to that at the Columbia Gorge Hotel, and at a fraction of the price. Built in 1913 and located in the heart of downtown Hood River, it was recently restored and boasts the casual elegance of a vintage hotel. You're greeted by brass rails, a street-side patio, and beveled-glass French doors as you arrive, and, inside, huge paned windows flood the high-ceilinged lobby with light. On winter nights a fire crackles in the fireplace. Italian meals are served in the hotel's casual dining room.

The guest rooms are all different and are furnished almost identically to the guest rooms at the Columbia Gorge Hotel. Canopy beds, ceiling fans, and oval floor mirrors capture a mood of elegance. Most third-floor rooms have skylit bathrooms, which makes them our favorites. The suites have full kitchens, and of course, river-view rooms are the most expensive.

Inn at the Gorge

1113 Eugene St., Hood River, OR 97031. ☎ **541/386-4429.** 1 rm, without bath; 3 suites. $60 double without bath; $78 suite. Rates include full breakfast. MC, V (add 5% surcharge). Closed early Oct–early May.

Though this bed-and-breakfast is housed in a 1908 Victorian home, it's still a casual sort of place catering primarily to sailboarding enthusiasts. Each of the three suites here has a kitchenette so you can save money on your meals while you're in town. There's a storage area for sailboarding and skiing gear, and mountain bikes are available for guests. The innkeepers are avid boardheads themselves and can steer you to the best spots for your skill level.

⑤ Vagabond Lodge

4070 Westcliff Dr., Hood River, OR 97031. ☎ **541/386-2992.** 39 rms, 5 suites. A/C TV TEL. $45–$65 double; $75 suite. AE, MC, V.

If you've got a banker's tastes but a teller's vacation budget, you can take advantage of the Vagabond Lodge's proximity to the Columbia Gorge Hotel and enjoy the latter's gardens and restaurant without breaking the bank. Actually, the back rooms at the Vagabond are some of the best in Hood River simply for their views (some have balconies). However, the motel grounds are also quite attractive. There are lots of big old oaks and evergreens, and natural rock outcroppings have been incorporated into the motel's landscaping.

NEARBY PLACES TO STAY

⑤ The Bingen School Inn

Humboldt and Cedar sts., Bingen, WA 98605 (just east of the turnoff for White Salmon). ☎ **509/493-3363** or 800/827-4331. $29 double ($39 June to mid-Sept); $11 dorm bed. MC, V.

Bingen is a lumber mill town just across the river from Hood River, and the Bingen School Inn, as its name implies, is an old schoolhouse that has been turned into a hostel. The folks who stay here come from all over the world, but share a love of the outdoors. Sailboarding is the main topic of conversation around the hostel, but when there aren't any winds, guests usually head off on their mountain bikes, catch a raft trip, hike, or practice their rock-climbing skills on the hostel's indoor climbing wall. Accommodations, in old school rooms, are very basic (beds are banged together from two-by-six lumber). There's a lounge and a laundry and plans to serve meals. This place is very basic, but if you're young at heart and traveling the Northwest on a backpacker's budget, you'll appreciate the atmosphere. Mountain bikes and sailboards can both be rented at the hostel.

Mio Amore Pensione

Little Mountain Rd., Trout Lake, WA 98650. ☎ **509/395-2264.** 4 rms, 2 with bath. $60–$135 double with bath; $80–$95 double without bath. Rates include full breakfast. MC, V.

Located about 23 miles up the valley of the White Salmon from the town of White Salmon, Trout Lake is a tiny community at the foot of Mount Adams and makes a great base of operations for exploring this beautiful and mountainous region. Mio Amore is the place to stay if you're up this way, and is a very worthy destination in its own right. The inn, housed in an old farmhouse, is situated on the banks of Trout Lake Creek. The huge beams you see in the living room were originally part of a nearby barn, but today they give this charming inn an old-world air. There's an outdoor spa at the edge of the creek. See "Where to Dine," below, for information on dining here.

WHERE TO DINE

The best restaurant in town is the dining room at the **Columbia Gorge Hotel** (see "Where to Stay," above, for details).

Bette's Place

416 Oak St. ☎ **541/386-1880.** All meals $4–$6. MC, V. Mon–Fri 5:30am–5pm, Sat–Sun 5:30am–4pm. AMERICAN.

Nothing more than a classic diner with overworked waitresses and unremarkable food, Bette's is where the boardheads hang out until the winds pick up. Breakfast and burgers are the specialties here.

The Mesquitery

1219 12th St. ☎ **541/386-2002.** Main courses $9–$16. MC, V. Wed–Fri 11:30am–2pm and 4:30–9:30 or 10pm, Sat–Tues 4:30–9:30 or 10pm. STEAK/SEAFOOD.

Located in the uptown district of Hood River, the Mesquitery is a small and cozy grill with a rustic interior. As the name implies, mesquite grilling is the specialty of the house. Chicken and ribs are most popular, but you can also get a sirloin steak or grilled fish. At lunch there are sandwiches made with grilled meats. If you aren't that hungry, this is a good place to put together a light meal from such à la carte dishes as shrimp burritos, fish tacos, and fettuccine pesto. For a starter, don't miss the jalapeño cheese bread pull-apart.

Purple Rocks Art Bar & Café

606 Oak St. ☎ **541/386-6061.** Main courses $10–$13.50. MC, V. Mon–Thurs 7am–4pm, Fri–Sun 7am–4pm and 6–10pm. INTERNATIONAL.

Java, jazz, and fine food are the basis for this self-proclaimed art bar and café, and there are plenty of café tables and jazz tunes on the stereo. The food is well prepared and ranges from filet mignon to gingered salmon. The salads are large and flavorful. There's a patio out front (a bit noisy from traffic) and a deck out back with a great view of the river.

✪ Sixth Street Bistro

509 Cascade St. ☎ **541/386-5737.** Reservations recommended. Main courses $8–$13. MC, V. Daily 11am–9pm. AMERICAN/INTERNATIONAL.

Just a block off Oak Street toward the river, the Sixth Street Bistro has an intimate little dining room and patio on the lower floor and a lounge with a balcony on the second floor. Each has its own entrance, but they share the same menu so there's a choice of ambience. There are numerous international touches such as chicken satay appetizers and a grilled-chicken salad with sesame-ginger dressing, and plenty of interesting pasta dishes such as Cajun fettuccine and phad thai. You'll find salmon (prepared in your choice of three different ways), blackened yellow-fin tuna, and garlic prawns, along with seasonal specials and a good list of burgers. It's worth stopping in just for coffee and dessert, both of which are provided by local shops.

Stonehedge
3405 Cascade St. ☎ **541/386-3940.** Reservations highly recommended. Main courses $13.50–$18.50. AE, CB, DC, DISC, MC, V. Wed–Sun 5–9pm. CONTINENTAL.

Built as a summer vacation home just after the turn of the century, the Stonehedge Inn is just west of downtown Hood River off Cascade Avenue, but it feels as if it were deep in the wilderness. Inside the old home, there's a small lounge with a bar taken from an old tavern, and several dining rooms, each of which has a slightly different feel. The menu sticks to traditional continental dishes, though there are occasional ventures into more creative territory with daily specials. For a starter, there's the house pâté. Veal chanterelle, made with fresh cream, brandy, and chanterelle mushrooms, and steak au poivre verts are two of the best choices on the menu. Casual attire is quite acceptable here.

A NEARBY PLACE TO DINE

⑤ Mio Amore
Little Mountain Rd., Trout Lake, WA. ☎ **509/395-2264.** Reservations required. Fixed-price dinner $25 and up (depending on market prices). MC, V. Daily with one seating at 7:30pm. NORTHERN ITALIAN.

Mio Amore is a bed-and-breakfast inn that also happens to be the finest restaurant for miles around. Owner and chef Tom Westbrook lived for five years in Italy and learned northern Italian cooking during his sojourn. Dinner includes an appetizer, sorbet, entrée, and dessert, and a respectable selection of wines is available to accompany your meal. Entrées include the likes of charcoal-grilled filet mignon in a cognac-peppercorn sauce, or shrimp sautéed in olive oil, garlic, and butter and flamed in orange brandy. Just a couple of tables are set up in the main rooms of the inn and socializing with other diners is almost *de rigueur*. Little Mountain Road is on the right just after the church and before you reach the gas station in Trout Lake.

HOOD RIVER AFTER DARK

Big Horse Brew Pub
115 State St. ☎ **541/386-4411.**

Located in a vertiginous old house above downtown, this brewpub has a limited selection of brews, but the views from the third floor can't be beat.

Full Sail Tasting Room
506 Columbia St. ☎ **541/386-2247.**

You have to walk past the brewery itself to get to this room at the back of an old industrial building a block off Hood River's main drag. There are big windows overlooking the river.

3 Mount Hood: Skiing, Hiking, Scenic Drives & More

60 miles E of Portland, 46 miles S of Hood River

At 11,235 feet, Mount Hood, a dormant volcano, is the highest point in Oregon. On clear days it forms a stunning backdrop for the high-rises of downtown Portland and beckons temptingly to anyone longing for a bit of alpine air. Winters are the busiest time of year on Mount Hood. With five downhill areas and many miles of cross-country trails, the mountain is a ski bum's dream come true. You have the country's largest night-skiing area, and you can even ski right through the summer at Timberline. Because its snowcapped summit is fairly easily reached by those with only a moderate amount of mountain-climbing experience, it's also the most climbed major peak in the United States.

One of the first settlers to visit Mount Hood was Samuel Barlow, who, in 1845, had traveled the Oregon Trail and was searching for an alternative to taking his wagon train down the treacherous waters of the Columbia River. Barlow blazed a trail across the south flank of Mount Hood and the following year he opened his trail as a toll road. The Barlow Trail, though difficult, was cheaper and safer than rafting down the river. The old trail still exists and is now a hiking and mountain-biking trail.

During the Great Depression the Works Progress Administration employed skilled craftsmen to build the rustic Timberline Lodge at the tree line on the mountain's south slope. Today the lodge is a National Historic Landmark and is the main destination for visitors to the mountain. The views from here, both of Mount Hood's peak and of the Oregon Cascades to the south, are superb and should not be missed.

ESSENTIALS

GETTING THERE   Government Camp, site of several ski areas, is on U.S. 26 near the junction with Ore. 35 from Hood River.

If you're not driving, **Amtrak** has service to Hood River. **Northwest Day Trips** (☎ 503/762-2757) provides winter van service from the Portland area to the ski resorts on Mount Hood. The one-way fare from the airport to Mount Hood is about $25.

VISITOR INFORMATION   Contact the **Mount Hood Information Center,** 65000 E. U.S. 26 (P.O. Box 819), Welches, OR 97067 (☎ 503/622-4822).

EXPLORING THE MOUNTAIN

Mount Hood is often visited as a day-long loop tour that includes the **Columbia Gorge National Scenic Area** as well. If you do this Mount Hood Loop clockwise, stopping in the gorge first, you'll approach the mountain on Ore. 35. This road, after passing through the orchards of the Hood River valley, climbs steadily.

About 10 miles south of Parkdale, you'll come to the turnoff for the **Cooper Spur Ski Area,** the oldest ski area on the mountain. Nearby is the historic **Cloud Cap Inn,** which was built in 1889 and, though no longer open to the public, is on the National Register of Historic Places.

Farther along Ore. 35, you crest the **Barlow Pass** at 4,157 feet, the highest point on the Mount Hood Loop. The **Pacific Crest Trail** crosses the road at the pass on its journey between Canada and Mexico. A little bit farther along you come to picturesque **Trillium Lake,** which is off the highway a short distance and has campgrounds, cabins, and picnic areas. Despite the fact that the Barlow Trail was safer than the Columbia River, it was not without its hazards, as the **Pioneer Woman's Grave** near Trillium Lake attests.

The nearby **White River** is a very popular cross-country ski area in winter. From here it's just a few more miles to **Government Camp** and the turnoff for Timberline Lodge.

If you're heading up to Mount Hood from Portland, take I-84 to the Troutdale and Gresham exit, and follow the signs for the Mount Hood Loop. There are several places to stop along the way to Timberline Lodge if you're not in a hurry. East of the town of Sandy you can visit the **Wasson Brothers Winery** and sample their fruit and berry wines. Right next door at **Janz Berry Farm,** a huge farm stand, you can stock up on picnic foods before continuing up the mountain. If you have a sweet tooth, drop by the **Oregon Candy Farm,** which has an incredible selection of homemade candies.

If you want to see another side of the mountain and have plenty of time, consider a visit to **Lost Lake,** one of the most beautiful lakes in the Oregon Cascades. It's up the winding Lolo Pass Road, which is paved for most of its way. At Lost Lake you'll find campgrounds, cabins, picnic areas, hiking trails, and a spectacular view.

East of Wemme, watch for the historical sign that marks the site of the **Barlow Trail** toll booth. If you're in the mood for a hike, you can hike the historic trail from this point. However, a prettier hike leads to **Mirror Lake,** which is almost to Government Camp and the turnoff for **Timberline Lodge.**

The lodge, besides being a historic mountain lodge with a fabulous view of Mount Hood (see "Where to Stay," below, for details), is surrounded by meadows that burst into bloom in midsummer. You'll also find snow here any time of year, and there's even summer skiing at **Timberline Ski Area.** Timberline Lodge is also the trailhead for several pleasant trails, including the **Timberline Trail,** which circles the mountain and is popular with backpackers. For more information on hiking in Mount Hood, contact the **Mount Hood National Forest,** Zig Zag Ranger District, 70220 E. U.S. 26, Zig Zag, OR 97049 (☎ **503/622-3191**).

Though both hiking and fishing are popular on Mount Hood, skiing attracts the biggest crowds. For information on skiing on Mount Hood, see "Outdoor Activities," in Chapter 10 on Portland.

Summers on Mount Hood, though not as busy as the ski season, do offer quite a few activities. At **Mt. Hood SkiBowl** (☎ 503/272-3206), you can speed down the alpine slide, go horseback riding, or take your mountain bike up to the top of the ski slopes on a chair lift and then ride down on miles of trails. However, hiking the mountain's many trails and fishing its streams and lakes are the most popular summer activities.

WHERE TO STAY

⑤ The Inn at Cooper Spur

10755 Cooper Spur Rd., Mount Hood, OR 97041. ☎ **541/352-6692** or 541/352-6037. 6 rms, 5 cabins, 3 suites. TV TEL. $78 double; $139 cabin or suite for two or four. Additional person $10 extra. AE, MC, V.

If you're looking to get away from it all, try an off-season stay at this surprisingly remote lodge. During ski season, though, you might find it difficult to get a reservation. The inn consists of a main building and a handful of modern log cabins that are certainly the more enjoyable rooms. These cabins have two bed-rooms and a loft area reached by a spiral staircase. There are full kitchens for those wishing to do their own cooking. The inn's restaurant serves decent meals at reasonable prices. Facilities include whirlpools, tennis court, croquet, basketball, and cross-country ski rentals.

✪ Mt. Hood Bed & Breakfast

8885 Cooper Spur Rd., OR 97041. ☎ 541/352-6885 or 800/557-8885. 3 rms, 1 cabin, 1 house. $75–$105 double with or without bath; $105 cabin; $225 house. Rates include full breakfast. No credit cards.

Located on a 42-acre working farm on the northeast side of Mount Hood, this B&B offers a quiet place to get away from it all. As an added bonus, you're only minutes away from a small ski area, and the mountain's major ski areas are less than 30 minutes away. We recommend either the Mount Hood Room or the Mount Adams Room, both of which have views of the respective mountains. An old log cabin on the property has also been renovated and makes for a very private accom-modation. Guests can help out on the farm as well as spend time in a barn that has a tennis court, basketball court, and sauna.

Mt. Hood Inn

87450 E. Government Camp Loop (P.O. Box 400), Government Camp, OR 97028. ☎ 503/272-3205 or 800/443-7777. 56 rms. TV TEL. $90–$135 double. Rates include continental breakfast. AE, DC, DISC, MC, V.

You'll spot this motel at the west end of town beside the Mt. Hood Brew Pub. The guest rooms have a contemporary rustic feel. The "king suites," which are the most expensive rooms, aren't really suites, but they do have two-person whirlpool tubs beside the king-size beds. Other rooms have refrigerators and microwaves. There's an indoor whirlpool, VCR and video rentals, and ski lockers.

Old Welches Inn

26401 E. Welches Rd., Welches, OR 97067. ☎ 503/622-3754. 3 rms, none with bath; 1 cottage. $65–$75 double; $120 cottage for two. Rates include full breakfast. AE, MC, V.

If you're a golfer and prefer the intimacy of a bed-and-breakfast to the impersonal feel of a big resort, the Old Welches Inn is the place for you. You'll be right across the road from the golf course with a great view of the mountains. The Old Welches Inn was built in 1890 and became the first summer resort and hotel on Mount Hood. Today the old white house with its bright-blue trim and shutters looks less like a hotel and more like the private residence it became in the late 1930s. The Salmon River runs right through the backyard. Skiing and hiking are only 15 minutes away.

The Resort at the Mountain

68010 E. Fairway, Welches, OR 97067. ☎ 503/622-3101 or 800/669-7666. Fax 503/622-2222. 160 rms, 73 suites. TV TEL. Mid-June to Sept, $95–$155 double; $175–$230 suite. Oct to mid-June, $87–$127 double; $155–$180 suite. Children 17 and under stay free in parents' room. Special packages available. AE, CB, DC, DISC, MC, V.

Calling the surrounding area "the Highlands of Oregon," the Resort at the Moun-tain has adopted a Scottish theme that emphasizes the resort's 27-hole golf course. Beautifully landscaped grounds that incorporate concepts from Japanese garden design hide the resort's many low-rise buildings. The guest rooms are large and all have either a balcony or a patio. Coffeemakers and special closets for ski gear are available in some rooms.

Dining/Entertainment: A casual dining room decked out in plenty of tartan overlooks the golf course. A more formal dining room serves a combination of Northwest, Scottish, and continental dishes at fairly reasonable prices.

Services: Room service (seasonal), mountain-bike rentals.

Facilities: 27-hole golf course, six tennis courts, outdoor swimming pool, whirlpool tub, fitness center, horseshoes, hiking and nature trails, volleyball, badminton, croquet, basketball, pro shop.

✪ Timberline Lodge

Timberline, OR 97028. ☎ **503/231-7979** or 800/547-1406. Fax 503/272-3710. 60 rms, 50 with bath. $62 double without bath. $92–$162 double with bath. AE, DISC, MC, V. Sno-park permit required to park in winter.

Constructed during the Great Depression as a WPA project, this classic mountain lodge overflows with craftsmanship. The grand stone fireplace, huge exposed beams, and wide plank floors of the lobby impress every first-time visitor. Details are not overlooked anywhere. Woodcarvings, imaginative wrought-iron fixtures, hand-hooked rugs, and handmade furniture complete the rustic picture. An exhibit in the lower lobby presents the history of the hotel, and tours of the hotel are also offered.

The rooms vary in size considerably, with the smallest rooms lacking private bathrooms. However, no matter which room you stay in, you'll be surrounded by the same rustic furnishings. Unfortunately, the room windows are not very large, but you can always retire to the Ram's Head lounge for a better view of Mount Hood.

Dining/Entertainment: The rustic dining room is short on mountain views, but the food is superb, if a bit pricey (see "Where to Dine," below, for details). There's a bar down in a dark dungeon of a place that shouldn't be missed. A bar on the mezzanine is a more open and airy place and also serves food.

Facilities: Ski lifts, ski school and rentals, outdoor pool, sauna, whirlpool, hiking trails.

WHERE TO DINE

In addition to the restaurants listed below, the **Mt. Hood Brew Pub,** 87304 E. Government Camp Loop (☎ **503/272-3724**), offers good microbrews and pub food. With at least six microbrews on tap, and a large selection of Northwest wines, you'll certainly find something to your liking.

Calamity Jane's

42015 U.S. 26, Sandy (next door to Janz Berry Farm). ☎ **503/668-7817.** Burgers $3.25–$11.25. AE, DISC, MC, V. Sun–Fri 11am–10pm, Sat 11am–11pm. BURGERS.

What, you ask, is a $11.25 hamburger? Well, at Calamity Jane's, it's a 1-pound pastrami-and-mushroom cheeseburger. That's right: 1 pound! If you think that's outrageous, wait until you see the other burgers listed on the menu. There's the peanut-butter burger, the George Washington burger (with sour cream and sweet pie cherries), the hot-fudge-and-marshmallow burger—even an unbelievably priced inflation burger. Not all the burgers at this entertaining and rustic eatery are calculated to turn your stomach: Some are just plain delicious. There are even pizza burgers.

Cascade Dining Room

In the Timberline Lodge, Timberline. ☎ **503/272-3710.** Reservations highly recommended on winter weekends. Main courses $15–$22.95. AE, DC, MC, V. Mon–Fri 8–10am, noon–2pm, and 6–8:30pm; Sat–Sun 8–10am, noon–2pm, and 5:30–9pm. NORTHWEST.

It may appear a bit casual from the lobby, and there are no stunning views of Mount Hood even though it's right outside the window, but the Cascade Dining Room is the best restaurant on Mount Hood. The menu features Northwest cuisine, though it's not as creative as at trendier restaurants around the region. For a starter, try the seafood sausage, pickled salmon, and sushi rice roll. The trio of powerful flavors combines for a tongue-tantalizing opening. Local rabbit is served with a red-curry sauce, and prime rib is served with a vibrant apple-horseradish sauce. There's a good wine selection, and desserts showcase the variety of local seasonal ingredients such as raspberries, pears, and apples.

Chalet Swiss

24371 E. Welches Rd., Welches. ☎ **503/622-3600.** Reservations recommended. Main courses $9–$18. AE, MC, V. Daily 5–9:30pm. Closed Mon–Tues in winter. SWISS/ CONTINENTAL.

The interior of this restaurant looks more like a Swiss barn than a Swiss chalet, with old wagon wheels, huge cowbells, and copper pots decorating the open-beamed dining room. Of course there's plenty of Swiss food on the menu. Start with either the raclette, a delicious melted cheese, or the Buendnerfleisch, which is a sort of Swiss prosciutto that's made from beef. If you opt for the latter, then by all means order the cheese fondue neuchateloise for an entrée. There's nothing quite as satisfying after a cold day on the slopes. The entrecôte (New York steak) romande, glazed with spicy herb butter, is tender and juicy, though certainly not for anyone worrying about cholesterol. There's an extensive wine list.

4 The Dalles

128 miles W of Pendleton, 85 miles E of Portland, 133 miles N of Bend

The Dalles, a French word meaning "flagstone," was given to this area by early 19th-century French trappers. These early explorers may have been reminded of stepping stones when they first gazed upon the flat basalt rocks that forced the river through a long stretch of rapids and cascades. These rapids, which were a barrier to river navigation, formed a natural gateway to western Oregon. Pioneers headed for the mild climate and fertile soils of the Willamette Valley would load their wagons onto rafts at this point and float downriver to the mouth of the Willamette and then up that river to Oregon City.

White settlers, the first of whom came to The Dalles as missionaries in 1838, were latecomers to this area. For more than 10,000 years Native Americans had inhabited this site because of the ease with which salmon could be taken from the river as it flowed through the tumultuous rapids. By the 1850s The Dalles was the site of an important military fort and had become a busy river port. Steamships shuttled from here to Cascade Locks on the run to Portland. The coming of the railroad in 1880, and later the flooding of the river's rapids, reduced the importance of The Dalles as a port town. However, cherry orchards, which were first planted near The Dalles in 1854, have become the mainstay of the local economy.

ESSENTIALS

GETTING THERE The Dalles is on I-84 at the junction of U.S. 197, which leads south to Antelope where it connects with U.S. 97.

Amtrak passenger trains stop in The Dalles at First and Federal streets.

VISITOR INFORMATION   Contact **The Dalles Convention & Visitors Bureau,** 404 W. Second St. (P.O. Box 1053), The Dalles, OR 97058 (☎ **541/ 296-6616** or 800/255-3385).

EXPLORING THE AREA

Long before settlers arrived in The Dalles, Lewis and Clark's expedition stopped here. The site of their camp is called **Rock Fort** and is one of the expedition's only documented campsites. You'll find the historic site west of downtown near The Dalles' industrial area. Take West Second Street west, turn right on Webber Street West, and then turn right again on Bargeway Road.

Some of The Dalles' most important historic buildings are to be seen at the **Fort Dalles Museum,** 15th and Garrison streets (☎ **541/296-4547**). Established in 1850, Fort Dalles was the only military post between Fort Laramie and Fort Vancouver. By 1867 it had become unnecessary, and after several buildings were destroyed in a fire, the fort was abandoned. Today there are several of the original buildings still standing, open daily in summer from 10am to 5pm, and in winter on Monday, Thursday, and Friday from noon to 4pm and on Saturday and Sunday from 10am to 4pm (closed the first two weeks of January). Admission is $3, free for children 17 and under.

Within a decade of the establishment of the fort, The Dalles became the county seat of what was the largest county ever created in the United States. Wasco County covered 130,000 square miles between the Rocky Mountains and the Cascade Range. The old **Wasco County Courthouse,** on West Second Street beside Mill Creek (☎ **541/296-6616**), a two-story wooden structure built in 1859, now houses a historical museum. It's open Tuesday through Saturday from 10am to 4pm (from 11am to 3pm in winter); admission is free.

It's hard not to notice the tall spire of **St. Peter's Landmark Church,** at the corner of West Third and Lincoln streets. The church was built in the gothic revival style in 1898, and its spire is topped by a 6-foot-tall rooster.

There are a couple of places where you can get a view of The Dalles and the Columbia Gorge. At **Sorosis Park,** on Scenic Drive, which forms the southern edge of town, you can get a panoramic view of both the town and the gorge. If you head west of town on old scenic loop highway (Ore. 30), you'll come to the **Governor Tom McCall Preserve** on Rowena Plateau. In addition to having spectacular views, this Nature Conservancy Preserve is known for its colorful **wildflower displays** between March and May.

Just east of town rises **The Dalles Lock and Dam** (☎ **541/296-1181**), which provides both irrigation water and electricity. The dam, which was completed in 1957, stretches for 1¹/₂ miles from the Oregon shore to the Washington shore. One of the main reasons this dam was built was to flood the rapids that made this section of the Columbia River impossible to navigate. Among the numerous rapids flooded by the dam were Celilo Falls, which, for thousands of years before the dam was built, were the most important salmon-fishing area in the Northwest. Each year thousands of Native Americans would gather here to catch and smoke salmon, putting the dried fish away for the coming winter. The traditional method of catching the salmon was to use a spear or net with a long pole. Men would build precarious wooden platforms out over the river and catch the salmon as they tried to leap up the falls. You can still see traditional Native American fishing platforms near the Shilo Inn here in The Dalles. The dam's **visitor center** has displays on both the history of the river and the construction of the dam. It's open April to September only, daily from 9am to 6pm; admission is free. To reach the visitor center, take Exit 87 off I-84 and turn right on Northeast Frontage Road.

WHERE TO STAY

Capt. Gray's Guest House

210 W. Fourth St., The Dalles, OR 97058. ☎ **541/298-8222** or 800/448-4729. 3 rms. A/C TEL. $50–$57.50 double. Rates include full breakfast. AE, MC, V.

Located just two blocks from the downtown business district, Capt. Gray's bed-and-breakfast is popular in the summer with visiting windsurfers. The guest rooms are large and filled with Victorian antiques, and one room even has a separate sitting room. The living room is a casual gathering place full of magazines and information on the region. This is a very laid-back sort of place.

Shilo Inn

3223 Brett Clodfelter Way, The Dalles, OR 97058. ☎ **541/298-5502** or 800/222-2244. 112 rms. A/C TV TEL. $58–$94 double. Rates include continental breakfast. AE, DC, DISC, ER, JCB, MC, V.

Though it's a couple of miles east of downtown, the Shilo Inn enjoys the most spectacular setting in town. Set on the banks of the Columbia River at the foot of The Dalles Dam, the motel is adjacent to the Native American ghost town of Lone Pine. The rooms are typical motel units, so it's definitely worth spending a little extra for a river-view room. The dining room and lounge offer moderately priced meals and views of the river. Room service is available and an outdoor pool, whirlpool tub, and sauna provide places to relax.

✪ Williams House Inn

608 W. Sixth St., The Dalles, OR 97058. ☎ **541/296-2889.** 2 rms, 1 suite. A/C TV. $65 double; $75 suite. Rates include continental breakfast. AE, DISC, MC, V.

Classic Victorian elegance awaits you at the Williams House Inn. Surrounded by a wrought-iron fence, green lawns, and colorful gardens, this mansion is listed in the National Registry of Historic Places. Gables, turrets, balconies, and a wrap-around porch are all decorated with myriad flourishes that rank this house among the finest Victorian homes in the West. Inside, Georgian and Victorian antiques and a collection of Chinese objets d'art should keep you moving from room to room as if this were a museum. The two upstairs rooms have private balconies that make them very special places for a romantic weekend. In summer you can enjoy breakfast out at the gazebo. Unfortunately, street noises make the huge front porch a bit noisy.

WHERE TO DINE

✪ Baldwin Saloon

First and Court sts. ☎ **541/296-5666.** Reservations accepted only for parties of six or more. Main courses $7–$18. MC, V. Mon–Thurs 11am–10pm, Fri–Sat 11am–11pm. Closed one hour earlier in winter. AMERICAN/CONTINENTAL.

Built in 1876, the Baldwin Saloon has one of the few remaining cast-iron facades in town. Brick walls, wooden booths, and a high ceiling (high enough to fit a loft with a piano) add to the old-time feel. Whether your tastes run to burgers or oysters Rockefeller, you'll find contentment issuing from the kitchen. Oysters are a house specialty and appear in numerous guises. *One last macabre note:* This building once served as a warehouse storing coffins. Bon appétit.

Ole's Supper Club

2620 W. Second St. ☎ **541/296-6708.** Reservations recommended. Main courses $8–$20. AE, MC, V. Tues–Thurs 4:30–9pm, Fri–Sat 4:30–10pm. PRIME RIB/CONTINENTAL.

Though it's located on a rather industrial stretch of road on the west side of town, this unassuming restaurant is The Dalles' best. The decor certainly won't distract you from your meal, and neither will the views out the windows. But, never mind—the food's great. Prime rib au jus is what has made this restaurant a local legend, and it comes in sizes for hearty appetites (10 ounces) and heartier appetites (16 ounces). The kitchen also does a respectable job on the steaks and seafood, but if you're only here for the day, go with the prime rib. An excellent selection of wines is available.

SIDE TRIPS FROM THE DALLES
KLICKITAT COUNTY, WASHINGTON

Across the river in Washington you can make a loop drive that takes you past several of the most interesting sites in the region. To visit the following attractions, cross the river from The Dalles and turn east on Wash. 14. At Maryhill, head north on U.S. 97 to Goldendale. In Goldendale, head west on Wash. 142, which takes you back to Wash. 14 west of the bridge to The Dalles.

Horsethief Lake State Park

Wash. 14. ☎ **509/767-1159.** Free admission. Apr–Oct, daily 9am–dusk. Closed Nov–Mar.

Located between The Dalles and Wishram on Wash. 14, Horsethief Lake is a popular fishing area and campground; however, long before the state park was designated, this area was a popular gathering spot for Native Americans. The park lies not far from the famous Celilo Falls, which were, before white settlers arrived, the most prolific salmon-fishing area in the Northwest. Each year for thousands of years Native Americans would gather here from as far away as present-day northern California and southern British Columbia. These Native Americans left signs of their annual visits, in the form of **petroglyphs,** on rocks that are now protected at Horsethief Lake State Park. Petroglyphs abound here, the most famous of which is Tsagaglalal ("she who watches"), which is a large face that gazes down on the Columbia River. Unfortunately, Tsagaglalal was vandalized a few years ago, and the only way to see this and other petroglyphs is on ranger-led walks held on Friday and Saturday mornings during the season the park is open. You must call ahead and make a reservation for these tours.

✪ Maryhill Museum and Stonehenge

35 Maryhill Museum Dr., Goldendale, WA. ☎ **509/773-3733.** Admission $5 adults, $4.50 seniors, $1.50 children 6–16. Mar 15–Nov 15, daily 9am–5pm. Closed Nov 16–Mar 14.

Atop a windswept bluff overlooking the Columbia River, at a spot more than 100 miles from the nearest city, eccentric entrepreneur Sam Hill built a grand mansion he called Maryhill. Though he never lived in the mansion, he did turn it into a museum that today is one of the finest, most eclectic, and least visited major museums in the Northwest. Exhibited here are an internationally acclaimed collection of sculptures and drawings by Auguste Rodin; an extensive collection of Native American artifacts, including rock carvings, beadwork, and baskets; the personal collection of Queen Marie of Romania; and vintage miniature French fashion mannequins. A few miles farther east from Maryhill, you'll come to Hill's concrete reproduction of Stonehenge, which he had built as a memorial to local men who died in World War I.

Goldendale Observatory

1602 Observatory Dr., Goldendale. ☎ **509/773-3141.** Free admission. Apr–Sept, Wed–Sun 2–5pm and 8pm–midnight; Oct–Mar, Sat 1–5pm and 7–9pm, Sun 1–5pm.

If you happen to be an amateur astronomer, you won't want to miss a visit to the Goldendale Observatory. The central 24^1/$_2$-inch reflector is one of the largest public telescopes in the country—large enough for scientific research. But instead it's dedicated to sharing the stars with the general public. The observatory is out in this remote part of the state because this region's dry weather and distance from city lights almost guarantees that every night will be a good night for stargazing.

Where to Stay & Dine

✪ Highland Creeks Resort

2120 Scenic Hwy. 97 (U.S. 97), Goldendale, WA 98620. ☎ **509/773-4026** or 800/458-0174. 23 rms. $46–$180 double. AE, MC, V.

Located in the ponderosa-pine forests north of Goldendale, this secluded resort is a popular weekend getaway for people from around the region. The remote location guarantees a peaceful and stress-free retreat, and if you book one of the creekside spa rooms, you can sit and soak while you listen to the rushing waters of the Little Kickitat River. Some rooms also have fireplaces, and all the rooms are very private, which makes this an excellent romantic getaway spot. Hiking trails and a sports court offer activities. The dining room, which overlooks the river, features Northwest cuisine, and often includes a few wild-game dishes. If you're looking to get away from it all in comfort, this is a good bet.

SHANIKO GHOST TOWN

Between 1900 and 1911 Shaniko was the largest wool-shipping center in the country, and claims to have been the site of the last range war between cattle ranchers and sheep herders. However, when the railroad line from the Columbia River down to Bend bypassed Shaniko, the town fell on hard times. Eventually, when a flood washed out the railroad into town, Shaniko nearly ceased to exist. Today the false-fronted buildings and wooden sidewalks make this Oregon's favorite and liveliest ghost town. Antiques shops, a wedding chapel, and a historic hotel make for a fun excursion or overnight getaway. Each year on the first weekend of August, the **Shaniko Days** celebration brings life to the town with stagecoach rides, shootouts, and plenty of crafts vendors.

Where to Stay & Dine

✪ Shaniko Historic Hotel

Fourth and E sts., Shaniko, OR 97057. ☎ **541/489-3441.** 18 rms. $56 double. Rates include full breakfast. DISC, MC, V.

This restored two-story brick hotel is a surprisingly solid little place in a ghost town full of glorified shacks. The faded elegance hints at the wealth that once made the fortunes of area sheep ranchers. An upstairs bridal suite is available for those who happen to be getting married in town, but otherwise, the rooms are simple and tend to be on the small side, although they do fit a queen-size bed and a rollaway bed. The hotel was restored in 1985 and the rooms were remodeled to include bathrooms and to be slightly larger than they were before.

The Oregon Coast 12

Stretching from the mouth of the Columbia River in the north to California's redwood country in the south, the Oregon coast is a shoreline of stunning natural beauty. In many spots along the coast, the mountains of the densely forested Coast Range rise straight from the ocean's waves to form rugged, windswept headlands still bearing the colorful names given them by early explorers—Cape Foulweather, Cape Blanco, Cape Perpetua. Offshore lie hundreds of monoliths and tiny islands that serve as homes to sea birds, sea lions, and seals. Lying between these rocky points are miles of sandy beaches. On the central coast there's so much sand that sand dunes rise as high as 500 feet.

To allow visitors to enjoy all this beauty, the state has created nearly 80 **state parks and waysides** between Fort Stevens State Park in the north and Winchuck Wayside in the south. Among the more popular activities at these parks are kite flying and beachcombing— but not swimming (the water is too cold).

Wildlife is abundant along the coast, and sea lions and seals can often be seen sunning themselves on rocks. The best places to observe these sea mammals are at Sea Lion Caves north of Florence and at Cape Arago State Park outside of Coos Bay. Gray whales are also regular visitors to the Oregon coast. Twice a year, during their migrations between the Arctic and the waters off Baja California, Mexico, the whales pass close by the coast and can be easily spotted from headlands such as Tillamook Head, Cape Meares, Cape Lookout, and Cape Blanco. The best time to spot whales is in late winter and early spring. At the Oregon Coast Aquarium in Newport, you can learn more about these and all the myriad other animals and plants that inhabit the diverse environments of the Oregon coast. Near the town of Reedsport, the Dean Creek meadows have been set aside as an elk preserve, and it's often possible to spot 100 or more elk grazing here.

Rivers, bays, and offshore waters are also home to some of the best **fishing** in the country. The rivers, though depleted by a century of overfishing, are still home to salmon, steelhead, and trout, most of which are now hatchery raised. Several charter-boat marinas up and down the coast offer saltwater fishing for salmon and bottom fish, and few anglers return from these trips without a good catch. **Crabbing and clamming** are two more productive coastal pursuits that can turn a trip to the beach into a time for feasting.

Oh, one last thing we forgot to mention. As you may have already heard, it rains a lot here. Bring a raincoat, and don't let a little moisture prevent you from enjoying one of the most beautiful coastlines in the world. In fact, the mists and fogs add an aura of mystery to the coast's dark, forested mountain slopes.

1 Astoria

95 miles NW of Portland; 20 miles S of Long Beach, WA; 17 miles N of Seaside

"Quaint it ain't" is a motto that was popular in Astoria a few years back, and those who have heard this description will be pleasantly surprised when they see this historic town at the mouth of the Columbia River. Sure, it has its seedy side, but it also has what may be the greatest concentration of historic Victorian homes in Oregon. These houses date to the 1870s when salmon canneries turned the town into the state's second-largest city. Today it's Astoria's history, old homes, and scenic location overlooking the mile-wide river mouth that give the city much of its appeal.

ESSENTIALS

GETTING THERE From Portland, take U.S. 30 west. From the north or south, take U.S. 101.

Astoria is served by **Pacific Transit System** buses (☎ 360/642-9418) from the Washington coast as far north as Raymond, Washington.

VISITOR INFORMATION Contact the **Greater Astoria–Warrenton Area Chamber of Commerce,** 111 W. Marine Dr. (P.O. Box 176), Astoria, OR 97103-0176 (☎ 503/325-6311).

GETTING AROUND If you need a taxi, contact **Yellow Cab** (☎ 503/325-3131).

FESTIVALS The **Astoria Regatta,** held each year in early August, is the city's biggest festival. As part of the festival you can catch a performance of the Astor Street Opry Company's *Shanghaied in Astoria,* a musical melodrama staged at the Elks Club, 453 11th St. (☎ 503/325-6104).

EXPLORING THE AREA
THE TOP ATTRACTIONS

Columbia River Maritime Museum
1792 Marine Dr. ☎ **503/325-2323.** Admission $5 adults, $4 seniors, $2 children 6–17. Daily 9:30am–5pm. Closed Thanksgiving and Dec 25.

The Columbia River, the second-largest river in the United States, was the object of centuries of exploration in the Northwest. Since its discovery in 1792, the Columbia has become as important to the region as the Mississippi is to the Midwest. Considered one of the finest maritime museums in the country, this museum contains within its architecturally striking wave-shaped building displays on all aspects of the river's maritime history. The Columbia Bar, an area of constantly shifting sands at the mouth of the river, and often high seas have made the Columbia one of the world's most difficult rivers to enter. Consequently, you'll see displays on shipwrecks, lighthouses, and lifesaving. Fishing, navigation, and naval history are also subjects of museum exhibits. Docked beside the museum and open to museum visitors is the lightship *Columbia,* the last seagoing lighthouse ship to serve on the West Coast.

The Oregon Coast

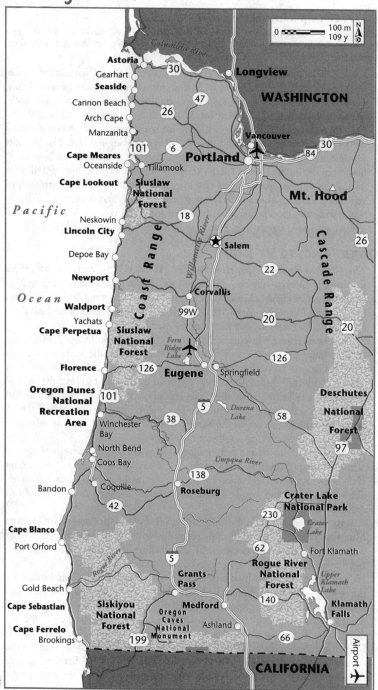

0 ___ 100 m
109 y

N

Columbia River

Astoria
Gearhart
Seaside
Cannon Beach
Arch Cape
Manzanita
Cape Meares
Oceanside
Cape Lookout

Pacific

Neskowin
Lincoln City
Depoe Bay
Newport

Ocean

Waldport
Yachats
Cape Perpetua

Florence

Oregon Dunes
National
Recreation
Area
Winchester
Bay
North Bend
Coos Bay
Bandon
Coquille

Cape Blanco
Port Orford

Gold Beach
Cape Sebastian
Cape Ferrelo
Brookings

Longview

WASHINGTON

Vancouver

Portland

Mt. Hood

Tillamook

Siuslaw
National
Forest

Coast Range

Cascade Range

Salem

Corvallis

Willamette River

Fern
Ridge
Lake

Siuslaw
National
Forest

Eugene

Springfield

Deschutes

National

Forest

Dorena
Lake

Umpqua River

Roseburg

Crater Lake
National Park

Crater
Lake

Fort Klamath

Upper
Klamath
Lake

Rogue River

Siskiyou
National
Forest

Oregon
Caves
National
Monument

Grants
Pass

Medford

Ashland

Rogue River
National
Forest

Klamath
Falls

Airport

CALIFORNIA

Airport

1931

30
47
26
6
101
18
99W
22
20
84
30
26
20
126
126
5
38
58
97
138
42
230
62
140
5
199
66

✪ Fort Clatsop National Memorial

Off U.S. 101 5 miles southwest of Astoria. ☎ **503/861-2471.** Admission $2 ($4 maximum per family). Labor Day to mid-June, daily 8am–5pm; mid-June to Labor Day, daily 8am–6pm. Closed Dec 25.

During the winter of 1805–06, Meriwether Lewis, William Clark, and the other members of the Corps of Discovery, having crossed the continent from St. Louis, camped at a spot near the mouth of the Columbia River. They built a log stockade and named their encampment Fort Clatsop after the local Clatsop peoples who had befriended them. Today's Fort Clatsop is a reconstruction of Lewis and Clark's winter encampment and is built near the site of the original fort. The 50-foot-square compound contains seven rooms, each of which is furnished much as it may have been during Lewis and Clark's stay. On weekends in late spring and daily during the summer, park rangers clad in period clothing give demonstrations of activities pursued by the explorers—from candle making and firearms use to buckskin sewing and food preparation. In the visitor center you can learn the history of the Corps of Discovery and Fort Clatsop before visiting the stockade itself.

OTHER THINGS TO SEE & DO

The **Clatsop County Historical Society** (☎ 503/325-2203) operates three museums in Astoria—the Flavel House Museum, the Heritage Museum, and the Uppertown Fire Fighters Museum—all open May to September, daily from 10am to 5pm; and October to April, daily from 11am to 4pm. Admission to all three museums is $5 for adults and $2.50 for children.

The **Flavel House Museum,** on the corner of Eighth and Duane streets, is the restored home of Capt. George Flavel, who made his fortune operating the first pilot service over the Columbia River Bar and was Astoria's first millionaire. In 1885 he built this Queen Anne–style Victorian mansion, which was the envy of every Astoria resident. Today the Flavel House is still the most elegant mansion in town and is preserved as a museum. The high-ceilinged rooms are filled with period furnishings that accent the home's superb construction. Of particular note is the ornate woodworking throughout the house.

The history of Astoria and surrounding Clatsop County are the focus of exhibits at the **Heritage Museum,** 1618 Exchange St., housed in Astoria's former City Hall. Native American and pioneer artifacts comprise the main exhibits, but there's also an art gallery and a collection of historic photos dating from the 1880s to the 1930s.

If you're interested in fire-fighting history, stop by the **Uppertown Fire Fighters Museum,** on the corner of 30th Street and Marine Drive. Housed in a former brewery building that was closed by Prohibition, the museum includes fire-fighting equipment dating from between 1877 and 1921.

Atop Coxcomb Hill, which is reached by driving up 16th Street and following the signs, you'll find the **Astoria Column.** Built in 1926, the column is patterned after Trajan's Column in Rome and stands 125 feet tall. On the exterior wall of the column a mural depicts the history of this area. It's 164 steps up to the top of the column, and on a clear day the view is well worth the effort. The column is open daily from dawn to dusk and admission is free. On the way up to the Astoria Column, stop by **Fort Astoria,** on the corner of 15th and Exchange streets. A log blockhouse and historical marker commemorate the site of the trading post established by John Jacob Astor's fur traders.

Fort Stevens State Park, 8 miles from Astoria at the mouth of the Columbia (☎ 503/861-2000), preserves a fort that was built during the Civil War to protect the Columbia River and its important port cities. Though Fort Stevens had the distinction of being the only mainland military reservation to be fired on by the Japanese, the fort was deactivated after World War II. Today the fort's extensive grounds include historic buildings and gun emplacements, a museum housing military artifacts, miles of bicycle paths and beaches, and a campground and picnic area. It's open in summer, daily from 10am to 6pm, and the rest of the year, Wednesday through Sunday from 10am to 4pm; admission is $3. At the north end of the park you can climb to the top of a viewing tower and get a good look at the South Jetty, which was built to make navigating the mouth of the Columbia easier. Also within the park you can see the wreck of the *Peter Iredale*, one ship that did not make it safely over the sandbars at the river's mouth.

If you'd like to see what area artists are up to, stop by the **Ricciardi Gallery,** 108 10th St. (☎ **503/325-5450**), which also has an espresso bar.

WHERE TO STAY

Columbia River Inn

1681 Franklin Ave., Astoria, OR 97103. ☎ **503/325-5044** or 800/953-5044. 5 rms. $70–$85 double. Rates include full breakfast. MC, V.

The exterior of this old Victorian home has been dolled up in shades of pink and blue in the fashion of the "painted ladies" of San Francisco. Inside, reproduction Victorian-era furnishings set the stage for a stay with friendly proprietor Karen Nelson. The inn's country decor was done by the owner, and if you see something you like, you just might be able to buy a similar item at the inn's Krafty's Korner gift shop. Each room is decorated differently, but they all have a little refrigerator and electric teapot. The Victorian Rose and River Queen rooms have the best views. In order to get private bathrooms into every room, some strange remodeling had to be done. In Amanda's Room, an odd little shower was tucked into one corner.

⑨ Crest Motel

5366 Leif Erickson Dr. (about 2 miles east of town on U.S. 30), Astoria, OR 97103. ☎ **503/325-3141.** 40 rms. TV TEL. $45.50–$78.50 double. AE, DISC, MC, V.

The Crest Motel sits high on a hillside overlooking Astoria and the river. The views, congenial atmosphere, and comfortable refurbished rooms have made this motel immensely popular. Keep in mind that the lower-priced rooms have no views—and since the views are the main reason to stay here, it's worth a bit of a splurge for a better room even if you're on a tight budget. The deluxe-view rooms are very large and have sliding glass doors and a patio or balcony. You'll also find a coffeemaker in your room and a whirlpool tub in a gazebo overlooking the river.

✪ Franklin Street Station Bed and Breakfast Inn

1140 Franklin St., Astoria, OR 97103. ☎ **503/325-4314** or 800/448-1098. 6 rms. $63–$115 double. Rates include full breakfast. MC, V.

Owned and operated by Renée Caldwell, the daughter of the Columbia River Inn's hostess, this bed-and-breakfast is three blocks from downtown Astoria. Though from the exterior this house doesn't seem to epitomize Victorian ornateness, inside you'll find rich wood accents and trim in every room. Built in 1900, the large house has been completely renovated and each of the guest rooms now has a private bathroom. The best room in the house, if you don't mind the climb, is the attic Captain's Quarters, which has a great view of the Columbia, a clawfoot tub, TV, VCR, stereo, and wet bar. The Columbia Room is another of our favorites because of its river-view deck.

Rosebriar Hotel

636 14th St., Astoria, OR 97103. ☎ **503/325-7427** or 800/487-0224. 10 rms, 1 cottage. TV TEL. $48–$109 double. Rates include continental breakfast. MC, V.

Originally built as a private home, the Rosebriar became a convent in the 1950s. In its current incarnation as a hotel and conference center, the Rosebriar is decorated in the style of a 1920s hotel. Ornate wainscoting, scrollwork ceilings, and lots of wood trim show the quality of workmanship that went into this home when it was built in 1902. The grand old Georgian mansion sits high above the river and high above the street, with commanding views from the two front rooms. If you're seeking that extra bit of privacy for a special occasion, ask for the carriage-house cottage, which has its own fireplace, whirlpool tub, and private patio.

Shilo Inn–Warrenton

1609 E. Harbor Dr., Warrenton, OR 97146. ☎ **503/861-2181** or 800/222-2244. 65 rms. TV TEL. $70–$96 double. AE, CB, DC, DISC, ER, JCB, MC, V.

Located just across the Youngs Bay Bridge and a little bit closer to the beach than other Astoria lodgings, the Shilo Inn is also the only place in town with an indoor swimming pool, whirlpool tub, sauna, steam room, and fitness center. The rooms here are large enough to be billed as minisuites and have microwaves, refrigerators, and wet bars. There's a restaurant and lounge across the parking lot from the hotel. The rooms on the upper floors have a view of the river.

WHERE TO DINE

In addition to the restaurants listed below, you might also want to check out **Josephson's,** 106 Marine Dr. (☎ **503/325-2190**), which is a local seafood-smoking company that sells smoked salmon by the pound, but that also has a take-out deli counter where you can get clam chowder, crab melts, and the like. **Victoria Dahl's Antiques & Espresso,** 2921 Marine Dr. (☎ **503/325-7109**), is a former dry-goods store that captures the spirit of Victorian Astoria better than any other restaurant in town. Ornate period furnishings surround you as you enjoy an espresso.

ⓢ Columbian Café

1114 Marine Dr. ☎ **503/325-2233.** Breakfast or lunch $3.25–$6.50; dinner $5–$10. No credit cards. Mon–Tues 8am–2pm, Wed–Thurs 8am–2pm and 5–8pm, Fri 8am–2pm and 5–9pm, Sat 10am–2pm and 5–9pm. VEGETARIAN.

This tiny place looks a bit like a cross between a college hangout and a seaport diner, and indeed the clientele reflects this atmosphere. There are only three or four booths and a lunch counter, and the café's reputation for good vegetarian fare keeps the seats full throughout the day. Crêpes are the house specialty and come with a variety of fillings, including black beans or curried bananas. Dinner offers a bit more variety and there are always a few specials. The crowd here is primarily young and hip.

Pier 11 Feed Store Restaurant

At the foot of 11th St. ☎ **503/325-0279.** Reservations recommended. Breakfast $2.50–$8; lunch $2.75–$9.50; dinner $10.50–$18. DISC, MC, V. Daily 7am–10pm. SEAFOOD.

Originally a freight depot for river cargo and one of the few buildings in town that was not destroyed by a fire in 1922, Pier 11 now houses a few small shops and this popular seafood restaurant. Nearly everyone gets a good view of the river through the restaurant's wall of glass, and if you're lucky you might spot some seals or sea lions frolicking just outside the window. Even if there are no seals, you can enjoy the view across the river mouth to the mountains in Washington and watch the ship traffic passing by. Meals are simply prepared and are usually quite good, although the restaurant does have an occasional off night. If you've never had razor clams, check to see if they're available when you visit.

The Ship Inn

1 Second St. ☎ **503/325-0033.** Main courses $4.50–$15.25. MC, V. Daily 11:30am–9:30pm. SEAFOOD.

A British couple who found that Astoria's weather made them homesick opened this fish-and-chips restaurant to share England's famous seafood with the Northwest. You can get full or half portions of halibut, cod, prawns, scallops, oysters, or squid served up with steaming-hot chips (french fries to us Yanks). You can also order a full dinner, which includes soup, salad, beverage, and ice cream as well. Meat eaters can try Cornish or chicken pasties, which are a sort of British meat pie. The restaurant lacks much decor, but there are big windows that take in a view of the bridge across the Columbia.

2 Seaside

17 miles S of Astoria, 79 miles W of Portland, 7 miles N of Cannon Beach

Seaside is a town with a split personality. On the one hand it's a historic beach resort dating from 1899, filled with quaint cottages and tree-lined streets that evoke a different era's ideas of what a seaside vacation should be. On the other hand it has all the trappings today's families associate with a beach vacation, including modern buildings filled with video arcades and souvenir shops. As the closest ocean beach to Portland, Seaside has long been a popular family destination; it's about as close as you can come to a Coney Island–style beach town in Oregon. Crowds and traffic are a way of life here on summer weekends, so if you're searching for a peaceful place to relax and unwind, Seaside is not for you. However, the nearby community of Gearhart, which has long been a retreat for wealthy Portlanders, is as quiet as any town as you'll find on this coast.

ESSENTIALS

GETTING THERE   Seaside is on U.S. 101 just north of the junction with U.S. 26 which connects to Portland.

VISITOR INFORMATION   Contact the **Seaside Chamber of Commerce,** 7 N. Roosevelt (P.O. Box 7), Seaside, OR 97138-0007 (☎ **503/738-6391** or 800/444-6740).

ENJOYING THE BEACH & SEASIDE'S OTHER ATTRACTIONS

Seaside's centerpiece is its 2-mile-long beachfront **Promenade** (or Prom), which was built in 1921. It's divided into the North Prom and the South Prom by the Turnaround, a local landmark at the west end of Broadway. Here at the Turnaround a bronze statue of Meriwether Lewis and William Clark marks the official end of the trail for the Lewis and Clark expedition.

Miles of **white-sand beach** begin just south of Seaside at the foot of the imposing Tillamook Head and stretch north to the mouth of the Columbia River. Though the waters here are quite cold and few people venture in farther than knee-deep, there are lifeguards on duty all summer, which is one reason Seaside is popular with families. With waters that never warm up, kite flying, beach cycling, and other nonaquatic activities prove far more popular than swimming.

In addition to the miles of sandy beach, there are, in the crowded downtown business district, all the video-and-skeeball arcades your kids will ever need. The **Seaside Aquarium,** Second Avenue and the Promenade (☎ 503/738-6211), is popular since you can feed the seals. Admission is $4.50 for adults and $2.25 for children.

All over town there are places that rent in-line skates, four-wheeled bicycles called surreys, and three-wheeled cycles for pedaling on the beach. Skates rent for $4 an hour, while cycles go for between $7 and $20 an hour depending on what sort you want.

If you prefer hiking to cycling, head south of town to the end of Sunset Boulevard where you'll find the start of the **Tillamook Head Trail,** which leads 6 miles over the headland to Indian Beach in **Ecola State Park.**

Golfers can play a round at the **Seaside Golf Club,** 451 Ave. U (☎ 503/738-5261), or the **Gearhart Golf Links,** on North Marion Street in Gearhart (☎ **503/738-3538**).

Though Seaside is the oldest beach resort in Oregon, there isn't much here to keep the history buff entertained. The **Lewis and Clark Salt Works,** a reconstruction of a fire pit used by members of the famous expedition, is on Lewis & Clark Way between the Promenade and Beach Drive, eight blocks south of Broadway. During the winter of 1805–06, while the expedition was camped at Fort Clatsop near present-day Astoria, Lewis and Clark sent several men southwest 15 miles to a good spot for making salt from seawater. It took three men nearly two months to produce four bushels of salt for the return trip to the east. Five kettles were used for boiling seawater, and the fires were kept stoked 24 hours a day. Ironically, Captain Clark felt no need for salt, though Meriwether Lewis and the rest of the men felt it was necessary for the enjoyment of their meager rations. Each year in July and August, the *Lewis and Clark Historical Drama* is presented on the banks of the Neawanna River in Seaside.

At the **Seaside Museum,** 570 Necanicum Dr. (☎ **503/738-7065**), you can see Native American artifacts dating back to A.D. 230 as well as more recent items of historic significance. It's open daily from 10:30am to 4:30pm; admission is $2. The adjacent **Butterfield Cottage** is decorated much as a summer cottage would have looked in 1912.

WHERE TO STAY

Ⓢ Gearhart Ocean Inn

67 N. Cottage St., Gearhart, OR 97138. ☎ **503/738-7373.** 11 rms. TV. $49–$79 double. MC, V.

Located in nearby Gearhart, this old motor court–style motel has been fully renovated with all the care that's usually lavished on Victorian homes. A taupe exterior with white trim gives the two rows of wooden buildings a touch of sophistication, and there are roses and Adirondack chairs adding character to the grounds, though a wide expanse of gravel parking lot does detract somewhat from the effect. The rooms all have lots of character and have been fully renovated. The most expensive rooms are two stories with hardwood floors, a kitchen, and even a garage. The decor is a combination of country cute and casual contemporary.

✪ The Gilbert Inn

341 Beach Dr., Seaside, OR 97138. ☎ **503/738-9770.** 10 rms, 4 apts. TV. $69–$115 double. Room rates include full breakfast. AE, MC, V.

One block from the beach and one block south of Broadway, on the edge of both the shopping district and one of Seaside's old residential neighborhoods, stands the Gilbert Inn, a big yellow Queen Anne–style Victorian house with a pretty little yard. Alexander Gilbert, who had this house built in 1892, was once the mayor of Seaside, and he built a stately home worthy of someone in such a high position. Gilbert made good use of the plentiful fir trees of the area; the interior walls and ceilings are constructed of tongue-and-groove fir planks. The current owners, Dick and Carole Rees, have decorated the house in country French decor that manages to enhance the Victorian ambience.

Riverside Inn Bed & Breakfast

430 S. Holladay Dr., Seaside, OR 97138. ☎ **503/738-8254** or 800/826-6151. 11 rms. TV. $50–$85 double. Rates include full breakfast. AE, DISC, MC, V.

Though it's located on busy Holladay Drive, the Riverside Inn is an oasis amid the traffic and businesses. Beautiful gardens frame the restored 1907 home and its attached cottages. Through the backyard flows the Necanicum River, and there's a sprawling multilevel deck for enjoying the riverside location. Inside, all the rooms are a bit different, with antique country decor and an emphasis on fishing collectibles. The Captain's Quarters room, way up on the third floor, features a skylight directly over the bathtub and has the feel of a well-appointed artist's garret. Another of our favorite rooms here is the Old Seaside, a two-room unit with its own private deck. If you're planning a long stay, there are some rooms with kitchenettes.

✪ Seaside Inn

581 S. Promenade, Seaside, OR 97138. ☎ **503/738-6403** or 800/772-PROM. Fax 503/738-6403. 13 rms. TV TEL. $95–$175 double. Rates include full breakfast. MC, V.

This small contemporary inn has added a touch of architectural interest to the traditional facades along the Prom, and inside you'll find other nontraditional touches. All the rooms are different. Our favorite is the rock 'n' roll room, which features a bed made from part of a 1959 Oldsmobile plus hula hoops and lava lamps. Other rooms are far less outrageous and are primarily calculated to put you in a romantic mood. Most rooms have ocean views and whirlpool tubs. Breakfast is served in the oceanfront lobby where there's also a bar for guests.

Shilo Inn–Seaside

30 N. Promenade (at Broadway), Seaside, OR 97138-6611. ☎ **503/738-9571** or 800/222-2244. Fax 503/738-0674. 113 rms. TV TEL. High season, $125–$275 double. Low season, $62–$150 double. AE, DISC, MC, V.

Located right on the Turnaround that marks the end of the trail for the Lewis and Clark expedition, the Shilo Inn is a very comfortable and modern beachfront resort hotel. If you expect to spend more time in the pool than on the beach, you should make this your first choice in Seaside—the recreation facilities here are the best in town. The indoor swimming pool, whirlpool tub, steam room, sauna, and exercise room all overlook the beach and are separated from the lobby by a wall of glass that lets people in the lobby look out at the ocean as well.

Oceanfront guest rooms all have large balconies and fireplaces so you can enjoy your stay no matter what the weather. These rooms also come with kitchenettes.

The hotel's dining room has a splendid view and serves seafood in the $10 to $15 range. Sunday brunch is especially popular. In the lounge there's nightly Top 40 dance music.

WHERE TO DINE

Dooger's Seafood & Grill

505 Broadway. ☎ **503/738-3773.** Reservations not accepted. Meals $5–$19. MC, V. Daily 11am–10pm. SEAFOOD.

For no-frills, simple, decent seafood in a family atmosphere, go to Dooger's. Prices are reasonable, especially at lunch, when you can order from a list of specials that includes steamers, calamari, or petrale sole accompanied by a salad topped with bay shrimp. Try their tasty clam chowder.

Miguel's

412 Broadway. ☎ **503/738-0171.** Reservations recommended on summer weekends. Main courses $6–$10. DISC, MC, V. Mon–Thurs noon–9pm, Fri–Sat noon–10pm, Sun 12:30–9pm. MEXICAN.

This small, family-run place diagonally across the street from Dooger's is a good choice for Mexican home-cookin'—they even bake their own tortilla chips, served with a chunky salsa. Along with the expected Mexican ingredients, such as rice, beans, and meat, they also use local seafood in dishes such as a fresh crab enchilada. The fish tacos are our favorite.

✪ Pacific Way Cafe and Bakery

601 Pacific Way, in Gearhart. ☎ **503/738-0245.** Sandwiches/salads $4.50–$9. MC, V. Wed–Sun 9:30am–4:30pm. BAKERY/SANDWICHES.

You'll find this former mom-and-pop grocery store in the center of nearby Gearhart. The present owners are admittedly mentally stuck in the 1930s—as the vintage interior of the restaurant will attest. Bakery items are delicious, especially the cinnamon rolls, marionberry scones, and pecan sticky buns, and along with an espresso they make a fine excuse for lounging in the flower-filled courtyard, weather permitting. Appetizing sandwich concoctions include hot Dungeness crab with garlic mayonnaise and pesto chicken.

Vista Sea Café

150 Broadway. ☎ **503/738-8108.** Pizzas $9–$22; sandwiches $4–$6.75. MC, V. Summer, daily 11:30am–9:30pm; winter, Fri–Tues 11:30am–7:30pm. PIZZA/SANDWICHES.

Whether you're in the mood for pizza or soup and a sandwich, you can't go wrong here. High-backed antique booths and a few tables in a bright and artistically decorated dining room give the café a touch of class, and big windows let in plenty of sunshine in the summer. Whatever you do, don't leave without trying the clam chowder, which is served with a delicious homemade beer bread. On the pizza menu you'll find such creations as pesto pizza and a veggie-and-bleu-cheese pizza.

3 Cannon Beach

7 miles S of Seaside, 112 miles N of Newport, 79 miles W of Portland

Cannon Beach is the Oregon coast's most renowned artists' community. So renowned has it become that in recent years the commercialization of the town has detracted quite a bit from the charm that originally attracted artists to the area.

Despite the crowds, Cannon Beach still has a village atmosphere, and summer throngs and traffic jams can do nothing to assault the fortresslike beauty of the rocks that lie just offshore. (In fact, Cannon Beach was named for several cannons that washed ashore after the sloop-of-war *Shark* wrecked on these rocks in 1846.) The most famous of these monoliths is **Haystack Rock,** which rises 235 feet above the water at the edge of the beach. Because of their resemblance to piles of hay, such offshore rocks are known generically as haystack rocks or sea stacks, but this is *the* Haystack Rock and is the most photographed rock on the Oregon coast. One glance up and down the beach at the many offshore sea stacks and it's easy to understand what has attracted artists and vacationers alike to tiny Cannon Beach.

ESSENTIALS

GETTING THERE   Cannon Beach is on U.S. 101 just south of the junction with U.S. 26.

VISITOR INFORMATION   Contact the **Cannon Beach Chamber of Commerce,** 207 N. Spruce St. (P.O. Box 64), Cannon Beach, OR 97110 (☎ **503/436-2623**).

GETTING AROUND   A **shuttle** operates Friday through Tuesday from 10am to 1pm and 2 to 6pm. It runs the entire length of town and passengers may board at any point. Donations for the ride are accepted.

FESTIVALS   Each year in early June, the **Sand Castle Day** contest turns the beach into one vast canvas for sand sculptors from all over the region, and in early November, the **Stormy Weather Arts Festival** celebrates the arrival of winter storms.

EXPLORING THE TOWN, THE COAST & NEARBY STATE PARKS

Seven miles of wide sandy **beach** stretch south from Cannon Beach, but it's the offshore rocks and not the abundance of sand that have made this beach so popular. Most of the rocks are protected as the nesting grounds of numerous species of sea birds. The most colorful of these is the **tufted puffin,** which you should be able to spot sitting on the rocks. Though Haystack Rock is the area's most famous monolith, another offshore rock is the site of the **Tillamook Rock Lighthouse,** which was built in 1879 and decommissioned in 1957.

Kite flying, surf fishing, and beachcombing are all popular Cannon Beach pastimes. If you've always dreamed of **riding a horse on the beach,** your dream can come true here in Cannon Beach. Guided rides are offered by the stables at the Sea Ranch R.V. Park. The price is $20 per hour and the rides head down Ecola Creek to the beach and then into Ecola State Park.

Ecola State Park, just north of town, offers the most breathtaking vantage point from which to soak up the view of Cannon Beach and Haystack Rock. The park also has several picnic areas perched on bluffs high above the crashing waves and a trail that leads 6 miles over Tillamook Head to Seaside. This was the southernmost point that Lewis and Clark explored on the Oregon coast. Admission is $3 per vehicle on weekends and holidays.

Three miles south of town is **Arcadia Beach Wayside,** one of the prettiest little beaches on the north coast. Four miles south of town is **Hug Point State Park,** which has picnic tables and a sheltered beach. **Oswald West State Park,** 10 miles south of Cannon Beach, is one of our personal favorites of all the parks on the

344   **The Oregon Coast**

Oregon coast. A short paved trail leads to a driftwood-strewn cobblestone beach on a small cove. Headlands on either side of the cove can be reached by hiking trails that offer splendid views. The waves here are popular with surfers, and there's a primitive campground that you must walk in to, though the walk is only a few hundred yards.

Saddle Mountain State Park, 25 miles east of Cannon Beach off of U.S. 26, is a favorite day hike in the area. A 2¹/₂-mile trail leads to the top of Saddle Mountain, from which there are breathtaking views up and down the coast. In the spring, rare wildflowers are abundant along this trail.

If you'd like to see a large herd of elk, continue another 12 miles east from the Saddle Mountain turnoff to the Jewel turnoff. From here, continue 10 miles north following the WILDLIFE signs to **Jewel,** where there's a large meadow frequented throughout most of the year by a large **herd of elk.** September and October are rutting season, when big bulls can be heard bugling and seen locking antlers.

For many Cannon Beach visitors, **shopping** is the town's greatest attraction. In the heart of town, along Hemlock Street, you'll find dozens of densely packed small shops and galleries offering original art, fine crafts, unusual gifts, and casual fashions.

Also on Hemlock Street, you'll find the **Coaster Theater** (☎ 503/436-1242), one of the best little playhouses in Oregon. In addition to plays, the theater stages performances of classical music and jazz. Tickets range from $12 to $15 and the box office is open Wednesday through Saturday from 1 to 5pm and one hour before a performance. The **Cannon Beach Gallery,** 1064 Hemlock St. (☎ 503/436-0744), mounts art exhibitions of consistent quality.

WHERE TO STAY

If you're heading here with the whole family or plan to stay a while, consider renting a house, cottage, or apartment. Offerings range from studio apartments to luxurious (and large) oceanfront houses and prices span an equally wide range. Contact **Cannon Beach Property Management** (☎ 503/436-2021), **Ecola Creek Management Company** (☎ 800/873-2749), or **Arch Cape Property Services** (☎ 503/436-1607) for more information.

At the north end of town, the **Sea Ranch R.V. Park,** 415 N. Hemlock St., Cannon Beach, OR 97110 (☎ 503/436-2815), offers sites for R.V.s and tents. The campground is green and shady and is right across the street from the entrance to Ecola State Park. Rates are $17 for full hookups and $13 for a tent. If you happen to be biking through, you can stay for $4 per person.

⑤ Cannon Beach Hotel

1116 S. Hemlock St., Cannon Beach, OR 97110. ☎ **503/436-1392.** 9 rms. TV TEL. May–Sept, $49–$119 double. Oct–Apr, $37–$89 double. Rates include continental breakfast. MC, V.

With its white picket fence, green shutters, and cedar-shingle siding, the Cannon Beach Hotel, though new, seems to have been on the Cannon Beach scene for ages and fits in perfectly with the town's atmosphere. The rooms vary in size, which means that even those on a budget can afford something here. However, the best rooms are those with fireplaces and whirlpool tubs, and two of these rooms have partial ocean views. Though it's not in the best location in Cannon Beach (there are parking lots all around the hotel), it's one of the best deals and has the ambience of a small European inn. Despite the small size, there's even room service here.

Hallmark Resort

1400 S. Hemlock St., Cannon Beach, OR 97110. ☎ **503/436-1566** or 800/345-5676. Fax 503/436-0324. 134 rms and suites. TV TEL. May–Sept, $99–$229 double. Oct–May, $49–$185 double. AE, CB, DC, DISC, MC, V.

Situated on a bluff at the south end of town, the Hallmark is the most luxurious hotel in Cannon Beach, and the wide range of rates reflects the variety of rooms available. The lowest rates are for nonview standard rooms and the highest rates are for oceanfront two-bedroom suites. In between these extremes are all manner of rooms, studios, and suites. The best values are the limited-view rooms, many of which have fireplaces and comfortable chairs set up to take in what little view there might be. Most rooms have a small refrigerator and coffeemaker, and some have kitchenettes. There are even a few cottages available through the hotel. Though the grounds aren't spacious, there are several little Japanese gardens tucked in some unlikely spots, so be sure to stroll around.

Services: Concierge.

Facilities: Indoor swimming pool, two whirlpool spas, sauna, meeting rooms.

The Sea Sprite

Nebesna St., Tolovana Park, OR 97145. ☎ **503/436-2266.** 10 rms. TV. May–Sept, $60–$130 double. Oct–May, $30–$130 double. MC, V.

This small motel is located in the Tolovana Park area south of Cannon Beach, and though it has been around for quite a few years, it still makes a great choice for families. All the rooms have kitchens and most have woodstoves. However, it's the views of Haystack Rock that convince most people that the Sea Sprite is aging gracefully. If you can do without the views and prefer more modern accommodations, the Sea Sprite also offers lodgings closer to downtown Cannon Beach at the Hearthstone Inn.

✪ Stephanie Inn

2740 S. Pacific St., Cannon Beach, OR 97110. ☎ **503/436-2221** or 800/633-3466. 46 rms, 4 suites. TV TEL. $109–$229 double; $250–$350 suite. Rates include full breakfast. Children 11 and under not accepted. AE, CB, DC, DISC, MC, V.

You're not likely to find a more classically romantic inn than the Stephanie anywhere on the Oregon coast. It's reminiscent of New England's country inns, with flowerboxes beneath the windows and neatly manicured gardens by the entry. Inside, the lobby feels warm and cozy with its river-rock fireplace, huge wood columns, and beamed ceiling. The guest rooms are equally cozy and are all individually decorated. All come with small refrigerators, wet bars, and VCRs, and most also have double whirlpool tubs and fireplaces. The higher you go in the three-story inn, the better the views and the more spacious the outdoor spaces (patios, balconies, and decks). Smoking is not permitted.

Dining/Entertainment: A bounteous buffet breakfast is served each morning in the second-floor dining room, which surprisingly does not have a view of the water. Creative prix-fixe dinners ($27) are also served (reservations are required).

Services: Complimentary afternoon wine, morning newspaper, video library, complimentary shuttle to downtown Cannon Beach, massages.

The Waves/Argonauta/White Heron Lodge

188 W. Second St., Cannon Beach, OR 97110. ☎ **503/436-2205** or 800/822-2468. 48 rms and suites. TV TEL. $69–$250 double. DISC, MC, V.

Variety is the name of the game in eclectic Cannon Beach, and the Waves plays the game better than any other accommodation in town. This lodge, only a block from the heart of town, consists of four dozen rooms, suites, cottages, and beach houses at the Waves and two other jointly managed lodges, the Argonauta and the White Heron Lodge. If clean and new appeal to you, try one of the rooms in the Garden Court, but our favorites are the cottages of the Argonauta. Surrounded by beautiful flower gardens in the summer, these old cottages overlook the beach and capture the spirit of Cannon Beach. For sybarites and romantics, there are fireplaces in some rooms and a whirlpool spa overlooking the ocean. If you want to get away from the crowds, ask for an apartment at the White Heron Lodge.

WHERE TO DINE

Bistro Restaurant
263 N. Hemlock St. ☎ **503/436-2661.** Reservations recommended. Main courses $14.50–$17.25. MC, V. Daily 5–9:30pm. Closed Wed in winter. NORTHWEST.

The best of Cannon Beach is rarely in plain view. Such is the case with the Bistro Restaurant. You'll see the restaurant's sign toward the north end of the shopping district, but the restaurant itself is set back a bit from the street behind a small garden and down a brick walkway. Step through the door and you'll think you've just stepped into a French country inn. Stucco walls, old prints of flowers, and fresh flowers on the tables are all the decor this tiny place can afford without growing cramped. But the simple decor allows diners to focus their attention on exquisitely prepared dishes such as grilled halibut on a bed of spinach and served with a raspberry sauce or a seafood stew made with fennel, leeks, tomatoes, curry, and saffron. Service can be unpredictable.

Café de la Mer
1287 S. Hemlock St. ☎ **503/436-1179.** Reservations recommended. Main courses $14.50–$25. AE, MC, V. Wed–Sun 5:30–9:30pm. FRENCH.

Almost directly across the street from the Hallmark Resort, down at the south end of Cannon Beach, you'll spot a Williamsburg-blue colonial-style building that houses Cannon Beach's most upscale restaurant. Pink tablecloths and burgundy napkins, slender wine glasses, and art deco wall sconces give the interior a contemporary styling not evident from the outside. The menu is pure French, with the likes of rack of lamb with homemade chutney, salmon with lemon and capers, and oysters in a tarragon sauce. Seafood also fills the appetizer menu, which, when we last visited, included tiger prawns with herb mayonnaise and smoked-salmon pâté.

Lazy Susan Café
126 Hemlock St. ☎ **503/436-2816.** Breakfast main dishes $3–$7.25; salads/sandwiches $5.50–$9.25. No credit cards. Mon and Wed–Sat 8am–3pm, Sun 8am–2pm. BREAKFAST/SANDWICHES.

Cannon Beach is a great place to be for breakfast. The air is invigorating and you can have delicious waffles or omelets at the Lazy Susan. Tucked into the back of a little brick courtyard shared with the Coaster Theater, the Lazy Susan is a quaint little cottage with unpainted siding, window boxes full of flowers in summer, and white Victorian railings leading up to the front door. If you slept in, there's always lunch, with such items as a broiled shrimp sandwich.

Midtown Café
1235 S. Hemlock St. ☎ **503/436-1016.** Breakfast $2.75–$7.95; lunch $4.25–$7.25. No credit cards. Wed–Fri 7am–3pm, Sat 7am–2pm, Sun 8am–2pm. NATURAL/INTERNATIONAL.

Located next door to the Café de la Mer, the Midtown Café is a diner for the health-conscious, gustatory globetrotters of the 1990s. This little place is only open for breakfast and lunch, but packed into those two meals are some of the most innovative dishes on this stretch of the coast. How about a burrito for breakfast, or some eclectic hippie soup? If you need a kick-start in the morning, try the chocolate-espresso smoothie. You can be sure that anything you order will be as fresh as possible. These folks even grind their own flour and make their own jams, marmalades, and ketchup. One meal and we're sure you'll be hooked.

4 Tillamook County

Tillamook: 75 miles W of Portland, 51 miles S of Seaside, 44 miles N of Lincoln City

Tillamook, a mispronunciation of Killamook, which was the name of the Native American tribe that once lived in this area, lies at the south end of Tillamook Bay. Surrounding the town are lush green pastures that are home to large herds of contented cows, and ever since the first settlers arrived in Tillamook in 1851, dairy farming has been the mainstay of the economy. Things haven't changed much over the years, but the town has managed to turn its dairy farming into a tourist attraction. No, this isn't the cow-watching capital of Oregon. It's home to the Tillamook County Creamery Association's cheese factory, which attracts more than 800,000 visitors every year. Tillamook is also a good base for exploring this section of the coast, and, as one of the closest coastal communities to Portland, it makes for a good day trip or quick getaway.

ESSENTIALS

GETTING THERE   Tillamook is on U.S. 101 at the junction with Ore. 6, which leads to Portland.

VISITOR INFORMATION   Contact the **Tillamook Chamber of Commerce,** 3705 U.S. 101 N., Tillamook, OR 97141 (☎ **503/842-7525**).

EXPLORING THE COUNTY

MANZANITA   As the crowds have descended on Cannon Beach, people seeking quiet, a slower pace, and fewer crowds have headed south to the community of Manzanita. Located south of Neahkanie Mountain, Manzanita enjoys a setting similar to Cannon Beach's but without the many haystack rocks. There isn't much to do in Manzanita except walk on the beach and relax, but in the nearby town of Nehalem, you'll find the **Nehalem Antique Mall** (☎ **503/368-7190**), one of the best antiques malls on the coast. Manzanita does, however, have a couple of the north coast's best restaurants (see "Where to Dine," below).

ROCKAWAY BEACH   Rockaway Beach has little of the picturesque scenery of Manzanita or Cannon Beach, but it does have plenty of wide sandy beach. The town has a rather run-down feel to its narrow strip of aging cottages, but is still quite popular with families who rent beach houses for their summer vacation. If you like smoked salmon, don't miss **Karla's Smokehouse,** 2010 U.S. 101 N. (☎ **503/355-2362,** or 800/522-8902 for mail order), which sells the best smoked fish on the coast. It's open Sunday through Thursday from 10am to 6pm and on Friday and Saturday from 10am to 7pm.

GARIBALDI   This little town is located at the north end of Tillamook Bay and is the region's main sport-fishing port. If you've got an urge to do some salmon or bottom fishing, this is the place to book a trip. Try **Troller Charters** (☎ **503/322-3666** or 800/546-3666), **Siggi-G Ocean Charters** (☎ **503/322-3285**), or **Garibaldi Charters** (☎ **503/322-0007** or 800/900-HOOK).

Garibaldi is also where you'll find the depot for the **Fun Run Express** (☎ 503/ **355-8667** or 503/355-8108) is an excursion train that runs along the coast to Rockaway Beach. The 28-mile trip has great views of the coast and stops at a winery for wine-tasting. The round-trip cost is $10 for adults and $5 for children 12 and under.

TILLAMOOK   Tillamook has long been known as one of Oregon's foremost dairy regions, and Tillamook cheese is ubiquitous throughout the state. So it's no surprise that the **Tillamook Cheese Factory,** on U.S. 101 just north of Tillamook (☎ **503/842-4481**), is the most popular tourist attraction in town. Not only can visitors observe the cheese-making process, but there's also a large store where all manner of cheeses and other edible gifts are available. The factory is open daily from 8am to 8pm in summer and 8am to 6pm in winter.

If the Tillamook Cheese Factory seems too crowded for you, head back toward town a short distance and you'll see the **Blue Heron French Cheese Company** on the same side of U.S. 101 (☎ **503/842-8281**). Located in a big old dairy barn, this store stocks the same sort of comestibles as the Tillamook Cheese Factory, though the emphasis is on locally made brie. It's open daily from 8am to 8pm in summer and 9am to 5pm in winter.

If you'd like to find out more about the cows that produce the milk for the cheese factories, the **Tillamook County Creamery Association** (☎ 503/ **842-5684**) offers tours of local dairy farms. Tours cost $8 for adults, $6 for children 5 to 16.

At the **Tillamook County Pioneer Museum,** 2106 Second St. (☎ 503/ **842-4553**), you'll find the expected hodgepodge of antique cars, old kitchen appliances, blacksmith's tools, and the like, but you'll also find an unusual natural-history display showing examples of different colors and where they're found in nature. The museum is open Monday through Saturday from 8am to 5pm and on Sunday from noon to 5pm (closed Monday October to March). Admission is $2 for adults, $1.50 for seniors, 50¢ for students 12 to 17.

A hangar built during World War II for a fleet of navy blimps is 2 miles south of town off U.S. 101 and lays claim to being the largest free-standing wooden building in the world. Statistics bear out the impressiveness of this building: 250 feet wide, 1,100 feet long, and 170 feet high. The blimp hangar now houses the **Naval Air Station Museum,** 6030 Hangar Rd. (☎ **503/842-1130**), which contains a respectable collection of old planes that you can tour daily from 9am to 6pm. Admission is $5 for adults, $2.50 for children 6 to 12.

If you're interested in outdoor activities, you can hike to **Munson Falls,** the tallest waterfall in the Coast Range, at Munson Creek County Park, 7 miles south of Tillamook off U.S. 101. The trail to the falls leads through a stand of old-growth forest. Golfers can play a round at the **Alderbrook Golf Course,** 7300 Alderbrook Rd. (☎ **503/842-6413**).

THE THREE CAPES SCENIC LOOP   The Three Capes Scenic Loop begins just west of downtown Tillamook and leads past Cape Meares, Cape Lookout, and Cape Kiwanda. These three capes offer some spectacular views and are great spots for whale watching in the spring or storm watching in the winter. Follow Third Street out of town and watch for the turnoff to the right, which will take you along the shore of Tillamook Bay. This road will take you around the north side of **Cape Meares,** where the resort town of Bayocean once stood. Built early in this century by developers with a dream to create the Atlantic City of the West, Bayocean was unfortunately constructed at the end of a sand spit that often felt the full force of winter storms. When Bayocean homes began falling into the ocean, folks realized that this wasn't going to be the next Atlantic City. Today there's no sign of the town, but the long sandy beach along the spit is a great place for a walk and a bit of birdwatching.

Just around the tip of the cape, you'll come to **Cape Meares State Park,** which is the site of the **Cape Meares Lighthouse.** The lighthouse is open to the public and houses a small museum. The views from atop this rocky headland are superb. Continuing around the cape, you come to the residential community of Oceanside, from where you have an excellent view of the **Three Arch Rocks** just offshore.

Three miles south of Oceanside, you'll come to tiny **Netarts Bay,** which is well known for its excellent clamming and crabbing. Continuing south, you come to **Cape Lookout State Park,** which has a campground, picnic areas, beaches, and several miles of hiking trails. The most breathtaking trail leads out 2^1/$_2$ miles out to the end of Cape Lookout, where, from several hundred feet above the ocean, you can often spot gray whales in the spring and fall.

Cape Kiwanda is the last of the three capes. At the foot of the cape's sandstone cliffs you'll find sand dunes and tide pools, and in the nearby town of Pacific City you can see Oregon's only beach-launched dory fishing fleet. South of Pacific City, the scenic loop rejoins U.S. 101.

NESKOWIN   The quaint little community of Neskowin is nestled at the foot of Cascade Head, 12 miles north of Lincoln City. The tiny cottages and tree-lined lanes have for decades been the summer retreats of inland families. Quiet vacations are the rule in Neskowin, where you'll find only condominiums and rental houses. Beach access here is provided at **Neskowin Beach State Park,** which faces Proposal Rock, a tree-covered haystack rock bordered by Neskowin Creek. If you'd like to go for a horseback ride on the beach, contact **Neskowin Stables,** 48490 Hawk Ave. (☎ **503/392-3277**).

The much larger **Cascade Head,** just to the south, is one of the highest headlands on the coast. Rising 1,770 feet from sea level, the headland creates its own weather and receives 180 days of rain a year. Lush forests of Sitka spruce and windswept clifftop meadows are home to a such a diversity of flora and fauna that the Nature Conservancy purchased much of the land here. Trails onto Cascade Head start about 2 miles south of Neskowin.

South of Cascade Head, you'll find the **Sitka Center for the Arts and Ecology** (☎ **503/994-5485**), which offers classes on various subjects.

WHERE TO STAY
In Manzanita

✪ The Inn at Manzanita
67 Laneda St. (on Manzanita's main street and just a few blocks from the beach), Manzanita, OR 97130. ☎ **503/368-6754.** 8 rms. TV TEL. $100–$140 double. Minimum stay two nights most of the summer and weekends year round. MC, V.

Searching for the perfect place for a romantic getaway? This is it. Right in the heart of Manzanita and within steps of a couple of the best restaurants on the northern Oregon coast, the Inn at Manzanita is our idea of the perfect place to celebrate an anniversary or any other special event. Double whirlpool tubs sit between the fireplace and the bed in every room, and balconies look out through shady pines to the ocean. The weathered cedar-shingle siding blends unobtrusively with the natural vegetation, and the grounds are planted with beautiful flowers for much of the year. A wet bar and small refrigerator let you chill a bottle of wine. If all this has you worrying that you'll forget about the outside world, never fear—a newspaper will be left at your door every morning.

IN OCEANSIDE

⑤ House on the Hill

1816 Maxwell Mountain Rd., Oceanside, OR 97134. ☎ **503/842-6030.** 16 rms. TV TEL. $55–$85 double; $60–$110 triple or quad. MC, V.

Set 250 feet above Oceanside's beach on a promontory jutting into the ocean, the House on the Hill is a collection of pale-blue two-story buildings, several of which look like truncated A-frames. The rooms here are large and the views are stunning, with the Three Arch Rocks directly offshore. Unfortunately, the price for such a dramatic location is the instability of the land. Over the years the cliffs below the motel have been eroding and current attempts to stabilize the cliff on the town side of the motel are meeting with resistance. Another bad winter storm could leave this place precariously balanced, so be sure to call ahead to see if it's still in business.

Ocean Front Cabins

1610 Pacific Ave. NW, Oceanside, OR 97134. ☎ **503/842-6081.** 7 cabins. $50–$65 cabin for two. MC, V.

The Ocean Front Cabins is a collection of funky old cabins, but if you don't mind swapping cramped quarters, paneled walls, and low ceilings for being only 100 feet from the beach with an unobstructed view of the waves and the Three Arch Rocks, then you might find these cabins perfect. Be forewarned however, that there's nothing standardized or fancy about the cabins. Young people, especially surfers, will be right at home here. A few have kitchenettes, which is a definite plus in a town with only one restaurant. These cabins are very popular, so call in February for summer reservations.

IN NESKOWIN

Neskowin Resort

48990 U.S. 101 S., Neskowin, OR 97149. ☎ **503/392-3191.** 30 condos, 10 suites. TV TEL. June–Sept, $79–$99 condo for two; $99–$115 suite. Sept–June, $45–$59 condo for two; $68–$79 suite. MC, V.

Most units at this condominium resort have views of Proposal Rock; the views, combined with the tranquillity of Neskowin, set this place in a totally different realm from hotels in nearby Lincoln City. All the units have kitchens, which makes this a popular choice with families. The resort's Raku Grille serves good seafood and there's an art gallery here also.

WHERE TO DINE
IN MANZANITA

Blue Sky Café

154 Laneda Ave. ☎ **503/368-5712.** Reservations highly recommended. Main courses $9–$22. No credit cards. Wed–Sun 5:30–9:30pm. NORTHWEST.

On the left as you approach the beach on the main street through town, you'll see a pale-gray beachy building with colorful raised flower beds in front. Inside, the decor is reminiscent of New Mexico, and more casual than Jarboe's across the street. We could make a dinner of the potted Montrachet cheese smeared on thick slabs of fresh-baked bread, with fresh herbs, sun-dried tomatoes, roasted garlic and fennel, niçoise olives, and olive oil, which is served as an appetizer. Entrées show influences from around the globe, and are particularly well integrated in the numerous fresh-fish dishes. Ahi tuna is served with a warm Vietnamese cabbage salad and coconut-jasmine rice, while salmon with caramelized shallots and bleu cheese is served over beet greens with lemon polenta, taking some of its flavors from the Mediterranean.

✪ Jarboe's in Manzanita
137 Laneda Ave. ☎ 503/368-5113. Reservations required. Main courses $16–$17.25; prix-fixe dinner $26. MC, V. Mon–Thurs 5–9pm, Fri–Sat 5–9:30pm. Closed Mon fall–spring. NORTHWEST.

Housed in a tiny restored beach cottage, Jarboe's is about as intimate as a restaurant gets; there are only a few tables in the two tiny dining rooms, which makes reservations imperative. The menu changes daily, but is always reliable. On a recent visit, chef Klaus Monberg teamed up a creamy fish bouillon with smoked shark. The house salad came accented with toasted hazelnuts, marinated mushrooms, and a choice of either Oregon bleu or Asiago cheese for a garnish. Mesquite-grilled silver salmon with wilted spinach, sweet beets, ginger, and chives was lightly flavored so that the flavor of the fish could shine through. Dessert might include the likes of poached pear with crème anglaise, vanilla pot de crème, chocolate cream cake with walnut meringue, or a grand dessert that includes all three.

IN BAY CITY

Artspace
U.S. 101 and Fifth St. ☎ 503/377-2782. Main courses $8–$14.50. No credit cards. Thurs–Sat noon–8pm. SEAFOOD/SANDWICHES.

Just off U.S. 101 several miles north of Tillamook, this place is a white-interiored gallery with a café tucked inside. The ambience is laid-back and offerings from the kitchen range from oysters Rockefeller to lemon chicken to stir-fries with prawns or beef. We like the curried chicken and apple sandwich, rounded out with a cup of the creamy oyster stew.

IN OCEANSIDE

Roseanna's Oceanside Café
1490 Pacific Ave. ☎ 503/842-7351. Reservations highly recommended. Main courses $11.50–$16; lighter meals $6.25–$12. MC, V. Tues–Wed 11am–9pm, Thurs–Mon 8am–9pm. SEAFOOD/INTERNATIONAL.

The decor here is nothing special, but hey, this is the only restaurant in Oceanside, and meals are reliable and the beach is right outside the windows. The wait for a table can be long, so make a reservation if possible. If you just want a quick snack, there are barstools at the front counter. The menu mixes the traditional with international influences without getting overly creative. Lunch prices are reasonable, with such offerings as a full-flavored cioppino soup or oyster sandwich, although the oysters in the latter were a bit skimpy. Angels on horseback (oysters wrapped in bacon and broiled) are one of our favorite appetizers. Entrées offer a choice of shellfish or fish with a choice of sauces. Cajun spices with a Dijon-citrus glaze can satisfy those who crave spiciness, while a cilantro-spiked peanut sauce hints of the Orient.

5 Lincoln City/Gleneden Beach

88 miles SW of Portland, 44 miles S of Tillamook, 25 miles N of Newport

Lincoln City is not really a city, but a collection of five little towns that stretch for miles along the coast. There's no specific downtown area, and though there may be more motel rooms here than anywhere else on the Oregon coast, there's little to distinguish any of the thousands of rooms. However, family vacationers looking for a long beach with lots of sand and steady winds for flying kites will find Lincoln City to their liking. Motel rates, though often high for what you get, are generally better than in beach towns that are long on charm. Likewise, restaurants catering to large families and small pocketbooks proliferate here. Such restaurants purvey hot meals rather than haute cuisine, and you can eat your fill of seafood without going broke.

Once referred to as "20 miracle miles," Lincoln City is no longer the miracle it once was. Miracle miles have become congested urban sprawl, and a summer weekend in Lincoln City can mean coping with bumper-to-bumper traffic. If at all possible, come during the week or during the off-season to avoid the crowds.

ESSENTIALS

GETTING THERE   Ore. 22 from Salem merges with Ore. 18 before reaching the junction with U.S. 101. From Portland, take Ore. 99W to McMinnville and then head west on Ore. 18.

VISITOR INFORMATION   Contact the **Lincoln City Visitor and Convention Bureau,** 801 SW U.S. 101, Suite 1, Lincoln City, OR 97367 (☎ **541/ 994-8378** or 800/452-2151).

GETTING AROUND   Car rentals are available from **U-Save Auto Rental** (☎ **541/994-6860**) and from **Robben Rent-A-Car** (☎ **541/994-5530** or 800/ 305-5530). If you need a taxi, contact **Lincoln Cab Co.** (☎ **541/996-2003**). Public bus service between the Otis Cafe and Newport is provided by **Lincoln County Transit** (☎ **541/265-4900** or 541/765-2177, ext. 4900), but is available on weekdays only.

FESTIVALS   Annual **kite festivals** include the Mother's Day Festival, the Stunt Kite Championship in July, and the International Fall Festival around Columbus Day weekend. In addition, Lincoln City hosts the annual **Cascade Head Music Festival** each June, and in July there's the annual **sandcastle festival.** On the nearby Siletz Indian Reservation, the **Siletz Pow Wows** takes place in August.

ENJOYING THE BEACH & THE OUTDOORS

Lincoln City's 7¹/₂-mile-long **beach** is its main attraction. However, cold waters and constant breezes conspire to make swimming a pursuit for Polar Bear Club members only. The winds, on the other hand, make this beach the best kite-flying spot on the Oregon coast. If you didn't bring your own kite, you can buy one at **Catch the Wind,** 266 SE U.S. 101 (☎ **541/994-9500**). Among the better beach-access points are the D River State Wayside on the south side of the river and the Road's End State Wayside up at the north end of Lincoln City.

Adding to the appeal of Lincoln City's beach is **Devil's Lake,** which drains across the beach by way of the D River, the world's shortest river. Boating, sailing, waterskiing, sailboarding, swimming, fishing, and camping are all popular lake activities. Access points on the west side of the lake include **Devil's Lake State Park,** Sixth Street (☎ 541/994-2002), which has a campground, and **Holmes Road Park**, which has a boat ramp and picnic tables. On the east side you'll find **East Devil's Lake State Park** 2 miles east on East Devil's Lake Road and **Sand Point Park** on View Point Lane near the north end of East Devil's Lake Road. Both of these parks have picnic tables and swimming areas.

Golfers have several options: the **Lakeside Golf & Racquet Club,** 3245 Club House Dr. (☎ 541/994-8442); the **Salishan Golf Resort,** U.S. 101 in Gleneden Beach (☎ 541/764-3632); **Hawk Creek Golf,** Neskowin (☎ 503/392-4120); and the **Neskowin Golf Club,** Neskowin (☎ 503/392-3377).

Cyclists can rent bikes at **David's Bicycle Rental,** 960 SE U.S. 101 (☎ 541/996-6001), or at **Blue Heron Landing,** 4006 W. Devils Lake Rd. (☎ 541/994-4708). If you want to challenge the waves, you can rent a surfboard or bodyboard at the **Oregon Surf Shop** (☎ 541/996-3957). Hikers should head north to **Cascade Head** where there are several miles of hiking trails on public and Nature Conservancy land. The trailheads are off Three Rocks Road (on the south side) and off Forest Road 1861 on the north side. Both trailheads are reached by heading north on U.S. 101.

If you're a gardener, schedule time to visit the **Connie Hansen Garden,** 1931 NW 33rd St. (☎ 541/996-2701). This cottage garden was created by one woman over a 20-year period. It's open on Wednesday, Saturday, and Sunday from 1 to 6pm or by appointment.

INDOOR PURSUITS

Shopping is probably Lincoln City's most popular recreational activity. **Factory Stores @ Lincoln City** on U.S. 101 is an outlet mall with Izod, London Fog, Eddie Bauer, Oshkosh B'Gosh, and Van Heusen among the shops.

Craft and gift shops also abound in Lincoln City. Among these is **Alder House II,** 611 Immonen Rd., the oldest glassblowing studio in Oregon. The shop and studio are open daily from 10am to 5pm between March 15 and November 30. Also on Immonen Road (which is just north of Salishan) is **Mossy Creek Pottery** (☎ 541/996-2415), with an imaginative selection of porcelain and stoneware by Oregon potters. You'll find several upscale shops and galleries, including the popular **Maveety Gallery** (☎ 541/764-2318), a little farther down the road at the Marketplace at Salishan.

Garden enthusiasts will also want to visit **Garden Arts & Gifts,** 3001 SW U.S. 101 (☎ 541/994-2660), a store full of beautiful garden accessories and garden-oriented art.

The only museum in town is the **North Lincoln County Museum,** 4907 SW U.S. 101 (☎ 541/996-6614), which has rooms decorated with historic artifacts and antiques from pioneer days. It's open Wednesday through Sunday from noon to 4pm; admission is free.

WHERE TO STAY

Lincoln City has plenty of vacation rental houses and apartments as well as all its motels and hotels. For information on renting a house or apartment, contact **Beachfront Vacation Rentals** (☎ 541/760-8654 or 800/224-7660) or **Pacific Retreats** (☎ 541/994-4833 or 800/473-4833).

There's a campground at **Devil's Lake State Park,** just off U.S. 101 north of the D River (☎ 541/994-2002). Campsite rates range from $15 to $17.

⑤ Cozy Cove

515 NW Inlet St., Lincoln City, OR 97367. ☎ **541/994-2950.** 69 rms. TV TEL. $46–$150 double. DC, DISC, MC, V.

Located near the mouth of the D River, the Cozy Cove offers some good deals among its wide range of guest rooms. The hotel is on a long, wide stretch of beach with easy access, and only a short walk away you'll find several good restaurants. Some rooms have fireplaces and balconies, while others have kitchens or whirlpool tubs or some combination of all of these amenities. There's a seasonal outdoor pool and a year-round whirlpool.

Dock of the Bay

1116 SW 51st St., Lincoln City, OR 97367. ☎ **541/996-3549** or 800/362-5229. 30 rms. TV TEL. June–Sept, $65–$120 double. Lower rates off-season. MC, V.

The southern end of Lincoln City is bordered by Siletz Bay, and it's here, right on the water, that you'll find these condominiums. From the waterfront rooms there are great views of the bay and its rocky islets. The beach here is protected, which makes it a good place for small children. Most rooms have kitchens, fireplaces, and balconies.

The Inn at Spanish Head

4009 SW U.S. 101, Lincoln City, OR 97367. ☎ **541/996-2161** or 800/452-8127. 120 rms, 35 suites. TV TEL. $99–$118 double; $168–$286 suite. Lower rates in winter. AE, DISC, MC, V.

Located down at the south end of Lincoln City, this hotel is surprisingly deceptive. From the parking lot it appears to be two stories tall, but what you can't see is that the hotel has another eight stories below the parking lot. You see, the Inn at Spanish Head is built into a steep cliff that rises up from the beach. This is a condominium resort and all the rooms are individually owned, which means there's a different decor in every room. However, the furnishings are reliably comfortable. Many rooms have kitchens and there are larger suites for family vacationers. Best of all, all the rooms have an ocean view.

Dining/Entertainment: The Panorama restaurant and lounge, on the 10th floor, provides a dizzying view and fresh seafood. Sunday brunch ($12.95) is also served here. In the Ocean View Lounge, there are happy-hour specials on weeknights.

Services: Room service, valet parking.

Facilities: Outdoor pool, whirlpool, sauna, coin laundry, game and recreation room.

✪ Salishan Lodge

7760 U.S. 101, Gleneden Beach, OR 97388. ☎ **541/764-3600** or 800/452-2300. 205 rms. TV TEL. Nov–Apr, $109–$201 double. May–Oct, $164–$236 double. Special packages available. AE, CB, DC, DISC, MC, V.

The largest and most luxurious resort on the coast, the Salishan Lodge is nestled amid evergreens on a hillside at the south end of Siletz Bay. Unfortunately, the resort is almost half a mile from the beach and on the inland side of U.S. 101. The guest rooms are spread out around the resort's 750 acres. The second-floor rooms are the more appealing here, with cathedral ceilings and stone fireplaces. For breathtaking views, you'll have to shell out top dollar for a Chieftain or Siletz Bay room.

Dining/Entertainment: See "Where to Dine," below, for a review of the Salishan Dining Room. There's also a less expensive restaurant as well as a coffee shop. The Attic Lounge features live piano music and dancing to Top 40 tunes in the evenings.

Services: Room service, laundry service.

Facilities: 18-hole golf course, driving range, pro shop, indoor pool, indoor and outdoor tennis courts, whirlpool, exercise room, saunas, children's games room, playground, walking trails.

Shilo Inn

1501 NW 40th Place, Lincoln City, OR 97367. ☎ **541/994-3655** or 800/222-2244. 186 rms and suites. TV TEL. June–Oct, $52–$186 double; $145–$229 suite. Lower rates off-season. AE, DC, DISC, MC, V.

Long and sprawling, the Shilo Inn, which bills itself as a convention center, is one of the more comfortable beach resorts in Lincoln City. You'll find the Shilo at the north end of town. The dunes here are quite low, so you can almost step out the door and onto the beach. The first-floor oceanfront rooms have patios, and most other rooms include such amenities as two phones and hairdryers. Some rooms also have microwaves and refrigerators.

Dining/Entertainment: The dining room has a long wall of glass overlooking the beach, and almost every table has a good view. In the lounge there is nightly dance music.

Services: Room service.

Facilities: Indoor pool, whirlpool, sauna, video-games room.

WHERE TO DINE
EXPENSIVE

✪ The Bay House

5911 SW U.S. 101. ☎ **541/996-3222.** Reservations recommended. Main courses $13–$25. AE, DISC, MC, V. Sun–Fri 5:30–9pm, Sat 5–9pm. Closed Mon–Tues Nov–May. NORTHWEST.

Overlooking Siletz Bay at the south end of town, the Bay House provides fine dining, great wildlife watching, and dramatic sunsets. A big wall of glass overlooks the bay and Salishan Spit. There are snowy linens on the tables and service is gracious. For starters, we have a weakness for the crostini with roast garlic, marinated goat cheese, and olive oil. Entrées include such unusual creations as Oregon mushrooms with shallots, garlic, and pine nuts in a marsala-wine sauce layered between handmade herb pasta.

Chez Jeanette

7150 Gleneden Beach Loop, Gleneden Beach. ☎ **541/764-3434.** Reservations highly recommended. Main courses $14–$25. AE, MC, V. Sun–Thurs 5:30–9pm, Fri–Sat 5:30–9:30pm. FRENCH.

You'll find Chez Jeanette south of Salishan Lodge on a side road that leads to Gleneden Beach. Just watch for the quaint little cottage on your left. Once inside, you'll swear you're in a French country inn. It would be a shame not to start your meal with the two house specialty appetizers: steamed mussels with a saffron sauce flavored with just a touch of Pernod and oysters with a bleu-cheese/sauterne sauce. The two sauces are as different as night and day: one soft and subtle, the other bright and brassy. Every night there are different seafood specials as well as a veal special and a pasta du jour.

The Dining Room at Salishan

U.S. 101, Gleneden Beach. ☎ **541/764-2371.** Reservations recommended. Main courses $16.25–$26.50. AE, CB, DC, DISC, MC, V. Daily 5:30–9pm. NORTHWEST.

Three levels and lots of windows assure every diner at this ever-popular restaurant a tranquillity-inducing view of the lush forest outside. Service is professional and unobtrusive, and the wine cellar, with more than 15,000 bottles, is positively legendary. Our favorite appetizer is the seafood sampler for two, which includes two types of smoked salmon, seafood boudin sausages, shrimp, and pickled black cod. Though the entrée menu includes such standards as sweetbreads and rack of lamb, we opt for more creative offerings such as Pacific abalone grilled and served with flowering Asian greens, lemongrass, ginger, and jasmine rice cakes.

MODERATE

⑨ Kyllo's Seafood Grill

1110 NW First Court. ☎ 541/994-3179. Reservations not accepted. Main courses $8–$19; lunch $4.50–$11. DISC, MC, V. Daily 11am–9:30pm. SEAFOOD.

Providing a touch of urban chic on a family-oriented beach, Kyllo's is housed in a very contemporary building that features concrete floors and walls, a big copper fireplace, plenty of deck space, and walls of glass to take in the view of the D River and the ocean. A colorful, narrow mural winds around the dining room, and there are unusual deconstructivist wall lamps. If all this sounds like you're going to be paying for the atmosphere, think again. Prices for such dishes as halibut with lemon-caper sauce, Cajun sautéed prawns, or calamari with aïoli sauce are quite reasonable. You might have to wait for a table if you come here on a summer evening.

INEXPENSIVE

Chameleon Cafe

2145 NW U.S. 101. ☎ **541/994-8422.** Main courses $6–$9. MC, V. Mon–Sat 11:30am–9pm. INTERNATIONAL/VEGETARIAN.

The Chameleon offers vegetarian meals and Mediterranean-style cuisine in a simple airy atmosphere with chameleons on the walls. Although the food here is primarily vegetarian, you'll also find occasional fish and chicken dishes, such as fish tacos, on the menu. We ordered the grilled marinated-eggplant sandwich with feta cheese, sun-dried and fresh tomatoes, and a thin slice of red onion, and when it arrived we could hardly be distracted enough to try our accompanying Caeser salad.

The Dory Cove Restaurant

5819 Logan Rd. ☎ **541/994-5180.** Main courses $7.50–$16.50; burgers $3.25–$8.50. MC, V. Mon–Sat 11:30am–9pm, Sun noon–8pm. Take the road that turns off U.S. 101 at the Lighthouse Pub. BURGERS/SEAFOOD.

Though the name suggests a seafood restaurant, and in fact the menu does include dozens of seafood dishes, this restaurant does burgers best. In fact, the menu lists half a page of different varieties, including oyster burgers and veggie burgers. The dining room is dark and almost always filled with locals and families on vacation. You'll find the Dory Cove up at the north end of Lincoln City in the area called Road's End.

✪ Otis Café

Ore. 18, Otis. ☎ 541/994-2813. Reservations not accepted. Breakfast $3–$7; lunch $3.25–$4.60; dinners $7–$9. AE, DISC, MC, V. Mon–Thurs 7am–3pm, Fri–Sat 7am–9pm, Sun 8am–9pm. AMERICAN.

Five miles north of Lincoln City, in the tiny town of Otis, is an equally tiny roadside diner with a reputation big enough to stop beach-bound traffic 4 miles shy of the coast. If you've ever seen the determination with which urbanites head for the beach on summer weekends, you can understand what a feat it is to get cars to stop before they've got sand in the treads of their tires. The black bread, cinnamon rolls, and fried red potatoes are legendary, and the mustard and killer salsa are homemade. Pies—marionberry, strawberry/rhubarb, walnut—have crusts for the noncholesterol conscious.

6 Depoe Bay

13 miles S of Lincoln City, 13 miles N of Newport, 70 miles W of Salem

Depoe Bay calls itself the smallest harbor in the world, and once you've seen the town's tiny harbor you'll have to agree. Though the harbor covers only 6 acres, it's home to more than 100 fishing boats. Even more fascinating than the harbor itself is the narrow channel that leads into it. The channel is little more than a crack in the solid rock wall that forms the coastline at this point. During stormy seas, it's almost impossible to get in or out of the harbor safely. Shell mounds and kitchen middens around the bay indicate that Native Americans have long called this area home. In 1894 the U.S. government deeded the land surrounding the bay to a Siletz Native American known as Old Charlie Depot, who had taken his name from an army depot at which he had worked. Old Charlie later changed his name, and when a town was founded here in 1927, it took the name Depoe Bay. Though most of the town is located a bit off the highway, you'll find, right on U.S. 101, a row of garish souvenir shops, which sadly mar the beauty of this rocky section of coast. Among these shops are several family restaurants and charter-fishing and whale-watching companies.

ESSENTIALS

GETTING THERE   From the north, the most direct route is Ore. 18/99W to Lincoln City and then south on U.S. 101. From the south take U.S. 20 from Corvallis to Newport and then go north on U.S. 101.

VISITOR INFORMATION   Contact the **Depoe Bay Chamber of Commerce,** 630 SE U.S. 101 (P.O. Box 21), Depoe Bay, OR 97341 (☎ **541/765-2889**).

WHAT TO SEE & DO

Aside from watching the boat traffic passing in and out of the world's smallest harbor, the most popular activity here, especially when the seas are high, is watching the **spouting horns** across U.S. 101 from Depoe Bay's souvenir shops. Spouting horns, which are similar to blowholes, can be seen all along the coast, but nowhere are they more spectacular than here at Depoe Bay. These geyserlike plumes occur in places where water is forced through narrow channels in basalt rock. As the channels become more restricted, the water shoots skyward under great pressure and can spray 60 feet into the air. If the surf is really up, the water can carry quite a ways, and more than a few unwary visitors have been soaked.

Just outside town is **Depoe Bay State Park,** with windswept lawns, picnic tables, and great views of buff-colored cliffs and spouting horns.

The road south from Depoe Bay winds its way through grand scenery of rugged splendor as it passes several small, picturesque coves. In a few miles you'll come to the **Otter Crest Scenic Loop,** which takes in some spectacular vistas and leads to Cape Foulweather, which was named by Capt. James Cook in 1778. This was Cook's first glimpse of land after leaving the Sandwich Islands (Hawaii), and the sighting initiated the first English claims to the region. The cape frequently lives up to its name; winds often surpass 100 m.p.h. Keep an eye out for the sea lions that sun themselves on offshore rocks near **Cape Foulweather.** Nearby **Beverly Beach State Park** includes a campground. Also on the loop is an overlook above the **Devil's Punchbowl,** a collapsed sea cave that during high tides or stormy seas becomes a churning cauldron of foam.

Sport fishing and whale watching draw most visitors to town these days. You can arrange for either at **Tradewinds** (☎ 541/765-2345 or 800/445-8730), beside the bridge, or **Dockside Charters** (☎ 541/765-2545 or 800/733-8915), down by the marina. Whale-watching trips run $9 for 1 hour and $16 for 2 hours, and fishing trips run $30 for 3 hours up to $108 for 12 hours of halibut fishing.

WHERE TO STAY

✪ Channel House

35 Ellingson St., Depoe Bay, OR 97341. ☎ **541/765-2140** or 800/447-2140. Fax 541/765-2191. 12 rms. TV TEL. $60–$80 double ocean-view, $120–$200 oceanfront. Rates include full breakfast. MC, V.

The narrow, cliff-bordered channel into diminutive Depoe Bay is one of the most challenging harbor entrances in Oregon, and perched above it is the Channel House, one of the coast's most luxurious and strikingly situated small inns. A contemporary building with lots of angles and windows, the Channel House offers large rooms, most of which have gas fireplaces and private decks with whirlpool tubs. You can sit and soak as fishing boats navigate their way through the channel below you.

✪ Inn at Otter Crest

Otter Crest Loop Rd., Otter Rock, OR 97369. ☎ **541/765-2111** or 800/452-2101. 93 rms and suites. TV TEL. $89–$109 double; $109–$249 suite. AE, DISC, MC, V.

The Inn at Otter Crest is one of the Oregon coast's premier resorts and reflects the region in both architecture and setting. The inn's numerous weathered-cedar buildings are surrounded by 35 acres of forests and beautifully landscaped gardens on a rocky crest above a secluded cove. If you want to get away from it all and enjoy a bit of forest seclusion on the beach, there's no better spot. Most rooms have excellent ocean views through a wall of glass that opens onto a balcony. Our favorite rooms are the loft suites, which have fireplaces, kitchens, and high ceilings. Service here is rather casual, in keeping with Northwest attitudes.

Dining/Entertainment: The Flying Dutchman is located downhill from the guest rooms near the resort's swimming pool. The menu focuses on local seafoods.

Facilities: Outdoor swimming pool, hot tub, sauna, tennis, hiking trails.

The Surfrider

3115 NW U.S. 101, Depoe Bay, OR 97341. ☎ **541/764-2311** or 800/662-2378. 41 rms. TV TEL. Summer and weekends, $75–$90 double. Off-season, $65–$80 double. AE, DC, DISC, MC, V.

Though it has been around for many years, this low-rise motel is still a family favorite on the Oregon coast. It's hidden from the highway, which gives it a secluded feel, and there are great views from the open bluff-top setting. You can choose between basic motel rooms and rooms with fireplaces, kitchens, or hot tubs. At the foot of a long staircase is a wide beach on a small cove. There's a dining-room lounge overlooking the ocean and an indoor swimming pool and hot tub.

WHERE TO DINE

In addition to the restaurants listed below, there's also the **Siletz Tribal Smokehouse,** on U.S. 101 south of the bridge (☎ **541/765-2286** or 800/828-4269). At this shop you can buy smoked salmon for around $11 to $17 per pound. The Smokehouse is run by the Confederated Tribes of the Siletz and is a great place to buy picnic fixings as you head out to the beach.

Oceans Apart

177 NW U.S. 101. ☎ **541/765-2513.** Reservations not accepted. Main courses $8–$12. MC, V. Daily 7:30am–8:30pm. AMERICAN/HAWAIIAN.

Oregon and Hawaii are oceans apart, but two things they have in common are spectacular coastlines and plenty of seafood. At Oceans Apart, which is little more than a clifftop shack, you get a mix of the two states—Hawaiian seafood and an Oregon coast view. Whether you stop by for breakfast, lunch, or dinner, you'll find a menu straight out of Honolulu. Tropical omelets, haole French toast, mahimahi paoa, kapaa baked snapper. Prices are very reasonable and you won't find the likes of these dishes for another 3,000 miles or so.

Tidal Raves

279 NW U.S. 101. ☎ **541/765-2995.** Reservations recommended. Main courses $9.25–$16; lunch $4.75–$9.25. MC, V. Daily 11am–9pm. SEAFOOD.

Up at the north end of Depoe Bay's strip of tourist shops is a newer restaurant that has folks raving. With its bright, uncluttered decor and big windows for taking in the view of wave-carved sandstone cliffs, Tidal Raves offers Depoe Bay diners something that's been missing from town—a contemporary restaurant with a view. Keep your eyes on those cliffs outside the windows and you just might see water spouting up through some of the famous blowholes. The menu offers plenty of straightforward seafood, but it also includes some creative preparations such as Thai prawns in a mild curry sauce and lemon-rosemary breast of chicken with cranberry relish.

7 Newport

23 miles S of Lincoln City, 58 miles W of Corvallis, 24 miles N of Yachats

The air smells of fish and shrimp, and freeloading sea lions doze on the docks while they wait for their next meal from the processing plants along the waterfront. Dockworkers unloading fresh fish mingle with vacationers licking ice-cream cones, and both fishing boats and pleasure craft ply the waters of the bay.

Newport got its start in the late 1800s as both an oystering community and one of the earliest Oregon beach resorts, and to this day many of the old cottages and historic buildings can still be seen. While the town's Nye Beach area has the feel of a turn-of-the-century resort, the downtown bayfront is, despite its souvenir shops, galleries, and restaurants, still a working port and home port for the largest commercial fishing fleet on the Oregon coast. The site of the Oregon Coast Aquarium and now the home of the killer whale that starred in the movie *Free Willy,* Newport is one of the most popular towns on the Oregon coast. Oysters are also still important to the local economy and are raised in oyster beds along Yaquina Bay Road east of town.

Though in recent years it has come close to matching the overdevelopment of Lincoln City, this fishing port on the shore of Yaquina Bay still manages to offer a balance of industry, history, culture, beaches, and family vacation attractions that makes it a popular destination.

ESSENTIALS

GETTING THERE   Newport is on U.S. 101 at the junction with U.S. 20, which leads to Corvallis.

VISITOR INFORMATION   Contact the **Greater Newport Chamber of Commerce,** 555 SW Coast Hwy., Newport, OR 97365 (☎ **541/265-8801** or 800/262-7844).

GETTING AROUND   Public bus service is provided by **Lincoln County Transit** (☎ **541/265-4900**), which operates from Lincoln City south to Yachats. If you need a taxi, call **Yaquina Cab** (☎ **541/265-9552**).

SEEING THE SIGHTS

✪ Oregon Coast Aquarium

2820 SE Ferry Slip Rd. ☎ **541/867-3474.** Admission $7.75 adults, $5.50 seniors and children 13–18, $3.30 children 4–12. Memorial Day–Labor Day, daily 9am–6pm; Labor Day–Memorial Day, daily 10am–5pm. Closed Dec 25.

Before you even make it through the doors of this modern aquarium, you begin to learn about life along the Oregon coast. Once inside, there are so many fascinating displays that it's easy to spend the better part of a day here. The stars of the aquarium are the playful sea otters, but the clown-faced tufted puffins, which are kept in a walk-through aviary, are big favorites as well. The sea lions sometimes rouse from their naps to put on impromptu shows, and the lucky visitor even gets a glimpse of a giant octopus with an arm span of nearly 20 feet. Artificial waves surge in a tank that reproduces, on a speeded-up scale, life in a rocky intertidal zone. And so far, you haven't even made it to the indoor aquarium displays. In these you'll find various coastal habitats and the life forms that inhabit them. There are examples of sandy beaches, rocky shores, salt marshes, kelp forests, and even the open ocean, where diaphanous jellyfish drift lazily on the currents. In January 1996, Keiko, the 7,700-pound killer whale who starred in *Free Willy,* was airlifted here from his cramped quarters in a Mexico City amusement park. He now lives in a state-of-the-art computerized pool that's five times as large as his old quarters. If he recovers his sagging health in his new home, environmentalists hope to return him to the wild.

Because this is the most popular attraction on the Oregon coast, lines to get in can be very long. Arrive early if you're visiting on a summer weekend.

OSU Hatfield Marine Science Center

2030 Marine Science Dr. ☎ **541/867-0100.** Admission $2 donation. Summer, daily 10am–5pm; the rest of the year, daily 10am–4pm.

Before the Oregon Coast Aquarium was built, Newport was already known as a center for marine science research. This facility, though primarily a university research center, also contains displays that are open to the public. Aquarium tanks exhibit examples of Oregon sea life and interpretive exhibits explain life in the sea.

Yaquina Bay Lighthouse

In Yaquina Bay State Park, 846 SW Government St. ☎ **541/867-7451.** Free admission. Memorial Day–Sept, daily 11am–5pm; Oct–Feb, Fri–Sun noon–4pm; Mar–Memorial Day, daily noon–4pm.

The Newport area has two lighthouses. The historic Yaquina Bay Lighthouse was built in 1871 and is both the oldest lighthouse in Oregon and the oldest building in Newport. This lighthouse is not the classic tower style, but is instead a two-story wood-frame house with the light on the roof. The building served as both home and lighthouse, but only operated until 1874 when the Yaquina Head Lighthouse was constructed. This latter lighthouse, located 3 miles north of here at Yaquina Head Outstanding Natural Area, was supposed to stand on Cape Foulweather, but heavy seas made it impossible to land there. Instead the light was built on Yaquina Head, and so powerful was the light that it supplanted the one at Yaquina Bay.

OTHER ATTRACTIONS: BEACHES, FISHING, SHOPPING & MORE

Beaches in the Newport area range from tiny rocky coves where you can search for agates to long, wide stretches of sand perfect for kite flying. Right in town you'll find the **Yaquina Bay State Park,** which borders on both the ocean and the bay and is home to the **Yaquina Bay Lighthouse.** North of Newport is **Agate Beach,** which was once known for the beautiful agates that could be found there. However, in recent years sand has covered the formerly rocky beach, hiding the stones from rock hunters. This beach has a stunning view of Yaquina Head, 3 miles north of Newport. Yaquina Head is an ancient volcano that's now preserved as the **Yaquina Head Outstanding Natural Area.** In addition to being the site of the **Yaquina Head Lighthouse,** it's home to thousands of nesting sea birds. Harbor seals can also be seen lounging on the rocks here, and in early winter and spring, gray whales can be spotted migrating along the coast. On the cobblestone beach below the lighthouse, you can explore tide pools at low tide. Two miles south of Newport, you'll come to **South Beach State Park,** a wide sandy beach with picnic areas and a campground (that also rents yurts). Another 4 miles south is **Ona Beach State Park,** a sandy beach with a picnic area under the trees. Another 2 miles will bring you to **Seal Rock State Park.**

Newport claims to be the Dungeness crab capital of the world, and if you'd like to find out if this claim is true, you can **rent crab rings and boats** at **Sawyer's Landing,** 4098 Yaquina Bay Rd. (☎ **541/265-3907**), or at the **Embarcadero Marina,** 1000 SE Bay Blvd. (☎ **541/265-5435**). Fishing for salmon and bottom fish can also be quite productive around here. You can charter a fishing boat on the bay front at **Newport Sportfishing,** 1000 SE Bay Blvd. (☎ **541/265-7558** or 800/828-8777). If you'd rather just go for a sail, contact **Newport Daysail Adventures,** 343 SW Bay Blvd. (☎ **541/265-7441**). Whale-watching tours are offered in season by **Marine Discovery Tours,** 345 SW Bay Blvd. (☎ **541/ 265-6200**). Another sport that's popular in the bay is **clamming.** Pick up a tide table at a local business and head out on the flats with your clam shovel and a bucket.

If you'd like to delve into local history, stop by the **Burrows House Museum,** 545 SW Ninth St. (☎ **541/265-7509**), and the affiliated Log Cabin Museum. The Burrows House was built in 1895 as a boardinghouse and now contains exhibits of household furnishings and fashions from the Victorian era. The **Log Cabin Museum,** 579 SW Ninth St., houses Native American artifacts from the local Siletz Indian Reservation, as well as exhibits on logging, farming, and maritime history. Both museums are open Tuesday through Sunday: June to September from 10am to 5pm and October to May from 11am to 4pm. The works of local and regional artists are showcased at the **Newport Visual Arts Center,** 239 NW Beach Dr. (☎ 541/265-6540), open daily: May to September from noon to 4pm and October to April from 11am to 3pm.

As one of the coast's most popular family-vacation spots, Newport has all the tourist traps one would expect. Billboards up and down the coast advertise the sorts of places that kids demand to be taken to. Tops on this list are **Ripley's Believe It or Not** and the **Wax Works Museum.** Across the street from these you'll find **Undersea Gardens,** where a scuba diver feeds the fish, including a giant octopus, in a large tank beneath a boat moored on the bayfront. All three attractions share the same address and phone number—Mariner Square, 250 SW Bay Blvd. (☎ 541/265-2206)—but not the same admission. You'll pay extortionate admission prices to all three, but it's either pay up or listen to the kids whine, right?

Golfers can head out to the **Agate Beach Golf Course,** 4100 N. Coast Hwy. (☎ 541/265-7331), north of town.

You'll find Newport's greatest concentration of interesting shops down on the bayfront. **Breach the Moon Gallery,** 434 SW Bay Blvd. (☎ 541/265-9698), features art glass and art with ocean and whale themes. Nearby is **Oceanic Arts,** 444 SW Bay Blvd. (☎ 541/265-5963), which sells interesting crafts, including wind chimes and lots of ceramics. The **Wood Gallery,** 818 SW Bay Blvd. (☎ 541/265-6843), specializes in wooden items including boxes and musical instruments. South of Newport, in Seal Rock, you'll find **Art on the Rocks,** 5667 NW Pacific Coast Hwy. (☎ 541/563-3920), which has an eclectic array of fine arts and crafts.

Toledo, a small historic town 12 miles east of Newport but still on Yaquina Bay, is home to a dozen or so antiques stores.

The **Newport Performing Arts Center,** 777 W. Olive St. (☎ 541/265-2787), hosts local and nationally recognized performers throughout the year. Tickets run $5–$20.

WHERE TO STAY

Embarcadero

1000 SE Bay Blvd., Newport, OR 97365. ☎ **541/265-8521** or 800/547-4779. Fax 541/265-7844. 87 rms. TV TEL. Summer, $97–$190 double. Lower rates off-season. AE, CB, DC, DISC, MC, V.

Located on Yaquina Bay, the Embarcadero is a condominium resort that offers Newport's most luxurious accommodations. The resort combines Northwest materials and landscaping and contemporary architecture, and is popular with the boating set, who tie up at the resort's marina. The three-story buildings have unobstructed views of Yaquina Bay, and the guest rooms have their own decks. The larger one- and two-bedroom suites have fireplaces and kitchens.

Dining/Entertainment: The Embarcadero dining room is one of the best restaurants in town and serves Northwest cuisine with an emphasis on seafood. Main-dish prices range from $12 to $20.

Services: Sport-fishing charters, boat rentals.

Facilities: Indoor pool, whirlpool, saunas, marina.

Shilo Inn

536 SW Elizabeth St., Newport, OR 97365. ☎ **541/265-7701** or 800/334-1049. 179 rms, 3 suites. TV TEL. $75–$160 double; $199–$395 suite. AE, CB, DC, DISC, ER, JCB, MC, V.

Perched on a bluff in the Nye Beach area of Newport, the Shilo Inn offers a wide variety of rooms sizes and rates, and every room comes with an ocean view. With more rooms than any lodging in town and a great location right on the beach, the Shilo is a good choice for clean, comfortable accommodations.

Dining/Entertainment: A café and a more formal dining room provide options when it comes time to eat. After dinner you can play a hand in the card room if you're so inclined.

Services: VCR and movie rentals, valet service, airport shuttle, complimentary morning newspaper and coffee.

Facilities: Two indoor pools, guest laundry.

✪ Starfish Point

140 NW 48th St., Newport, OR 97365. ☎ **541/265-3751.** Fax 541/265-3040. 6 condo apts. $140–$160 apt for two. Off-season rates available. Two-night weekend minimum. AE, DISC, MC, V.

Located north of town in a grove of fir trees on the edge of a cliff, the Starfish Point condominiums are our favorite rooms in the area. Each of the six condos has two bedrooms and two baths spaced over two floors. Between the two floors you'll find a cozy sitting area in an octagonal room that's almost all windows. This room is in addition to the spacious living room with its unusual wicker furniture, fireplace, stereo, VCR, and Asian accent pieces. The bathrooms here are extravagant affairs with two-person whirlpool tubs, skylights or big windows, and hanging plants.

A path leads down to the beach, and to the north is Yaquina Head, one of the coast's picturesque headlands. You're a ways out of town here, so you might want to cook your own meals and savor the solitude.

✪ Sylvia Beach Hotel

267 NW Cliff St., Newport, OR 97365. ☎ **541/265-5428.** 20 rms. $55–$125 double. Rates include full breakfast. AE, MC, V.

This eclectic four-story green-shingled hotel pays homage to literature. The rooms are named for different authors, and in the rooms you'll find memorabilia, books, and decor that reflects these authors' lives, times, and works. The Agatha Christie Room, the hotel's most popular, seems full of clues, while in the Edgar Allan Poe Room, a pendulum hangs over the bed and a stuffed raven sits by the window. Among the writers represented are Tennessee Williams, Colette, Hemingway, Alice Walker, Jane Austen, F. Scott Fitzgerald, Emily Dickinson, and even Dr. Seuss. There's also a resident cat.

The Tables of Content restaurant downstairs is a local favorite. The four-course reservation-only dinners are served at 7pm Sunday through Thursday and at 6 and 8:30pm on Friday and Saturday. For an extremely reasonable $16.50, you'll be served the likes of black-bean soup, Greek salad, scallops in saffron sauce, wild rice, fresh vegetables, a chocolate-berry trifle, and coffee or tea. Hot wine is served in the library at 10pm each evening.

⑤ Vikings Motel

729 NW Coast St., Newport, OR 97365. ☎ **541/265-2477.** 14 cabins, 22 condo apts. TV. $55–$75 one-bedroom cabin for two; $65–$95 two-bedroom cabin for two; $85–$225 condo apt for two. AE, DC, DISC, MC, V.

Though there are more of the new condominiums here than old cabins, the cabins are still most appealing, especially if you're on a budget. Certainly not for everyone, these rustic old places are rather dark and eclectically furnished but are right on the beach and are comfortable nonetheless. Most cabins come with kitchens, which makes them an even better deal. Built in 1925 and modeled after Cape Cod cottages, the cabins are reminiscent of times gone by when families spent their annual vacation clamming, fishing, and beachcombing. The most popular accommodation here is a room called the Crow's Nest, which has a great view. The condos are clean, modern, and individually decorated and have kitchens.

WHERE TO DINE

Our two favorite restaurants in town are **Tables of Content** at the Sylvia Beach Hotel and the **Embarcadero dining room** at the Embarcadero condominium resort. See "Where to Stay," above, for details.

Canyon Way Restaurant & Bookstore

1216 SW Canyon Way. ☎ **541/265-8319.** Reservations recommended. Main courses $13.50–$21; lunch $4–$9.50. AE, DISC, MC, V. Mon 11am–3pm, Tues–Thurs 11am–3pm and 5–8:30pm, Fri–Sat 11am–3pm and 5–9pm. CONTINENTAL/CAJUN.

Located just up the hill from Bay Boulevard, this big pink building is a combination restaurant, deli, bookstore, and gift shop. A vaguely southwestern exterior, patios, and attractive flower gardens make this a very relaxing spot for lunch or dinner. Pastas and sauces, which are available to go, are made fresh daily and wind up in such flavorful combinations as pasta with shrimp in basil-cream sauce. At dinner you can start things off with oysters on the half shell or the house pâté, and then follow up with prawns Provençal, mussels bordelaise, bouillabaisse, or the like.

Mo's

622 SW Bay Blvd. ☎ **541/265-2979.** Reservations not accepted. Complete dinner $6–$9. MC, V. Daily 11am–9pm. SEAFOOD.

Established in 1942, Mo's has become so much of an Oregon coast institution that it has spawned not only an annex across the street but several other restaurants up and down the coast. Clam chowder is what made Mo's famous, and you can get it by the bowl, by the cup, or family style. You can even get clam chowder base to go. Basic seafood dinners are fresh, large, and inexpensive, and the seafood-salad sandwiches are whoppers. There are also such dishes as cioppino, gazpacho with shrimp, and slumgullion (clam chowder with shrimp). There's a good chance you'll have to wait in line if it's lunch or dinner time.

Rogue Ales Public House

748 SW Bay Blvd. ☎ **541/265-3188.** Reservations not accepted. Sandwiches $3.50–$4.75; pizzas $6.75–$19. MC, V. PUB GRUB.

The fresh ales brewed by this microbrewery are not only delicious to drink, but they also end up in a number of the pub's most popular dishes. The chili is made with Logger Ale. The pizza dough is made with Rogue Stout. The English bangers are served with a beer mustard, and the oyster shooters come with an ale sauce. You'll find the pub downtown on the bay.

The Whale's Tale

Bay Blvd. and Fall St. ☎ **541/265-8660.** Reservations recommended. Main courses $9–$18. AE, DISC, MC, V. Mon–Fri 8am–9pm, Sat–Sun 9am–10pm. SEAFOOD.

Opened in the 1970s and still owned by its founder, the Whale's Tale is a tried-and-true place for locals who seek it out for the clam chowder and such great breakfasts as pancakes topped with fresh fruit or huevos rancheros. Lunch and dinner include Greek salads, catch of the day with fruit salsa, veggie lasagne, or grilled oysters. In keeping with the location, the theme is nautical, and service is friendly, whether you're a long-time customer or just visiting.

Yuzen

U.S. 101, Seal Rock. ☎ **541/563-4766.** Reservations recommended on weekends. Main courses $8.50–$24; lunch $4.50–$11.50. MC, V. Tues–Sun 11am–2pm and 4–9pm. JAPANESE.

Located 8 miles south of Newport in Seal Rock, this Japanese restaurant is in an unlikely looking Tudor house. A long menu includes such unusual dishes as octopus salad and smoked eel, but also includes sushi, sashimi, teriyaki salmon steak, and several special dinners. If you plan ahead you can even order a special chef's-choice feast that can be prepared for budgets from $15 to $50.

DRIVING ON TO YACHATS WITH A STOP IN WALDPORT

Located at the mouth of the Alsea River 8 miles north of Yachats, Waldport is a popular **fishing** spot with anglers who head upriver to catch salmon, steelhead, and cutthroat trout. Crabbing and clamming are also good here in the Alsea Bay. To learn a little more about the area, visit the **Historic Alsea Bay Bridge Interpretive Center,** 620 NW Spring St. (☎ 541/563-2133).

WHERE TO STAY

Cliff House Bed & Breakfast

Adahi Rd., Waldport, OR 97394. ☎ **541/563-2506.** 3 rms, 1 suite. TV. $110–$125 double; $225 suite. Rates include full breakfast. MC, V.

The setting of this B&B, perched on the edge of a cliff overlooking the mouth of the Alsea River and 8 miles of beach, should be enough to take your breath away. The guest rooms are beautifully decorated, and depending on which room you take, you may find a four-poster bed, a wood stove, huge skylights, a wall of windows overlooking the ocean, or, should you stay in the Bridal Suite, a huge bathroom with mirrored ceiling, double whirlpool tub, and double shower. There's a hot tub and massages are available.

8 Yachats

26 miles S of Newport, 26 miles N of Florence, 138 miles SE of Portland

Located on the north side of 800-foot-high Cape Perpetua, the village of Yachats (pronounced *Yah*-hots) is known as something of an artists' community. When you get your first glimpse of the town's setting, you, too, will likely agree that there's more than enough beauty here to inspire anyone to artistic pursuits. Yachats is an Alsi Native American word meaning "dark waters at the foot of the mountains," and that sums up perfectly the setting of this small community (pop. 650). The tiny Yachats River flows into the surf on the south edge of town, and to the east stand steep, forested mountains. The shoreline on which the town stands is rocky, with little coves here and there where you can find agates among the pebbles paving the beach. Tide pools offer hours of exploring, and in winter, storm waves create a spectacular show. Uncrowded beaches, comfortable motels, and one of the coast's best restaurants all add up to a great spot for a quiet getaway.

ESSENTIALS

GETTING THERE From the north, take Ore. 34 west from Corvallis to Waldport and then head south on U.S. 101. From the south, take Ore. 126 west from Eugene to Florence and then head north on U.S. 101.

VISITOR INFORMATION   Contact the **Yachats Area Chamber of Commerce,** 441 U.S. 101 (P.O. Box 728), Yachats, OR 97498 (☎ 541/547-3530).

EXPLORING THE AREA

Looming over tiny Yachats is the impressive bulk of Cape Perpetua, which, at 800 feet high, is the highest spot on the Oregon coast. Because of the cape's rugged beauty and diversity of natural habitats, it has been designated the **Cape Perpetua Scenic Area.** The **Cape Perpetua Visitor Center** (☎ 541/547-3289) is located up a steep road off U.S. 101 and houses displays on the natural history of the cape and the Native Americans who harvested its bountiful seafoods for thousands of years. The visitor center is open daily from 9am to 5pm in summer and on weekends only the rest of the year; admission is free. Within the scenic area are 18 miles of hiking trails, tide pools, ancient forests, scenic overlooks, and a campground. If you're here on a clear day, be sure to drive to the top of the cape for one of the finest vistas on the coast. Waves and tides are a year-round source of fascination along these rocky shores. A spouting horn sends geyser-like plumes of water skyward, and at the Devil's Churn, waves boil through a narrow opening in the rocks. Cape Perpetua's tide pools are some of the best on the coast.

If you're looking for wide sandy beach, continue south to the **Stonefield Beach Wayside, Muriel Ponsler Memorial Wayside,** or **Carl G. Washburne Memorial Park.** The last offers 2 miles of beach, hiking trails, and a campground.

Between April and October each year, **fishing** in Yachats takes on an unusual twist. It's during these months that thousands of smelts, a sardinelike fish, spawn in the waves that crash in the sandy coves just north of Yachats. The fish can be caught using a dip net, and so popular are the little fish that the town holds an annual **Smelt Fry** each year on the second weekend in July. **Gray whales** also come close to shore near Yachats. You can see them in the spring from Cape Perpetua, and throughout the summer several take up residence at the mouth of the Yachats River. Stawberry Hill Wayside, south of Cape Perpetua, is another good place to spot whales, and sea lions can also be seen lounging on the rocks offshore from this wayside.

A couple of historic buildings in the area are also worth a visit if you're spending any amount of time here in Yachats. The **Little Log Church by the Sea,** on the corner of Third and Pontiac streets, is now a museum housing displays on local history. The church was built in 1927 and is in the shape of a cross. Nine miles up Yachats River Road you'll find a **covered bridge** that was built in 1938 and is one of the shortest in the state.

Yachats has two interesting crafts galleries worth visiting: **Earthworks Gallery,** 2222 U.S. 101 N. (☎ 541/547-4300), and the **Back Porch Gallery,** U.S. 101 and Fourth Street (☎ 541/547-4500).

WHERE TO STAY

In addition to the hotels listed below, there are also plenty of rental homes available in Yachats. Contact **Yachats Village Rentals,** 230 Aqua Vista Dr. (P.O. Box 44), Yachats, OR 97498 (☎ 541/547-3501), which has houses ranging from $100 to $125 per night.

Adobe Motel Resort
1555 U.S. 101 N., Yachats, OR 97498. ☎ **541/547-3141** or 800/522-3623. 98 rms, 12 suites. TV TEL. Summer, $58–$95 double; $95–$150 suite. AE, CB, DC, DISC, MC, V.

The Adobe has long been a Yachats favorite. The setting, on a windswept rocky headland on the edge of town, affords great views up and down the coast. Our favorite rooms are the fireplace rooms, which also have some of the best ocean views. Other rooms have balconies or whirlpool tubs. The least expensive rooms are those facing the hills to the east of town. In front of the hotel at low tide there are tide pools to explore and tiny beaches where you can find agates among the pebbles. There's no pool but there is a whirlpool.

The Adobe dining room is a circular room with the best ocean views for miles around. The menu is, of course, primarily seafood. A separate two-floor lounge offers similar views.

ⓢ Shamrock Lodgettes

105 U.S. 101 S., Yachats, OR 97498. ☎ **541/547-3312** or 800/845-5028. Fax 541/547-3843. 13 rms, 6 cabins. TV. $67–$90 double; $86–$106 cabin for two. AE, CB, DC, MC, V.

This collection of classic log cabins at the mouth of the Yachats River bewitched us the first time we saw it. Spacious lawns and old fir trees give the rustic cabins a relaxed old-fashioned appeal that just begs you to kick back and forget your cares for the duration. Each log cabin has a tile entry, hardwood floors, a kitchenette, a stone fireplace, and a big picture window that takes in a view of either the beach or the river—but other than that they're pretty basic. The motel rooms are more up-to-date and also have fireplaces and views. Some rooms also have whirlpool tubs. A health spa features an exercise room, hot tub, and sauna. Massages are also available.

NEARBY PLACES TO STAY

Gull Haven Lodge

94770 U.S. 101, Florence, OR 97439. ☎ **541/547-3583.** 8 rms, 5 with bath. $35–$49 double without bath, $60–$85 double with bath. MC, V.

Rustic and cozy, the Gull Haven Lodge is a great place to hole up with family or friends. Opt for either the North Up or South Up room and you'll find yourself ensconced in a room with two walls of glass overlooking the ocean. Window seats and wood stoves will keep you comfortable even on a cool damp day, and when the weather's good, you're only a short trail away from the beach. Despite its lack of a private bath, the Shag's Nest cottage is the lodge's most popular room. This private elfin cottage is across the grass from the main lodge and perched on the edge of the bluff. You can lie in bed gazing out to sea with a fire crackling in the fireplace, but you'll have to walk back to the main lodge for a bathroom. If you're looking for a good value and rooms that are a little bit out of the ordinary, this is the place. No smoking.

✪ Ziggurat Bed & Breakfast

95330 U.S. 101, Yachats, OR 97498. ☎ **541/547-3925.** 1 rm, 2 suites. $110–$125 double. No credit cards.

Located 6¹/₂ miles south of Yachats on a wide, flat stretch of beach, the Ziggurat is an architectural gem on this jewel coast. The four-story pyramidal contemporary home rises on the edge of the dunes and a salmon stream. The interior is every bit as breathtaking as the architectural design, with contemporary art and international artifacts on display. A maze of rooms and stairways leads to the two huge first-floor suites, the larger of which covers more than 700 square feet. In these fascinating spaces you'll find slate floors, walls of windows, spacious bathrooms, private saunas, and contemporary furnishings—in short, they're the most stunning rooms on the coast. Up at the apex of the pyramid is the third room, which has a half bath in the room plus a full bath two flights below. This room has two decks and the best views in the house. Those who appreciate contemporary styling will find the Ziggurat to be their favorite lodging on the coast.

WHERE TO DINE

One of Yachats' most popular restaurants is the dining room at the **Adobe Motel Resort** (see "Where to Stay," above, for details). For light breakfasts or espresso, try the **New Morning Coffee House,** which is right on the highway.

✪ La Serre

Second Ave. and Beach St. ☎ **541/547-3420.** Reservations highly recommended. Main courses $8.50–$23. AE, MC, V. Mon and Wed–Sat 5–9pm, Sun 9am–noon and 5–9pm (also Tues 5–9pm July–Aug). Closed Jan. CONTINENTAL.

La Serre has for years served up the best food in the area. Although the greenhouse setting is attractive, if you're like us you'll be immediately distracted by the dessert table just inside the front door. Hanging from the ceiling are more plants and lots of old Japanese glass floats, the sort that frequently wash up on the shores of this coast. You could start your dinner with some Manhattan clam chowder, a delicious surprise here on the West Coast. The entrée menu includes everything from a simple shrimp sandwich to filet mignon to fisherman's stew, a gentle tomato-flavored cioppino with so much fish, shrimp, clams, crab, and oysters in it that you don't know where to start first. The desserts are as good as they look: Pear crunch, hazelnut cheesecake with raspberry sauce, and a wickedly rich flourless chocolate cake are all outstanding.

DRIVING ON TO FLORENCE

Traveling south from Cape Perpetua, you pass several waysides and parks providing picnic areas, campgrounds, and access to the beach. Of these, **Devils Elbow State Park** offers the most breathtaking setting. Situated on a small sandy cove, the park has a stream that flows across the beach on its route to the ocean. Just offshore stand several haystack rocks, and visible from the beach is **Heceta Head Lighthouse,** the most photographed lighthouse on the Oregon coast. Heceta (pronounced Huh-*see*-tuh) Head is a rugged headland that's named for Spanish explorer Capt. Bruno Heceta.

A mile farther south you'll come to **Sea Lion Caves,** 91560 U.S. 101 (☎ **541/ 547-3111**), which is the largest sea cave in the United States. It's also the only year-round mainland home for Steller's sea lions. Hundreds of these large mammals reside in the cave and on a nearby rock ledge, where they spend the day lounging and barking up a storm. Though the bulls can weigh as much as a ton and measure up to 12 feet long, the seal pups often capture the attention of visitors with their antics. During the fall and winter the sea lions move into the cave, which measures more than 300 feet long and 120 feet high. A combination of stairs, pathway, and elevator lead down from the bluff-top gift shop to a viewpoint in the cave wall. The cave was discovered in 1880, and since 1932 has been one of the most popular stops along the Oregon coast. Admission is $6 for adults, $4 for children 6 to 15. The cave is open daily from 9am until one hour before dark.

Another 6 miles south is the **Darlingtonia Wayside,** a small botanical preserve protecting a bog full of *Darlingtonia californica* plants, an insectivorous pitcher plant that's also known as the cobra lily. You'll find this interesting preserve on Mercer Lake Road.

9 Florence & Oregon Dunes National Recreation Area

50 miles S of Newport, 50 miles N of Coos Bay, 60 miles W of Eugene

Florence, home of the Oregon Dunes National Recreation Area, has long been a popular summer vacation spot for families. Sand dunes, beaches, the Siuslaw River, and 17 freshwater lakes combine to provide an abundance of recreational opportunities. However, popularity means crowds, and in the summer months campgrounds around here stay full and traffic can be bumper-to-bumper through town.

In spring you can avoid the crowds and enjoy the beauty of rhododendrons blossoming by the thousands all around the region. Rhododendrons are so much a symbol of Florence that the town holds a **Rhododendron Festival** each year on the third weekend of May.

Along Florence's Siuslaw River waterfront, many old buildings have been restored. The charming character of this neighborhood, with its interesting shops and restaurants, is all the more appealing when compared to the unsightly sprawl along U.S. 101.

ESSENTIALS

GETTING THERE   Florence is on U.S. 101 at the junction with Ore. 126 from Eugene.

VISITOR INFORMATION   Contact the **Florence Area Chamber of Commerce,** 270 U.S. 101, Florence, OR 97439 (☎ **541/997-3128**).

SEEING THE SIGHTS & ENJOYING THE OUTDOORS

Florence's **Old Town,** on the north bank of the Siuslaw River, is one of the most charming historic districts on the Oregon coast. The restored wood and brick buildings capture the flavor of a 19th-century fishing village, and many of the buildings now house interesting shops, galleries, and restaurants. Nearby, the **Siuslaw Pioneer Museum,** 85294 U.S. 101 S. (☎ **541/997-7884**), displays pioneer and Native American artifacts from this area. It's open Tuesday through Sunday from 10am to 4pm (closed in December); admission is by donation.

Despite the charm of Old Town Florence, it's the wide sandy beaches and dunes of the nearby coast that are the area's main attraction. Beginning just south of town is the 47-mile-long **Oregon Dunes National Recreation Area,** which includes more than 14,000 acres of dunes. This is the largest area of sand dunes on the West Coast and contains dunes more than 500 feet tall.

The first Oregon dunes were formed between 12 and 26 million years ago by the weathering of inland mountain ranges. Though the dunes are in constant flux, they reached their current size and shape about 7,000 years ago after the eruption of Mount Mazama formed Crater Lake.

Water currents and winds are the factors responsible for the dunes. Currents move the sand particles north each winter and south each summer, while constant winds off the Pacific Ocean blow the sand eastward, piling it up into dunes that are slowly marching east. Over thousands of years the dunes have swallowed up forests, leaving some groves of trees as remnant tree islands.

Fresh water trapped behind the dunes has formed numerous freshwater lakes, many of which are now ringed by campgrounds and vacation homes. These lakes are popular for fishing, swimming, and boating. The easiest place to get an overview of the dunes is at the **Dunes Overlook,** 10 miles south of Florence. If you'd like to explore the dunes, you have many options. **Jessie M. Honeyman State Park,** 3 miles south of Florence, is a unique spot with a beautiful forest-bordered lake and towering sand dunes. The park offers camping, picnicking, hiking trails, and access to Cleawox and Woahink lakes. There are also 16 Forest Service campgrounds within the recreation area. For more information on the dunes, contact the **Oregon Dunes National Recreation Area,** 855 Hwy. Ave., Reedsport, OR 97467 (☎ **541/271-3611**).

About half the sand dunes are open to **off-road vehicles** and throngs of people flock to this area to roar up and down the dunes. If you'd like to do a little off-roading in the dunes, you can rent a miniature dune buggy for around $35 to $40 an hour from **Sand Dunes Frontier** (☎ **541/997-3544**), which has its facilities 4 miles south of Florence. Alternatively, you can leave the driving to someone else and take a guided tour by four-wheel-drive truck.

C&M Stables, 90241 U.S. 101 N. (☎ **541/997-7540**), located 8 miles north of Florence, offers rides either on the beach or through the dunes. Rides last one to two hours, and prices range from $18 to $28. A more unusual excursion can be had on the **Seahorse Stagecoach** (☎ **541/999-0319**), a horse-drawn wagon that makes trips on the beach.

At the same time that stagecoaches were plying the beaches of Oregon, paddlewheelers were plying its rivers. The *Westward Ho!,* a half-scale replica of an 1850s stern-wheeler, revives the days of riverboat travel with its various **river cruises.** Regular cruises cost $15 for adults, $5 for children 4 to 12; the dinner cruise is $33. The *Westward Ho!* operates Wednesday through Sunday between May and September; other months the schedule is more limited.

If being on the river has you thinking about catching some fish, contact **Speer's Guide Service** (☎ **541/997-6644** or 800/997-6690). These folks can take you to where the fish are biting no matter what month of the year.

If golf is your sport, try the **Ocean Dunes Golf Links,** 3345 Munsel Lake Rd. (☎ **541/997-3232**).

WHERE TO STAY

Driftwood Shores Surfside Inn

88416 First Ave., Florence, OR 97439-9112. ☎ **541/997-8263** or 800/422-5091. 136 rms. TV TEL. Summer, $73–$110 double. Lower rates off-season. AE, CB, DC, DISC, MC, V.

Located north of Florence's Old Town district, this is the only oceanfront lodging in the area. As such, it's popular year round, so be sure to book early if you decide to stay here. The rooms vary in size and amenities, but all have ocean views and balconies. Most also have kitchens, which makes this a great place for a family vacation. There's an indoor pool and whirlpool, and the Surfside Restaurant and Lounge serves reasonably priced seafood and steaks with a view from every table.

✪ The Johnson House

216 Maple St., Florence, OR 97439. ☎ **541/997-8000.** 6 rms, 3 with bath. $75–$105 double. Rates include full breakfast. MC, V.

A white house behind a white picket fence conjures up classic images of small-town America, and with Old Town Florence only a block away, it's easy to maintain the image (if you can tune out the summer crowds). The Johnson House is the oldest home in Florence, and has been completely renovated. Today it's filled with antiques. The guest rooms are bright and cozy and there's a comfortable parlor where guests can gather to swap stories of their day's outings. The breakfasts are elaborate and filling.

River House Motel
1202 Bay St., Florence, OR 97439. ☎ **541/997-3933.** 40 rms. Summer, $64–$120 double. Off-season, $42–$110 double. AE, DISC, MC, V. Free parking.

Overlooking the Siuslaw River drawbridge and sand dunes on the far side of the river, the River House is only one block from the heart of Florence's Old Town district. This modern motel offers comfortable and attractive rooms, most of which have views and balconies. The largest and most expensive rooms are those with a double whirlpool tub. There's also an indoor hot tub available to all guests.

WHERE TO DINE

Bridgewater Seafood Restaurant
1297 Bay St. ☎ **541/997-9405.** Reservations recommended. Main courses $5–$19.50. MC, V. Mon–Thurs 11am–8:30pm, Fri–Sat 11am–9:30pm, Sun 11am–9pm. AMERICAN/CAJUN.

In a restored building in Old Town, this eclectic eatery combines a Wild West storefront facade with a tropical interior complete with wicker furniture and potted plants. In the summer there's patio dining, and any time of year the lounge area is a cozy place to wait out the rain. The menu is long and lists everything from jambalaya to scallops St. Jacques. However, we prefer to stick to the Cajun dishes.

✪ Traveler's Cove
1362 Bay St. ☎ **541/997-6845.** Main courses $11–$13. AE, DISC, MC, V. Mon–Thurs 9am–5pm, Fri–Sun 9am–8pm. INTERNATIONAL.

This eclectic eatery is at the back of an unusual little import shop right on the waterfront in Old Town Florence. Lunch is the main meal here, with lots of good sandwiches, a crab quiche, and both chicken and vegetarian chilis. The dinner menu is brief but includes such dishes as Thai chicken skewers and crab enchiladas. The hot apple dumplings are rich and heavy and go well with an espresso in the middle of the afternoon.

Windward Inn
3757 U.S. 101 N. ☎ **541/997-8243.** Reservations recommended. Main courses $9–$20. AE, DISC, MC, V. Daily 7am–9pm (sometimes later Fri–Sat). AMERICAN/CONTINENTAL.

With all the sophistication of an elegant historic hotel, the Windward is Florence's biggest and most luxurious restaurant, but way back in 1932 it was just a road-side diner and gas station. Today a small dining room and a few decorative antique gas pumps are all that remain of these humble beginnings. Each dining room has a slightly different atmosphere. In the lounge you'll find a marble floor and a long bar. The menu is almost exclusively seafood from start to finish. The blackened Cajun oysters make a good starter and among the entrées, the broiled herbed scallops and salmon filet poached in riesling, butter, and dill are good choices.

DRIVING ON TO COOS BAY WITH STOPS IN GARDINER, REEDSPORT & WINCHESTER BAY

Gardiner, Reedsport, and Winchester Bay are all on the shores of Winchester Bay and each has a very distinct character. **Gardiner** was founded in 1841 when a

Boston merchant's fur-trading ship wrecked near here, and is the oldest of the three towns. An important mill town in the 19th century (there's still a mill in the middle of town), Gardiner has several stately Victorian homes.

Two miles farther along the bay, you come to **Reedsport,** where you can stop in at the **Umpqua Discovery Center,** on the waterfront (☎ **541/271-4816**). This modern museum contains displays on the history and ecology of the area. It's open in summer, daily from 10am to 6pm; in winter, Wednesday through Sunday from 10am to 4pm. Admission is $3 for adults, $1.50 for children 5 to 12. Docked out-side the center is the *Hero,* a 125-foot-long research vessel that was built in 1968 for service in Antarctica. It's open daily from 10am to 4pm; admission is $3 for adults, $1.50 for children 5 to 12, and combination tickets are available. If you want to get out on the water, you can take a jet-boat tour with **Umpqua Jet Adventures,** 423 Riverfront Way (☎ **541/271-5694** or 800/353-8386), which offers two-hour trips at $15 for adults and $8 for children.

At the **Dean Creek Elk Viewing Area,** 1 mile east of town on Ore. 38, you can spot 100 or more elk grazing on 1,000 acres of meadows that have been set aside as a preserve. During the summer months, the elk tend to stay in the forest where it's cooler.

While in Reedsport, you can also stop in at the headquarters of the Oregon Dunes National Recreation Area, which is right on the highway as you pass through town.

The town of **Winchester Bay** is almost at the mouth of the Umpqua River and is known for its large fleet of charter-fishing boats. The fishing boats are moored at Salmon Harbor marina, where a stroll along the docks is almost certain to turn up a boat willing to take you out **fishing** for salmon, bottom fish, steelhead, striper, or sturgeon. While you're in Winchester Bay, be sure to have a look at the historic **Umpqua River Lighthouse.** The original lighthouse was at the mouth of the Umpqua River and was the first lighthouse on the Oregon coast. Across the street is a **whale-viewing platform** (best viewing months are November to June), and 100 yards up the road is the **Coastal Visitors Center,** 1020 Lighthouse Rd. (☎ **541/271-4631**), which is housed in a former Coast Guard station and contains historical exhibits and an information center. Also nearby is the very pretty **Umpqua Lighthouse State Park,** the site of the 500-foot-tall sand dunes that are the tallest in the United States. The park offers picnicking, hiking, and camping amid forests and sand dunes.

For more information on this area, contact the **Reedsport/Winchester Chamber of Commerce,** U.S. 101 and Ore. 38 (P.O. Box 11-B), Reedsport, OR 97467 (☎ **541/271-3495,** or 800/247-2155 in Oregon).

10 Coos Bay, North Bend & Charleston

85 miles NW of Roseburg, 48 miles S of Florence, 24 miles N of Bandon

Coos Bay, North Bend, and Charleston are together known as Oregon's bay area, and with a combined population of 35,000 people, the bay area is the largest urban center on the Oregon coast. Coos Bay and North Bend are the bay's com-mercial center and have merged into a single large town, while nearby Charleston maintains its distinct character as a small fishing port. As the largest natural harbor between San Francisco and Puget Sound, Coos Bay has long been an important port. Logs and wood products are the main export, but with the controversy over raw log shipments to Japan and the continuing battle to save old-growth forests in the Northwest, Coos Bay's days as a timber-shipping port may be numbered. In response to the economic downturn of the port, the bay area is gearing up to attract more tourists. Plans are underway to beautify the waterfront and improve public access to this area. Even if it isn't the most beautiful town on the Oregon coast, Coos Bay does have quite a few tourist amenities, including several good restaurants, moderately priced motels, and even a few B&Bs, that make it a good place to spend a night. And a closer look turns up, not far away, a trio of state parks that are, in our opinion, the most beautiful on the coast.

ESSENTIALS

GETTING THERE   From the north, take Ore. 99 from just south of Cottage Grove. This road becomes Ore. 38. At Reedsport, head south on U.S. 101. From the south, take Ore. 42 from just south of Roseburg.

The North Bend–Coos Bay Municipal Airport is served by Horizon Air.

VISITOR INFORMATION   Contact the **Bay Area Chamber of Commerce,** 50 E. Central Ave. (P.O. Box 210), Coos Bay, OR 97420 (☎ **541/269-0215** or 800/824-8486).

GETTING AROUND   If you need a taxi, contact **Coos Yellow Cab (☎ 541/ 267-3111).** Car rentals are available from **Hertz** and **Enterprise Rent-a-Car** at the North Bend–Coos Bay Municipal Airport.

FESTIVALS   Each year during the last two weeks of July, the **Oregon Coast Music Festival (☎ 541/267-0938** or 800/676-7563) brings a wealth of music to the area. Classical, jazz, bluegrass, swing, blues, and pops are all part of the festival, which is held in different locations around the bay area.

EXPLORING A MEMORABLE STRETCH OF COASTLINE

Southwest of Coos Bay you'll find three state parks and a county park that together preserve some of the most breathtaking shoreline anywhere in the Northwest. Walkers should note that the three state parks are connected by a trail that makes an excellent day hike.

Start your exploration of this beautiful stretch of coast by heading southwest on the Cape Arago Highway. In 10 miles you'll come to **Sunset Bay State Park (☎ 541/888-4902).** This park has one of the few beaches in Oregon where the water actually gets warm enough for swimming (although folks from warm-water regions may not agree). Sunset Bay is almost completely surrounded by sandstone cliffs, and the entrance to the bay is quite narrow. Together these two factors allow the waters of the bay to warm up a bit more than the waters of other beaches on the coast. Picnicking and camping are available in the park, and there are lots of tide pools to explore.

Another 3 miles brings you to **Shore Acres State Park (☎ 541/888-3732),** once the estate of local shipping tycoon Louis J. Simpson, who spent years developing his gardens. His ships would bring him unusual plants from all over the world, and eventually the gardens grew to include a formal English garden and a Japanese garden with a 100-foot lily pond. The gardens and his home, which long ago was torn down, were built atop sandstone cliffs overlooking the Pacific and a tiny cove. Rock walls rise up from the water and have been sculpted by the waves into unusual shapes. During winter storms, wave watching is a popular pastime here. The water off the park is often a striking shade of blue, and **Simpson Beach,** in the little cove, is the prettiest beach in Oregon. A trail leads down to the beach.

The third of this trio is **Cape Arago State Park** (☎ 541/888-3732). Just offshore from the rugged cape, several rocky islands offer a sunbathing spot for hundreds of seals (including elephant seals) and sea lions. Their barking can be heard from hundreds of yards away, and though you can't get very close to the seals, with a pair of binoculars you can see them quite well. The best viewing point is at **Simpson Reef Viewpoint.** On either side of the cape are coves with quiet beaches, although the beaches are closed from March 1 to June 30 to protect the seal pups. Tide pools along these beaches offer hours of fascination.

Bastendorff Beach County Park (☎ 541/888-5353), north of Sunset Bay at the mouth of Coos Bay, offers a long, wide beach that's popular with surfers. Four miles down Seven Devils Road from Charleston, you'll find the **South Slough National Estuarine Reserve** (☎ 541/888-5558). An interpretive center (open from 8:30am to 4:30pm, daily in summer and Monday through Friday in other months) set high above the slough provides background on the importance of estuaries. South Slough is in the process of being restored after many years of damming, diking, and reclamation of marshlands by farmers. A hiking trail leads down to the marshes.

Coos Bay and North Bend are the southern gateway to the **Oregon Dunes National Recreation Area** (see Section 9 of this chapter), and from North Bend you can see the dunes on the far side of Coos Bay. If you'd like to explore the dunes, there are several local companies offering all-terrain-vehicle (ATV) rentals and guided tours. Some of the best rates are offered by **Pacific Coast Recreation,** 4121 U.S. 101 (☎ 541/756-7183), located 5 miles north of North Bend and operates its tours in World War II surplus transport vehicles. The tours cost $12 for adults and $8 for children. ATVs rent for $20 to $25 per hour.

Charleston is the bay area's charter-fishing marina. If you'd like to do some sport fishing, contact **Bob's Sport Fishing** (☎ 541/888-4241 or 800/628-9633) or **Betty Kay Charters** (☎ 541/888-9021 or 800/752-6303).

Dune-buggy rentals are available from **Spinreel Dune Buggy Rentals,** 9122 Wildwood Dr. (☎ 541/759-3313), north of North Bend. Rates for ATVs start at $30 an hour.

Golfers can choose between the **Kentuck Golf Club,** 675 Golf Course Lane (☎ 541/756-4464), north of North Bend off East Bay Drive, or the **Sunset Bay Golf Course,** 11001 Cape Arago Hwy. (☎ 541/888-9301), a nine-hole course near Sunset Bay State Park.

In addition to all the outdoor recreational activities around the bay area, there are also a few small museums. The **Coos Art Museum,** 235 Anderson St. (☎ 541/267-3901), hosts changing exhibits. It's open Tuesday through Sunday from 11am to 4pm; admission is by donation. The **Coos County Historical Society Museum,** 1220 Sherman St., North Bend (☎ 541/756-6320), contains artifacts pertaining to the history of Coos County and southern coastal Oregon. Here you can also pick up copies of walking-tour brochures that will guide you to the historic buildings of both North Bend and Coos. It's open Tuesday through Saturday from 10am to 4pm; admission is $1 for adults, 25¢ for children 5 to 12.

At Coos Bay you enter myrtle-wood country. The myrtle tree grows only along a short section of coast in southern Oregon and is prized by woodworkers for its fine grain and durability. A very hard wood, it lends itself to all manner of platters, bowls, goblets, sculptures, and whatever. All along this section of coast you'll see myrtle-wood factories and shops where you can see how the raw wood is turned into finished pieces. The **House of Myrtlewood,** on U.S. 101 south of Coos Bay

(☎ 541/267-7804), is one of the bigger myrtle-wood factories. The **Real Oregon Gift,** 3955 Coast Hwy. 101 (☎ 541/756-2220), 5 miles north of North Bend, is another large factory and showroom. If you'd like to see some myrtle trees in their natural surroundings, visit **Golden and Silver Falls State Park** (☎ 541/269-0215), which is 25 miles northeast of Coos Bay on Coos River Road (take the Allegany exit off U.S. 101). Here in addition to seeing myrtle trees, you can hike to two 100-foot-high waterfalls.

Despite its industrial appearance, Coos Bay supports a surprisingly well-developed performing-arts scene. The **Little Theater on the Bay** (☎ 541/756-4336), which has its theater on Sherman Avenue in North Bend, has been around since 1947 and does four productions per year. **On Broadway Thespians,** On Broadway Theater, 226 S. Broadway, Coos Bay (☎ 541/269-2501), offers 12 productions a year, including classical and contemporary dramas and musicals.

WHERE TO STAY

If you're looking for cheap accommodations, you won't do any better than the **Motel 6,** 1445 Bayshore Dr., Coos Bay, OR 97420 (☎ 541/267-7171), charging $39 double.

Coos Bay Manor Bed & Breakfast Inn

955 S. Fifth St., Coos Bay, OR 97420. ☎ **541/269-1224,** or 800/269-1224 outside Oregon. 5 rms, 1 with bath. $60 double without bath, $70 double with bath. Rates include full breakfast. No credit cards.

This restored home in a quiet residential neighborhood in downtown Coos Bay was built in the colonial style in 1912. The guest rooms are large and vary from a Victorian room full of ruffles and lace to the masculine Cattle Baron's Room, which has bear and coyote rugs. This latter room is also the only one with a private bath.

Edgewater Inn

275 E. Johnson St., Coos Bay, OR 97420. ☎ **541/267-0423** or 800/233-0423. Fax 541/267-4343. 82 rms. A/C TV TEL. $68–$115 double. AE, DISC, MC, V.

This is Coos Bay's only waterfront hotel, and though the water it fronts on is only a narrow stretch of the back bay, you can watch ships in the harbor. Pilings and exposed beams used in the portico reflect the local logging-and-shipping economy. The guest rooms are large and furnished with blond-wood bureaus and headboards. The deluxe rooms are particularly well designed, with a breakfast bar, coffeemaker, minirefrigerator, extra-large TV, two sinks, lots of counter space, and a hairdryer in the bathroom. Other deluxe rooms have in-room spas. Most rooms also have balconies overlooking the water (and industrial areas). Facilities include an indoor pool, a hot tub, an exercise room, and a fishing and ship-viewing dock.

Red Lion Coos Bay

1313 N. Bayshore Dr., Coos Bay, OR 97420. ☎ **541/267-4141** or 800/547-8010. Fax 541/267-2884. 143 rms. A/C TV TEL. $80–$90 double. AE, CB, DC, DISC, MC, V.

This is the largest and most luxurious hotel in Coos Bay, and even so, it's quite reasonably priced. As the town's only convention lodging, the Red Lion is often full, so if you decide this is the place for you, book early. With its acres of parking and sprawling two-story buildings, the hotel is none too attractive, but if it's big-hotel amenities you want, it's got them. The guest rooms are larger than in most similar hotels, which makes rooms here a good choice for families. There's a dining room serving steaks and seafood and a lounge with a DJ playing classic and contemporary dance tunes. Services include room service, valet service, and a free airport shuttle. Facilities include an outdoor pool.

WHERE TO DINE

In addition to the restaurants listed below, you might want to check out **Kaffe 101,** 1950 Sherman St. (☎ **541/756-1065**), which serves espresso, pastries, and ice cream.

Blue Heron Bistro

100 Commercial Ave. ☎ **541/267-3933.** Reservations recommended. Main courses $7.25–$12.45. MC, V. Daily 8am–8pm (sometimes later). INTERNATIONAL.

A casual café, espresso bar, deli, and international restaurant all rolled up in one— that's what you'll find at the Blue Heron in the heart of downtown Coos Bay and right on U.S. 101. Add to this one of the largest assortments of imported beers on the coast and a dynamite breakfast menu and you have the sort of place that's perfect for breakfast, lunch, or dinner. From Belgian waffles to German Bratwurst (nitrite free) to Indonesian satay to blackened red snapper, the Blue Heron cruises the world in search of tastebud-tantalizing dishes. If you've got some friends with you, don't miss the Greek antipasto plate.

Kum-Yon's

835 S. Broadway. ☎ **541/269-2662.** Reservations recommended. Main courses $3.50–$20. AE, MC, V. Mon–Fri 11am–10pm, Sat–Sun 11:30am–10pm. ASIAN.

Though the Japanese, Koreans, and Chinese have never lived together in complete harmony, here at Kum-Yon, at least their respective cuisines do. Located right on U.S. 101 near downtown, Kum-Yon's is a rather plain restaurant that puts its energy into preparing excellent meals. Whether you're in the mood for sushi, bulgogi, or kung pao chicken, you'll leave sated and contented after a meal here.

Portside

8001 Kingfisher Dr., Charleston. ☎ **541/888-5544.** Reservations recommended. Main courses $11–$25. AE, MC, V. Daily 11:30am–11pm. SEAFOOD.

Charleston is home to Coos Bay's charter and commercial fishing fleets, and so it should come as no surprise that it's also home to the area's best seafood restaurant. Under different names, this restaurant has been in business for more than 30 years and has developed quite a reputation. Check the daily sheet to see what just came in on the boat. Preparations tend toward traditional continental dishes, of which the house specialty is a bouillabaisse marseillaise that's just swimming with shrimp, lobster, crab legs, butter clams, red snapper, scallops, and prawns—a seafood symphony.

11 Bandon

24 miles S of Coos Bay, 85 miles W of Roseburg

Once known primarily as the cranberry capital of Oregon, Bandon is now better known as an artists' colony. It's also set on one of the most spectacular pieces of coastline in the state. Just south of town, the beach is littered with boulders, monoliths, and haystack rocks that seem to have been strewn by some giant hand. Sunsets are stunning—it's easy to see why artists were drawn here.

Just north of town the Coquille River empties into the Pacific, and at the river's mouth stands a picturesque and historic lighthouse. The lighthouse was one of only a handful of Bandon buildings to survive a fire in 1936 that destroyed nearly the entire town. If you're a fan of old architecture, head over to the nearby town of Coquille, which is known for its turn-of-the-century Victorian homes.

ESSENTIALS

GETTING THERE   From Roseburg, head west on Ore. 42 to Coquille where you take Ore. 42S to Bandon, which is on U.S. 101.

VISITOR INFORMATION   Contact the **Bandon Chamber of Commerce,** 300 S. Second St. (P.O. Box 1515), Bandon, OR 97411 (☎ **541/347-9616**).

FESTIVALS   In September, the impending harvest is celebrated with the **Bandon Cranberry Festival.**

OUTDOOR ACTIVITIES & BANDON ATTRACTIONS

Head out of Bandon on Beach Loop Road and you'll soon see why rock watching is one of the area's most popular pastimes. Wind and waves have sculpted monoliths along the shore into contorted spires and twisted shapes. The first good place to view the rocks is at **Coquille Point,** at the end of 11th Street. From here you can see Table Rock and the Sisters. From the **Face Rock Viewpoint** you can see a face gazing skyward. Nearby stand a dog, a cat, and kittens. An ancient Chinook tribal legend tells how a young woman, Ewauna, swam into the sea and, while gazing at the moon, was seized by a sea monster. Her dog, cat, and kittens tried to save her but to no avail, and they were all turned into stone. A trail leads down to the beach from the viewpoint, so you can go out and explore some of the rocks that are left high and dry by low tide. South of the rocks, along a flat stretch of beach backed by sand dunes, there are several beach access areas, all of which are within **Bandon State Park.**

Bandon calls itself the **Storm-Watching Capital of the World,** and if you haven't yet been initiated into this wintertime activity, Bandon is the place to learn the ropes. Winter storms come blowing in off the Pacific with great regularity here on the Oregon coast, and with the storms often come huge waves. The waves crashing against the cliffs and rocks near Bandon put on a dramatic performance. One of the best places for storm watching is at the Face Rock Viewpoint on Beach Loop Road.

At Bandon, as elsewhere on the Oregon coast, **gray whales** migrating between the Arctic and Baja California, Mexico, pass close to the shore and can often be spotted from land. The whales pass Bandon between December and February on their way south and between March and May on their way north. Early morning, before the wind picks up, is the best time to spot whales. Coquille Point, at the end of 11th Street, and the bluffs along Beach Loop Road are the best vantage points.

More than 300 species of birds have been spotted in the Bandon vicinity, making this one of the best spots in Oregon for **birdwatching.** The **Oregon Islands National Wildlife Refuge,** which includes 1,400 rocks and islands off the state's coast, includes the famous monoliths of Bandon. Among the birds that nest on these rocks are tufted puffins, rhinoceros auklets, storm petrels, and gulls. In the **Bandon Marsh National Wildlife Refuge,** at the mouth of the Coquille River, is another good spot for birdwatching. In this area you can expect to see grebes, mergansers, buffleheads, plovers, and several birds of prey. Most beloved of local birds is the colorful tufted puffin, which you'll see illustrated on all manner of souvenirs around town.

Stormy Weather

"And the forecast for the weekend at the coast calls for high winds and heavy rain as another storm front moves in off the Pacific Ocean." This sort of weather forecast would keep most folks cozily ensconced at home with a good book and a fire in the fireplace, but in Oregon, where storm watching has become a popular winter activity, it's the equivalent of "Surf's up!"

Throughout the winter, Oregon's rocky shores and haystack rocks feel the effects of storms that originate far to the north in cold polar waters. As these storms slam ashore, sometimes with winds topping 100 m.p.h., their huge waves smash against the rocks with breathtaking force, sending spray flying. The perfect storm-watching days are those rare clear days right after a big storm, when the waves are still big but the sky is clear. After a storm is also the best time to go beachcombing—it's your best chance to find the rare hand-blown Japanese glass fishing floats that sometimes wash ashore on the Oregon coast.

So popular is storm watching that some bed-and-breakfast inns keep lists of people who are interested in storms and will give potential guests a call when the waves reach impressive proportions. There's also a storm-watchers club in Bandon.

Among the best storm-watching spots on the coast are the South Jetty at the mouth of the Columbia River in Fort Stevens State Park, Cannon Beach, Cape Meares, Depoe Bay, Cape Foulweather, Devil's Punchbowl on the Otter Crest Scenic Loop, Seal Rock, Cape Perpetua, Shore Acres State Park, Cape Arago State Park, Bandon, and Cape Sebastian.

Among the best lodgings for storm-watching are the Inn at Otter Crest north of Depoe Bay, the Channel House in Depoe Bay, the Cliff House in Waldport, the Adobe Motel Resort in Yachats, and the Sunset Motel in Bandon, The coast's best restaurants for storm watching are Tidal Raves in Depoe Bay, the dining room of the Adobe Motel Resort in Yachats, and Lord Bennett's at the Sunset in Bandon.

Other local attractions include the **Bandon Historical Society Museum** (☎ 541/347-2164), which is housed in a historic Coast Guard Station on First Street in the old town district. The museum contains Native American artifacts, historic photos, displays on lifesaving, and other examples of Bandon history. It's open Tuesday through Saturday from noon to 4pm; admission is $1.

Across the river from the museum is the historic **Coquille River Lighthouse,** which was built in 1896 and is open to the public daily: in summer from 7am to 8pm, and in winter from 8am to 5pm. The lighthouse is one of the only lighthouses to ever be hit by a ship—in 1903 an abandoned schooner plowed into the light. In December the lighthouse is decorated with Christmas lights. You'll find the lighthouse in **Bullards Beach State Park** (☎ 541/347-2209), which has long sandy beaches but no rocks. Fishing, crabbing, and clamming are all very popular in the park. You'll also find a campground and picnic area.

The **West Coast Game Park,** 7 miles south of town on U.S. 101 (☎ 541/347-3106), bills itself as America's largest wild animal petting park and is a must for families. Depending on what young animals they have at the time of your visit, you might be able to play with a leopard or bear cub. It's open daily from 9am to 7:30pm in summer, with shorter hours in other months. Admission is $6.50 for adults, $5.25 for children 7 to 12, $2 for children 2 to 6.

Bandon is the cranberry capital of Oregon, and each year in September the impending harvest is celebrated with the **Bandon Cranberry Festival.** Cranberry bogs can be seen along U.S. 101 both north and south of town.

If you're interested in exploring the Coquille River, contact **River Run Kayak Tours,** 1130 Baltimore St. (☎ **541/347-1884**), which runs 2¹/₂-hour flat-water kayak trips for $20 per person. If you'd rather ride a horse down the beach, contact **Bandon Beach Riding Stables,** on Beach Loop Drive south of Face Rock (☎ **541/347-3423**). The **Bandon Face Rock Golf Course,** 3235 Beach Loop Dr. (☎ **541/347-3818**), offers a very challenging nine holes not far from the famous Face Rock.

SHOPPING

Shopping is Bandon's main attraction these days, and in the historic old town district just off U.S. 101, you'll find many interesting shops and galleries in restored buildings. Most of the buildings date back only to 1936, when all but four of Bandon's commercial buildings were destroyed in a fire.

Nearly a dozen galleries selling artworks by regional artists give validity to Bandon's reputation as an arts community. Among our favorite Bandon galleries are the **210 Second Street Gallery,** 210 Second St. (☎ **541/347-4133**), which is the largest gallery on the Oregon coast and represents nearly 100 artists who work in a variety of media; **Campbell's Glassworks,** 275 E. Second St. (☎ **541/347-9810**), which does custom stained-glass designs and also sells a variety of glass gifts; and **Spirit of Oregon,** 112 Second St. (☎ **541/347-4311**), offering hand-thrown ceramics.

At the **Bandon Cheese Factory,** located right on U.S. 101 in the middle of town (☎ **541/347-2456**), you can watch cheese being made, try some samples, and maybe pick up some fixings for a picnic on the beach. A few blocks away, **Cranberry Sweets,** on the corner of First Street and Chicago Avenue (☎ **541/347-9475**), sells handmade candies. Some of the candies are made from cranberries, but there are also many noncranberry candies among the 200 varieties available.

If you haven't yet visited a myrtle-wood factory and showroom, you can visit **Seagull Myrtlewood** (☎ **541/347-2248**), 3 miles south of town at the intersection of U.S. 101 and Beach Loop Road, or **Zumwalt's Myrtlewood Factory** (☎ **541/347-3654**), 6 miles south of town on U.S. 101.

WHERE TO STAY

Riverboat Bed & Breakfast

P.O. Box 2485, Bandon, OR 97411 ☎ **541/347-1922** or 800/348-1922. 8 rms. $125 double. Rates include full breakfast. MC, V.

This modern sternwheeler is one of the most unique B&Bs on the Oregon coast and is docked just across the Coquille River from Bandon. The guest rooms here are small, as you'd expect on any boat, but they all have big windows and private bathrooms. A parlor on the main deck provides a space for gathering to meet other guests or just enjoy the feel of being aboard an old-fashioned riverboat. Breakfast is served during a 90-minute cruise up the river.

Sea Star Guesthouse and AYH Hostel
370 First St. and 375 Second St., Bandon, OR 97411. ☎ **541/347-9632.** 8 rms, 39 dorm beds. TV. $35–$75 double; $12 per night dorm bed for members, $15 for nonmembers. MC, V.

The guesthouse, a two-story contemporary beach home overlooking Bandon's marina, is your best choice for accommodations in the old town waterfront district. All four downstairs rooms here (three of which are actually suites) have views of the harbor, but the upstairs rooms are the better choices. These have skylights and open beams. The larger of the two has a loft sleeping area, while the smaller has a four-poster bed.

Dorms in the hostel are small, so if you're traveling with some friends, you might get one all to yourself. There are four family rooms as well. Guests can use a small lounge and kitchen.

⑤ Sunset Motel
1755 Beach Loop Rd., Bandon, OR 97411. ☎ **541/347-2453** or 800/842-2407. Fax 541/347-3636. 58 rms, 14 cabins/condos. TV TEL. $40–$50 economy double, $56–$66 ocean-view double, $80–$110 oceanfront double; $80–$190 cabin/condo. AE, DISC, MC, V.

Nowhere in Oregon will you find a better ocean view than here at the Sunset Motel, where you'll also find everything from economy motel rooms to contemporary condos, rustic cabins, and classic cottages. Dozens of Bandon's famous rock spires, sea stacks, and monoliths rise from the beach or just offshore in front of the motel, making sunsets from the Sunset truly memorable. If you want modern accommodations, opt for the Vern Brown addition rooms, but if you want something romantic and private, try to get one of the cottages, several of which were built back in the 1930s or 1940s. The adjacent Lord Bennet Restaurant has some of the best food in town, and there's no question about its having *the* view in Bandon. A hot tub, video rentals, and guest laundry round out the motel's amenities.

Windermere
3250 Beach Loop Rd., Bandon, OR 97411. ☎ **541/347-3710.** 17 rms. TV. $55–$89 double. Lower rates off-season. AE, MC, V.

Turning into the Windermere's driveway on a gray blustery day, you can almost hear a voice calling for "Heathcliff." The *Wuthering Heights* setting is a combination of moorlike surroundings and the English cottage–style architecture of this 60-year-old beach getaway. Set on the edge of a wide sand beach, the Windermere has seen better years, but for families on a budget or anyone who enjoys old-fashioned accommodations, the rooms here are quite adequate. All the rooms have oceanfront decks, and some have sleeping lofts or kitchens.

WHERE TO DINE

Andrea's Old Town Café
160 Baltimore Ave. ☎ **541/347-3022.** Reservations recommended. Main courses $11–$17; lunch $4–$8. No credit cards. Mon–Sat 9am–3pm and 5:30–9pm, Sun 10:30am–2:30pm (brunch) and 5:30–9pm. Closed Sun–Thurs night in winter. INTERNATIONAL.

Though it looks as if it's just another ducks-and-chicks, country-cute family restaurant from the outside and a well-worn natural-foods college café on the inside, Andrea's is neither. This restaurant defies classification. By day it's an ever-popular omelet-and-sandwich place where the hangtown fry omelet, made with oysters and ham, is a breakfast must and the seafood sandwiches, such as the Cajun oyster sandwich, are simply outstanding. At night, a daily changing menu takes over and you might find scallops dijonaise, sesame chicken with plum sauce, or prawns with a bleu-cheese sauce. Friday is pizza night at Andrea's, and the pizzas are the best on the beach.

Harp's

130 Chicago St. ☎ **541/347-9057.** Reservations highly recommended. Main courses $10–$16. AE, MC, V. Summer, daily 5–10pm; fall–spring, Tues–Sat 5–9pm. ITALIAN.

A weathered cedar-shingle exterior and a front door framed by an assemblage of driftwood may say "old crab shack," but the forest-green interior and intimate dining rooms are signs of a new incarnation. Harp's has what many Oregonians consider the best Italian food on the coast, and we certainly have to agree. It starts with the appetizers, which aren't your usual antipastos, nor are they exclusively Italian. We like the smoked game hen, which is smoked and basted with Kahlúa and honey. The house onion soups, made with sweet onions and vermouth, also shouldn't be missed. This is cranberry country, and if you didn't opt for the game-hen appetizer, try the entrée, which is served with a garlic-and-cranberry sauce. The poached salmon with capers and vermouth is a superb combination of subtle flavors, as is the charcoal-broiled halibut with hot pistachio sauce.

Lord Bennett's at the Sunset

1695 Beach Loop Rd. ☎ **541/347-3663.** Reservations recommended. Main courses $11.75–$17; lunch $5–$8. AE, DISC, MC, V. Daily 11am–3pm and 5–10pm (until 9pm in winter). CONTINENTAL.

Lord Bennett's is the only restaurant in Bandon overlooking the bizarre beachscape of contorted rock spires and sea stacks, and as such, would be a must for a meal. However, great continental meals make the restaurant doubly worthwhile. Sunsets are an absolute must at Lord Bennett's, and since sunsets come late in the summer, you might want to eat a late lunch the day you plan to eat here. We suggest starting dinner with some steamed clams before moving on to such main courses as poached oysters bordered with a mushroom duxelle and covered with anise-flavored mornay sauce. There's a decent wine list and desserts that are both beautiful and delicious.

Sea Star Bistro

375 Second St. ☎ **541/347-9632.** Reservations recommended. Main courses $9–$15. AE, MC, V. Daily 8am–9pm. PACIFIC RIM/SOUTHWEST.

Small and casually elegant, the Bistro is housed in a restored cottage just off U.S. 101. Skylights and big front windows brighten the room. Everything is home-made using the best and freshest ingredients available. Whether you order a Greek omelet for breakfast, an eggplant, red pepper, and feta cheese sandwich for lunch, or paella for dinner, you'll be delighted by the sunny flavors served here. Before starting a meal, be sure to stroll over to the dessert case and see what tempting baked delicacies are available.

DRIVING ON TO GOLD BEACH WITH STOPS IN CAPE BLANCO & PORT ORFORD

Cape Blanco is the westernmost point in the contiguous United States. First discovered by Spanish explorer Martín de Aguilar in 1603, it's now the **Cape Blanco State Park** (☎ **541/332-6774**) and the site of the **Cape Blanco Lighthouse.** The lighthouse was built in 1870 and is the oldest continuously operating light in Oregon. Not far from the lighthouse is the **Hughes House Museum,** a restored Eastlake Victorian home that was built in 1898 and is furnished with period antiques. It's open May to September only, Thursday through Monday from 10am to 4pm and on Sunday from noon to 4pm. The park also offers hiking, picnicking, camping, and a beach.

If you're interested in sailboarding, check out the **Floras Lake Windsurfing School,** at the Floras Lake B&B, 92870 Boice Cope Rd. (☎ 541/348-2573), which offers rentals and lessons. You'll find Floras Lake west of U.S. 101 south of the community of Langlois.

The nearby town of **Port Orford,** little more than a wide spot in the road, actually has a very long history. Named by Capt. George Vancouver on April 5, 1792, this natural harbor became the first settlement on the Oregon coast, when, in 1851, settlers and soldiers together constructed Fort Orford. For a good view of Port Orford and this section of coast, drive up to the **Port Orford Heads Wayside** where you'll find a short trail out to an overlook. The route to the way-side is well marked.

Six miles south of Port Orford, you come to **Humbug Mountain State Park** (☎ 541/332-6774), where Humbug Mountain rises 1,756 feet from the ocean's waves. A pretty campground is tucked into the lee of the mountain and a trail leads to the summit.

Another 6 miles brings you to a place the kids aren't going to let you pass. The **Prehistoric Gardens,** 36848 U.S. 101 S. (☎ 541/332-4463), is a lost world of life-size dinosaur replicas. Though they aren't as realistic as those in *Jurassic Park,* they'll make the kids squeal with delight. The gardens are open daily from 8am to dusk; admission is $5 for adults, $4 for students 12 to 18, $3 for children 5 to 11.

WHERE TO STAY & DINE

Floras Lake House Bed & Breakfast

92870 Boice Cope Rd., Langlois, OR 97450. ☎ **541/348-2573.** 4 rms. $95–$125 double. Rates include full breakfast. DISC, MC, V.

Located south of Bandon near the community of Langlois, this contemporary B&B is close to the shore of Floras Lake, which is popular for sailboarding. The inn even offers sailboard rentals and lessons. The guest rooms all have views of the lake, and the two more expensive rooms have fireplaces. Across the back of the house are several large decks that provide plenty of lounging areas.

Home by the Sea

44 Jackson St., Port Orford, OR 97465-0606 ☎ **541/332-2855.** Fax 541/332-7585. 2 rms. $70–$75 double. Rates include full breakfast. MC, V.

Set high atop a bluff overlooking the ocean, this contemporary B&B offers large guest rooms with some of the best views on the coast. Pet birds fill the house with their songs, and in the downstairs living room area you'll still get that million-dollar view. The inn is a block off U.S. 101 and is within walking distance of several restaurants.

Sixes River Hotel & Restaurant

93316 Sixes River Rd., Sixes, OR 97476. ☎ **541/332-3900** or 800/828-5161. 5 rms. $75 double. Rates include full breakfast. MC, V.

About 6 miles north of Port Orford, near the turnoff to Cape Blanco State Park, stands the last remaining building in Sixes, once an active logging-and-mining community. Built in 1895 and recently restored, the Sixes River Hotel is surrounded by farmland. The guest rooms are simply furnished and sport a country decor. The inn makes a good base for exploring the coast and nearby state parks.

The restaurant is one of the finest on the south coast. The menu is limited and much of the produce is organically grown here on the farm. Reservations are required and main-course prices range from $11 to $14.

12   Gold Beach

54 miles N of Crescent City, Calif.; 32 miles S of Port Orford

In California, gold prospectors of the mid-19th century had to struggle through rugged mountains in search of pay dirt, but here in Oregon they could just scoop it up off the beach. The black sands at the mouth of the Rogue River were high in gold (as were the river and other nearby streams), and it was this gold that gave the town its name. The white settlers attracted by the gold soon came in conflict with the local Rogue River (or TuTuNi) native peoples. Violence erupted in 1856, but within the year the Rogue River Indian Wars had come to an end and the Native Americans were moved to a reservation. The Native Americans had for centuries found the river to be a plentiful source of salmon, and when the gold played out, commercial fishermen moved in to take advantage of the large salmon runs. The efficiency of their nets and traps quickly decimated the local salmon population, and a salmon hatchery was constructed to replenish the runs. In the 20th century sport fishing on the Rogue River became so famous that it attracted western author Zane Grey. His novel *Rogue River Feud* chronicles the conflict that arose between the sport fishermen and the commercial fishermen.

Today the area is more peaceful, but it's still the Rogue River that draws visitors to Gold Beach.

ESSENTIALS

GETTING THERE   From the north, take Ore. 42 west from Roseburg to Bandon and then head south on U.S. 101. From the south, the only route to Gold Beach is from California via U.S. 101.

VISITOR INFORMATION   Contact the **Gold Beach Chamber of Commerce,** 1225 S. Ellensburg Ave., Suite 3, Gold Beach, OR 97444 (☎ **541/ 247-7526** or 800/525-2334).

WHAT TO SEE & DO: FISHING, HIKING, COASTAL SCENERY & MORE

Gold Beach itself is a wide sandy beach, but just a few miles to the south, the mountains once again march into the sea, creating what many say is the single most spectacular section of coastline in Oregon.

Though it's only 34 miles from Gold Beach to the town of **Brookings,** you can easily spend the whole day making the trip. The first place to stop is at **Cape Sebastian,** 5 miles south of Gold Beach. This headland was named by a Spanish explorer in 1603 and towers 700 feet above the ocean. Between December and March, this is a good vantage point for whale watching. A 2-mile trail leads down to the water. In another 2 miles you come to **Meyers Creek,** where you can get a closer look at some of the rugged rock formations that make this coastline so breathtaking. This is also a good clamming beach. **Pistol River,** 2 miles farther south, is an area of sand dunes and perfect waves that's popular with surfers and boardsailors. This was the site of a battle during the Rogue River Indian Wars of

1856. Five more miles brings you to **Whiskey Creek,** which is the site of many tide pools. Less than a mile farther you come to the **Arch Rock Viewpoint,** a picnic area with a stunning view of an offshore monolith that has been carved into an arch by the action of the waves. In another 2 miles, you come to the **Natural Bridge Viewpoint.** These two arches were formed when a sea cave collapsed. In 2 more miles you cross the **Thomas Creek Bridge,** which at 345 feet high is the highest bridge in Oregon. In a little more than a mile, you come to **Whalehead Beach State Park,** where a pyramidal rock just offshore bears a striking resemblance to a spy-hopping whale. There's a better view of Whalehead Rock half a mile south. In another mile and a half you'll come to **House Rock Viewpoint,** which offers sweeping vistas to the north and south. At **Cape Ferrelo Viewpoint** and **Lone Ranch State Park** just to the south, you'll find a grassy headland. Three more miles brings you to **Harris Beach State Park** (☎ **541/469-2021**), the last stop along this coast. Here you'll find picnicking and camping and a good view of **Goat Island,** which is the Oregon coast's largest island.

Since 1895 mail boats have been traveling up the Rogue River from Gold Beach to deliver mail and other freight to remote homesteads. Back when this route was initiated, it took four days to make the 64-mile round-trip run, but today you can cover the same length of river in just six hours in powerful hydrojet boats that use water jets instead of propellers and have a very shallow draft, which allows them to cross rapids and riffles only a few inches deep. Along the way you may see deer, black bear, river otters, and bald eagles. A running narration covers the river's colorful history. Three different trips are available ranging in length from 64 to 104 miles. Two companies operate these trips. **Rogue River Mail Boat Trips** (☎ 541/247-7033 or 800/458-3511) leaves from a dock a quarter mile upriver from the north end of the Rogue River Bridge. **Jerry's Rogue River Jet Boats** (☎ 541/247-4571 or 800/451-3645) leaves from the Port of Gold Beach on the south side of the Rogue River Bridge. Departures are between 7:30 and 8am (with afternoon departures in summer), and fares range from $30 to $75 for adults and $12 to $35 for children. The price of lunch is only included in the 104-mile run.

An alternative to the jet-boat trips is to do a white-water rafting trip down the Rogue. These are offered by **Rogue White Water Rafting** (☎ **541/247-6022** or 541/247-6504). The four-hour float costs $65 for adults and $30 for children.

Fighting salmon and steelhead are what have made the Rogue River famous, and if you'd like to hire a guide to take you to the best **fishing** holes, you've got plenty of options. Some guides to check out include **Rogue River Outfitters** (Denny Hughson) (☎ **541/247-2684**), and **Steve Beyerlin,** 94575 Chandler Rd. (☎ **541/247-4138** or 800/348-4138). A half day of fishing will cost you around $100 and a full day will cost around $125. Clamming and crabbing can also be quite productive around Gold Beach.

Jerry's Rogue River Museum (☎ **541/247-4571**), located at the Port of Gold Beach and affiliated with Jerry's Jet Boat Tours, is actually the more modern and informative of the town's two museums. It focuses on the geology and cultural and natural history of the Rogue River. It's open daily from 7am to 7pm; admission is free. At the diminutive **Curry County Historical Museum,** 920 S. Ellensburg Ave. (☎ **541/247-6113**), you can learn more about the history of the area and see plenty of Native American and pioneer artifacts. The admission-free museum is open June to September, Tuesday through Saturday from noon to 4pm; the rest of the year, on Saturday from noon to 4pm.

Golfers can play a round at **Cedar Bend Golf Course,** 12 miles north of Gold Beach off U.S. 101 (☎ **541/247-6911**). If you'd like to go horseback riding, contact **Indian Creek Trail Rides,** half a mile up Jerry's Flat Road in Wedderburn (☎ **541/247-7704**).

Hikers have an abundance of options in the area. At the **Schrader Old-Growth Trail,** about 8 miles up Jerry's Flat Road near the Lobster Creek Campground, you can hike through an ancient forest and see for yourself the majestic trees that so many people in the Northwest are fighting to save. In spring, the **Lower Illinois River Trail,** 27 miles up South Bank Road and another 3¼ miles up County Road 450, is abloom with wildflowers. Backpackers can hike the **Lower Rogue River Trail,** which is 40 miles long and parallels the river most of the way. If you don't want to carry a heavy pack, seven lodges along the river provide meals and accommodations. You can combine a hike along this trail with a jet-boat ride up the river. The **Oregon Coast Trail,** which extends (in short sections) from California to Washington, has several segments both north and south of Gold Beach. The most spectacular sections of this trail are south of town at Cape Sebastian and in **Samuel H. Boardman State Park.** For more information on hiking in the Gold Beach area, contact the Gold Beach Chamber of Commerce (see above) or the **Siskiyou National Forest,** 200 NE Greenfield Rd., Grants Pass, OR 97526 (☎ **541/471-6516**).

WHERE TO STAY

Ireland's Rustic Lodges

1120 S. Ellensburg Ave., Gold Beach, OR 97444. ☎ **541/247-7718.** 28 rms, 9 cottages, 3 houses. TV. $40–$61 double. No credit cards.

The name sums it all up—rustic cabins set amid shady grounds that are as green as Ireland. Though there are some modern motel rooms here, they just can't compare to the quaint old cabins, which have stone fireplaces, paneled walls, and unusual door handles made from twisted branches. Built in 1922, the cabins are indeed rustic and are not for those who need modern comforts. The mature gardens surrounding the cabins are beautiful any time of year but particularly in late spring.

Jot's Resort

94360 Waterfront Loop, Gold Beach, OR 97444. ☎ **541/247-6676** or 800/367-5687. 140 rms. TV TEL. Summer, $80–$90 double; $115–$250 condo apt. Off-season, $50–$75 double; $85–$200 condo apt. AE, DC, DISC, MC, V.

Stretching along the north bank of the Rogue River, Jot's offers a wide variety of room sizes and rates, but every room has a view of the water and the Rogue River Bridge. The deluxe rooms here are the most attractively furnished, while the condos could stand a good remodeling. This place has a definite fishing orientation and is very popular with families. The dining room and lounge offers reasonably priced meals. Fishing guides, deep-sea charters, boat and bicycle rentals, and jet-boat trips can all be arranged, and there are indoor and outdoor pools, a whirlpool, a sauna, and a boat dock and marina.

✪ Tu Tu Tun Lodge

96550 North Bank Rogue, Gold Beach, OR 97444. ☎ **541/247-6664.** Fax 541/247-0672. 16 rms, 2 suites, 2 houses. TEL. $125–$160 double; $170–$180 suite; $195–$275 house. Lower rates in winter. MC, V.

Tu Tu Tun is the most luxurious lodging on the south coast, and the main lodge building incorporates enough rock and natural wood to give it that rustic feel without sacrificing any modern comforts. The immense fireplace in the lounge is the center of activity. On warm days, the patio overlooking the river is a great spot for relaxing and sunning, and on cold nights logs crackle in a fire pit.

The guest rooms are large and beautifully furnished with slate-topped tables and tile counters. Each room has a private patio or balcony, and should you get an upstairs room, you'll have a high ceiling and an excellent river view. Some rooms also come with a fireplace or outdoor soaking tub.

Dining/Entertainment: The dining room overlooks the river and serves four-course fixed-price dinners ($32.50) focusing on Northwest cuisine. For those heading out on the river, box lunches are available.

Services: Fishing guides and boat rentals arranged.

Facilities: Outdoor pool, four-hole pitch-and-putt golf course, horseshoe courts, games room with pool table, dock, hiking trails.

NEARBY FISHING LODGES

As one of the most famous fishing rivers in the United States and as one of the first designated National Wild and Scenic Rivers in the country, the Rogue River has a number of rustic fishing lodges, several of which can only be reached by boat. These lodges are popular with rafting companies and fishing guides heading downstream from the Grants Pass area. Fishing lodges are, in general, rustic riverside retreats with small guest rooms and dining rooms serving fixed menus. In the tiny rural community of **Agness,** at the end of a 35-mile winding, but paved, road from Gold Beach, you'll find several lodges that can be reached by car.

Paradise Bar Lodge

P.O. Box 456, Gold Beach, OR 97444. ☎ **541/247-6022**, 247-6504, or 800/525-2161. 14 rms. $260–$380 double. Rates include all meals. MC, V.

You can fly in, hike in, raft in, or jet-boat in, but you can't drive in, and as far as we're concerned, that's reason enough for a trip to the Paradise Bar Lodge. Located 52 miles upriver from Gold Beach and 13 miles from the nearest road access, the lodge was built in the early 1960s, but the area was first homesteaded in the early 1900s. The lodge buildings are up above the river on an open hill and command a sweeping view of the river's turbulent waters. Basic rooms and more spacious cabins, some with loft sleeping areas, are available. Though steelhead and salmon and white water are the main topics of discussion here, it's still a great place to get away from it all with a bit of comfort. Hiking trails lead along the banks of the river and up to the top of nearby Deak's Peak.

Facilities: Airstrip, volleyball court, croquet equipment, horseshoes, driving range and putting green, museum.

Santa Anita Lodge

36975 Agness-Illahe Rd., Agness, OR 97406. ☎ **541/247-6884.** 8 rms, 3 with bath. $200 double. Rates include all meals. AE, MC, V.

Built in the 1930s and reopened as a lodge in 1992, the Santa Anita Lodge captures the essence of the Rogue River experience in its classic fishing-lodge decor. Though the exterior is unremarkable, step through the door and you'll enter a different world—massive timbers, wood stoves and stone fireplaces, and a trophy room filled with the mounted heads of the original owner's big-game hunting expeditions around the world. A huge deck overlooks the river and a meadow where elk and bear are often seen. Deer and wild turkeys are regular visitors to the lodge grounds, and best of all, the fishing is great right in front of the lodge. The three guest rooms with private baths also have walls of glass and wood stoves in the rooms. Even if you aren't into fishing, these rooms would be ideal for a quiet getaway.

WHERE TO DINE

The best meals in Gold Beach are served in the dining room at **Tu Tu Tun Lodge** (see "Where to Stay," above, for details).

Nor'wester

Port of Gold Beach. ☎ **541/247-2333.** Reservations accepted only for parties of five or more. Main courses $12–$40. MC, V. Daily 5–9pm. SEAFOOD.

Large portions of simply prepared fresh seafood are the mainstay of the menu at this dockside restaurant where you can watch fishing boats in the mouth of the Rogue River. The steak-and-seafood combinations here are popular choices for big appetites, but we prefer the handful of continental dishes such as coquilles St-Jacques and snapper à la meunière.

DRIVING ON TO THE REDWOODS WITH STOPS IN BROOKINGS & HARBOR

Brookings and Harbor together comprise the southernmost community on the Oregon coast. Because of the warm year-round temperatures, this region is known as the Oregon Banana Belt, and you'll see palm trees and other cold-sensitive plants thriving in gardens around town. The area is also home to a native azalea that is celebrated each Memorial Day weekend with an **Azalea Festival.** May is usually the time to see the wild azaleas in bloom and the best place to see them is at **Azalea State Park** near the south end of Brookings. The myrtle tree, yet another plant unique to the south coast, is preserved at **Loeb State Park,** which is also the site of Oregon's largest grove of coast redwoods. This is as far north as the redwoods naturally grow. The park is 10 miles northeast of Brookings on the north bank of the Chetco River. For more information on this area, contact the **Brookings/ Harbor Chamber of Commerce,** P.O. Box 940, Brookings, OR 97415 (☎ **541/ 469-3181** or 800/535-9469).

WHERE TO STAY

Best Western Beachfront Inn

16008 Boat Basin Rd., Harbor, OR 97415. ☎ **541/469-7779** or 800/468-4081. Fax 541/469-0283. 78 rms. TV TEL. $69–$105 double. AE, CB, DC, DISC, MC, V.

The Beachfront Inn is the only oceanfront accommodation in this area. Most rooms are fairly large and all have ocean views, balconies, microwaves, and mini-refrigerators. The more expensive rooms also have whirlpool tubs with picture windows over them. There's an outdoor pool and a whirlpool.

✪ Chetco River Inn

21202 High Prairie Rd., Brookings, OR 97415. ☎ **541/469-8128** or 800/327-2688. $75–$85 double. Rates include full breakfast. MC, V.

Set on 35 very secluded acres on the banks of the Chetco River, this contemporary B&B caters primarily to anglers but also makes a great weekend retreat for anyone looking to get away from it all. Before you can get away, first you'll have to find the lodge, which is 16 miles from town up North Bank Road (the last

3 miles are on gravel). The lodge makes use of alternative energies and is connected to the outside world by a radio phone only. If you don't feel like leaving the woods, you can arrange to have dinner here at the lodge.

South Coast Inn Bed & Breakfast

516 Redwood St., Brookings, OR 97415. ☎ **541/469-5557** or 800/525-9273. Fax 541/ 469-6615. 3 rms, 1 cottage. $74–$94 double. Rates include full breakfast. AE, DISC, MC, V.

Although the guest rooms here are fairly plain, the location of this 1917 craftsman bungalow makes it a good choice for anyone seeking a B&B in the Brookings area. Two of the guest rooms have good views, and the cottage, across the garden from the main house, offers a more private setting. Guests have use of a large living room full of antiques, where a fire often crackles in the stone fireplace. Although the weather here never gets really cold, there are also a sauna and whirlpool.

WHERE TO DINE

Bistro Gardens

1103 Chetco Ave. ☎ **541/469-9750.** Reservations recommended. Main courses $10–$17. MC, V. Mon–Fri 11:30am–2pm and 5–9pm, Sat 5–9pm. ITALIAN.

This unpretentious little spot in an older shopping center at the north end of town is easy to miss. It's small, but the lavender walls give it a touch of daring, an indicator of what you'll find on the menu. It's not typical Brookings fare. There are Dungeness crab cakes or tomato-and-basil soup for starters, and such dishes as king salmon baked with oysters and topped with pesto cream, or oysters with peppers and pasta to round out the meal. Several versions of Caesar salads include one with Dungeness crab.

Chive's

1025 Chetco Ave. ☎ **541/469-4121.** Reservations recommended. Main courses $12–$16. MC, V. Wed–Sat 11am–2pm and 5–9pm, Sun 9:30am–2:30pm (brunch) and 2:30–9pm. NORTHWEST.

If you've just reached Oregon from California and are looking for your first bite of Northwest cuisine, this is a good choice. Leaded glass and coral-pink walls make this place a bit more formal than the Bistro Gardens, above. Here you might try a salad with pear, endive, and watercress dressed with goat cheese and walnuts, and follow it up with roast rack of lamb with minted couscous, sweet peppers, and mizuna greens. At brunch egg dishes prevail, finished off by a light dessert such as yogurt and berry parfait.

Rubio's

1136 Chetco Ave. ☎ **541/469-4919.** Complete dinner $7.25–$13. AE, DISC, MC, V. Tues–Sun 11am–9pm (to 8pm in winter). MEXICAN.

A wild paint job makes Rubio's, up at the north end of town, unmistakable, and if you can stand the traffic noise and the weather is clear, you can eat out on the front patio. Inside this old cottagelike building, the lace curtains, red tablecloths, and Mexican music are reassuring after the rush of traffic on the highway. The fiery salsa is a Brookings legend and is available to go. You can order a fixed-price dinner combination or create your own Mexican banquet by mixing and matching various dishes. The chiles rellenos are outstanding.

The Willamette Valley   13

For more than 150 miles, from south of Eugene to the Columbia River at Portland, the Willamette River (pronounced Wih-*lam*-it) flows between Oregon's two major mountain ranges. Protected from winter winds by the Cascade Range to the east and tempered by cool moist air flowing off the Pacific Ocean, which lies to the west on the far side of the Coast Range, the Willamette Valley enjoys a mild climate that belies its northerly latitudes. It was along the banks of the Willamette that Oregon's first towns sprang up, and today the valley is home to Oregon's largest cities, its most productive farmlands, the state capital, and the state's two major universities.

The Willamette Valley was the Eden at the end of the Oregon Trail, a fabled land of rich soils, mild winters, and plentiful rains. Families were willing to walk 2,000 miles across the continent for a chance at starting a new life. The valley became the breadbasket of the Oregon country, and today, despite the urban sprawl of Portland, Salem, and Eugene, the Willamette Valley still produces an agricultural bounty unequaled in its diversity. Although the region offers history and culture, its idyllic rural scenery and prolific farms are what enchant most visitors. Throughout the year you can sample the produce of this region at farms, fruit stands, and wineries. In spring commercial fields of tulips and irises paint the landscape with bold swaths of color. In summer there are farm stands near almost every town, and many farms will let you pick your own strawberries, raspberries, blackberries, peaches, apples, cherries, and plums. In the autumn you can sample the filbert and walnut harvest, and at any time of year you can do a bit of wine tasting at dozens of wineries.

1   The Wine Country

McMinnville: 38 miles SW of Portland, 26 miles NW of Salem

If it hadn't been for Prohibition, wine connoisseurs might be comparing California wines to those of Oregon rather than vice versa. Oregon wines had already gained a national reputation when the state voted in Prohibition. It would be a few years before more liberal California would adopt Prohibition, and in the interim the Golden State got the upper hand. Oregon wines didn't begin to make themselves known again until the 1970s, but by then Napa

Valley was a household name. Perhaps someday Willamette Valley wineries will be as well known—in fact, they're already winning awards.

The Willamette Valley is on the same latitude as the great wine regions of France and the weather is quite similar—plenty of spring rains, then long, hot summer days and cool nights. Unfortunately, wineries here must contend with the potential specter of dark clouds and early autumn rains. These rains can sometimes wreak havoc on Willamette Valley wines, but most years, the grapes get harvested before the rains begin to fall.

ESSENTIALS

GETTING THERE   You'll find the heart of wine country between Newberg and McMinnville on Ore. 99W, which heads southwest out of Portland.

VISITOR INFORMATION   Contact the **Greater McMinnville Chamber of Commerce,** 417 N. Adams St., McMinnville, OR 97128 (☎ **503/472-6196**), or the **Newberg Area Chamber of Commerce,** 115 N. Washington St., Newberg, OR 97132 (☎ **503/538-2014**).

FESTIVALS   The most prestigious festival of the year is the **International Pinot Noir Celebration** (☎ **800/775-4762**), held each year on the last weekend in July. The three-day event, which is usually sold out months in advance, includes tastings, food, music, and seminars. At the **Vintage Festival** in Newberg each September, vintage cars, airplanes, motorcycles, bicycles, and boats are on display.

TOURING THE WINERIES

Heading southwest from Portland on Ore. 99W, you soon leave the urban sprawl behind and enter the rolling farm country of Yamhill County. These hills, on the north side of the Willamette Valley, provide almost ideal conditions for growing wine grapes, and a patchwork quilt of vineyards, interspersed with orchards and woodlands, now blankets the slopes. The views from these hills take in the Willamette Valley's fertile farmlands as well as the snowcapped peaks of the Cascades. Between Newberg and Dundee you'll find more than 20 vineyards, wineries, and tasting rooms. If you're willing to drive a bit farther, you'll find still more wineries and vineyards to the north near Hillsboro and Forest Grove and to the south around Salem. Wines produced at these vineyards include Pinot noir, Pinot gris, chardonnay, gewürztraminer, riesling, Muller-Thurgau, and several sparkling wines.

Most, but not all, wineries maintain tasting rooms that are open to the public, usually between 11am or noon and 5pm. During the summer most tasting rooms are open daily, but in other months they may be open only on weekends or by appointment. If you're interested, you're almost always welcome to tour the facilities. For the dilettante an afternoon of wine tasting can be a very educational experience, while for the oenophile it provides a chance to uncover some rare gems.

Most wineries also have a few picnic tables, so if you bring some goodies with you and then pick up a bottle of wine, you'll be set for a great picnic. At some wineries you'll be asked to pay a sampling fee. At others the selections of the day can be sampled free but there's a fee for sampling other vintages. Still others charge for sampling any premium reserve wines. Many wineries have celebrations, festivals, music performances, and picnics throughout the summer.

The Willamette Valley

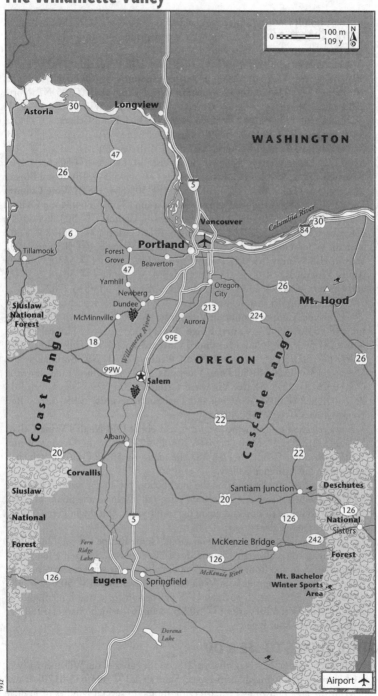

0   100 m
    109 y

Astoria
Longview
WASHINGTON
30
47
26
6
Tillamook
Vancouver
Columbia River
84
30
Portland
Forest Grove
Beaverton
47
Yamhill
Oregon City
26
Mt. Hood
Newberg
Dundee
McMinnville
Aurora
213
224
26
18
99E
OREGON
99W
Salem
Siuslaw National Forest
Willamette River
Coast Range
Cascade Range
22
Albany
Corvallis
22
Siuslaw
20
National
Santiam Junction
Deschutes
Forest
20
126
126
National
Sisters
Fern Ridge Lake
McKenzie Bridge
242
5
126
Forest
126
McKenzie River
Mt. Bachelor Winter Sports Area
Eugene
Springfield
Dorena Lake

Airport ✈

1932

The **Yamhill County Wineries Association,** P.O. Box 871, McMinnville, OR 97218 (☎ **503/434-5814**), publishes a free map and guide to the local wineries. You can pick up copies at any winery.

Area wineries with tasting rooms include: **Rex Hill Vineyards,** 30835 N. Ore. 99W, Newberg (☎ 503/538-0666); **Veritas Vineyards,** 31190 NE Veritas Lane, Newberg (☎ 503/538-1470); **Autumn Wind Vineyard,** 15225 NE North Valley Rd., Newberg (☎ 503/538-6931); **Champoeg Wine Cellars,** 10375 Champoeg Rd. NE, Aurora (☎ 503/678-2144); **Duck Pond Cellars,** 23145 Ore. 99W, Dundee (☎ 503/538-3199); **Argyle,** 691 Ore. 99W, Dundee (☎ 503/538-8520); **Torii Mor Winery,** 18325 NE Fairview Dr., Dundee (☎ 503/538-2279); **Lange Winery,** 18380 NE Buena Vista Rd., Dundee (☎ 503/538-6476); **Knudsen Erath,** Worden Hill Road, Dundee (☎ 503/538-3318); **Sokol Blosser Winery,** 5000 Sokol Blosser Lane, Dundee (☎ 503/864-2282); **Wine Country Farm Cellars,** 6855 Breyman Orchards Rd., Dayton (☎ 503/864-3446); **Château Benoit Winery,** 6580 NE Mineral Springs Rd., Carlton (☎ 503/864-2991); **Elk Cove Vineyards,** 27751 NW Olson Rd., Gaston (☎ 503/985-7760); **Yamhill Valley Vineyards,** 16250 Oldsville Rd., McMinnville (☎ 503/843-3100); **Kristin Hill Winery,** 3330 SE Amity Dayton Hwy., Amity (☎ 503/835-0850); **Amity Vineyards,** 18150 Amity Vineyards Rd. SE, Amity (☎ 503/835-2362); and **Cuneo Cellars,** 9360 SE Eola Hills Rd., Amity (☎ 503/835-2782).

Within 30 to 45 minutes north you'll find quite a few more wineries. These include: **Cooper Mountain Vineyards,** 9480 SW Grabhorn Rd., Beaverton (☎ 503/690-0027); **Laurel Ridge Winery,** 46350 David Hill Rd., Forest Grove (☎ 503/359-5436); **Montinore Vineyards,** 3663 SW Dilley Rd., Forest Grove (☎ 503/359-5012); **Oak Knoll Winery,** 29700 SW Burkhalter Rd., Hillsboro (☎ 503/648-8198); **Ponzi Vineyards,** 14665 SW Winery Lane, Beaverton (☎ 503/628-1227); **Shafer Vineyard Cellars,** 6200 NW Gales Creek Rd., Forest Grove (☎ 503/357-6604); and **Tualatin Vineyards,** 10850 Seavey Rd., Forest Grove (☎ 503/357-5005).

For a selection of area wines, you can visit either **Old Noah's Wine Cellar,** 511 E. Third St., McMinnville (☎ 503/434-2787), or the **Oregon Wine-Tasting Room,** 19700 SW Ore. 18, Sheridan (☎ 503/843-3633), which is adjacent to the Lawrence Gallery.

So as not to get pulled over by the local police, you might want to limit the number of wineries you visit to between three and five in an afternoon. This will also allow you time to stop and enjoy the countryside. You might even consider having a designated driver.

You can also do your wine tasting on a tour. **Grape Escape** (☎ **503/282-4262**) offers tours to three different wineries for $60 per person, including lunch and transportation to and from Portland. You can also see the wine country from the air on a hot-air balloon ride with **Vista Balloon Adventures** (☎ **503/625-7385** or 800/622-2309), which charges $175 per person for a one-hour flight, or through **Rex Hill Vineyards** (☎ **503/538-0666**), which charges $180 per person for a one-hour flight.

OTHER THINGS TO SEE & DO

Seven miles south of Newberg off Ore. 219, on the banks of the Willamette River, is **Champoeg** (pronounced Sham-*poo*-ee) **State Park** (☎ **503/633-8170**). It was here, in the area known as French Prairie (home to several families of French Canadian settlers), that the region's first pioneers voted in 1843 for the formation of a provisional American government. This occurred at a time when the British, in the form of the Hudson's Bay Company, exercised a strong control over the Northwest. The park includes a campground, bike path, picnic area, a historic home, a log cabin, and a visitor center that traces Champoeg's history from its days as an Native American village up through its pioneer farming days. Park admission is $3.

Near downtown Newberg, the **Hoover-Minthorn House Museum,** 115 S. River St. (☎ **503/538-6629**), preserves the childhood home of Herbert Hoover, the 31st president of the United States. It's open March to November, Wednesday through Sunday from 1 to 4pm; February and December, on Saturday and Sunday from 1 to 4pm (closed January). Admission is $2 for adults, $1.50 for seniors and students, 50¢ for children 5 to 11.

The **Evergreen Air Venture Museum** is scheduled to open early in 1996 and will be the new home of Howard Hughes's famous "Spruce Goose" flying boat.

In Dundee, you'll find **Red Hills Pottery,** 9545 NE Red Hills Rd. (☎ **503/538-5918**), where Donna Gettel produces beautiful wood-fired porcelain ware. To reach this pottery studio, take Ninth Street north, then turn right on Fairview Drive and right again on Red Hills Road. West of Dundee, the **Laube Orchards Fruit Stand,** 18400 N. Ore. 99W (☎ **503/864-2672**), sells a wide selection of produce and gourmet foods from around the area. If your tastes run to vintage furniture from the 1940s and 1950s, check out **Viva Gallery,** on Ore. 99W on the east side of Dundee (☎ **503/538-4349**). Anyone looking for deals will want to visit the **Tanger Factory Outlet Center,** on Ore. 18 at Norton Lane in McMinnville.

Between Dundee and McMinnville, you'll find the town of Lafayette, which is home to the **Yamhill County Historical Museum and Barn,** on the corner of Sixth and Market streets (☎ **503/864-2589**). The museum, which houses a collection of pioneer memorabilia, is open on Saturday and Sunday from 1 to 4pm (Wednesday through Sunday in summer). Also in Lafayette is the **Lafayette Schoolhouse Antique Mall,** Ore. 99W (☎ **503/864-2720**), which is located in a 1910 schoolhouse and is filled with more than 100 dealers.

McMinnville, which is home to Linfield College, a small liberal arts college with an attractive campus, is the largest town in wine country. Here, you can pick up a guide to the historic buildings of downtown McMinnville from the McMinnville Chamber of Commerce (see "Essentials," above, for address).

West of McMinnville, a few miles on Ore. 18, you'll find the **Lawrence Gallery** (☎ **503/843-3633**) near the town of Sheridan. This large art gallery has a sculpture garden, water garden, and several rooms full of artworks by regional artists; it's open daily. If you like chocolate, you might want to head down to Amity and stop in at the **Brigittine Monastery,** 23300 Walker Lane (☎ **503/835-8080**), which is known for making a heavenly fudge. The fudge and truffles are on sale at the guest reception area, which is open daily but closes for lunch.

WHERE TO STAY
IN NEWBERG

Partridge Farm Bed & Breakfast
4300 E. Portland Rd., Newberg, OR 97132. ☎ **503/538-2050.** 4 rms, 1 with bath. May–Oct, $60–$70 double without bath; $95 double with bath. Nov–Apr, $55–$65 double without bath; $85 double with bath. Rates include full breakfast. MC, V.

Under the same ownership as the Rex Hill Winery, this old yellow farmhouse feels secluded even though it's right on busy Ore. 99W. Shade trees, beautiful gardens full of perennials, berry hedges, and fruit trees give Partridge Farm a relaxing country atmosphere that, on a sunny afternoon, positively begs to be enjoyed with a glass of wine and a good book. Inside there's a hint of French country sophistication. Downstairs is a spacious room with a private bath. Upstairs are three more guest rooms that share a bathroom. All are furnished with period antiques that complement the mood of this turn-of-the-century home.

Springbrook Hazelnut Farm

30295 N. Ore. 99W, Newberg, OR 97132. ☎ **503/538-4606** or 800/793-8528. 5 rms, 3 with bath. $90 double without bath; $90–$125 double with bath. Rates include full breakfast. No credit cards.

Only 20 miles from Portland, this working farm is a convenient rural getaway for anyone who craves a slower, old-fashioned pace. The four craftsman-style buildings are all listed on the National Register of Historic Places and include the main house with its four rooms and a carriage house that serves as a spacious suite. Original artwork abounds in the boldly decorated main house and gives the inn a decidedly sophisticated air. Both of the main buildings overlook the pond and lovely back garden. In addition, you'll have access to a swimming pool and tennis courts, and through the hazelnut orchard you'll find Rex Hill Vineyards.

In Dundee

⑤ Wine Country Inn

6855 Breyman Orchards Rd., Dayton, OR 97114. ☎ **503/864-3446.** 4 rms, 1 suite. $65–$85 double; $125 suite. $55–$75 double. Rates include full breakfast. No credit cards.

This bed-and-breakfast inn has one of the best views in the area, and with its 5 acres of grape vines, should satisfy all those wishing to steep themselves in the atmosphere of wine country. When this 1910 farmhouse was renovated and converted into a B&B, the owners even gave the facade the look of a French farmhouse. Two of the rooms have good views, as do the breakfast room and the deck that runs the entire length of the house. You can spend your days hiking, mountain biking, and taking horse-drawn–buggy rides nearby.

In McMinnville

Best Western Vineyard Inn Motel

2035 S. Ore. 99W, McMinnville, OR 97128. ☎ **503/472-4900** or 800/285-6242. Fax 503/434-9157. 65 rms. A/C TV TEL. $45–$95 double. Rates include continental breakfast. AE, CB, DC, DISC, MC, V.

This modern hotel is one of the first in the area to actively cater to the growing numbers of oenophiles who are touring Oregon's wine country. Purple and lavender are the predominant colors here, and there are wine posters throughout the hotel. The guest rooms are very comfortable and most are quite spacious. You'll find a microwave and a refrigerator in every room. An indoor pool, exercise room, and whirlpool provide a bit of exercise and relaxation in the evening. You'll find the Vineyard Inn at the west end of McMinnville.

Steiger Haus

360 Wilson St., McMinnville, OR 97128. ☎ **503/472-0821.** 5 rms. $70–$100 double. Rates include full breakfast. MC, V.

Spinning and weaving are the passions of the Steigers, and you'll find many examples of their craft (including a sun-room weaving studio) around the inn, which is set on tree-shaded grounds not far from downtown McMinnville. The contemporary three-story building sports lots of windows and decks, and depending on which room you choose, you may enjoy a superb view of the garden through a bay window or perhaps have a nice deck for afternoon lounging. The most expensive room has its own fireplace. We like the treetop room the best.

✪ Youngberg Hill Farm B&B

10660 Youngberg Hill Rd., McMinnville, OR 97128. ☎ **503/472-2727.** 5 rms. $110 double Sun–Thurs, $120 double Fri–Sat. Rates include full breakfast. Seventh night is free for weekly stays. MC, V (add 3%). Closed Nov–April.

With its modern home overlooking the Willamette Valley, Cascades, and Coast Range and its vineyard-covered hillsides, the Youngberg Hill Farm is the quintessential wine country B&B. Two of the guest rooms have their own fireplaces and large decks wrap around both floors of the inn. If you can get six people together, you may be able to arrange a specially prepared gourmet dinner accompanied by wines from the inn's own wine cellar. There always seems to be something going on no matter what the season, whether it's grape harvest in October, lambing in March, or blackberry picking in August.

IN YAMHILL

Flying M Ranch

23029 NW Flying M Rd., Yamhill, OR 97148. ☎ **503/662-3222.** Fax 503/662-3202. 28 rms, 7 cabins. $50–$70 double; $75–$150 cabin for one to six; $10 campsite. Picnicking $3. AE, DC, DISC, MC, V.

If you feel like mixing a bit of wine-country touring with the Wild West, the Flying M Ranch is the place for you. Located 4 miles down a gravel road at the foot of the Coast Range, this ranch on the North Yamhill River caters to folks who want to do a bit of horseback riding and play at being cowboys. The center of ranch activity is the big log lodge where every inch of wall space seems to display hunting trophies from musk-ox and buffalo heads to bearskins and even a stuffed cougar.

Dining/Entertainment: Inside the lodge there's a large dining room overlooking the Yamhill River. The menu features plenty of cowboy standards as well as a few dishes you'd only expect from a big-city restaurant. In the lounge you can marvel at the bar, which is made from a 6-ton log, or you can do a bit of western dancing to the resident cowboy singer.

Services: Horseback riding, hayrides.

Facilities: Airstrip, swimming pond, tennis courts, basketball court, volleyball courts, horseshoes.

WHERE TO DINE
IN DUNDEE

Alfie's Wayside Country Inn

1111 Ore. 99W, Dundee. ☎ **503/538-9407.** Reservations recommended. Main courses $13–$33. AE, MC, V. Sun–Thurs noon–2:30pm and 5–9pm, Fri–Sat noon–2:30pm and 5–10pm. CONTINENTAL.

Unlike California, Oregon does not have very many pink houses, so Alfie's, a big pink Dutch colonial home turned into a restaurant, comes as quite a shock as you pass through Dundee. You just can't miss it! Inside, the pink theme continues with pink napery and pink frosted-glass globes over the candles on the tables. In summer you might dine on the second-floor deck or the covered patio out front, though traffic noises can be a bit intrusive in the latter area. On most nights the menu lists close to 20 entrées, ranging from roast prime rib to frogs' legs to rack of lamb. You should also try a dish or two off the much shorter appetizer menu—perhaps escargots bourguignons or pâté de foie truffée.

Ⓢ Red Hills Provincial Dining

276 Ore. 99W. ☎ **503/538-8224.** Reservations recommended. Main courses $11.50–$15.75; lunch $3.50–$7.25. No credit cards. Wed–Fri 11:30am–2pm and 5–9m, Sat–Sun 5–9pm. CONTINENTAL/NORTHWEST.

Located in a 1920s craftsman bungalow on the east side of town, this restaurant serves Mediterranean-influenced food that's well paired with the wines of the region. The dinner menu changes every two weeks and is limited to five or six appetizers and an equal number of main courses. Local wines and produce make frequent appearances in such dishes as venison pâté with hazelnuts, dark rum, and mushrooms or salmon with a wild-ginger/Pinot gris sauce. Lunches display a welcome creativity too, with focaccia sandwiches a mainstay. There's a very good selection of wines available (also sold retail). If you bring your own wine, there's a $5 corkage fee.

✪ Tina's

760 Ore. 99W, Dundee. ☎ **503/538-8880.** Reservations recommended. Dinner $14–$19. AE, MC, V. Mon 5–9pm, Tues–Fri 11:30am–2pm and 5–9pm, Sat 5–9pm, Sun 3:30–8pm. CONTINENTAL/NORTHWEST.

Dundee isn't a very big town, and Tina's, a little cube of a place right beside Ore. 99W, isn't a very big restaurant. Inside there are 10 small tables, which makes this place popular with couples. The menu is short, with fewer than 10 entrées available each night, and is constantly changing but you'll always find a good selection of seafood. There are usually almost as many desserts available as there are entrées.

IN McMINNVILLE

In addition to the restaurants listed below, you can get good, inexpensive meals at the **Golden Valley Brewery & Pub,** 980 E. Fourth St., McMinnville (☎ **503/ 472-BREW**), which is gaining a reputation for its Red Thistle Ale.

✪ Nick's Italian Café

521 E. Third St. ☎ **503/434-4471.** Reservations recommended. Five-course fixed-price dinner $29. No credit cards. Tues–Thurs 5:30–9pm, Fri–Sat 5:30–10pm, Sun 5–8pm. NORTHERN ITALIAN.

There's nothing in Nick's narrow storefront windows to indicate that this is one of the best restaurants around. However, when you step through the door and are immediately confronted by the rich tones of carved-and-polished wood, you'll know that this is someplace special. Each evening there's a fixed-price five-course dinner. For example, dinner might start with an artichoke served with tarragon mayonnaise, followed by minestrone soup. A fresh-fennel salad served with tomatoes and kalamata olives is followed by a pesto, chanterelle mushroom, and hazelnut lasagne. For the entrée, there's a choice among three dishes—say, salt-grilled salmon, sirloin steak stuffed with prosciutto and lappi cheese and served with a marsala sauce, or grilled pork loin with fresh rosemary and garlic.

Sir Hinkleman's

729 E. Third St. ☎ **503/472-1309.** Reservations recommended. Lunch $5.50–$9; dinner $8–$17. MC, V. Mon 11am–4pm, Tues–Thurs 11am–8pm, Fri–Sat 11am–9pm. CONTINENTAL.

Down at the east end of Third Street, in an old Victorian home surrounded by a white picket fence, you'll find an elegant little restaurant. Surprisingly, prices here are much more reasonable than the decor would indicate. The menu includes such offerings as marinated teriyaki steak and grilled chicken with Dijon-caper sauce. Be sure to have a look at the day's wine offerings as you enter.

IN SHERIDAN

Augustine's

19706 Ore. 18. ☎ **503/843-3225.** Reservations recommended. Main courses $13–$17. DISC, MC, V. Sun–Mon and Wed–Thurs 11am–8pm, Fri–Sat 11am–9pm. INTERNATIONAL.

There isn't much on Ore. 18 once you leave McMinnville, but right on the high-way near Sheridan, upstairs from an art gallery, you'll find another of the wine country's favorite restaurants. If you're heading for the beach on a Friday night, Augustine's is an excellent place to stop for dinner, but be sure you have a reser-vation. The smoked-seafood platter—which usually includes salmon, halibut, and trout garnished with red onions, capers, and cream cheese—is a great start to dinner here. When it comes to main courses, we like the scampi Mediterranean, which is made with sun-dried tomatoes, Greek olives, and capers. The pork tenderloin with plum-wine sauce is a completely different taste sensation.

DRIVING ON TO THE BEACH

During the busy summer months beach-bound and returning drivers in the know always make a stop at the **Strawberry Patch** in Grande Ronde. This roadside produce stand is fabled for its shortcake, which is served with whatever fresh fruit happens to be in season.

2 Salem

47 miles S of Portland, 40 miles N of Corvallis, 131 miles W of Bend, 57 miles E of Lincoln City

Home to Willamette University, Salem has become the third-largest city in Oregon (pop. 100,000), and running the state has become the city's main occu-pation. True to its origins (it was founded by a Methodist missionary), the city still wears its air of conservatism like a minister's collar. No one has ever accused Salem of being too raucous or rowdy. Though it's the seat of state government, the city feels more like a small midwestern college town than a Pacific Rim capital. When school is out for the summer and the legislature is in recess, the city becomes a ghost town, and even when everyone's in town the city hardly seems charged with energy. The quiet conservatism does, however, give the city a certain charm that's not found in the other cities of the Willamette Valley.

Salem's roots date back to 1834, when Methodist missionary Jason Lee, who had traveled west to convert Native Americans, founded Salem, making it the first American settlement in the Willamette Valley. In 1842, one year before the first settlers crossed the continent on the Oregon Trail, Lee founded the Oregon Institute, the first school of higher learning west of the Rockies. In 1857 the first textile mill west of the Mississippi opened here, giving Salem a firm industrial base. However, despite all these historic firsts, Oregon City and Portland grew much faster and quickly became the region's population centers. Salem seemed doomed to backwater status until the year 1859 when Oregon became a state and Salem was chosen to become the state capital.

ESSENTIALS

GETTING THERE   Salem is on I-5 at the junction of Ore. 22, which heads west to connect with Ore. 18 from Lincoln City and southeast to connect with U.S. 20 from Bend.

Amtrak has passenger rail service to Salem. The station is at 13th and Oak streets.

VISITOR INFORMATION   Contact the **Salem Convention & Visitors Association,** 1313 Mill St. SE, Salem, OR 97301 (☎ **503/581-4325** or 800/874-7012; fax 503/581-4540).

GETTING AROUND   Car rentals are available from **Hertz, Budget,** and **National.** If you need a taxi, contact **Salem Keizer Yellow Cab** (☎ 503/362-2411). Public bus service throughout the Salem area is provided by **Salem Area Transit** (☎ **503/588-BUSS**), which goes by the name of Cherriots.

FESTIVALS   Two of the biggest events of the year in Salem are the **Oregon State Fair,** which is held from late August to early September, and the **Salem Arts Festival,** the largest juried art fair in Oregon.

WHAT TO SEE & DO
HISTORIC BUILDINGS & NEIGHBORHOODS

If you're interested in touring Salem's historic neighborhoods, stop by the **Salem Visitors Center** at Mission Mill Village and pick up copies of the **walking-tour** brochures for the Gaiety Hill/Bush's Pasture Park Historic District and the Court-Chemeketa Residential Historic District. There are also several **restored homes** in the Riverfront Park on Water Street, and on the tree-shaded campus of Willamette University just across State Street from the Capitol Mall.

Mission Mill Village
1313 Mill St. SE. ☎ **503/585-7012.** Admission $5 adults, $4.50 seniors, $2 children. Daily 10am–4:30pm. Closed Jan 1, Thanksgiving, and Dec 25.

The sprawling red Thomas Kay Woolen Mill, a water-powered mill built in 1889, has become one of the most fascinating attractions in Salem. The restored buildings house exhibits on every stage of the wool-making process, and in the main mill building the water-driven turbine is still in operation producing electricity for these buildings. Also on these neatly manicured grounds are several other old structures (including the **Jason Lee House,** which was built by Salem's founder in 1841 and is the oldest frame house in the Northwest), a café, and a collection of interesting shops. The **Marion Museum of History,** also on the grounds, houses exhibits on the history of the area with a particularly interesting exhibit on the local Calapooyan tribespeople. Because this complex also houses the **Salem Visitors Information Center,** it should be your first stop in town.

Oregon State Capitol
900 Court St. (Visitor Services Center). ☎ **503/986-1388.** Free admission. Mon–Fri 7:30am–5:30pm, Sat 9am–4pm, Sun noon–4pm. Closed national holidays.

Stark and boxy, the Oregon State Capitol was built in 1938 of white Italian marble and is topped by *The Oregon Pioneer*, a 23-foot-tall gilded statue. Inside the building, which is open to the public, there are murals of historic Oregon scenes. Tours of the capitol are available.

Bush House and Bush Barn Art Center

600 Mission St. SE. ☎ **503/363-4714** (Bush House) and 503/581-2228 (Bush Barn Art Center). Bush House, $2.50 adults, $2 students and seniors, $1 children; Bush Barn Art Center, free. Bush House, May–Sept, daily noon–5pm; Oct–Apr, Tues–Sun 2–5pm. Bush Barn Art Center, Tues–Fri 10am–5pm, Sat–Sun 1–5pm. Closed major holidays.

Sitting at the top of a shady hill, this imposing Italianate Victorian home was built between 1877 and 1888. Inside the Bush House you can see the original furnishings, including 10 fireplaces and even the original wallpaper. The house is surrounded by 100 acres of parkland known as Bush's Pasture Park. Also on the grounds are the oldest greenhouse conservatory in Oregon and the Bush Barn Art Center. The latter includes a sales gallery as well as exhibition spaces that feature changing art exhibits.

Historic Deepwood Estate

1116 Mission St. SE. ☎ **503/363-1825.** Admission $2 adults, $1.50 seniors, 75¢ children. May–Sept, Sun–Fri noon–4:30pm; Oct–Apr, Sun–Mon, Wed, and Fri 1–4pm.

While the Bush House is huge and imposing, the Deepwood Estate home, a Queen Anne–style Victorian is light and airy, a delicate jewel box of a house. Numerous lightning rod–topped peaked roofs and gables create the complex lines that give this house its elegance. Built in 1894 and set amid nearly 6 acres of shady gardens and forest, this historic home is renowned for its wealth of stained-glass windows and golden oak moldings.

PARKS, GARDENS & FLOWER FIELDS

Each year between mid-May and early June the countryside around Salem bursts into color as commercial iris fields come into bloom. The two biggest growers open their farms during bloom time. **Cooley's Gardens,** 11553 Silverton Rd. NE (☎ **503/873-5463**), with 250 acres and more than three million irises, is the world's largest bearded iris grower. To reach the gardens, take the Market Street exit and drive east to Lancaster Road; at Lancaster, turn left and drive north to Silverton Road where you make a right turn. It's less than 10 miles on Silverton Road. **Schreiner's Iris Gardens,** 3625 Quinaby Rd., Brooks (☎ **503/393-3232**), also has 250 acres of irises, and is an equally impressive sight. To reach Schreiner's, take the Brooks exit off I-5 north of Salem.

   Located 26 miles east of Salem on Ore. 214, **Silver Falls State Park (☎ 503/873-8681**) is the largest state park in Oregon. Hidden in the lush canyons and dark old-growth forests of this park are 10 silvery waterfalls. You can walk behind a couple of them, and all are connected by various loop trails. You can spend an afternoon or several days exploring the park. Camping, swimming, picnicking, bicycling, and horseback riding are all popular activities.

WINE TOURING

Wineries in the Salem area that are open to the public on a regular basis include the following: **Bethel Heights Vineyards,** 6060 Bethel Heights Rd. NW, Salem (☎ 503/581-2262); **Chateau Bianca,** 17485 Ore. 22, Dallas (☎ 503/623-6181); **Cristom Vineyards,** 6905 Spring Valley Rd. NW, Salem (☎ 503/375-3068); **Ellendale Winery,** 1 Main St., Rickreall (☎ 503/623-5617); **Eola Hills Wine Cellars,** 501 S. Pacific Hwy., Rickreall (☎ 503/623-2405); **Flynn Winery,**

2200 Pacific Hwy. W., Rickreall (☎ 503/623-8683); **Honeywood Winery,** 1350 Hines St. SE, Salem (☎ 503/362-4111); **Oak Grove Orchards,** 6090 Crowley Rd., Rickreall (☎ 503/364-7052); **Orchard Heights Winery,** 6057 Orchard Heights NW, Salem (☎ 503/363-0375); **Redhawk Vineyard,** 2995 Michigan City Rd. NW, Salem (☎ 503/362-1596); **St. Innocent Winery,** 2701 22nd St. SE, Salem (☎ 503/378-1526); **Schwarzenberg Vineyards,** 11975 Smithfield Rd., Dallas (☎ 503/623-6420); **Stangeland Winery,** 8500 Hopewell Rd. NW, Salem (☎ 503/581-0355); **Willamette Valley Vineyards,** 8800 Enchanted Way SE, Turner (☎ 503/588-9463); and **Witness Tree Vineyards,** 7111 Spring Valley Rd. NW, Salem (☎ 503/585-7874).

ESPECIALLY FOR KIDS

The Gilbert House Children's Museum

116 Marion St. NE. ☎ **503/371-3631.** Admission $4. Tues–Sat 10am–5pm, Sun noon–4pm.

A. C. Gilbert was the inventor of the Erector Set, the perennially popular children's toy that has inspired generations of budding engineers, and here in the restored Gilbert house, kids can learn all about engineering, art, music, drama, science, and nature through fun hands-on exhibits.

Enchanted Forest

8462 Enchanted Way SE. ☎ **503/363-3060.** Admission $4.95 adults, $4.75 seniors, $4.25 children 3–12. Mar 15–Sept, daily 9:30am–6pm. Closed Oct–Mar 14. Take I-5 7 miles south of Salem to Exit 248.

Classic children's stories come to life at this amusement park for kids. In addition to Storybook Land, English Village, and a mining town, there's a haunted house, a bobsled run, and a comedy theater.

OUTDOOR ACTIVITIES

The nearest ski area is **Hoodoo Ski Area** (☎ 541/822-3799), 82 miles east on Ore. 22 and Ore. 126 at Santiam Pass. There are three chair lifts and a rope tow, and a variety of runs for all levels of experience. Lift tickets are $22 for adults and $16 for children. Night skiing is available.

Public golf courses in the Salem area include the **McNary Golf Course,** 6255 River Rd. N., Keizer (☎ **503/393-4653**), and the **Salem Golf Club,** 2025 Golf Course Rd. S., Salem (☎ **503/363-6652**).

WHERE TO STAY

Best Western Mill Creek Inn

3125 Ryan Dr. SE, Salem, OR 97301. ☎ **503/585-3332** or 800/528-1234. Fax 503/375-9618. 109 rms. A/C TV TEL. $67–$86 double. AE, CB, DC, DISC, MC, V.

With a surprisingly elegant little lobby and an easily accessible location, the Mill Creek Inn is a good choice. It's located just off I-5 at the Mission Street exit, which is not nearly as congested as the Market Street freeway exit. The guest rooms are large, and the "king rooms" come with sofa and wet bar. Services include a free airport shuttle, VCR and movie rentals, and free coffee in lobby. An indoor pool, whirlpool, sauna, and exercise room provide recreational opportunities.

✪ Marquee House

333 Wyatt Ct. NE, Salem, OR 97301. ☎ **503/391-0837.** 5 rms, 3 with bath. $48 double without bath, $65–$75 double with bath. Rates include full breakfast. MC, V.

Fans of old movies will want to make this their address in Salem. All the rooms are named for well-known movies and are furnished to reflect the movie theme. We like the Topper Room with its black-tie theme and the Blazing Saddles Room with its Wild West decor. This B&B is located on a narrow lane in a quiet residential neighborhood and has Mill Creek running through the back yard.

Phoenix Inn

4370 Commercial St. SE, Salem, OR. ☎ **503/588-9220** or 800/445-4498. 88 rms. A/C TV TEL. $65–$99 double. Rates include continental breakfast. AE, CB, DC, DISC, MC, V.

This is the best hotel in Salem these days and is popular with legislators and business travelers. The rooms (called "minisuites" here) are in fact quite large and well designed for both business and relaxation. There are two phones (free local calls), hairdryers, microwave ovens, refrigerators, and wet bars in all the rooms. The top-end rooms also have whirlpool tubs. Facilities include an indoor pool, whirlpool, and exercise room.

WHERE TO DINE

If you have a sweet tooth, you won't want to miss **Konditorei,** 310 Kearney St. SE (☎ 503/585-7070), which sells an amazing selection of extravagant cakes and pastries. If you're just looking for a good place to spend the evening with friends, check out the **Willamette Brew Pub & Eatery,** 120 Commercial St. (☎ 503/ 363-8779), a popular microbrewery offering good ales and simple meals.

Allesandro's Park Plaza

325 High St. SE. ☎ **503/370-9951.** Reservations recommended. Main courses $7.75–$25. AE, DC, MC, V. Mon–Thurs 11:30am–2pm and 5:30–9pm, Fri 11:30am–2pm and 5:30–10pm, Sat 5:30–10pm. SOUTHERN ITALIAN.

Located on a pretty little park just south of Salem's shopping district, the Park Plaza is Salem's best Italian restaurant. The building housing the restaurant looks like little more than a parking garage, but inside you'll find a half-timbered Tudor-look dining room where classical music plays softly on the stereo. Service is very professional even though the atmosphere is fairly casual. Chef Alessandro Fasani's sauces are made fresh daily from the finest of ingredients, including fresh herbs and the best of Northwest seafood. The wine list features moderately priced Italian and Oregon wines.

Court Street Dairy Lunch

347 Court St. ☎ **503/363-6433.** Reservations not accepted. Meals $4–$7. No credit cards. Mon–Fri 7am–2pm. BURGERS.

In business since the 1920s, the Court Street Dairy Lunch is the quintessential burger place and a Salem institution. Burgers and sandwiches "just like Mom used to make" are the attraction. The specialties of the house are the ranch burger and ranch dog, marionberry pie, and chocolate malts.

DaVinci Italiano Ristorante

180 High St. SE. ☎ **503/399-1413.** Reservations recommended on weekends. Main courses $8.25–$15. AE, DISC, MC, V. Mon–Fri 11:30am–2pm and 5–9pm, Sat–Sun 5–9pm. ITALIAN.

Wonderful aromas often greet diners in this casual eatery in a restored downtown building. The ambience is early 20th century, with a pressed-tin ceiling and lots of oak and exposed brick. Those aromas are soon followed, after you take a seat at your table, by a delicious bread and olive oil in which to dip it. Menu offerings run the gamut from traditional fare to designer pizzas and more unusual dishes such as ravioli with chestnuts.

Karma's Café

1313 Mill St. SE. ☎ **503/370-8855.** Meals $3.50–$6. Mon–Fri 9am–4:30pm, Sat 10am–4:30pm. DELI.

We can't imagine a more pleasant place to lunch on a sunny summer afternoon in Salem. The deck in front of Karma's sandwich shop is right in the middle of Mission Mill Village and overlooks the big red mill. You can hear water flowing through the stream and are almost completely surrounded by history. Soups, salads, and sandwiches are the fare here.

✪ Morton's Bistro Northwest

1128 Edgewater St. W. ☎ **503/585-1113.** Reservations recommended. Main courses $13–$20. MC, V. Tues–Sat 5–10pm. NORTHWEST.

This romantic little bistro on the west side of the Willamette River serves up the most imaginative meals in Salem. The menu changes regularly depending on the whim of the chef, the availability of ingredients, the season, and even the weather. On a recent summer evening, flavors ranged from the subtle scents of saffron- and fennel-steamed mussels to the firey flavors of penne diablo made with crab and andouille sausage. Other summer standouts included chicken in a bourbon-cream sauce and a mixed grill of smoked pork loin and chicken sausage with grilled polenta and apple chutney.

SALEM AFTER DARK

The Oregon Symphony performs in Salem between September and May, with concerts held at Smith Auditorium on the campus of Willamette University. For more information, contact the **Oregon Symphony Association** (☎ **503/364-0149**). There are also regularly scheduled performances by touring companies at the historic **Elsinore Theater** (☎ **503/375-0279**).

3 Corvallis & Albany

40 miles S of Salem, 45 miles N of Eugene, 55 miles E of Newport

Corvallis, whose name is Latin for "heart of the valley," is set amid flat farmlands in the center of the Willamette Valley and is home to Oregon State University, a noted center for agricultural research. The fields around Corvallis produce much of the nation's grass-seed crop, and in late summer, after the seed has been harvested, the remaining stubble is burned. The field burnings often blanket the valley with dense black smoke, making driving quite difficult along certain roads.

Nearby Albany, 13 miles northeast, was a prosperous town in territorial days. Located on the banks of the Willamette River, the town made its fortune as a shipping point in the days when the river was the main transportation route for the region. More than 500 historic homes make Albany the best-preserved town in the state.

ESSENTIALS

GETTING THERE   Albany is on I-5 at the junction with U.S. 20, which heads east to Bend and west to Newport. Corvallis is 12 miles west of I-5 at the junction of U.S. 20, Ore. 99W, and Ore. 34.

VISITOR INFORMATION   Contact the **Corvallis Convention & Visitors Bureau,** 420 NW Second St., Corvallis, OR 97330 (☎ **541/757-1544** or 800/334-8118), or the **Albany Visitors Association,** 300 SW Second Ave. (P.O. Box 965), Albany, OR 97321 (☎ **541/928-0911** or 800/526-2256).

GETTING AROUND   If you need a taxi, call **A-1-Taxi** (☎ 541/754-1111). Public bus service around the Corvallis area is provided by the **Corvallis Transit System** (☎ 541/757-6998).

FESTIVALS   Da Vinci Days, held each year in mid-July, is Corvallis's most fascinating festival. The highlight of this celebration of art, science, and technology is the **Kinetic Sculpture Race** in which competitors race homemade, people-powered vehicles along city streets, through mud, and down the Willamette River. Prizes are given for engineering and artistry. Though Albany celebrates its Victorian heritage with a July **Victorian Week** and a **Victorian Christmas Celebration,** the **Albany Timber Carnival,** held each year on the Fourth of July, is the town's biggest celebration. This festival is the largest of its kind in the world and attracts logging contestants from around the world.

EXPLORING CORVALLIS

You can pick up a self-guiding walking tour booklet to the **Oregon State University campus** at the information kiosk at the corner of 14th and Jefferson streets. Off campus, you'll find the **Corvallis Arts Center,** 700 SW Madison Ave. (☎ 541/754-1551), housed in an old church; it's open Tuesday through Sunday from noon to 5pm; admission is free. The arts center schedules changing exhibits of works by regional artists, and the gift shop has a good selection of fine crafts.

To learn more of the history of the area, take U.S. 20 6 miles west to **Philomath,** which is the county seat of Benton County. Here you'll find the historic Benton County Courthouse, a stately 1888 building still in use today. Nearby is the **Benton County Historical Museum,** 1101 Main St. (☎ 541/929-6230). The museum building itself was built in 1867 as part of Philomath College. The museum contains primarily exhibits on early pioneer life, but also includes a collection of Native American artifacts.

SEEING THE HISTORIC SIGHTS IN ALBANY

Albany is a hidden jewel that lies right on I-5 but is overlooked by most motorists because the only thing visible from the Interstate is a smoke-belching wood-pulp mill. Behind the industrial screen lies a quiet town that evokes days of starched crinolines and straw boaters. Throughout the mid- to late 19th century Albany experienced prosperity as it shipped agricultural and wood products downriver to Oregon City and Portland. Though every style of architecture popular during that period is represented in the buildings of downtown Albany's historic districts, it is the town's many elegant Victorian homes that capture the attention of visitors. Stop by the **Albany Visitors Association** or the **information gazebo** at the corner of Eighth and Ellsworth streets and pick up a guide to the town's historic buildings. Each year, on the last Saturday of July, many of the historic homes are opened to the public for a **Summer Historic Homes Tour,** and on the third Sunday in December, they are opened for a **Christmas Parlour Tour.** Two sparkling white 1890s churches—the **Whitespires Church** and **St. Mary's Church**—were built in the gothic revival style and are quite striking. The **Monteith House,** 518 Second Ave. SW (☎ 541/928-0911), built in 1849, is the town's oldest frame building; it's open June to September only, Wednesday through Saturday from 1 to 4pm; admission is free. It was here that the Oregon Republican party was formed.

To learn more about Albany's past, stop in at the **Albany Regional Museum,** 302 Ferry St. SW (☎ 541/967-6540), which is in the basement of the Albany library. It's open June to September, Wednesday through Sunday from noon to 4pm; September to May, on Wednesday and Saturday from noon to 4pm. Admission is free. The **Albany Fire Museum,** 120 34th St. SE (☎ **541/967-4302**), houses historical fire-fighting equipment and is open by appointment only.

While touring the historic districts, you can stop in at more than a dozen antiques stores, most of which are on First and Second streets downtown.

WINE TOURING

If you'd like to do a bit of wine tasting while you're in the Corvallis area, you can stop in at any of the following wineries and vineyards: **Airlie Winery,** 15305 Dunn Forest Rd., Monmouth (☎ 503/838-6013); **Serendipity Cellars Winery,** 15275 Dunn Forest Rd., Monmouth (☎ 503/838-4284); **Springhill Cellars Winery,** 2920 NW Scenic Dr., Albany (☎ 541/928-1009); or **Tyee Wine Cellars,** 26335 Greenberry Rd., Corvallis (☎ 541/753-8754). You can get a guide to these wineries and vineyards by contacting the **Oregon Winegrowers Association,** Southern Willamette Chapter, P.O. Box 1591, Eugene, OR 97440.

OUTDOOR ACTIVITIES

If you're a birdwatcher, the **William L. Finley National Wildlife Refuge,** 12 miles south of Corvallis on Ore. 99W, is a good place to add a few more birds to your life list. Head west 16 miles from Corvallis on Ore. 34 and you'll come to **Mary's Peak,** the highest peak in the Coast Range. A road leads to the top of the mountain.

WHERE TO STAY
IN CORVALLIS

✪ Hanson Country Inn

795 SW Hanson St., Corvallis, OR 97333. ☎ **541/752-2919.** 4 rms, 2 with bath. $65 double without bath; $75 double with bath. Rates include full breakfast. MC, V. Take Western Boulevard to West Hills Road; Hanson Street is on the right just past the fork onto West Hills Road.

Situated atop a knoll on the edge of town and surrounded by 5 acres of fields and forests, this B&B feels as if it's out in the country yet is within walking distance of the university and downtown Corvallis. The Dutch colonial–style farmhouse was built in 1928 and features loads of built-in cabinets, interesting woodwork, and lots of windows. The decor is in a pastel country motif, and one of the two rooms with a private bath also has its own sitting room.

Shanico Inn

1113 NW Ninth St., Corvallis, OR 97330. ☎ **541/754-7474** or 800/432-1233. Fax 541/754-2437. 76 rms. A/C TV TEL. $47–$60 double. Rates include continental breakfast. AE, DC, DISC, MC, V.

Located about a mile from the university campus, the Shanico Inn is a pleasant motel with shady grounds. The guest rooms are standard-issue motel, but they're clean and comfortable. There's an outdoor pool and an adjacent 24-hour restaurant.

IN ALBANY

Brier Rose Inn

206 Seventh Ave. SW, Albany, OR 97321. ☎ **541/926-0345.** 4 rms, 1 with bath. $49–$59 double without bath; $69 double with bath. Rates include full breakfast. MC, V.

This turreted Queen Anne–style Victorian B&B is on a busy corner in the heart of Albany's historic district. With its balconies, bay windows, curving porches, stained glass, and numerous styles of siding, it's a classic example of Victorian excess. Common areas are filled with period antiques, though the guest rooms are more simply furnished.

WHERE TO DINE
IN CORVALLIS

The Gables

1121 NW Ninth St. ☎ 541/752-3364. Reservations recommended. Main courses $11–$36. AE, DISC, MC, V. Mon–Sat 5–9pm, Sun 5–8pm. CONTINENTAL.

Since 1958 this has been where college students take their visiting parents. The cuisine is reliable if none too creative. Steaks and prime rib are the pillars of the Gables, though seafood is also available. Both the pâté maison and the smoked salmon are good starter choices. If you can get here between 5 and 6pm Monday through Thursday, or Friday from 5 to 5:30pm, smaller dinners are served at smaller prices.

Nearly Normal's

109 NW 15th St. ☎ **541/753-0791.** Reservations not accepted. Main dishes $3.95–$7.25. No credit cards. Mon–Fri 8am–9pm, Sat 9am–9pm. VEGETARIAN/INTERNATIONAL.

Housed in an old bungalow half a block from campus, Nearly Normal's is your basic college town standby, an international and natural-foods eatery. Nearly Normal's serves up filling portions of food that spans the globe from tempeh Reubens to scarlet pesto to felafel to Grandma Nina's spaghetti. If it's sunny out, try to get a seat out back in the patio area planted with apple trees and kiwi vines. As often as possible ingredients are organically grown.

IN ALBANY

✪ Novak's Hungarian Paprikas

2835 Santiam Hwy. ☎ **541/967-9488.** Reservations recommended. Main courses $7.25–$14. AE, MC, V. Sun–Fri 11am–9pm, Sat 4–9pm. HUNGARIAN.

From the outside, Novak's looks as if it could be a car-repair garage, especially when considering the surrounding neighborhood. However, as soon as you walk through the door you'll be hit with the Hungarian hospitality of the Novak family, who came to the United States from Hungary in 1957. The tongue-twisting dishes on the menu challenge the long-held belief that Eastern European cuisine means meat and potatoes. More often than not, Hungarian pearl noodles or fresh bread accompany dishes here. The homemade pork sausage is very good, though the chicken paprika, in its creamy red sauce, is probably the restaurant's most popular dish.

4 Eugene & Springfield

40 miles S of Salem, 71 miles N of Roseburg, 61 miles E of Florence

Though Eugene is the second-largest city in Oregon (pop. 110,000), you're more likely to spot tie-dyed T-shirts than silk ties on its downtown streets. This lively laid-back character is due in large part to the presence of the University of Oregon, the state's liberal arts college. The U of O, as it's known here in Oregon, has helped the city develop a very well rounded cultural scene at the heart of which is the grandiose, glass-gabled Hult Center for the Performing Arts. On the university's tree-shaded 250-acre campus you'll also find an art museum, a natural-history museum, and a science museum. Eugene has been known for years as a home to liberal-minded folks who have adopted alternative lifestyles. Though 1960s nostalgia has produced a new wave of hippies all over the country in the past few years, many flower children here in Eugene never grew up. At the Saturday Market, a weekly outdoor craft market, you can see the works of many of these colorful and creative spirits.

ESSENTIALS

GETTING THERE   Eugene is located just off I-5 at the junction with I-105, which connects Eugene and Springfield, and Ore. 126, which leads east to Bend and west to Florence. Ore. 58 leads southeast to connect with U.S. 97 between Klamath Falls and Bend. Ore. 99W is an alternative to I-5.

The **Eugene airport** is located 9 miles northwest of downtown off Ore. 99W. It's served by Alaska Airlines, Horizon, SkyWest, United, and United Express.

Amtrak passenger trains stop in Eugene. The station is at East Fourth Avenue and Willamette Street.

VISITOR INFORMATION   Contact the **Convention & Visitors Association of Lane County, Oregon,** 115 W. Eighth Ave., Suite 190 (P.O. Box 10286), Eugene, OR 97440 (☎ **541/484-5307** or 800/547-5445).

GETTING AROUND   Car rentals are available at the Eugene airport from **Hertz, Budget, Avis,** and **National.** If you need a taxi, contact **Eugene Yellow Cab** (☎ **541/343-7711**). **Lane Transit District (LTD)** (☎ **541/687-5555**) provides public transit throughout the metropolitan area and out to a number of nearby towns including McKenzie Bridge, which is up the scenic McKenzie River; some routes do not run on Sunday. You can pick up bus-route maps and other information at the **LTD Customer Service Center** at the corner of Tenth Avenue and Willamette Street. LTD fares are 80¢ for adults, 40¢ for seniors and children 5 to 11.

FESTIVALS   The **Eugene Celebration** (☎ **541/687-5215**), held the third weekend in September, is a three-day celebration that includes a wacky parade and the crowning of the annual Slug Queen. In mid-July, all the region's hippies, both young and old, show up in nearby Veneta for the **Oregon Country Fair** (☎ **541/343-4298** or 541/343-6554), a showcase for music and crafts.

SEEING THE SIGHTS
HISTORIC NEIGHBORHOODS & TOWNS

At the Convention & Visitors Association of Lane County, Oregon (see "Essentials," above) you can pick up walking-tour brochures to Eugene's **East Skinner Butte Historic Landmark District** (a neighborhood of historic homes) and the University of Oregon campus.

Nearby there are also a few interesting small towns. In **Coburg,** you'll find a historic district of restored homes and an 1877 inn that now houses a collection of antiques dealers. Coburg holds its **Coburg Golden Years Festival** each year in July.

In **Cottage Grove** there are several covered bridges and Oregon's gold-mining history is on view at the **Cottage Grove Museum** and in the nearby **Bohemia Mining District** above Dorena Lake. Gold-rush days are celebrated here each July with the **Bohemia Mining Days.**

The town of **Brownsville,** 25 miles north of Eugene, has a historic business district, many old Victorian homes, and the **Linn County Historical Museum.**

MUSEUMS

University of Oregon Museum of Natural History
1680 E. 15th Ave. ☎ **541/346-3024.** Admission $1. Wed–Sun noon–5pm.

This modern museum is housed in a building designed to resemble a traditional Northwest coast Native American longhouse. Ancient peoples and even more ancient animals that once roamed the Northwest are the main focus of the museum, but exhibits also cover worldwide traditional cultures. Of particular interest, especially to kids, is a full skeleton of a saber-toothed tiger.

University of Oregon Museum of Art
1430 Johnson Lane. ☎ **541/346-3027.** Free admission. Wed–Sun noon–5pm.

You'll find the university's art museum just east of 14th Avenue and Kincaid Street on the U of O campus. Asian art is the museum's strong point, and primitive African art, Indian sculptures, Russian icons, and Persian miniatures round out the international collections. Contemporary art of the Northwest is also represented. Throughout the year there are changing exhibits.

Lane County Historical Museum
740 W. 13th Ave. ☎ **541/687-4239.** Admission $2 adults, $1 senior citizens, 75¢ children 3–17. Wed–Fri 10am–4pm, Sat–Sun noon–4pm.

The Willamette River valley was one of the first regions of the Northwest to be settled, and at this museum you'll find displays on early pioneer life along the river.

Springfield Museum
590 Main St. ☎ **541/726-2300.** Admission $1 adults. Wed–Fri 10am–4pm, Sat noon–4pm.

More area historical artifacts, here focusing on the industrial, logging, and agricultural heritage, are on display in this renovated 1908 Pacific Power & Light building. The collection of old photos is very evocative.

Maude Kerns Art Center
1910 E. 15th Ave. ☎ **541/345-1571.** Admission by donation. Tues–Fri 10am–5pm, Sat–Sun 1–5pm.

The works of contemporary local, regional, and national craftspeople are the subjects of changing exhibits at this small gallery. You'll find this art center just up the street from the Museum of Natural History.

Oregon Air and Space Museum
90377 Boeing Dr. ☎ **541/461-1101.** Admission $3 adults, $1 children 6–17. Thurs–Sun noon–5pm.

Located near the Eugene airport, the museum focuses on the history of aviation in Oregon. Numerous aircraft, including an F-4 Phantom, an F-86F, and an L-19, are on display.

Willamette Science & Technology Center (WISTEC)
2300 Leo Harris Pkwy. ☎ **541/687-3619.** Admission $3 adults; $2 seniors, college students, and children 3–17; free for children 2 and under. Wed–Sun noon–6pm (extended hours in summer).

With loads of cool hands-on exhibits, this is the place to bring the kids to teach them about science. You might even learn something yourself. This building also houses a planetarium that offers changing features throughout the year.

The Bridges of Lane County

In Robert James Waller's runaway hit novel *The Bridges of Madison County*, photographer Robert Kincaid hales from the Puget Sound area, but *National Geographic* sends him all the way to Madison County, Iowa, to photograph covered bridges. Kincaid could have saved himself a lot of miles on that beat-up old pickup truck if he had just headed south into Oregon, where he would have found the largest concentration of covered bridges west of the Mississippi. We're sure there are plenty of lonely farm wives in Oregon, too.

Today there are 53 covered bridges still standing in Oregon, down from more than 300 as recently as the 1930s. The oldest covered bridge is the Upper Drift Creek Bridge near Lincoln City, which dates back to 1914, but there are also bridges built as recently as 1988. Built of wood and covered to protect them from the rain and extend their life, the covered bridges of Oregon are found primarily in the Willamette Valley, where early farmers needed safe river and stream crossings to get their crops to market. The highest concentration of covered bridges is to be found in Lane County, which stretches from the crest of the Cascade Range all the way to the Pacific Ocean and is home to 20 covered bridges. This gives Lane County the distinction of having more covered bridges than any county west of the Appalachians.

To do a bit of covered bridge touring, head southeast from Eugene on Ore. 58. for 5 miles, turn left on Parkway Road, and go 3 miles north. Turn southeast on Jasper-Lowell Road and in 4 miles turn onto Place Road where you'll find the Pengra Bridge, which was restored in 1994. Another 4½ miles on the Jasper-Lowell Road will bring you to the Unity Bridge. Continuing into the town of Lowell, you can visit the Cannon Street Bridge, a pedestrian bridge built in 1988. South of Lowell on the Jasper-Lowell Road you'll find the Lowell Bridge. When the Jasper-Lowell Road reaches Ore. 58, turn east and continue 21 miles to Westfir, where you'll find the Office Bridge, which at 180 feet in length is the

PARKS & GARDENS

Alton Baker Park, on the north bank of the Willamette River, is the city's most popular park and offers jogging and biking trails. Across the river, **Skinner Butte Park** on the north side of downtown Eugene, includes a 12-mile bike path. Nearby are the **Owen Memorial Rose Gardens.** At the **Mount Pisgah Arboretum,** Frank Parish Road, south of town off Seavey Loop Road, you can hike 5 miles of trails through meadows and forests.

WINE TOURING

Eugene is at the southern limit of the Willamette Valley wine region, and there are more than half a dozen wineries and vineyards within 30 miles of the city. Those with tasting rooms open on a regular basis include **Broadley Vineyards,** 265 S. Fifth St., Monroe (☎ 541/847-5934); **Alpine Vineyards,** downtown Alpine (☎ 541/424-5851); **Hinman Vineyards,** 27012 Briggs Hill Rd., Eugene (☎ 541/345-1945); **Rainsong Vineyards,** 92989 Templeton Rd., Cheshire (☎ 541/998-1786); and **Secret House Vineyards,** 88324 Vineyard Lane, Veneta (☎ 541/935-3774).

longest covered bridge in Oregon. Heading back toward Eugene on Ore. 58, watch for Lost Creek Road, 11 miles east of I-5. After 1.8 miles on Lost Creek Road, turn onto Rattlesnake Road. In half a mile, turn south on Lost Valley Lane to Parvin Road and the Parvin Bridge.

Another good bridge route begins in Cottage Grove. Here in town, you can see the Centennial Bridge, a pedestrian bridge on Main Street. This bridge was built in 1987 from timbers salvaged from a dismantled covered bridge. From here, cross the river and drive three-quarters of a mile south on South River Road to the Chambers Bridge. This is the only remaining covered railroad bridge in Oregon. Head back into Cottage Grove and take Row River Road 2¹/₂ miles to Layng Road. In 1.4 miles you'll come to the Currin Bridge. Continuing another 1.2 miles south on Layng Road will bring you to the Mosby Creek Bridge. Continue south and turn left on Mosby Creek Road. You'll soon come to Garoutte Road, where you'll see the Stewart Bridge. Drive 2¹/₂ miles north on Garoutte Road and turn right onto Shoreview Drive. Follow this road 6.7 miles to the Dorena Bridge.

You can get a map and guide to Lane County's covered bridges from the **Convention & Visitors Association of Lane County, Oregon,** 115 W. Eighth Ave., Suite 190, Eugene, OR 97440 (☎ **541/484-5307** or 800/547-5445). Another easy covered bridge tour begins in Albany, which is in Linn County (north of Lane County). Contact the **Albany Visitors Association,** 300 SW Second Ave., Albany, OR 97321 (☎ **541/928-0911** or 800/526-2256), for a map and guide to this tour, which visits 10 covered bridges. If you still haven't had enough covered bridges, there are seven more near Roseburg, south of Eugene. Brochures available from the **Roseburg Visitors & Convention Center,** 410 SE Spruce St., Roseburg, OR 97470 (☎ **541/672-9731** or 800/444-9584), will guide you to the area's covered bridges.

OUTDOOR ACTIVITIES

With two rivers, the McKenzie and the Willamette, flowing through the city, it isn't surprising that Eugene has quite a bit of water-oriented activities. You can rent canoes, kayaks, rafts, and pedal boats at **River Runner Supply,** 2222 Centennial Blvd. (☎ **541/343-6883** or 800/223-4326), which is in Alton Baker Park. Rates range from $4 to $6 per hour. For more exciting river running, contact **Oregon Whitewater Adventures** (☎ **541/746-5422** or 800/820-RAFT), which offers white-water-rafting trips starting at $45 per person. A slightly tamer white-water experience can be had on the pontoon platform boats of **McKenzie Pontoon Trips** (☎ **541/741-1905**).

The calmer waters of **Fern Ridge Reservoir,** 12 miles west of Eugene on Ore. 126, attract sailboarding enthusiasts. Sailing, powerboating, waterskiing, and swimming are also popular.

The nearest snow skiing is at **Willamette Pass Ski Area** (☎ **541/484-5030** or 800/444-5030 for information, 541/345-SNOW for skiing conditions), 69 miles southeast of Eugene on Ore. 58, where you'll find 18 downhill runs and 12¹/₂ miles (20km) of groomed cross-country trails. The ski area is open daily between mid-November and mid-April. Night skiing is available on Friday and Saturday nights from late December to March. Adult lift tickets range from $16 to $22.

Eugene is Oregon's best bicycling city, and if you'd like to see why, you can rent a bike at **Pedal Power Bicycles,** 535 High St. (☎ **541/687-1775**). This store has road bikes, mountain bikes, and tandems.

Hikers and backpackers will find miles of trails in the **Willamette National Forest,** which lies to the east along both Ore. 58 and Ore. 126. For more information, contact the Willamette National Forest, 211 E. Seventh Ave. (P.O. Box 10607), Eugene, OR 97440 (☎ **541/465-6521**).

Golfers have plenty of Eugene options, including the following: the **Fiddler's Green Golf Club,** 91292 Ore. 99N (☎ 541/689-8464); the **Oakway Golf Course,** 2000 Cal Young Rd. (☎ 541/484-1927); the **Riverridge Golf Course,** 3800 N. Delta Hwy. (☎ 541/345-9160); and out in the town of Blue River, 45 miles east on Ore. 126, the **Tokatee Golf Club,** 54947 McKenzie Hwy., Blue River (☎ 541/822-3220, or 800/452-6376), which is considered one of the best golf courses in Oregon.

SHOPPING

You can shop for one-of-a-kind crafts at Eugene's **Saturday Market** (☎ 541/686-8885), which covers more than two downtown blocks beginning at the corner of Eighth Avenue and Oak Street. The bustling outdoor arts-and-crafts market was founded in 1970. Good, inexpensive food, fresh produce, and live music round out the offerings of this colorful event. The market is held every Saturday from 10am to 5pm between April and December.

Other days of the week, you can explore the **Market District,** a six-block area of restored buildings that now house unusual shops, galleries, restaurants, and nightclubs. The **Fifth Street Public Market,** 296 E. Fifth St. (☎ 541/484-0383), at the corner of Fifth Avenue and High Street, is the centerpiece of the area, and has a courtyard that almost always features some sort of free entertainment. Directly across Fifth Avenue is the 5th & Pearl building, which houses the city's best restaurant (Chanterelle), a couple of music stores, and an antiques shop, among others. **Station Square,** a block west on Fifth Avenue, is a modern upscale mall designed to look like an old train station.

WHERE TO STAY
VERY EXPENSIVE

Eugene Hilton Hotel

66 E. Sixth Ave., Eugene, OR 97401. ☎ **541/342-2000** or 800/HILTONS. Fax 503/342-6661. 271 rms, 12 suites. A/C TV TEL. $130–$150 double; $190–$340 suite. AE, CB, DC, DISC, MC, V.

Eugene's only high-rise hotel is located directly adjacent to the Hult Center for the Performing Arts in downtown Eugene. Travertine marble floors and lots of glass blocks give the lobby an atmosphere of modern sophistication as befits the top hotel in Oregon's second-largest city. Try to get a room on an upper floor so you can enjoy the views. If you need plenty of room, there are minisuites that have sleeping alcoves.

Dining/Entertainment: The hotel's coffee shop is just off the lobby, while the more formal dining room is up on the 12th floor and offers great views. The Lobby Bar is a convenient place for an after-work drink, and up on the top floor is a more lively nightclub.

Services: Room service, free airport shuttle, complimentary health-club membership.

Facilities: Indoor pool, exercise room, whirlpool, saunas.

✪ Valley River Inn

1000 Valley River Way, Eugene, OR 97401. ☎ 541/687-0123 or 800/543-8266. 257 rms, 8 suites. A/C TV TEL. $135–$155 double; $195–$300 suite. AE, CB, DC, DISC, MC, V.

Though it's a few minutes' drive from downtown and the university, the Valley River Inn claims an envious location on the bank of the Willamette River. The low-rise hotel is lushly landscaped to evoke the green forests of the Northwest, and though all the rooms are large and have a balcony or patio, the riverside rooms have the best views.

Dining/Entertainment: Sweetwater's Restaurant, with its long wall of glass overlooking the river, is one of the city's best restaurants and serves primarily Northwest cuisine; entrées are $13 to $23. In the same large room is a more casual bar and grill with live contemporary music most evenings.

Services: Concierge, room service, free airport shuttle, discount membership at Downtown Athletic Club, bicycle rentals.

Facilities: Outdoor pool, whirlpool, saunas.

MODERATE

✪ The Campbell House

252 Pearl St., Eugene, OR 97401. ☎ 541/343-1119 or 800/264-2519. Fax 541/343-2258. 13 rms, 12 with bath. TV TEL. $70–$75 double without bath; $70–225 double with bath. AE, MC, V. Rates include full breakfast.

Located only two blocks from the Market District and set on Skinner's Butte overlooking the city, this large Victorian home was built in 1892 and now offers convenience and comfort. The guest rooms here vary considerably in size and price so there's something to fit all tastes and budgets. Breakfasts are served in a sunny room with a curving wall of glass, and there's also a parlor with a similar glass wall. Several of the guest rooms on the first floor have high ceilings, and down in the basement is a pine-paneled room with a fishing theme and another with a golf theme. The upstairs rooms have plenty of windows, and in the largest room you'll find wood floors and a double whirlpool tub.

Red Lion Inn–Eugene

205 Coburg Rd., Eugene, OR 97401. ☎ 541/342-5201 or 800/547-8010. 138 rms. A/C TV TEL. $69–$90 double. AE, CB, DC, DISC, MC, V.

Located just off the I-105 off-ramp for downtown Eugene, this Red Lion is fairly small and unpretentious compared to many other Red Lions. The guest rooms have all been remodeled, and the bathrooms are quite spacious. The rooms that overlook the courtyard and pool are quieter and have small balconies. There's a small coffee shop on one side of the lobby and on the opposite side is a more formal restaurant and lounge. A complimentary airport shuttle and outdoor pool are available.

INEXPENSIVE

Angus Inn

2121 Franklin Blvd., Eugene, OR 97401. ☎ 541/342-1243, or 800/456-6487. 81 rms. A/C TV TEL. $40–$54 double. AE, DC, DISC, MC, V.

Each guest room at this older motel has been remodeled and has newer carpets and furnishings. Some rooms have showers only while others have shower-tub combinations. You'll also have access to a swimming pool, sauna, whirlpool tub, and exercise room, and there are even some rental bicycles. There's also a steakhouse on the premises. Coffee and fruit are available each morning.

Best Western New Oregon Motel

1655 Franklin Blvd., Eugene, OR 97403. ☎ **541/683-3669** or 800/528-1234. 128 rms. A/C TV TEL. $54–$75 double. AE, CB, DC, DISC, ER, MC, V.

Although the motel looks a bit old from the outside, you'll be pleasantly surprised when you open your room door and find all new furnishings and a modern bathroom complete with built-in hairdryer. If you're in need of a bit of exercise or relaxing, you'll find racquetball courts, an indoor swimming pool, a whirlpool tub, saunas, an exercise room, and a sundeck.

WHERE TO DINE
EXPENSIVE

Ambrosia

174 E. Broadway. ☎ **541/342-4141.** Reservations recommended for parties of six or more. Main courses $10–$14. AE, MC, V. Sun–Thurs 11:30am–9:30pm, Fri–Sat 11:30am–10:30pm. NORTHERN ITALIAN.

The white-tiled entry, exposed brick walls, pressed-tin ceiling, and ornately carved wooden back bar all combine to give Ambrosia a genuine historical appeal. The menu offers quite a few tempting dishes. Pasta fans will enjoy the creamy farfalle (bow ties) with prosciutto, sun-dried tomatoes, red-pepper flakes, and Parmesan. Many of the entrées are familiar dishes such as lemon chicken or scampi, but the chicken with fontina cheese, fresh basil, and a roasted-pepper sauce is a delicious and unusual dish.

Chanterelle

207 E. Fifth St. ☎ **541/484-4065.** Reservations highly recommended. Main courses $12–$22. AE, DC, MC, V. Tues–Thurs 5–10pm, Fri–Sat 5–11pm. CONTINENTAL.

This small continental restaurant is located in one of downtown Eugene's many restored old industrial buildings that have been turned into chic shopping centers. There are few surprises on the menu, just tried-and-true recipes prepared with reliable expertise and served with gracious attentiveness. Escargots bourguignons, oysters Rockefeller, coquilles St-Jacques, tournedos of beef, and steak Diane are just some of the familiar dishes on the Chanterelle menu. You'll also find emu, moose, and buffalo on the menu. A long wine list offers plenty of choices for the perfect accompaniment to your meal.

MODERATE

✪ Zenon Café

898 Pearl St. ☎ **541/343-3005.** Reservations not accepted. Main courses $9.75–$14.75. AE, MC, V. Mon–Thurs 8am–11pm, Fri–Sat 8am–midnight, Sun 10am–11pm. INTERNATIONAL.

Urbanites visiting Eugene will be glad to know that they can find sophistication even in such a small city. The interior of this trendy (and noisy) café is black on black, with just a hint of bare wood for accent. The menu, which changes daily, is long and emphasizes whatever flavor combinations are currently in vogue. The globe-trotting menu assures all adventurous eaters of finding something they've never tried before. Before you ever reach your table, though, you'll have to run the gamut of the dessert case, which usually flaunts around 20 irresistible cakes, pies, tortes, and other pastries.

INEXPENSIVE

Mekala's
296 E. Fifth Ave. ☎ **541/342-4872.** Reservations recommended. Main courses $6.50–$15. MC, V. Mon–Thurs 11am–9pm, Fri 11am–10pm, Sat noon–10pm, Sun noon–9pm. THAI.

Located on the second floor of the Fifth Street Public Market, Mekala's has only a hint of Thai decor. Separated from the main dining room by several French doors is a patio dining area with a few tables. Brick floors give the restaurant a feel of age. The menu is quite long and includes a substantial vegetarian section. On a cool evening nothing warms better than a big bowl of thom yom kung, a sour-and-spicy shrimp soup. The homoke soufflé, made with coconut milk and various seafoods, is an unusual and delicious dish that rarely turns up on Thai menus in this country.

Mona Lizza
830 Olive St. ☎ **541/345-1072.** Main courses $8.75–$14. AE, DC, MC, V. Daily 11:30am–11:30pm. ITALIAN.

Affiliated with the Eugene City Brewery and the West Bros. Bar-B-Que, next door, this restaurant offers good pizzas, pasta, and microbrew ales. The dark brick-and-wood interior has a classic publike feel. Pool tables and dart boards keep customers entertained. The dessert case just inside the front door may have you thinking about a salad instead of a big plate of pasta.

⊖ Poppi's Anatolia
992 Willamette St. ☎ **541/343-9661.** Reservations accepted only for parties of six or more. Main course $6.50–$11.25. MC, V. Mon–Thurs 11:30am–9:30pm, Fri 11:30am–10pm, Sat 11:30am–3pm and 5–10pm, Sun 5–9:30pm. GREEK/INDIAN.

This cozy little café on the downtown pedestrian mall serves an unusual combination of cuisines and with its funky atmosphere and low prices sums up everything a good college-town restaurant should be. Plates are piled high with the flavors of the East. The Greek dishes definitely get the nod for best fare here, and the appetizer list is particularly satisfying.

EUGENE AFTER DARK

To find out what's happening in town, pick up a copy of the free *Eugene Weekly,* which is available at restaurants and shops around town. The huge glass gables of the **Hult Center for the Performing Arts,** Seventh Avenue and Willamette Street (☎ **541/687-5000**), are an unmistakable landmark of downtown Eugene. Each year this sparkling temple of the arts manages to put together a first-rate schedule of performances by visiting companies and performers, as well as the Eugene Symphony Orchestra, the Eugene Ballet Company, the Eugene Opera, and other local and regional companies. Tickets run $6 to $35. During the summer the center hosts the Oregon Bach Festival, Oregon's Festival of American Music, and the Eugene Festival of Musical Theatre. Summer concerts are also held at the Cuthbert Amphitheater. October through May there are free Thursday lunchtime concerts.

NIGHTCLUBS, BARS, COFFEE HOUSES & BREW PUBS

In addition to the places listed below, you'll find several microbreweries in Eugene. These include the **High Street Brewery & Cafe,** 1243 High St. (☎ 541/345-4905), and the **East 19th Street Cafe,** 1485 E. 19th St.(☎ 541/342-4025), both of which are McMenamin's brewpubs; **West Bros. Bar-B-Que Eugene City Brewery,** 844 Olive St. (☎ 541/345-8489); **Steelhead Brewery & Cafe**, 199 E. Fifth Ave. (☎ 541/686-2739); and **Fields Restaurant & Brewpub,** 13th Avenue and Oak Street (☎ 541/341-6599).

Cafe Paradiso

115 W. Broadway. ☎ **541/484-9933.**

This is one of Eugene's most popular coffeehouses and has an eclectic schedule of live music, including open-mike nights. Good coffee and voluptuous scones.

✪ Jo Federigo's Café & Bar

259 E. Fifth Ave. ☎ **541/343-8488.**

Housed in a historic granary building, Jo Federigo's is both a popular restaurant and Eugene's favorite jazz club. There's live music nightly, and Monday is open-mike night.

Oregon Electric Station

Fifth Ave. and Willamette St. ☎ **541/485-4444.**

This building dates back to 1914, and with a wine cellar in an old railroad car, lots of oak, and a back bar that requires a ladder to access all the various bottles of premium spirits, it's the poshest bar in town. There's live jazz on Friday and Saturday nights.

DRIVING ON TO BEND

Ore. 126 east of Eugene follows the scenic McKenzie River, passing through some of the most spectacular sections of the Cascades in its upper reaches, and during the summer Ore. 126 connects to Ore. 242, the most breathtaking pass in the Oregon Cascades. See "A Scenic Drive Along the Cascade Lakes Highway" under the "Bend" section of Chapter 15 for details on this scenic section of highway. There's also plenty to see along Ore. 126. Several state parks provide access to the river and near the towns of Vida and McKenzie Bridge, you can see historic covered bridges (see the box in this chapter for details). Just east of McKenzie Bridge, which is 55 miles east of Eugene, you'll find **Belknap Lodge & Hot Springs** (☎ 541/822-3512), where you can soak in a hot mineral swimming pool. At Belknap Springs, Ore. 126 heads north and Ore. 242 heads east. Continuing north, you'll find access to the **McKenzie River Trail,** which parallels the river on the far bank. There are several campgrounds along this stretch of road. Five miles south of the junction with Ore. 20, you'll come to two picturesque waterfalls—**Sahalie Falls** and **Koosah Falls.** Both north and south of these falls, you drive along the edge of lava flows that are best seen from Ore. 242 in summer.

WHERE TO STAY & DINE

Log Cabin Inn

56483 McKenzie Hwy., McKenzie Bridge, OR 97413. ☎ **541/822-3432.** 8 cabins. $65–$75 cabin for two. DISC, MC, V.

Situated on 6¹/₂ acres in the community of McKenzie Bridge, this log lodge was built in 1906 after the original 1886 lodge burned to the ground. In the lodge's heyday, its guests included President Herbert Hoover, Clark Gable, and the duke of Windsor. Today you can stay in rustic log cabins, all but one of which have their own fireplaces. The one cabin without a fireplace does, however, have a kitchen, which the others do not. The lodge's restaurant is renowned for the quality of its meals, which include such game as wild boar, venison, and buffalo.

Southern Oregon 14

Roughly defined as the region from the California line to just north of Roseburg and lying between the Coast Range and the Cascades, southern Oregon is a mountainous area that seems more akin to northern California than to the rest of Oregon. Here the Cascade Range, Coast Range, and Siskiyou Mountains converge in a jumble of peaks.

It was gold that first brought white settlers to this area and it was timber that kept them here. The gold is all played out now but the legacy of the gold-rush days, when stagecoaches traveled the rough road between Sacramento and Portland, remains in picturesque towns such as Jacksonville and Oakland.

Southern Oregon is quite a hike from the nearest metropolitan areas. From Ashland, the southernmost city in the region, it's a six-hour trip to either Portland or San Francisco. Despite this distance from major cities, Ashland is renowned for its **Oregon Shakespeare Festival,** which annually attracts tens of thousands of theatergoers. The festival, which now stretches across most of the year, has turned a sleepy mill town into a facsimile of Tudor England. Not to be outdone, the nearby historic town of Jacksonville offers performances by internationally recognized musicians and dance companies throughout the summer.

However, it is rugged beauty and the outdoors that draw most people to the region. Crater Lake National Park, Oregon's only national park, hides within its boundaries a sapphire jewel formed by the massive eruption of Mount Mazama less than 7,000 years ago. In this same area rise two of the most fabled fly-fishing rivers in the country. Ever since Zane Grey wrote of the fighting steelhead trout and salmon of the Rogue and Umpqua rivers, fly fishermen have been casting their lines in hopes of hooking a few of these wily denizens of the Cascade Range's cold waters.

In addition to the sources of information listed below in each individual city section, you can get information on all of southern Oregon by contacting the following regional tourism associations: **Southern Oregon Visitors Association,** P.O. Box 1645, Medford, OR 97501-0731 (☎ **541/779-4691**), or the **Southern Oregon Reservation Center,** 87 Third St. (P.O. Box 477), Ashland, OR 97520 (☎ **541/488-1011** or 800/547-8052).

1 Ashland & the Oregon Shakespeare Festival

285 miles S of Portland, 50 miles W of Klamath Falls, 350 miles N of San Francisco

It was the Fourth of July 1935. In a small Ashland theater built by the Chautauqua Movement, Angus Bowmer, an English professor at Southern Oregon State College, was staging a performance of Shakespeare's *As You Like It.* The Depression had dashed any hopes local businessman Jesse Winburne had of turning Ashland, a quiet mill town in the rugged Siskiyou Mountains, into a mineral-springs resort. However, before the Depression struck, Winburne had managed to construct beautiful Lithia Park. Neither man's love's labor was lost, and today their legacies have turned the town into one of the Northwest's most popular destinations.

Each year more than 300,000 people attend performances of the Oregon Shakespeare Festival, a nine-month-long repertory festival that was born of Bowmer's love of the Bard. Though Ashland never became a mineral-springs resort, Lithia Park, through which still flow the clear waters of Winburne's dreams, is the town's centerpiece. Over the years the festival has attracted all manner of artists to settle in Ashland, giving the town a cosmopolitan air. With the growing popularity of the festival, fine restaurants and bed-and-breakfast inns opened to cater to the theatergoers. It seems amazing that a small town roughly 300 miles from San Francisco or Portland could become a cultural mecca, but that's the power of the Bard.

ESSENTIALS

GETTING THERE   Ashland is located on I-5. From the east, Ore. 66 connects Ashland with Klamath Falls.

The nearest airport is the **Rogue Valley International Airport** in Medford, which is served by Horizon Air and United Airlines. A taxi from the airport to Ashland will cost around $14.

VISITOR INFORMATION   Contact the **Ashland Chamber of Commerce,** 110 E. Main St. (P.O. Box 1360), Ashland, OR 97520 (☎ **541/482-3486**).

GETTING AROUND   If you need a taxi, call **Yellow Cab** (☎ **541/482-3065**). Car-rental companies with offices at the Rogue Valley International Airport include **Avis** and **Budget** (also in Ashland). Public bus service in the Ashland area is provided by the **Rogue Valley Transportation District** (☎ **541/779-2877**).

FESTIVALS   The month-long yuletide **Holiday Festival of Lights** held each year in December is Ashland's other big annual festival.

THE OREGON SHAKESPEARE FESTIVAL

The raison d'être of Ashland, the Oregon Shakespeare Festival is an internationally acclaimed theater festival with a season that stretches from February to October. The season typically includes four works by Shakespeare plus eight other classic or contemporary plays. These plays are performed in repertory with as many as four being staged on any given day.

The festival complex, often referred to as "the bricks" because of its brick courtyard, is in the center of town and contains three theaters. The visually impressive outdoor **Elizabethan Theatre,** which is modeled after England's 17th-century Fortune Theatre, is used only in the summer and early fall. The **Angus Bowmer**

Southern Oregon

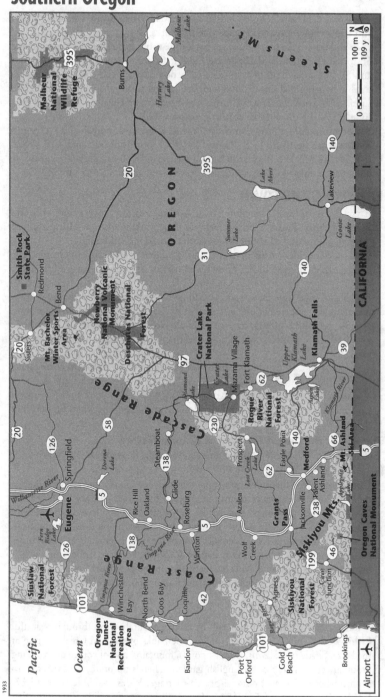

1933

Theatre is the festival's largest indoor theater. The **Black Swan** is smallest theater and stages contemporary and experimental works.

In addition to the plays, there are **backstage tours** (tickets are $8 for adults and $6 for children) and a **Shakespeare Exhibit Center** (admission is $2 for adults and $1.50 for children) that houses a collection of props and costumes that were used in past productions. Throughout the festival season there are also talks and special performances. The opening of the Elizabethan Theatre is celebrated each June in Lithia Park with the elaborate Feast of Will.

For more information and upcoming schedules, contact the **Oregon Shakespeare Festival,** 15 S. Pioneer St. (P.O. Box 158), Ashland, OR 97520 (☎ **541/482-4331**). Regular tickets range from $18.50 to $28.50, box seats are $40.50, standing room costs $10, and previews range from $14.75 to $22.75.

EXPLORING THE TOWN

If you'd like to learn a bit more about Ashland's history, take a tour with **Old Ashland Story Tours,** which offers one-hour walking tours at 10am Monday through Saturday. Tickets are $5 for adults and $2 for children.

At the **Schneider Museum of Art,** on the campus of the Southern Oregon State College, 1250 Siskiyou Blvd. (☎ **541/552-6245**), art exhibits change every month or two.

Ashland's first fame came from its healing mineral waters and today you can still relax and be pampered at one of the city's day spas. The **Ashland Spa,** 27 Third St. (☎ **541/482-6086**), and the **Beach House,** 625 Beach St. (☎ **541/482-0196**), both offer various body treatments, skin care, mineral baths, and massages.

If you'd like to taste some local wines, stop by the **Ashland Vineyards,** 2775 E. Main St. (☎ **541/488-0088**), just east of town on the far side of I-5, or **Weisinger's,** 3150 Siskiyou Blvd. (☎ **541/488-5989**), just south of town. Cabernet sauvignon, merlot, and chardonnay are among the wines produced in the area.

The Pacific Northwest Museum of Natural History

1500 E. Main St. ☎ **541/488-1084.** Admission $6 adults, $5 seniors, $4.50 children 5–15. Apr–Oct, daily 9am–5pm; Nov–Mar, daily 10am–4pm.

Using interactive exhibits, computer programs, sights, sounds, and even smells, this modern museum serves as an introduction to the natural history of the Pacific Northwest. The museum is entered through a mock-up of a lava tube, and from that point on, visitors must use all their senses to learn about everything from old-growth forests to coastal tidepools. One of the most fascinating exhibits comes compliments of the adjacent U.S. Fish and Wildlife Forensics Laboratory, which investigates wildlife crime. Kids can learn a lot in the Discovery Center, and there are tips on how to improve the natural environment of your own back yard.

OUTDOOR ACTIVITIES

A memorable part of your visit will be a long, leisurely stroll through beautiful **Lithia Park.** This 100-acre park follows the banks of Ashland Creek starting at the Plaza. Shade trees, lawns, flowers, ponds, fountains, and of course the babbling brook are reminiscent of an English garden. There's no more romantic way to explore the park than by horse-drawn carriage. Rides available from **Lithia Carriage Company** (☎ **541/482-2484**). A 20-minute ride costs $20 for the first two people and $25 for three or more people.

Summertime thrill seekers shouldn't pass up the chance to do some **white-water rafting** on the Rogue or Klamath River while in southern Oregon. Trips are offered between May and October by several companies. Try **Noah's World of Water,** 53 N. Main St. (☎ **541/488-2811** or 800/858-2811), or **The Adventure Center,** 40 N. Main St. (☎ **541/766-4932** or 800/444-2819), both of which offer trips lasting from half a day to four days. Prices range from $40 to $600 per person, depending on the length and type of the trip. The former company also offers salmon- and steelhead-fishing trips and the latter offers downhill bike rides from the top of Mount Ashland and guided cross-country ski trips.

Mountain **bikes** can be rented at **Ashland Mountain Supply,** 31 N. Main St. (☎ 541/488-2749), and the folks at this shop can point you in the direction of good rides.

Miles of hiking trails, including the **Pacific Crest Trail,** can be found up on Mount Ashland in the **Siskiyou Rogue River National Forest.**

Horseback riding is available at **Circle C Stables,** 1275 Old Hwy. 99 (☎ 541/ 482-7463), and **Mountain Gate Stables,** 4399 Ore. 66 (☎ 541/482-8873). Rides start at $15 for one hour.

In the winter there's good downhill and cross-country skiing at **Mt. Ashland Ski Area,** 15 miles south of Ashland (☎ 541/482-2897 for information or 541/ 482-2754 for snow report). Lift tickets range from $10 to $24. You can rent skis and pick up ski-trail maps at **Ashland Mountain Supply,** 31 N. Main St. (☎ 541/488-2749).

SHOPPING

Ashland has the best shopping in southern Oregon. Interesting and unusual shops line **East Main Street,** so when the curtains are down on the stages, check the windows of downtown.

Art galleries abound in Ashland. Our favorites are the **Hanson Howard Gallery,** 82 N. Main St. (☎ 541/488-2562), for contemporary art, and the **American Indian Art Gallery,** 27 N. Main St. (☎ 541/488-2731), for Native American pieces. If your tastes run to Asian arts, visit the **Silk Road Gallery,** 296 E. Main St. (☎ 541/482-4553), which sells Oriental rugs, art, and jewelry.

If you plan to head out into the surrounding wilderness areas, a visit is in order to the **Northwest Nature Shop,** 154 Oak St. (☎ 541/482-3241), for maps and guides.

WHERE TO STAY

Ashland, because of its Shakespearean theme, has become a very popular spot to open a bed-and-breakfast inn. At last count, there were more than 50 bed-and-breakfasts in town, many of which are only open during the festival season. For a more comprehensive list of inns, contact the **Ashland B&B Reservation Network,** P.O. Box 1051, Ashland, OR 97520-0048 (☎ 541/482-BEDS or 800/944-0329).

If all you're looking for is a clean, comfortable room for the night, the **Super 8 Motel–Ashland,** 2350 Ashland St., Ashland, OR 97520 (☎ 541/482-8887 or 800/800-8000), is the most reliable bet in town, charging $42 to $67 double.

EXPENSIVE

Best Western Bard's Inn

132 N. Main St., Ashland, OR 97520. ☎ **541/482-0049** or 800/528-1234. Fax 503/ 488-3259. 79 rms. A/C TV TEL. June–Oct, $96–$115 double. Oct–May, $38–$58 double. AE, CB, DC, DISC, MC, V.

If you prefer motels to bed-and-breakfast inns, the Bard's Inn should be your first choice in Ashland. The rooms are large and comfortable, and those in the new annex have patios or balconies, though these rooms can get a bit of traffic noise. The older rooms have all been refurbished and have minirefrigerators. An outdoor pool and hot tub provide a bit of relaxation, and there's an acceptable restaurant as well. However, what makes this motel most attractive is that it's only two blocks from the festival theaters.

Chanticleer Bed & Breakfast Inn

120 Gresham St., Ashland, OR 97520. ☎ and fax **541/482-1919.** 6 rms. A/C TEL. High season, $120–$160 double. Winter, $95–$105. Rates include full breakfast. MC, V.

As one of the oldest bed-and-breakfast inns in Ashland, the Chanticleer has long been a favorite of theatergoers. The 1920s craftsman bungalow is only three blocks from "the bricks," and equally close to all the downtown shops and restaurants. European country styling gives the inn an old-world charm that allows you to immerse yourself in the Shakespeare experience. The guest rooms are decorated with antiques, Persian carpets, and down comforters, and there are always fresh flowers all around. You can even pick up a script from the evening's play and reread your favorite passages. The rooms look out on either the garden or the valley. Breakfasts are a lavish affair and can be served either in bed or in the dining room overlooking the mountains. Throughout the day there are always treats on hand as well.

Country Willows

1313 Clay St., Ashland, OR 97520. ☎ **541/488-1590** or 800/WILLOWS. Fax 541/488-1611. 6 rms, 1 suite. $90–$120 double; $155 suite. Rates include full breakfast. Lower rates Nov–Apr. MC, V.

Just outside town and surrounded by 5 acres of rolling hills and pastures, the Country Willows bed-and-breakfast offers the tranquillity of a farm only minutes from excellent restaurants and the theaters. If you're looking for a very special room, consider the Sunrise Suite, in a renovated barn behind the main house; it has pine paneling, a high ceiling, a king-size bed, a gas fireplace, and best of all, an old-fashioned tub for two with its very own picture window and skylight. Rooms in the restored farmhouse are smaller, but some offer excellent views across the valley. Ducks, geese, goats, and sometimes horses call the farm home, and there's a 2-mile hiking trail that starts at the back door.

Fox House Inn

269 B St., Ashland, OR 97520. ☎ **503/488-1055.** 2 rms. A/C TV TEL. $130 double. Rates include full breakfast. Lower rates off-season. No credit cards.

The Fox House has the air of a Victorian dollhouse. Compared to other houses of this vintage it's a mere cottage, but the inn more than makes up for its size with elegant Victorian furnishings, unusual touches such as working antique telephones, and private hot tubs. There are also clawfoot bathtubs in both bathrooms. Unlike many Victorian B&Bs, this inn has avoided the Laura Ashley look and instead opted for the dark colors and fabrics (burgundy velvet curtains) that were popular 100 years ago. The "bricks" is only three blocks away.

✪ Mt. Ashland Inn

550 Mt. Ashland Rd., Ashland, OR 97520. ☎ **541/482-8707** or 800/830-8707. 5 rms. $85–$130 double. Rates include full breakfast. Discounts available Nov–Apr. MC, V.

Located on 160 acres on the side of Mount Ashland, this massive log home commands distant panoramas from its forest setting. Though the inn is only 15 minutes from downtown Ashland, you're in a different world up here. The Pacific Crest Trail, which stretches from Canada to Mexico, passes through the front yard, and just a few miles up the road is the Mount Ashland Ski Area. Whether you're in the area for an active vacation or a few nights of theater, this lodge makes a very special base of operations. The decor is straight out of an Eddie Bauer catalog with plenty of special touches such as handmade furniture and stained glass, Oriental rugs, and, in one guest bathroom, a stone wall with a built-in waterfall.

✪ The Winchester Country Inn

35 S. Second St., Ashland, OR 97520. ☎ **541/488-1113.** 18 rms. TEL. June–Oct, $125–$170 double. Oct–June, $89–$115 double. Rates include full breakfast. DISC, MC, V.

Though it calls itself a country inn, the Winchester is right in the heart of downtown Ashland, within a few blocks of the theaters. However, with its massive old shade trees, gazebo, and English cottage garden, you'd never guess you were in town. The rooms are comfortably furnished with antiques and modern bath fixtures, including sinks built into old bureaus in some rooms. We prefer the upstairs rooms, which get quite a bit more light than the basement rooms. There are also rooms in the building next door, and these are as well designed as those in the main house. A decanter of sherry in each room is a welcome touch upon returning from the theater. For fine dining, you need go no further than the inn's first-floor dining room, which is one of the best restaurants in town.

MODERATE

Ashland Hills Inn

2525 Ashland St., Ashland, OR 97520-1478. ☎ **541/482-8310** or 800/547-4747. 159 rms, 85 suites. A/C TV TEL. June–Oct, $89–$99 double; $175–$250 suite. Oct–June, $42–$75 double; $100–$225 suite. AE, CB, DC, DISC, MC, V.

Set on the outskirts of Ashland a few miles from downtown, the Ashland Hills Inn is the area's premier lodging and the only local hotel offering resort-style amenities. Set on sprawling, attractively landscaped grounds, the inn combines a Northwest aesthetic with urban sophistication and glitz. This translates into large rooms, most with balconies or patios, bathrooms with two sinks, and great views of the surrounding countryside. The dining room serves Northwest regional dishes, and in the adjacent lounge you can watch the big game on TV. A lighter menu is available in the lounge. Services include room service, complimentary morning coffee and newspaper, free airport shuttle, a library of bestsellers, and valet/laundry service. A swimming pool, hot tub, tennis courts, guest bicycles, and jogging trail provide plenty of recreational options.

INEXPENSIVE

The Ashland Hostel

150 N. Main St., Ashland, OR 97520. ☎ **541/482-9217.** 40 dorm beds. $11 dorm bed for members, $13 for nonmembers. No credit cards.

Located in a historic home just three blocks from the plaza, this official AYH hostel stays busy most of the year with students here to study theater. There are seven dorms, two private rooms, a common room, a recreation room, a dining room, a kitchen, a laundry, and a bike-storage area.

⑤ Columbia Hotel

262¹/₂ E. Main St., Ashland, OR 97520. ☎ **541/482-3726.** 24 rms, 4 with bath. June–Oct, $46 double without bath, $74 double with bath. Oct–June, $39 double without bath, $54 double with bath. MC, V.

Inexpensive accommodations are difficult to find in Ashland, but if you don't mind walking down the hall to the bathroom, you'll save a lot of money by staying at the Columbia. Located at the top of a flight of squeaky stairs, this historic hotel is of a style once popular throughout the West. The guest rooms are individually decorated with a country flavor. The four rooms with private bathrooms are extremely spacious and have sitting areas and brass beds. If the heat is getting to you, request a room with air conditioning. All in all, the Columbia feels like a bed-and-breakfast without the breakfast.

WHERE TO DINE
EXPENSIVE

✪ Chateaulin

50 E. Main St. ☎ **541/482-2264.** Reservations recommended. Main courses $14.50–$24. AE, DISC, MC, V. Daily 5–9:30pm. FRENCH.

Exposed brick walls and old champagne bottles give this restaurant a casually elegant appearance that's accented by lace curtains, burgundy tablecloths, and dark-wood furnishings. The menu is almost as traditional as the decor, so you can start your meal with escargots, French onion soup, or house pâté and then move on to loin of lamb with a sauce of red wine, demiglaze, fresh thyme, shallots, and roasted garlic, or crêpes Florentine made with spinach, shallots, shiitake mushrooms, and Parmesan cheese. A separate café menu caters to smaller appetites. The restaurant's wine list features 100 selections from Oregon, California, and France.

Monet

36 S. Second St. ☎ **541/482-1339.** Reservations recommended. Main courses $11.75–$20.50. MC, V. Summer, Sun–Mon 5:30–8:30pm, Tues–Sat 11:45am–1:45pm and 5:30–8:30pm; winter, Tues 5:30–8:30pm, Wed–Sat 11:45am–1:45pm and 5:30–8:30pm. Closed Jan. FRENCH.

Though the big white house across the street from the Winchester Inn looks rather plain from the outside, when you step through the door you'll find the colors of Monet enlivening the impeccably set dining room. On warm, sunny days you may wish to dine in the garden surrounded by many of the same flowers that appear in Monet's famous garden. The cuisine is modern French. You might find smoked salmon wrapped around avocado mousse and served with a lemon vinaigrette as a starter, and baked pork tenderloin in a kiwi-cream sauce as an entrée. There's always a good selection of salads, available in appetizer or entrée portions.

✪ New Sammy's Cowboy Bistro

2210 S. Pacific Hwy., Talent. ☎ **541/535-2779.** Reservations highly recommended. Main courses $15–$22. No credit cards. Thurs–Sun 5–9pm. NORTHWEST.

Unmarked yet unmistakable, New Sammy's is a tiny shack of a place in nearby Talent. If it weren't for the fact that the building looks as if the owners got their paint at a Sherwin Williams going-out-of-business sale, you'd drive right past. In fact, lots of folks do drive right past, convinced that this just can't be the place. Be bold. Open the door. Things look different inside.

The menu, however, is as imaginative as the exterior paint job, and every-thing is as fresh as it gets, with lots of organic produce from local growers. This is a mom-and-pop operation (mom cooks and pop serves), so be sure to make a reservation.

Primavera Restaurant & Gardens

241 Hargadine St. ☎ **541/488-1994.** Reservations recommended in summer. Main courses $15–$19.50. MC, V. Wed–Sun 5–8:30pm. FRENCH/ITALIAN.

In keeping with Ashland's theatrical theme, this restaurant has adopted a very dramatic decor, with autumnal colors, carved columns, and theatrically lit paintings inspired by old Ballet Russe posters. A handsome garden at the back makes a fine place to dine before attending a performance. The menu changes daily and is limited to a few choice treatments of beef, chicken, or fish, and a vegetarian dish. The produce used here is largely organic, and they also make their own bread, sausage, and ice cream. Don't forget to leave room for a finale such as orange-lavender sorbet with biscotti.

The Winchester Inn

35 S. Second St. ☎ **541/488-1115.** Reservations required. Main courses $15–$24; Sun brunch $6.75–$11. DISC, MC, V. Mon–Sat 5:30–8:30pm, Sun 9:30am–1:30pm (brunch) and 5:30–8:30pm. INTERNATIONAL.

The Winchester Inn's reputation is far reaching, so if you want to dine here, make reservations as early as possible. The dining rooms take up half the first floor of Ashland's favorite in-town country bed-and-breakfast and overlook the English cottage garden. In summer there is dining on the porch and deck, which is just that much closer to the gardens, but any time of year you'll enjoy a dinner here. The menu draws on such varied cuisines as French, Chinese, Italian, and Mexican, but all end up superbly prepared and bursting with flavor. For a starter, try the smoked salmon, which is smoked on the premises. Any time of year the duck à la bigarade, made with fresh seasonal fruit, brandy, duck stock, and caramel, is a fragrant and unusual delicacy. Desserts make frequent and delicious use of Oregon's bounty of fresh fruits. Sunday brunch is the perfect way to finish a weekend of theater before heading home.

MODERATE

✪ Cucina Biazzi

568 E. Main St. ☎ **541/488-3739.** Reservations recommended in summer. Four-course prix-fixe dinner $17–$19. MC, V. Summer, daily 5:30–8:30pm; winter, daily 6–7:30pm. ITALIAN.

The owners have transformed this slightly run-down Ashland bungalow on the outskirts of town into a rustic Italian cottage, with romantic touches such as lace curtains and chianti bottles dripping with candle wax. The menu here, inspired by available seasonal ingredients, changes every one or two weeks, but you might find that the antipasto course is a salad of Tuscan white beans, mushrooms, marinated artichokes, asiago cheese, and other tempting ingredients. The pasta course might include ravioli tossed with basil pesto or cheese ravioli with lobster in a lemon, cream, and white-wine sauce. If you like your Italian food hot, try the bistecca alla chimi churri, grilled sirloin with parsley, garlic, and jalepeño pesto. For al fresco dining, there's an intimate low-walled patio in the back.

Thai Pepper

84 N. Main St. ☎ **541/482-8058.** Reservations recommended. Main courses $9–$13. MC, V. Mon 5:30–9pm, Tues–Thurs 11:30am–2pm and 5:30–9pm, Fri–Sat 11:30am–2pm and 5–9:30pm, Sun 5–8:30pm. THAI.

You'll find the Thai Pepper down a flight of stairs at the north end of Main Street about a block from the plaza. If it's a sunny day, you can sit out on the patio and listen to Ashland Creek burbling past. The menu here is rather short and the names of the dishes don't exactly sound Thai. But this isn't to say that the menu doesn't include the best that Thai cooking has to offer—it does. It's hard to pass up dishes with names such as Evil Jungle (sweet-and-spicy coconut beef curry) and Tiger Cries (grilled beef with serrano peppers, garlic, and lime sauce).

INEXPENSIVE

Ashland Bakery Cafe

38 E. Main St. ☎ **541/482-2117.** Main courses $9–$10; breakfast $3–$6; sandwiches $3.25–$7. MC, V. Mon 7am–4pm, Tues–Sun 7am–8:30pm. INTERNATIONAL.

You'll find this café right in the hub of downtown Ashland. It's usually mobbed at breakfast with people reading newspapers and sipping coffee while patiently waiting for their huevos rancheros, tofu scrambles, avocado-and-cheese omelets, and blueberry pancakes. At lunch or dinner it's a good place for a quick sandwich, pizza, or pasta dish. Check out the bakery case for the giant oatmeal-raisin cookie or pecan cookies to assuage between-meal cravings.

Five Rivers

139 E. Main St. ☎ **541/488-1883.** Main courses $5.50–11.50. MC, V. Daily 11am–2:30pm and 5:30–10pm. INDIAN.

Located on the second floor overlooking Main Street and across from the chamber of commerce office, Five Rivers has plenty of succulent and fragrant dishes to choose from, including tandoori chicken, prawn biriyani (prawns with saffron basmati rice, raisins, and nuts), and lamb kebabs. The all-you-can-eat lunch buffet is a bargain at $5.50, and includes chicken tikka, curries, and vegetarian selections.

ASHLAND AFTER DARK

The Oregon Shakespeare Festival may be the main draw, but Ashland is overflowing with talent begging to express itself. From experimental theater to Broadway musicals, the town sees an amazing range of theater productions. To find out what's going on while you're in town, pick up a free copy of either the *Ashland Gazette,* a monthly, or *Sneak Preview,* a biweekly.

Theaters and theater companies in the area include the **Actor's Theatre,** Miracle Playhouse, 101 Talent Ave., Talent (☎ **541/535-5250**); the **Oregon Cabaret Theatre,** First and Hargadine streets (☎ **541/488-2902**), a professional dinner theater; the **Theatre Arts Department of Southern Oregon State College,** 1250 Siskiyou Blvd. (☎ **541/552-6348**), which stages well-regarded student productions; the **Ashland Community Theatre,** 125 E. Main St. (☎ **541/ 482-7532**), staging new and old popular plays; the **Cygnet Theatre Group** (☎ **541/488-2945**), a children's theater company; the **Lyric Theatre Company** (☎ **541/482-3531**), which stages professional musical theater; and the **Camelot Theatre Company** (☎ **541/482-9350**), a musical dinner-theater company.

Nontheater performing-arts companies include the **Rogue Valley Symphony** (☎ **541/488-2521**) and the **Rogue Opera** (☎ **541/552-6400**).

Throughout the summer there are numerous outdoor events, some free and some not, at the **Lithia Park band shell.** You can pick up a schedule of events at the **Ashland Chamber of Commerce Visitors & Convention Bureau,** 110 E. Main St. (☎ **541/482-3486**).

A SIDE TRIP TO KLAMATH FALLS

Klamath Falls, 65 miles east of Ashland, is set in a wide windswept expanse of lakes and high desert. However, the region has a history that stretches back more than 14,000 years. The presence of water (in the form of large lakes) in this dry region attracted not only wildlife but human life as well. Native Americans lived on the banks of the Klamath Basin's lakes from which they harvested fish, birds, and various marsh plants. Two local museums have extensive collections of Native American artifacts that have been found in this area over the years.

Before exploring this region, stop by the **Klamath County Department of Tourism,** 1451 Main St. (☎ **503/884-0666** or 800/445-6728), and pick up copies of the Upper Klamath Lake Tour Loop and Lower Klamath Loop Tour brochures. These two brochures outline **driving tours** that take in many of the region's most interesting attractions, including state parks, historic sites, and the best vistas around.

Klamath Falls made its name as a railroad shipping point and a boom in the 1920s and 1930s left the city with a surprising collection of art deco–influenced commercial buildings. Most notable of these is the **Ross Ragland Theater,** 218 N. Seventh St. (☎ **541/884-LIVE**), a former 1940s movie palace built in the art deco style that manages to book numerous name acts every year. You can get a free walking map of historic buildings from the visitors association.

Anyone with an interest in Native American artifacts or western art will find a trip to the **Favell Museum of Western Art and Indian Artifacts,** 125 W. Main St. (☎ **541/882-9996**), reason enough to visit Klamath Falls. It's open Monday through Saturday from 9:30am to 5:30pm; admission is $4 for adults, $3 for seniors, $2 for children 6 to 16. On display are thousands of arrowheads, including one made from fire opal, obsidian knives, slave killers, spear points, stone tools of every description, baskets, pottery, even ancient shoes and pieces of matting and fabric. Though the main focus is on the Native Americans of the Klamath Basin and Columbia River, there are artifacts from Alaska, Canada, other regions of the United States and Mexico. Few museums anywhere in the country have such an extensive collection and the cases of artifacts can be overwhelming, so take your time. The other half of the museum's collection is western art by more than 300 artists, including 13 members of the famous Cowboy Artists of America. Paintings, bronzes, photographs, dioramas, and woodcarvings capture the Wild West in realistic, romantic, and even humorous styles.

At the **Klamath County Museum,** 1451 Main St. (☎ **541/883-4208**), more Native American artifacts, this time exclusively from the Klamath Lakes area, are on display. A history of the Modoc Indian Wars chronicles the most expensive campaign of the American West. Also of particular interest here are the early 20th-century photos of local photographer Maud Baldwin. The admission-free museum is open Monday through Saturday: in summer from 9am to 5:30pm and in winter from 8am to 4:30pm.

In this dry region between the Cascades and the Rocky Mountains there are few large bodies of water, so the lakes and marshes of the Klamath Basin are a magnet for birds. In the winter the region hosts the largest concentration of **bald eagles** in the Lower 48. More than 300 eagles can be seen at the **Bear Valley National Wildlife Refuge** near the town of Worden, 11 miles south of Klamath Falls. Other avian visitors and residents include white pelicans, great blue herons, sandhill cranes, egrets, geese, ducks, grebes, bitterns, and osprey. For more information on birdwatching in the area, contact the Klamath County Department of Tourism (see above).

If you want to get out and paddle around one of the local lakes, check out the **Upper Klamath Canoe Trail,** which begins near the junction of Ore. 140 and West Side Road northwest of Klamath Falls. The canoe trail wanders through marshlands on the edge of Upper Klamath Lake. For more information, contact the **Winema National Forest,** Klamath Ranger District, 1936 California Ave., Klamath Falls, OR 97601 (☎ **541/885-3400**).

WHERE TO DINE

Chez Nous

3927 S. Sixth St. ☎ **541/883-8719.** Reservations recommended. Main courses $11–$23. AE, CB, DC, MC, V. Tues–Sat 5–10pm. FRENCH/AMERICAN.

Though Sixth Street is one of Klamath Falls' main roads and this section is lined with motels and other modern buildings, you'll find Chez Nous in a quaint little house that dates back to the early 1900s. The old-fashioned elegance of the house is a fitting setting for the fine meals served here. The menu features primarily traditional fare such as escargots de Bourgogne and French onion soup for starters and salmon with béarnaise sauce and veal Oscar for entrées.

Saddle Rock Cafe

1012 Main St. ☎ **541/883-3970.** Main courses $5.50–$10.50. MC, V. Daily 11am–8pm. AMERICAN/ITALIAN.

Right downtown in an old brick building with green awnings, you'll find a casual yet interesting dining spot. Exposed brick walls and pink tablecloths give the restaurant a bit of urban sophistication. Though there are several pasta dishes and steaks on the menu, we prefer the seafood dishes such as scallops and baby shrimp in a spicy tomato sauce served over pasta or the simply prepared shrimp sautéed in white wine and garlic.

2 Jacksonville & Medford: A Slice of Oregon History

16 miles N of Ashland, 24 miles E of Grants Pass

Jacksonville is quite literally a snapshot of southern Oregon history. Because it became a forgotten backwater after the Great Depression, more than 80 buildings from its glory years as a gold-boom town in the mid-1800s stood untouched. The entire town has been restored, thanks to the photos of pioneer photographer Peter Britt, who moved to Jacksonville in 1852 and operated the first photographic studio west of the Rockies. His photos of 19th-century Jacksonville have provided preservationists with invaluable 100-year-old glimpses of many of the town's historic buildings. Britt's name has also been attached to the **Britt Festivals,** another southern Oregon cultural binge that rivals the Oregon Shakespeare Festival in its ability to stage first-rate entertainment.

Though thousands of eager gold seekers were lured into California's Sierra Nevada by the gold rush of 1849, few struck it rich. Many of those who were smitten with gold fever and were unwilling to give up the search for the mother lode headed out across the West in search of golder pastures. At least two prospectors hit pay dirt in the Siskiyou Mountains of southern Oregon in 1851, at a spot that would soon be known as Rich Gulch. Within a year Rich Gulch had become the site of booming Jacksonville, and within another year the town had become the county seat and commercial heart of southern Oregon. Over the next half century

Jacksonville developed into a wealthy town with brick commercial buildings and elegant Victorian homes. However, in the 1880s the railroad running between Portland and San Francisco bypassed Jacksonville in favor of an easier route 5 miles to the east. It was at this spot that the trading town of Medford began to develop.

Despite a short rail line into Jacksonville, over the years more and more business migrated to the main railway in Medford. Jacksonville's fortunes began to decline and, by the time of the Depression, residents were reduced to digging up the streets of town for the gold that lay there. In 1927 the county seat was moved to Medford, and Jacksonville was left with its faded grandeur and memories of better times.

Off the beaten path, forgotten by developers and modernization, Jacksonville inadvertently preserved its past in its buildings. In 1966 the entire town was listed on the National Register of Historic Places, and Jacksonville, with the aid of Britt's photos, began a renaissance that today makes it a historical showcase. Together the Britt Festivals and Jacksonville's history combine to make this one of the most fascinating towns anywhere in the Northwest.

ESSENTIALS

GETTING THERE   Medford is right on I-5 30 miles north of the California state line, and Jacksonville is 5 miles west on Ore. 238.

The **Rogue Valley International Airport,** at 3650 Biddle Rd., Medford, is served by Horizon Air and United Airlines.

VISITOR INFORMATION   Contact the **Jacksonville Chamber of Commerce,** 185 N. Oregon St. (P.O. Box 33), Jacksonville, OR 97530 (☎ **541/ 899-8118**), or the **Greater Medford Visitors & Convention Bureau,** 101 E. Eighth St., Medford OR 97501 (☎ **541/779-4847**).

THE BRITT FESTIVALS

Each summer between mid-June and early September, people gather several nights a week for folk, pop, country, jazz, and classical music concerts and modern dance performances. The Britt Festivals is a celebration of music and the performing arts featuring internationally renowned performers. The setting for the performances is an amphitheater on the grounds of Britt's estate. Located only a block from historic California Street, the ponderosa pine–shaded amphitheater provides not only a great setting for the performances, but a view that takes in distant hills and the valley far below.

Both reserved and general-admission **tickets** are available for most shows. If you opt for a general-admission ticket, arrive early to claim a prime spot on the lawns behind the reserved seats—and be sure to bring a picnic. For information, contact the festival at P.O. Box 1124, Medford, OR 97501 (☎ **541/773-6077** or 800/88-BRITT). Tickets range from $8 to $35.

MUSEUMS & HISTORIC HOMES

With more than 80 buildings listed on the National Register of Historic Places, Jacksonville boasts that it's the most completely preserved historic town in the nation. Whether or not this claim is true, there certainly are enough restored old buildings to make the town a genuine step back in time. Along California Street you'll find restored brick commercial buildings that now house dozens of interesting shops, art galleries, and boutiques. On the side streets you'll see the town's many Victorian homes.

Jacksonville Museum of Southern Oregon History

206 N. Fifth St. ☎ **541/773-6536.** Admission $3 in summer, $2 in winter. Memorial Day–Labor Day, daily 10am–5pm; Labor Day–Memorial Day, Tues and Sun noon–5pm, Wed–Sat 10am–5pm.

In order to get some background on Jacksonville, make this museum your first stop in town. Housed in the old county courthouse, which was built in 1883, the museum has displays on the history of Jacksonville, including 19th-century photos by Peter Britt. Your ticket also gets you into the adjacent Children's Museum, which is housed in the former jail.

Jeremiah Nunan House

635 N. Oregon St. ☎ **541/899-1890.** Admission $5 adults, $4 seniors, $3 children. June–Sept, Mon and Thurs–Sat 10:30am–5pm; Nov–Dec, Fri–Sun 10:30am–5:30pm. Tours every hour on the hour. Closed Jan–May and Oct.

Of the many elegant Victorian homes in town, few are more ornate than the Jeremiah Nunan House. Long known as the Catalog House, the Queen Anne–style Nunan home was ordered in 1892 from a catalog and shipped from Knoxville, Tennessee, in 14 boxcars. The Nunan House has been completely restored and furnished with period antiques.

Beekman House

470 E. California St. ☎ **541/773-6536.** Beekman House, $3; Beekman Bank, free. Beekman House, Memorial Day–Labor Day only, daily 1–5pm. Beekman Bank, Memorial Day to late Sept only, daily 9am–4:30pm.

At the 1876 Beekman House, history comes alive as actors in period costume portray the family of an early Jacksonville banker. The turn-of-the-century **Beekman Bank,** 101 W. California St., is also open to the public.

Southern Oregon History Center

106 N. Central Ave. ☎ **541/773-6536.** Free admission. Mon–Fri 9am–5pm, Sat noon–5pm.

Located in downtown Medford, this large museum is a repository for thousands of artifacts pertaining to the history of this region.

Butte Creek Mill

402 N. Royal Ave., Eagle Point. ☎ **541/826-3531.** Free admission. Mon–Sat 9am–5pm.

In nearby Eagle Point, you can visit Oregon's only operating waterpowered flour mill. The Butte Creek Mill was built in 1873 and its millstones are still grinding out flour. After looking around at the workings of the mill, you can stop in at the mill store and buy a bag of flour or cornmeal.

OTHER ATTRACTIONS

Pears and roses both grow well in the Jacksonville and Medford area, and these crops have given rise to two of the country's best known mail-order businesses. **Harry and David's Original Country Store,** 2836 S. Pacific Hwy. (☎ 541/776-2277), is the retail outlet of a specialty fruit company specializing in mail-order Fruit-of-the-Month Club gift packs. You'll find the store just 1 mile south of Medford at Exit 27 off I-5. You can tour the Harry and David's packing house and then wander through the store in search of bargains. Associated with this store is the **Jackson and Perkins rose test garden** and mail-order rose nursery.

For an overview of Jacksonville's historic buildings, consider a **trolley tour** of town. These leave daily in summer between 10am and 4pm from the corner of Third and California streets; tickets are $4 for adults and $2 for children. For a more elegant tour of town, contact the **Jacksonville Carriage Service** (☎ 541/482-2484). Their tours cost between $15 and $30 per couple.

If you'd like to take a guided tour of the surrounding countryside, contact **Applegate Valley Excursions** (☎ 541/776-9803). Their half-day tours ($10 for adults and $5 for children) include stops at an elk ranch, a winery, a ghost town, and other sites of interest. Each fall in early October, the Jacksonville Boosters Club sponsors a **homes tour** that allows glimpses into many of Jacksonville's most lovingly restored old homes. Contact the Jacksonville Chamber of Commerce for details.

When the Britt Festivals have closed up shop for the year, you can still catch Dixieland jazz at the annual **Medford Jazz Jubilee,** which is held in early October. Three-day passes are $35 to $40.

OUTDOOR ACTIVITIES

Rafting and fishing on the numerous fast-flowing, clear-water rivers of southern Oregon are two of the most popular sports in this region, and Medford makes a good base for doing a bit of either, or both. **Rogue Excursions Unlimited,** White City (☎ 541/826-6222 or 800/460-3865), and **River Trips Unlimited,** 4140 Dry Creek Rd., Medford (☎ 541/779-3798), are two companies operating in the Medford area. Fishing trips cost between $85 and $130 per person for a day's fishing, while a day of rafting will cost around $60. Three- and four-day rafting trips cost $425 to $550.

If you're here in the spring, you can catch the colorful **wildflower displays** at Table Rocks. These mesas are just a few miles northeast of Medford, and because of their great age and unique structure, create a variety of habitats that allow the area to support an unusual diversity of plants. For more information, contact the **Bureau of Land Management,** Medford District Office (☎ 541/770-2200).

Information on hiking and backpacking in the area can be obtained from the **Rogue River National Forest,** 333 W. Eighth St. (P. O. Box 520), Medford, OR 97501 (☎ 541/858-2200).

For a different perspective on this region, try a hot-air balloon ride with **Sunrise Balloon Adventures** (☎ 541/776-2284) or **Oregon Adventures Aloft** (☎ 541/582-0700 or 800/238-0700).

WHERE TO STAY
IN JACKSONVILLE

Jacksonville Inn

175 E. California St., Jacksonville, OR 97530. ☎ **541/899-1900.** 8 rms, 1 cottage. A/C. $80–$125 double; $175 double in cottage. Rates include continental breakfast. AE, CB, DC, DISC, MC, V.

Located right on historic California Street in the heart of the town's restored business district, the Jacksonville Inn is best known for its gourmet restaurant, but upstairs there are eight antique-filled rooms that offer traditional elegance mixed with some modern amenities. Room 1, with its queen-size canopy bed and whirlpool tub for two, is the house favorite. Many rooms have exposed brick walls. Modern bathrooms complement the antique furnishings.

✪ Old Stage Inn

883 Old Stage Rd., Jacksonville, OR 97530. ☎ **541/899-1776** or 800/US-STAGE. 4 rms, 2 with bath. A/C. $75–$90 double without bath, $95–$110 double with bath. Rates include full breakfast. MC, V.

There simply is no better place to stay in southern Oregon. This huge 1857 Greek revival farmhouse sits surrounded by shade trees and lawns a mile north of downtown Jacksonville. In the front parlor, a baby grand piano, fireplace, and gaming table hold promises of long relaxing evenings. Upstairs, three guest rooms offer spaciousness that's enhanced by 11-foot ceilings. In the Bybee Suite, a reproduction antique king-size canopy bed, clawfoot tub, marble fireplace, and a dark and romantic color scheme may convince you to lock yourself in your room and never come out. The two rooms with shared bath are by no means small, and if you balk at the idea of a shared bath, wait till you get a look at the common bathroom, which has a double whirlpool tub. Out behind the main house, in a restored cottage, is another spacious room that also happens to be wheelchair accessible (a rarity in bed-and-breakfasts). Breakfast includes four courses.

Orth House

105 W. Main St., Jacksonville, OR 97530. ☎ **541/899-8665.** Fax 503/899-9146. 2 rms, 1 suite. A/C. $95 double; $175 suite. Rates include full breakfast. MC, V.

This yellow house with its gray trim stands behind majestic old shade trees on a corner one block off busy California Street. The picket fence, old buggy on the lawn, and inviting front porch cry out small-town Americana. Inside, a Victorian sensibility reigns. Small rooms are cheek by jowl with unusual antiques. There's even a small museum room that serves as a guest parlor. What you wouldn't expect in such an antique-filled home are all the little high-tech features that make a stay here just a little bit unusual. Old photos on the walls can talk and tell you their stories, and bird recordings wake you in the morning if the real birds aren't singing. You can choose a room with a clawfoot tub or a whirlpool.

ⓢ The Stage Lodge

830 N. Fifth St., Jacksonville, OR 97530. ☎ **541/899-3953** or 800/253-8254. 27 rms, 2 suites. A/C TV TEL. $67–$72 double; $135 suite. Lower rates Oct–Apr. AE, DC, MC, V.

Jacksonville has plenty of bed-and-breakfast inns, but it's short on moderately priced motels. Filling the bill for the latter category is a motel designed to resemble a 19th-century stage stop, with gables, clapboard siding, and turned-wood railings along two floors of verandas. These details allow the lodge to fit right in with all the original buildings in town. The rooms are spacious and comfortable, and have a few nice touches such as ceiling fans, TV armoires, and country decor.

IN MEDFORD

In addition to the B&B listed below, you'll find dozens of inexpensive chain motels clustered along I-5. These include the **Best Western Medford Inn,** 1015 S. Riverside Ave., Medford, OR 97501 (☎ **541/773-8266**), charging $48 to $85 double; **Comfort Inn,** 1100 Hilton Rd., Medford, OR 97504 (☎ **541/772-9500**), charging $60 to $85 double; and **Motel 6,** 950 Alba Rd., Medford, OR 97504 (☎ **541/773-4290**), charging $35 double.

Under the Greenwood Tree

3045 Bellinger Lane, Medford, OR 97501. ☎ **541/776-0000.** 5 rms. A/C TEL. $95–$125 double. Rates include full breakfast. No credit cards.

Located just west of Medford and taking its name from the 300-year-old oaks that shade the front yard, this bed-and-breakfast offers a step back in time to the days of iced tea on the veranda, croquet on the lawn, and stolen kisses behind the barn. Romance and Americana are the themes here at Under the Greenwood Tree, and you'll find plenty of both. The guest rooms are filled with antiques, and two have separate sitting rooms. Throughout the house you'll find antique quilts and Oriental carpets, which give the inn a touch of country class. Out back is a huge deck overlooking the gazebo, garden, and barns. On the inn's surrounding 10 acres of land, you can explore old barns and granaries. A three-course breakfast and afternoon tea are served.

WHERE TO DINE
IN JACKSONVILLE

Bella Union

170 W. California St. ☎ **541/899-1770.** Main courses $8.50–$18. AE, MC, V. Daily 11am–10pm. ITALIAN/AMERICAN.

For casual dining or someplace to just toss back a cold beer or sip an Italian soda, the Bella Union is Jacksonville's top choice. The lounge hearkens back to the days when the Bella Union was one of Jacksonville's busiest saloons, and in the back of the building are a garden patio and a large bright room that displays works by local artists. However, it's the main dining room up front that's most popular. Old wood floors, storefront windows, and exposed brick walls conjure up images of gold miners out on the town. Meals range from pizzas to a delicious house chicken that's marinated in Gorgonzola and walnut pesto.

Jacksonville Inn

175 E. California St. ☎ **541/899-1900.** Reservations recommended. Main courses $6–$13 at lunch, $11–$40 at dinner; Sun brunch $7–$14. MC, V. Mon 5–10pm, Tues–Sat 7:30–10:30am and 11:30am–10pm, Sun 7:30–9pm. CONTINENTAL.

Old-world atmosphere, either in the basement rathskeller or in the more elegant upstairs dining room, sets the mood for reliable continental fare. Together the cuisine and the decor attract a well-heeled clientele that prefers familiar dishes perfectly prepared rather than adventurous combinations that may or may not hit the mark. However, if surf and turf or veal scaloppine don't excite your taste buds, don't despair—search out the chicken breast with artichoke hearts and feta cheese or the hazelnut prawns with dill beurre blanc. Pears are a mainstay of the local economy and show up frequently in both entrées and desserts. The inn's wineshop gives diners access to a cellar boasting more than 700 wines.

IN MEDFORD

Samovar Restaurant

101 E. Main St. ☎ **541/779-4967.** Reservations recommended on weekends. Main courses $7–$13. MC, V. Mon 7:30am–3pm, Tues–Sat 7:30am–3pm and 5–9pm. RUSSIAN/MIDDLE EASTERN.

At this restaurant run by a Russian couple, you'll find soft lights, tablecloths, and classical music—an unexpected scene in downtown Medford. Bakery products made with whole grains, fresh produce, and low-fat poultry and meats are the mainstay ingredients for dishes such as a bracing and delicious borscht, with cabbage, tomatoes, and beets (and topped with sour cream, of course). Other Russian and Middle Eastern favorites are blintzes, piroshki (flaky dough pies stuffed with cheese or meat), stuffed cabbage, and skewered kebabs of lamb or chicken. To top off your meal, baklava and Russian and Napoleon tortes are available from the bakery to eat in or take out.

Streams

1841 Barnett Rd. ☎ **541/776-9090.** Reservations recommended on weekends. Main courses $7–$13. AE, DISC, MC, V. Mon–Fri 11:30am–2pm and 4:30–9pm, Sat–Sun 4:30–9pm (5–9:30pm daily in winter). INTERNATIONAL/NORTHWEST.

Streams serves "food that doesn't sit in your stomach like a lead weight"—that is, light and wholesome dishes such as pasta and vegetables, fettuccine with sausage or smoked salmon, toasted almonds, vegetables, and rosemary cream (they make their own pasta, by the way). On the more robust side, charcoal-broiled steaks and pork with apples, mushrooms, cider, and cinnamon can also be enticing. Streams is located just east of I-5.

A FUN TOURIST TRAP ALONG THE DRIVE TO GRANTS PASS

About midway between Medford and Grants Pass and just 4 miles off I-5 is one of Oregon's most curious attractions—the **Oregon Vortex and House of Mystery,** 4303 Sardine Creek Rd. (☎ **541/855-1543**). This classic tourist trap is guaranteed to have the kids, and some adults, oohing and aahing in bug-eyed amazement at the numerous phenomena that defy the laws of physics. People grow taller as they recede. You, and the trees surrounding the House of Mystery, lean toward magnetic north rather than stand upright. Seeing is believing—or is it? Open March to May and in September and October, daily from 9am to 5pm; June to August, daily from 9am to 6pm (closed November through January). Admission is $6 for adults, $4.50 for children 5 to 11.

3 Grants Pass: A Great Base for Enjoying the Outdoors

63 miles S of Roseburg, 40 miles NW of Ashland, 82 miles NE of Crescent City

IT'S THE CLIMATE proclaims a sign at the entrance to Grants Pass, and with weather almost as reliably pleasant as California's, the town has become a popular base for outdoor activities of all kinds. With the Rogue River running through the center of town, it's not surprising that most local recreational activities focus around the water. Located at the junction of I-5 and U.S. 199, Grants Pass is also the last large town in Oregon if you're heading over to the redwoods, which are about 90 miles southwest on the northern California coast. A similar distance to the northeast, you'll find Crater Lake National Park, so Grants Pass makes a good base if you're trying to see a lot of this region in a short time.

ESSENTIALS

GETTING THERE   Grants Pass is at the junction of I-5 and U.S. 199.

The **Rogue Valley International Airport,** at 3650 Biddle Rd. in Medford, is served by Horizon Air and United Airlines.

VISITOR INFORMATION   Contact the **Grants Pass–Josephine County Chamber of Commerce,** 1501 NE Sixth St. (P.O. Box 970), Grants Pass, OR 97526 (☎ 541/476-7717 or 800/547-5927).

FESTIVALS   Boatnik, held Memorial Day weekend, is Grants Pass's biggest annual festival and includes boat races on the Rogue River as well as lots of festivities at Riverside Park.

OUTDOOR ACTIVITIES: RAFTING, FISHING, HIKING & MORE

Grants Pass is located midway between the source and the mouth of the **Rogue River** and is an ideal base for river-oriented activities. The Rogue, first made famous by western-novelist and avid fly-fisherman Zane Grey and recently the location for scenes in the film *The River Wild,* is now preserved for much of its length as a National Wild and Scenic River. Originating in Crater Lake National Park, the river twists and tumbles through narrow gorges and steep mountains as it winds its way to the coast at Gold Beach. The most famous section of the river is 250-foot-deep **Hellgate Canyon,** where the river narrows and rushes through a cleft in the rock. The canyon can be seen from an overlook on Merlin-Galice Road, which begins at Exit 61 off I-5. From the Interstate it's about 10 miles to the canyon overlook.

Several companies offer **river trips** of varying length and in various watercraft. You can even spend several days rafting the river with stops each night at riverside lodges. If you have only enough time for a short trip on the river, we'd recommend a jet-boat trip up to Hellgate Canyon, the most scenic spot on this section of the river. **Hellgate Excursions,** 953 SE Seventh St. (☎ 541/479-7204 or 800/648-4874), operates four different jet-boat trips, with prices ranging from $21 to $39.

Local **white-water rafting** companies offer half-day, full-day, and multiday trips, with multiday trips stopping either at rustic river lodges or at campsites along the river banks. Rafting companies include **Rogue Wilderness,** 325 Galice Rd. (☎ 541/479-9554 or 800/336-1647); **Galice Resort,** 11744 Galice Rd. (☎ 541/476-3818); **Orange Torpedo Trips,** 209 Merlin Rd. (☎ 541/479-5061); and **Rogue River Raft Trips,** Morrison's Lodge, 8500 Galice Rd. (☎ 541/476-3825). Rates are around $40 for a half day, $50 for a full day, $175 to $225 for a two-day camping trip, and as $550 to $660 for a four-day lodge-to-lodge trip. Two-day lodge trips start around $225 per person and four-day camping trips are $435.

At several places near town, you can **rent rafts and kayaks** of different types and paddle yourself downriver. Try **White Water Cowboys,** 209 Merlin Rd., Merlin (☎ 541/479-0132); or **Galice Resort Store,** 11744 Galice Rd., Merlin (☎ 541/476-3818). Rental rates are between $20 and $65 per day.

If **fishing** is your passion, the steelhead and salmon of the Rogue River already haunt your dreams. To make those dreams a reality, you'll want to hire a guide to take you where the fish are sure to bite. Rogue Wilderness and Rogue River Raft Trips, both mentioned above, offer guided fishing trips of one to four days. Expect to pay between $100 and $125 for a day of fishing.

Hikers and backpackers will find a 180,000-acre botanical wonderland in the **Kalmiopsis Wilderness** of the Siskiyou National Forest. The wilderness area is west of Cave Junction. For more information, contact the **Siskiyou National Forest,** 200 NE Greenfield Rd. (P.O. Box 440), Grants Pass, OR 97526 (☎ 541/471-6500).

If you'd like to do a bit of horseback riding, try **Lake Selmac Trail Rides,** Selma (☎ 541/597-4989), which is 23 miles south of Grants Pass on U.S. 199.

Golfers can play a round at the **Red Mountain Golf Course,** 324 N. Schoolhouse Creek Rd. (☎ 541/479-2297), which is 15 minutes north of Grants Pass, or at the **Dutcher Creek Golf Course,** 4611 Upper River Rd. (☎ 541/474-2188).

Fans of horse racing can bet on the ponies at **Grants Pass Downs** at the Josephine County Fairgrounds (☎ 541/476-3215) on U.S. 199 west of town. The season runs from Memorial Day to the Fourth of July.

OTHER ATTRACTIONS & ACTIVITIES

Though most people visiting Grants Pass are here to enjoy the mountains and rivers surrounding the town, history buffs can pick up a free map of the town's historic buildings at the Tourist Information Center. Two small art museums— the **Grants Pass Museum of Art,** 304 SE Park St. (☎ 541/479-3290), in Riverside Park, and the **Wiseman Gallery,** 3345 Redwood Hwy., at Rogue Community College (☎ 541/471-3500, ext. 224)—offer changing exhibits of classic and contemporary art by local and national artists.

Wildlife Images Rehabilitation and Education Center, 11845 Lower River Rd. (☎ 541/476-0222), is dedicated to nurturing injured birds of prey and other wild animals back to health. The center is located 13 miles south of Grants Pass and is open for tours Tuesday through Sunday at 11am and 1pm by reservation only. Admission is by donation.

Riverside Park, in the center of town, is a popular place to play, especially in the warmer months when people come to cool off in the river.

It seems you're never far from a winery in the Northwest, and Grants Pass is no exception. **Rogue River Winery,** 3145 Helms Rd. (☎ 541/476-1051), is about 7 miles west of town just off U.S. 199. Other nearby wineries include **Foris,** 654 Kendall Rd. (☎ 541/592-3752), and **Bridgeview,** 4210 Holland Loop Rd. (☎ 541/592-4688), both of which are near Cave Junction, 32 miles southwest of Grants Pass. Cabernet sauvignon, merlot, chardonnay, riesling, and Muller-Thurgau are the most common varietals produced in this region. You'll see signs for these wineries along U.S. 199 and Ore. 46.

The concentration of theatrical talent down in Ashland seems to be spreading throughout southern Oregon. Here in Grants Pass, you can catch good community theater in the staging of musicals by the **Rogue Music Theatre** (☎ 541/479-2559), with its summer performances in an outdoor amphitheater on the campus of Rogue Community College just south of town on U.S. 199. Another local company, **Barnstormers Little Theatre,** 112 NE Evelyn St. (☎ 541/479-3557), stages contemporary and classic dramas and comedies.

WHERE TO STAY

Paradise Ranch Inn
7000-D Monument Dr., Grants Pass, OR 97526. ☎ 541/479-4333. Fax 503/479-7821. 18 rms, 1 cottage, 1 house. A/C. $40–$90 double; $70–$100 cottage; $400 house (or $90–$125 per room). Rates include continental breakfast. MC, V.

Rolling green hills, white wooden fences, a big barn converted into a lounge—the Paradise Ranch Inn has all the trappings of a classic guest ranch. Add to the picture-perfect setting a golf course, several ponds and lakes, tennis courts, a swimming pool, and a gourmet restaurant and you have the makings of a relaxing resort. The guest rooms are furnished in a very traditional style.

Dining/Entertainment: The inn's dining room overlooks the golf course, a lake, and the nearby mountains. You can dine inside or out on the deck. The continental cuisine is some of the best in southern Oregon, and entrée prices are in the $12 to $20 range.

Facilities: Swimming pool, golf course, tennis courts, jogging path, whirlpool, volleyball, fishing lake, bicycles, boating.

⑤ Riverside Inn Resort & Conference Center

971 SE Sixth St., Grants Pass, OR 97526. ☎ **541/476-6873** or 800/334-4567. Fax 503/ 474-9848. 174 rms. A/C TV TEL. $55–$175 double. AE, CB, DC, DISC, MC, V.

Located in downtown Grants Pass, the Riverside Inn is, as the name implies, right on the bank of the Rogue River. A weathered wood exterior and cedar-shingle roof give the two-story inn a bit of Northwest flavor, though the setting between two busy bridges is not exactly idyllic. Luckily, a park across the river means the views from most rooms are quite pleasant.

The inn sprawls across three blocks, and rooms vary in age and quality. Our favorites are the fireplace rooms in the west section. Avoid the rooms near the road, which can be quite noisy. Though the river-view rooms are a bit more expensive than nonview rooms, they're certainly worth the price.

The inn's restaurant and lounge offer a great view of the river and some of the best meals in town.

NEARBY PLACES TO STAY

✪ Morrison's Rogue River Lodge

8500 Galice Rd., Merlin, OR 97532. ☎ **541/476-3825** or 800/826-1963. 4 rms, 9 cabins. $160–$240 double in rooms or cabins. Rates include all meals. MC, V. Closed Dec–Apr.

If you're in the area to do a bit of fishing or rafting, we can think of no better place to stay than at Morrison's. Perched on the banks of the Rogue, this fishing lodge epitomizes the Rogue River experience. The main lodge is a massive log building that's rustic yet comfortable, and has a wall of glass that looks across wide lawns to the river. There are bed-and-breakfast–style accommodations in this building, but we prefer the spacious cabins. These latter stand beneath grand old trees and all have good views of the river. Fireplaces will keep you warm and cozy in the cooler months.

Dining/Entertainment: The dining room serves surprisingly creative four-course dinners. For nonguests, dinner is available for $18 to $25. Reservations are required.

Services: Fishing guides, rafting trips.

Facilities: Outdoor pool, tennis courts, putting green, private beach.

Pine Meadow Inn

1000 Crow Rd., Merlin, OR 97532. ☎ **541/471-6277** or 800/554-0806. 3 rms. A/C. $95–$110 double. Rates include full breakfast. No credit cards.

This modern farmhouse B&B sits between a meadow and a pine forest on 9 acres of land near the Rogue River. The setting is secluded and very relaxing, with a hot tub and koi pond in the back yard. The guest rooms are furnished with antiques and have fresh flowers on the guests' arrival. Two rooms have mountain views, while the third overlooks the gardens and forest.

⑤ Wolf Creek Tavern

P.O. Box 97, Wolf Creek, OR 97497. ☎ **541/866-2474.** 8 rms. $55–$75 double. DISC, MC, V.

Originally opened in the 1870s on the old stagecoach road between Sacramento and Portland, the Wolf Creek Tavern is a two-story clapboard building with wide front verandas along both floors. Today the inn, which is 18 miles north of Grants

Pass and just off I-5, is the oldest hotel in Oregon. Owned by the Oregon State Parks and Recreation Division, the inn was completely restored in 1978 and reopened in 1979. The interior is furnished in period antiques dating from the 1870s to the 1930s. The ladies' parlor downstairs features 1870s vintage antiques, a piano, and old photos. On a winter's night there's no cozier spot than by the fireplace here. The guest rooms are small and simply furnished much as they may have been in the early 1900s. The spartan guest rooms are more than compensated for by the excellent meals served in the inn's dining room. Waitresses in 19th-century costumes serve the likes of Cornish pasties, coquilles St-Jacques, chicken Kiev, and filet mignon.

CAMPGROUNDS

There are several county-operated campgrounds near Grants Pass. These include **Indian Mary Park,** near Galice on Merlin-Galice Road; **Schroeder Park,** off Ore. 199 (the Redwood Highway) only a mile or so out of town; and **Whitehorse Park,** on Lower River Road about 2¹/₂ miles out of town. There are also two national forest campgrounds near the entrance to **Oregon Caves National Monument.**

WHERE TO DINE

Hamilton House

344 NE Terry Lane. ☎ **541/479-3938.** Reservations recommended. Main courses $7.50–$15. AE, MC, V. Daily 5–9pm. CONTINENTAL.

You'll find this attractive old house tucked in between the Walmart and the Fred Meyer just off E Street. The Hamilton House does a respectable job and there's no denying that the garden views through most of the windows add to a meal. In summer there's also patio dining. The menu includes a torta of creamed cheeses layered with pesto and dried tomatoes that makes a great start to a meal. We prefer the chicken and seafood dishes here. You'll find such entrées as spicy pasta jambalaya; scampi made with basil, sherry, and capers; and chicken piccata sautéed in lemon and wine with capers.

Legrand's Bakery/Restaurant

323 NE E St. ☎ **541/471-1554.** Main courses $9–$17; lunch $4–$10. MC, V. Mon–Thurs 11am–2:30pm and 5–9pm, Fri–Sat 8:30am–2:30pm and 5–10pm, Sun 8:30am–2:30pm and 5–9pm. INTERNATIONAL.

Housed in a small bungalow, Legrand's has a genteel but casual French ambience that make it the place to go in Grants Pass for anything from a croissant to duck à l'orange. For lunch, simple and satisfying standards such as curried chicken salad on crusty bread or pasta primavera are served. It's difficult not to ogle the pastry case, which contains the likes of fruit tarts and margarita cake made with tequila.

Matsukaze

1675 NE Seventh St. ☎ **541/479-2961.** Main courses $6.50–$15. DISC, MC, V. Mon–Thurs 11am–2pm and 5–9pm, Fri 11am–2pm and 5–9:30pm, Sat 5–9:30pm. JAPANESE.

This little restaurant is a Grants Pass favorite and is always busy. Casual, friendly, and very reasonably priced, Matsukaze is a surprising treat for travelers visiting this area. If you're not too hungry, you might want to opt for some airy tempura or one of the light dinners. But if you're ravenous, there's the "Killer Hawaiian" steak, a 10-ounce rib eye rubbed with rock salt and garlic and served with wild mushrooms. To finish off your meal, there's the traditional green-tea ice cream, a definite must in the summer.

✪ Meadowview Country Cottage Cafe & Tea Room

2315 Upper River Road Loop. ☎ **541/471-8841.** Salads/sandwiches $4–$7. DISC, MC, V. Mon–Sat 11am–4pm. Drive west on G Street and look for the sign; it's 1¹/₂ miles from downtown Grants Pass. SALADS/SANDWICHES.

Located out in the country and surrounded by flower and vegetable gardens, this casual restaurant provides a glimpse of the good life, Grants Pass style. If you like gardens, you'll especially enjoy a meal here in high summer when the gardens are bursting with life. Lunch (often busy and popular with groups) and high tea are served inside or outside on the lawn. The café uses organically grown produce.

✪ Pongsri's

1571 NE Sixth Ave. ☎ **541/479-1345.** Main courses $5.50–$7.50. MC, V. Tues–Sun 11am–9pm. THAI/CHINESE.

Located in a nondescript old shopping center near the Grants Pass Visitor Information Center, Pongsri's is a tiny Thai restaurant that's considered by many locals to serve the best food in town. The long menu includes plenty of choices, including lots of seafood. The shrimp satay appetizer consists of 10 succulent jumbo shrimp served with a piquant peanut sauce. If you like shrimp as much as we do, you'll also opt for the tom yum gung, a sour-and-spicy soup that's guaranteed to clear your sinuses. Vegetarians have lots of options here too, and the lunch special for $3.25 just can't be beat.

A SIDE TRIP TO OREGON CAVES NATIONAL MONUMENT

High in the rugged Siskiyou Mountains a clear mountain stream cascades through a narrow canyon, and here stands one of southern Oregon's oldest attractions. Known as the marble halls of Oregon and first discovered in 1874, the Oregon Caves are 50 miles south of Grants Pass. The caves, which stretch for 3 miles under the mountain, were formed by water seeping through marble bedrock. The slight acidity of the water dissolves the marble, which is later redeposited as beautiful stalactites, stalagmites, draperies, soda straws, columns, and flowstone.

Guided tours of the caves take about an hour and a half. Back up above ground there are several miles of hiking trails that start near the cave entrance.

For information, contact **Oregon Caves National Monument,** 19000 Caves Hwy. (☎ 541/592-2100). Admission is $5.75 for adults, $3.50 for children 6 to 11. It's open in May and June, daily from 9am to 5pm; June to September, daily from 8am to 7pm; and in September and October, daily from 8:30am to 5pm. From Grants Pass, head south on U.S. 199 to Cave Junction, pick up Ore. 46 east, and follow the signs.

WHERE TO STAY

Oregon Caves Château

P.O. Box 128, Cave Junction, OR 97523. ☎ **541/592-3400.** 22 rms. $59–$79 double. MC, V. Closed Jan–Feb.

A narrow road winds for 20 miles south into the Siskiyou National Forest climbing through deep forests before finally coming to an end in a narrow, steep-walled canyon. At the very head of this canyon stands the Oregon Caves Château, a rustic six-story lodge built in 1934. Huge fir beams support the lobby ceiling and two marble fireplaces beckon (it can be cool here any time of year). About the only thing that's missing from this alpine setting is a view. Because the lodge is in a canyon surrounded by tall trees, there are no sweeping vistas. The guest rooms, unfortunately, have rather unattractive furnishings, but you can spend your time in the attractive lobby. A 1930s-style soda fountain serves burgers, shakes, and other simple meals, while in the main dining room dinners of steaks and seafood are available.

WHERE TO DINE

✪ Pizza Deli & Brewery

249 N. Redwood Hwy. ☎ **541/592-3556.** Sandwiches $2.50–$4.25; pizzas $2.90–$17. No credit cards. Mon–Sat 10am–10pm, Sun noon–9:30pm. PIZZA/DELI.

If you're a fan of microbrewery ales, a pleasant surprise awaits you in the crossroads community of Cave Junction. This very casual combination pizza parlor and deli also happens to be a respectable little brewery specializing in British ales. The rich and flavorful ales go great with the pizzas, several of which are made with locally made sausage. And for fans of the unusual, there's a pizza with smoked sausage and sauerkraut and another with avocado and sprouts.

EXPLORING NORTH OF GRANTS PASS

There are a number of interesting options as you head north from Grants Pass along I-5 toward Eugene. If you've got a sweet tooth, you may want to pull off the Interstate at Exit 86 (Azalea) and check out **Heaven on Earth,** 703 Quines Creek Rd. (☎ **541/837-3596**), which serves legendary cinnamon rolls, blackberry pies, and turnovers.

THE ROSEBURG AREA

Wildlife Safari

Off Ore. 42, just outside Winston (south of Roseburg). ☎ **541/679-6761.** Admission $11.75 adults, $9.75 seniors, $6.75 children 3 and over, free for children 2 and under. Summer, daily 9am–7pm; winter, daily 9am–4pm.

This 600-acre drive-through nature park is home to wild animals from around the world. You'll come face to face with curious bears, grazing gazelles and zebras, shy ostriches, and even lumbering elephants and rhinos. In addition to the drive through the park, you can ride an elephant, visit the educational center, or attend an animal show. Signs as you approach let you know that convertibles are not allowed in the lion or bear enclosures (but rental cars are available).

Douglas County Museum of History & Natural History

Douglas County Fairgrounds. ☎ **541/440-4507.** Free admission. Tues–Sat 10am–4pm, Sun noon–4pm.

South of town at the Douglas County Fairgrounds you'll find this surprisingly large and well-designed museum. The unusual, large building that houses it resembles an old mining structure or mill. Inside are displays on the history and natural history of the region. Pioneer farming and mining displays interpret the settlement of the region, but it's the saber-tooth tiger skeleton that really grabs people's attention.

A DETOUR EAST OF ROSEBURG ALONG THE NORTH UMPQUA

Ore. 138, which heads east out of Roseburg, leads to Diamond Lake and the north entrance to Crater Lake National Park, but it's also one of the state's most scenic highways. Along much of its length, you'll follow the **North Umpqua River,** which is famed among anglers for its fly fishing.

Your first stop out of Roseburg on Ore. 138 should be at the **Colliding Rivers Viewpoint,** 12 miles east of Roseburg in the town of Glide. Oregon abounds in waterfalls and white-water rivers, but this is the only place in the state where rivers collide. The North Umpqua River rushing in from the north slams into the white water of the Little River, which flows from the south. The two rivers create a churning stew that's forced westward toward the Pacific Ocean.

Farther along this road, you'll be paralleling the North Umpqua River, a wild river well-known among anglers for its steelhead fishing. There are several picnic areas on the banks of the river, and trails provide access to the water. Continuing on, you pass several waterfalls, including **Toketee Falls,** one of the most photographed waterfalls in the state. After leaving the banks of the river, the highway continues on to **Diamond Lake,** one of the most popular recreational spots in the state. Just beyond this lake is the north entrance to Crater Lake National Park.

If you'd like to do a bit of **fishing** on the Rogue River, you can cast a fly wherever the water looks fishy, or you can contact river and fishing guide **Jerry Q. Phelps** (☎ **541/672-8324**), who can take you to holes where you're almost certain to hook a steelhead or salmon. Rates are $100 to $150 per day for one person and $150 to $200 per day for two people.

If you'd rather just paddle the river in a kayak or raft, contact **North Umpqua Outfitters** (☎ **541/673-4599**) or **Oregon Ridge & River Excursions** (☎ **541/496-3333**). Rates are around $45 for a half-day trip.

Where to Stay & Dine

✪ Steamboat Inn

Steamboat, OR 97447-9703. ☎ **541/498-2411.** Fax 541/498-2411*2. 12 rms, 2 suites. $85–$125 double; $195 suite. MC, V.

Although it's located more than 50 miles northwest of Crater Lake, this inn on the bank of the North Umpqua River is one of the region's finest lodgings. The lodge appeals most to anglers but the gourmet meals served here each evening have become legendary and now attract many gastronomes. Dinners are multicourse affairs served in a cozy dining room.

If you aren't springing for one of the suites, which have their own soaking tubs overlooking the river, your best bet will be the streamside cabins. These rooms are beside the main lodge and feature a comfortably rustic styling and decks that overlook the river. The hideaway cottages are more spacious but don't have river views and are half a mile from the lodge (and the dining room). There's a fly-fishing shop on the premises.

OAKLAND

About 15 miles north of Roseburg is the historic town of Oakland, which is listed on the National Register of Historic Places. Though the town was founded in the 1850s, most of the buildings here date from the 1890s. A stroll through town soaking up the atmosphere is a pleasant way to spend a morning or an afternoon. You can pick up a self-guided walking-tour map at the **Oakland Museum,** 130 Locust St. (☎ **541/459-4531**), which is housed in an 1893 brick building and contains collections of historic photos, old farm tools, household furnishings, and clothing from Oakland's past. The admission-free museum is open daily from 1 to 4:30pm.

Where to Stay

The Beckley House Bed & Breakfast

338 SE Second St., Oakland, OR 97462. ☎ **541/459-9320.** 2 rms. $65–$80 double. Rates include continental breakfast. No credit cards.

If you enjoy the atmosphere in Oakland, maybe you'll want to stick around and spend the night at the Beckley House B&B. This Queen Anne–style Victorian home dates back to the late 1800s and is furnished with period antiques.

Where to Dine

✪ Tolly's

115 Locust St. ☎ **541/459-3796.** Main courses $7–$19. AE, MC, V. Soda fountain, daily 9am–5pm. Dining room, Tues–Sun 5–9pm. AMERICAN.

Since 1964 folks from all over the region have been dropping in on Oakland to have dinner or just a root-beer float or sundae here at Tolly's. Housed in a store-front on Locust Street, Tolly's is both an elegant restaurant and an old-fashioned soda fountain. You can hop onto a stool at the counter and linger over a cold malted-milk shake in a tall glass, or head upstairs for a dinner of steak or perfectly prepared salmon. Attached to the restaurant are both an antiques shop and an art gallery.

A SERIOUS ICE CREAM STOP IN RICE HILL

Consider yourself very lucky if you happen to be driving north from Roseburg on I-5 on a hot summer day. Respite from the heat lies just off the Interstate at the Rice Hill exit ramp where you'll find the legendary **K-R Drive Inn,** where every scoop of ice cream you order is actually a double scoop! Consider this before you order a double scoop of rocky road. The K-R is open daily from 9:30am to 9pm.

4 Crater Lake National Park

71 miles NE of Medford, 83 miles E of Roseburg, 57 miles N of Klamath Falls

At 1,932 feet deep, Crater Lake is the deepest lake in the United States (in fact, it ranks seventh in the world). But depth alone is not what has made this one of the most visited spots in the Northwest—it's the startling sapphire-blue waters. They've mesmerized visitors ever since a prospector searching for gold stumbled on the high mountain lake in 1853. The lake and its surroundings became a national park in 1902 and to this day it's still the only national park in Oregon.

The caldera (crater) that today holds the serene lake was born in an explosive volcanic eruption 7,700 years ago. When the volcano now known as Mount Mazama erupted, its summit (thought to have been around 12,000 feet high) collapsed, leaving a crater 4,000 feet deep. It has taken thousands of years of rain and melting snow to create the cold, clear lake we now know as Crater Lake, which today is surrounded by crater walls nearly 2,000 feet high.

The drive into the park winds through forests that hold not a hint of the spectacular sight that lies hidden among these mountains. With no warning except the signs leading to Rim Village, you suddenly find yourself gazing down into a vast bowl full of blue water. Toward one end of the lake, the cone of Wizard Island rises from the lake. This island is the tip of a volcano that has been slowly building since the last eruption of Mount Mazama.

ESSENTIALS

GETTING THERE   If you're coming from the south on I-5, take Exit 62 in Medford and follow Ore. 62 for 75 miles. If you're coming from the north, take Exit 124 in Roseburg and follow Ore. 138. From Klamath Falls, take U.S. 97 north to Ore. 62.

VISITOR INFORMATION   For more information, contact **Crater Lake National Park,** P.O. Box 7, Crater Lake, OR 97604 (Tel. **541/594-2211**).

For more information on activities just outside the park, contact the **Diamond Lake Ranger District,** HC 60, Box 101, Idleyld Park, OR 97447 (☎ **541/ 498-2531**); the **Umpqua National Forest,** 2900 NW Stewart Pkwy. (P.O. Box 1008), Roseburg, OR 97470 (☎ **541/672-6601**); or the **Diamond Lake Visitor Center,** Chemult, OR 97731 (☎ **541/793-3310**).

ADMISSION   Park admission is $5 per vehicle and $3 per person for pedestrians and cyclists.

SEEING THE HIGHLIGHTS

After your first breathtaking view of the lake, you may want to stop by one of the park's two visitor centers—**Steel Information Center** and the **Rim Village Visitor Center.** Though the park is open year round, in winter, when deep snows blanket the region, only the road to Rim Village is kept clear. During the summer (roughly beginning in late June), the **Rim Drive** provides many viewpoints as it makes a 39-mile-long circuit of the lake.

There are many activities available in the park, but the most popular are **boat trips** around the lake. These tours last two hours and begin at Cleetwood Cove, which is at the bottom of a very steep 1-mile trail that descends 700 feet from the rim to the lakeshore. Before deciding to take a boat tour, be sure you're in good enough physical condition to make the steep climb back up to the rim. Also, be sure to bring warm clothes, as it can be quite a bit cooler on the lake than it is on the rim. A naturalist on each boat provides a narrative on the ecology and history of the lake, and all tours include a stop on Wizard Island. Tours are offered from late June to mid-September and cost $10 for adults and $5.50 for children.

Other park activities include children's programs, campfire ranger talks, history talks, and guided walks.

Many miles of **hiking and cross-country skiing trails** can be found within the park, but the mile-long **Cleetwood Trail** is the only trail that leads from the rim to the lake. It's a steep and tiring hike back up from the lake. Although it's a rigorous 2¹/₂-mile hike, the trail to the top of **Mount Scott** is the park's most rewarding hike. Shorter trails with good views include the 0.8-mile trail to the top of the **Watchman,** which overlooks Wizard Island, and the 1.7-mile trail up **Garfield Peak.** The short **Castle Crest Wildflower Trail** is best hiked in late July and early August. Backpackers can hike the length of the park on the **Pacific Crest Trail (PCT),** which is in the process of being rerouted so that it travels along the rim (currently the PCT gives the lake a wide berth).

In winter cross-country skiing is popular on the park's snow-covered roads and in the backcountry. The **Diamond Lake Resort Cross Country Ski Center** (☎ **800/733-7593**) in Diamond Lake offers snowcat ski tours on the north side of the park. These tours are $35 per person.

NEARBY ATTRACTIONS & ACTIVITIES

Surrounding Crater Lake National Park are several national forests that offer a bounty of outdoor recreational activities. Among the most popular spots in the region is **Diamond Lake,** which is located only a few miles north of the national park's north entrance. At almost a mile in elevation, Diamond Lake is set at the foot of jagged Mount Thielsen, which is known as the "lightning rod of the Cascades." The lake offers swimming, boating, fishing, camping, hiking, biking, and snowmobiling and skiing in winter.

Although there's no downhill ski area in the vicinity, **Mount Bailey Snowcats** (☎ 541/793-3333) provides access to untracked snow on the slopes of nearby Mount Bailey. A day of snowcat skiing runs $160. Cross-country skiers will find rentals and groomed trails at the **Diamond Lake Resort Cross Country Ski Center** (☎ 800/733-7593).

Near the community of Union Creek, west of the park, are the **Rogue River Gorge** and a natural bridge. The gorge is only a few feet wide in places and has an easy trail running alongside. The natural bridge is formed by a lava tube through which flows the Rogue River.

WHERE TO STAY & DINE

✪ Crater Lake Lodge

400 Rim Village Dr., Crater Lake, OR 97604. ☎ **541/594-2511.** Fax 541/594-2622. 71 rms. $99–$169 double. MC, V. Closed mid-Oct to mid-May.

This lodge on the rim overlooking Crater Lake reopened in mid-1995 after a complete reconstruction. The old lodge was in such bad shape when renovation began that only 10% was salvaged. However, despite the loss of most of the original building, this lodge has the look and feel of a historic mountain lodge yet now has modern conveniences as well. Among the lodge's few original features are the stone fireplace and ponderosa pine–bark walls in the Great Hall. Slightly more than half the guest rooms overlook the lake, and although most of the rooms have modern bathrooms, there are eight rooms with clawfoot bathtubs. The dining room serves creative Northwest cuisine and provides a view of both Crater Lake and the Klamath River basin.

Diamond Lake Resort

Diamond Lake, OR 97731. ☎ **541/793-3333** or 800/733-7593. 40 rms, 10 studios, 42 cabins. TV. $56 double; $58 studio for two; $88–$135 cabin. MC, V.

Located on the shores of Diamond Lake near the north entrance to the national park, this resort has long been a popular family vacation spot, and with Mounts Thielsen and Bailey flanking the lake, this is one of the most picturesque settings in the Oregon Cascades. The variety of accommodations provides plenty of choices, but our favorites are the lakefront cabins. These have great views of the lake and mountains. If you want to do your own cooking, you'll find kitchenettes in both the cabins and studios. The lodge offers several dining options.

Boat and mountain-bike rentals are available, and there's a small sandy beach at the resort. In winter the resort is popular with both downhill and cross-country skiers as well as snowmobilers.

Mazama Village Motor Inn

P.O. Box 128, Crater Lake, OR 97604. ☎ **541/594-2511.** Fax 541/594-2622. 40 rms. $59–$74 double. MC, V. Closed Nov–May.

Though the Mazama Village Motor Inn isn't on the rim of the crater, it's just a short drive away. The modern motel-style guest rooms are housed in 10 steep-roofed buildings that look much like traditional mountain cabins. A laundry, gas station, and general store make Mazama Village a busy spot in the summer.

⑤ Prospect Historical Hotel and Motel

391 Millcreek Rd., Prospect, OR 97536. ☎ **541/560-3664** or 800/944-6490. Fax 503/560-3825. 23 rms. $50–$80 double. DISC, MC, V.

This hotel, located in the tiny hamlet of Prospect, 30 miles from Crater Lake's Rim Village, is a combination of an 1889 vintage hotel and a modern motel. The old hotel is a big white building with a wraparound porch on which are set several bent-willow couches. The small rooms in the historic hotel have few furnishings, but they do have a country styling that gives them a bit of charm. If you stay in one of these rooms, a continental breakfast is included. The motel rooms are much larger and feature such modern conveniences as televisions and telephones, and some of these rooms also have kitchenettes. An elegant dining room is well known for its excellent meals. Sunday brunch is particularly popular. The dinner menu includes such dishes as Jamaican jerk chicken, rack of lamb, and shrimp scampi. Entrée prices range from $9 to $15.

Union Creek Resort

56484 Ore. 62, Prospect, OR 97536. ☎ **541/560-3339** or 541/560-3565. 9 rms, 15 cabins. $38–$48 double; $45–$80 cabin for two. MC, V.

Located almost across the road from the Rogue River Gorge, the resort has been catering to Crater Lake visitors since the early 1900s. Today there are both lodge rooms and cabins available, and most have been updated in recent years. Most of the cabins have kitchenettes. Tall trees shade the grounds of the rustic resort, which is right on Ore. 62 about 23 miles from Rim Village. Across the road from the cabins and lodge building is Beckie's Café, which serves home-style meals and is best known for its pies.

CAMPGROUNDS

Tent camping and RV spaces are available on the south side of the park at the **Mazama Village Campground,** where there are 198 sites ($11 per night). There are also 16 tent sites available at **Lost Creek Campground** ($10 per night) on the park's east side. These campgrounds are open from June to October. Reservations are not accepted at either campground If you're a backpacker, there's camping in the park's backcountry.

Four miles north of the park's north entrance, Diamond Lake has three **U.S. Forest Service campgrounds**–Diamond Lake, Broken Arrow, and Thielsen View–with a total of 450 campsites. Here you'll also find the **Diamond Lake RV Park** (☎ **541/793-3318**) 4 miles north of the park's north entrance.

15 Central & Eastern Oregon

On the west side of the Cascade Range, rain is as certain as death and taxes. But cross the invisible dividing line formed by the mountains and you leave the deluge behind. Central and eastern Oregon bask under blue skies nearly 300 days of the year—in fact, they get so little rain that the region is considered a desert. Such a natural attraction is a constant enticement to Oregonians living west of the Cascades. They head east in summer for hiking, fishing, rafting, and camping, and in winter they descend on Bend and the nearby ski slopes of Mount Bachelor. This vast region is crossed by few roads and takes time to explore, but outdoors enthusiasts will be rewarded.

1 Bend: Skiing, Hiking, Fishing, Mountain Scenery & More

160 miles SE of Portland, 241 miles SW of Pendleton

Situated on the banks of the Deschutes River, this town was originally named Farewell Bend but said goodbye to its Farewell in 1905 at the insistence of postal authorities. Lumber mills supported the local economy for much of Bend's history, but today retirees, skiers, and lovers of the outdoors are fueling the town's growth.

Today, with only about 30,000 residents, Bend is still the largest city east of the Oregon Cascades, and the surrounding area has more resorts than any other location in the state. To understand why a small town on the edge of a vast high desert could attract so many vacationers, just look to the sky. It's blue. And the sun is shining. For the webfoots who spend months under gray skies west of the Cascades, that's enough of an attraction.

However, Bend doesn't end with sunny skies; it also offers the biggest and best ski area in the Northwest—Mount Bachelor. Several other mountains—the Three Sisters and Broken Top among them—provide a breathtaking backdrop for the city, and their pine-covered slopes, many lakes, and trout streams attract hikers, mountain bikers, sailors, and anglers. A lively downtown area filled with interesting shops, excellent restaurants, and attractive Drake Park (which is named for the city's founding father, A. M. Drake, and not for the ducks that are the park's major attraction) complement the outdoor offerings of the area, and it's sometimes difficult to tell which is more popular.

Central and Eastern Oregon

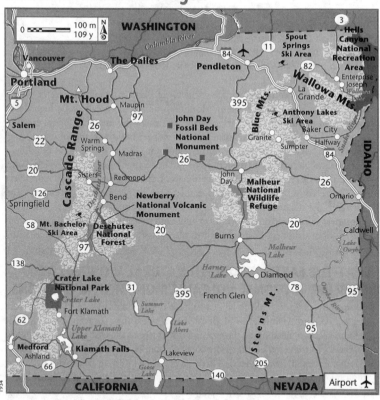

ESSENTIALS

GETTING THERE Bend is at the junction of U.S. 97, which runs north and south, and U.S. 20, which runs east to west across the state. From the Portland area, the most direct route is by way of U.S. 26 to Madras and then south on U.S. 97.

The **Redmond Municipal Airport,** 16 miles north of Bend, is served by Horizon Airlines, Alaska Airlines, and United Airlines. The **Redmond Airport Shuttle** (☎ **541/382-1687** or 800/955-8267) operates vans between the airport and Bend. There are also taxis operating from the airport.

CAC Transportation (☎ **541/382-1687**) operates a shuttle van between the Portland International Airport and Bend.

VISITOR INFORMATION Contact the **Bend Chamber of Commerce,** 63085 N. U.S. 97, Bend, OR 97701-5765 (☎ **541/382-3221**).

GETTING AROUND Car rentals are available from **Budget,** 2060 U.S. 20 E. (☎ **541/383-2642**), and **Hertz,** 1045 SE Third St. (☎ **541/388-1535**). If you need a taxi, call **Owl Taxi Service** (☎ **541/382-3311**).

FESTIVALS The **Cascade Festival of Music** held each June in Drake Park is Bend's biggest festival.

A MUSEUM NOT TO MISS

✪ The High Desert Museum

59800 S. U.S. 97. ☎ **541/382-4754.** Admission $6.25 adults, $5.75 students and seniors, $3 children 5–12. Daily 9am–5pm. Closed Jan 1, Thanksgiving, and Dec 25. Take U.S. 97 6 miles south of Bend.

Bend lies on the westernmost edge of the Great Basin, a region that stretches from the Cascade Range to the Rocky Mountains and is often called the high desert because of its elevation and lack of water. Through the use of historical exhibits, live animal displays, and reconstructions of pioneer buildings, the museum brings the cultural and natural history of the region into focus. In the main building is a walk-through timeline of western history. The natural history of the region comes alive in the Desertarium where live animals of the region can be observed in very natural settings. The frolicking river otters and slow-moving porcupines are, however, the star attractions. Throughout the day informative talks are scheduled. A pioneer homestead and a forestry exhibit with a steam-driven sawmill round out the outdoor exhibits. Throughout the year, classes, workshops, and lectures are held at the museum.

WHAT THE EARTH WROUGHT: NATURAL WONDERS AT NEWBERRY NATIONAL VOLCANIC MONUMENT & ENVIRONS

From snow-covered peaks to lava caves, past volcanic activity and geologic history are everywhere visible around Bend. For a sweeping panoramic view of the Cascade Range, head up to the top of **Pilot Butte** at the east end of Greenwood Avenue. From the top of this cinder cone, you can see Mount Hood (11,235 feet), Mount Jefferson (10,495 feet), Three-Fingered Jack (7,848 feet), Mount Washington (7,802 feet), North Sister (10,094 feet), Middle Sister (10,053 feet), South Sister (10,354 feet), Broken Top (9,165 feet), and Mount Bachelor (9,075 feet). All these peaks are volcanic in origin, even Mount Bachelor, which is the site of the Northwest's largest ski resort.

To the south of Bend lies a region of relatively recent volcanic activity that has been preserved as the **Newberry National Volcanic Monument.** The best place to start an exploration of the national monument is at the **Lava Lands Visitor Center,** 58201 S. U.S. 97 (☎ **541/593-2421**), 11 miles south of Bend. Here you can learn about the titanic forces that sculpted this region. An interpretive trail outside the center wanders through a lava flow at the base of 500-foot-tall **Lava Butte,** an ominous black cinder cone. In summer, a shuttle bus ($1.50 for adults, 75¢ for children) will take you to the summit of the cinder cone. From here you have another outstanding view of the Cascades, and can explore the crater on another trail.

A mile to the south, you'll find the **Lava River Cave.** The cave was formed by lava flows and is actually a long tube or tunnel. The cave is more than a mile long and takes about an hour to explore. Admission is $1.50 for adults, $1 for children 13 to 17, plus $1.50 for lantern rentals. When lava flowed across this landscape, it often inundated pine forests, leaving in its wake only molds of the trees. At **Lava Cast Forest,** 9 miles down a very rough road off U.S. 97 south of Lava River Cave, a paved trail leads past such molds. Continuing farther south on U.S. 97 will bring you to the turnoff for the **Newberry Crater** area, the centerpiece of the monument. Covering 500 square miles, the crater contains Paulina and East lakes, both of which are popular with boaters and anglers, and numerous volcanic features, including an astounding flow of obsidian. Today there are rental cabins and campgrounds within the national monument, and 150 miles of hiking trails.

If, after thoroughly exploring all the local volcanic features, you still want to see more geologic wonders, head south 75 miles or so to **Fort Rock State Park** and the nearby **Hole-in-the-Ground,** both of which are off Ore. 31. These unusual volcanic features were formed when lakes of molten lava encountered groundwater and exploded with great violence. The walls of Fort Rock rise straight out of the flat landscape and form almost a full circle. Hole-in-the-Ground is a mile-wide crater 200 to 300 feet deep.

. . . AND MORE ATTRACTIONS

North of Bend 40 miles is the **Cove Palisades State Park** (☎ 541/546-3412) on Lake Billy Chinook, a man-made lake that flooded canyons formed by the Metolius, Crooked, and Deschutes rivers. The palisades for which the park is named are nearly vertical walls of basalt that rise several hundred feet above the lake waters. This is a very popular recreation area offering boating, fishing, swimming, picnicking, and camping. There are even houseboats available for rent from **Chinook Water Chalets, Inc.,** P.O. Box 40, Culver, OR 97734 (☎ 541/546-2939). Rates range from $1,000 to $1,850 per week.

To learn more about the history of central Oregon, stop by the **Des Chutes Historical Center,** 129 NW Idaho Ave. (☎ 541/389-1813), which is housed in a 1914 stone school building at the south end of downtown. It's open Tuesday through Saturday from 10am to 4:30pm; admission is free.

The same clear skies that attract vacationers to central Oregon have also attracted astronomers. At **Pine Mountain Observatory** (☎ 541/382-8331), 35 miles east of Bend off U.S. 20, you, too, can gaze at the stars and planets through a 15-inch telescope. It's open to the public May to September only, on Friday and Saturday from dusk; admission is $2.

In the resort community of Sunriver, 18 miles south of Bend, you'll find the **Sunriver Nature Center,** 17620 River Rd. (☎ 541/593-4394). With its frequent nature-oriented activities, raptor rehabilitation area, and observatory, the center is a great place to bring the kids for the day. It's open on Sunday and Monday from 9am to 4pm and Tuesday through Saturday from 9am to 5pm (shorter hours in winter). Admission is $2 for adults, $1 for children 12 and under.

If you'd like to have a guide show you around the area, contact **Wanderlust Tours** (☎ 541/389-8359 or 800/661-5878), which offers trips to many of the region's attractions. Full-day tour rates range from $32 to $52.

SKIING & OTHER WINTER SPORTS

If downhill skiing is your passion, you probably already know about the fabulous skiing conditions and myriad runs of **Mount Bachelor Ski & Summer Resort** (☎ 800/800-8334 for a snow report), located 22 miles west of Bend on the Cascades Lakes Highway. With a 3,100-foot vertical drop, 60 runs, 11 lifts, six day lodges, and skiing from November to July, it's no wonder that this is the training area for the U.S. Ski Team.

Lift tickets can be purchased for the day or on a point system that allows you to make a few runs and come back another day or share the rest of your points with a friend. Day lift tickets are $33 for adults, $18 for children 7 to 12, and free for children 6 and under.

Cross-country skiers will also find plenty of trails to choose from. Just be sure to stop by a ski shop and buy a **Sno-Park** permit before heading up to the cross-country trailheads, the best of which are along the Cascades Lakes Highway leading to Mount Bachelor ski area. At the ski area itself, there are 90 miles (55km) of groomed trails. Passes to use these trails are $9.50 for adults and $4.50 for children. Ski shops abound in Bend and nearly all of them rent both downhill and cross-country equipment. If you're heading to Mount Bachelor, you can rent equipment there, or try the **Powder House,** 311 SW Century Dr. (☎ 541/389-6234), on the way out of Bend heading toward Mount Bachelor.

The **Mount Bachelor Super Shuttle** (☎ 541/382-2442) operates between Bend and the ski resort and leaves from the corner of Colorado Avenue and Simpson Street, where there's a large parking lot.

If you've had enough skiing, how about a **sled-dog ride?** At **Oregon Trail of Dreams** (☎ 541/382-2442 or 800/829-2442) you can take a 1¹/₂-hour sled-dog ride and then learn about the care of sled dogs. Rates are $60 for adults and $30 for children. All-day and overnight trips are also available.

SUMMER ACTIVITIES

Both hiking and mountain biking are available at Mount Bachelor in the summer, when a chair lift operates to the 9,065-foot top of the mountain; the fare is $9 for adults, $6.50 for seniors, $4.50 for children 7 to 12, and and free for children 6 and under. From here you can hike or ride a mountain bike down. Bike rentals and guided tours are available.

HIKING   Hiking is one of the most popular summer activities here, but keep in mind that high-country trails may be closed by snow until late June or early July.

Just to limber up or for a quick breath of fresh air, head up to the north end of Northwest First Street where you'll find a 3-mile-long trail along the Deschutes River. However, our favorite trail is the **Deschutes River Trail,** which parallels the Deschutes for several miles. To reach the trail, head 10 miles west on the Cascade Lakes Highway (Century Drive) and, after the Inn of the Seventh Mountain, turn left on Forest Road 41 and follow the signs to Lava River Falls.

The **Three Sisters Wilderness,** which begins just over 20 miles from Bend or Sisters, offers secluded hiking among rugged volcanic peaks. Permits are required for overnight trips in the wilderness area and are currently available at trailheads. For more information contact the **Bend/Fort Rock Ranger Station,** 1230 NE Third St. (☎ 541/388-5664), or the **Sisters Ranger Station** (☎ 541/549-2111) in Sisters for trail maps and other information.

MOUNTAIN BIKING   Mountain biking is fast becoming one of the most popular activities in central Oregon. When the snow melts, the cross-country ski trails become mountain-bike trails. Stop by the Deschutes National Forest Office to find out about trails open to mountain bikes. The most scenic trail open to mountain bikes is the Deschutes River Trail mentioned above.

Guided mountain-bike rides in Newberry National Volcanic Monument are offered by **High Cascade Descent Guide Service** (☎ 541/389-0562). Rates range from $37 to $50, depending on the length of the ride. An easy downhill ride includes stops at waterfalls and a natural water slide. Guided rides are also offered by **Pacific Crest Pedalers** (☎ 541/593-8369), with rates ranging from $30 to $60.

HORSEBACK RIDING   Horseback riding is available through **Saddleback Stables** (☎ 541/593-1221, ext. 4420) in Sunriver, where an hour ride will cost

$22. **Black Butte Stables** (☎ 541/595-2061), near Sisters, offers a variety of rides with an hour ride costing $22.

WHITE-WATER RAFTING   The Deschutes River, which passes through Bend, is the most popular river in Oregon for white-water rafting, although the best sections of river are 100 miles north of here. Both **Hunter Expeditions** (☎ 541/389-8370) and **Rapid River Rafters** (☎ 541/382-1514 or 800/ 962-3327) offer full-day trips on the Lower Deschutes for $60 to $65. At the **Inn of the Seventh Mountain** (☎ 541/382-8711, ext. 601), you can arrange a half-day trip for only $27.

From Bend it's also possible to do trips down the McKenzie River on the west side of the Cascades. These trips are offered by **Black Paw Rafting Co.** (☎ 800/572-RAFT) and **Ouzel Outfitters** (☎ 541/385-5947). Full-day trips cost around $85.

SAILBOARDING   There's good sailboarding at Sunset View Beach on **Elk Lake.** Board rentals and lessons are available here from **Cascade Lakes Windsurfing** (☎ 541/389-8759).

FISHING   If the fish beneath the white water are more important to you than the water itself, you may want to do a bit of angling while you're in the area. The Metolius and Deschutes rivers are both popular for fly fishing, and if you're not familiar with these rivers, you may want to hire a guide to show you where to hook into a big one. **John Garrison** (☎ 541/593-8394) and **Rick Wren** (☎ 541/ 382-1264 or 800/952-0707) are two local guides who both charge between $125 and $150 for a day of fishing. **High Cascade Descent** (☎ 541/389-0562) charges only $60 to $65 for a day of fishing. Fly-fishing supplies are available at **The Fly Box,** 1293 NE Third St. (☎ 541/388-3330).

HOT-AIR BALLOONING   How about floating above the rivers and trees in a hot-air balloon. The **Morning Glory Balloon Company** (☎ 541/389-8739) offers one-hour trips for $175 per person.

GOLF   For many of central Oregon's visitors, Bend's abundance of sunshine means only one thing—plenty of rounds of golf at more than 20 area golf courses. **Resorts with courses** include Sunriver, the Inn of the Seventh Mountain, and the Riverhouse (see "Where to Stay," below), and Black Butte Ranch and Eagle Crest (see "Where to Stay" in the section on side trips from Bend, at the end of this section). Greens fees at these courses range from $36 to $49. Other courses open to the public include **Mountain High Golf Course,** China Hat Road (☎ 541/ 382-1111), and **River's Edge Golf Course,** 3075 N. U.S. 97 (☎ 541/389-2828).

WHERE TO STAY
EXPENSIVE

✪ Sunriver Lodge & Resort
P.O. Box 3609, Sunriver, OR 97707. ☎ **541/593-1221** or 800/547-3922. Fax 541/ 593-5458. 299 rms, 77 suites, and 108 condos. A/C TV TEL. $110–$129 double; $175–$195 suite; $184–$274 two- to four-bedroom condo. Lower rates off-season. AE, CB, DC, DISC, MC, V.

This sprawling resort has a wealth of activities available for active vacationers. Most of the accommodations overlook both the golf course and the mountains. Our favorite rooms are the loft suites, which have stone fireplaces, high ceilings, and rustic log furniture. In fact, these are the nicest rooms at any of the area's resorts.

Lots of pine trees shade the grounds and there are 30 miles of paved bicycle paths connecting the resort's many buildings (two bicycles come with every room).

Dining/Entertainment: Meadow's, the resort's main dining room, displays Northwest creativity, with entrée prices in the $10 to $20 range. The adjacent lounge offers a cozy fireplace. A more casual restaurant offers the same view, and a separate lounge features live country and Top 40 music and a great deck. Golfers have two choices for quick meals or a drink.

Services: Concierge, room service, aerobics classes, tennis clinics, horseback riding, fishing-gear rentals, massage, children's programs, white-water rafting, shopping service.

Facilities: Two golf courses, two pools, 28 tennis courts, indoor miniature golf, ice-skating rink, canoes, bicycles, pro shop.

MODERATE

Best Western/Entrada Lodge

19221 Century Dr., Bend, OR 97702. ☎ **541/382-4080** or 800/528-1234. 79 rms. A/C TV TEL. $55–$89 double. Rates include continental breakfast. AE, CB, DC, DISC, MC, V.

Located a few miles west of Bend on the road to the Mount Bachelor ski area, this motel charges a little more for the peace and quiet that you won't find at in-town choices. Tall pine trees shade the grounds and the Deschutes National Forest borders the property. The popular Deschutes River Trail is only a mile away. Facilities include an outdoor pool and a whirlpool.

⑤ Inn of the Seventh Mountain

18575 SW Century Dr., Bend, OR 97709. ☎ **541/382-8711** or 800/452-6810, 800/874-9402 in western Canada. 269 rms, 159 suites. A/C TV TEL. $65–$109 double; $139–$285 suite. AE, CB, DC, DISC, MC, V.

This resort is the closest accommodation to Mount Bachelor and is especially popular with skiers in the winter. In summer an abundance of recreational activities turns the resort into a sort of summer camp for families. The guest rooms are done in a country decor and come in a wide range of sizes. Many have balconies and/or kitchens. Our favorites are the rooms perched on the edge of the wooded Deschutes River canyon.

Dining/Entertainment: Two restaurants, one serving creative meat-and-potato meals, provide options at mealtimes. The fireside lounge is popular for après-ski gatherings.

Services: Tennis clinics, golf lessons, massage, children's summer camp, teen program, arts-and-crafts classes, white-water rafting, float trips, canoe trips, patio boat cruises, horseback riding, hayrides, mountain-bike rentals, rentals of VCRs, movies, and video games.

Facilities: 18-hole golf course, indoor and outdoor pools, whirlpools, indoor and outdoor tennis courts, pickleball courts, roller-skating rink, ice-skating rink, hiking/jogging trails, miniature golf course, playing fields, volleyball, basketball, horseshoes, playgrounds, horse stables.

Mount Bachelor Village Resort

19717 Mount Bachelor Dr., Bend, OR 97702. ☎ **541/389-5900** or 800/452-9846. 80 condos. A/C TV TEL. $68–$105 condo for two; $105–$285 one- to three-bedroom condo. Minimum stay two nights; discounts for three nights or longer. AE, MC, V.

Most of Bend's resorts cater to families in the summer months and consequently can be very noisy and crowded. If you'd rather be able to hear the wind in the trees, this condominium resort is the place to check out. All the rooms have separate bedrooms, and many have fireplaces and kitchens. Views aren't too great unless you get one of the condos on the edge of the bluff, but there are balconies. The River Ridge condos are newer and have the better views.

Dining/Entertainment: The restaurant in the athletic club just down the hill from the condos features a brick oven and offers innovative meals. There's also a fireside lounge up by the swimming pool.

Facilities: Outdoor pool, whirlpool, tennis courts, athletic club, nature trail.

☉ The Riverhouse

3075 N. U.S. 97, Bend, OR 97701. ☎ **541/389-3111** or 800/547-3928. 220 rms, 30 suites. A/C TV TEL. $61–$72 double; $99–$165 suite. AE, CB, DC, DISC, MC, V.

Located at the north end of town on the banks of a narrow stretch of the Deschutes River, the Riverhouse is an economical choice for anyone who wants the amenities of a big resort. We like the ground-floor rooms that allow you to step off your patio and almost jump in the river. However, the rooms on the upper floor have a better view of this rocky stretch of river. All in all, we'd say that this is the best deal in Bend. Book early.

Dining/Entertainment: A formal dining room serves continental dishes along with a view of the river, and there's an inexpensive Mexican restaurant as well. The lounge features a variety of live entertainment. Quick meals and drinks are available poolside.

Services: Room service, complimentary coffee, a welcoming drink.

Facilities: 18-hole golf course, indoor and outdoor pools, whirlpools, sauna, exercise room, pro shop.

INEXPENSIVE

Bend Riverside Motel

1565 NW Hill St., Bend, OR 97709. ☎ **541/389-2363** or 800/284-2363. 100 rms. A/C TV TEL. $49–$99 double. AE, DISC, MC, V.

You won't find better-placed budget lodging in Bend, and if you don't mind rooms that are just a little out of the ordinary for a motel, you'll probably be happy staying here. Located on the banks of the Deschutes and bounded by Pioneer Park, this renovated older motel is only a few blocks from most of Bend's best restaurants. The cheapest rooms lack views and are rather cramped, so we recommend opting for a deluxe room in the newer section of the motel. The slightly more expensive studio units also have fireplaces and kitchens. Facilities include an indoor pool, whirlpool, sauna, and tennis court.

WHERE TO DINE

The Bend area's best meals are to be had at **Meadows Dining Room** at Sunriver Lodge (see "Where to Stay," above, for details). Coffee addicts will want to spend time at the **Café Paradiso,** 945 NW Bond St. (☎ **541/385-5931**), a popular hangout that combines elegance and funkiness. For good handcrafted ales and pub food, stop by the **Deschutes Brewery and Public House,** 1044 NW Bond St. (☎ **541/382-9242**).

EXPENSIVE

Le Bistro

1203 NE Third St. ☎ **541/389-7274.** Reservations recommended. Main courses $10.50–$19. AE, DISC, MC, V. Daily 5–9pm. FRENCH.

Located on busy Third Street, and housed in a converted church, is Le Bistro, Bend's only French restaurant. The interior decor simulates a French sidewalk café, and you'll either like it or find it tacky. But the food is quite good and the prices are reasonable. The menu is primarily tried-and-true standards such as escargots, French onion soup, and boeuf bourguignon, but there are also a few more intriguing dishes. Seafood Wellington is a satisfying mix of scallops, prawns, shrimp, and lobster in a puff pastry, and the rack of lamb is fragrant with rosemary.

MODERATE

Pine Tavern Restaurant

967 NW Brooks St. ☎ **541/382-5581.** Reservations highly recommended. Main courses $8.75–$17.50. AE, CB, DC, DISC, MC, V. Mon–Sat 11:30am–2:30pm and 5:30–9:30pm, Sun 5:30–9:30pm. STEAK/PRIME RIB.

Opened in 1936, the Pine Tavern Restaurant has been a local favorite for generations, and neither the decor nor the view has changed much over the years. Knotty pine and cozy booths give the restaurant an old-fashioned feel, while the 200-year-old ponderosa pines growing up through the center of one dining room provide a bit of grandeur. Most people ask for a table in the back room, which overlooks Mirror Pond. The menu is designed to appeal to a wide range of tastes and many of the dishes meet American Heart Association guidelines. Teriyaki chicken, Cajun-style scallops and shrimp, and pork satay are three favorites from around the world. It's popular with families.

✪ Rosette

150 NW Oregon St. ☎ **541/383-2780.** Reservations recommended. Main courses $14–$17.50. MC, V. Mon 5:30–9pm, Tues–Thurs 11:30am–1:30pm and 5:30–9pm, Fri 11:30am–1:30pm and 5:30–9:30pm, Sat 5:30–9:30pm. NORTHWEST/CONTINENTAL.

Offering downtown's most innovative cuisine, Rosette is a rather spartan place. However, the lack of distractions allows you to focus your attention on the artful creations that come from the kitchen. The menu changes regularly, and on a recent night included a pork tenderloin with a sauce of tarragon, apple brandy, and cream. We like the appetizers so much that we're willing to forgo an entrée in favor of two or three different starters such as Dungeness crab cakes with tangy remoulade or panko-crusted oysters with chile-ginger sauce.

✪ Yoko's Japanese Restaurant

1028 NW Bond St. ☎ **541/382-2999.** Reservations recommended. Main courses $10–$15.50. MC, V. Tues–Fri 11:30am–2pm and 5–9:30pm, Sat 5–9:30pm. JAPANESE.

Simple Japanese furnishings give Yoko's a sense of serenity, though it can be bustling on a busy night. You can order one of Yoko's special rolls from the sushi bar or start your meal with an order of gyoza, seasoned pork wrapped in a thin Japanese noodle. Although such standard dishes as chicken teriyaki and shrimp tempura are available, there are also less well known dishes such as kare, a hot-and-spicy curry stew. For the hearty appetite, and for visual appeal, you can't beat Yoko's special boat dinner which carries a cargo of beef-and-chicken teriyaki, crisp tempura, a choice of traditional sushi or sashimi, and fresh fruit.

INEXPENSIVE

Ⓢ Baja Norte

801 NW Wall St. ☎ **541/385-0611.** Main courses $3–$6. MC, V. Daily 11am–9pm. MEXICAN.

This colorful Mexican fast-food spot makes its own tortillas and fills them with tasty fillings. You can get chunky fish tacos or thick quesadillas covered with various toppings (we like the artichoke quesadilla). The icy margaritas are a big hit in summer. These meals are big, so bring a good appetite. The crowd here is generally young and athletic.

Café Santé

718 NW Franklin St. ☎ **541/383-3530.** Meals $4–$6.50. No credit cards. Daily 7am–3pm. VEGETARIAN.

The Santé is a bright and airy little café that stays packed all through breakfast and lunch, and on weekends can have quite a waiting line out the door. The bacon is made of tempeh, the cheese is low-sodium, the tuna is dolphin safe, organically grown foods are used as often as possible, and the juices are fresh squeezed. For breakfast, we like the thick slabs of French toast, and at lunch the tempeh fajitas are a good bet.

Mexicali Rose

301 NE Franklin Ave. ☎ **541/389-0149.** Main courses $6.25–$10. AE, MC, V. Sun–Thurs 5–10pm, Fri–Sat 5–10:30pm. MEXICAN.

Mexicali Rose has been Bend's most popular Mexican restaurant for years, despite its location on a corner of congested Third Street. Amid all the fast-food places, car dealers, and shopping centers, this restaurant's stone building still manages to stand out. The menu includes all the standard Mexican dishes plus a few that aren't so common. Try the chingalinga appetizer, which is a sort of Mexican eggroll. Crab enchiladas are a tasty entrée, and the picados (beef or chicken with vegetables in a spicy sauce) are another good choice.

SIDE TRIPS FROM BEND
THE SISTERS & REDMOND AREA

The small town of Sisters takes its name from the nearby **Three Sisters mountains,** and there's no better view of these peaks than from this little town of fewer than 1,000 people.

Ponderosa pine forests and wide meadows surround Sisters, giving it a classic western setting that the town has cashed in on in recent years. Modern buildings sport false fronts and covered sidewalks, though the predominantly pastel color schemes are more 1990s than 1890s. Once just someplace to stop for gas on the way to Bend, Sisters is now a destination in itself.

Shopping is the town's raison d'être, and western and Native American themes predominate in the galleries and clothing stores. The **Folk Arts Co.,** 138 W. Hood St. (☎ **541/549-9556**), displays the town's most eclectic collection of art by regional artists.

During the annual **Sisters Outdoor Quilt Show** on the second Saturday in July, buildings all over town are hung with quilts. The **Sisters Rodeo,** held the second weekend of June, also attracts large crowds.

For more information on the Sisters area, contact the **Sisters Area Chamber of Commerce,** P.O. Box 430, Sisters, OR 97759 (☎ **541/549-0251**).

One of the most breathtaking sections of road in the state begins just west of Sisters. **Ore. 242,** which is only open in the summer, climbs to **McKenzie Pass,** from which there's a sweeping panorama of the Cascades. Making the view all the more spectacular are the **lava fields** that surround the pass. These are some of the most recent lava flows in Oregon. An observation building made of lava rock provides sighting tubes so you can identify all the visible peaks.

Just west of Sisters off U.S. 126 near the community of Camp Sherman, you can see the springs that form the headwaters of the Metolius River.

Sisters also makes a good starting point for **hiking or mountain biking** in the Deschutes National Forest. Stop by the **Sisters Rangers Station** (☎ 541/549-2111) at the west end of town for information and trail maps. During the summer, you can rent bikes in town at **Mountain Supply** (☎ 541/549-3251), at 148 Hood St., for about $9 per day. **Flyfishers** (☎ 541/595-2073) can set you up with equipment and guide you to the best **fly-fishing** spots on the Metolius River.

Sisters is surrounded by wilderness, and there are 18 trailheads scattered around the Sisters area that all lead into the wilderness areas of **Mt. Washington, Mt. Jefferson,** and **Three Sisters.** These glacier-scoured volcanic ridges along the Cascades range contain over 100 miles of trails for primitive hiking.

East of Terrebonne, you'll find **Smith Rock State Park,** yet another of central Oregon's many geological wonders. Jagged rock formations tower above the Crooked River here and attract rock climbers from around the world. If you want to try climbing, contact **First Ascent Climbing School & Guide Service** (☎ 541/548-5137), which offers group ($40 per day), semiprivate ($65 to $80 per day), and private ($135 per day) climbing lessons. **Vertical Ventures** (☎ 541/389-7937) also offers rock-climbing classes at similar prices. Even if you prefer to stay on horizontal ground, you can appreciate the majesty of this rugged canyon wall. There are picnic tables, a primitive campground used almost exclusively by rock climbers, and hiking trails that lead through the canyon and up to the top of the rocks. The view of the Cascades framed by Smith Rock is superb.

If you haven't yet had your fill of viewing rocks, stop by the **Petersen Rock Gardens,** 7930 SW 77th St., Redmond (☎ 541/382-5574), 9 miles north of Bend just off U.S. 97. This 4-acre folk-art creation consists of buildings, miniature bridges, terraces, and tiny towers all constructed from rocks. The gardens, built between 1935 and 1952 by a Danish immigrant farmer, are open daily from 9am to dusk; admission is by donation.

If you're a fan of rail travel, consider an excursion on the **Crooked River Railroad Company Dinner Train,** 525 SW Sixth St. (☎ 541/548-8630). The 38-mile, 2¹/₂-hour rail excursion travels from Redmond to Prineville and back. Restored dining cars are the elegant setting for the four-course dinners. Friday is hoedown night, Saturday is murder-mystery night, and then on Sunday there's a brunch run. Fares are $50 to $69, and reservations are required.

One local attraction that appeals to kids is **Reindeer Ranch at Operation Santa Claus,** located 2 miles west of town on Ore. 126 (☎ 541/548-8910). This is the largest reindeer ranch in the United States and is home to more than 100 reindeer. It's open daily and admission is free.

Where to Stay

✪ Black Butte Ranch

P.O. Box 8000, Black Butte Ranch, OR 97759. ☎ **541/595-6211** or 800/452-7455. Fax 541/595-2077. 19 rms, 16 condos, 65 homes. TV TEL. $80–$130 double; $160–$225 condo or house. AE, DISC, MC, V.

This gated resort 8 miles west of Sisters is built on a former ranch and offers stunning views of the Cascade peaks across the meadows of a wide valley. With its two golf courses and wide range of scheduled activities and recreational opportunities,

Black Butte appeals primarily to families. The condos and homes are set amid open lawns between the forest and the meadows, and most have fireplaces and kitchens. Large decks and sliding glass doors let you enjoy the views no matter what the weather.

Dining/Entertainment: The Lodge restaurant is built around a huge old ponderosa, and large windows provide nearly every table with a view of the mountains or the lake. The menu is equally divided between steaks and seafood. A cozy lounge is upstairs from the dining room. A poolside café provides casual family dining.

Services: Canoe rentals, bicycle rentals, horseback riding, white-water rafting, nature walks, children's programs.

Facilities: Two 18-hole golf courses, outdoor pool, tennis courts, recreation center, sports field, 16 miles of bike and jogging trails, pro shop, sports shop.

Conklin's Guest House

69013 Camp Polk Rd., Sisters, OR 97759. ☎ **541/549-0123.** 5 rms, 3 with bath. $60–$70 double without bath, $70–$110 double with bath. Rates include full breakfast. No credit cards.

Surrounded by meadows and with an unobstructed view of the mountains, Conklin's bed-and-breakfast is an excellent choice for anyone who has become enamored of Sisters' western charm. The inn's country decor fits right in with the town, and a duck pond and a trout pond provide a bit of a farm feel. There's even a swimming pool, and breakfast is served in a tile-floored sun room. Our favorite room has a big old clawfoot tub surrounded by windows that look out to the Cascades. This room also has its own little balcony.

⑤ Inn at Eagle Crest

P.O. Box 1215, Redmond, OR 97756. ☎ **541/923-2453**, or 800/682-4786. 80 rms, 20 suites. A/C TV TEL. $60–$88 double; $85–$235 suite. AE, DISC, MC, V.

Less than 20 miles north of Bend is another sprawling resort that attracts sun worshipers and golfers. The landscape is much drier here than around Bend and is dominated by scrubby junipers that give Eagle Crest the feel of a desert resort. The rooms overlook the golf course rather than the mountains, which should give you an idea of most guests' priorities. Facilities here are, unfortunately, geared primarily toward owners of homes and condos.

Dining/Entertainment: The restaurant is located on the opposite side of the golf course from the main building, so you'll have to walk or drive. The decor here is very traditional and the menu sticks to traditional continental dishes.

Services: Tennis clinics, horseback riding, massage, aerobics classes, bicycle rentals, complimentary airport shuttle, babysitting, teen club.

Facilities: Two golf courses, outdoor pool, hot tub, indoor and outdoor tennis courts, playing field, jogging trails, beauty salon.

✪ Metolious River Resort

P.O. Box 1210, Camp Sherman, OR 97730. ☎ **541/595-6281** or 800/81-TROUT. 11 cabins. $120–$140 double in cabins. Lower rates off-season. MC, V.

These new shake-sided two-story cabins 14 miles west of Sisters are exceptional, offering modern amenities and styling with a bit of a rustic feel. Peeled log beds, wood paneling, river-stone fireplaces, and green roofs give the cabins a quintessential western appearance. Set on the banks of the spring-fed Metolious River not far from the river's source, the cabins are particularly popular with trout anglers. Despite the name, this is hardly a resort—it's a secluded getaway that will be appreciated by anyone looking for peace and quiet.

Where to Dine

Hotel Sisters and Bronco Billy's Saloon

101 Cascade St. ☎ **541/549-RIBS.** Reservations recommended. Meals $9–$19. MC, V. Daily 11am–9pm. AMERICAN.

Though it's no longer a hotel, the Hotel Sisters does serve up some Wild West grub in the form of belt-loosening platters of barbecued ribs, chicken breasts, and hot links. The decor, with its Victorian wallpaper and lace curtains, is a bit too fussy for a rib house, but step through the swinging saloon doors into the bar and you'll find genuine western atmosphere, including a buffalo head on the wall.

✪ Kokanee Café

Camp Sherman. ☎ **541/595-6420.** Reservations recommended. Main courses $10–$17. MC, V. Mon–Fri 5–9pm, Sat–Sun 9am–9pm. Closed Nov–Mar. NORTHWEST.

The Kokanee Café is located adjacent to the Metolius River Resort in Camp Sherman, about 15 miles west of Sisters. This out-of-the-way place is one of the best restaurants in the region and serves Northwest cuisine with an Oregon slant. The decor is contemporary rustic with an open-beamed ceiling and wrought-iron chandelier. Out back there's a deck under the ponderosa pines. The menu is short and includes daily chalkboard specials such as chicken–apple sauce sausage and fresh-grilled ahi with olive-rosemary butter. The always-interesting dessert menu might include champagne sorbet with raspberry sauce or chocolate suicide cake.

You might also like to know that the restaurant has two rooms for rent on the second floor. They go for around $50 double.

WARM SPRINGS

✪ The Museum at Warm Springs

U.S. 26, Warm Springs. ☎ **541/553-3331.** Admission $5. Daily 10am–5pm.

The Confederated Tribes of the Warm Springs Reservation, comprised of Warm Springs, Wasco, and Paiute Native Americans, opened this impressive museum in 1993 after decades spent amassing an outstanding collection of regional Native American artifacts. For thousands of years these tribes have inhabited this region and adapted to its environment. Various styles of traditional houses have been reconstructed at the museum and serve as backdrops for displays on everything from basketry and beadwork to fishing and root gathering. Exhibits on traditional drumming, singing, and dancing are of particular interest.

Where to Stay & Dine

Kah-Nee-Ta Resort

P.O. Box K, Warm Springs, OR 97761. ☎ **541/553-1112** or 800/554-4SUN. 139 rms, 4 suites, 25 cottages, 21 tepees. A/C TV TEL. $115–$130 double; $185–$295 suite; $105–$200 cottage; $50 tepee. AE, CB, DC, DISC, MC, V.

This unusual resort 65 miles north of Bend is one of central Oregon's most popular sunny-side destinations. Operated by the Confederated Tribes of the Warm Springs Reservation, on whose land the resort is built, Kah-Nee-Ta offers a wide range of accommodations from hotel rooms to cottages to R.V. sites to tepees. The main lodge is a contemporary building atop a bluff that commands a brilliant vista of the high desert. The Warm Springs Native Americans and the reservation both take their names from the hot springs that come welling out of the ground here at Kah-Nee-Ta.

Dining/Entertainment: Two dining rooms serve traditional Native American dishes as well as other Northwest specialties. Over in the camping area are a snack bar and a more casual restaurant. During the summer months a traditional salmon bake is held on Saturday evening and is followed by traditional Native American dancing. There are also dance performances on Sunday afternoon. If you'd like to do your own dancing, check out the lounge.

Services: Resort shuttle, bicycle rentals, kayak rentals, horseback riding, massage, fishing-rod rentals.

Facilities: Casino, golf course, naturally heated outdoor pool, mineral baths, fitness center, games room, tennis courts.

A SCENIC DRIVE ALONG THE CASCADE LAKES HIGHWAY

During the summer the Cascade Lakes Highway is the most popular excursion out of Bend. Formerly known as Century Drive because it was a loop road of approximately 100 miles, this National Forest Scenic Byway is an 87-mile loop that packs in some of the finest scenery in the Oregon Cascades. Along the way are a dozen lakes and frequent views of the jagged Three Sisters peaks and the rounded Mount Bachelor. The lakes provide ample opportunities for boating, sailboarding, fishing, swimming, and picnicking.

The first area of interest along the highway is **Dutchman Flat,** just west of Mount Bachelor. This minidesert is caused by a thick layer of pumice that can support only a few species of plants. A little farther and you come to **Todd Lake,** a pretty little lake offering swimming, picnicking, and camping.

West of the Green Lakes trailhead is an area known as **Devils Garden,** where several springs surface on the edge of a lava flow. On a boulder here you can still see a few **Native American pictographs.** Apollo astronauts trained here before landing on the moon.

Elk Lake is popular with windsurfers. There are cabins, a lodge, and campsites around the lake. **Hosmer and Lava lakes** are both well known as good fishing lakes, while spring-fed **Little Lava Lake** is the source of the Deschutes River. **Cultus Lake,** with its sandy beaches, is a popular swimming lake. At the **Crane Prairie Reservoir** you can observe osprey between May and October. The **Twin Lakes** are examples of volcanic maars (craters) that have been filled by springs. These lakes have no inlets or outlets.

At the **Central Oregon Welcome Center,** 63085 N. U.S. 97 in Bend (☎ **541/ 382-3221**), you can pick up a guide to the Cascade Lakes Highway. From mid-November to late May this road is closed because of snow beyond the Mount Bachelor ski area.

DRIVING ON TO EASTERN OREGON

If you're heading east from Bend, you have two choices—U.S. 26 or U.S. 20. The former provides access to the fossil beds and painted hills of John Day Fossil Beds National Monument and the latter provides access to the best birdwatching in the Northwest at Malheur National Wildlife Refuge.

ALONG U.S. 20: THE JOHN DAY FOSSIL BEDS NATIONAL MONUMENT & MORE

The **John Day Fossil Beds National Monument,** consisting of three separate units, preserves a 40-million-year fossil record that indicates this region was once a tropical or subtropical forest. From tiny seeds to extinct relatives of the rhinoceros and elephant, an amazing array of plants and animals have been preserved in one of the world's most extensive and unbroken fossil records.

To see fossil plants in their natural state, visit the **Clarno Unit,** 60 miles north of U.S. 20. Here ancient mudflows inundated a forest. At the **Painted Hills Unit,** along the John Day River near Mitchell, you won't see any fossils but you will see strikingly colored rounded hills. The bands of color were caused by the weathering of volcanic ash under different climatic conditions. At the **Sheep Rock Unit,** stop by the **Visitor Center** (☎ **541/987-2333**), where you can get a close-up look at some fossils and watch a paleontologist at work; it's open daily in summer from 8:30am to 6pm (hours vary in other months). Afterward, head to **Blue Basin,** where there's an interpretive trail.

For more information, contact the **John Day Fossil Beds National Monument,** 420 W. Main St., John Day, OR 97845 (☎ **541/575-0721**).

In the town of John Day, the fascinating little **Kam Wah Chung & Co. Museum** (☎ **541/575-0028**), adjacent to City Park, is well worth a visit. It preserves the home and shop of a Chinese doctor who, for much of the first half of this century, administered to his fellow countrymen who were laboring here in John Day. The building looks much as it might have at the time of the doctor's death and contains an office, pharmacy, general store, and living quarters. It's open May to October only, Monday through Thursday from 9am to noon and 1 to 5pm, and on Saturday and Sunday from 1 to 5pm. Admission is $2 for adults, $1.50 for seniors, and $1 for children.

Where to Stay

Best Western John Day Inn

315 W. Main St., John Day, OR 97845. ☎ **541/575-1700** or 800/528-1234. 39 rms. $51–$93 double. AE, CB, DC, DISC, MC, V.

If you should decide to break your trip, you'll find that this is the most convenient and comfortable lodging in the area. The two-story motel is located in downtown John Day and has an indoor pool and whirlpool. A few of the rooms even have their own whirlpool tubs.

ALONG U.S. 26: WILDLIFE WATCHING & MORE

U.S. 26 is the southern route across eastern Oregon and passes through ranch country in the driest part of the state. Because water is scarce here in the high desert, it becomes a magnet for wildlife wherever it appears. Three marshy lakes—Malheur, Harney, and Mud—south of Burns provide such an ideal habitat for birdlife that they have been designated the **Malheur National Wildlife Refuge.** The shallow lakes surrounded by thousands of acres of marshlands form an oasis that annually attracts more than 300 species of birds, including waterfowl, shorebirds, songbirds, and raptors. Some of the more noteworthy birds that are either resident or migratory at Malheur are trumpeter swans, sandhill cranes, white pelicans, great blue herons, and great horned owls. Of the more than 58 mammals that live in the refuge, the most visible are mule deer, antelopes, and coyotes.

The refuge headquarters is 32 miles south of Burns on Ore. 205, but the refuge stretches for another 30 miles south to the crossroads of Frenchglen. The **visitor center,** where you can find out about recent sightings and current birding hotspots, is open weekdays only, while a **museum** housing a collection of nearly 200 stuffed-and-mounted birds is open daily. Camping is available at two campgrounds near Frenchglen. For more information on the refuge, contact **Malheur**

National Wildlife Refuge, HC-72, Box 245, Princeton, OR 97721 (☎ 541/ 493-2612).

Steens Mountain, a different sort of desert oasis, is 30 miles southeast of Frenchglen on a gravel road that's usually open only between July and October. Even then the road is not recommended for cars with low clearance, but if you have the appropriate vehicle, the mountain is well worth a visit. Rising more than 9,500 feet high, Steens Mountain is a fault-block mountain, which means that it was formed when one side of a geological fault line rose in relationship to the other side of the fault. In the case of Steens Mountain, the east slope is a precipitous escarpment that falls away to the Alvord Desert a mile below. The panorama out across southeastern Oregon is spectacular. The mountain rises so high that it creates its own weather, and on the upper slopes the sagebrush of the high desert gives way to juniper and aspen forests. From Frenchglen there's a 66-mile loop road that leads to the summit and back down by a different route.

More wildlife-viewing opportunities are available at the **Hart Mountain National Antelope Refuge,** which is a refuge for both pronghorn antelope, the fastest land mammal in North America, and California bighorn sheep. The most accessible location for viewing antelope is the refuge headquarters, 49 miles southwest of Frenchglen on gravel roads. Primitive camping is available at **Hot Springs Campground.** For more information, contact the **Hart Mountain National Antelope Refuge,** P.O. Box 111, Lakeview, OR 97630 (☎ 541/947-3315).

Note: When traveling in the desert, always keep your gas tank topped off and carry water for both you and your car.

Where to Stay & Dine

☉ Frenchglen Hotel

Frenchglen, OR 97736. ☎ **541/493-2825.** 8 rms, none with bath. $45–$49 double. MC, V. Closed Nov 16–Mar 15.

Frenchglen is in the middle of nowhere, so for decades the Frenchglen Hotel has been an important way station for travelers passing through the region. Today this historic hotel is owned by the Oregon State Parks. The two-story hotel is 60 miles south of Burns on the edge of Malheur National Wildlife Refuge and is one of the few lodgings in this remote corner of the state. Though the historic setting will appeal to anyone with an appreciation for pioneer days, the hotel is most popular with birdwatchers. The guest rooms are on the second floor and are small and simply furnished. This hotel is often booked up months in advance. Three meals a day will cost $20 to $25 per person, and the hearty dinners are quite good.

Hotel Diamond

Diamond Lane, Diamond, OR 97722. ☎ **541/493-1898.** 6 rms, 1 with bath. $45–$65 double. MC, V.

Located 54 miles south of Burns off Ore. 205, the Hotel Diamond is on the opposite side of the Malheur Wildlife Refuge from Frenchglen. Built in 1898, this hotel serves as lodging, general store, post office, and gas station for the remote community of Diamond. Completely restored in the late 1980s, the hotel is now open year round. There's a big screened porch across the front and a green lawn complete with croquet court and horseshoe pits. There are also bicycles available. Inexpensive meals are served to guests only.

✪ McCoy Creek Inn

McCoy Creek Ranch, HC 72, Box 11, Diamond, OR 97722. ☎ **541/493-2131.** 4 rms. $75 double. Rates include full breakfast. MC, V.

Of the three lodges in this area, the McCoy Creek Inn is the most remote and most luxurious. Set on a working cattle ranch that has been run by the same family for five generations, the inn consists of three rooms in the main house plus one more in the bunkhouse. McCoy Creek runs right through the property and its canyon is full of wildlife. You can hike the trails or splash in the stream or feed the farm animals if you're so inclined. Steens Mountain rises up from the ranch and the Malheur National Wildlife Refuge is nearby. A hot tub provides the perfect end to a long day of exploring the high desert.

2 Pendleton

125 miles E of The Dalles, 52 miles NW of La Grande, 40 miles S of Walla Walla, WA

Pendleton, located at the foot of the Blue Mountains in northeastern Oregon, prides itself on being a real western town, and as the site of one of the largest and oldest rodeos in the West, it has a legitimate claim. In the 1840s the first settlers passed this way on the Oregon Trail, and in the 1850s gold strikes created boom towns in the nearby mountains. Sheep ranching and wheat farming later became the mainstays of the local economy, and by the turn of the century Pendleton was a rowdy town boasting dozens of saloons and legal bordellos.

Today Pendleton is a much quieter place that few people notice as they rush by on the Interstate. But those who do pull off find a quiet town with a downtown historic district that includes attractive brick commercial buildings and some stately old Victorian homes. However, once a year, during the Pendleton Round-Up, the raucous good old days come back to life.

ESSENTIALS

GETTING THERE   I-84 runs east to west through Pendleton. From the south take U.S. 395, and from the north Ore. 11, which leads to Walla Walla, Washington.

The **Pendleton Municipal Airport** is located about 4 miles west of downtown Pendleton and is served by Horizon Airlines.

Amtrak trains stop in Pendleton at the intersection of South Main Street and Frazer Avenue (there's no station).

VISITOR INFORMATION   Contact the **Pendleton Chamber of Commerce,** 25 SE Dorion, Pendleton, OR 97801 (☎ **541/276-7411** or 800/547-8911).

THE PENDLETON ROUND-UP

The Pendleton Round-Up, held the second week of September each year, is one of the biggest rodeos in the country and has been held since 1910. In addition to daily rodeo events, there's a nightly pageant that presents a history of Native American and pioneer relations in the area. After the pageant there's live country-and-western music in the Happy Canyon Dance Hall. A country-music concert and a parade round out the Round-Up. The Hall of Fame, under the south grandstand, holds a collection of cowboy and Indian memorabilia. The city is packed to overflowing during the Round-Up week, so if you plan to attend, reserve early. Tickets sell for $5 to $13 and should be ordered as far in advance as possible. For more information, contact the **Pendleton Round-Up,** P.O. Box 609, Pendleton, OR 97801 (☎ **541/276-2553** or 800/457-6336).

OTHER THINGS TO SEE & DO

If you happen to be in town any other week of the year, there are still a few things worth doing. This is the home town of **Pendleton Woolen Mills,** the famed manufacturer of Native American–inspired blankets and classic sportswear. At this mill the raw wool is turned into yarn and then woven into fabric before being shipped off to other factories to be made into clothing. Tours are offered Monday through Friday at 9am, 11am, 1:30pm, and 3pm. Also at the mill is a salesroom that's open Monday through Friday from 8am to 4:45pm and on Saturday from 9am to 1pm (8am to 2pm in summer).

On **Pendleton Underground Tours,** 37 SW Emigrant Ave. (☎ 541/ 276-0730), the shady underside of old Pendleton is laid bare. You'll go under the streets of the city to see where gamblers, drinkers, Chinese laborers, and prostitutes caroused in the days when Pendleton was the entertainment capital of the Northwest. Tours are offered daily from 9am to 5pm; tickets are $10. Up above ground, a separate tour will show you a former bordello (prostitution was legal until early in this century).

If you'd like to walk around historic downtown Pendleton, the chamber of commerce offers a **self-guided walking tour** brochure.

At the **Umatilla County Historical Museum,** 108 SW Frazer Ave. (☎ 541/ 276-0012), you can learn about the region's more respectable history. The museum is housed in the city's 1909 vintage railway depot and contains exhibits on the Oregon Trail and Pendleton Woolen Mills as well as a display of beautiful Native American beadwork. The museum is open Tuesday through Saturday from 10am to 4pm; admission is by donation.

You can see **Oregon Trail wagon ruts** just outside the town of Echo, 20 miles west of Pendleton.

WHERE TO STAY

In addition to the hotel below, there's a **Motel 6,** 325 SE Nye Ave., Pendleton, OR 97801 (☎ 541/276-3160), charging $35 double; and the **Best Western Pendleton Inn,** 400 SE Nye Ave., Pendleton, OR 97801 (☎ 541/276-2135), charging $59 to $69 double. Both are located at Ore. 11 off I-84 (see the Appendix for toll-free phone numbers).

Red Lion Motor Inn

304 SE Nye Ave., Pendleton, OR 97801. ☎ **541/276-6111** or 800/547-8010. 170 rms. A/C TV TEL. $79–$94 double. AE, CB, DC, DISC, MC, V.

This is the largest and most luxurious lodging in Pendleton and is located south of town along I-84. As the city's only convention hotel, it's frequently booked up, especially during the Pendleton Round-up. The rooms are large and many have balconies overlooking spacious lawns and a lake. You'll find a formal dining room, a coffee shop, and a lounge featuring live entertainment, as well as a swimming pool and hot tub. There's also a free airport van.

WHERE TO DINE

Crabby's Underground Saloon and Hole in the Wall Kitchen

220 SW First St. ☎ **541/276-8118.** Reservations not accepted. Main courses $8–$17. DISC, MC, V. Mon–Sat 11am–3pm and 5–10pm. STEAK.

Down a flight of stairs and behind a heavy wooden door that used to lead to a walk-in freezer is a dark and friendly saloon with stone walls that look as if they were blasted from the bedrock. Back during Prohibition a lot of saloons went underground, but today this is the only one in town that evokes Pendleton's wilder days. Crabby's is known as much for its steak dinners and lunch buffet as for the cold drinks it serves.

The Great Pacific Wine and Coffee Company
403 S. Main St. ☎ **541/276-1350.** Sandwiches $2–$5. MC, V. Mon–Fri 8:30am–6pm, Sat 9:30am–5pm. DELI.

If you happen to be in town at lunch or need an espresso to get you the rest of the way across the hot Oregon plains, this is the place. Sandwiches come on croissants or bagels and there are also daily soups. Cookies, muffins, truffles, and other sweets round out the menu.

Raphael's Restaurant & Lounge
233 SE Fourth St. ☎ **541/276-8500.** Reservations recommended. Main courses $10–$20. MC, V. Tues–Fri 11:30am–1:30pm and 5–9pm, Sat 5–9pm. AMERICAN/CONTINENTAL.

Housed in one of Pendleton's most elegant old homes and right across the street from City Hall, Raphael's is the city's only upscale restaurant. The house's original oak and mahogany trim can be seen throughout the restaurant, but aside from this bit of elegance, the decor is far plainer than the exterior would suggest. A regular menu that includes such dishes as hot-and-spicy Cajun shrimp salad, sautéed prawns, and chicken-fried steak is complemented by a specials list that might include lightly smoked prime rib seasoned with various herbs.

3 La Grande, Baker City & the Blue Mountains

La Grande: 260 miles E of Portland, 52 miles SE of Pendleton
Baker City: 41 miles SE of La Grande, 75 miles NW of Ontario

Oregon Trail history, ghost towns, hot springs, and mountain scenery are today the main attractions of this remote corner of Oregon. Though pioneers traveling the Oregon Trail in the 1840s had found a place to rest in the Powder River Valley, site of today's Baker City, one of the most difficult sections of the trail still lay ahead of them—the crossing of the Blue Mountains. Today the Blues are no longer the formidable obstacle they once were, but they are among the least visited mountains in Oregon. However, back 1861 a gold strike in these mountains started a small gold rush that brought gold prospectors flocking to the area and left the region with several ghost towns. Although the gold has run out, the Blue Mountains still offer recreational activities, including skiing and soaking in hot springs, and both La Grande and Baker City make good bases for exploring this relatively undiscovered region.

ESSENTIALS
GETTING THERE   Both La Grande and Baker City are on I-84. La Grande is at the junction of Ore. 82, which heads northeast to Joseph and Wallowa Lake. Baker City is at the junction with Ore. 7, which runs southwest to John Day, and Ore. 86, which runs east to the Hells Canyon National Recreation Area.

   Amtrak trains stop in La Grande at Depot and Jefferson streets and in Baker City at 2803 Broadway.

VISITOR INFORMATION   Contact the **Baker County Visitor & Convention Bureau,** 490 Campbell St., Baker City, OR 97814 (☎ **541/523-3356** or 800/523-1235), or the **La Grande–Union County Chamber of Commerce,** 1912 Fourth St., Suite 200, La Grande, OR 97850 (☎ **541/963-8588** or 800/848-9969).

SEEING THE SIGHTS

If the Oregon Trail Interpretive Center leaves you fired up to learn more about pioneer days, there are a few other places you might want to stop in Baker City. The **Oregon Trail Regional Museum,** on the corner of Campbell and Grove streets (☎ **541/523-9308**), has a large collection of stagecoaches and an extensive mineral collection. It's open May to October only, daily from 9am to 5pm; admission is $2. The **Eastern Oregon Museum,** on Third Street in nearby Haines (☎ **541/856-3233**), is another small museum cluttered with all manner of artifacts of regional historic significance. It's open April to October only, daily from 9am to 5pm; admission is by donation. At the **U.S. Bank** on Main Street in Baker City, you can see a collection of gold that includes a nugget that weighs in at 80.4 ounces.

✪ Oregon Trail Interpretive Center

Ore. 86, Baker City. ☎ **541/523-1843** or 800/523-1235. Free admission. Apr–Oct, daily 9am–6pm; Nov–Mar, daily 9am–4pm. Closed Jan 1 and Dec 25.

Today, atop sagebrush-covered Flagstaff Hill just north of Baker City, stands a monument to what became the largest overland migration in North American history. Between 1842 and 1860 an estimated 300,000 people loaded all their worldly belongings onto wagons and set out to cross the continent to the promised land of western Oregon. Their route took them through some of the most rugged landscapes on this continent, and many perished along the way.

This museum commemorates the journeys of these hardy souls, who endured drought, dysentery, and starvation in the hopes of a better life at the end of the Oregon Trail. Through the use of interactive exhibits that challenge your ability to make the trip, diary quotes, a life-size wagon-train scene, and lots of artifacts from the trail, the center takes you through every aspect of life on the trail. Outside, a trail through the sagebrush leads to ruts left by the wagons on their journey west.

HISTORIC HAMLETS & GHOST TOWNS

If you have an interest in Victorian architecture, be sure to visit the town of **Union,** 11 miles southeast of La Grande on Ore. 203. Union was the first settlement in the Grande Ronde Valley and flourished as a trading center and county seat of Union County. Today the small town has numerous large Victorian homes in various states of restoration. Stop by the **Union County Museum,** 311 S. Main St. (☎ **541/562-6003**), to learn more about the town's historic buildings. It's open May to October only, Monday through Friday from 1 to 5pm; admission is free.

In the town of **Elgin,** 18 miles north on Ore. 82, you can take in a film or live performance at the restored **Elgin Opera House,** which was built in 1912.

The mountains of this region are dotted with **ghost towns** that appeared and disappeared with the gold. At the Baker City Chamber of Commerce information center, you can pick up a guide to two dozen historic towns, most of which are now ghost towns in various states of decay. **Sumpter,** 30 miles west of Baker City on Ore. 7, is a historic community that has a few too many people to be called a ghost town. Gold here was dredged from the valley floor and the **Sumpter Dredge State Park** preserves the ominous-looking dredge that between 1935 and 1954 ate its way up the valley in its own little pond. The **Sumpter Valley Railroad** (☎ 541/894-2268) operates a classic steam train on a 5-mile run from west of Phillips Lake to the Sumpter Dredge on Saturday and Sunday from late May to late September; fares are $8 for adults, $6 for children 6 to 16. The train chugs its way slowly through an eerie landscape of dredge tailings that have created hundreds of ponds that are now home to quite a bit of wildlife.

Continuing west on a winding county road for another 14 miles will bring you to **Granite,** another ghost town that also has a few flesh-and-blood residents. The weatherbeaten old buildings on a grassy hillside are the epitome of a western ghost town, and most buildings are marked. You'll see the old school, general store, saloon, bordello, and other important town buildings.

OUTDOOR ACTIVITIES: SKIING, HIKING, HOT SPRINGS & MORE

In winter there is **downhill skiing** in excellent powder snow at **Anthony Lakes Mountain Resort** (☎ 541/856-3277), 40 minutes west of Baker City. Daily lift tickets are $20. The smaller **Spout Springs** ski area, 40 miles north of La Grande on Ore. 204 (☎ 541/566-2164), offers downhill and cross-country skiing and usually has good powder snow also. Daily lift tickets are $15.

Cross-country skiing and **snowmobiling** are also popular winter sports around these parts, so stop by the tourist information center in La Grande or Baker for information on where you can pursue these sports.

In summer there are plenty of nearby trails to hike or mountain bike, and the Spout Springs ski area stays open for mountain biking. Contact the **Wallowa-Whitman National Forest,** 1550 Dewey Ave. (P.O. Box 907), Baker City, OR 97814 (☎ 541/523-1205), or the **Malheur National Forest,** 139 NE Dayton St., John Day, OR 97845 (☎ 541/575-1731), for details.

If you're interested in **birdwatching,** head out to the **Ladd Marsh Wildlife Area,** 6 miles south of La Grande off I-84 at the Foothill Road exit. This wetland is home to Oregon's only breeding population of sandhill cranes.

The hot springs of this region have been attracting people since long before the first white settlers arrived and you can still soak away your cares at several of these springs. Each has a very different character, but all are pleasant places to relax. **Lehman Hot Springs,** in Ukiah, 38 miles west of La Grande on Ore. 244 (☎ 541/427-3015), claims the best location. It's surrounded by forested mountains and features a large swimming pool, campsites, two cabins ($75 per night), and nearby hiking and cross-country ski trails. It's open daily in summer from 10am to 9pm; in other months there are shorter hours and it's closed Tuesday and Wednesday; admission is $5.

In the town of Cove, 13 miles east of La Grande on Ore. 237, you can go for a swim in a hot springs–fed swimming pool at **Cove Hot Springs** (☎ 541/568-4890), which is open daily throughout the summer.

WHERE TO STAY
IN THE BAKER CITY AREA

In addition to the two B&Bs listed below, you'll find several inexpensive chain motels in Baker City. These include the **Best Western Sunridge Inn,** 1 Sunridge

Lane, Baker City, OR 97814 (☎ **541/523-6444**), charging $57 to $76 double; the **Quality Inn,** 810 Campbell St., Baker City, OR 97814 (☎ **541/523-2242**), charging $44 to $61 double; and the **Super 8 Motel,** 250 Campbell St., Baker City, OR 97814 (☎ **541/523-8282**), charging $43 to $49 double.

A'Demain Bed & Breakfast

1790 Fourth St., Baker City, OR 97814. ☎ **541/523-2509.** 2 rms. $55–$65 double. Rates include full breakfast. No credit cards.

Set on a tree-lined street and built of brick, this is Baker City's most appealing bed-and-breakfast inn. An octagonal turret anchors one corner of the house and heavy stone columns support the porch. If the turret captures your attention as much as it did ours, you'll want to spend a bit extra to stay in the suitelike room, which includes the second-floor turret room, as well as a small private balcony. The downstairs room is smaller.

Sumpter Bed & Breakfast

344 NE Columbia St., Sumpter, OR 97877. ☎ **541/894-2229,** or 800/640-3184 in Oregon. 4 rms. $45 double. Rates include full breakfast. No credit cards.

Big and drafty and authentically old-fashioned, this B&B was once used as a hospital when this was a booming mining town. This is a pretty laid-back and informal place—no stuffy lace curtains or pastel-print wallpaper—and if you need modern comforts, you may want to give it a miss. However, we liked the genuine western atmosphere of both the inn and the town.

IN LA GRANDE

In addition to the B&B listed below, there are several inexpensive chain motels in La Grande. These include the **Comfort Inn,** 1711 21st St., La Grande, OR 97850 (☎ **541/963-3100**), charging $57 to $100 double; the **Best Western Pony Soldier Inn,** 2612 Island Ave., La Grande, OR 97850 (☎ **541/963-7195**), charging $62 to $78 double; and the **Super 8 Motel,** 2407 E. R Ave., La Grande, OR 97850 (☎ **541/963-8080**), charging $44 to $49 double.

Stang Manor Bed & Breakfast

1612 Walnut St., La Grande, OR 97850. ☎ **541/963-2400.** 3 rms, 1 suite. $70–$90 double; $90 suite. Rates include full breakfast. MC, V.

This Georgian colonial mansion, built in the 1920s, looks a bit like the White House and is filled with beautiful woodwork and comfortable guest rooms. A couple of the guest rooms have the original bathroom fixtures, including a footed bathtub. The best deal here is the three-room suite, which has a fireplace and sun porch that has been converted into a sleeping room. Breakfasts are elegant affairs served in the formal dining room.

WHERE TO DINE
IN THE BAKER CITY AREA

Front Street Coffee Co. & Café

1840 Main St. ☎ **541/523-7536.** Reservations not accepted. Meals $5–$8. MC, V. Mon–Sat 7am–4pm. SANDWICHES/MEXICAN.

Gourmet sandwiches, large-and-filling salads, hearty breakfasts, Mexican dishes, and espresso are the staples at this antique-filled café. With exposed brick walls and big black-and-white tile floor, the café is a bit of a mix between an urban coffee shop and an old-fashioned country diner.

Haines Steakhouse

910 Front St., Haines. ☎ **541/856-3639.** Reservations recommended. Main courses $9–$18. AE, DC, DISC, MC, V. Mon and Wed–Fri 5–10pm, Sat 4–10pm, Sun 1–9pm. STEAK.

Thick, juicy steaks are the specialty of the house here, but it's the decor as much as the food that attracts people. Log walls and booths, a chuck-wagon salad bar, buffalo and elk heads mounted on the walls, even a totem pole and an old buggy keep diners gazing around them as they eat.

Pizza à Fetta

1915 Washington Ave. ☎ **541/523-3641.** Pizzas $10–$20. MC, V. Mon–Sat 11am–8 or 9pm. PIZZA.

When you've just got to have a pizza and you want more than pepperoni or sausage, this is the place. Bleu cheese, sheep's-milk feta, montrachet, sun-dried tomatoes, kalamata olives, chorizo, and pancetta are the sort of toppings available here.

IN LA GRANDE

La Grande Centennial House

1606 Sixth St. ☎ **541/963-6089.** Reservations recommended. Main courses $9–$17. DISC, MC, V. Tues–Fri 11:30am–2pm and 5–9pm, Sat 5–9pm. CONTINENTAL.

Housed in an 1890 Victorian home, this is La Grande's most elegant restaurant. The menu sticks to familiar territory—escargots, veal piccata, chicken Cordon Bleu. Lunches here are a great deal.

Mamacita's

110 Depot St. ☎ **541/963-6223.** Main courses $4.25–$10. No credit cards. Tues–Fri 11am–2pm and 5:30–9pm, Sat–Sun 5:30–9pm. MEXICAN.

This small, low-key Mexican place has a short but varied menu. Fire-eaters should try the hot salsa verde.

Ten Depot Street

10 Depot St. ☎ **541/963-8766.** Reservations recommended. Main courses $8–$14. AE, MC, V. Mon–Fri 11:30am–2:30pm and 5:30–10pm, Sat 5:30–10pm. STEAK/SEAFOOD.

Housed in a historic brick commercial building, this restaurant has a classic turn-of-the-century feel, complete with a saloon on one side. Although the steaks are what most people come for, the salads are large and flavorful and there are even some vegetarian dishes.

4 Hells Canyon National Recreation Area & the Wallowa Mountains

Joseph: 355 miles E of Portland, 80 miles E of La Grande, 125 miles N of Baker City

Hells Canyon, which lies just to the east of the Wallowas, was carved by the Snake River and is the deepest canyon in the United States. Bounded on the east by the Seven Devils Mountains and on the west by the Wallowa Mountains, Hells Canyon is 8,000 feet deep in some places and serves as the boundary between Oregon and Idaho. Here in this remote gorge you can choose from a wide variety of outdoor activities—and you won't have to fight crowds.

The Wallowa Mountains, which stand just south of the town of Joseph, are a glacier-carved range of rugged beauty that has been called the Alps of Oregon and the Little Switzerland of America. Though the range is small enough in area to drive around in a day, it's big on scenery. In the northeast corner of the mountains lies Wallowa Lake, which was formed when glacial moraines blocked a valley that had been carved by the glaciers. With blue waters reflecting the rocky peaks, the lake has long attracted visitors.

In recent years, the town of Joseph has become a center for the casting of bronze sculptures with western themes, and there are now several art galleries in the area. With its natural beauty, recreational opportunities, and artistic bent, this corner of the state today has more to offer than any other area in eastern Oregon.

ESSENTIALS

GETTING THERE   Ore. 82 connects Joseph to La Grande in the west, and Ore. 3 heads north from nearby Enterprise to Lewiston, Idaho, by way of Wash. 129.

VISITOR INFORMATION   Contact the **Joseph Chamber of Commerce,** P.O. Box 13, Joseph, OR 97846 (☎ **541/432-1015**), or call the **Hells Canyon Recreation Report** (☎ **800/521-9102**) or **Northeast Oregon Vacationlands** (☎ **800/523-1235**).

FESTIVALS   The rowdy **Chief Joseph Days** over the last full weekend in July, **Jazz on the Lake** in mid-July, and the **Alpenfest** on the third weekend after Labor Day are the biggest annual events in the area.

HELLS CANYON NATIONAL RECREATION AREA

The rugged gorge lives up to its name in the blazing hot summer months, but boating, swimming, and fishing are all very popular despite the heat. Below Hells Canyon Dam, the Snake River is turbulent with white water and is a designated National Wild and Scenic River. Few roads lead into the canyon, and most of these are only recommended for four-wheel-drive vehicles. Much of Hells Canyon is wilderness and is accessible only by boat, on horseback, or on foot.

To get an overview of the canyon, drive to the Hells Canyon overlook, 30 miles northeast of Halfway on Forest Road 39. From here you can gaze down into the canyon—but you won't be able to see the river. To get a bottom-up view of the canyon, take Ore. 86 to Oxbow and continue across the river into Idaho to the Hells Canyon Dam. Stop at the **Hells Canyon Creek Information Station** to learn more about the canyon. For further information, you can also contact **Hells Canyon National Recreation Area,** 88401 Ore. 82, Enterprise, OR 97828 (☎ **541/426-4978**).

The best way to see Hells Canyon is by white-water raft or in a jet-boat. Both sorts of trip can be arranged through **Hells Canyon Adventures,** Oxbow (☎ **541/ 785-3352** or 800/422-3568). If you'd like to try pedaling a mountain bike in Hells Canyon, contact **Hells Canyon Bicycle Tours,** Joseph (☎ **541/432-2453**), which charges $75 for a day-long ride.

While in this area, you can learn about bison at **Clear Creek Gardens and Game** (☎ **541/742-6558**). This ranch outside the town of Halfway offers tours during which you get to see their bison up close, learn more about bison and their cultural significance to the Plains native peoples, and even get a taste of buffalo meat. Tours are offered May to September only, Wednesday through Sunday at 10am and 3pm for $6.

"I Will Fight No More Forever"

The Wallowa Mountains and Hells Canyon areas were once the homeland of the Nez Perce people. The Nez Perce land, which encompassed rolling hills covered with lush grasses, was perfect for raising horses, and sometime in the early 1700s the tribe came to own horses that were descended from Spanish stock and had been traded northward from the American Southwest. They began selectively breeding this strange new animal, emphasizing traits of speed and endurance. Their horses were far superior to those used by other tribes and became known as Appaloosas. The area where these horses were first bred is now the Palouse Hills country of eastern Washington.

The Nez Perce had befriended explorers Lewis and Clark in 1805 and had remained friendly to white settlers when other Native Americans were waging wars. However, the Nez Perce's neutrality was rewarded with treaties that twice cut the size of their reservation in half. When one band refused to sign a new treaty and relinquish its land, the stage was set for one of the great tragedies of Northwest history.

En route to a reservation in Idaho, several Nez Perce braves ignored orders from the tribal elders and attacked and killed four white settlers to exact revenge for the earlier murder by whites of a father of one of the braves. This attack brought the ire of settlers, and the cavalry was called in to hunt down the Nez Perce. Tribal elders decided to flee to Canada, and, headed by Chief Joseph (also known as Young Joseph), 700 Nez Perce, including 400 women and children, began a 2,000-mile march across Idaho and Montana on a retreat that lasted four months.

Along the way several skirmishes were fought, and when the cavalry finally succeeded in defeating the Nez Perce, these people were only 40 miles from Canada. At their surrender, Chief Joseph spoke the words for which he has long been remembered: "Hear me my Chiefs, I am tired; my heart is sick and sad. From where the sun now stands, I will fight no more, forever."

The town of Joseph is named after Chief Joseph, and on the outskirts of town you'll find the grave of his father, Old Joseph. Young Joseph is buried on the Colville Indian Reservation in central Washington. Not far from Joseph, near Lewiston, Idaho, you can learn more about the Nez Perce at Nez Perce National Historical Park.

THE WALLOWA MOUNTAINS & WALLOWA LAKE

Down at the south end of Wallowa Lake, you'll find **Wallowa Lake State Park** (☎ 541/432-4185), where there's a swimming beach, picnic area, and campground. Adjacent to the park is the **Wallowa Lake Marina** (☎ 541/432-9115), where you can rent a canoe, rowboat, paddleboat, or motorboat. This end of the lake has an old-fashioned mountain resort feel, with pony and kiddie rides, go-cart tracks, and the like.

For a different perspective on the lake, ride the **Wallowa Lake Tramway** (☎ 541/432-5331) to the top of 8,200-foot Mount Howard. It operates in spring and summer, daily from 10am to 4pm; the fare is $10 for adults, $9 for seniors, and $5 for children 10 and under. The views from the top are excellent and take in Wallowa Lake and the surrounding jagged peaks. There are 2 miles of walking trails on the summit, and food is available at the **Summit Deli & Alpine Patio.**

If you'd like to head into the **Eagle Cap Wilderness** to the popular **Lake Basin** or anywhere else in the Wallows, you'll find the trailhead less than a mile past the south end of the lake. For more information on hiking in the Wallows, contact the **Eagle Cap Ranger District** of the Wallowa-Whitman National Forest, Enterprise, OR 97828 (☎ **541/426-4978**).

Horse packing into the Wallows is a popular activity, and rides of a day or longer can be arranged through **Eagle Cap Wilderness Pack Station,** 59761 Wallowa Lake Hwy., Joseph (☎ **541/432-4145** or 800/681-6222); **High Country Outfitters,** Joseph (☎ **541/432-9171**); or **Cornucopia Wilderness Pack Station,** Route 1, Richland (☎ **541/893-6400,** or in summer 541/ 742-5400).

If you'd like to try llama trekking and let these South American beasts of burden carry your pack, contact **Hurricane Creek Llama Treks,** 63366 Pine Tree Rd., Enterprise (☎ **541/432-4455** or 800/528-9609), or **Wallowa Llamas,** Route 1, Halfway (☎ **541/742-2961** or 541/742-4930). Trips range in price from $285 to $770.

In winter, the Wallows are popular with cross-country and backcountry skiers. Check with at the ranger station in Enterprise for directions to trails or contact the **Eagle Cap Nordic Club** (☎ **541/432-3281**). You'll also find a small downhill ski area and groomed cross-country trails at **Ferguson Ridge,** which is 9 miles southeast of Joseph on Tucker Down Road. **Wing Ridge Ski Tours,** Joseph (☎ **541/426-4322**), leads experienced skiers on hut-to-hut ski tours.

JOSEPH

Though the lake and mountains are the main attraction of this area, the presence of several bronze foundries in the area has made this a sort of western art community. You'll find several galleries as you stroll along Main Street in Joseph. Of particular interest is the **Nez Perce Crossing Gallery and Museum** at the west end of town. In addition to housing bronzes by artist Dave Manuel, the museum includes an outstanding collection of Native American artifacts and John Wayne memorabilia.

Other Joseph galleries include the **Bronze Coast Gallery,** 2 S. Main St. (☎ **541/432-1290**), and the **Wildhorse Gallery,** 508 N. Main St. (☎ **541/ 432-4242**). If you'd like to see how all these intricate bronze statues are made, visit **Valley Bronze of Oregon,** 307 W. Adler St. (☎ **541/432-7551**), which is a working bronze foundry and has a gallery at 018 Main St. (☎ **541/432-7445**). You can also stop in at the **Wallowa County Museum,** also on Main Street (☎ **541/426-3811**), and see some genuine pioneer artifacts daily from 10am to 5pm from Memorial Day to late September.

WHERE TO STAY
In Joseph/Wallowa Lake

Chandlers' Bed, Bread, and Trail Inn
700 S. Main St., Joseph, OR 97846. ☎ **541/432-9765** or 800/452-3781. 5 rms, none with bath. $60 double. Rates include full breakfast. MC, V.

Located right in Joseph, Chandler's is a contemporary home with cedar-shingle walls and a boardwalk that leads through a rock garden to the front door. Inside you'll find a high-ceilinged living room with open-beam construction, folk art, quilts, and an "early attic" decor. Three of the rooms have mountain views, and there are also three sitting areas for guests to use. In warm weather, breakfast is served in a gazebo in the garden.

Eagle Cap Chalets

59879 Wallowa Lake Hwy., Joseph, OR 97846. ☎ **541/432-4704.** 23 rms, 9 cabins, 5 condos. TV. $46–$51 double in rms; $47–$57 double in cabins; $55–60 double in condos. AE, DC, DISC, MC, V.

This is the most comfortable and best-placed budget lodging in the area. Set under tall pines just a short walk from hiking trails and the lake, the rooms here vary from motel style to rustic-though-renovated cabins. Siding on all the buildings makes them appear to be built of logs. The cabins and condos have kitchens and are ideal for families or small groups.

✪ Wallowa Lake Lodge

60060 Wallowa Lake Hwy., Joseph, OR 97846. ☎ **541/432-9821.** 22 rms, 8 cabins. May–Sept, $70–$114 double; $65–$120 cabin. Oct–Apr, $50–$80 double; $55–$85 cabin. DISC, MC, V.

This rustic two-story lodge at the south end of Wallowa Lake was built in the 1920s and is surrounded by big pines and a wide expanse of lawn. Big comfortable chairs fill the lobby, where folks often sit by the stone fireplace in the evening. The guest rooms are divided between those with carpeting and modern bathrooms and those with hardwood floors, original bathroom fixtures, and antique furnishings. All but two of the latter type have two bedrooms each, and there are also two rooms with balconies overlooking the lake. We prefer the rustic rooms. The cabins all have a certain rusticity but are comfortable and have full kitchens. The dining room serves a limited menu of well-prepared dishes that make use of local produce and meats.

In Enterprise

⑤ Outbound Inn

507 S. River St., Enterprise, OR 97828. ☎ **541/426-6457.** 3 rms, none with bath. $48–$54 double. Rates include full breakfast. MC, V.

This casual B&B tends to attract a youngish crowd who come to explore the Wallowas and Hells Canyon but who don't want to camp out. The guest rooms are comfortable but not fancy. Hosts Jeff Irish and Michele Chapin can help you plan your explorations of the area, and will start you off with a hearty breakfast.

In Halfway

The Birch Leaf Lodge

Rte. 1, Box 91, Halfway, OR 97834. ☎ **541/742-2990.** 2 rms, neither with bath. $65–$75 double. MC, V.

Located on a 42-acre farm on the outskirts of Halfway, the Birch Leaf Farm is a tranquil spot in a valley surrounded by the peaks of the Wallowa Mountains. Orchards, pastures, and even several ponds and marshes make the farm a great place to explore, and the birdwatching is great. The guest rooms are small, but comfortable and simply furnished. The big country breakfast includes local jams and honey from the farm. In winter there's excellent cross-country skiing here.

✪ Pine Valley Lodge

163 N. Main St., Halfway, OR 97834. ☎ **541/742-2027.** 2 rms, neither with bath. $65–$75 double. No credit cards.

This amazing little lodge is a Wild West fantasy created by two artists. With handmade furniture and western collectibles scattered all about, the lodge is a fascinating place to just wander around in. The two small guest rooms are on the second floor and combine rustic furnishings with the artistic endeavors of the owners. The downstairs common rooms also double as a restaurant in the evenings (see "Where to Dine," below, for details). All in all, this place is unique.

A GUEST RANCH IN THE WILDERNESS

Minam Lodge

Eagle Cap Wilderness Pack Station, High Country Outfitters, 59761 Wallowa Lake Hwy., Joseph, OR 97846. ☎ **541/432-9171** or 800/681-6222. 6 rms. $190–$290 per person for two days and one night. Rates include all meals and transportation to and from the ranch. MC, V.

Located on the Minam River in the Eagle Cap Wilderness, and only accessible on foot or on horseback or by small plane, Minam Lodge is a rustic getaway for those who love the great outdoors and enjoy horseback riding, hiking, fishing, and hunting. The rustic log cabins are set atop a low hill and have wood stoves for warmth and fairly large windows to let in the sunshine and views.

WHERE TO DINE

In Joseph/Wallowa Lake

The dining room at the **Wallowa Lake Lodge** is the best restaurant in the area (see "Where to Stay," above, for details).

Vali's Alpine Restaurant and Delicatessen

59811 Wallowa Lake Hwy. ☎ **541/432-5691.** Reservations required. Main courses $7–$11. No credit cards. Tues–Sun 10am–noon and 5:30–9pm. Closed weekdays from Labor Day to Memorial Day. EASTERN EUROPEAN.

Just past the Wallowa Lake Lodge you'll find this little restaurant, which specializes in the hearty fare of Eastern Europe. Stuffed cabbage, Hungarian goulash, chicken paprikas, schnitzel, and apple strudel should help you stay warm on cold mountain evenings.

In Halfway

✪ The Halfway Supper Club

In the Pine Valley Lodge, 163 N. Main St. ☎ **541/742-2027.** Reservations recommended. Main courses $14–$18. No credit cards. Wed–Sun 6–8pm. CONTINENTAL.

Located in the wonderfully eclectic and rustic Pine Valley Lodge, this restaurant serves the most creative cuisine in this corner of the state. The meals, which include the likes of lamb chops with rosemary and lemon and coq au vin (here known as hunter's chicken), are served amid handmade furniture and painted pillows and wall coverings by the owners. This place is well worth a drive if you're staying anywhere in the vicinity.

Appendix: Useful Toll-Free Numbers

MAJOR AIRLINES

Alaska Airlines	800/426-0333
Aero México	800/237-6639
America West	800/235-9292
American	800/433-7300
Continental	800/525-0280
Delta	800/221-1212
Northwest	800/225-2525
Southwest	800/435-9792
TWA	800/221-2000
United	800/241-6522
USAir	800/428-4322

CAR-RENTAL COMPANIES

Alamo	800/327-9633
Avis	800/331-1212
Budget	800/527-0700
Dollar	800/800-4000
Hertz	800/654-3131
National	800/227-7368
Thrifty	800/367-2277

MAJOR CHAIN MOTELS

Best Western	800/528-1234
Comfort Inns	800/228-5150
Days Inns	800/329-7466 (800/DAYS-INN)
Econo Lodges	800/424-4777
Embassy Suites	800/362-2779 (800/EMBASSY)
Hampton Inns	800/426-7866 (800/HAMPTON)
Hilton	800/445-8667
Holiday Inns	800/465-4329 (800/HOLIDAY)
La Quinta Inns	800/531-5900
Marriott	800/228-9290

Marriott Residence Inn	800/331-3131
Motel 6	505/891-6161
	(no 800 number)
Quality Inns	800/228-5151
Radisson	800/333-3333
Ramada	800/272-6232
Rodeway Inns	800/424-4777
Sheraton	800/325-3535
Super 8 Motels	800/800-8000
Travelodge	800/578-7878
Wyndham	800/996-3426

Index

FROMMER'S COMPLETE TRAVEL GUIDES

(Comprehensive guides to sightseeing, dining and accommodations, with selections in all price ranges—from deluxe to budget)

FROMMER'S $-A-DAY GUIDES

(Dream Vacations at Down-to-Earth Prices)

FROMMER'S COMPLETE CITY GUIDES

(Comprehensive guides to sightseeing, dining, and accommodations in all price ranges)

FROMMER'S FAMILY GUIDES

(Guides to family-friendly hotels, restaurants, activities, and attractions)

FROMMER'S WALKING TOURS

*(Memorable strolls through colorful and historic neighborhoods,
accompanied by detailed directions and maps)*

FROMMER'S AMERICA ON WHEELS

*(Guides for travelers who are exploring the U.S.A. by car, featuring a brand-new
rating system for accommodations and full-color road maps)*

FROMMER'S SPECIAL-INTEREST TITLES

Arthur Frommer's Branson!	P107	Frommer's Where to Stay U.S.A.,	
Arthur Frommer's New World		11th Ed.	P102
of Travel (avail. 11/95)	P112	National Park Guide, 29th Ed.	P106
Frommer's Caribbean Hideaways		USA Today Golf Tournament Guide	P113
(avail. 9/95)	P110	USA Today Minor League	
Frommer's America's 100 Best-Loved		Baseball Book	P111
State Parks	P109		

FROMMER'S BEST BEACH VACATIONS
*(The top places to sun, stroll, shop, stay, play, party, and swim—with each
beach rated for beauty, swimming, sand, and amenities)*

California (avail. 10/95)	G100	Hawaii (avail. 10/95)	G102
Florida (avail. 10/95)	G101		

FROMMER'S BED & BREAKFAST GUIDES
*(Selective guides with four-color photos and full descriptions of
the best inns in each region)*

California	B100	Hawaii	B105
Caribbean	B101	Pacific Northwest	B106
East Coast	B102	Rockies	B107
Eastern United States	B103	Southwest	B108
Great American Cities	B104		

FROMMER'S IRREVERENT GUIDES
*(Wickedly honest guides for sophisticated travelers
and those who want to be)*

Chicago (avail. 11/95)	I100	New Orleans (avail. 11/95)	I103
London (avail. 11/95)	I101	San Francisco (avail. 11/95)	I104
Manhattan (avail. 11/95)	I102	Virgin Islands (avail. 11/95)	I105

FROMMER'S DRIVING TOURS
*(Four-color photos and detailed maps outlining
spectacular scenic driving routes)*

Australia	Y100	Italy	Y108
Austria	Y101	Mexico	Y109
Britain	Y102	Scandinavia	Y110
Canada	Y103	Scotland	Y111
Florida	Y104	Spain	Y112
France	Y105	Switzerland	Y113
Germany	Y106	U.S.A.	Y114
Ireland	Y107		

FROMMER'S BORN TO SHOP
*(The ultimate travel guides for discriminating
shoppers—from cut-rate to couture)*

Hong Kong (avail. 11/95)	Z100	London (avail. 11/95)	Z101